P9-EEP-461

Physiological Psychology

SECOND EDITION

Physiological Psychology

MARVIN SCHWARTZ
University of Cincinnati

PRENTICE-HALL, INC., ENGLEWOOD CLIFFS, NEW JERSEY 07632

Library of Congress Cataloging in Publication Data

Schwartz, Marvin.
Physiological psychology.

Bibliography: p.
Includes index.
1. Psychology, Physiological. I. Title.
[DNLM: 1. Psychophysiology. WL102 S399p]
QP360.S38 1978 152 77-17438
ISBN 0-13-674895-3

Printed in the United States of America

10 9 8 7 6 5 4 3 2 1

Prentice-Hall International, Inc., *London*
Prentice-Hall of Australia Pty. Limited, *Sydney*
Prentice-Hall of Canada, Ltd., *Toronto*
Prentice-Hall of India Private Limited, *New Delhi*
Prentice-Hall of Japan, Inc., *Tokyo*
Prentice-Hall of Southeast Asia Pte. Ltd., *Singapore*
Whitehall Books Limited, *Wellington, New Zealand*

FOR

BARBARA, JEFF, PAUL, AND DAVID

Contents

2 Genetics and Behavior 40

3 Development of Behavior 74

7 Emotion 241

8 Hunger and the Regulation of Eating 286

11 Motivation: Implications of Brain Stimulation 405

Preface

This book was designed as an introduction to physiological psychology. It is also a revision of a prior edition, and as such is designed to fulfill several intentions. Most obviously, a revision is aimed at updating the material covered. During the course of its writing, I have been amazed at how much the field of physiological psychology has changed in the five years since the first edition was published. Not only has a plethora of empirical facts emerged—more important is the evolution in some of the basic concepts of the discipline. Just about every topic area discussed in the earlier edition has undergone some change, and this new information appears to have contributed greatly to our understanding of behavior. In presenting the material in this text, I have tried to give some indication of this evolutionary process. In order to do this, it was often necessary to show how theories and concepts were built up on the basis of existing findings and subsequently analyzed and revised. If this approach tends to leave the reader without a feeling of closure or assurance about many things, it is, however, a realistic description of the process. A textbook is a cross-sectional view of the state of a science undergoing continuous revision and I have tried to provide the reader with a glimpse of that process.

A revision is also an opportunity to add to the topics covered, and I have done that too. However, this book still remains a selected sampling of the material that might be discussed. Both instructors and students using this book will undoubtedly be aware of omissions. I hope it is not begging the question when I suggest that these provide the opportunity for supplementary materials and independent lectures and reading.

Above all, however, a revision should be an opportunity to improve on the performance of the original effort. I have, therefore, tried to keep uppermost in mind the goal of presenting a true introduction to physiological psychology, suitable for use by students without a background in the basic biological sciences. The only assumption is that they do have some background in psychology. Thus, I have tried to be more consistent about defining and illustrating new terms and concepts and I hope the writing style is better.

A revision should also retain the best of the older effort. I believe that this is represented by the fundamental premise on which the first edition was written: The book should be about *behavior*. The orientation is, as much as possible, toward behavioral problems rather than toward physiology per se. Each chapter addresses a problem or problems pertinent to the psychologist's interest in understanding behavior. I have attempted to show how a physiological approach can promote that understanding.

And, finally, a revision requires the cooperation of critics, both sympathetic and otherwise inclined. Drs. John Renfrew, Northern Michigan University, Jerry Koppman, San Diego State University, Bernard Schiff, University of Toronto, Eugene Eisman, University of Wisconsin-Milwaukee, Lawrence O'Kelly, Michigan State University, and Freya Weizenbaum, Virginia Polytechnic Institute, read portions of the draft and Dr. Elizabeth K. Adkins, Cornell University, reviewed the entire second draft. I acknowledge that I have not always followed their advice, but each of them should be able to detect segments of the work which he or she materially influenced. I thank each of them sincerely. And to Ms. Olive Beard, I can only say that I have never been more pleased with any effort to put together a manuscript.

M.S.

Physiological Psychology

1

Introduction

Psychology may be simply defined as the science of behavior. Although it has important historical roots within physiology, over the past 100 to 150 years psychology has, for the most part, pursued an independent course, developing its own unique methods and procedures. In fact, much of psychological theorizing over this period has been devoted to emancipating psychology from its physiological roots. The typical psychological investigation involves the relationship between the environment, past and present, and responses. For the most part, little consideration is given to physiological variables within the organism—indeed, such consideration is sometimes even deemed undesirable (B. F. Skinner, 1963). One branch of the discipline, physiological psychology, has, however, consistently maintained a relationship to the parent discipline. Essentially, the thesis of physiological psychology is that our understanding of behavioral processes can be enhanced by consideration of organismic variables.

The pros and cons of adopting a physiological approach to behavioral problems have been argued extensively, and it is not our purpose to indulge in a philosophical analysis of the issues here.[1] It is enough to say that in

[1]A brief summary of these issues will be found in Schwartz (1967).

common with all other psychologists, the physiological psychologist's prime interest is in the understanding of *behavior*. He maintains, however, that an understanding of the structure, organization, and functioning of the biological mechanism that produces that behavior will help to clarify it.

Within this biological framework, the psychologist is apt to be highly selective about what is considered pertinent. Psychologists are not likely to show much interest in the dynamics of oxygen exchange in the lungs, but they certainly have been very interested in the behavioral capacities of individuals who have been subjected to oxygen deprivation (Gottfried, 1973). Obviously, then, the specific biological interests of the physiological psychologist are subject to rapid change. As new research developments demonstrate their behavorial relevance, new areas of physiological interest open for the psychologist. A few years ago, most psychologists would have been unconcerned with cardiac functioning; today, cardiac functioning is central to the area of biofeedback and behavorial modification (Chapter 7).

Foremost, this book is about behavior. Its intention is to relate behavior to its biological foundations. To fulfill this intention, it will be necessary to become acquainted with terms, structures, procedures, etc., from the biological sciences. On the other hand, this text cannot provide basic training in the biological sciences, only an initial, general familiarity; thus we shall be more concerned with the general properties of biological mechanisms than with the details of their chemistry or anatomy. We begin with some introductory descriptive material pertaining to the nervous system, to which we will add throughout the remaining chapters. Our aim is a general understanding of its structure and functioning and the methods by which it can be studied. We shall also be concerned with its interactions with other physiological systems, particularly with the hormonal system.

THE NERVOUS SYSTEM

The nervous system is grossly divided into two parts: the central nervous system and the peripheral nervous system.[2] The *central nervous system* (CNS) is made up of the brain and the spinal cord. In this text, our focus will be mainly on the brain. Our first consideration will be a description of the gross physical features of the brain.

The Brain

Figure 1.1 presents, for comparison, diagrams of the human brain and the cat brain. Those areas of the visible surface, the *cortex* (rind or covering), devoted to sensory and motor functions are also roughly indicated. (Note

[2]Gardner (1968) provides an excellent introduction to the anatomy of the nervous system in greater detail than can be presented here.

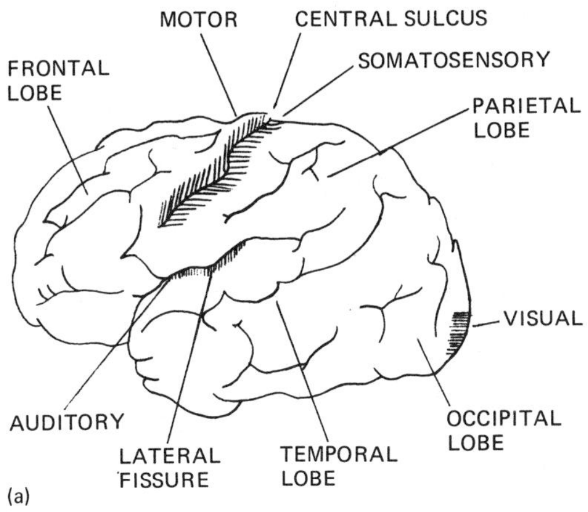

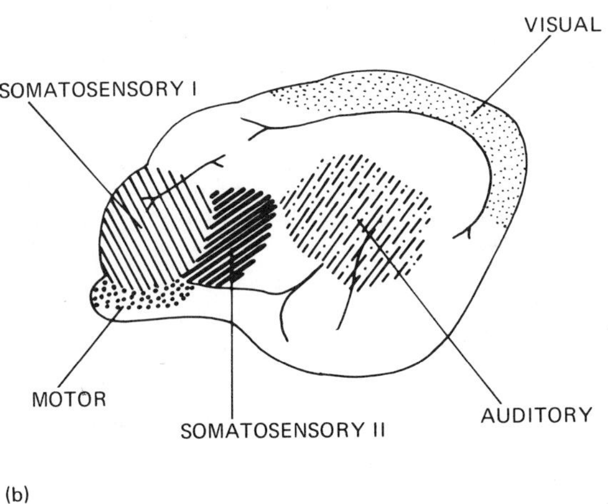

Figure 1.1. Diagrams of the brains of (a) human and (b) cat.

that the diagrams are not drawn to scale.) The most obvious difference between these brains is their comparative size—the human brain weighs in the neighborhood of 1500 grams, while the cat brain weighs less than one-tenth as much. Second, the cat brain is relatively smooth in appearance, while the human brain is characterized by a large number of convolutions (*gyri*) and depressions (*fissures*, or *sulci*). These convolutions and depressions allow the human brain to have a large cortical surface area relative to its volume, in the same way that crumpling a piece of paper makes it take up less space but does not change its actual surface area.

Figure 1.1 also indicates the location of the sensory receiving areas within the *lobes* formed by the major fissures. For example, the visual areas in humans are in the occipital lobe, the auditory in the temporal lobe, and so on. Finally, as the diagrams indicate, a much larger proportion of the cat's

Figure 1.2. Anatomical terms used to indicate position and direction.

brain is devoted to sensory and motor functioning. Presumably the greater volume of the remaining, or *association,* cortex in people has something to do with the differences between the functional capacities of cat and human.

Locating Points in the Brain

In order to begin dealing with the nervous system, we have to know how to orient ourselves with respect to it, i.e., to specify location. Anatomists employ a convenient, general vocabulary for indicating direction. Basically, we need terms to indicate whether a structure is toward the front, back, sides, or middle. Figure 1.2 summarizes terms which describe this. *Dorsal* means toward the spinal column; *ventral,* toward the stomach, or, in four-legged animals, toward the undersurface. The top of the head in humans and other two-legged animals is considered to be dorsal even though it is at a right angle to the spine. *Medial* means toward the middle; *lateral* indicates displacement away from the midline, toward the sides. Directions toward the head are indicated by several equivalent terms: *anterior, rostral,* or

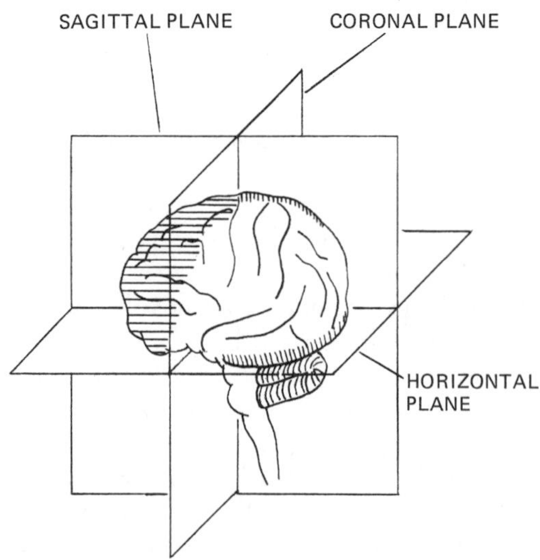

Figure 1.3. Planes providing a coordinate system for mapping the brain.

cephalic. Conversely, directions toward the tail of the animal are indicated by *posterior* or *caudal*.

This system enables us, once we have a point of reference, to describe where a structure is located in relation to that reference. For example, one could describe the eyes of an animal like the rat as located on the head, in a position that is anterior to and somewhat more medial than the ears, and also caudal and dorsal to the mouth.

The terms that we have just described are adequate for indicating general, relative position; for experimental work, however, points must be located more precisely in space—a coordinate system in three dimensions is necessary. Such a coordinate system, corresponding to the x, y, and z axes of geometry, is illustrated in Figure 1.3 along with the appropriate nomenclature. Thus, the *sagittal* plane bisects the brain along the anterior-posterior direction; planes parallel to the sagittal are generally referred to as *parasagittal*; a *horizontal* plane divides the brain into dorsal and ventral portions; a

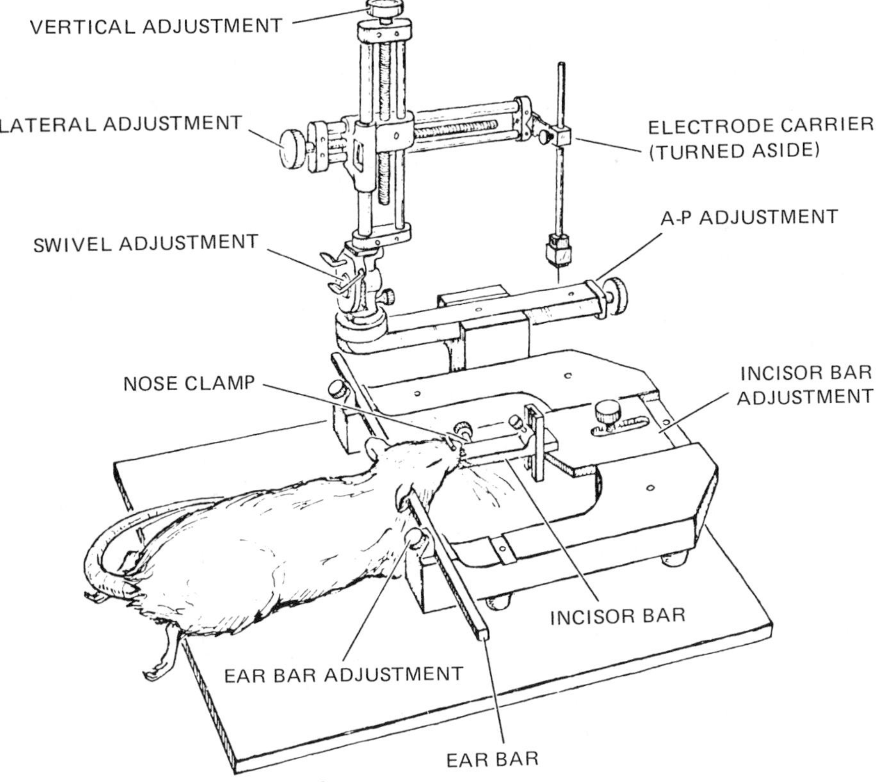

Figure 1.4. Rat in a stereotaxic instrument in preparation for implantation of electrodes.

coronal or *frontal* plane divides the brain into rostral and caudal portions. If these planes could be fixed in reference to the brain, all that would be necessary to locate any point within the brain would be to make measurements along such fixed planes. Figure 1.4 illustrates a device, a *stereotaxic instrument*, designed to accomplish this.

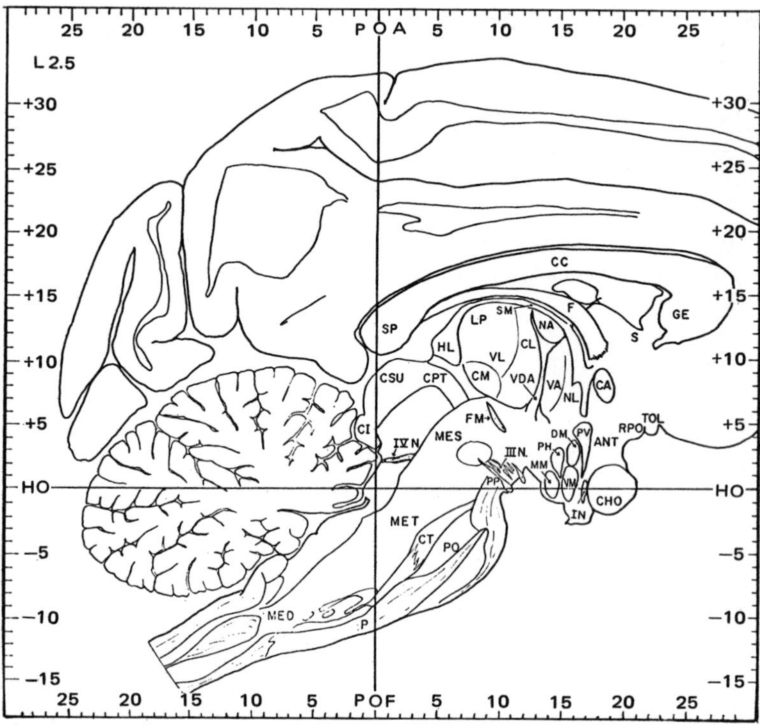

Figure 1.5. Diagram of a parasagittal section 2.5 mm lateral to the midline of the brain of a rhesus monkey. *ANT*, anterior hypothalamic area; *CA*, anterior commissure; *CC*, corpus callosum; *CHO*, optic chiasm; *CI*, inferior colliculus; *CL*, central lateral nucleus; *CM*, center median nucleus; *CPT*, posterior commissure; *CSU*, superior colliculus; *CT*, trapezoid body; *DM*, dorsomedial hypothalamic nucleus; *F*, fornix; *FM*, habenulopeduncular tract; *GE*, genu of the corpus callosum; *HL*, habenular nuclei; *LP*, lateral posterior nucleus; *MED*, medulla; *MES*, midbrain; *MET*, pons; *MM*, mammillary body; *NA*, anterior nucleus; *NL*, reticular nucleus; *P*, pyramid; *PH*, posterior hypothalamic area; *PO*, pons; *PP*, cerebral peduncle; *PV*, periventricular nucleus; *RPO*, preoptic area; *S*, septal region; *SM*, medullary stria; *SP*, splenum of the corpus callosum; *TOL*, lateral olfactory tract; *VA*, ventral anterior nucleus; *VDA*, mammillothalamic tract; *VL*, ventral lateral nucleus; *VM*, ventromedial nucleus; I *N*, optic nerve; III *N*, oculomotor nerve; IV *N*, trochlear nerve. [From Russell, G. V., Hypothalamic, preoptic and septal regions of the monkey. In D. E. Sheer (Ed.), *Electrical Stimulation of the Brain*. Austin: The University of Texas Press, 1961, pp. 232–250. Copyright 1961 by the University of Texas Press.]

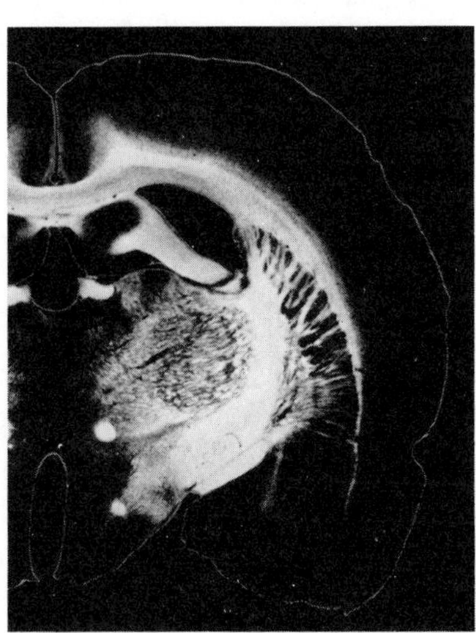

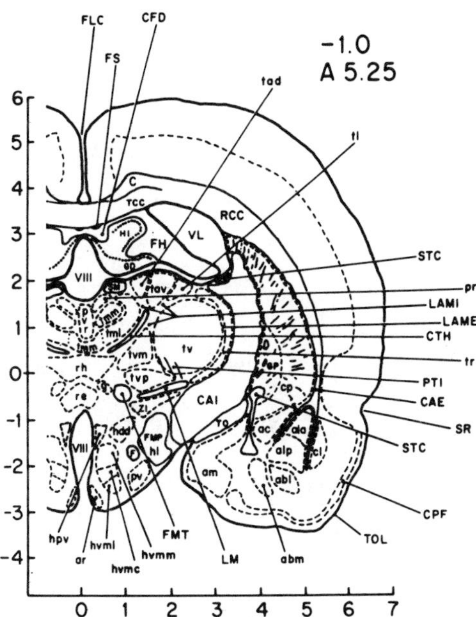

Figure 1.6. Coronal section of the rat brain. The section passes through the corpus callosum dorsally and the hypothalamus ventrally. (From Skinner, J. E. *Neurosciences: A Laboratory Manual.* Philadelphia: W. B. Saunders Company, 1971.)

Stereotaxic instruments come in a variety of designs and are suitable for use with a variety of animals, including humans. In essence, however, they are designed simply to hold the skull, and the enclosed brain, in some convenient fixed position so that each brain of that species is oriented in the same way, permitting the same procedures to be applied from animal to animal. Typically, this is accomplished by inserting support bars into the ear canals and clamping the upper jaw. Figure 1.5 is a diagram of a parasagittal section of the monkey brain with superimposed coordinates measuring anterior-posterior and dorsal-ventral directions.

By cutting across the brain, in a coronal plane, the internal structure of the brain at a given anterior-posterior level may be seen. Such a coronal plane, passing through the hypothalamus of the rat, is illustrated in Figure 1.6. It was taken from one of several brain *atlases* that are available. Here, one-half the figure is an enlarged photograph of the actual brain tissue, and the other half is a schematic indicating the structure delineated by anatomists. The hypothalamus is an anatomical area to which we shall have reference in connection with motivational processes, sleep, and emotion; it is located between −1 and −3 on the vertical scale and between 0 and 2 on the horizontal scale. In Chapter 13, "Cognitive Functioning and Integration," we shall be concerned with the corpus callosum; this is shown as TCC

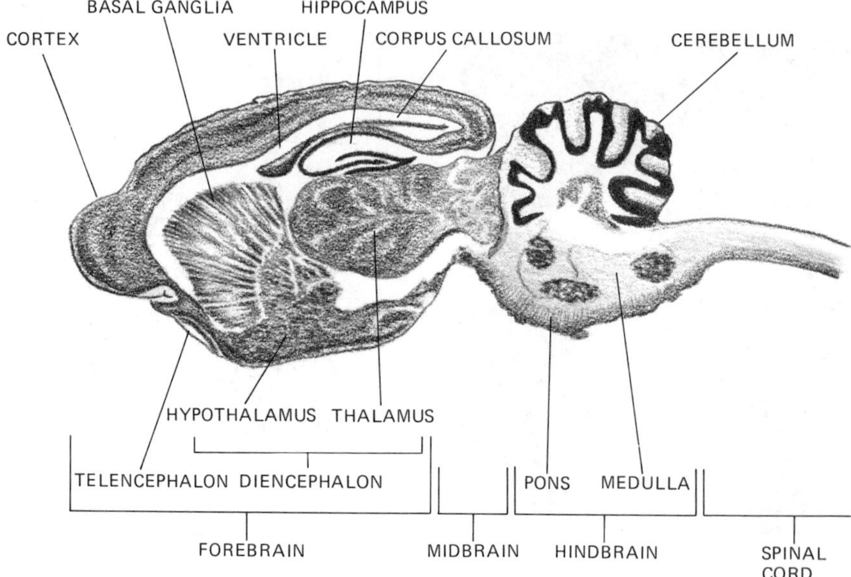

Figure 1.7. Drawing of a lateral view of the rat brain.

in the diagram and straddles the midline dorsally. The corpus callosum is a bundle of neural fibers connecting the two hemispheres of the brain. Note that these scales are in millimeters—some of these structures are quite small.

Adult laboratory animals like the rat and cat have brains that are quite uniform in size and topography, permitting the construction of atlases that can be used with all varieties of these animals. Dogs, on the other hand, have brains that vary greatly in size according to the size and weight of the breed; individual atlases for each breed are, therefore, necessary.

In summary, with the use of a holder and micrometer device that are part of the stereotaxic instrument, the coordinate system we have described enables the experimenter to reach any predesignated part of the brain with a suitable probe. We shall discuss such probes below, in connection with research techniques employed by physiological psychologists.

Divisions of the Brain

Anatomists divide the brain into major divisions—*hindbrain, midbrain* or *mesencephalon,* and *forebrain.* These, along with some distinguishing anatomic landmarks, are illustrated in Figure 1.7, an enlarged drawing of the rat brain. The hindbrain (*medulla* and *pons*) and the midbrain together are sometimes referred to as the *brainstem.*

The forebrain has two major subdivisions, the *diencephalon* and the *telencephalon.* The diencephalon is comprised of the *thalamus* and the *hypothalamus.* The thalamus resembles a pair of footballs joined together, side by side, at the midline of the brain; the area where they are joined is called the *massa intermedia.* Functionally, much of the thalamus is involved in the transmission of sensory information to the cortex from more peripheral locations through so-called *relay nuclei.* The hypothalamus is located ventral to the thalamus and, as we have indicated, is extremely important in motivational mechanisms.

The telencephalon is composed of three parts. Most prominent is the *neocortex,* that part of the brain visible from the sides and top. The *limbic system* and the *basal ganglia* are the other two parts. We will discuss the limbic system in connection with emotionality and motivational mechanisms. It is a complex of interrelated structures whose location in the brain's space is schematized in Figure 1.8. Generally, it occupies space over and around the diencephalon, with portions extending into the temporal lobe. It has extensive interconnections with the neocortex, hypothalamus, and the brainstem. The basal ganglia are a set of structures also located within the brain, rostral and lateral to the thalamus; they are prominent in the regulation of motor activities but have also assumed importance because

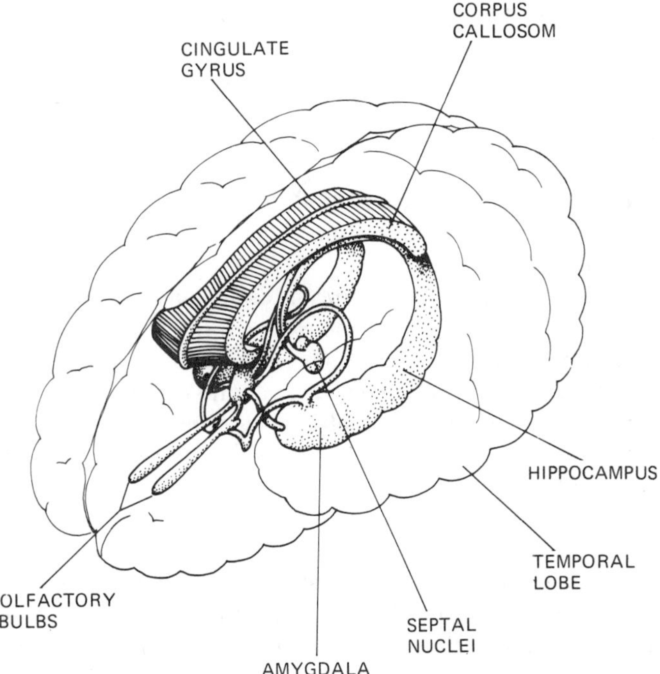

Figure 1.8. Diagram of the location of the limbic system within the human brain.

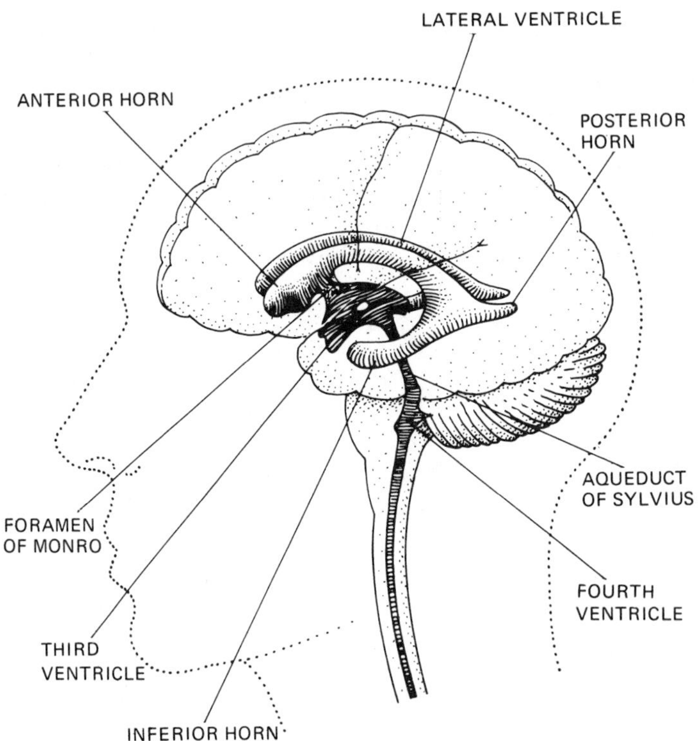

Figure 1.9. Schematic diagram of the location of the ventricular system within the brain.

they are affected by certain drugs used in the treatment of schizophrenia. These motor side effects seem to imply something about the chemistry of schizophrenia.

The brainstem will be important in discussions of several topics of interest to us as psychologists. It contains structures that feature prominently in discussions of sleep and arousal mechanisms, motivation and reinforcement, and emotion. Several important anatomic systems have origins in or pass through the brainstem. We shall discuss some of these systems shortly but first we shall complete our description of the gross structure of the CNS.

Ventricular System

The brain is not a solid mass of cells; rather, it contains a system of spaces or *ventricles* and their interconnections (*foramen*); these contain *cerebrospinal fluid*. Figure 1.9 schematizes this aqueduct system that presumably plays a part in the nutrition of the brain and spinal cord. In the developing infant, exececessive production of cerebrospinal fluid can result in enlargement of the ventricles and increased pressure on the brain and skull. This, in turn, causes enlargement and deformation of the head, a condition known as *hydrocephaly* and accompanied by severe mental retardation. If diagnosed early, it can be relieved by draining the excess fluid.

The ventricles appear as open spaces on coronal sections of the brain. In Figure 1.6 note one of the lateral ventricles (VL) about 3 mm above the horizontal plane and about 2.5 mm lateral to the midline. The third ventricle (VIII) is on the midline and, because of its shape in the rostral-caudal direction, we can see it twice—at 2 mm above and 2 mm below the horizontal plane.

The Spinal Cord

The brain forms one part of the CNS; the spinal cord forms the other. Figure 1.10 depicts the general appearance of the spinal cord—its exact configuration varies over the length of the cord. The central, H-shaped region contains the cell bodies of the neural elements forming the cord. The surrounding, homogeneous white area is really not homogeneous at all—it consists of many distinct neural tracts that ascend and descend in the cord. Basically, the cord is a transmission cable with internal connections, receiving and sending information between the periphery and the brain. Input to the cord comes via the nerves entering the dorsal portions (*dorsal roots*) of the cord; output leaves the cord over nerves exiting in the ventral portions of the cord (*ventral roots*). Note that the peripheral nerves are mixed—*afferent* (incoming, sensory) and *efferent* (outgoing, motor) branches divide just prior to their respective points of contact with the cord.

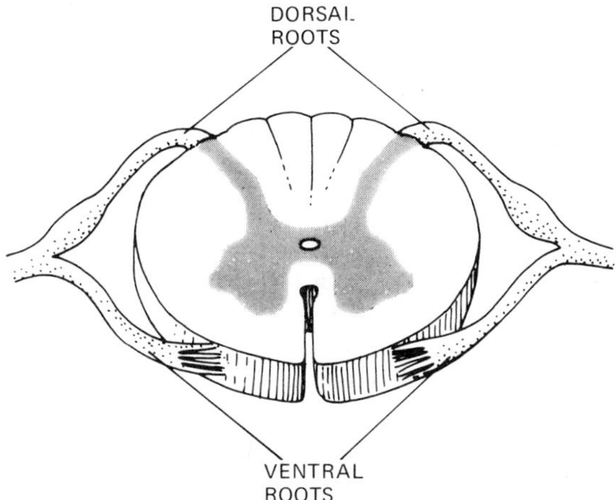

Figure 1.10. Schematic diagram of the general plan of the spinal cord.

The simplest afferent-efferent connections, in the form of spinal reflexes such as the knee jerk, occur in the cord. Input, from a tendon-tap, for instance, enters in the dorsal root, makes a connection, and exits through the ventral root, resulting in the muscular response. More complicated afferent-efferent connections, such as might be involved in instrumental learning, apparently require intervening activity by the brain. One issue, then, is can the spinal cord learn anything? Since the brain and cord are both composed of similar appearing neural elements, what is the intrinsic difference between them, i.e., what allows the brain to function in much more complex behavior? We shall touch on these questions in Chapter 12, dealing with physiological mechanisms in learning.

Brain Systems

We have just completed a brief survey of the gross structure of the CNS. However, another way of understanding the brain has to do with "systems"; that is, there are elements within the total structure that can be grouped in terms of their specific structure and function. A moment's reflection reminds us that there must be such systems involved, for example, in the reception of stimulus information from the environment or for the control of motor output. Actually, many such systems, often less obvious ones, have been identified. Frequently, their initial identification was based on anatomy; that is, certain structures are closely interconnected anatomically and those connections imply a functional unity. Not infrequently, the reverse has been the case—the discovery of functional relations between structures implied the existence of anatomic connections and these have only subsequently been discovered. And, finally, some systems have been discovered on the basis of their chemistry—similarity in chemical specification of certain neural elements suggests integration of their functioning.

We have mentioned the limbic system in passing. Its anatomic interconnections suggested a functional organization. Initially, damage to that system seemed to produce alterations in emotionality. Subsequent experimentation suggests that this may be too simple a view of the functions of the limbic system. We shall discuss some of these issues in Chapter 7.

Traveling through the central core of the brainstem is a meshwork of fine neural fibers that forms another prominent system, the *reticular system* (see Figure 5.1). Initially, the attention of psychologists was drawn to the reticular system because of experiments indicating its functional role in the processes of sleep and arousal. Later experiments suggested a role in perception. Initially, the system was conceived to be relatively homogenous in both structure and function; later research has indicated that the reticular system contains structurally and functionally differentiable mechanisms. In Chapters 5 and 6, which deal with attention and perception, and sleep and arousal, respectively, we shall discuss these aspects of reticular functioning.

Recently, it has become possible to identify the chemical transmitters operating in different neural systems. The existence of chemical differentiation between neural systems suggests functional differences. Theories implicating different chemical systems in schizophrenia and manic-depressive psychosis are being intensively investigated at the present time. Similar theories have been formulated in connection with hunger, thirst, sexual, and aggressive motivations. Again, we shall discuss such formulations in later chapters.

There are several points to be made in connection with these and other brain systems. First, of course, is to acknowledge their existence and that they provide fruitful hypotheses about brain functioning. In fact, it would be possible to organize the subject matter of this text around the functioning of these systems. However, befitting a psychology text, the organization adopted revolves around *behavioral* topics rather than anatomic or chemical systems. Second, as has already been implied, none of these systems can be characterized as having a single, psychological function—they operate over diverse behaviors and influence a variety of presumed psychological variables. And, finally, as we shall see, there is not always a straightforward

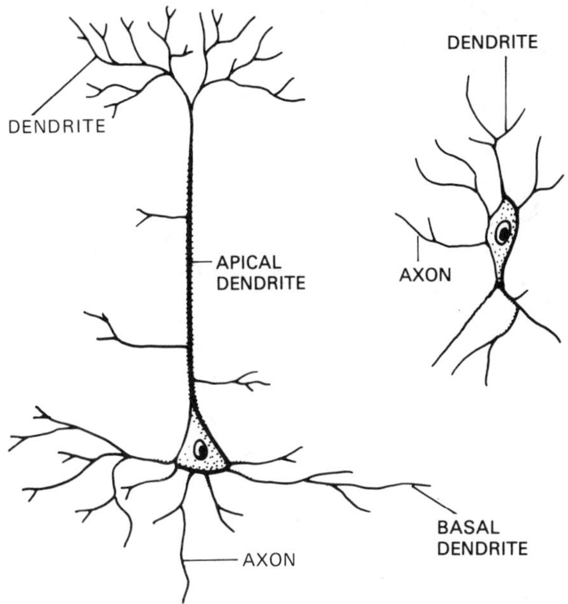

Figure 1.11. Drawings of two neurons.

relationship between psychological concepts like emotion and motivation and physiological concepts such as neural excitation and inhibition. Part of both the fun and the difficulty of physiological psychology is the necessity for clarifying the relationship between theoretical concepts from different disciplines.

Neural Tissue

We have looked at the gross structure of the brain and have at least been introduced to its functional organization. Here, we will begin to look at the units comprising the tissue of the nervous system. This tissue consists of individual *neurons*—cell bodies and their associated fibers. Neurons come in a variety of types and shapes. Figure 1.11 shows two examples. Each neuron has three parts: the *dendrites*, the cell body or *soma*, and the *axon*. The dendrites are specialized to receive extracellular influences, either from other cells or from the environment; the axons are specialized to transmit impulses from the neuron to other cells.

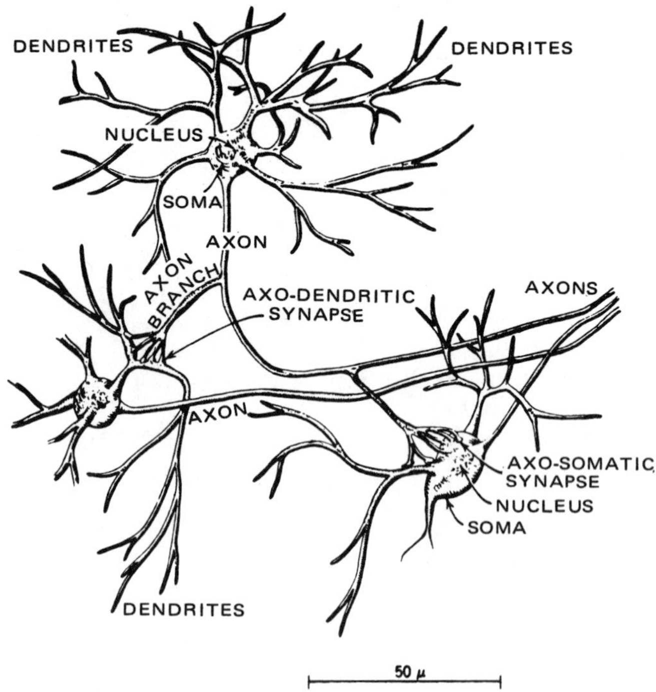

Figure 1.12. Diagrammatic representation of three neurons. (From Stevens, C. F. *Neurophysiology: A Primer.* N.Y.: John Wiley, 1966. Copyright © 1966, John Wiley & Sons. Reprinted by permission of John Wiley & Sons, Inc.)

Figure 1.12 is a schematic representation of how neurons may make contact with each other. In some instances, the contact is between the axons of one neuron and the dendrites of the other (axo-dendritic); in other instances, the contact is between the axon and the cell body or soma (axo-somatic). Axons and dendrites can be quite short (thousandths of an inch) but some axons are several feet long.

There are approximately 10 billion neurons in the CNS, but there are also some 5 to 10 times as many smaller *glial cells* surrounding them. Apparently, glial cells do not partake directly in neural conduction, although it is possible to record electrical potentials from them. Their function is not well understood, but they are presumed to take part in a variety of activities, including nutrition, disposal of dead tissue, and providing support for neural tissue. It has been suggested that they may have a direct role in the storage of information in the brain.

The Peripheral Nervous System

While the brain and spinal cord constitute the CNS, the nervous tissue lying outside of the CNS composes the *peripheral nervous system*.

There are differences in terminology between the two systems; for example, bundles of axons collected together are called *nerves* in the peripheral system; in the CNS they are referred to as *tracts*. Neuronal cell bodies occur in clusters; in the CNS such clusters are generally called *nuclei*, while they are called *ganglia* in the peripheral system. As we saw in Figure 1.10, peripheral nerves generally are mixed nerves in that they include both afferent and efferent fibers.

The peripheral nervous system has two divisions, the *somatic* and *autonomic*. The somatic system involves afferents from the sensory organs and efferent fibers innervating the skeletal muscles. We shall discuss the sensory portions of the somatic system in Chapter 4, where we will be concerned with how information from the environment is coded in the brain.

The *autonomic* system consists of ganglia and fibers innervating the internal organs, smooth muscles, and glands. These are shown with their innervations in Figure 1.13. The functioning of the autonomic nervous system in emotions will be our concern in Chapter 7; here we will briefly describe its organization.

The autonomic system is itself divided into two parts, the *sympathetic* and the *parasympathetic* systems. Generally, the two systems exert opposing influences on the same glands and smooth muscles. Sympathetic influence tends to cause activation and energy expenditure, while parasympathetic influence tends to be energy conserving. Figure 1.13 shows the organization of the sympathetic and parasympathetic connections to these peripheral organs. Parasympathetic innervation comes from either sacral spinal nerves

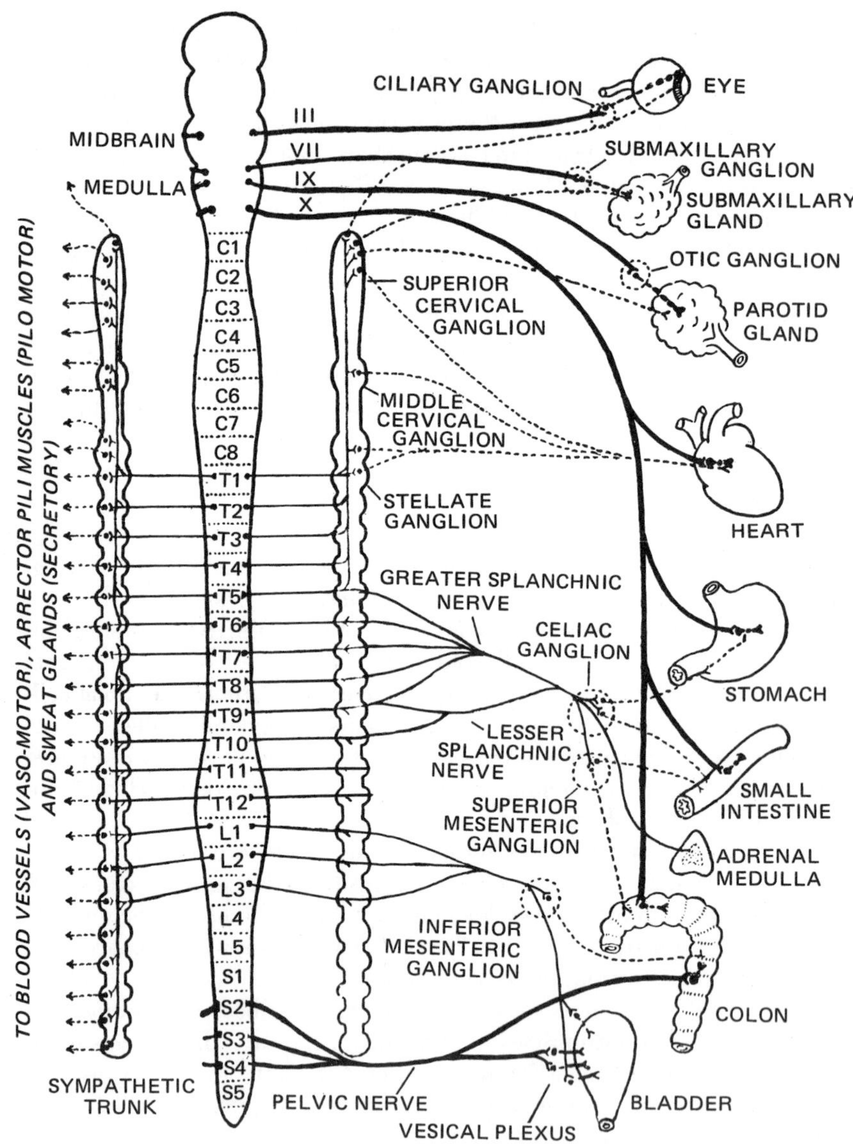

Figure 1.13. General principles of autonomic innervation. Sympathetic system in light lines; parasympathetic system in heavy lines. C = Cervical; T = Thoracic; L = Lumbar; S = Sacral. (From Copenhaver, W. M. and Johnson, D. D. *Bailey's Textbook of Histology*. Baltimore: Williams & Wilkins Co., 1953. © 1953 The Williams & Wilkins Co., Baltimore.)

or cranial (brainstem) nerves and is indicated by the heavy lines in the diagram. Sympathetic figures leave the spinal cord in the thoracic and lumbar regions only (lighter lines). Notice that sympathetic fibers always go first to a ganglion before reaching a target organ. The *sympathetic chain*, lying parallel to the thoracic and cervical spinal cord, is a chain of such ganglia. There are also some ganglia that exist separately from the chain, closer to the target organ; these ganglia are known as *plexuses.* In contrast to the sympathetic ganglionic arrangement, the parasympathetic ganglia are all located near or on the target organs.

NEURAL FUNCTIONING

To this point we have been mainly concerned with a structural description of some salient features of the nervous system. We will now turn to some considerations of actual neural functioning. It should be quite clear, however, that we will be dealing with extremely complex processes in only a summary fashion; to do more would go far beyond the needs and intent of the present text.

Spike Discharge

Neurons are cells. The cellular parts can be divided into a cell body, one or more dendrites, and an axon; but the peculiar characteristics of neural cells seem to derive from processes associated with the cellular membrane. Neural cells exist in a fluid environment. That environment contains chemical substances in the form of electrically charged particles or ions. The cell membrane is porous to certain of these ions, allowing them to pass in and out of the cell, but it restricts the passage of other ions. The result of this is that in the *resting state* of the neuron, ions with one type of electrical charge predominate outside the cell membrane, while other ions predominate inside the cells, and the membrane is said to be *polarized.* Current theory and experiments indicate an excess of sodium ions (positively charged) outside the membrane. Because of the difference in ionic distribution, there is, in the resting condition, a measurable electrical potential, the *resting potential*, across the membrane. This is a negative potential, typically in the range of 50 to 100 millivolts (a millivolt is one-thousandth of a volt). Negative means that the inside of the cell membrane is more negative than the outside. Neural activity involves changes in the membrane potential: If the resting potential becomes sufficiently less negative, it reaches a threshold and the membrane depolarizes—the neuron is said to "fire"; there is a breakdown in the resting potential, and sodium ions enter the cell and then leave again. These pro-

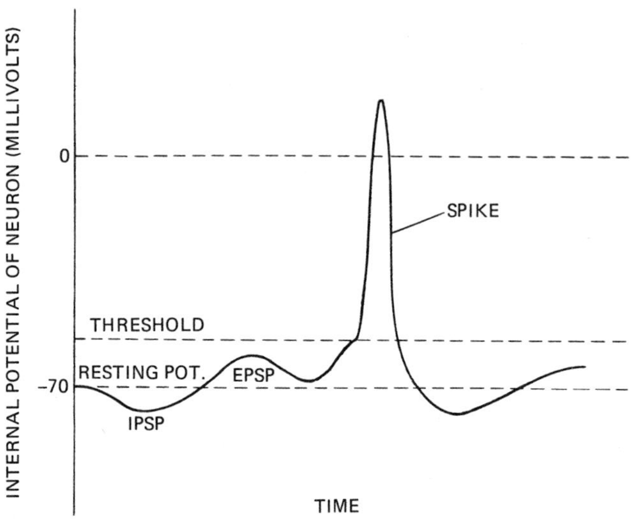

Figure 1.14. Schematic of potential changes in a neuron. EPSP (excitatory postsynaptic potential) and IPSP (inhibitory postsynaptic potential) are graded potentials. The spike potential is the only potential that is propagated along the axon.

cesses occur over a period of a millisecond (msec)—thousandth of a second—or less. It appears that some sort of "pump" restores the resting condition again by driving the sodium ions out of the cell.

The membrane activities that we have sketched produce an electrically recordable *spike* discharge of the neuron. Such a spike is shown in Figure 1.14. When such a spike occurs, it takes place at its maximum or not at all. This constitutes the so-called *all-or-none law* of neural discharge. The magnitude of potential change that can be recorded depends on the diameter of the neural fiber and the surrounding chemical conditions; with constant chemical conditions and a fiber of a given size, the spike is of a constant size. Since individual spike discharges are of a constant size, they cannot "code" or indicate the intensity of the stimulus that elicited them. But stimulus intensity is indicated in two ways: A more intense stimulus will discharge a single neural element more often and units with higher thresholds for discharge will be triggered by higher intensity stimuli, resulting in more units firing.

Spike discharges travel down the length of an axon because successive portions of the axon depolarize. This process is affected by the *myelin sheath*, a fatty covering that develops over all but very small diameter nerve axons in the vertebrate nervous system. This sheath is interrupted at intervals up to two millimeters apart by constrictions where the myelin is either very thin or absent (the *nodes of Ranvier*). The development of the myelin sheath may be quite protracted, with completion of the process occurring during postnatal development in some instances. The myelin cover seems to act as an insulator. Since this is the case, the depolarization process that we have just sketched takes place at a succession of nodes of Ranvier as the spike propagates along the axon. In effect, in a myelinated fiber, the spike "jumps" from node to node instead of traversing the intervening length of the fiber. The functional result of this is to speed up the conduction process in myelinated fibers—conduction velocity may be up to 20 times faster in such fibers, and on the order of 100 to 120 meters/sec in the fastest fibers. There is an inverse relationship between fiber diameter and conduction velocity—small diameter fibers conduct more slowly.

It is important to note also that, having discharged once, neurons go through a complex cycle during which they discharge with relatively more or less ease. A neuron is said to be *refractory* when it will not discharge again, to be relatively refractory when it will discharge again but only in response to greater stimulus energy, and to be in a supernormal condition if it will discharge more easily than in the resting condition.

Graded Potentials

The spike potential is only one type of electrical phenomenon recordable from neural tissue; a second class of electrical events is the *graded potential.* Unlike the spike discharge, which is all-or-none, graded potentials can be of varying size. They also differ from spikes in that they are a "local" phenomenon—they are not propagated along the axon like the spike, but are confined to a particular locus. Graded potentials induced from two different sources may also combine algebraically to produce total potentials of greater or lesser size.

Local graded potentials influence whether subsequent spike discharge will occur (Figure 1.14). For example, graded changes that make the membrane potential more negative are inhibitory (IPSP—inhibitory postsynaptic potential) i.e., they move the membrane potential further from the threshold for discharge; graded changes reducing the negativity of the membrane potential bring it closer to the threshold for discharge and are, therefore, excitatory (EPSP).

Graded potentials appear in two contexts: As the result of environmental stimulation in sensory receptors, they initiate the sensory transmission processes we will be concerned with in Chapter 4. They also appear in connection with the transmission of excitation between individual neurons—transmission across the synapse—which we will discuss next. In brief then, graded potentials may be excitatory or inhibitory and change the neuron's capability for producing a spike discharge.

Synaptic Transmission

Each neuron is a separate structural unit; where neurons impinge on each other, they are actually separated by a gap, the *synapse*. This gap is on the order of 100 *Angstroms* (one Angstrom $= 10^{-10}$ meter). How neural activity is transmitted across the synapse is one of the most important questions of neurophysiology. The evidence indicates that such transmission is generally chemically mediated. (Some nonmammalian synapses involve electrical transmission.) Transmitter substances are synthesized and stored in vesicles in the presynaptic nerve endings (Figure 1.15). The arrival of the neural impulse at these endings results in the release of transmitter substances into the synaptic space, where the transmitter reacts with a postsynaptic receptor. The result is an alteration in the resting condition of the postsynaptic membrane, which may be either excitatory or inhibitory. The number and location of synapses and the timing of synaptic events are important in determining the end result of such activity. In other words, if close to each other in space or time, the resulting graded potentials have an opportunity to combine, enhancing the effect that could be achieved by any single synapse.

Figure 1.16 illustrates the high density and distribution of synaptic endings. The delay introduced by chemical transmission across the synapse is on the order of .5 to 1.0 msec.

Chemical Transmitters. Most of what is known about synaptic transmitters has been derived from the study of the peripheral nervous system, but a variety of presumed transmitters has been located in the brain. It is

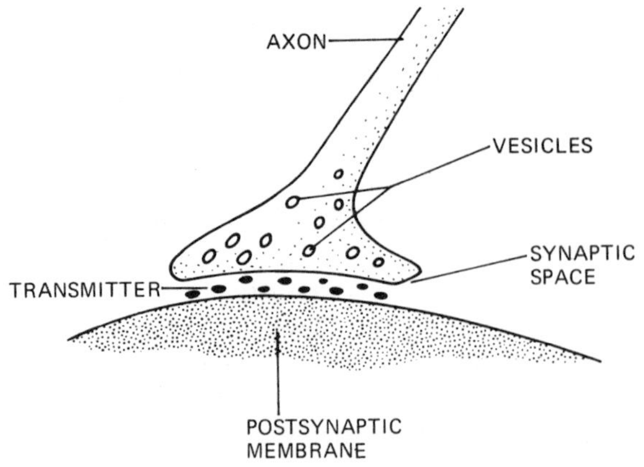

Figure 1.15. Synaptic transmission (greatly simplified).

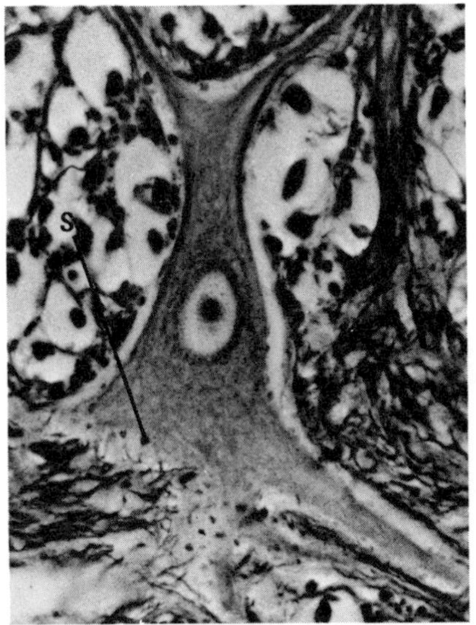

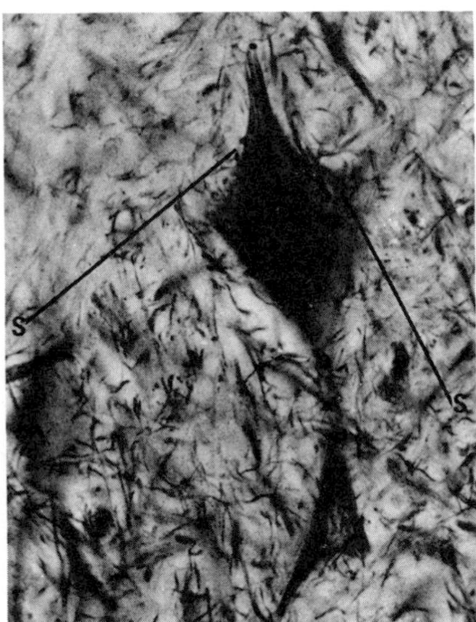

Figure 1.16. Photomicrographs of nerve cells stained with silver. That at the left is from medulla oblongata and shows synaptic endings, S, at the edge of the cell body and dendrites. The cell on the right, from the spinal cord, is cut through the edge so that the nucleus is not included. Synaptic endings, S, occur on its surface. The left-hand leader ends between two synaptic endings. (From Gardner, E. *Fundamentals of Neurology*. Philadelphia: W. B. Saunders Company, 1968.)

assumed that their central function is similar to their function in the peripheral nervous system. One of the problems in studying transmitter functions in the CNS is the dense packing of CNS neurons; on the other hand, the relative isolation of peripheral neurons allows specific input-output relations to be studied which can be approched only indirectly in the CNS.

Neural transmitters and substances that influence their functioning share the properties of organic compounds; i.e., chemical compounds of carbon. Hydrocarbons, for example, contain only carbon and hydrogen. Two hydrocarbon compounds both of which contain the same number of carbon and hydrogen atoms may have different functional properties because the structural arrangements of the carbon and hydrogen atoms within the molecule differ. A basic hydrocarbon structure is the benzene ring shown in Figure 1.17a. When oxygen is added to this structure, the result is the *catechol* structure shown in Figure 1.17b. The *catecholamines* are comprised of catechol attached to an amine group. Amines are derived from ammonia (NH_3) by replacing one of the hydrogens in ammonia by an organic group. Figure 1.18a shows the catecholamines of interest to us—*epinephrine*, *norepinephrine*, and *dopamine*; all are presumed to be synaptic transmitters.

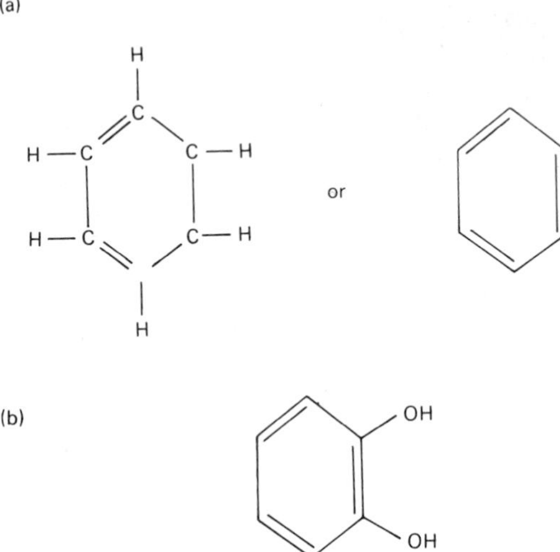

Figure 1.17. (a) Carbon and hydrogen arrangement in the benzene ring. This ring structure is symbolized at the right, omitting the hydrogen and carbon designations. (b) Addition of oxygen to the benzene ring produces the catechol structure.

Another modification, addition of nitrogen, results in the *indolamines*, the most important for us being *serotonin* (Figure 1.18b). Yet another amine of interest for its synaptic functioning is *acetylcholine* (Figure 1.18c).

Note the similarity of structure among the catecholamines. The diagram in Figure 1.19 indicates that these catecholamines are all metabolic products of a substance known as phenylalanine. We will also encounter phenylalanine, and another of its metabolic products, phenylpyruvic acid, in Chapter 2; they are involved in a genetic disorder whose behavioral consequence is mental retardation. Finally, we should note that these compounds do *not* constitute a comprehensive list of the possible neural transmitters: Several amino acids are likely substances with transmitter properties, among them gamma-aminobutyric acid (GABA) and glutamic acid.

Body Chemistry. The hormones, vitamins, and other chemical substances that occur naturally in the body and are necessary for the maintenance of life are called *essential metabolites*. "Each essential metabolite performs its special functions in living things by acting as a substrate for some special enzyme or receptor. These enzymes and receptors contain active centers which are parts of the molecule made so that they will combine in reversible fashion with the substrate and hold it in such a position as to activitate it. When so activited, it reacts with a new molecule or undergoes some decomposition within itself" (Wooley, 1962, p. 13).

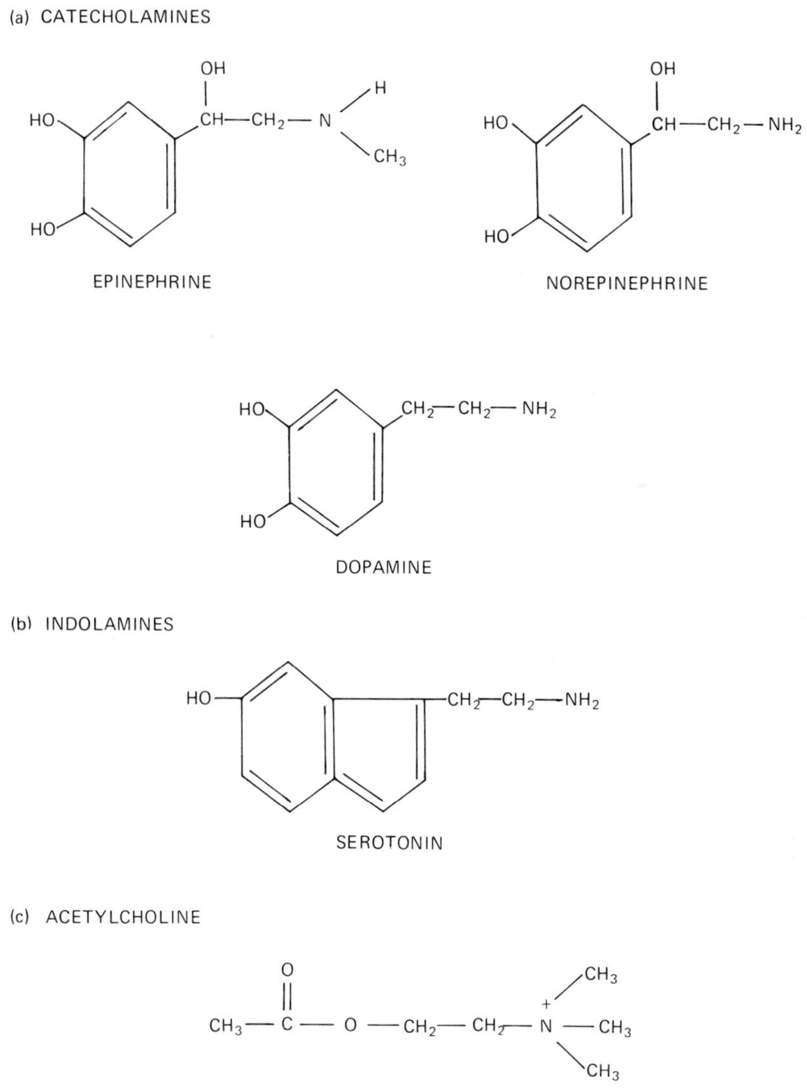
(a) CATECHOLAMINES
OH
HO
CH—CH2—N
H
CH3
HO
EPINEPHRINE
OH
HO
CH—CH2—NH2
HO
NOREPINEPHRINE
HO
CH2—CH2—NH2
HO
DOPAMINE
(b) INDOLAMINES
HO
CH2—CH2—NH2
SEROTONIN
(c) ACETYLCHOLINE
O
CH3—C—O—CH2—CH2—N—CH3
+
CH3
CH3

Figure 1.18. Chemical structure of some amines of interest for their action as neural transmitters.

An *anti*metabolite is a molecule shaped sufficiently like a metabolite so as to enable it to combine with the active center of the enzyme or receptor; the antimetabolite thereby excludes the metabolite from its normal functioning. The result of this exclusion is a deficiency of the essential metabolite. The analogy appropriate here is that of a lock and key: If a damaged key

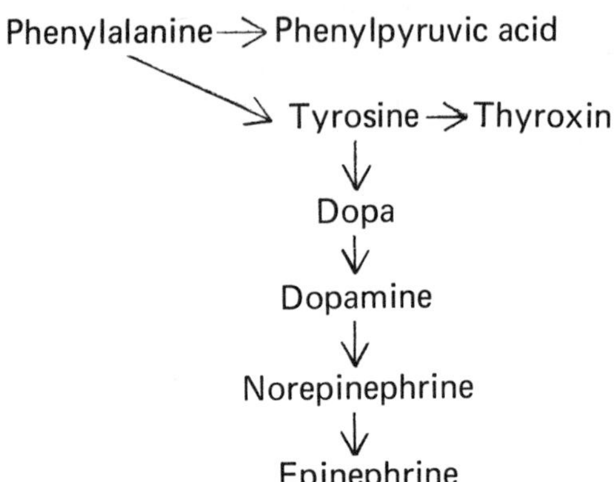

Figure 1.19. The amino acid phenylalanine is metabolized to three hormones—thyroxin (thyroid hormone), norepinephrine, and epinephrine—as well as phenylpyruvic acid.

(antimetabolite) is sufficiently similar to the normal one, the lock can open and no disruption of the process occurs; but with a damaged key the lock may require forcing—the metabolic process is slowed down with consequent disruption of the system. In fact, the damaged key may simply prevent the lock from opening at all.

Antimetabolities may either occur naturally or be man-made products of the chemistry laboratory. LSD (lysergic acid diethylamide) is one antimetabolite whose name may be familiar to you. It results in hallucinations and a mental state that has been likened to schizophrenia. It is also of interest to us because of its chemical structure, which has a partial resemblance to the structure of serotonin. It is known that LSD exerts an antimetabolite function in peripheral, smooth muscles; it is hypothesized that its hallucinogenic properties result from a similar central action. Thus, metabolites and antimetabolites compete with each other for sites of activity.

The outcome of metabolite-antimetabolite competition depends on the relative concentrations of the two substances, not their absolute levels. If an essential metabolite partakes in more than one bodily process, an antimetabolite can have varying effects, depending on the specific reaction observed; the substance might act like an antimetabolite in one reaction but might be just as effective as the metabolite itself in another reaction. In other words, the total body or total brain levels of a metabolite may not be nearly so important as the amount available at a specific brain site and whether the antimetabolite disrupts the process at that site. And, again, one process that antimetabolites can disrupt is neural transmission.

Transmission Systems. The basic apparatus of synaptic transmission consists of two neurons with the axon of one juxtaposed to the dendrites or soma of the other, separated by the synaptic space (Figure 1.15). To this must be added the chemical transmitter and the mechanisms for its production and release, the postsynaptic receptors, and the system designed to inactivate the transmitter.

Two synaptic transmitters, acetylcholine and norepinephrine, have been isolated and identified as such in the peripheral nervous system. To date, no presumed transmitter has been definitively proven to act in such a capacity within the CNS. However, the presumption is strong that some substances do function in that capacity. Synapses believed to employ acetylcholine are referred to as *cholinergic* and those apparently employing norepinephrine are called *adrenergic*. These designations reflect the fact that it is a class of agents, rather than a single one, that is capable of activating these synapses. It is also probable that some or all of the intermediaries involved in the production of these agents are also capable of functioning as transmitters. Many of these substances have been demonstrated to occur within the brain, which is at least the first step in demonstrating that they act as transmitters.

After crossing the synaptic space and influencing the postsynaptic receptor, the transmitter must be cleared from the system. Without this clearance, the synapse would be blocked from sending discrete "messages" across. This clearing is mainly accomplished by inactivating the transmitter with an enzyme. In the case of acetylcholine, the enzyme is *acetylcholine esterase*. Finally, there are certain drugs that block either synthesis or utilization of the transmitters or of the inactivating enzymes. As we shall see in subsequent chapters, the employment of drugs as antimetabolities allows for manipulation of these presumed synaptic events in an effort to change behavior.

THE ENDOCRINE SYSTEM

Working in conjunction with the nervous system to control bodily functions and behavior is the endocrine system. *Endocrine*, or ductless, glands secrete hormones directly into the blood stream.[3] The two systems may cooperate in that neural changes produce rapid effects while endocrine changes sustain long-term effects. The neural transmitters are hormones chemically. The ductless glands include the *hypophysis* (or *pituitary*), *pineal*, *thyroid*, *parathyroids*, *adrenals*, and the *ovaries* and *testes*. Figure 1.20 shows their general locations.

Because of its central role in the endocrine system, the hypophysis is sometimes termed the "master" gland. It is located at the base of the brain, just ventral to the hypothalamus, to which it is structurally and functionally attached (Figure 1.21). Functionally, it consists of two parts, the anterior

[3]In contrast, *exocrine* or duct glands produce secretions into special ducts that do not enter the blood stream. They include sweat, tear, salivary, and pancreas glands.

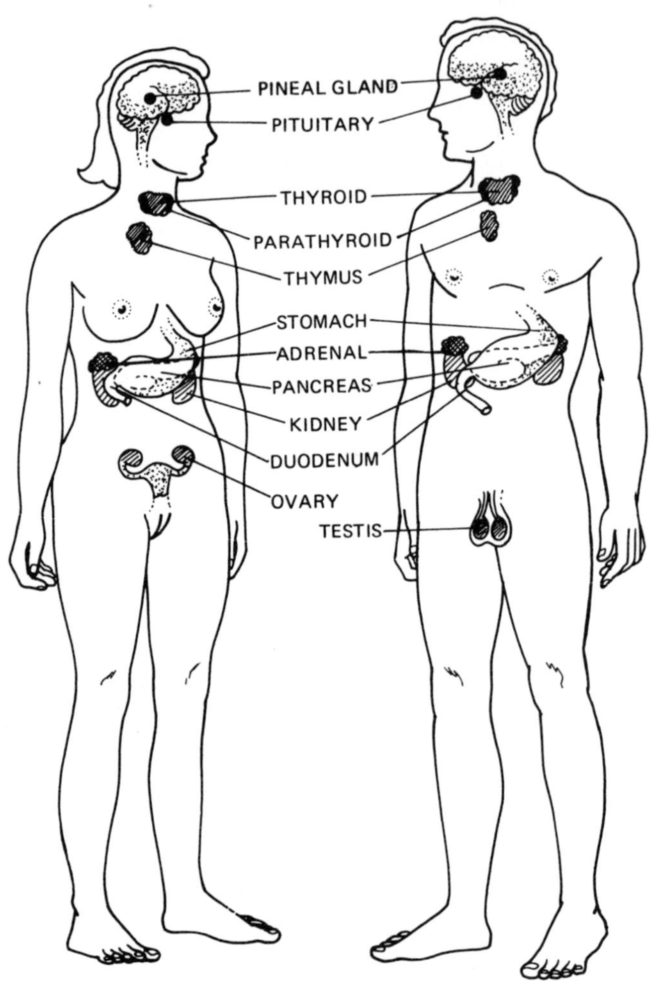

Figure 1.20. Location of the major glands of the body.

adenohypophysis and the posterior *neurohypophysis*. While both parts secrete hormones, the anterior part secretes them in response to hormones circulating in the blood (it does not have any direct neural connections). The neurohypophysis receives innervation from the hypothalamus along the *infundibular* stalk, attaching the pituitary to the hypothalamus.

The anterior pituitary secretes a number of *trophic* hormones—hormones that promote the activity of other endocrine glands. Among these are a number of gonadotrophic hormones, particularly those which stimulate the function of the ovaries. In addition, trophic hormones include one that plays a role in regulation of body growth, one that functions in metabolism through the thyroid and thymus glands, and another, ACTH, which acts on the adrenal gland. ACTH (adrenocorticotrophic hormone) will be of concern when we consider the topic of emotions (Chapter 7).

The neurohypophysis secretes hormones that have effects on the blood pressure (raising it by constricting the vessels), effects on other smooth muscles, and an *antidiuretic* effect of inhibiting the excretion of urine through the kidneys. We will be particularly concerned with this mechanism when we consider water regulation and thirst (Chapter 10).

Of the other endocrine glands, we will single out only the adrenal for specific discussion here. The adrenal gland consists of two parts, a cortex and medulla. The adrenal cortex plays a vital role in metabolism, being active in maintaining the sodium-potassium balance and carbohydrate utilization. The adrenal medulla secretes epinephrine and norepinephrine, the same substances encountered in neural transmission. As hormones from the adrenal, they act on the cardiovascular system to increase blood pressure. Epinephrine does this by increasing cardiac output, while norepinephrine does it by producing a general constriction of the blood vessels. Both hormones also raise blood sugar levels.

EXPERIMENTAL TECHNIQUES

Our discussion thus far has already revealed some of the techniques that the physiological psychologist employs in making his experimental observations. In essence, the various experimental procedures applied to the brain can all be conceived as falling into one or another of four types—lesions, stimulation (either electrical or with drugs), electrical recording, and chemical analysis. We will discuss each of these in turn.

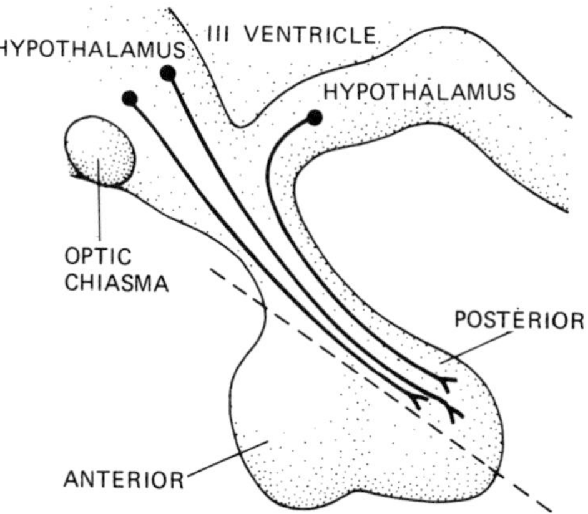

Figure 1.21. General arrangement of the hypophysis or pituitary gland.

Experimenters and their tools are not infallible; experimenters make measuring errors, electrodes bend, and not all animals conform exactly to the atlas for that species. These and other possible sources of error make it mandatory that the intended loci of experimental manipulations be checked against their actual placements. We will, therefore, begin by briefly indicating some commonly used anatomic controls.

Anatomic Controls

We have already sketched the stereotaxic method for reaching locations within the depths of the brain. Once the experimental observations have been made, the animals are sacrificed and the brains are prepared for examination. Such preparation will ordinarily require that the brains be "fixed" or preserved to retain their structure, and frozen or embedded in a medium to make them amenable to the cutting of very thin sections of tissue. Because fixed brains are generally colorless, they are usually treated in such a manner as to differentially stain the tissue. Certain chemical treatments selectively stain different aspects of the tissue, making the visualization of these features much easier. Thus, techniques have been developed to stain cell bodies only as against fibers, or neural cells as against glial cells. *Nissl* methods stain only cell bodies. *Weil* or *Weigert* methods are used to stain fibers. The latter methods are common, but anatomists have developed a large variety of other methods, each of which is designed to deal with special problems. Thus, for instance, *Nauta's* method is designed to stain degenerating neural terminals.

It is of interest to note, however, that the photograph of Figure 1.6 is actually of an unstained section. It has been found that such a section can be placed in a photographic enlarger and printed as if it were a photographic negative; the resulting picture shows fibers in good detail, and this, then, is a good rapid means of locating electrode placements.

Lesions

A psychologist using experimental *lesions*, or intentional damage designed to inactivate some neural tissue, basically is asking what happens to the behavior of interest when a portion of the brain is removed or inactivated. Further, he is also concerned with *interpreting* the "what happens" in theoretical terms. Thus, he might ask whether the changes in behavior can be conceptualized as a "sensory" or a "motivational" change, for instance. As we shall see, such interpretations may not always follow in a straightforward manner.

Lesions may be produced with a variety of techniques. One determiner of technique is the accessibility of the site of the intended lesion. If the site is on the surface of the brain or spinal cord, simply exposing the surface may permit ready access, and the operation can be carried out under the operator's visual control. Cortical tissue can be removed in this manner with a simple suction system. Fiber tracts may be cut with a knife or spatula, or even by pulling through a strong thread. In less readily accessible locations, the sterotaxic procedure can be employed to reach the desired location and direct current (DC) passed through the tissue to be destroyed; such a lesion is termed *electrolytic.* Very-high-frequency alternating currents can also be used to produce lesions because of the heat that is generated in the brain tissue. In a more sophisticated approach, several X-ray or other radiation sources, or ultrasonic sound waves, may be brought to a common focus. Individually, each source is subthreshold for producing damage, but where they are brought to a common focus they produce damage. Such techniques have the advantage of not leaving a track of damaged tissue along the path needed to reach the lesion site; they do, however, require extensive and expensive equipment. Finally, lesions may be produced through the use of chemicals which destroy the tissue. Each of these techniques has problems associated with controlling the extent of the lesion; obviously, it is hoped to keep the lesion confined to the desired location. This, then, provides additional reason for actually verifying the extent of the lesion after the experimental observations have been made.

The techniques described above produce permanent damage; several methods have also been developed for producing reversible lesions. This may be accomplished through the use of chemicals that are subsequently dissipated. Reversible cooling of neural tissue will also temporarily deactivate the tissue. But measures such as these are less precisely controlled in that their spatial extent can only be calculated rather than verfied directly.

Lesion experiments must also contend with another set of issues—the age of the animal when the lesion is made and the length of the recovery period. For instance, lesions of the sensory cortex in adult animals result in the loss of some discriminative abilities; the same lesions in infant animals may not result in such losses when these animals mature. Similarly, effects that are believed to be produced by lesions have sometimes been found to change if the animals are given a sufficiently long recovery period. How to interpret these changes is a difficult problem. In some instances they may represent recovery from debilitation, or surgical shock, but they may also represent some more profound "reorganization" of the CNS in the remaining neural tissue. Obviously, the placement of a lesion tells something about the functioning of the lesioned area, but it also reveals something about the functioning of the *remaining* tissue.

STIMULATION

In contrast to lesion methods, which are designed to inactivate neural tissue, the various stimulation techniques are designed to activate the tissue. Such "activation" can result in either excitatory or inhibitory effects. A gross

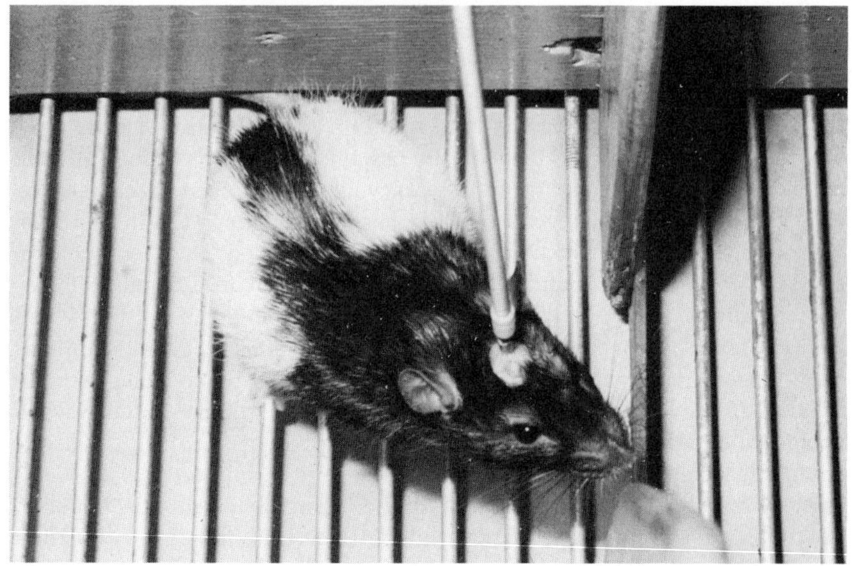

Figure 1.22. Rat with chronically implanted brain electrodes for stimulation and/or recording. (Courtesy of Dr. Robert Stutz)

example of such opposite effects is that, depending on the locus, electrical stimulation may be used either to put an animal to sleep or to awaken it. Stimulation can be accomplished either electrically or chemically. Electrical stimulation is convenient, rapid, and relatively simple to apply. Chemical stimulation, on the other hand, may indicate something about the synaptic transmitters involved.

Electrical stimulation is typically accomplished through metal wires that are insulated except at the tips and lowered into the brain stereotaxically. Unlike the currents employed in making lesions, stimulating currents are typically of low or medium frequencies; 60-cycle alternating current or brief (1 to 2 msec) square-wave pulses at around 100 pulses/sec are commonly used; they frequently are applied in bursts. Stimulation currents generally range from 10 to about 200 microamperes (μ amps = millionths of an ampere).

In addition to injecting drugs into the blood stream, *chemical stimulation* can be introduced directly into the brain itself through stereotaxically placed tubes or *cannulae*. In a common technique, crystalline chemicals are tamped into a tube that is then introduced into the brain by sliding it into such a cannula. The depth of penetration is controlled by cutting the tubes to the appropriate length beforehand. Cannulae can be used to bring chemicals into direct contact with neural tissue or to introduce the chemicals into the ventricular system from which they may then diffuse.

In this regard, it might also be noted that many substances do not reach the brain when injected—there is a so-called *blood-brain barrier*. Apparently the structural properties of such substances prevent their penetration of the small blood vessels of the brain. Normally, such a barrier must serve a protective function; for experimental work, it can prove troublesome. However, it is often possible to circumvent the barrier by injecting the metabolic precursor of the substance, i.e., its essential "building block" may pass the barrier.

With many of the stimulation techniques, and with the recording techniques that will be discussed shortly, it is often desirable to implant electrodes and cannulae in a permanent manner. This allows repeated access to the brain of the animal that has recovered from the operative procedures used to implant the devices.This can be accomplished by cementing or screwing parts of the implanted device to the skull of the animal. Electrical attachments can then be made by simply plugging the animal into the laboratory apparatus. Figure 1.22 depicts such a chronically prepared animal.[4] Such animals may provide useful experimental data over many months. The implants seem to cause the animal no disturbance at all.

Electrical Recording

Single Cell and Gross Recordings

As has been implied, considerable information about the functioning of the nervous system can be obtained from electrical recordings. Clinically, this is very well exemplified by the use of such recordings in the diagnosis of epilepsy and certain brain tumors.

The electrical activity that we are concerned with is of extremely low amplitude, typically in the microvolt range (millionths of a volt, μ v), so that in addition to electrodes for picking up the activity, amplification equipment is required. Furthermore, display equipment is needed to show changes over time. We shall give a brief, nontechnical introduction to each of these aspects of the recording problem.[5]

The electrical activity that we have so far considered is that of single neural cells or single "units." In order to record such activity, the diameter of the electrodes must approximate the area involved in the potential being

[4] For the specifics of actually preparing such animals and for some of the basic procedures for preparing brains for examination, the reader is referred to the extremely useful manual by J. E. Skinner (1971).

[5] The *Handbook of Psychophysiology* (Greenfield & Sternbach, 1972) contains presentations concerned with the more specific aspects of recording electrical activity in different central and peripheral systems.

recorded—if the electrode is too large the activity of the individual neural elements cannot be distinguished. Electrodes for such recordings are called *microelectrodes*. For intracellular recording, the electrodes must be capable of penetrating the cell with a minimum of damage; their tip diameters are usually less than 1 μ (micron = one millionth of a meter). For extracellular recording, the tips are usually no larger than 2 to 5μ. Microelectrodes may be either metal or glass pipettes filled with a conducting electrolyte. Their construction requires special care. Examples of single cell recordings appear in Figure 4.28 (p. 152).

More frequent is the use of *gross* electrical recordings—recordings from large populations of neurons rather than single cells. Instead of the spikes characteristic of single cell discharge, such recordings appear oscillatory and wavelike (Figure 1.23). The origins of such potentials are still obscure and the subject of some controversy; however, they generally seem to be the result of the summation of graded potentials from the millions of synapses in the vicinity of the electrodes. Such recordings can be obtained from a variety of electrode styles. Metal wires similar to those used for stimulating the brain may be used for implantation within the brain or such activity can be recorded from silver or gold discs pasted to the scalp. Scalp electrodes are the way in which the human electroencephalogram (EEG) is typically recorded and were employed to obtain Figure 1.23. The figure also indicates some generally standard locations for placing scalp electrodes.

In Figure 1.23, it will be noticed that to obtain a recording, electrodes from two locations on the head were employed. This is so because any electrical circuit ultimately describes a loop; electricity must be able to complete an entire circuit. Similarly, in recording from the brain there must be at least two electrodes involved. Ideally, one would like one of these electrodes to be at a zero electrical potential so that changes in the other electrode could be referred to it in an absolute sense. Practically speaking, it is not possible to attain this ideal. In *monopolar* recordings, one electrode is placed on some *relatively* neutral or "indifferent" location, such as the ear, while the other is placed on the scalp; with animals, the bone over the frontal sinus or some similar location is generally used in conjunction with an electrode implanted on or in brain tissue. In *bipolar* recordings, both electrodes are on or over active neural tissue. Usually they are closely spaced; with implanted depth electrodes they may be as little as .5 mm apart, while with EEG scalp leads they may be several centimeters apart. Bipolar stimulating and recording electrodes are employed in an effort to better localize the effects of interest.

With physiological amplifiers, in either monopolar or bipolar records, what is recorded is the voltage *difference* between electrodes. Thus, in either instance, unless special attempts are made to ascertain which electrode is the source, a voltage change *could* come from either electrode. In monopolar recordings with the ear as a reference, it is still possible, for

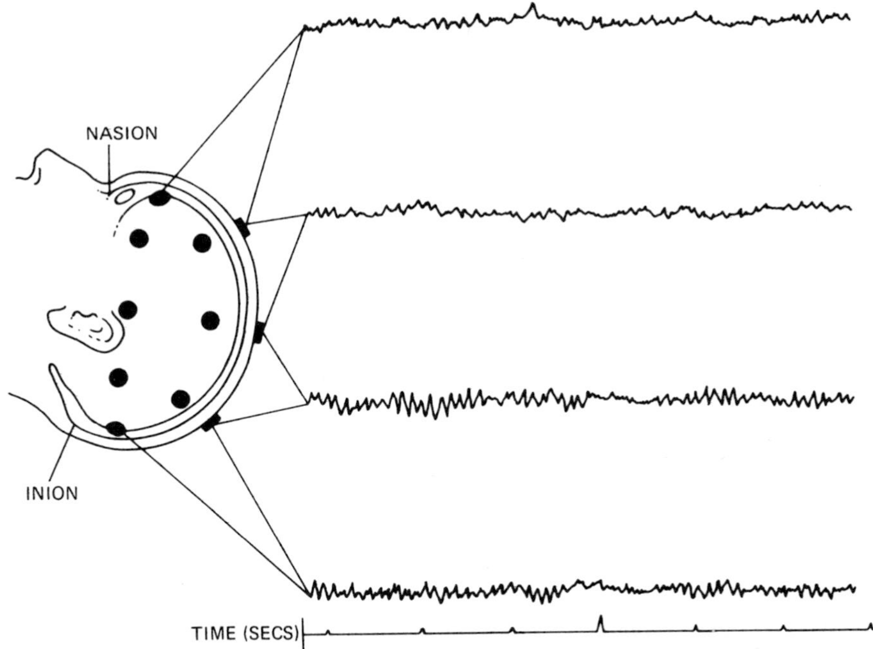

Figure 1.23. EEG from a human subject and scalp locations of the electrodes.

instance, to pick up high voltage signals from the temporal lobe in the reference electrode. Furthermore, since it is voltage differences which are detected, voltage changes must be specified in a relative manner. In other words, one electrode is said to be, for instance, negative with respect to another—both may actually be positive with respect to zero, but one less so than the other. Finally, the electrodes and amplifier must be connected in a specific, or at least known, fashion: Hooked up one way, relative negativity at an active electrode may cause an upward pen deflection of the recorder; hooked up in the opposite manner, negativity would be indicated by a downward pen deflection. The way the hookup is made is entirely arbitrary, but it must be specified. Generally, EEG convention is that negative is up (just the opposite of what is employed in physics), but this is not always followed for other types of recordings, and recordings should specify the convention.

Amplifiers and Display Equipment

Given electrodes suitable for picking up the potentials of interest, the next step is to amplify those potentials to the point where they are large enough to drive the display and storage equipment necessary for visualizing them. The amplification factor necessary here is generally more than 10,000. And the characteristics of the amplifiers need to be taken into account. We have spoken of spike discharges or oscillatory potentials. Spike discharges are typically very rapid events; oscillatory potentials may be quite slow. Typical recordings of the EEG will be concerned with potentials that recur with frequencies ranging from about 1 to 50 cycles per second. Some potentials of interest, however, change very slowly, if at all, and are generally known as DC (direct current), steady state potentials, or slowly changing potentials. Generally amplifiers differ in their ability to handle the entire range of frequencies that might be of interest—a given amplifier might be capable of recording one frequency range but not another. The point here is that knowledge of the characteristics of the amplifiers employed and the nature of the phenomena to be observed is necessary to make intelligent use of such equipment.

After appropriate amplification, the electrical signals require display. EEG recordings are typically displayed on a chart with the paper driven by a constant speed motor, and the ink record is produced by a pen on the arm of a galvanometer. The result is a permanent record of voltage changes over time. However, the necessity for pens imposes a limitation on the frequencies recordable; pens have inertia and this limits usage of even the finest pens to frequencies of less than 100 cycles/sec. The cathode-ray oscilloscope is an essentially inertialess instrument and, therefore, does not have this limitation. However, in order to obtain permanent records, the face of the tube must be photographed. Electrical activity can also be permanently stored on magnetic tape; FM tape is particularly useful because of the range of frequencies that can be handled. Tape has the added advantage of being compatible with data analysis via computer. In the earlier days of clinical EEG recording, data analysis was generally a matter of applying the eyeball to the recording and looking for distinctive or characteristic features. Today the use of sophisticated computer analysis enables much more refined handling of electrical data.

Spontaneous and Evoked Potentials

The electrical activity of the CNS is generally characterized as either "spontaneous" or "evoked." Spontaneous activity is that which is recorded in the absence of any known environmental stimulus. As we shall see, the CNS is constantly active even in the most quiescent of behavioral conditions—such activity is a fundamental characteristic of living neural tissue. The EEG provides an example of such spontaneous activity. Evoked activity, on the other hand, can be directly attributed to the presence of an environmental stimulus; it is a response to that stimulus. Tracing such activity through the nervous system has, for instance, been of fundamental importance in tracing sensory pathways through the CNS. Though the use of evoked responses has traditionally been a tool of the neurophysiologist, in recent years

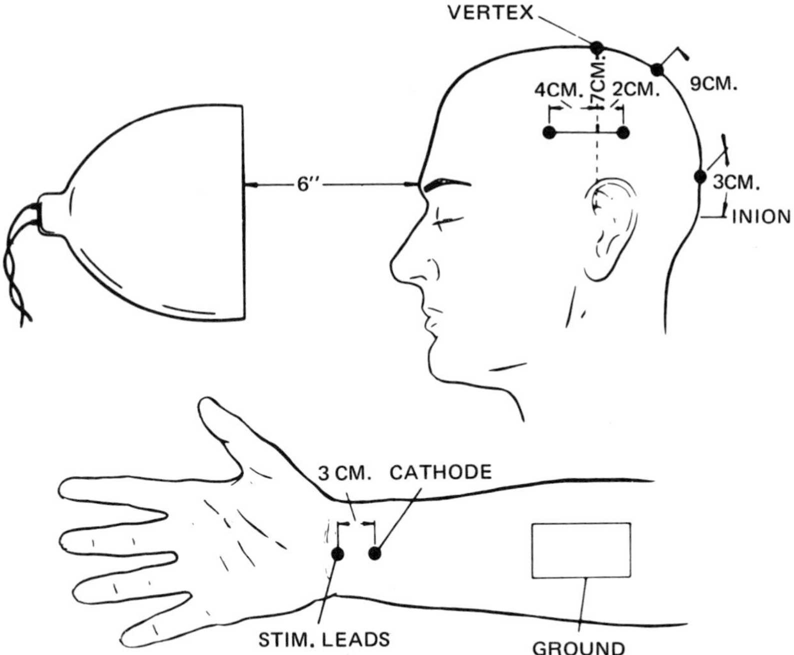

Figure 1.24. Diagram of arrangements for stimulating and recording light- and somatosensory-evoked responses in the human.

psychologists have employed them increasingly in their studies of learning and perception.

With electrodes placed on the sensory cortex of an animal, the recording of evoked responses to sensory stimuli presents little difficulty. The responses will show some variability but are relatively large and apparent against the background of spontaneous EEG. The situation becomes more complex when the comparable experiment is attempted on the intact human subject. Figure 1.24 diagrams the arrangements for stimulating and recording light- and somatosensory-evoked responses with scalp electrodes in the human. Somatosensory responses may be obtained by stimulating the median nerve in the wrist electrically and recording from over the somatosensory cortex; for photic stimulation, a bright strobe light is often used and the EEG is recorded from over the occipital lobe. With such maximal photic stimulation, the subject's eyelids are closed to avoid possible retinal damage (in studies of visual perception, tachistoscopic presentation of dimmer flashes is employed). Under these conditions, evoked responses are detected only with difficulty, if at all, in the EEG. The reason for this is the amplitude of the responses compared to that of the spontaneous EEG. With scalp electrodes, some components of the evoked response in humans average about 3 to 5 μ v—15 μ v is quite large—in contrast to a background of

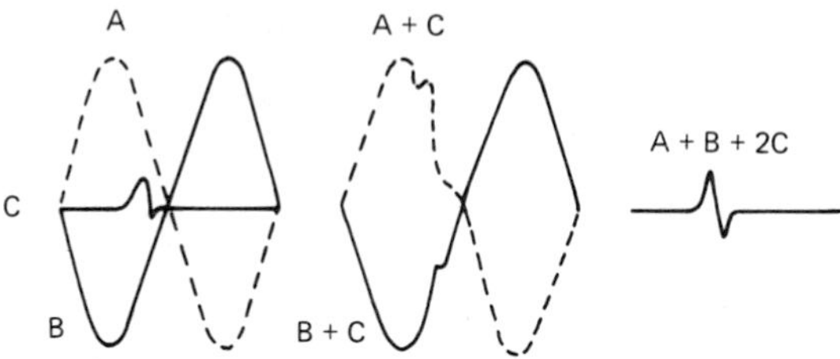

Figure 1.25. Idealized conception of the averaging process used to record evoked responses in human subjects.

spontaneous activity that may average 50 μ v or more. In short, the evoked responses are obscured by the "noise" of the spontaneous EEG. The spontaneous activity and the evoked responses each have properties, however, which make it possible to get around this situation with special processing of the raw EEG data.

Evoked responses have a characteristic latency—they are said to be "time-locked" to the occurrence of the stimulus. The spontaneous activity bears no such relationship to the stimulus; that is, the stimulus can occur at any phase of the spontaneous EEG. Furthermore, the spontaneous EEG is a cyclical process. Figure 1.25 conceptualizes how these properties may be employed to retrieve the evoked response from the "noise" of the spontaneous EEG. *A* and *B* are representative of two spontaneous EEG waves; *C* is representative of the evoked response that we are trying to record. When superimposed on *A* and *B*, *C* is distorted and difficult to detect. If *C* is evoked many times, however, and the activity following each stimulus is stored and added together, the spontaneous EEG will cancel itself out in the long run. This is idealized in the diagram by making *A* and *B* exactly out of phase with each other. By contrast, the evoked responses, because they have a consistent time and phase relationship to the stimulus, will tend to add up. In practice, this result is typically approximated with 50 to 100 presentations of the stimulus. It should be clear, though, that what is obtained is a summed or "average" evoked response—the sum and average differ only in that the latter is divided by *n*, the number of stimulus presentations. Thus, though we may speak of *the* evoked response under these recording conditions, we are in fact referring to a composite of many responses.

Prior to about 1960, no equipment was commercially available for carrying out this averaging process, and laboratories engaged in such recordings built their own apparatus. Today small, special digital computers as well as larger, general-purpose computers are employed. But it is instructive to look at how an earlier device was employed to carry out this processing.

An oscilloscope ordinarily displays voltage changes by varying the excursion of the trace in the vertical direction. However, such voltage changes can also be shown by varying the brightness of the trace—the brighter the beam, the higher the voltage. Thus, a straight line moving across the face of the scope indicates time, and the brightness of that line indicates voltage. Each sweep of the line can be triggered by the occurrence of a stimulus; successive sweeps can be slightly displaced, vertically, from the preceding ones. A photograph of the face of the scope would show a series of lines, varying in lightness and darkness. Figure 1.26 shows a Polaroid transparency

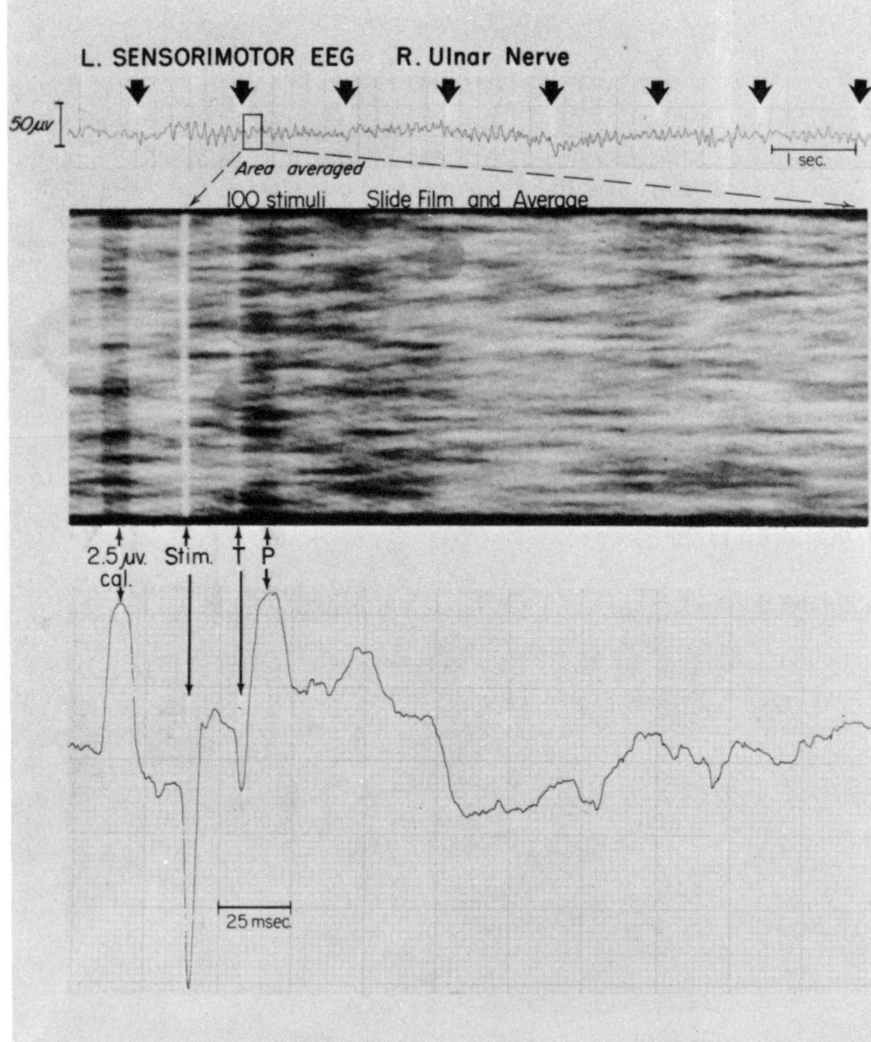

Figure 1.26. Photographic technique for recording average evoked responses. The top trace is a strip of EEG obtained during stimulation (arrows) of the ulnar nerve. The bottom trace is an optical readout of the average of 100 stimulations recorded on transparency film. See text for further explanation.

of such a process. The film has stored on it the results of 100 stimulations. The top trace is a strip of EEG recorded during the stimulation process; the arrows indicate the occurrence of stimuli. The EEG was used to vary the brightness of the trace; that is, the trace was filmed for the time span indicated by the small rectangle on the EEG tracing. The "addition" of the individual filmed traces was accomplished by passing a light beam through a slit which moves over the transparency from left to right; that is, the amount of light reaching a photocell through the film is proportional to the varying shades of exposure of the transparency. The output of the photocell is plotted below the film; the excursions of this plot, then, correspond to an integration of the voltage changes across all the original traces. *T* and *P* on this plot correspond to the trough and peak of the initial component of the complex response obtained. The film is instructive in that it shows quite graphically: (1) Only those features of an evoked response which are fairly consistent from trace to trace appear with any prominence in the final average response. (2) The initial components, especially *T*, have an extremely consistent latency, indicated by the sharp line across the film. (3) The relative amplitude of such responses is small—the average response is some 3 μ v in maximal excursion, while the EEG averages about 8 or 10 times this.

The recent development of convenient and reliable instrumentation for the recording of evoked responses from human subjects enables experimenters to carry out some types of research that were previously confined to animals. In the study of perception, for instance, this has added a whole new dimension to the kinds of research possible.

Chemical Analysis

In addition to the use of chemical stimulation techniques, it is also possible to assay the brain for its chemical composition. When analytic methods are applied to intact, functioning organisms, they are called *in vivo* methods; when analysis is carried out on isolated tissues that are maintained in solutions of nutrients and oxygen, they are termed *in vitro*. *In vitro* methods are in some sense artificial but they allow for strict control of conditions. Both approaches have been used in behaviorally relevant research. Such experiments generally take the form of looking for changes in chemical composition of the brain as a result of the application of some behavioral treatments. A number of changes have been reported as a result of a variety of environmental exposures and specific learning situations.

SUMMARY

Physiological psychology consists of a complex of subspecialties drawn from a broad range of biological and behavioral endeavors. This book attempts to introduce the reader to this vast area by presenting some selected examples of the research and problems encountered. In each of the subsequent chapters, we will consider one problem area. The topics chosen were selected primarily for their *behavioral* interest. It is hoped that they illustrate how a physiological approach can enhance this behavioral focus. No introductory chapter can substitute for training in the multitude of subspecialties encountered within physiological psychology. What we have presented here is, we hope, the basic minimal orientation and vocabulary necessary to go further.

It is hoped that this book accomplishes two purposes. The primary one is simply to convey to the average student of psychology what the physiological enterprise encompasses; a second purpose is to stimulate some portion of this larger group to go on to further study in this area.

REFERENCES

COPENHAVER, W. M., & JOHNSON, D. P. *Bailey's textbook of histology.* Baltimore: Williams and Wilkins, 1958.

GARDNER, E. *Fundamentals of neurology.* Philadelphia: W. B. Saunders, 1968.

GOTTFRIED, A. W. Intellectual consequences of perinatal anoxia. *Psychological Bulletin,* 1973, *88*, 231–242.

GREENFIELD, N. S., & STERNBACH, R. A. *Handbook of psychophysiology.* New York: Holt, Rinehart & Winston, 1972.

RUSSEL, G. V. Hypothalamic, preoptic, and septal regions of the monkey. In D. E. Sheer (ed.), *Electrical stimulation of the brain.* Austin, Texas: University of Texas Press, 1961, pp. 232–250.

SCHWARTZ, M. Physiological psychology: Or can a science over 95 afford to be "grubo"? *Psychological Bulletin,* 1967, *67*, 228–230.

SKINNER, B. F. The flight from the laboratory. In M. G. Marx (ed.), *Theories in contemporary psychology.* New York: Macmillan, 1963, pp. 323–338.

SKINNER, J. E. *Neuroscience: A laboratory manual.* Philadelphia: W. B. Saunders, 1971.

STEVENS, C. F. *Neurophysiology: A primer.* New York: Wiley, 1966.

WOOLEY, D. W. *The biochemical bases of psychoses, or the serotonin hypothesis about mental disease.* New York: Wiley, 1962.

2

Genetics and Behavior

Psychologists tend to stress that behavior is changeable and they emphasize the power of environmental manipulations for producing changes in behavior. These attitudes are a heritage from the early behaviorists (cf. Chaplin & Krawiec, 1968) and are illustrated in the extreme by Watson's (1930, p. 82) famous boast that if he had complete control over its environment, he could take any normal infant and make him into a specialist in any type of occupation whatsoever. These attitudes also illustrate a strong tendency to undervalue or ignore any biological contribution to, or limitation on, behavior. Genetic influences on behavior probably have been the most slighted and misunderstood of such biological variables. Physiological psychology starts with the assumption that behavior is a biological phenomenon. As such, it is incumbent on us to examine its basis in genetics.

It is not unusual to see a son who strongly resembles his father. On the other hand, many closely related individuals do not look alike. The science of *genetics* attempts to furnish an explanation for both the similarities and the differences among individuals. For the most part, genetics has been concerned with similarities and differences in physical characteristics. Psychologists are more interested in asking whether there is any truth to such commonplace ideas as "Johnny inherited his father's temper." This chapter will discuss some of the hereditary influences on behavior and the ways in which such influences are expressed.

BASIC MECHANISMS OF HEREDITY

Except for simple organisms which reproduce by fission or the splitting apart into two individuals, the development of a new individual begins with the merging of two cells. A male sperm and a female ovum combine to form a single new cell, the *zygote*. The zygote contains information that directs the further development of the cell into a complex, multicellular organism. These developmental blueprints are contained in the *chromosomes* of the new organism. Chromosomes are colored fibers that can be seen under the microscope in the zygote or any cell of the developed organism. They contain the chemical regulators which determine the growth and development of the new cell.

Chromosomes

Every species of living organism has a characteristic number of chromosomes; humans have 46, the laboratory rat 42. The total number of chromosomes is called the *diploid* complement of chromosomes. Chromosomes come in paired sets—23 such sets in humans. One member of each pair is supplied by the original male cell and one by the original female cell. Thus, each sex cell contains only half the diploid number of chromosomes, termed the *haploid* number, and corresponding chromosomes, or *homologues*, are obtained from each sex cell to form the diploid complement.

While each species has a typical chromosome complement that exhibits definite characteristics of size, shape, and number of chromosomes, deviation from these characteristics may occur (see Figure 2.1). *Polysomy* (the presence of more than two homologues for a given pair of chromosomes), *translocation* (the transfer of part of one chromosome to a nonhomologous chromosome), and *deletion* (or the loss of part of a chromosome) are some of the aberrations that may occur.

Genes

Genes are the units responsible for the mechanisms of heredity. While chromosomes can be directly observed, the presence of genes on the chromosomes is only inferred. That is, breeding experiments which produce offspring with varying observable traits or *phenotypes*—for example, eye

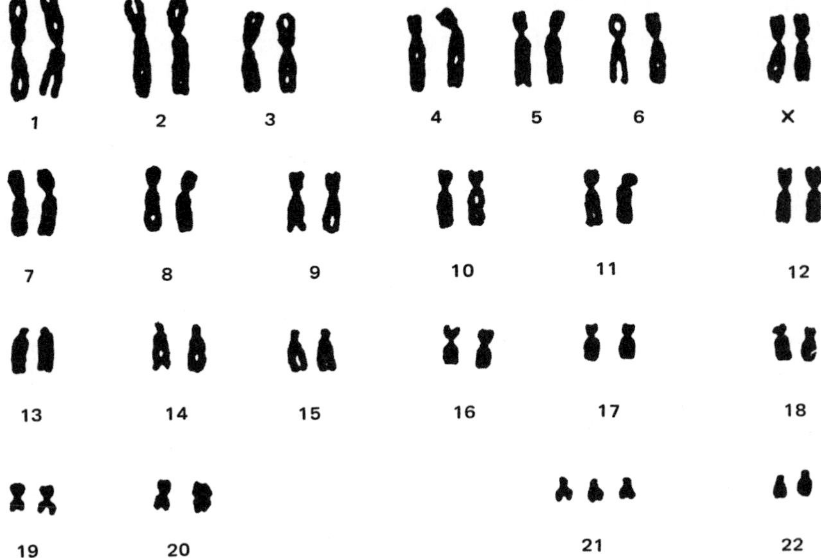

Figure 2.1. In the normal human there are 23 pairs of chromosomes. In the female subject whose chromosomes are illustrated here, there is an extra chromosome in the set numbered 21. The extra chromosome appears in one variety of mental deficiency, Down's syndrome, or mongolism. (From Ferguson-Smith, M. A. and Johnston, A. W. Chromosome abnormalities in man. *Annals of Internal Medicine*, 1960, 53, 361.)

color—lead to the inference that the parents must have had certain *genotypes*, or genetic constitutions. As we shall see, however, it is entirely possible for two individuals to appear the same although their genotypes differ.

Different forms of phenotype—for example, brown or blue eyes—are produced by different forms (*alleles*) of the responsibile genes. Each gene has a definite location on a specific chromosome. Since chromosomes come in pairs, at least two genes, one from each pair, will determine any particular phenotype. The individual is said to be *homozygous* for a gene location when the two genes are identical; when the genes are different, the individual is said to be *heterozygous*. In some instances—for example, eye color—where the individual is heterozygous, the effects of one of the genes predominate, while the effects of the other are hidden. An individual with one gene for brown eyes and one for blue eyes will have brown eyes; brown is said to be *dominant* and blue *recessive*. The dominance of one gene over another may not be absolute, however, and some effects of a recessive gene may show phenotypically.

If an individual homozygous for blue eyes marries one homozygous for brown eyes, all their children will have brown eyes, since brown is dominant. However, the children will carry the blue gene, and it will be transmittible to their offspring. If two heterozygous individuals have children, the possible eye colors of the offspring are illustrated in Figure 2.2. These offspring may be either brown- or blue-eyed, but they are more likely to be brown-eyed; that is, there are three ways for them to have brown eyes and only one way to have blue eyes. If one parent is heterozygotic and the other homozygotic blue-eyed, the chances of their children having blue eyes are altered—in this instance, chances are that half of them would have blue eyes.

Of course, it is only in the long run, with many children of heterozygous parents, that we can make statistical predictions as to the number of brown- and blue-eyed children. The mechanisms in Figure 2.2 operate in all cases in exactly the same way, but they illustrate only the *possible* combinations of genes; the *actual* outcome in any individual is the result of random combinations of genes.

Twins

In the production of the cells for sexual reproduction (the process is called *meiosis*), the total number of chromosomes is split in half, and the chromosomes are assorted to the sperm and ova *independently within pairs*. So the sex cells contributed by each human parent came from among 2^{23} chromosomal combinations. The chances of two children of the same parents having identical heredities (genotypes) is thus less than 1 in 70 trillion. The

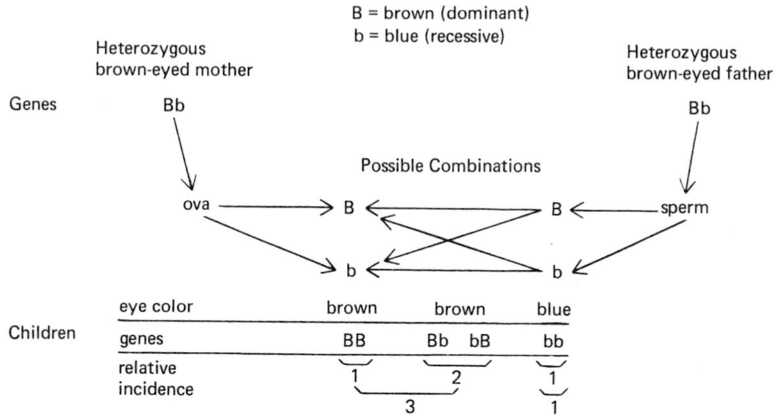

Figure 2.2. Possible combinations of genes and phenotypes in a simple two-allele situation starting with heterozygous parents. Gene for brown eye color (B) is dominant; gene for blue eye color (b) is recessive. Statistically, it would be expected that such parents would have brown- and blue-eyed children in a ratio of 3:1, but only one-fourth of all the children would be homozygous for brown eyes.

only exceptions to this are identical, or *monozygotic*, twins. They share identical genotypes because they originally derived from a single cell that subsequently split to form two individuals. Fraternal, or *dizygotic*, twins, on the other hand, are the result of nearly simultaneous fertilization of two ova; they are no more alike in genotype than siblings from separate pregnancies.

Sex-linked Characteristics

There is one exception to the rule that chromosomes come in homologous pairs. The sex of an individual is determined by two chromosomes; in the female these are homologous in the usual manner—females have two X chromosomes—but males have one X and a nonhomologous Y chromosome. In effect, then, males carry only one allele for genes on the sex chromosomes. Since males receive the X chromosome from the female parent, the result is that chracteristics carried on the X chromosome will always show phenotypically in male offspring, even if they are recessive in the mother. Characteristics of this sort are called *sex-linked*. Color-blindness is one such recessive sex-linked characteristic.

Polygenetic Inheritance

For simplicity, eye color was employed in discussing the mechanisms of heredity because it involves only a single gene pair. For most behavioral characteristics, however, this is likely to be an oversimplification. It is generally considered more probable that quantitative variations between individuals in psychological characteristics result from determination by several genes. This is called *polygenic* inheritance. Intellectual performance, for instance, is probably dependent on more than one pair of genes.

As an example of the complexity of polygenetic inheritance, suppose just three gene pairs were involved in the transmission of a particular characteristic. Many alternative genotypes would be possible: AABBCC,[1] AABBCc, aabbCC, aabbcc are only a few examples of the possibilities. The alternative genotypes would show quantitative variation in the appearance of the phenotype.

Another important point should be raised in this connection. Two individuals might show quantitatively equivalent phenotypes—say, in rats, equal brightness in solving a maze—even though their genotypes might be different. Quantitatively equivalent behaviors can be produced by different mechanisms and the genotypical differences could represent meaningful psychological variables, such as perceptual differences or motivational differences (McClearn, 1967).

[1]Capital and lower case letters represent the respective alleles.

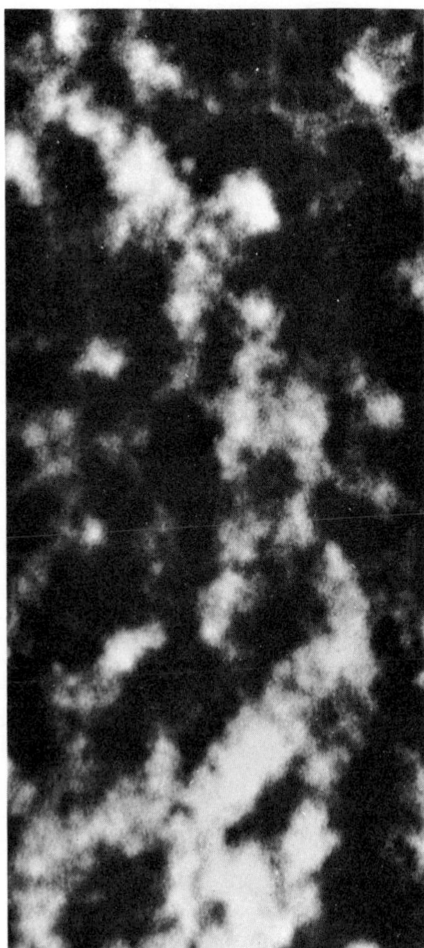

Figure 2.3. Photomicrograph of part of a DNA molecule from a pea plant (magnification about 4,000,000 times). This picture was generously provided by Dr. Jack Griffith. With it, the first visual confirmation was obtained of the hypothesis that the DNA molecule is shaped like a twisted ladder (see Figure 2.4).

Statistical Predictions

The basic mechanisms that we have just illustrated were worked out by Gregor Mendel over a hundred years ago by crossbreeding strains of garden peas. Four major points deserve emphasis: (1) Genetic information is contained in units or "packets"; (2) these individual packets or genes occur in pairs which are separable and independently distributed to different offspring; (3) the offspring get a random assortment of alleles from each parent; (4) when two phenotypes are controlled by genes on different, nonhomologous chromosomes, the inheritance of each of the two phenotypes is independent of the other. These facts enable the geneticist to employ the laws of probability to make statistical predictions about the distribution of phenotypes among offspring.

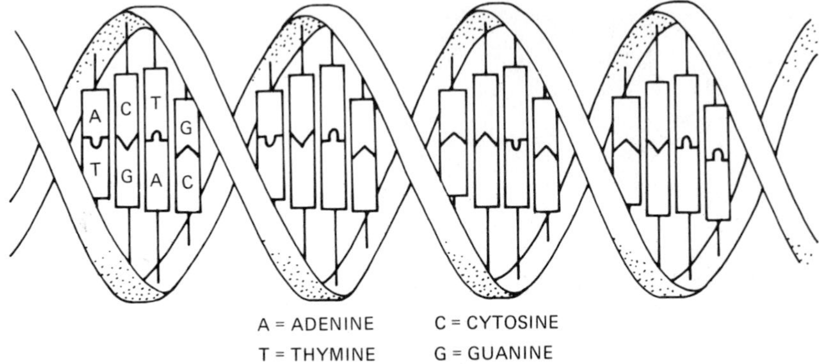

Figure 2.4. Diagrammatic model of the DNA molecule. Note that adenine and thymine link in two orders and that cytosine and guanine also link in two orders. The result is a four-letter code that allows DNA to replicate itself or to transcribe a message to RNA molecules.

BIOCHEMISTRY OF GENE ACTION

Some recent developments are leading to an understanding of the ways in which genetic action occurs. The present summary is intended to convey only the highlights (see, for example, Caspari, 1967).

Genes are constituted of deoxyribonucleic acid (DNA). The structure of the DNA molecule is shaped like a twisted rope ladder (see Figure 2.3). The long strands of the ladder consist of a regular alternation of sugars and phosphates. The rungs of the ladder consist of four organic nitrogen-containing bases: adenine, guanine, cytosine, and thymine. Because of their structure, these bases combine only in specific combinations: adenine and thymine form one combination, and cytosine and guanine another. The result is diagrammed in Figure 2.4.

This arrangement accomplishes two functions: (1) It can replicate itself; the arrangement of the components on one half of the ladder strictly specifies the arrangement on the other half and, when the molecule separates into halves, each serves as the template for the synthesis of its complement. (2) The arrangement of the bases over a set of rungs in the ladder constitutes a four-letter code in which the information is specified for the development of the phenotypic characteristics of the organism. This is carried out through the structure of protein molecules that will be synthesized. The synthesis of protein involves three varieties of ribonucleic acid (RNA)—transfer, ribosomal, and messenger RNA. In brief, such synthesis calls for the "transcription" of the genetic messages of the DNA to messenger RNA and "translation" from messenger RNA into protein. Transcription occurs in the nucleus of the cell. Messenger RNA then migrates to the cytoplasm and attaches itself to ribosomes where the proteins are synthesized. Proteins are involved in the basic biochemical processes in the body, particularly as enzymes catalyzing the reactions. In this way, the information contained in the genetic code is finally brought to actuality in bodily processes.

Genes may change from one form into another. Such changes, or *mutations*, may arise spontaneously, from unknown causes, or they may be induced. One way they may be induced is by exposure to ionizing radiation. Mutations appear to be changes in the genic material, DNA, and involve changes in the base sequences on the rungs of the DNA ladder. Such changes may result in the production of a protein that cannot carry out its enzymatic function; the reaction is, therefore, blocked. Where the product of the reaction is vital to the life of the organism, it will die unless the missing product is supplied from the environment—as, for example, when insulin must be given to diabetics. It should also be noted that where an enzymatic reaction is blocked, more than a simple lack of the end product of the reaction is likely to be manifested in the phenotype. Thus, there will probably be an accumulation of the substrate from which the product would normally be produced, and this residue may have consequences of importance, as we shall see on page 59 in the discussion of phenylketonuria.

GENETIC–ENVIRONMENTAL INTERACTION

In order to present the mechanisms of genetic transmission, we have been speaking in a shorthand manner. For instance, we have referred to a gene for blue eyes as though the characteristic of having blue eyes were heritable. But, of course, blue eyes are not inherited—genes are inherited. The *combined* action of genes and some environmental circumstances will produce an individual with blue eyes.

Dobzhansky (1962) gives the following examples that clearly emphasize this point. *Diabetes mellitus*, a genetically based disorder, is due to a failure of the pancreas to secrete enough insulin for normal utilization of blood sugars. Its complications can lead to death. When diabetes is diagnosed, a reduction in dietary sugars and starches and sometimes insulin injections are prescribed. The diabetes is thus "cured" by the manipulation of environmental factors. Neither dietary restrictions nor insulin injections alter or cure the "diabetic genes," but the organism responds to the changed environment with appropriate carbohydrate metabolism. Therefore, is diabetes a "genetic" or an "environmental" disease? Conversely, diseases such as malaria, syphilis, and influenza are induced by the action of environmental agents—a specific infectious agent causes the disease. In an environment free of the agent, the individual is free of the disease. However, such agents only infect certain genotypes—few animals other than humans contract these diseases. In addition, not all humans are equally susceptible to influenza or malaria, and it is probable that such variation in reactivity to these diseases is, in part at least, genetic.

Generally, then, genes determine the limits of phenotypical variation that *could* be seen and the specific environment to which those genes are exposed determines which of the possible phenotypes actually occurs. If, across a variety of environments, a specific genotype shows a relatively uniform phenotype, we would conclude that this phenotype is largely determined by genetic considerations; i.e., that it has a high *heritability*. Alternatively, if variations in the phenotype occurred across the variety of environments, we would seem to have a phenotype where heritability is low. Theoretically at least, these considerations suggest that it should be possible to use statistical procedures to estimate the proportions of total phenotypical variance attributable to genetic mechanisms, to environmental mechanisms, to their interaction and to any errors of measurement. In fact, much research has been devoted to this type of analysis. Thus, for instance, the heritability of IQ scores—the proportion of phenotypic variance attributable to genetic variation among individuals—has been estimated as ranging from .60 to .80. That is, IQ variation is estimated to depend largely on genetic variation.

But the adequacy of such estimates is completely dependent on the range of values of the data employed to make the estimates. This is illustrated in Figure 2.5. These curves are designed to show the phenotypic scores of two hypothetical genotypes over a range of environments to which they may be exposed. In one case, Genotype 1, there is relatively little

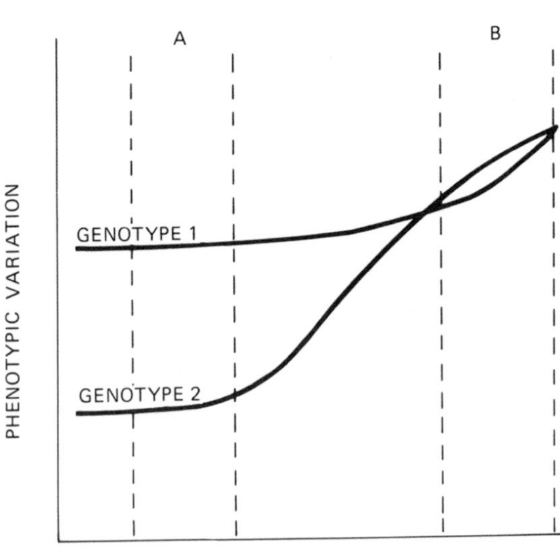

Figure 2.5. Variation in phenotypical scores of two hypothetical genotypes exposed to a large range of environmental variation.

phenotype variation across different environments; in the second case, there is a much larger change in phenotypic scores as environment is changed. If a given experiment attempts to measure the heritability of the phenotypical variation over a relatively limited range of the possible environments (region A in the diagram), phenotypic variance will be largely attributed to differences in genotype. However, if the experiment employs a different limited range (region B of the diagram), the phenotypic variation would be much smaller and mainly attributable to environmental variations. Note that the diagram also suggests the possibility that phenotypic scores may reverse the direction of their mean differences—in region A genotype 1 shows superior scores while in region B genotype 2 shows superior scores. The point of all this, then, is to emphasize that most studies which estimate heritability in human populations are based on limited samples of the *possible* genetic–environmental interactions. In agricultural experiments it may be feasible to test a large range of possible environments and to vary genotype to a great extent. Under such circumstances, and with controlled breeding, very productive strains can be developed. However, even in agricultural experiments, the environmental component must be taken into account. Witness the fact that strains of corn and cattle that are excellent producers in the U.S. or Europe may be entirely unsuitable for African or Asian conditions. In the human context, most studies simply cannot examine the variety of environments let alone the genetic factors that contribute to phenotypic variation. The latter include the genetic context (the other genes present) in which the relevant alleles occur and the total population of genes from which the sampels were drawn. Thus, heritability estimates are likely to change from experiment to experiment with manipulation of this variables.

A related issue that has unnecessarily troubled psychologists for a long time is the heredity–environment controversy—how much of this phenotypic variation is attributable to heredity and how much is to environmental factors? The reasoning presented here should make it obvious that both genetic and environmental factors contribute to phenotypic variation. The more relevant question is: What are the functional mechanisms involved in producing variation among individuals? What are the mechanisms through which environmental factors interact with basic biological processes (Anastasi, 1958)? Such a focus assumes that all behavior has a biological component if we are, after all, biological organisms. Our basic question in physiological psychology may thus be reformulated: What are the mechanisms through which the environmental–organismic interaction takes place?

The reasoning presented here should also serve to counter the generally prevalent notion that if some behavior has an inherited component, there is not much that can be done about it—it is fixed and unalterable. Such pessimism is unjustified. There are many examples, some relevant for psychologists, indicating that hereditary factors can be offset.

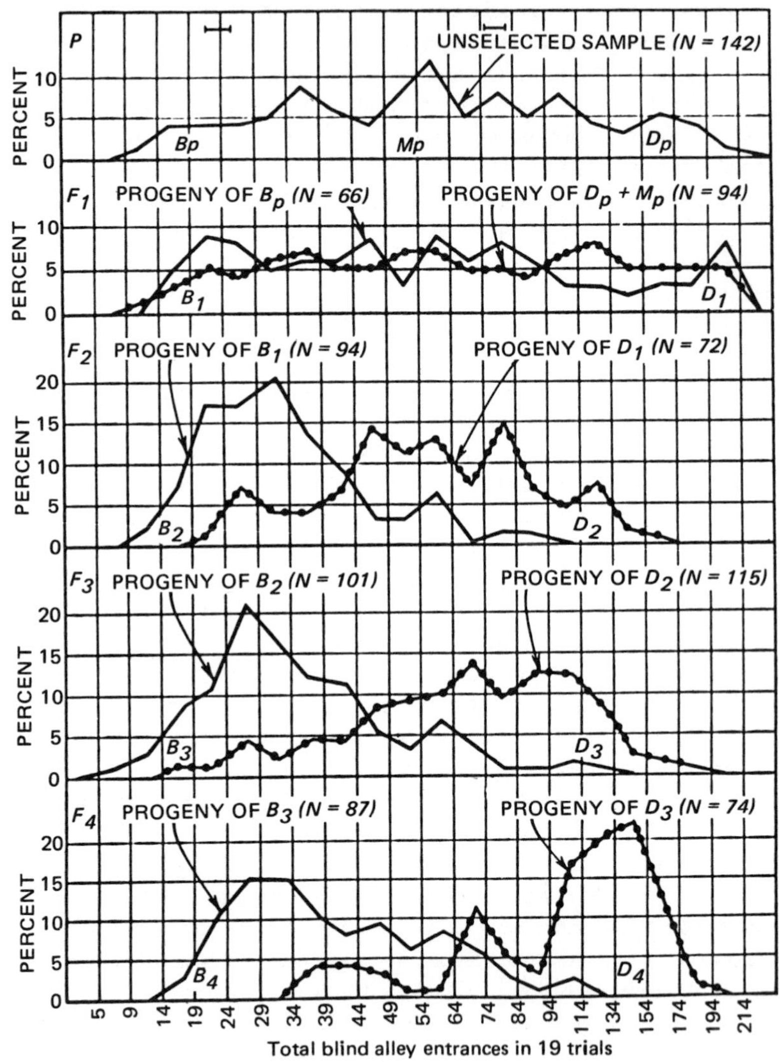

Figure 2.6. Selective breeding for maze-learning ability in rats. [From Tryon, R. C. Individual differences. In F. A. Moss (Ed.), *Comparative Psychology*. Englewood Cliffs, N.J.: Prentice-Hall, 1942.]

BEHAVIORAL–GENETIC RESEARCH

The scientist interested in the genetic aspects of behavior is concerned with answering four basic questions. First, a genetic factor implies that a characteristic (in this case a behavioral one) is transmitted from generation to generation. As a first step in establishing the genetic influence, such transmission must be shown. The other questions, which are not necessarily

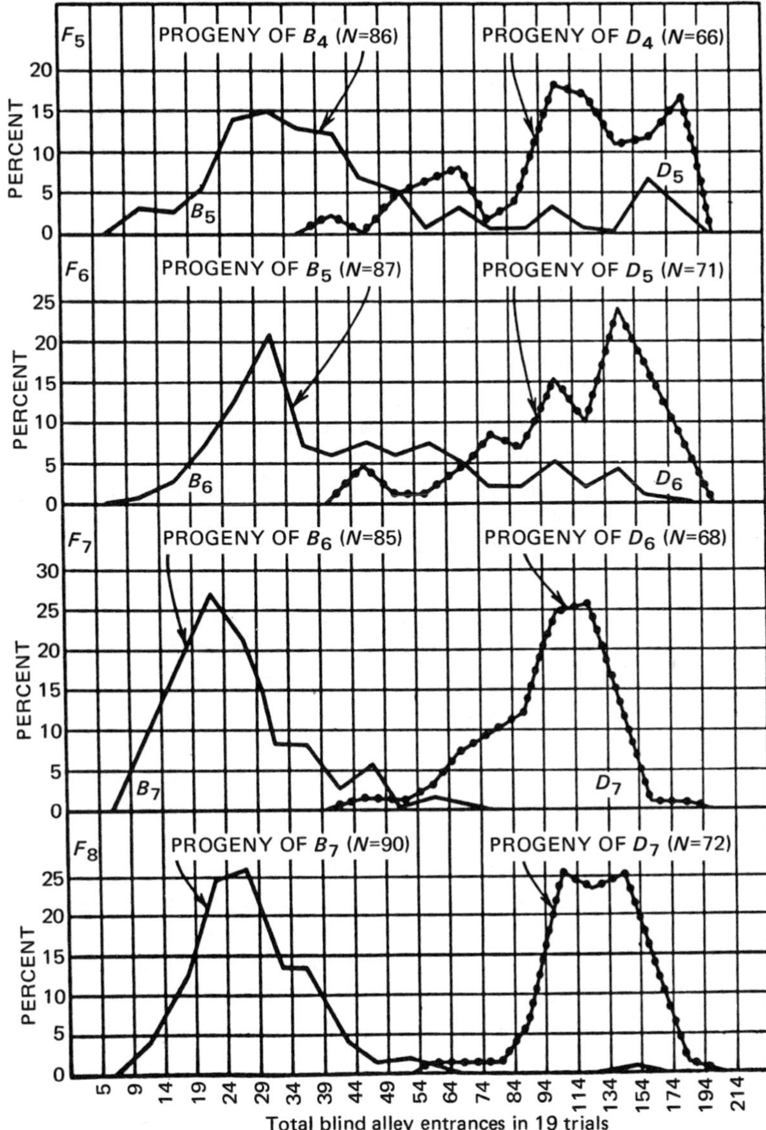

taken up in this order, are: (1) The nature and number of the genetic factors involved—Are there one or more sets of alleles? Is there linkage with other characteristics? What are the dominant and recessive relationships? (2) The chromosome or chromosomes involved—Which are the specific chromosomes, and what is the locus of the relevant genes on these chromosomes? (3) The mechanisms through which the genes act to produce their functional effect—Are there changes in biochemical processes, electrical properties of the nervous system, anatomy of the organism? These questions have not yet been successfully answered about those behaviors already under investigation. Generally, we know the least about the numbers of genes and their loci. Following are several methods through which answers to these questions may be sought.

Selective Breeding

The method of selective breeding for the characteristic under investigation is the most pertinent and conclusive alternative. If it can be shown that separate populations, disparate in the characteristic under investigation, can be produced through selectively allowing certain matings to occur, one has the strongest evidence for genetic involvement in determining the phenotype.

Probably the most often quoted behaviorally relevant example of such a selective breeding experiment is Tryon's (1942) breeding of maze-bright and maze-dull rats. Tryon tested an unselected sample of rats in a 17-unit multiple T-maze. The brightest rats in each of the brightest litters were then mated with each other, and the dullest rats in each of the dullest litters were mated with each other. Each successive generation of rats was subjected to the same test and breeding schedule. Figure 2.6 shows the results after eight generations. It can be seen that performance in this situation was gradually but markedly altered until there was practically no overlap in the error scores of the two groups of animals.

There can be little doubt that the behavioral performance on this maze task was influenced by genetic factors. However, the interpretation of the experiment does require additional comment. First, it cannot be assumed that the selective breeding produced a strain of rats that was homozygous for the quality of maze-bright and another homozygous for maze-dull. Two factors mitigate against this conclusion. Foremost is the breeding schedule that Tryon employed. In order to end up with homzygosity for either characteristic, he should have used the single brightest pair (and the single dullest pair) of animals from one litter in any generation to form the parental stock for each succeeding generation. At best, Tryon's procedure would result in several heterogeneous sublines within the bright animals, and several other sublines within the dull. Furthermore, even under the more rigorous selection conditions, homozygosity would require more generations of inbreeding. However, for our purposes an even more important qualification must be made. It cannot be assumed that Tryon succeeded in breeding for the rat equivalent of "intelligence." The performance of animals bright and dull on his maze test may be modified simply by changing the spacing of trials (McGaugh, Jennings, & Thompson, 1962). Also, the performance in other testing situations may not correlate very well with this test. While it is obvious that the behavior on the test was genetically influenced, it is also obvious that the theoretical points made earlier (Figure 2.5) do apply.

Other behavioral characteristics that have been subjected to selective breeding experiments include activity in a revolving activity wheel and emotionality in rats, mating ability, the tendency of *Drosophila* (fruit flies) to orient toward light and gravity, and aggressiveness in chickens (see DeFries, 1967). An experiment on selective breeding for open field activity in mice (DeFries, Hegmann, and Halcomb, 1974) illustrates how behaviors correlated with the one for which selection was specific may also change—defecation scores were three times higher in low-activity mice. As a caution, it should also be noted that breeding experiments indicate it is possible for related groups of animals to show similar behavior even though their genotypes and inheritance modes differ. Thus, for example, in *Peromyscus* (deer mice) audiogenic seizures (sound–induced epileptic "fits") are dominant, while in *Mus musculus* (house mice) they are recessive (Hall, 1951).

Strain Differences

Everyone is at least superficially familiar with behavioral differences that appear characteristic of different breeds of a species—for instance, beagles and Saint Bernards. The existence of such characteristic differences in activity, temperament, and vocalization suggests that such differences may have a genetic foundation. Studies that take advantage of the existence of different strains of animals may then be profitably undertaken in lieu of or in preparation for breeding experiments. While the inferences from strain difference experiments may be very strong, they cannot be as conclusive as those from breeding experiments; nonetheless, they do provide a convenient means of starting the investigation of genetic factors in behavior. This method has been applied to differences in wildness, susceptibility to audiogenic seizures, aggressiveness, and temperature preferences (see Hall, 1951). Myers (1959) has shown that strain differences in rats may show complicated interactions with conditions of training in avoidance learning, and Bovet, Bovet-Nitti, and Oliverio (1969) have studied several inbred strains of mice in a variety of learning tasks under different training conditions with the imposition of drugs and environmental manipulations. It is an understatement to say that strain differences may reflect genetic differences important in determining a variety of behavioral responses.

Pedigree and Twin Studies

In the absence of the ability to do controlled-breeding and strain-difference experiments in humans, great reliance has been placed on "pedigree" and twin studies.

Pedigree studies follow the incidence of a particular behavior characteristic or accomplishment in a particular family. For instance, Johann Sebastian Bach's family tree reveals an extremely disproportionate number

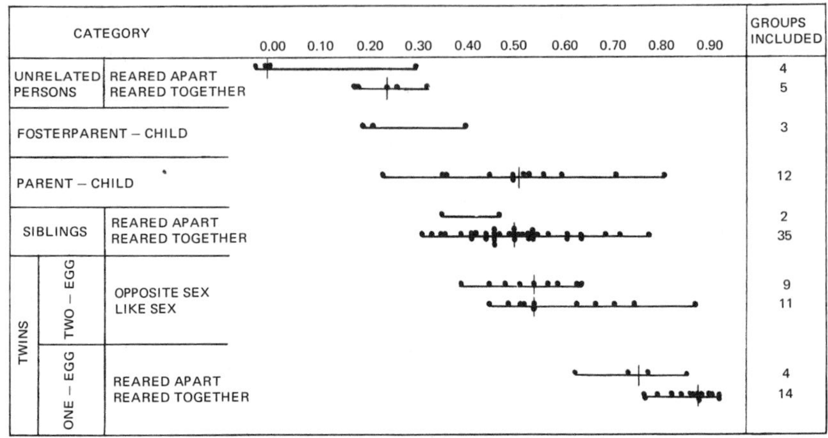

Figure 2.7. Correlation coefficients for "intelligence" test scores from 52 studies. Some studies reported data for more than one relationship category; some included more than one sample per category, giving a total of 99 groups. Over two-thirds of the correlation coefficients were derived from IQs, the remainder from special tests (for example, Primary Mental Abilities). Midparent-child correlation was used when available, otherwise mother-child correlation. Correlation coefficients obtain in each study are indicated by dark circles; medians are shown by vertical lines intersecting the horizontal lines, which represent the ranges. (From Erlenmeyer-Kimling, L. and Jarvik, L. F. Genetics and intelligence: A review. *Science*, Dec. 1963, *142*, 1477–1479. Copyright 1963 by the American Association for the Advancement of Science.)

of competent musicians among his male relatives (Sandiford, 1938). Similar studies of intellectual attainment or deficiency were once quite common. The major defect of such studies is that they are not able to separate the influence of family environment from the possible genetic influence—living in an environment of musical geniuses may promote musical interests and talents.

Erlenmeyer-Kimling and Jarvik (1963) surveyed the results obtained in 52 separate studies correlating intelligence test scores among persons of varying degrees of genetic relationship. Figure 2.7 illustrates their findings. As they point out, many of the studies taken individually are probably subject to a variety of criticisms. On the other hand, the data are striking in showing, despite a relatively large variability within categories, a uniform trend toward increasing intellectual resemblance with increasing genetic relationship. The results do at least suggest that intellectual performance is strongly influenced by hereditary factors.

More recently, Munsinger (1975) surveyed the available literature concerning the IQs of adopted children. The general theoretical reason behind such studies is that they allow for comparison of the correlations between the IQs of adopted and natural children and the IQs of their adoptive and natural parents. Such correlations theoretically permit assessment of the relative genetic and environmental contributions to IQ scores. Munsinger shows that many of the existing studies suffer from serious defects. Among these are selection biases in the placement of children in adoptive homes, confounding of genetics and environment by late separation from the natural parent or late placement in the adopting home, unreliable measurement of IQ scores, and lack of reliable information on parents, particularly the biological fathers. Munsinger's analysis suggested a correlation between adopting parents' IQ and the child's IQ of only .19 while that between parents and their biological children was .58.[2] But while noting the strong genetic determination of IQ, Munsinger also points out that studies such as this do not yet answer questions relating to sex linkage, gene dominance, gene-environment interaction, or the number of polygenes involved in the heredity of intelligence.

A longitudinal study of early mental development in twins also supports a strong hereditary component (Wilson, 1972). Infant twins were given developmental tests periodically throughout the first two years of life. Subsequently they were divided into monozygotic and dizygotic groups on the basis of blood-types. Infant development is typically not a smooth process but rather is characterized by periods of accelerated growth intermingled with periods of relative drift. As a consequence, test scores at any one point in time may correlate poorly with those of some other time. The test scores of individual infants in this study confirmed this. But when within-pair correlations at different times were computed, the correlations were much larger. That is, twin *A*'s test score at any one time was a better predictor of *B*'s performance at the same time than it was of *A*'s performance at a different time. Furthermore, these correlations were much larger for monozygotic twins than for dizygotic pairs. That is, in monozygotic twins there was a high degree of agreement in the spurts and lags of development. From these results it was concluded that infant mental development is largely determined by genetic factors, and that it probably requires unusual environmental conditions to cause a major deviation in this developmental process.

The study of twins provides us with the closest approach to controlled studies available in research on humans. Fraternal twins are no more alike genetically than any other pair of siblings; identical twins, on the other hand, do share a common heredity. While identical twins may be treated more alike than fraternals because they look alike, all twins at least share the influence of common intrauterine environment, being born into families of the same size, with parents of the same age, experience, and socioeconomic status. Of course, brothers and sisters born singly, cannot be as similar on any of these factors. Comparisons, then, between fraternals and identicals on

[2]It is beyond the scope of this discussion to pursue the details (see Munsinger, 1975), but these results are approximately what one would expect assuming the heritability estimate of .70 mentioned earlier (p. 48).

behavioral performances of various kinds may be extremely illuminating for differentiating hereditary and environmental influences. Painstaking diligence has also made it possible to find samples of twins who have been reared apart; these pairs may then be compared to samples in which the children have been reared together.

Nonetheless, in many instances the study of twins is fraught with difficulties. These are especially apparent in studies of mental illness: Twins studies are dependent, in large part, on records that may vary widely from institution to institution in their accuracy, reliability, and availability; psychiatric diagnoses also vary, both in criteria and in reliability of classification; a statement that an individual does not currently have a history of mental disorder does not preclude the possibility that he or she may subsequently develop that disorder. Much of the research on mental disorder in twins is still fraught with controversy. For those who desire to review the matter in depth, Rosenthal (1970) has provided an excellent comprehensive treatment. Generally, it may be said, however, that with respect to schizophrenia there is a much higher *concordance*—both twins alike, both with schizophrenia—in monozygotic twins than in dizygotic twins. Estimates vary but monozygotic twins exhibit concordance in some 50 percent of the cases in the more recent and better documented studies, while dizygotic twins are concordant in only 10 to 15 percent of the cases. This much higher concordance in monozygotic twins is suggestive of extremely potent genetic factors operating in the production of schizophrenia. Whether one or more genes is involved, the role of dominant and recessive characteristics of the genes, whether there is linkage to other characteristics, and so forth—all remain matters of theoretical controversy. Most importantly, the mechanisms through which any genetic contribution is made to the production of schizophrenia have not yet been identified. This aspect of the heritability of schizophrenia will be discussed in Chapter 14.

Environmental and Experiential Factors

It seems fairly clear that in using any of the methodological approaches available for research in genetics, a primary concern is that the effects attributed to the operation of genetic factors are, indeed, properly designated as such. Thus environmental and experiential factors must be carefully controlled. Generally, the problem that plagues work in this area is that genetic and social relationships tend to be highly correlated. In the study of mental disorders, for instance, the closer the genetic relationship, the higher the concordance in mental disorder; yet close genetic relationships, as in families, are generally accompanied by a similarity of social environment. Some recent studies of the incidence of mental disorders have attempted to deal directly with this problem. The data of Table 2.1, abstracted from a paper by Heston (1970), are particularly pertinent.

Table 2.1 **Some results of a study of individuals born to schizophrenic mothers and reared in adoptive or foster homes, and of controls born to normal parents and similarly reared**

Item	*Control*	*Experimental*	*Probability (Fisher's Test)*
Number of subjects	50	47	
Number of males	33	30	
Age	36.3	35.8	
MHSRS, means[1]	80.1	65.2	.0006
Number with schizophrenia	0	5	.024
Number with mental deficiency (IQ 70)[2]	0	4	.052
Number with anti social personalities	2	9	.017
Number with neurotic personality disorders	7	13	.052
Number with more than one year in penal or psychiatric institutions	2	11	.006
Number of felons	2	7	.054
Number discharged from armed forces on psychiatric or behavioral grounds	1	8	.021

[1]The MHSRS (Menninger Health-Sickness Rating Scale) is a global rating of psychopathology going from 0 to 100 with decreasing psychopathology.

[2]One mental defective was also schizophrenic; another had an antisocial personality.

(From Heston, 1970, p. 251)

In this study, subjects in both groups were permanently separated from their biological mothers in the first month of life; thus, the significant excess of schizophrenics among the children of schizophrenic mothers seems difficult to explain on other than genetic grounds. Perhaps even more important is the indication that members of this group also display significant excesses of other, nonschizophrenic behavioral disorders and problems. This finding led Heston to speculate that the heritability here involves a more general disorder. While an identical twin of a schizophrenic has about one chance in two of being schizophrenic, Heston claims only about 13 percent of such twins are clearly normal.

In some instances there is a fairly obvious source of possible nongenetic influence; in others, this is not evident. For example, in studying the inheritance of emotionality in animals, an important control would be to cross-foster the neonatal animals—that is, raise some of the animals with the natural mother and some with a foster mother. This procedure would allow for the assessment of postnatal maternal environment. It is entirely conceivable that, even in animals, differences in caring for the young exist between "nervous" and "non-nervous" mothers. In addition, there may be essential differences in the milk given by such mothers. If such differences are not taken into account, their effects might be mistakenly attributed to the operation of genetic influences.

Prenatal Environment

There is a tendency to consider that environmental effects are always postnatal effects. But one should not overlook the fact that even in rigidly controlled crossbreeding experiments, certain prenatal *nongenetic* factors may not easily be distinguishable from genetic influences. Beach (1955) cites a particularly clear example. Mice may be selectively bred for high or low susceptibility to audiogenic seizures. Crossbreeding such high- and low-susceptible animals results in animals that are intermediate in susceptibility between the parental strains. Such results would seem to support the inference of genetic factors in determining this behavior. However, the incidence of seizure may be altered without changing the genetic constitution. Fertilized ova may be transplanted from females of one strain and introduced into the uterus of the other. This has been done with seizure-susceptible females serving as donors and seizure-resistant females serving as hosts. The offspring in such transplant experiments are less susceptible to seizures than their genetic strain would indicate, though more susceptible than the strain of their foster mothers. In other words, such a study indicates the operation of factors in the fetal environment that contribute to the "degree" of susceptibility to seizures. These might include differences in maternal hormones, oxygenation, or nutrition. Too often we are inclined to think that the life of the individual begins at birth and that environmental factors are all postnatal.

Uniformity of Environment

Finally, a high degree of uniformity of behavior may reflect not genetic uniformity but uniformity in the environment. We may become more aware of the effects of uniformity in the environment in the near future. For instance, are any human behavioral characteristics determined not simply by genetic constitution but also by the fact that the species normally inhabits a planet with an atmosphere and gravitational pull of a certain average value?

Without any genetic changes, if human children are ever born on some distant planet, they could prove to be surprisingly different in ways that are now unforeseen.

HEREDITARY DISORDERS OF INTELLIGENCE

In this section we will briefly review two hereditary disorders, phenylketonuria and Down's syndrome (mongolism), both of which have a profound behavioral effect—mental retardation. Phenylketonuria is of considerable interest in that much research has been directed to clarifying the biochemistry of the disorder. It is unique in being readily diagnosed and treated; in many respects it serves as a model for insight into other similar disorders. Although it is known that phenylketonuria is transmitted by a single recessive gene, more precise mapping has not been accomplished to date. By contrast, much less is known about the biochemical mechanisms in Down's syndrome, but more is known about the particular chromosomes involved in producing the disorder. Together the two disorders illustrate current research trends.

Phenylketonuria

In phenylketonuria (PKU), there is a deficiency in phenylalanine hydroxylase, a liver enzyme necessary for the conversion of phenylalanine to tyrosine (cf. Figure 1.19). The result is an accumulation of phenylalanine. One effect of this accumulation is its conversion to a number of other products which are then excreted in the urine. A second effect is that the disruption in tyrosine production probably impairs production of several biochemical precursors and their resulting synaptic transmitters. Finally, and probably unrelated to the mental symptoms, is an inhibition in production of melanine, which results in the observable characteristics of lighter skin pigmentation and hair color. Each of the effects summarized here is part of a complex chain of events and may involve several preceding and subsequent steps (see Hsia, 1967).

Behaviorally, the history of patients with PKU may show a wide range of abnormalities. These include severe vomiting in the first weeks of life, smaller than average stature and weight, mild to marked reduction in head size, epileptic seizures, posturing and ticlike movements, and EEG abnormalities even in the absence of clinical seizures. A large majority of untreated PKU patients show IQ scores below 50.

The biochemical abnormality in PKU is treated by restricting phenylalanine intake in the diet, thus preventing its buildup in the body. PKU is readily diagnosed in infants, and the prompt administration of the restricted diet seems to avoid the retardation and other symptoms. Such treatment seems also to be ineffective when it is begun after the child reaches six years of age. How long the child need remain on the diet is a matter of conjecture at the present time.

Given the complex biochemical alterations that occur in PKU, it is not surprising that no satisfactory answer is yet available about just which changes are criticial for the variety of symptoms that appear. The PKU syndrome offers an excellent example of the complex changes traceable to a single gene which results in a deficiency in a single enzyme.

Down's Syndrome

Individuals with Down's syndrome (mongolism) are characterized physically by obliquely placed eyes, a round face, short stature, and abnormalities of the extremities. They are pleasant and affectionate but generally have IQ scores below 50. The incidence of Down's syndrome is a function of the age of the mother: Below 35 years of age, the incidence is less than 1 per 1,000; this rises sharply to 30 per 1,000 for mothers over 45. While a genetic involvement has been long suspected in the etiology of this disorder, it was not until 1959 that this could be conclusively shown by the dramatic demonstration of actual chromosomal anomalies. The research on heritable aspects of this disorder has been summarized by Jarvik, Falek, and Pierson (1964).

Two types of chromosomal anomalies have been identified in Down's syndrome. In the first variety, individuals affected with Down's syndrome were found to have 47 chromosomes instead of the usual complement of 46 (see Figure 2.1). As indicated earlier, in the production of sex cells, the chromosomal complement of 46 is reduced to 23 per sex cell. For some as yet unknown reason, one pair of chromosomes (number 21 in the standardized numbering system employed by geneticists) fails to divide (the nondisjunctive or trisomic variety), and this results in sex cells that contain 24 chromosomes. When such a cell unites with a normal cell, the result is an individual with 47 chromosomes. In the second variety of Down's syndrome, patients had the normal complement of 46 chromosomes; however, extra chromosomal material was found attached to one of the other chromosomes. Again, chromosome 21 is implicated, and in this variety it is translocated, usually to a chromosome in the 13-14-15 group. In both instances, then, the presence of excess chromosomal material from chromosome 21 is implicated in the etiology of the disorder.

Figure 2.8 diagrams the chromosomal conditions in the two varieties of Down's syndrome. It can be seen from the figure that the two varieties have different implications. As far as the nondisjunctive variety is concerned, an individual either has Down's syndrome or does not. In the translocation variety, however, a more complex situation prevails: An individual may be

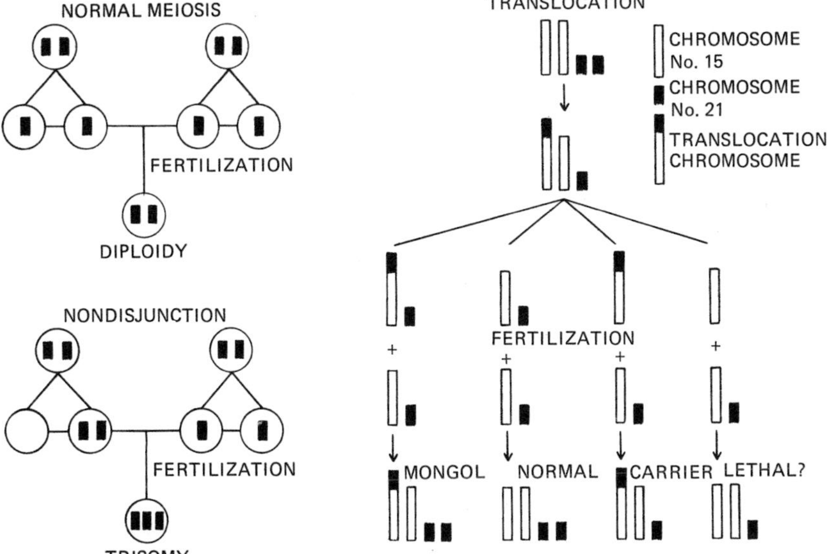

Figure 2.8. Meiosis, nondisjunction, and translocation. In normal meiosis, diploid number of chromosomes is reduced to haploid number. Fertilization reconstitutes the diploid complement. In mongolism resulting from nondisjunction, chromosome pair number 21 fails to separate during meiosis, and fertilization results in trisomy number 21. In mongolism due to translocation, the genetic material of chromosome number 21 is attached to another chromosome—for example, number 15. The independent assortment of chromosomes produces four possible combinations: mongol, normal, carrier, lethal. (From Jarvik L.F., Falek, A., and Pierson, W.P., Down's syndrome: The heritable aspects. *Psychological Bulletin*, 1964, *61*, 388–398. Copyright 1964 by the American Psychological Association. Reprinted by permission.)

(1) normal, (2) exhibit Down's syndrome, or (3) may be phenotypically normal but be a carrier of the disorder. (The other possibility—individuals with missing chromosome 21 material—has not been found and is presumed not to be viable.) The presence of Down's syndrome in a relative, then, entails two different probabilities of having a child similarly afflicted: In an individual whose own chromosomes are normal, the probability is less than .002 percent; in an individual who is a carrier, the probability is better than 30 percent.

Implications

PKU and Down's syndrome illustrate how genetic factors may have very direct behavioral consequences—both disorders result in extremely low IQ scores. Logically, one would hope that it would be possible to elucidate the processes through which the genetic disturbances result in mental deficiency in the two disorders. But an important part of such an analysis must occur at the behavioral level. That is, what are the behavioral, functional components that contribute to these low IQ scores? For instance, are the low IQ scores of Down's syndrome composed of functional deficits different from those involved in the low IQ scores of PKU? Unfortunately, neither Down's syndrome nor PKU produces a specific deficit—both are heterogeneous disorders in that they produce a generalized functional incapacity, and comparison of them at a behavioral level is not likely to be particularly informative. In tracing the mechanisms involved in a physiological disorder, having a specific behavioral "marker" of the disorder provides an index by which the investigator can measure the effects of any proposed mechanisms. The measure here, IQ, is so heterogeneous behaviorally as to promise little help in "dissecting" the physiological mechanisms.

SEX CHROMOSOME ANOMALIES

Nondisjunction and other chromosomal anomalies also occur in association with the sex chromosomes. Nondisjunction may result in sex chromosome constitutions such as XXY or XYY or XXYY. In addition, deletion of chromosomes can occur and produce XO, where "O" refers to a missing chromosome. *Mosaicism*—a mixed chromosmal pattern, with some cells showing one pattern and other cells showing a different pattern—can also occur, such as XO/XXX. These are but a few of the many variations that are known to occur. Most of these anomalies have implications for the sexual functioning of the individual. However, mental development and other socially relevant behaviors are also concerned.

Genetics and Sexual Identification

In ordinary discourse, one has little problem with identifying males and females; the existence of a variety of anomalies points up some of the problems that can occur, however. There are at least seven criteria that can be applied to the identification of an individual's sex (Jones & Scott, 1971):

1. Sex chromosomes
2. Gonadal microscopic structure
3. Morphology of the external genitalia
4. Morphology of the internal genitalia
5. Hormonal status
6. Sex of rearing
7. Gender role of the individual

Generally, of course, all these criteria agree. The existence of a variety of ways in which development can deviate from normal, however, makes it possible for some to exhibit a high degree of dissonance. There are a relatively large number of ways in which this can happen and we will discuss only some examples and their general behavioral implications (for a fuller discussion, see Money & Ehrhardt, 1972).

Fetally Androgenized Genetic Females

Some years ago a condition of prenatal masculinization was inadvertently produced in some genetic females because certain hormones were administered to the pregnant mothers in order to avoid miscarriages. Such children showed varying degrees of masculination of their external genitalia. Of interest here are those children who were diagnosed, underwent surgical feminization, and were reared as girls. Another group of fetally androgenized females consists of individuals with XX chromosomal complements who are exposed to androgenic stimulation via secretion of an improper hormone by the adrenal gland. The time course of this hormonal release is such that the internal development of the fetus is appropriately female for the most part, but the external genitalia become masculinized.

These two variants of genetic females exposed to androgenization are of interest for their behavioral development. Of particular interest is the characterization of these girls as tomboys in contrast to normal control girls. Tomboyism did not necessarily imply a dissatisfaction with the feminine role, however, and none of the girls entertained notions of sexual reassignment. There was a relative downplay of interest in maternal activities and a general subordination of such interests to career interests. These girls are also reported to have rather markedly higher IQ levels. There were no indications of lesbianism.

Turner's Syndrome

In the absence of androgen (male hormones), the genetic male differentiates genitally as a female. In the absence of estrogen (female hormones), the genetic female differentiates as a female. Thus, irrespective of genetic sex, the development of the remaining male organic characteristics requires androgen. In Turner's syndrome, the fetus has no gonadal hormones whatsoever, and will look like a girl genitally and so will be assigned and reared as a girl. (Turner's syndrome basically involves the loss of one chromosome or a mosaic variant of this.) Pubertal difficulties will arise, however, in the absence of estrogen treatment. That is, such girls will not show the expected pubertal changes and it will be difficult for them to establish the psychosocial adjustments appropriate to pubertal development. Accompanying these specifically sexual characteristics, there may be a variety of physical abnormalities, particularly short stature; such individuals are rarely more than five feet tall.

Generally, Turner's syndrome girls have a completely feminine gender identification. Thus, feminine gender identification does not appear dependent on prenatal gonadal hormones. In contrast, as noted earlier, there are some changes in role *behavior* associated with prenatal androgenization in genetic females, even though basic identification is not altered.

Fetally Nonandrogenized Genetic Males

Feminization of genetic males occurs in a genetic disorder that may be sex-linked and which results in an inability to utilize androgen. In the normal male, the testes secret androgen and lesser amounts of estrogen. In this disorder, the inability to utilize androgen results at puberty in the estrogen bringing about a complete feminization of the bony structure and outer contours of the body and normally feminine growth of the breasts. The androgen insensitivity in fetal life causes suppression of masculine development and many affected babies are indistinguishable from genetic females, but usually there are signs that the baby is not a gonadally normal female. Most such children are assigned as females for rearing and apparently adjust readily to a female gender role despite the incapacity with respect to child bearing. Thus, their genetic status as males and the histology of their gonads apparently is irrelevant to their psychosocial status as females.

Klinefelter's Syndrome

This disorder is present in persons who are phenotypically male prior to puberty. Genotypically, most of these patients show an XXY pattern. Early development is generally quite normal, but the first indication of any problem arises during puberty with the development of feminine breasts. This and infertility constitute the major complaints. There may also be mental deficiency, which seems to be correlated with the number of X chromosomes—the most severely retarded patients showing XXXXY patterns. Treatment of the disorder consists primarily of surgical removal of the breasts; hormonal therapy is not effective in either the breast or fertility problem. Basically, these patients have a male identification, and sexual identity per se, aside from possible embarrassment over the breasts, is not a problem.

Conclusions

Basically, then, a variety of disorders may result in discrepancies among the several indicators of sex in the development child. It is clear that none of these indicators is absolutely determining and, in fact, stress is placed on the relative plasticity of sexual determination (Money & Ehrhardt, 1972; Jones & Scott, 1971). The literature is replete with cases where sexual determination was ambiguous in early childhood and where various surgical repairs were performed and sex of rearing was assigned; in fact, cases with similar diagnosis and etiology have often been assigned opposite sex rearing. Within the physical limitations inherent in all such cases, the sex role identity of these patients then seems to develop relatively normally and appropriate for the assignment. Apparently a successful outcome depends on the following conditions (Money & Ehrhardt, p. 142): (1) The parents must show no ambiguity as to whether they are rearing a boy or girl once the decision as to assigned sex is reached; (2) appropriate corrective surgery should be begun as soon as possible; (3) at the usual age of puberty, and in accord with physical growth, the gender-appropriate hormonal therapy should be administered; any additional corrective surgery should also be initiated at this time; (4) appropriately age-graded information about the child's condition and the prognosis should be given throughout the developmental years. Money and Ehrhardt claim that it is those patients who are treated ambiguously who ultimately decide that they were assigned the wrong sex and request reassignment.

The above conclusions are based on experience with a relatively large number of cases given sophisticated medical and psychological attention. However, recently, 24 cases of anomolous sexual development in genetic males have been identified in an isolated community in the Dominican Republic (Imperato-McGinley, Guerrero, Gautier, & Peterson, 1974). In brief, these genetic males appear to carry recessive genes which result in an abnormal chemistry of testosterone (one androgen) and prevent its conversion to a hormone responsible for certain aspects of masculine physical development. At birth, there is ambiguity of the external genitalia, so that 18 of these individuals were reared as girls. At puberty, however, there is growth of the phallus and other signs of virilization, owing to the presence of endogenous testosterone. These cases are of interest because it is claimed that despite their sex of rearing, these 18 individuals changed gender identity at puberty and adopted a masculine psychosexual orientation. These data seem to indicate that testosterone is related to male sex drive and that sex of rearing has a lesser role in the presence of testosterone. In contrast, the syndromes reviewed earlier, which imply that sex of rearing is of greater importance, all seem to involve genetic females or individuals lacking androgen in early development. The present cases appear unique in that potent androgens were present early in development of genetic males and again at puberty. Thus, it is possible that the greatest flexibility in psychosexual identification may be limited to genetic females. We shall return to this hypothesis in discussin the role of hormones in CNS development in Chapter 10.

Generally, however, the data reviewed illustrate the complexities of the genetic–environment interaction. In some instances, environmental factors include some of physiological origin—the existence of anomolous hormonal conditions. In other instances, environmental factors may be more psychological and social in origin—gender expectations and rearing practices. In any event, it is clear that genetic influnces alone are not the exclusive determinants of sexual identification.

The XYY Syndrome

Although comparable to the cases we have just considered, individuals with an XYY chromosomal pattern are of interest for reasons other than their sex role. It has been claimed that a much greater than expected incidence of such chromosomal patterns occurs in criminal populations. The maximum rate of occurrence of this pattern at birth is around .5 percent; the incidence in institutions for criminals has been reported as at least five times that rate (Hook, 1973; Jarvik, Kloden, & Matsuyama, 1973).

Individuals with the XYY pattern have been described as likely to be strikingly tall, have abnormal internal and external genitalia, to be mentally dull with IQs between 80 and 95, and to have a high incidence of epileptiform disorders. Their criminal offenses have a very high rate of extreme aggression. These men are described as being "driven" in their acts of aggression and as showing such behavior early in development (see Jarvik et al. for one case description). The evidence is scanty, but the XYY anomaly does not appear to be transmitted to the offspring of such individuals; on the other hand, there may be a heritable predisposition to chromosomal nondisjunction.

It should be clear that the large majority of violent crimes are committed by individuals with normal chromosomal patterns. In addition, individuals with XYY patterns have been identified who are not particularly tall nor criminal in behavior. The issue here, then, is whether XYY individuals are more likely to commit crimes. A survey of the literature available (Hook, 1973; Jarvik et al., 1973) suggests that the incidence of XYY patterns in penal and combined mental-penal institutions is higher than would be expected from birth rates and that this higher incidence is likely to be limited to this type of institution in particular. In addition, a study by Walzer and Gerald (1975) indicates that neither the XYY nor the XXY pattern is associated with paternal social class. XYY apparently occurs much more frequently in the white population than in blacks. So far the XYY chromosomal pattern has not been generally accepted as a legal defense in court.

A recent report (Witkin et al., 1976) suggests that the elevated crime rate of XYY individuals may be related to their lower intelligence rather than any aggressive tendencies. However, statistical adjustment for intelligence did not completely compensate for the higher incidence of crimes in the XYY groups. More important, perhaps, is that the crimes committed by XYYs in this study were *not* aggressions against people for the most part but were rather crimes against property. There is also the possibility that XYYs of lower intelligence may be more readily apprehended than other criminals.

The XYY chromosomal pattern raises a number of perplexing social questions. What, if anything, should be told to parents of a child who is discovered to have the XYY pattern? Since it is also possible to determine the chromosomal pattern of unborn infants, is abortion of an XYY fetus justified? In order to understand the XYY pattern and its implications, more research is required. But the fear of unjustifiably stigmatizing individuals has led some advocacy groups to force the abandonment of studies designed for long-term follow-up of babies with the chromosomal aberration.

Very little is known of the mechanisms operating here. There are some indications XYY individuals have mild EEG abnormalities but the evidence is far from conclusive. It has been suggested (Jarvik et al., 1973) that the Y chromosome may contain factors controlling "normal" male aggression; that is, the predisposition to aggressiveness would differ in different individuals. The presence of a second Y chromosome would of course add to that predisposition. Now, if the genes on the Y chromosome predispose to minimal aggression, then a double dose of such a chromosome would not necessarily lead to unusual aggressive behavior. In another individual, however, the second Y chromosome might lead to extreme aggression. At the present time, particularly with research suspended, it is extremely doubtful that we can readily validate any such notion.

RACIAL DIFFERENCES

The history of American psychology includes a long and stormy chapter devoted to the question of racial differences. Are there racial differences, for instance, in mental abilities that can be attributed to genetic differences? The literature in this area has been reviewed many times (e.g., Loehlin, Lindzey, & Spuhler, 1975), and it will not be our purpose to go over this ground here. However, a few comments from the standpoint of the considerations that have been presented here are certainly in order.

The vast bulk of the literature, and the contemporary controversy on this subject, centers around estimates of the heritability of IQ. Our discussion earlier should make it clear that such controversy is, at best, of doubtful value. It is apparently the case that there is an average IQ difference of some 15 points between American whites and blacks. This fact of itself does not justify attributing the difference to genetic factors. Even if obtained heritability estimates *within* each of the two groups are comparable, the *between* group differences could be due to environmental differences. Without the ability to assess the full range of genotypes available in each population and without the ability to test the interaction of those genotypes with the full range of possible environments, the question will remain a matter for conjecture.

It is obvious that the research in this area falls short of the precision demanded in laboratory investigation. There have not been, of course, any selective breeding experiments, and the existing research basically attempts to follow a strain difference model. There are several respects in which the analogy of "strains" and "race" does not hold, however. The existence of strains of animals depends on reproductive isolation between strains, that is, lack of matings between the groups. This simply has not been the case for most racial groupings, particularly for American whites and blacks. The result has been that racial designations, implying mainly differences in skin color, actually are arbitrary cultural distinctions. Our society imposes a definition that operates in one direction only—the degree of intermingling of genes between blacks and whites that permits the categorization "white" is both very small and unspecified. The matter is further complicated by the confounding of these factors with sociocultural and socioeconomic differences.

Hirsch (1967) raises another point that has not been well recognized—a factor that might be termed "biological confounding." Correlation between two behavioral traits can lead to the inference that there is a dependence between them at the genetic level when, in fact, there is not. Where genes are independent, all the possible combinations of their separate alleles should show a chance distribution *if there is random mating* within the population. In fact, we know that this assumption of random mating definitely is not true in human populations. Random mating would involve every conceivable kind of heterosexual mating equally often between members of the same and different generations and between related and nonrelated individuals—geography and economic and social considerations would not enter into the choice of partners. Clearly this has never occurred, nor is it likely to occur, in human populations. In the absence of random mating, "statistically significant but biosocially unimportant correlations between functionally independent traits may be maintained indefinitely. Many of the trait correlations that distinguish racial, ethnic, and national groups can be of just this fortuitous nature, maintained by reproductive isolation and nonrandom idiosyncratic systems of mating" (Hirsch, 1967, p. 125).

If any productive work is to be done in this area of research, it may be that it awaits technical and biochemical developments that would enable the identification of individuals by whether or not they carry specific genes. The racial designation would then become superfluous. Under these conditions, it might be possible to assess in what ways, if any, the presence of those genes makes a difference for any particular behavior.

EVOLUTION

The genetic mechanisms that we have been considering find their most profound expression not in the phenotype of successive individuals but in the long-term development of the species, through evolution. It is through evolution that the characteristics of entire species are determined.

In capsule form, Darwin's theory of evolution indicates that there is a process of *natural selection* through which certain characteristics are perpetuated and others tend to be eliminated from the population. The selective process is applied by environmental pressures; that is, characteristics adaptive to the demands of the environment are retained in the population, while maladaptive characteristics tend to be eliminated. This is "survival of the fittest." Several misunderstandings have grown up around the idea of survival of the fittest, and these have become the cornerstones of certain social and economic proposals. Survival of the fittest used to be generalized to include a rationale for a capitalistic system unfettered by governmental restrictions. More up-to-date is the argument that advances in medical care and our generally protective civilization are interfering with and even stopping the process of evolution. By interfering with natural selection and survival of the fittest, it is argued, we are developing into a species that is losing its physical and mental strength and is degenerate when compared with our ancestors. Eugenics programs are suggested as a means of preventing the accumulation of genetically determined afflictions in the gene pool.

Survival and adaptation, insofar as they pertain to evolutionary mechanisms, refer to genetic survival rather than to the life of the individual. In other words, the genes of the individual who has a child and then dies at the age of 20 have survived. The genes of the childless individual who dies at 80 have not. Survival of the fittest means the perpetuation of genes in the population, and any single gene carried by an individual "dies" if it is not part of the random assortment that is passed on to his progeny. Thus, analogies between evolutionary mechanisms and economics and politics are of doubtful validity at best.

But human beings do continue to evolve. Dobzhansky (1962, 1967) has discussed the fallacy of the view that cultural changes have stopped the process of biological evolution. Cultural influences certainly affect the directions that biological evolution will take, but they should be viewed simply as environmental influences like any other; they shape the process of natural selection. It is clear that the environment to which humans must currently adapt is not the same one presented to our prehistoric ancestors. It should also be clear that present-day members of the species are relatively better suited for adapting to that environment than were our remote ancestors. Any discussion of eugenics and similar programs designed to improve the species would take us too far from present purposes; suffice it to say that, in general, all these programs founder on the problem of what qualities should be selected. These programs require a prediction of what will be best for mankind in the distant future; once past some obvious platitudes like "intelligence," the requirements of the programs are vague.

Finally, hereditary mechanisms are basically conservative; that is, they generally operate to produce similarity between parent and offspring. However, the built-in process of mutation ensures that change will occur within the system. Mutation rates in Homo sapiens have been estimated as ranging from 1/10,000 to 1/100,000 for a given gene per generation. Estimating 20,000 genes per person, and employing the conservative estimate of mutation rate, one person in five will carry one or more *newly* arisen mutant genes (Dobzhansky, 1962). Even though most of these mutations are inconsequential for the individual, they add up to considerable potential for change within the pouplation.

SUMMARY

Genetic influences operate through cellular chemical processes. In this manner, they influence cellular functioning. Cellular function in turn determines the function of organ systems; and the characteristics of organ systems limit individual functioning. In human beings, relatively prolonged developmental and learning processes, and the sociocultural nature of the individual's adaptation also influence individual functioning. Thus, while the chain of events linking genetic influences and human behavior is quite direct, it is a long chain and subject to environmental forces at every link. Thus it should come as no surprise if the relationships between genetics and specific behaviors are unclear and complicated. Genetic analysis does indicate, however, that the mechanisms accounting for the genetic determination of physical characteristics may be applied to behavioral characteristics as well. In regard to human behavior, however, the analytic problems are compounded by the probable polygenetic determination of most of the behaviors of greatest interest and the confusion of genic differences with social, cultural, and economic differences. A failure to appreciate fully the *interactive* nature of the gene–environment relationship has also resulted in largely fruitless concerns about how much phenotypic variance in behaviors is attributable to one or the other component of the interaction. A much more productive approach directs attention instead to the mechanisms of the interaction.

Recent advances in microbiology and biochemistry hold forth promise that real progress in analyzing the genetic influences on behavior can be made. Chromosomal analysis of Down's and the XYY syndromes at least suggest that it may be possible to identify the chromosomes involved in relatively discrete behavioral categories. We hope it may not be too long a step to the identification of specific gene locations on the chromosomes. In addition, disorders such as PKU are serving as a model for tracing the biochemical mechanisms through which genic influences are exerted. Animal strains with comparable genetic disorders are being developed and provide a means to study mechanisms and potential treatments. Genetic analysis demonstrates the fundamental truth of the idea that behavior is a biological process.

REFERENCES

Anastasi, A. Heredity, environment and the question "how?" *Psychological Review*, 1958, *65*, 197–208.

Beach, F. A. The descent of instinct. *Psychological Review*, 1955, *62*, 401–410.

Bovet, D., Bovet-Nitti, F., & Oliverio, A. Genetic aspects of learning and memory in mice. *Science*, 1969, *163*, 139–149.

Caspari, E. W. Gene action as applied to behavior. In J. Hirsch (ed.), *Behavior-genetic analysis*. New York: McGraw-Hill, 1967, pp. 112–134.

Chaplin, J. P., & Krawiec, T. S. *Systems and theories of psychology*, 2nd ed. New York: Holt, Rinehart & Winston, 1968.

DeFries, J. C. Quantitative genetics and behavior: Overview and perspective. In J. Hirsch (ed.), *Behavior-genetic analysis*. New York: McGraw-Hill, 1967, pp. 322–339.

DeFries, J. C., Hegmann, J. P., & Halcomb, R. A. Response to 20 generations of selection for open-field activity in mice. *Behavioral Biology*, 1974, *11*, 481–495.

Dobzhansky, T. *Mankind evolving*. New Haven: Yale University Press, 1962.

Dobzhansky, T. Changing man. *Science*, 1967, *155*, 409–415.

Erlenmeyer-Kimling, L., & Jarvik, L. F. Genetics and intelligence: A review. *Science*, 1963, *142*, 1477–1479.

Ferguson-Smith, M. A., & Johnston, A. W. Chromosomal abnormalities in man. *Annals of Internal Medicine*, 1960, *53*, 359–371.

Hall, C. S. The genetics of behavior. In S. S. Stevens (ed.), *Handbook of experimental psychology*. New York: Wiley, 1951, pp. 304–329.

HESTON, L. L. The genetics of schizophrenia and schizoid disease. *Science*, 1970, *167*, 249–256.

HIRSCH, J. Behavior-genetic, or "experimental," analysis: The challenge of science versus the lure of technology. *American Psychologist*, 1967, *22*, 118–130.

HOOK, E. B. Behavioral implications of the human XYY genotype. *Science*, 1973, *179*, 139–150.

HSIA, D. Y. The hereditary metabolic diseases. In J. Hirsch (ed.), *Behavior-genetic analysis*. New York: McGraw-Hill, 1967, pp. 176–193.

IMPERATO-MCGINLEY, J., GUERRERO, L., GAUTIER, T., & PETERSON, R. E. Steroid 5 α-reductase deficiency in man: An inherited form of pseudohermaphroditism. *Science*, 1974, *186*, 1213–1215.

JARVIK, L., FALEK, A., & PIERSON, W. P. Down's syndrome (mongolism): The heritable aspects. *Psychological Bulletin*, 1964, *61*, 388–398.

JARVIK, L. F., KLODEN, V., & MATSUYAMA, S. S. Human aggression and the extra Y chromosome: *Fact* or *fantasy*? *American Psychologist*, 1973, *28*, 674–682.

JONES, H. W., JR., & SCOTT, W. W. *Hermaphroditism, genital anomalies and related endocrine disorders*. Baltimore: Williams and Wilkins, 1971.

LOEHLIN, J. C., LINDZEY, G., & SPUHLER, J. N. *Race differences in intelligence*. San Francisco: Freeman, 1975.

MCCLEARN, G. Genes, generality and behavior research. In J. Hirsch (ed.), *Behavior-genetic analysis*. New York: McGraw-Hill, 1967, pp. 307–321.

MCGAUGH, J. L., JENNINGS, R. D. & THOMPSON, C. W. Effect of distribution of practice on the maze learning of decendants of the Tryon maze-bright and maze-dull strains. *Psychological Reports*, 1962, 9, 147–150.

MONEY, J., & EHRHARDT, A. A. *Man & woman, boy & girl*. Baltimore: Johns Hopkins University Press, 1972.

MUNSINGER, H. The adopted child's I.Q.: A critical review. *Psychological Bulletin, 1975*, *82*, 623–659.

MYERS, A. K. Avoidance learning as a function of several training conditions and strain differences in rats. *Journal of Comparative and Physiological Psychology*, 1959, *52*, 381–386.

ROSENTHAL, D. *Genetic theory and abnormal behavior*. New York: McGraw-Hill, 1970.

SANDIFORD, P. *Foundations of educational psychology*. New York: Longmans, Green, 1938.

TRYON, R. C. Individual differences. In F. A. Moss (ed.), *Comparative Psychology*. New York: Prentice-Hall, 1942, pp. 330–365.

WALZER, S. AND GERALD, P. S. Social class and frequency of XYY and XXY. *Science*, 1975, *190*, 1228–1229.

WATSON, J. B. *Behaviorism*. New York: Norton 1930.

WILSON, R. S. Twins: Early mental development. *Science*, 1972, *175*, 914–917.

WITKIN, H. A., MEDNICK, S. A., SCHULSINGER, F., BAKKESTROM, E., CHRISTIANSEN, K. O., GOODENOUGH, D. R., HIRSCHHORN, K., LUNDSTEEN, C., OWEN, D. R., PHILIP, J., RUBIN, D. B., & STOCKING, M. Criminality in XYY and XXY men. *Science*, 1976, *193*, 547–556.

3

Development of Behavior

For the most part, psychologists use relatively mature organisms as subjects for their research. Interest centers on how such organisms modify their behavior, and learning processes tend to be emphasized. But mature organisms have had a developmental history and responses seen in the adult will depend on that history. An important part of that history is concerned with the development of the human nervous system; the behavorial capacities of the individual are dependent on this process. The study of immature organisms can thus show the variations possible in the development of the nervous system. Some of the questions to which we will direct our attention are: How is it that the human nervous system is so similar across the species? To what extent are we "prewired" to produce certain behaviors? Aside from gross abnormalities of development, to what extent may the development of the nervous system be altered, and, if it can be altered, what are the influences capable of such alterations? Are there critical periods in the development of the individual—periods during which events have irrevocable consequences for later behavior? Can we compensate for any alterations in normal development? This chapter will indicate some directions that research has taken in seeking answers to such questions.

NEURAL DEVELOPMENT

It is obvious that the capacities of the developing organism will be affected by the stage of its physical development. Genetic processes and uniformity of environment typically produce a pattern of physical and behavioral development characteristic of the species. Many organisms, from amphibians to humans, have been studied to plot the course of such development. Most of these studies have been concerned with the timing of the appearance of certain responses and with their patterning (see Marler & Hamilton, 1967). But the uniformities such studies show are dependent on uniformities in the development of the nervous system. How do the nerves "know" where to grow? How specific are the synapses that nerves make? To what extent are the functional properties of nervous connections determined by experiential factors?[1]

Chemical Coding

Generally, the growth and specification of neuronal connections would seem to be under chemical control. Because of chemical specificity, the advancing tips of growing nerve fibers synapse with only particular neurons out of the various ones that they encounter during their growth. Some neurons probably have their destinations and connections highly specified by such chemical coding. Other neurons probably are incompletely specified and have relatively indeterminate connections.

During embryological development, neuronal specification increases and connections become more rigidly determined. There probably are *critical periods* for this process; that is, there is a flexiblilty of connections prior to a definite stage in development and a lack of such flexibility following it. Such time periods are quite circumscribed. In some instances at least, final specification of the functional role of the neuron is induced by the peripheral connection, and this, apparently, is transmitted back to the central synapses (Sperry, 1951; Jacobson, 1969).

[1]There are also well-known disturbances of these developmental processes, such as those caused by disease (for example, German measles) or drugs (for example, thalidomide). In addition, spurred by concern with the effects of drugs such as thalidomide and environmental pollutants, a new field of *behavioral teratology* is emerging. Teratology is a subfield of the neurological sciences; it studies the development of CNS monstrosities under the influence of toxic agents. Behavioral teratology is particularly concerned with the possibility that some agents or some doses of agents, ineffective in producing gross CNS structural damage, still may produce behavioral effects. These problems will not be reviewed here.

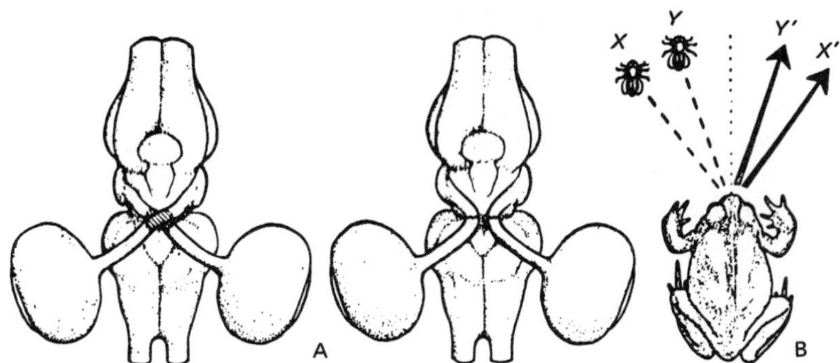

Figure 3.1. Contralateral transfer of retinal projection on the brain. A: By excising the optic chiasma and cross-uniting the four optic nerve stumps as diagrammed, the central projection of the two retinas can be interchanged. B: After optic-nerve regeneration, the animals respond as if everything viewed through either eye were being seen through the opposite eye. For example, when a lure is presented at X or at Y, the animal strikes at X′ or at Y′, respectively. [From Sperry, R. W., Mechanisms of neural maturation. In S. S. Stevens (Ed.), *Handbook of Experimental Psychology.* N.Y.: John Wiley, 1951. Copyright © 1951, John Wiley & Sons. Reprinted by permission of John Wiley & Sons, Inc.]

The physiochemical processes responsible for the formation and specification of connections are largely hypothetical at the moment; the statements we have just made are reasonable inferences based on the available experimentation. We will discuss some examples of that experimentation. They illustrate the complex role that presumed chemical specificity plays in determining the structure of the nervous system and the resulting patterns of response.

Cross-Connection of Optic Nerve

Sperry (1951) has described a large series of experiments by himself and others which support the ideas that neuronal connections are chemically specified and that they are uninfluenced by their functional adaptiveness. Much of this early work was carried out on adult amphibians. Their capacity for neural regeneration illustrates the basic concepts.

Figure 3.1 diagrams the results of one such experiment on frogs. The optic nerves were cut and cross-connected to the nerve stumps of the opposite eye, so that after nerve regeneration the retina was projected to the brain on the side opposite to normal development. After recovery, the frog responded as if what was seen through his left eye was still coming through the right eye, and vice versa. He struck at objects as if their locations were in the opposite direction. It must be emphasized that such maladaptive responses do not show adjustment with experience; even after protracted experience, the frog persisted in striking in the wrong direction.

Examination of the regenerating tissue in preparations similar to this indicates that there is extreme intermixing of regenerating fibers in the scar tissue. Additionally, the cut nerve stumps can be physically rotated before the connections are made and the regenerating fibers still reestablish their functional connections in a predictable, orderly manner. This type of result would seem to indicate that such regeneration is not simply mechanically guided down the original pathways; the regenerating fibers apparently "seek" chemically specified destinations.

These experiments indicate that in the adult animal neuronal connections are specified in a very particular manner. That such specification occurs in the original neural connections in the developing animal is illustrated in the next set of experiments.

Rotation of the Eye

Jacobson (1969) has experimented with the toad during various stages of embryological development before connections between the retina of the eye and the brain are formed. In the adult animal, maps may be made to indicate the locations of corresponding points on the retina and midbrain visual areas in the *tectum* or roof of the midbrain; that is, points in the tectum

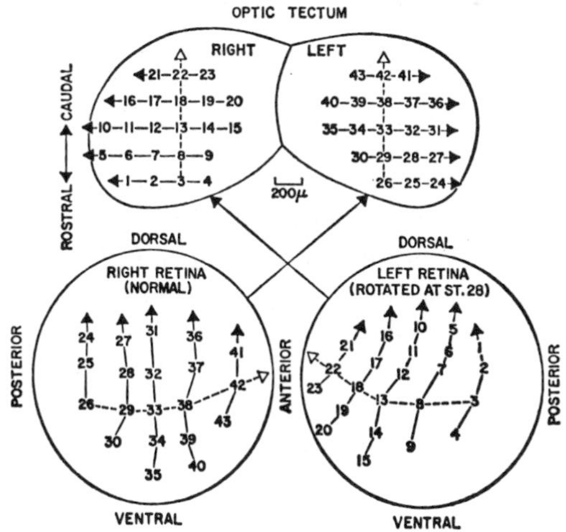

Figure 3.2. Map of the retinotectal projection in an adult toad, in which the left eye had been inverted dorsoventrally and anteroposteriorly (rotated 180 degrees) at larval stage 28–29. The projection from the inverted eye is normal. Each number on the tectum represents the position at which a microelectrode recorded action potentials in response to a small spot of light at the position shown by the same number on the retina. (From Jacobson, M., Development of specific neuronal connections. *Science*, Feb. 1969, *163*, 543–547. Copyright 1969 by the American Association for the Advancement of Science.)

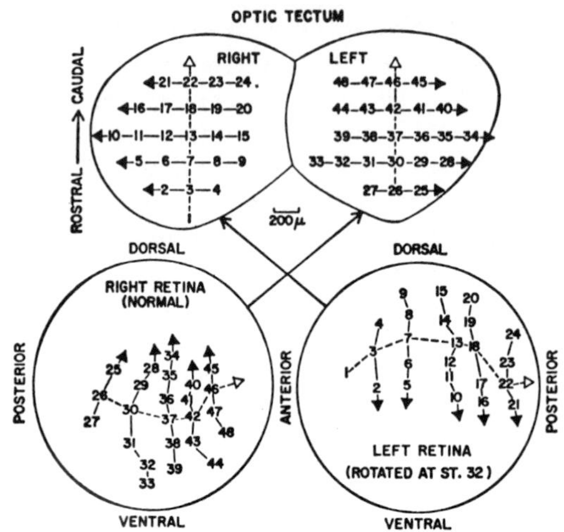

Figure 3.3. Map of the retinotectal projection in an adult toad, to the left tectum from the normal right eye, and to the right tectum from the left retina, which had been inverted at larval stage 32. The projection from the left retina is totally inverted. For the significance of the numbers on the tectum, see Figure 3.2. (From Jacobson, M., Development of specific neuronal connections. *Science*, Feb. 1969, *163*, 543–547. Copyright 1969 by the American Association for the Advancement of Science.)

are specified which respond selectively to stimulation of points on the retina.[2] In these experiments, the left eye was rotated 180 degrees before a given stage of larval development. The maps in Figure 3.2 show that, despite the rotation of the eye, the connections between the retina and midbrain that developed later were entirely normal. Figure 3.3 shows that this is not the case if the eyeball rotation is done at a later stage—in this instance, only 10 hours later. Here the adult projection from the retina is totally inverted.

Thus, it appears that the growing nerve fibers are unspecified before a given stage and will form connections appropriate to a new eye position; but after this stage they are specified, and the animal has inverted vision if the eye is rotated.

Translocated Eyes

In normal development, the eyes are located anterior to the brain; retinal fibers growing into the brain advance in a caudal direction. But what happens if the eyes are moved early in development? In frog embryos, it is possible to move the developing eyes to a position normally occupied by ear tissue. In such a preparation, Constantine-Paton and Capranica (1975) caused the optic nerve to enter the hindbrain rather than along the normal

[2] In those phyla more primitive than mammals, the midbrain tectum carries out sensory functions that are subserved by the cortex in mammals.

route through the diencephalon to the optic tectum. Instead of growing into the tectum, in these animals, the optic fibers grew caudally and penetrated the spinal cord. It should be noted that the translocated eyes themselves were externally normal and the retinas were microscopically and electrophysiologically normal. These results suggest that in the normal animal there is a three-dimensional gradient system to which the optic fibers are responsive and which guides the development of the visual pathway in space. In these experiments, the optic fibers were not in contact with that guidance system.

Tectal Lesions in Neonate Hamsters

Recently, comparable experiments have shown that similar conclusions can be extended to the mammalian brain. Schneider and Jhaveri (1974) have summarized some of the pertinent experiments. The hamster is born with a relatively immature nervous system and its brain takes an additional three months to reach full size. Figure 3.4 diagrams one of the experimental procedures and its results. On the left of the diagram are the normal connections between the eye and the tectum (superior colliculus—SC) of the ham-

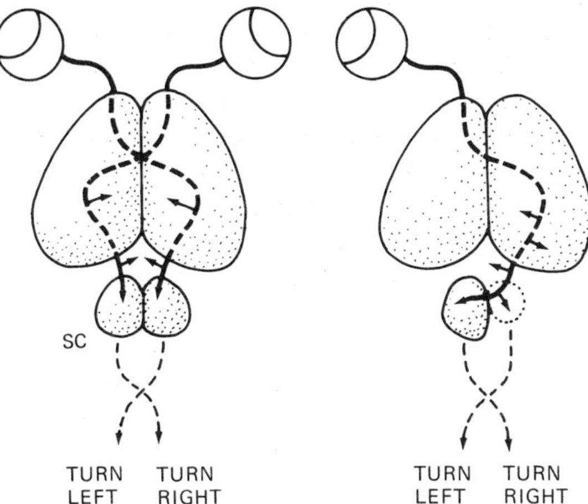

Figure 3.4. Axonal pathways in the Syrian hamster critical in the control of visually elicited turning of the head. (Left) Top view of eyes, cerebral hemispheres, and superior colliculi (SC); the latter are displaced caudally for the sake of the diagram. (Right) Similar view of the brain of a hamster in which the right eye and the superficial layers of SC were ablated at birth. Axons from the remaining eye not only form anomalous connections in the diencephalon, but also form an abnormal pattern of termination in the midbrain tectum, some ending in the area of early surgical damage, others recrossing to the left SC. (From Schneider G.E., and Jhaveri, S.R. Neuroanatomical correlates of spared or altered function after brain lesions in the newborn hamster. In D.G. Stein, J.J. Rosen, and N. Butters (eds.), *Plasticity and Recovery of Function in the Central Nervous System.* New York: Academic Press, 1974, 65–110.)

ster; connections in the right side of the tectum normally mediate turning of the head toward the left in response to visual stimulation in the left eye. On the right of the diagram are the anatomical and behavioral results of removing the right eye and destroying the superficial layers of the superior colliculus in neonate animals. Anomalous connections—connections not normally seen—were found in the mature animal. Of major concern here is the fact that some of these involve the recrossing of optic fibers to the left superior colliculus and result in the animal turning right, instead of left, to stimulation in parts of the left visual field. Similar lesions made in mature animals result in a deficit in orientational movements; however, such animals do not turn in the wrong direction and the anomalous connections are not found.

Functional Adjustments

We see here that in the early stages of development some degree of "plasticity" of the CNS is exhibited. That is, before some specific stage of development, the growth of the system itself can compensate for gross interference. Thus, as in the case of rotation of the eye, the subsequently established neural connections are entirely normal. Following a "critical period," that plasticity is lost and the development of the system does not provide compensation for the distortion. Furthermore, once the critical periods are passed, experimental animals with atypical connections do not show any tendency to compensate for their anomalous connections by making appropriate *functional* adjustments; despite opportunity for learning to make the correct responses, they fail to do so. Similarly, adult rats with sensory nerves of the hind limb crossed to the opposite side of the body, or with muscles of the leg transposed, fail to learn to make the adjustments necessary to compensate for the inappropriate sensory-motor relationships (Sperry, 1958). And chicks wearing distorting prisms (E. Hess, 1956) are unable to correct their pecking behavior to compensate for a seven-degree shift of the visual image. Such results would seem to indicate that specific functional adaptations are greatly dependent on the presence of specific neuronal connections.

This conclusion must be tempered, however, in view of the results of experiments with human subjects. Humans can learn to adjust to a variety of sensory-motor distortions of the visual field introduced by distorting prisms (Held & Freedman, 1963). Where the human subject has opportunity to experience the correlation of feedback from his own movements with distorted visual input, he shows appropriate adaptation; where the opportunity for such movement is restricted or the subject is passively moved rather than initiating the movements himself, adaptation is absent.

Whether the animal experiments and those with humans are comparable remains an unanswered question. It may be that distortions of sensory input from environmental manipulations—like the introduction of prisms—are not the equivalent of distortions produced by lesions as in the frog and hamster experiments. But the difference between chicks and humans in learning to adapt to visual distortion produced by prisms suggests a species difference in inherent plasticity of the nervous system. There is evidence that only mammals are capable of such functional adjustments (see Taub, 1968).

It is generally agreed that lesions in younger animals are less disruptive of normal behavioral capacities but determination of the critical periods for such plasticity of the CNS is as yet strictly empirical. As a consequence, there are conflicting findings. Thus, for instance, Wetzel, Thompson, Horel, and Meyer (1965) reported that visual pattern discrimination learning is normal in cats with neonatal visual cortical lesions; such lesions in mature cats prevent this performance. But Bland and Cooper (1969) found that rats lesioned neonatally and as adults were equally debilitated in pattern discrimination. This discrepancy could have occurred because there are species differences in when the visual system loses its plasticity or simply because of procedural differences in the experiments.

Finally, adult humans and other higher animal forms do show varying degrees of functional recovery from the effects of CNS lesions. Thus, after some lesions there may be almost complete recovery of speech where the patient was initially *aphasic*, or incapable of speech. Similarly, varying degrees of sensory-motor recovery have been demonstrated among humans and animals. What is not clear is the mechanisms of that recovery and the limiting factors. We shall now turn to a brief discussion of this issue.

Recovery of Function After Lesions

Much material suggests that after some critical stage of development neuronal connections are rigidly determined. Moreover, there has been a long-standing belief that the mammalian CNS is not capable of regenerating damaged neurons. (Limited regeneration of peripheral axons has been substantiated, however.) In contrast, it has also been obvious that functional recovery, at least to a limited extent, is a fact. What, then, accounts for such recovery?

This problem is certainly important for the clinical rehabilitation of patients with CNS damage. It also has theoretical implications for the question of the localization of learning and memory in the CNS, which we will address in Chapter 12.

Several possibilities, none mutually exclusive, have been suggested to account for functional recovery. One suggests that some of the functioning lost immediately after CNS damage results from "shock" to neurons that are not actually permanently lost; recovery from that shock gives the appearance of partial recovery. Another suggests that the remaining neurons in the relevant circuitry somehow become "supersensitive" and thereby pick up the burden, giving the appearance of recovery. A behaviorally oriented hypothesis suggests that recovery can be attributed to altered functional strategies; the lost behavior *is* lost but it is replaced by new, more or less equivalent behavior, not utilizing the destroyed neurons. A fourth approach suggests that recovery is mediated through "vicarious functioning." That is, portions of the brain not previously utilized for this purpose now take over in the absence of the normally utilized neurons; i.e., they substitute.

While all of these possibilities may have some validity, of principal concern here is the appearance of data that at least question or alter the original assumption that damaged CNS neurons do not replace themselves. The previously cited hamster experiment is one such piece of evidence. Much of the material on this issue has been reviewed in a symposium volume edited by Stein, Rosen, and Butters (1974); we will sketch only the highlights.

There seems to be growing agreement that at least two forms of regenerative growth can occur in the CNS of mammals (Moore, 1974). In one form, the distal parts of severed axons degenerate while the proximal parts, near the cell body, begin a growth process that results in replacement of the damaged axons. In the other form, collateral sprouting occurs; that is, axons in the *remaining* innervation to a damaged structure show growth of their terminal fibers, and this new growth replaces that lost from degeneration of the severed axons. Figure 3.5 diagrams the two possibilities.

In reviewing the experiments with hamsters, Schneider (1974) suggested that the formation of new terminals and their location may be influenced by a variety of factors: (1) Invasion of vacated terminal space—new terminals grow into locations that are available, i.e., they "compete" for the terminal space, thus placing limits on the growth that is possible; (2) a "pruning" effect—growing axons tend to sprout in other branches when some of the original branches are lost; (3) an axon ordering factor—growing axons tend to arrange their growth in appropriate topographical order even if the total space available is reduced; (4) mechanical influences—the physical layout can cause a deflection of growing fibers, resulting in a disruption of an orderly arrangement of their terminal distribution.

The interactions among these and other possible factors, such as differences among cell types, are undoubtedly complicated. Thus, it may very well be the case that the limitations on mammalian CNS regenerative processes stem from the very fact that regeneration *does* occur. Thus, in the densely packed brains of mammals the regenerative process may be severely self-limiting and dependent on precisely where the lesion occurs, its configuration, the nature of the remaining tissue, etc. In addition, it is possible that the regenerative growth may itself stymie behavioral recovery; the reasoning here is that an anomalous growth may prevent restoration of the behavior that was lost. Devor (1975) reported an experiment that is relevant

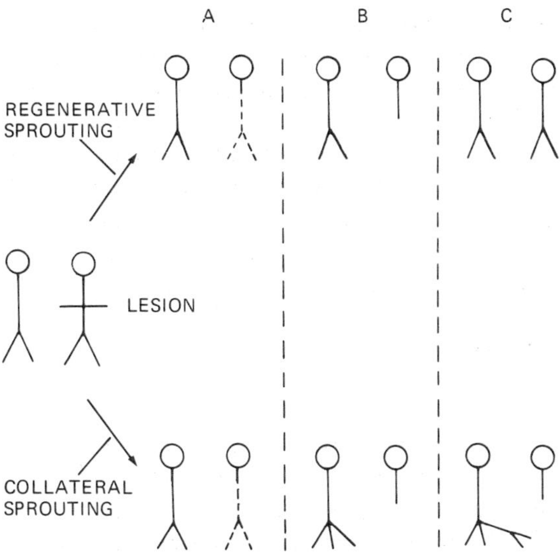

Figure 3.5. Possible modes of replacing axon terminals lost as a result of lesions. Dotted lines indicate degeneration. A, B, and C indicate successive stages in growth. (After Moore, R.Y. Central regeneration and recovery of function: The problem of collateral reinnervation. In D.G. Stein, J.J. Rosen, and N. Butters (eds.), *Plasticity and Recovery of Function in the Central Nervous System.* New York: Academic Press, 1974, 111–128.)

here. In the male hamster, mating is dependent on the sense of smell; thus transection of the lateral olfactory tract in the forebrain (which carries afferents for smell) eliminates mating. If the cut is made early in life, however, mating is spared. Partial section in adult animals does not interfere with mating, but similar partial cuts in neonatal males do impair mating in adulthood. These behavioral differences seem to be accounted for by the differential patterns of rearranged axonal connections in the lateral olfactory tract that were seen postsurgically in the several groups of animals.

Other recent advances in the field of neural growth and regeneration include drug treatments that promote nerve growth (e.g., Crain & Peterson, 1975) and the discovery that growth after lesions may be capable of supporting electrophysiological function (Lynch, Deadwyler, & Cotman, 1973). These are all new and exciting concepts and data—only further work can determine their ultimate practical and theoretical significance.

INSTINCTS

This section will examine some aspects of the concept of innate, or instinctive, behavior (see Beach, 1955). At issue here is whether such behavior is unlearned.

The concept of instinct actually covers several aspects of a behavioral sequence. A given pattern of movements—the behavior—may be said to be instinctive. On the other hand, the motive force—the drive or "go"—energizing the behavior may be said to be instinctive. *Or* both these aspects may be lumped together by a description of the presumptive goal object; for example, nest-building may be characterized as instinctive. However, it is important to distinguish these aspects, because some of their underlying mechanisms may be dependent on innate factors while others are not Central to modern instinct theory is the concept of the fixed action pattern.

The Fixed Action Pattern

The *fixed action pattern* is conceptualized as a sequence of coordinated movements that appear without the necessity for learning on the part of an animal. It is also a consummatory act rather than a reflex. The actions of digging in the ground, tamping nuts into it, and covering them are cited as examples of such a fixed action pattern of squirrels (E. Hess, 1962).

The fixed action pattern is typically preceded by appetitive behavior. *Appetitive behavior* is variable search behavior that is subject to learning; the goal of appetitive behavior is the discharge of the fixed action pattern. When appetitive behavior brings the animal into contact with certain stimuli, *innate releasing mechanisms* are triggered, and the fixed action pattern occurs. The appearance of this set of responses is dependent on the time since they were last discharged; that is, there is an accumulation of motivation, or *action specific energy*. If there is no opportunity to display the consummatory act (the fixed action pattern), action specific energy may accumulate to the point of spilling over, producing *displacement*, or *vacuum*, activities—that is, acts outside the normal context of behavior (see Zeigler, 1964). Animals raised in social isolation perform these consummatory responses; hence, they must be innate (however, see Moltz, 1965). The question is whether there is any neurophysiological evidence for such patterns.

Neurophysiological Evidence

In a variety of animal species, electrical stimulation of particular brain structures may elicit complex behavioral sequences. As early as 1928, W. R. Hess (summarized by Akert, 1961) was able to evoke an affective defense reaction in cats from stimulation of the brain. When the hypothalamus is stimulated, the defense behavior starts with arousal and assumption of a defensive posture. Angry vocalization proceeds to retraction of the ears, hissing and spitting, and may culminate in a well-directed attack. This sequence terminates at any point when the electrical stimulus is stopped. (Because the behavior is dependent on the electrical stimulation, it is called *stimulus-bound* behavior.) Similarly, Hess and others have elicited sleep from thalamic and brainstem structures. Eating and gnawing (Miller, 1957) and mating (Vaughan & Fisher, 1962) have also been elicited from hypothalamic stimulation.

Unlearned Behavior

It should be pointed out that all the above examples involved the use of adult animals that would certainly have had ample opportunity to learn any elements of the responses requiring learning. In other words, these data do not necessarily support the notion that fixed action patterns are innate. Two experiments by Roberts and his co-workers bear on this issue. In the first experiment (Roberts & Kiess, 1964), cats were pretested for spontaneous attack on rats (not all cats attack rats, and there is evidence that it is a learned response; see Kuo [1930]). Only cats that did not exhibit spontaneous attack were employed for later experimentation. In these animals, electrical stimulation of the hypothalamus elicited attack behavior; even after repeated experience of this sort, attack occurred only during stimulation. In the second experiment (Roberts & Berquist, 1968), attack behavior resulting from hypothalamic stimulation was compared in normal cats and those cats raised in social isolation. Isolates displayed all the elements present in the attack of control animals, albeit in less persistent and vigorous form. In another experiment, vigorous male copulatory behavior was elicited from female opossums with electrical stimulation of the hypothalamus (Roberts, Steinberg, & Means, 1967).

At the very least, then, one can conclude that there are organized neural circuits available and that although they may not be normally utilized, they can be activited by central brain stimulation. More strongly, the data suggest that these are innately organized circuits; whether they achieve behavioral expression may be determined by experiences during early development.

Goal Objects

It should be noted that in all the above instances of behavior evoked by central stimulation, the occurrence of the behavior was dependent on the availability of the appropriate goal objects. The behavior is not automatic but rather appears to be dependent upon the presence of specific goal objects. For instance, Roberts and Carey (1965) found that gnawing in rats elicited by hypothalamic stimulation is dependent on the presence of a chewable piece of material that splinters. The material is ejected from the mouth rather than eaten; if stimulated while engaged in eating, the animals leave the food and proceed to chew a block of wood. Again, such behavior is limited to the duration of the electrical stimulus.

Reinforcing Properties

Roberts' group has also shown that the elicitation of such responses has reinforcing properties. Animals will learn to make differential maze responses during electrical stimulation in order to gain access to the appropriate goal objects; in the absence of stimulation, maze performance was random. Roberts and Carey (1965, p. 323) suggest that "the execution of many behaviors controlled by the hypothalamus may be postively reinforcing when a readiness to perform them has been aroused by humoral or neural input." Stemming as it does from a different theoretical background, this suggestion is impressive in its similarity to the notion of the fixed action pattern. If the similarity is borne out by further experimentation, it may well be that we shall see a rapproachement between instinct and learning theorists.

Evidence of Plasticity

There is some evidence that stimulus-bound behavior has more plasticity than the above experiments would indicate. Valenstein, Cox, and Kakolewski (1968, 1969) reported data showing that there is a great deal of variety in the behavior evoked by hypothalamic stimulation. They suggested that such variety indicates that stimulus-bound behavior may not be dependent on the existence of fixed neural circuits. In their experiments, rats with electrodes in the hypothalamus were stimulated in the presence of food, water, and wooden blocks. Individual animals displayed stimulus-bound behavior to one of these goal objects—that is, some animals ate, while others drank or gnawed during the electrical stimulus only. The chosen goal object was then removed, and electrical stimulation continued with the nonpreferred objects remaining. After some hours of such intermittent stimulation, the animals showed response to one of the remaining goal objects. On reintroduction of the originally preferred goal object, the animals responded to both the new and old goal objects. These experiments imply that the elicitation of behavior from hypothalamic stimulation is not the result of fixed, unmodifiable neural circuits. Furtherfmore, Valenstein et al. (1969) reject the interpretation (Wise, 1968, 1969) that their result is due to changing thresholds for excitation of separate, fixed neural circuits. This issue will be discussed in greater detail in Chapter 11.

Conclusions

In short, then, it is apparent that is is possible to evoke a variety of behaviors, some of which may not normally be displayed by the animal, with central brain stimulation. It is not clear if the underlying neuronal circuits for such behavior are genetically fixed or whether they are modified through experience.

NUTRITION

The physical aspects of malnutrition in both human beings and animals have been studied for some time. Malnutrition retards physical growth in infants, and such retardation may never be recovered in spite of later dietary supplementation. A variety of biochemical abnormalities parallel the physical retardation. Depressed metabolism of phenylalanine to tyrosine (see Chapter 2 on PKU, p. 59) is one such consequence of malnutrition in infants. Generally, malnourished children show biochemical development corresponding to that of younger children of the same weight and height (Eichenwald & Fry, 1969; Cravioto, 1968).

Studies of Mental Development in Humans

Recently, studies have been directed at the possible impairment of mental development that might accompany the physical effects of malnutrition in infancy. For instance, *kwashiorkor* is a disease caused by protein deficiency. It is commonly found in infants not weaned until the second or third year of life. Such children are generally apathetic and lack the curiosity and response to the environment normally found in children of that age (Eichenwald & Fry, 1969).

But whether malnutrition is a direct cause of mental deficiency and whether such deficiency is permanent seems to be very much a matter of controversy. Kaplan (1972) made a comprehensive review of the studies then available. She concluded that mental deficiency is a direct consequence of malnutrition and that it is mediated in two ways: (1) Malnutrition directly affects the CNS and thus results in learning difficulties; and (2) malnutrition creates disturbances in the child's social experiences and opportunities for learning and these further compound the learning difficulties. The CNS is most vulnerable during the period of its maximal development; i.e., during gestation and the first few years of life. Kaplan suggested that malnutrition operates on the CNS by increasing the probability of prematurity, lowering the birth weight, and affecting the children of previously malnourished mothers through increased pregnancy complications.

In a reply to Kaplan, Warren (1973) sharply disagreed. In essence, he argued that the retrospective nature of the studies cited by Kaplan prevented attainment of appropriate controls and confounded malnutritional effects with environmental factors; that is, malnourished children generally come from socially and culturally deprived homes, and their parents tend to be in the lower intelligence range and show a high degree of illiteracy. In addition, the children in these studies generally have come from hospitalized populations, where they have been subjected to deprivation of learning opportunities and immobilized in bed. Warren also argues that the short-term nature of the studies also precludes any conclusions about the permanence of specific effects. He suggests suspending judgment until long-term, prospective studies can be completed. Several are currently being carried out.

Two studies that have become available since these reviews were written are of particular interest since they avoid some of the difficulties we have mentioned. The first of these (Stein, Susser, Saenger, & Marolla, 1972) took advantage of famine conditions that existed in Holland during World War II. The Dutch famine was unique in that it was sharply circumscribed in both time and place; it resulted from a combination of war and weather conditions in a particular area of Holland. In the famine area, official food rations reached a low of 450 calories per day while outside the famine area consumption almost never fell below 1300 calories per day. Furthermore, Dutch birth records were so accurate that it was possible, almost 20 years later, to locate specific male individuals born in and immediately around the famine period, either in or outside the famine locale. And, finally, the study looked at the military induction testing of these individuals. Thus, the study could compare the intellectual test performance of 19-year-old males whose periods of gestation and birth either were or were not touched by the famine. Briefly, careful analysis showed an expected relationship between social class variables and intellectual performance but failed to reveal any association between exposure to famine conditions and intellectual performance. One possible source of error in this study might have been some systematic increase in the rations of pregnant women if their families shared part of their own rations with them; Stein and Susser (1973) discount this, however, in view of the fact that maternal weights immediately after birth were some four standard deviations below the norm in those mothers exposed to the famine. It is also possible that increased infant mortality because of the famine was selective in eliminating children who might have later showed intellectual deficit; this hypothesis implies some sort of threshold effect for which the authors could find no evidence.

The second study of interest concerns the remedial effects of environmental enrichment. Winick, Meyer, and Harris (1975) studied three groups of Korean children who were adopted into American middle-class homes prior to the age of three and who had been in the U.S. for at least six years. The three groups were composed of girls who had been exposed to different nutritional conditions prior to receiving care by the adoption agency. The focus of this study is the fact that the children were not returned to a socially deprived environment subsequent to treatment for malnutrition. Again, in brief, all groups of children at least reached American IQ norms—the malnourished group had a mean IQ of 102. However, the best nourished group had an IQ mean of 112, which is significantly higher. The authors note, however, that this is also above the IQ level of middle-class American children. Thus it may be that the IQ attainments of all groups reveal both the effects of malnutrition and the ameliorative effects of the select character of the adoptive parents and the environment they provided. Note that Levitsky and Barnes (1972) showed that learning deficits in rats caused by malnutrition could be compensated for by enriching the environment to which such rats were exposed (see p. 102).

There can be no doubt that malnutrition causes severe and lasting retardation in physical development. But whether it has any direct consequence for any lasting retardation of intellectual development seems unsettled.

We will not review the animal literature relating to this topic; it is sufficient to indicate that malnutrition in young animals has been shown to result in retardation of development (see Kaplan [1972] and Salas and Cintra [1975] for some pertinent references). While such studies are free of the control problems that plague studies in humans, their applicability to the human problem of intellectual development is only inferential.

One animal study of particular interest, however, concerns prenatal nutrition. In this study (Butcher, 1970), pregnant rats were fed a diet containing an increased phenylalanine percentage, along with an inhibitor of the enzyme involved in metabolism of phenylalanine. This diet was designed to simulate in the mothers the biochemical abnormalities associated with phenylketonuria in humans. Postnatally, the mothers' experimental diet was discontinued, and at weaning the pups were put on a normal diet. At 50 days of age they showed a significant decrement in learning a water maze and its reverse path. These results indicate that during fetal development an imbalance in nutrition may have serious consequences for learning ability in the mature animal; the implications for human phenylketonuric mothers are obvious.

SENSORY SUPPORT OF DEVELOPMENT

The nature and extent of early experience have been shown to influence sensory discrimination, feeding behavior, reproductive functioning, learning, and social behavior (Beach & Jaynes, 1954; Marler & Hamilton, 1967). As a result of the demonstration of such influences, there is a tendency to equate "experience" with "learning." A variety of evidence from both human and animal studies indicates, however, that such need not be the case; quite apart from any learning that may occur, normal development and functioning of the organism is dependent on the reception of an optimal sensory input. In the absence of such input, sensory systems may show abnormalities of development.

Visual Deprivation

Because of the relative ease with which it may be controlled, most research on the effects of sensory deprivation has involved visual deprivation. Riesen (1950), for instance, has described the behavior of chimpanzees reared from birth to 16 months of age in almost total darkness; subsequently, they were given varying periods of limited access to light. Briefly, these studies showed that many visual functions—such as visual pursuit of moving objects, coordination of the two eyes, convergent fixation, and the recognition of objects—develop only after prolonged experience in the use of the eyes. If deprivation is maintained for too long, it may be impossible for the chimpanzee to develop these functions. It is becoming increasingly clear that physiological disturbances occur in the absence of visual input and they result in behavioral deficits.

In a survey of the literature in this area, Riesen (1966) reports that light deprivation produces a variety of changes in cell dimensions, number of cells, etc., throughout the visual system. The specific findings are a function not only of the animal's age at deprivation, but also probably of the species employed. Age, severity of deprivation, and length of deprivation are implicated in determining the reversibility of the changes. Considerable recovery of function may be demonstrated by animals allowed sufficient exposure to light; however, instances of failure to show reversibility have also been reported. Riesen's comprehensive review also covers differences in neurochemical activity and electroencephalographic activity that have been found in light-deprived animals. Generally, then, "the effect of early and prolonged sensory deprivation is to interfere with neural growth and function. Conversely, the use of sensory neurons results in the development to larger size, more complex structure, and increased physiological and behavioral reactivity" (Riesen, 1966, p. 140). As examples of some recent research in this area, we shall briefly review three provocative experiments by Torsten Wiesel and David Hubel.

Monocular Visual Deprivation

An experiment by Wiesel and Hubel confirmed and extended a previous finding. It had been shown that in the normal kitten about 80 percent of the cells in the visual cortex are responsive to stimulation of either eye. In kittens raised with one eye sutured closed, however, very few cells are responsive to stimulation of the deprived eye. On the basis of these results, one would expect that suturing both eyes would produce profound deficits in cell responses. Wiesel and Hubel (1965a) raised kittens in normal surroundings for two and one-half to four and one-half months of age with both eyes sutured. Contrary to expectation, only about one-fourth of the cells sampled were unresponsive to light stimulation. The cortex was not normal, however, in that many cells that responded did so in atypical fashion. Cell changes were found in the lateral geniculate nucleus (see Chapter 4) but not in the retina or cortex. The results imply that the ill effects of closing one eye were avoided in part by closing both. This suggests that the functional integrity of the system is not dependent merely on the amount of stimulation in the particular pathway but on the interrelationships between the two eyes.

Binocular Function

In a second experiment, Hubel and Wiesel (1965) retested these notions in a different manner. By cutting one muscle of the eyeball, the proper alignment of the two eyes was precluded in four kittens 8 to 10 days after birth. This procedure permits normal input to the two eyes but not their appropriate coordination. The naturally occurring condition is called *strabismus*. In another procedure, two kittens were raised for 10 weeks with an opaque contact occluder covering one eye one day and the other eye the next. Again, normal binocular function was precluded, but here the possibility of antagonistic interaction between the eyes was reduced. In both groups of animals, visual functioning, behaviorally, with either eye covered appeared to be normal, and in the second group the eyes moved together without strabismus with both uncovered. Responses of cells in the visual cortex were then tested and were found to be normal in all but one respect—there was again a marked reduction in cells that were responsive to stimulation of both eyes. In other words, the cells responded to stimulation of one or the other eye but not both, as they would in normal animals. Cellular examination disclosed no obvious pathology of the lateral geniculate or cortex. The results again suggest that the maintenance of a synapse depends not only on the amount of incoming impulse activity but also on a normal relationship between activities in different afferent pathways.

Recovery

The third experiment (Wiesel & Hubel, 1965b) attempted to assess whether recovery from these deficits was possible. Here various kittens had one or both eyes sutured for the first three months of life. The eyes were then surgically opened (in two monocular animals, the deprived eye was opened and the normal eye was closed). The animals were tested after their eyes had been opened for 3 to 15 months. Although the kittens showed some minor behavioral recovery, all remained severely handicapped. Cell abnormality of the lateral geniculate did not show any improvement, and cortical responses were still generally atypical. The capacity to recover from the effects of early monocular or binocular visual deprivation thus appears to be severely limited.

Additional Research

These seminal experiments have been followed in recent years by a large volume of research. For instance, Blake and Hirsch (1975) found that allowing kittens to use only one eye at a time not only reduces the proportion of binocularly activated cortical cells, but also severely reduces the adults cats' binocular depth perception. Not all studies are in agreement, however. For instance, Hirsch and Spinelli (1970) reported that cats raised from birth with one eye viewing horizontal lines and one eye viewing vertical lines showed no cells sensitive to oblique lines. (Some cells in the visual system are preferentially sensitive to lines of different orientation; this topic will be discussed in Chapter 4, p. 150.) Cortical units were selectively sensitive to the orientation experienced by the particular eye. Several studies have confirmed this finding. However, Stryker and Sherk (1975), using similar procedures, did not find any bias toward line orientations presented during rearing. They suggested that previous results were due to a variety of sampling artifacts. On the other hand, Leventhal and Hirsch (1975) reported that neurons that are preferentially sensitive to oblique contours are present only in cats exposed to them early in life. In contrast, cells preferentially responsive to horizontal or vertical lines do not require a specific input for maintenance or development—they seem to be genetically determined.

Obviously, further definition of these empirical contradictions is necessary. Grobstein and Chow (1975) have reviewed much of this material and have tried to bring some theoretical ordering to it. They emphasize, first of all, that the visual pathways are not completely developed before visual experience begins. Second, their review suggests that many of the changes resulting from restricting visual experience in young animals may not be the result of deterioration of function but rather a delay in the development of those functions. They cite evidence suggesting that in animals with restricted experience there may be a large proportion of "uncommitted" and nonresponding neurons—neurons that, without the restrictive experience, would have become further differentiated in functioning. Thus, they suggest that the genetic program permits a range of possible realizations and individual experience acts to specify the outcome of this range. It is as if the visual system (and all the CNS?) were constructed so as to be generally capable of certain functions but is intrinsically inadequately specified to ensure the precise "tuning" of the system. Trying out the system, testing it in the visual world, gives the opportunity for the fine adjustments to be made.

We should also mention that some research has discovered a degree of plasticity of visual neural functioning among adult animals possibly similar to that seen in neonates (Creutzfeldt & Heggelund, 1975; Brown & Salinger, 1975). Finally, lesions and restricted experience apparently produce their effects by modifying the patterns of excitation in the neural circuitry. Thus, functions seemingly lost actually may only be suppressed or inhibited. Witness the remarkable finding that lesions can sometimes *restore* a function that was previously lost because of restricted experience or a prior, first lesion (e.g., Sherman, 1974a, b). It remains to be seen, however, what the tradeoff is in terms of the functions lost as a result of the second lesion; i.e., are such losses relatively trivial in comparison to the function regained?

Sensory Deprivation in Humans

That humans are subject to similar influences in the development of their visual systems is indicated by the report that corrective surgery is most effective if performed early in children with congenital strabismus; with a late postnatal onset in the strabismus, there is no advantage if the surgery is performed early (Banks, Aslin, & Letson, 1975). Children between one and three years of age seem to be most sensitive to abnormal binocular experience.

Support for the proposition that continued sensory input is also necessary for the maintenance of functional integrity in the adult human organism comes from work on sensory deprivation (see Zubeck, 1969). Generally, the behavioral results of deprivation of sensory input may include hallucinations, intellectual and perceptual deterioration, and increased susceptibility to propaganda; subjects find the situation to be extremely unpleasant and often are capable of enduring only short periods of such confinement. It should also be noted, however, that the occurrence of hallucinatory phenomena during deprivation is by no means invariant. A number of studies have failed to isolate the causes of such hallucinations (see Vernon, Marton, & Peterson, 1961), and others question whether they are the result of sensory deprivation per se (see Arnhoff, Leon, & Brownfield, 1962; Zuckerman & Cohen, 1964).

For our purposes, however, it is pertinent to note the physiological changes concomitant to those behavioral changes that have been reported. A number of studies (see Zubeck, Welch, & Saunders, 1963; Zubeck & Welch, 1963) indicate that a consistent concomitant of sensory deprivation is the slowing of occipital lobe electrical activity. This reduction is actually greater in deprivation of *patterned* sensory input than under conditions of total deprivation (Zubeck & Welch, 1963). EEG-slowing is greatest at the end of deprivation periods and may persist for a period of time equaling the deprivation time. Post-isolation losses in motivation are also reported, and they are correlated with the degree of EEG-slowing. The long-term effects of isolation on the galvanic skin response appear to be a decrease in skin resistance (greater arousal). Other measures, notably biochemical, have also been secured under these conditions, but their results do not appear as consistent.

Conclusions

Generally, there is clear and consistent evidence that normal development of the nervous system requires sensory support, and that in the absence of such support the nervous system shows extensive anatomical and functional abnormality, which may not be remedied later. In addition, continued normal functioning in the adult organism is probably dependent on maintenance of sensory input.

It should be clear that no attempt is made here to separate learning and maturational factors; obviously, animals that are visually deprived postnatally are necessarily deprived of the opportunity of learning to deal with visual stimulation. It would seem fruitless to belabor this issue.

EARLY EXPERIENCE

If there is one statement with which most psychologists will agree, it is that the early experience of organisms is extremely important for their later behavior. The evidence supporting this belief comes from every subfield of psychology, and the belief need not be further elaborated at this point. What is of interest to us, however, is whether we can begin to delineate the physiological mechanisms that might mediate the effects of such experience.

Critical Periods

A key concept in this research area is that of *critical periods*. The concept of critical periods stems from embryological experiments. The induction of monstrosities or the effects of transplantion of tissue from one site to another are dependent on the development stage of the embryo—certain effects are achieved only within a restricted stage of development. We have already encountered this in connection with our discussion of CNS development (p. 75). When applied to behavioral development, the critical period concept is used in a similar manner. It implies that during some period of time the organism has a greater sensitivity to certain experiences than it has either before or afterward. For example, during a relatively restricted period, the individual might be better able to learn a particular response, or be more susceptible to the effects of certain kinds of environmental influence, than either before or after. There are developmental changes in the central and autonomic nervous systems that probably underlie such behavioral critical periods.

Learning

Studies ranging over motor learning in young children, the learning of species-specific song patterns in birds, fighting in mice and dogs, and sexual behavior in rats, guinea pigs, primates, and children have all been cited to indicate that there are critical periods for the learning of various behaviors (Scott, 1962). Each of these behaviors appears to have an associated period during which learning is optimal. But it may be that memory, rather than learning per se, is the issue. Thus, 18-day-old rats showed nearly 100 percent retention of an avoidance response when tested immediately after training but only chance performance when tested at 21- and 42-day retention intervals. In contrast, 54- and 100-day-old rats showed little or no performance decrement at any retention interval (Campbell & Campbell, 1962). Campbell and Spear (1972) discuss the paradox that this presents—early experiences are generally believed to have a disproportionate influence on adult behavior but at the same time specific events occurring early in life are less likely to be remembered than if they occurred in adulthood. There are several CNS changes that might be relevant to the development of memory and the resolution of this paradox.

Generally, neonatal mammals have little or no myelinization of their neurons (see Chapter 1). The development of the myelin covering can be a protracted process and differs in time in different species and in different brain locations in the same species. In humans, the process may last beyond the first decade of life in some cortical locations; in the rat, the process generally overlaps that associated with the development of long-term memory. Similarly, the neural cells undergo a continuing differentiation and growth process. Figure 3.6 illustrates this in the rat. There are also developmental changes in the EEG, in the availability of the different neural synaptic transmitters, and in DNA and RNA content. Thus, it is at least reasonable to conjecture that memory changes in the developing animal are related to such physiological changes.

A study by Purpura (1974) may be pertinent here. Purpura reported that genetically normal but retarded children showed abnormally long, thin, dendritic spines on the cortical neurons. Normal children show a predominance of short, thick, and stubby-appearing spiny processes. He also suggested that the degree of loss of the normal spines is related to age and severity of the mental retardation.

One of the major problems in pursuing these relationships is that many biological changes logically related to learning and memory occur concurrently. Thus, determining which are *functionally* related will be a complicated enterprise.

Socialization

Socialization of animals, or the formation of attachments between animals of the same or different species, would seem to involve the functioning of the autonomic nervous system. An older S-R learning theory approach to the socialization process assumed that socialization begins with the feeding situation, on the premise that feeding, as primary reinforcement, is the basis of acquired drives and rewards. Studies of socialization in puppies (Scott, 1962), Harlow's classic studies on infant monkeys reared with "surrogate" mothers (e.g., Harlow & Zimmerman, 1959), and studies of imprinting in young birds (e.g., E. Hess, 1964) all indicate that this is at least not a sufficient explanation. All these studies suggest the operation of significant changes in the development of intrinsic emotional response mechanisms.

Puppies that were hand-fed, fed by machine, or were rewarded or punished by differential social treatment, all demonstrated attraction to and dependence on human handlers. The evidence indicates that any strong emotional response will speed up the socialization process. In puppies this process starts at about 3 weeks of age and reaches a peak at about 6 to 7 weeks, the time when puppies bark or whine when in isolation or strange places. Puppies raised without human contacts through the critical period show extreme fear and may be very difficult to train.

In Harlow's experiments, newborn macaque monkeys were separated from their mothers and raised with "surrogate" mothers—cloth-covered or wire cylinders—either of which could be equipped with bottle holders and nursing tubes. An initial measure of affectional attachment was the time the monkey spent on each of the two types of mothers. Regardless of feeding conditions, infant animals to the age of 165 days spent an average of more than 15 hours per day in contact with the cloth mother. Differential warmth was not a factor, for infants ignored a heating pad that was available. These data suggest that the contact comfort provided by the cloth-covered surrogate far outweighs feeding as a significant variable in establishing infant–mother relationships. Additional evidence is provided by the fact that when fear-evoking stimuli were introduced, the infants overwhelmingly fled to the

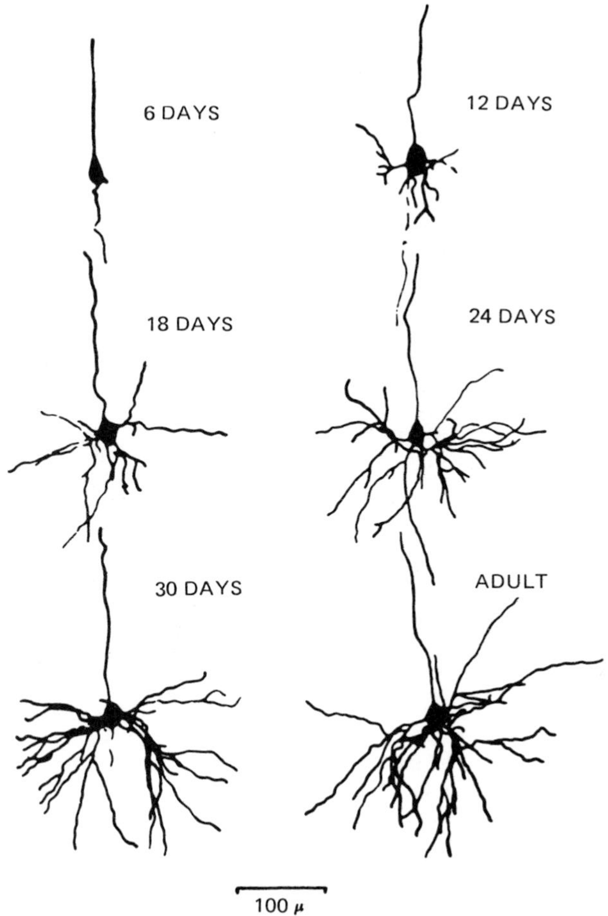

Figure 3.6. Characteristic changes in appearance of pyramidal cells in the rat from six days of age to maturity. (From Eayrs, J.T., and Goodhead, B. Postnatal development in the cerebral cortex of the rat. *Journal of Anatomy*, 1959, 93, 385–411.)

cloth mothers, again regardless of feeding conditions. Infants raised only with wire mothers rushed away from fearful objects but did not cling to the wire mother; rather they clutched themselves, rocked, and vocalized. These and other experiments (Harlow & Zimmerman, 1959) emphasize the role of contact comfort in establishing infant–mother relationships.

Peer and sex relationships in monkeys are also disrupted by social isolation. Infant monkeys subjected to total social deprivation for the first 3 months—no mothering or peer contacts—showed a state of emotional shock on release from deprivation but quickly established effective peer relationships. But monkeys similarly isolated for 6 to 12 months showed impaired

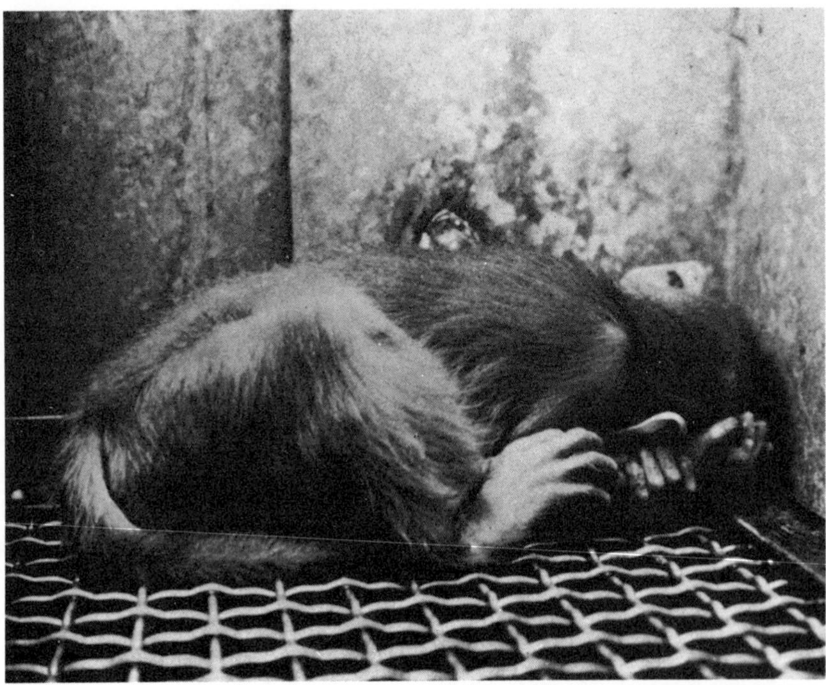

Figure 3.7. Rhesus monkey viewed immediately after raising the wall of the isolation chamber where it was confined from birth to 12 months of age. The monkeys typically retreat to a back corner of the box and display a crouching posture, which includes some form of self-clutching and shielding of the eyes. Such postures are also common during confinement and continue after the animals are housed in wire-mesh cages in the nursery. (From Harlow, H.F. and Harlow, M. Learning to love. *American Scientist,* 1966, *54,* 244–272.)

interactions with control age mates (Figure 3.7). Monkeys raised without peer contacts are extremely deficient in adult sexual performance. Females raised without mothers are themselves deficient, abusive, and unloving in their behavior toward their infants if they do become pregnant (Harlow, 1962). Here, the failure to learn specific responses may be in part responsible, but the atypical emotional responses of these animals is also striking.

Imprinting and Emotions

The influence of emotional factors, not simply the learning of certain responses, seems to play an important part in the *imprinting process.* Although use of the term has been extended, imprinting originally referred to the process whereby young birds form an attachment to the parent. Soon after hatching, precocial birds (birds capable of independent existence) become attached to and follow the first moving object in their immediate environment (normally this is the parent). If something or someone else is substituted for the parent bird, the attachment is formed for the new object and the parent is ignored. One important characteristic of this process is that it has a critical period, from hatching to about 36 hours, peaking at about 16 hours. It should also be noted that many aspects of adult behavior that are not operative during the stage when imprinting occurs are nonetheless, thought to be influenced by it.

Much controversy has circulated about the question of whether the process of forming the attachment in imprinting is the same or different from conventional associative learning. E. Hess (1964) has listed a number of features which seem to distinguish imprinting from associative learning. Moltz (1960), Rajecki (1973), and Hoffman and Ratner (1973), in contrast, attempt to place imprinting within the more conventional learning models of attachment. It is interesting that both sides emphasize the influence of emotional and arousal processes in the formation of attachments. Generally, the periodicity, or limited time course of imprinting, seems to be a function of the variation in development of emotional and arousing mechanisms.

Infantile Stimulation

The third area from which evidence for critical period effects comes is the influence of infantile stimulation on adult emotionality. The results of many experiments generally point to the conclusion that infant animals exposed to a variety of handling, gentling, and stress experiences are less emotional, better at avoidance-learning tasks, and survive stress better than control animals in tests during adulthood; critical periods for such effects have been suggested.

In the typical experiment (e.g., Denenberg, 1962), groups of infant rats are exposed to treatments like handling, electric shock, or cooling at different times, typically within the first 10 days of life. As Adults, such groups may show differential body weights, avoidance-response performance, emotionality,[3] and survival duration in response to terminal food and water deprivation. Generally, such treatments result in animals that are less emotional and withstand adult stress conditions better. Similarly, Ader and Conklin (1963) showed that pregnant rats that were handled produced less

[3]"Emotionality" is typically tested in rats with the open field test: The apparatus consists of a large, enclosed space that is marked off in squares; generally, the more the rat moves about, particularly in the center squares, and the less he defecates and urinates in the apparatus, the less emotional he is considered to be.

emotional offspring than controls, when the offspring were tested at 45 or 100 days of age. This was true even if the pups were cross-fostered to other mothers. On the other hand, prenatal maternal anxiety caused increased emotionality in the offspring rats (Thompson, 1957). In this study, anxiety was induced by giving avoidance training with strong shock prior to pregnancy and blocking the avoidance (without shock) after the females became pregnant.

Criticisms of the Critical Period Hypothesis

Recent data suggest that the critical period for socialization may not be that "critical," either in the sense of being irreversible or in the sense of circumscribing a specific time limit (Mason & Kenney, 1974). In this study, the subjects were young monkeys that had previously experienced a variety of infant socialization experiences; some had been raised with their natural mothers, others with peers, and still others with surrogate mothers. After varying periods of such experiences, they were gradually introduced to living exclusively with adult female dogs. At first, most monkeys reacted with fear, distress vocalizations, and withdrawal. These behaviors usually disappeared quickly, however (a matter of hours), and the animals ended up in frequent contact, clinging to each other, playing and resting together, and grooming each other. Formal tests of the exclusiveness of the attachment were also carried out after 6 to 8 weeks of cohabitation. Generally, the familiar dog was preferred in all tests over unfamiliar surrogates, other dogs and even other monkeys. The varying prior exposure conditions did not affect these results; that is, even monkeys previously exposed to other monkeys preferred the familiar dog. Thus, prior strong attachment bonds did not preclude the formation of new attachments of equal strength. And the notion that the formation of such attachments is restricted sharply in time is also questionable in the light of these results.

Fuller (1967) has emphasized that isolation may simply act to inhibit normal adaptations. On release from isolation, the animal is overwhelmed by his environment, preventing any adaptation to it. He found that if measures are taken to avoid the stress of emergence from isolation—for example, if puppies are stroked and handled and given tranquilizers—many of the deficits attributed to the isolation itself may be alleviated.

Finally, Harlow and others deemphasize the criticality of any particular period. For Harlow, socialization consists of a great variety of behaviors and these are mutually interdependent; it would be difficult to isolate one particular period as critical for any social relationship. Schneirla and Rosenblatt (1963) stress the interdependence of maturational processes with specific experiences—normally each age period contributes to a complex *progression* in the patterns of adjustment. It seems likely that the importance of whether critical periods can be isolated will diminish with knowledge of the physiological mechanisms that are involved.

Mechanisms of Changing Emotionality

Generally, then, a variety of handling, stimulating, and social rearing procedures are accompanied by marked changes in the emotional behavior of the animals so exposed. It is not clear whether there is any common mechanism operating in each of these manipulations or whether any of these are direct or indirect effects; for instance, the effects of handling infant pups could be due to disruption of the mother's care of the infants, cooling of the animals, or "stress" (Russell, 1971). However, all do seem to have the common end result of influencing the sympathetic division of the autonomic nervous system, and in particular, the hypothalamic-pituitary-adrenal system. The effects of handling have been particularly studied and may provide a model. For instance, Levine, Haltmeyer, Karas, and Denenberg (1967) compared adult male rats handled during the first 20 days of infancy to nonhandled animals on open field behavior and adrenal-cortical-hormonal output following open field testing. Generally, handled rats were more active, defecated less, and had a lesser adrenal-cortical hormone response to the test than nonhandled animals in the open field. Thus, one would conclude that both behaviorally and physiologically, the handled rats showed less emotional reaction to the test. It is of interest that the resting levels of adrenal hormone did not differ; that is, these results indicate a difference in *responsiveness* to the stress of the test situation rather than a difference in level.

Levine and Mullins (1966) reviewed findings such as these on developmental changes in endocrine gland responses in infant animals (for instance, that adrenal ascorbic acid response to cold appears earlier in rats that have been handled), and proposed the following mechanism of action to account for the effects of infantile stimulation. In the adult animal, adrenal-cortical activity seems to be under at least partial control by a homeostatic feedback system or *hormonostat*. The concentration of adrenal-cortical hormones in the blood is monitored in the central nervous system and compared to some "setting." If the concentration deviates from the setting, ACTH (adrenocorticotrophic hormone of the pituitary) is increased or decreased, causing the appropriate compensatory output of the adrenals. The setting of the hormonostat is not fixed but depends on the demands of the environment and the state of the organism. The sensitivity of the hormonostat to demands on the organism is reflected in the range of output values that the adrenals can show; that is, can the organism respond in a graded fashion to demands of varying severity? It is hypothesized that handling at a critical state in the maturation of this system, by causing variation in the concentration of adrenal hormones, modifies the setting point of the hormonostat so that adrenal output can vary in a graded manner in the adult animal. In the nonhandled animal, there is less variation in the adrenal output at this critical stage, and this results in less flexibility of response in the adult. Such animals operate at resting levels or at levels close to maximum on exposure to even moderate stress from the environment.

Some support for this model comes from the demonstration that concurrent norepinephrine and chlorpromazine injections mitigate the effects of early extra stimulation (Young, 1964). Parallel evidence for similar mechanisms involving the gonadal system is also marshaled by Levine and Mullins (1966); these data will be discussed in Chapter 10.

Generally, then, handling, stimulating, and social rearing procedures seem to influence whether an "appropriate" response to environmental stimulation occurs later in life. Specifically, early experiences influence whether the emotional response mechanisms are capable of differentiating their responses in a manner suitable to the environmental circumstances. For instance, in response to electric shock administered at 60 days of age, mice handled in infancy showed more elevated plasma norepinephrine levels than nonhandled mice, whereas epinephrine levels were similar in the two groups. In contrast, when subjected to defeat by trained fighter mice, epinephrine levels were higher in the handled mice while norepinephrine levels were similar (Hucklebridge & Newell, 1973). Kety (1967, p. 106) has suggested that "epinephrine is secreted primarily in situations of uncertainty, in which fight or flight may be the appropriate response, and this agent would have adaptive functions. Norepinephrine appears to be secreted in those situations in which the outcome is inevitable or unavoidable and muscular activity would be inappropriate or useless." In other words, secretion of these substances is an indicator of how the animal copes with his environment! We will return to the concept of coping in Chapter 7.

Environmental Enrichment

Stemming from Hebb's (1949) theory of perceptual development, a number of experiments in the early fifties investigated the effects of early perceptual experience in rats on their adult performance (for example, Forgays & Forgays, 1952; Forgus, 1954). Generally, such studies have shown that rats reared in small, restricted enclosures are inferior to rats reared in a complex, free environment on tests of problem solving, form discrimination, and the like. Complex or "enriched" environments generally consist of large boxes or cages containing a variety of "toys" such as blocks, marbles, swings, inclined planes, and platforms. The intent is to provide the experimental animals with an opportunity for varied visual and motor involvement with the environment.

Effects on Brain Chemistry and Anatomy

A series of studies employing this basic environmental manipulation have been carried out by an interdisciplinary group of investigators representing psychology, biochemistry, and anatomy. Summaries of this research are available in Rosenzweig (1966), Bennett, Diamond, Krech, and Rosenzweig (1964); and Walsh and Cummins (1975), among others. The intent of these studies is to examine the effects on brain chemistry and anatomy of environmental manipulation. Remember that neural information is transmitted across synapses through the release of chemical substances; the chemical transmitter is then inactivated by action of an enzyme. Acetylcholine and acetylcholinesterase constitute one of several hypothesized synaptic transmission systems. The studies under consideration here were conducted under the hypothesis that enriched environmental experience would increase the rate of liberation of acetylcholine, and this in turn would result in increased production of acetylcholinesterase, the latter actually being amenable to measurement. After several experiments had been carried out, it was discovered that the data suggested that changes in brain anatomy were also occurring.

The general plan of these experiments was to put rats into differential environments at weaning (about 25 days of age) for 80 days. One group of animals received enriched experience with a complex environment. A second group was kept in an isolated condition, with the animals housed singly in a dimly lit, quiet room. Other control animals were kept in colony conditions, three animals to a cage, exposed to no special treatment except the normal activities going on in the room.

Acetylcholinesterase activity was measured for the cortex, the remainder of the brain, and for portions of the cortex; i.e., visual versus somesthetic cortex. Environmental enrichment increased acetylcholinesterase activity by small but significant amounts—the largest increases, about 3.5 percent, were in the visual cortex. Comparing enriched and isolated animals, the total cortex increased in weight by some 4.6 percent, although the enriched animals were actually 7 percent smaller in body weight at the end of the experiment. Animals receiving enriched experience were also significantly different from the colony controls, indicating that the differences did not result from a decrement produced by the stress of isolation. Other experiments indicate that differential handling and locomotor activity did not produce the differences in enzymatic activity and brain weight. In addition, the effects are not confined to young animals, for they can also be produced in mature, colony-reared animals given later enrichment. Finally, the results do not seem to reflect a general alteration in brain chemistry; the pattern of results was not duplicated when other chemicals were measured.

Other investigators (see Walsh & Cummins [1975] for references) have found that environmental enrichment leads to larger brains and increased cell body size, dendritic formation, and number of glial cells. Walsh and Cummins suggest that the activation of arousal mechanisms may be a major mediator for producing these changes.

Behavioral Changes

The relationships between results at the chemical level and the behavioral changes resulting from enrichment are obscure, however. Thus, Brown (1971) found learning improvements and cholinesterase changes after certain enrichment experiences, but the biochemical changes dissipated over a period of time more rapidly than did the behavioral improvements. Furthermore, the various enrichment experiences employed differed somewhat in their resulting pattern of biochemical changes, although behavioral improvements were similar with all enrichment procedures.

These experiments suggest, then, that the brain will respond to environmental manipulations with small but significant increases in chemical activity and brain anatomy, but the precise meaning of these changes will require further investiation.

The Issue of Generalizability

To the degree that the results discussed in this chapter can be generalized to human development and behavior, they obviously have important implications. However, the degree to which such generalization is warranted is as yet not certain. In fact, some words of caution should be directed to the fact that most of the data discussed were obtained from laboratory-bred animals whose early lives were spent in small, relatively barren cages with little opportunity for locomotion and exploration; they grew up in a relatively impoverished environment. It is probable that these conditions contribute to some of the effects discussed in this chapter—in fact, the environmental enrichment experiments manipulate just this variable. In other words, the effects discussed here may not be generalizable to nonlaboratory animals in the sense that their normal habitats may supply more nearly optimal conditions for development where enrichment would be superfluous (also see Kavanau, 1964). Furthermore, many writers have pointed to the changes in rats as a result of domestication. As a result, they bear little anatomical and physiological resemblance in many important respects to their wild forebears. Lockard (1968) summarized these differences and concluded that the albino laboratory rat is particularly unsuitable for most psychological and physiological experimentation. For instance, here we have been particularly interested in emotional reactivity and adrenal mechanisms in its development; the laboratory rat is characterized by particularly small adrenals compared to wild rats. On the other hand, Boice (1973) has taken some of the same facts and has argued that they imply that the domesticated rat is, in fact, a good analogue for civilized man. While we must be cautious in the pursuit of analogies based on findings in animals, neither can they be totally disregarded.

SUMMARY

That the behavior of an organism is dependent on its developmental history seems to be a self-evident proposition. Starting with the development of the nervous system, there is evidence that the growth and destination of neural fibers is under endogenous chemical control. Despite dramatic interventions on the part of experimenters, there seems to be a great deal of regularity and relative invariance in this process. Neurons grow and make their functional connections seemingly without influence from experiential determinants. On the other hand, there is also evidence that the maintenance of the functional integrity of at least some organisms is dependent on the presence of stimulation from the environment and the nature of such stimulation. Furthermore, CNS damage does not necessarily result in permanent functional losses. Such evidence suggests some form of continuing CNS plasticity. Presumably, some neurons also alter their functional properties during learning.

Roughly, at least, it might appear that "involuntary," reflexive behavior is mediated by neurons characterized by endogenous control. From this, one could very easily leap to the conclusion that there is something different about neurons or snyapses mediating "voluntary," learned behavior. It is too easy to make this inference because there is no precise way of delimiting "voluntary" from "involuntary." What, for instance, is "voluntary" about the kitten's coordination of its two eyes? Yet functional neural changes occur in the absence of the opportunity for such coordination. Again, why is it that humans can learn to compensate for distorted visual input but chicks apparently do not? Clearly, answers to such questions are dependent on specification of the functional properties of the neurons involved.

There are similar difficulties in discussing instinctive behavior. Some evidence exists for genetically fixed, neural circuits mediating specific consummatory behavior; but it is uncertain whether these circuits are in fact fixed.

Experiments on early experience do suggest that anatomical and biochemical changes may take place in at least the rat brain as a result of differential environmental treatment. On the other hand, there is controversy over the existence of critical periods. But with clarification of the physiological mechanisms operating in early experience effects, the importance of this issue will diminish.

It should also be clear that the various factors reviewed separately here do not operate in isolation. There are likely to be interactions among them and interactions imply the possibility of compensating effects, e.g., environmental enrichment might offset nutritional or emotional deficits.

Psychologists have tended to emphasize learning processes as a factor in postnatal development. But the material reviewed in this chapter emphasizes that the basic response capacities of the neonate are not fully determined at birth. The brain, emotional response systems, and even the sensory capacities of the organism are subject to further modifications which are dependent on the nature of the environmental conditions to which they are exposed. Indeed, such experience seems to determine to a large degree what the organism is capable of learning.

REFERENCES

ADER, R., & CONKLIN, P. M. Handling of pregnant rats: Effects on emotionality of their offspring. *Science*, 1963, *142*, 411–412.

AKERT, K. Diencephalon. In D. E. Sheer (ed.), *Electrical stimulation of the brain.* Austin, Texas: University of Texas Press, 1961, pp. 288–310.

ARNHOFF, F. N., LEON, H. V., & BROWNFIELD, C. A. Sensory deprivation: Its effects on human learning. *Science*, 1962, *138*, 899–900.

BANKS, M. S., ASLIN, R. N., & LETSON, R. D. Sensitive period for the development of human binocular vision. *Science*, 1975, *190*, 675–677.

BEACH, F. A. The descent of instinct. *Psychological Review*, 1955, *62*, 401–410.

BEACH, F. A., & JAYNES, J. Effects of early experience upon the behavior of animals. *Psychological Bulletin*, 1954, *51*, 239–263.

BENNETT, E. L., DIAMOND, M. C., KRECH, D., & ROSENZWEIG, M. R. Chemical and anatomical plasticity of the brain. *Science*, 1964, *146*, 610–619.

BLAKE, R., & HIRSCH, H. V. B. Deficits in binocular depth perception in cats after alternating monocular deprivation. *Science*, 1975, *190*, 114–116.

BLAND, B. H., & COOPER, R. M. Posterior neodecortication in the rat: Age at operation and experience. *Journal of Comparative and Physiological Psychology*, 1969, *69*, 345–354.

BOICE, R. Domestication. *Psychological Bulletin*, 1973, *80*, 215–230.

BROWN, C. P. Cholinergic activity in rats following enriched stimulation and training: Direction and duration of effects. *Journal of Comparative and Physiological Psychology*, 1971, *75*, 408–416.

Brown, D. L., & Salinger, W. L. Loss of X-cells in lateral geniculate nucleus with monocular paralysis: Neural plasticity in the adult cat. *Science*, 1975, *189*, 1011–1012.

Burghardt, G. M., & Hess, E. H. Food imprinting in the snapping turtle, *Chelydra serpentina*. *Science*, 1966, *151*, 108–109.

Butcher, R. E. A behavioral deficit associated with maternal phenylketonuria in rats. *Nature*, 1970, *226*, 555–556.

Campbell, B. A., & Campbell, E. H. Retention and extinction of learned fear in infant and adult rats. *Journal of Comparative and Physiological Psychology*, 1962, *55*, 1–8.

Campbell, B. A., & Spear, N. E. Ontogeny of memory. *Psychological Review*, 1972, *79*, 215–236.

Constantine–Paton, M., & Capranica, R. P. Central projection of optic tract from translocated eyes in the leopard frog *(Rana pipiens)*. *Science*, 1975, *189*, 480–482.

Crain, S. M., & Peterson, E. R. Development of specific sensory-evoked synaptic networks in fetal mouse cord-brainstem cultures. *Science*, 1975, *188*, 275–278.

Cravioto, J. Nutritional deficiencies and mental performance in childhood. In D. C. Glass (ed.), *Environmental influences, biology and behavior series*. New York: Rockefeller University Press, 1968, pp. 3–51.

Creutzfeldt, O. D., & Heggelund, P. Neural plasticity in visual cortex of adult cats after exposure to visual patterns. *Science*, 1975, *188*, 1025–1027.

Denenberg, V. H. An attempt to isolate critical periods of development in the rat. *Journal of Comparative and Physiological Psychology*, 1962, *55*, 813–815.

Devor, M. Neuroplasticity in the sparing or deterioration of function after early olfactory tract lesions. *Science*, 1975, *90*, 998–1000.

Eayrs, J. T., & Goodhead, B. Postnatal development in the cerebral cortex of the rat. *Journal of Anatomy*, 1959, *93*, 385–401.

Eichenwald, H. F., & Fry, P. C. Nutrition and learning. *Science*, 1969, *163*, 644–648.

Forgays, D. G., & Forgays, J. W. The nature of the effect of free environmental experience in the rat. *Journal of Comparative and Physiological Psychology*, 1952, *45*, 322–328.

Forgus, R. H. The effect of early perceptual learning on the behavioral organization of adult rats. *Journal of Comparative and Physiological Psychology*, 1954, *47*, 331–336.

Fuller, J. L. Experiential deprivation and later behavior. *Science*, 1967, *158*, 1645–1652.

Grobstein, P., & Chow, K. L. Receptive field development and individual experience. *Science*, 1975, *190*, 352–358.

Harlow, H. F. The heterosexual affectional system in monkeys. *American Psychologist*, 1962, *17*, 1–9.

Harlow, H. F., & Harlow, M. Learning to love. *American Scientist*, 1966, *54*, 244–272.

Harlow, H. F., & Zimmermann, R. R. Affectional responses in the infant monkey. *Science*, 1959, *130*, 421–432.

Hebb, D. O. *Organization of behavior.* New York: Wiley, 1949.

Held, R., & Freedman, S. J. Plasticity in human sensorimotor control. *Science*, 1963, *142*, 455–462.

Hess, E. Space perception in the chick. *Scientific American*, 1956, *195*, 71–80.

Hess, E. Ethology: An approach toward the complete analysis of behavior. *New directions in psychology*, I. New York: Holt, Rinehart & Winston, 1962, pp. 157–266.

Hess, E. Imprinting in birds. *Science*, 1964, *146*, 1128–1129.

Hirsch, H. V. B., & Spinelli, D. N. Visual experience modifies distribution of horizontally and vertically oriented receptive fields in cats. *Science*, 1970, *168*, 869–871.

Hoffman, H. S., & Ratner, A. M. A reinforcement model of imprinting: Implications for socialization in monkeys and men. *Psychological Review*, 1973, *80*, 527–544.

Hubel, D. H., & Wiesel, T. N. Binocular interaction in striate cortex of kittens reared with artificial squint. *Journal of Neurophysiology*, 1965, *28*, 1041–1059.

Hucklebridge, F. H., & Newell, N. W. Effect of infantile handling upon catecholamine response to acute noxious stimulation in adulthood. *Behavioral Biology*, 1973, *9*, 563–579.

Jacobson, M. Development of specific neuronal connections. *Science*, 1969, *163*, 543–547.

Joffe, M. J. Genotype and prenatal and premating stress interact to affect adult behavior in rats. *Science*, 1965, *150*, 1844–1845.

Kaplan, B. J. Malnutrition and mental deficiency. *Psychological Bulletin*, 1972, *78*, 321–334.

Kavanau, J. L. Behavior: Confinement, adaptation, and compulsory regimes in laboratory studies. *Science*, 1964, *143*, 490.

Kety, S. S. Psychoendocrine systems and emotion: Biological aspects. In D. C. Glass (ed.), *Neurophysiology and emotion.* New York: Rockefeller University Press, 1967, pp. 103–108.

KUO, Z. Y. The genesis of the cat's responses to the rat. *Journal of Comparative Psychology*, 1930, *11*, 1–35.

LEVENTHAL, A. G., & HIRSCH, H. V. B. Cortical effect of early selective exposure to diagonal lines. *Science*, 1975, *190*, 902–904.

LEVINE, S., HALTMEYER, G. C., KARAS, G. G., & DENENBERG, V. H. Physiological and behavioral effects of infantile stimulation. *Physiology and Behavior*, 1967, *2*, 55–59.

LEVINE, S., & MULLINS, R. F., JR. Hormonal influences on brain organization in infant rats. *Science*, 1966, *152*, 1585–1592.

LEVITSKY, D. A., & BARNES, R. H. Nutritional and environmental interactions in the behavioral development of the rat: Long-term effects. *Science*, 1972, *176*, 68–71.

LOCKARD, R. B. The albino rat: A defensible choice or a bad habit? *American Psychologist*, 1968, *23*, 734–742.

LYNCH, G., DEADWYLER, S., & COTMAN, C. Postlesion axonal growth produces permanent functional connections. *Science*, 1973, *180*, 1364–1366.

MARLER, P. R., & HAMILTON, W. J., III. *Mechanisms of animal behavior.* New York: Wiley, 1967.

MASON, W. A., & KENNEY, M. D. Redirection of filial attachments in rhesus monkeys: Dogs as mother surrogates. *Science*, 1974, *183*, 1209–1211.

MILLER, N. E. Experiments on motivation. *Science*, 1957, *126*, 1271–1278.

MOLTZ, H. Imprinting: Empirical basis and theoretical significance. *Psychological Bulletin*, 1960, *57*, 291–314.

MOLTZ, H. Contemporary instinct theory and the fixed action pattern. *Psychological Bulletin*, 1965, *72*, 27–47.

MOORE, R. Y. Central regeneration and recovery of function: The problem of collateral reinnervation. In D. G. Stein, J. J. Rosen, & N. Butters (eds.), *Plasticity and recovery of function in the central nervous system.* New York: Academic Press, 1974, pp. 111–128.

PURPURA, D. Dendritic spine "dysgenesis" and mental retardation. *Science*, 1974, *186*, 1126–1128.

RAJECKI, D. W. Imprinting in precocial birds: Interpretation, evidence, and evaluation. *Psychological Bulletin*, 1973, *79*, 48–58.

RIESEN, A. H. Arrested vision. *Scientific American*, 1950, *183*, 16–19.

RIESEN, A. H. Sensory deprivation. In E. Stellar (ed.), *Progress in physiological psychology.* New York: Academic Press, 1966, pp. 117–147.

ROBERTS, W. W., & BERQUIST, E. H. Attack elicited by hypothalamic stimulation in cats raised in social isolation. *Journal of Comparative and Physiological Psychology*, 1968, *66*, 590–595.

ROBERTS, W. W., & CAREY, R. J. Rewarding effect of performance of gnawing aroused by hypothalamic stimulation in the rat. *Journal of Comparative and Physiological Psychology,* 1965, *59*, 317–325.

ROBERTS, W. W., & KIESS, H. O. Motivational properties of hypothalamic aggression in cats. *Journal of Comparative and Physiological Psychology,* 1964, *58*, 187–193.

ROBERTS, W. W., STEINBERG, M. L., & MEANS, L. W. Hypothalamic mechanisms for sexual, aggressive, and other motivational behaviors in the oppossum, *Didelphis virginiana. Journal of Comparative and Physiological Psychology,* 1967, *64*, 1–16.

ROSENZWEIG, M. R. Environmental complexity, cerebral change, and behavior. *American Psychologist,* 1966, *21*, 321–332.

RUSSELL, P. A. "Infantile stimulation" in rodents: A consideration of possible mechanisms. *Psychological Bulletin,* 1971, *75*, 192–202.

SALAS, M., & CINTRA, L. Development of the electrocorticogram during starvation in the rat. *Physiology and Behavior,* 1975, *14*, 589–593.

SCHNEIDER, G. E., & JHAVERI, S. R. Neuroanatomical correlates of spared or altered function after brain lesions in the newborn hamster. In D. G. Stein, J. J. Rosen, and N. Butters (eds.), *Plasticity and recovery of function in the central nervous system.* New York: Academic Press, 1974, pp. 65–110.

SCHNEIRLA, T. C., & ROSENBLATT, J. S. "Critical periods" in the development of behavior. *Science*, 1963, *139*, 1110–1115.

SCOTT, J. P. Critical periods in behavioral development. *Science*, 1962, *138*, 949–958.

SHERMAN, S. M. Visual fields of cats with cortical and tectal lesions. *Science*, 1974, *185*, 335–357. (a)

SHERMAN, S. M. Monocularly deprived cats: Improvement of the deprived eye's vision by visual decortication. *Science*, 1974, *186*, 267–269. (b)

SPERRY, R. W. Mechanisms of neural maturation. In S. S. Stevens (ed.), *Handbook of experimental psychology.* New York: Wiley, 1951, pp. 236–280.

SPERRY, R. W. Physiological plasticity and brain circuit theory. In H. Harlow & C. N. Woolsey (eds.), *Biological and biochemical bases of behavior.* Madison: University of Wisconsin Press, 1958, pp. 301–424.

STEIN, D. G., ROSEN, J. J., & BUTTERS, N. (eds.). *Plasticity and recovery of function in the central nervous system.* New York: Academic Press. 1974.

STEIN, Z., & SUSSER, M. LETTER. *Science*, 1973, *180*, 134–135.

STEIN, Z., SUSSER, M., SAENGER, G., & MAROLLA, F. Nutrition and mental performance. *Science*, 1972, *178*, 708–713.

STRYKER, M. P., & SHERK, H. Modification of cortical orientation selectivity in the cat by restricted visual experience: A reexamination. *Science*, 1975, *190*, 904–906.

TAUB, E. Prism compensation as a learning phenomenon: A phylogenetic perspective. In S. J. Freedman (ed.), *The neuropsychology of spatially oriented behavior*. Homewood, Ill.: Dorsey Press, 1968, pp. 77–106.

THOMPSON, W. R. Influence of prenatal maternal anxiety on emotionality in young rats. *Science*, 1957, *125*, 698–699.

VALENSTEIN, E. S., COX, V. C., & KAKOLEWSKI, J. W. Modification of motivated behavior elicited by electrical stimulation of the hypothalamus. *Science*, 1968, *159*, 1119–1121.

VALENSTEIN, E. S., COX, V. C., & KAKOLEWSKI, J. W. Hypothalamic motivational systems: Fixed or plastic neural circuits. *Science*, 1969, *163*, 1084.

VAUGHAN, E., & FISHER, A. E. Male sexual behavior induced by intracranial electrical stimulation. *Science*, 1962, *137*, 758–760.

VERNON, J., MARTON, T., & PETERSON, E. Sensory deprivation and hallucinations. *Science*, 1961, *133*, 1808–1812.

WALSH, R. N., & CUMMINS, R. A. Mechanisms mediating the production of environmentally induced brain changes. *Psychological Bulletin*, 1975, *82*, 986–1000.

WARREN, N. Malnutrition and mental development. *Psychological Bulletin*, 1973, *80*, 324–328.

WETZEL, A. B., THOMPSON, V. E., HOREL, J. A., & MEYER, P. M. Some consequences of perinatal lesions of the visual cortex in the cat. *Psychonomic Science*, 1965, *3*, 381–382.

WIESEL, T. N., & HUBEL, D. H. Comparison of the effects of unilateral and bilateral eye closure on cortical unit responses in the kitten. *Journal of Neurophysiology*, 1965, *28*, 1029–1040. (a)

WIESEL, T. N., & HUBEL, D. H. Extent of recovery from the effects of visual deprivation in kittens. *Journal of Neurophysiology*, 1965, *28*, 1060–1072. (b)

WINICK, M., MEYER, K. K., & HARRIS, R. C. Malnutrition and environmental enrichment by early adoption. *Science*, 1975, *190*, 1173–1176.

WISE, R. A. Hypothalamic motivational systems: Fixed or plastic neuralcircuits? *Science*, 1968, *162*, 377–379.

WISE, R. A. Plasticity of hypothalamic motivational systems. *Science*, 1969, *165*, 929–930.

WYNNE-EDWARD, V. C. Population control and social selection in animals. In D. C. Glass (ed.), *Genetics, Biology and behavior series*. New York: The Rockefeller University Press, 1968, pp. 143–163.

YOUNG, R. D. Drug administration to neonatal rats: Effects on later emotionality and learning. *Science*, 1964, *143*, 1055–1057.

ZEIGLER, H. P. Displacement activity and motivational theory: A case study in the history of ethology. *Psychological Bulletin*, 1964, *61*, 362–376.

ZUBECK, J. P. (ed.). *Sensory deprivation: Fifteen years of research*. New York: Appleton-Century-Crofts, 1969.

ZUBECK, J. P., & WELCH, G. Electroencephalographic changes after prolonged sensory and perceptual deprivation. *Science*, 1963, *139*, 1209–1210.

ZUBECK, J. P., WELCH, G., & SAUNDERS, M. G. Electroencephalographic changes during and after 14 days of perceptual deprivation. *Science*, 1963, *139*, 490–492.

ZUCKERMAN, M., & COHEN, N. Sources of reports of visual and auditory sensations in perceptual-isolation experiments. *Psychological Bulletin*, 1964, *62*, 1–20.

4

Sensory Processes

This chapter and the next, taken together, address the problem of how we receive and process information from the environment. Psychologists sometimes divide this problem into two subproblems: sensation and perception. This distinction suggests that *sensation* refers to those receptor processes that are involved in the conversion of stimulus energy from the environment into the neural events the organism is equipped to handle. *Perception* "follows" this conversion by applying some sort of interpretive or organizing process to the raw stimulus events. As we shall see, this distinction is somewhat artificial and not entirely in keeping with the empirical facts. Nonetheless, it does provide a means for organizing the problem and we shall follow it for that purpose. Generally, then, this chapter will focus on that part of the total problem dealing with reception of stimulus energy from the environment and its conversion into neural processes. More specifically, we shall be concerned with the question of how environmental stimuli are "coded" in the nervous system. In the next chapter we will concentrate on how the oranism utilizes that information; for instance, how it selectively responds to the myriad environmental stimuli that reach it.

Historically, scientific psychology began with the study of sensory processes—psychophysics—during the mid 1800s (Boring, 1929).

Psychophysics basically involves exposing subjects to a variety of stimulus events and drawing inferences about the structure and functioning of their sensory apparatus from the relationship between the stimuli and the subjects' reports of their sensations.[1] These inferences quite often have taken the form of presumed physiological properties. For instance, if subjects can be shown to be capable of differentiating between red and blue lights, there should be a receptor or a system capable of mediating the differentiation; if some subjects cannot differentiate red and green, it is inferred that they have some defect in their receptor systems. The validation of such inferences has led to some of the most precise psychological information available. For instance, human sensitivity to light of different wavelengths is almost perfectly related to the light absorption characteristics of pigments in the retina of the eye.

ACTIVATION OF SENSORY SYSTEMS

Sensory processes begin with the activation of a *receptor*. Basically, a receptor is a transducer—a converter of energy from one form to another. A TV set converts invisible electromagnetic radiation into visible energy so that the transmission may be received by the human eye. Similarly, the eye contains receptors which act as transducers in that they convert visual energy into neural impulses. In the eye, these receptors are the rods and cones in the retina. The hair cells of the cochlea of the ear are another example. Along with the receptors, there may be a more or less complex *accessory* apparatus, such as the cornea, lens, and iris of the eye, or the external ear, ossicles, and tympanic membrane of the auditory system. Accessory apparatus serves to focus, amplify, or conduct the stimulus energy to the receptors. Either through accessory apparatus or directly, the stimulus activates the receptor which then produces an electrical potential. This *receptor potential* is a *graded* potential; that is, the size of the potential is proportional to the sensory input to the system. The processes by which this graded potential is produced are largely unknown in most sensory systems.

In close proximity to each receptor is a sensory neuron, separated from it by a snyapse. The receptor potential results in graded activity across the synapse in the dendrite of the neuron. If this graded potential reaches sufficient size, the *threshold*, an all-or-none spike discharge will be propagated along the sensory fiber into the CNS. There are also efferent neural pathways that terminate on the receptor systems and serve to modulate or "gate" the influx of information from the receptors to the CNS. Thus, the CNS need

[1]Generally psychophysics employs human subjects and the data are the subjects' reports of their sensations but, with appropriate training procedures, animals have also been employed in many of the same tasks.

not passively accept the incoming information from the various sensory receptors; it may selectively exert a filtering or dampening action on the input. We will discuss these mechanisms in the next chapter.

CODING OF SENSORY INFORMATION

It is obvious, of course, that we receive light through the eyes, sound through the ears, etc. But each sensory system is composed primarily of nerve tissue, and it is "messages" in nerve tissue that are received by the brain. Thus, it is not "redness" or "heat" that is directly received by the brain, but rather a message about the stimulus. How does the brain "know" which messages are about redness and which about heat? What we have here is an elementary example of coding. That is, redness and heat are coded, kept separate, by virtue of the fact that they stimulate different sensory systems. Furthermore, a variety of physical energies is capable of stimulating any specific sensory system. If the system responds, however, the sensations evoked are appropriate for that system; for example, pressure on visual receptors produces visual sensations.

In 1826, Johannes Müller formulated these facts into his doctrine of *specific nerve energies.* Müller recognized that all sensory stimulation is perceived via the nerves, and that the sensory quality is dependent on which nerve is stimulated rather than how it is stimulated. He also recognized that different sensory nerves terminate in different locations within the brain and the location in the brain might also affect sensory quality. Although different cortical locations do show differences in structure, just what distinguishes visual cortex, say, from auditory cortex, is still not clear.

Coding Within Sensory Systems

In the above example the question concerned keeping different stimulus energies from getting mixed together; the means for doing this is the simple one of separating the sensory systems physically. But within a given form of stimulus energy, the energy may have a variety of characteristics—for example, light of different colors or sounds of different pitch. How does the nervous system maintain these differences so that the organism may make differential responses to them? What the organism has with which to work are nerves and nerve impulses; thus nerves and nerve impulses must be coded so as to preserve the varying qualities of the environmental stimuli. How each sensory system accomplishes this, then, is the basic interest of this chapter.

Many sensory experiences seem to be composed of a combination of certain basic "qualities," such as reds and blues in the visual system or salty

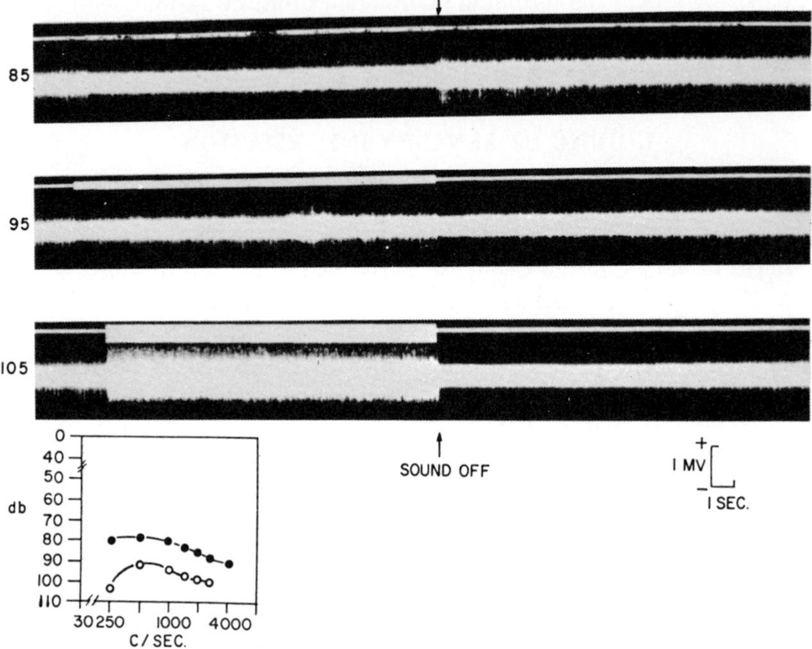

Figure 4.1. Response pattern of a single unit of cochlear nucleus of the cat to tones of different intensity. With lowest intensity (85 db), tone onset inhibited the unit's spontaneous discharge; offset produced a transient increase in discharge. With 95 db, onset did not materially alter the spontaneous firing, but offset produced temporary inhibition. With 105 db, there was increased discharge with onset and a longer inhibition to offset. Note that the insert graph indicates these effects were relatively independent of tone frequency (filled circles = inhibition, open circles = activation). (From Starr, A. Suppression of single unit activity in cochlear nucleus of the cat following sound stimulation. *Journal of Neurophysiology,* 1965, *28,* 850–862.)

and sweet in taste. This suggests that there may be some fundamental receptors which, in combination, may result in the variety of sensations possible in each modality. That is, one fundamental means of coding within a sensory system may be through stimulation of specialized sensory units. The search for such basic sensory units has been a major preoccupation for sensory psychologists for some 150 years. As we shall see, there is still controversy about this in some sensory systems.

In addition, all stimuli can be characterized according to their intensity, duration, and locus of stimulation. *Intensity coding* is the combined result of changes in frequency of firing in single neural elements plus increased numbers of elements firing (see Chapter 1). The simple start and stop of firing can code *duration,* but this may be augmented in the CNS by units that specifically respond to the cessation of stimulation. *Locus of stimulation* is of particular importance in systems with extended receptor surfaces, such as the skin and retina. The coding function is accomplished because the general spatial relations among receptive elements—that is, their topographical layout—are maintained in the CNS. The same principle apparently operates in part for the coding of pitch in the auditory system.

The precision of the topographic arrangement of neurons is exquisitely demonstrated in the sensory areas of the cortex. Cells generally are organized into vertical columns. In the visual cortex bundles of fibers from the thalamus are aligned to form a series of bands, each of which is related to one eye. In the somatosensory cortex, the individual columns are related to a single modality of sensation (see Jones, Burton, & Porter [1975], for some references and details).

Some stimuli also have the characteristics of shape and movement. It seems obvious that the pattern of receptive elements that is being stimulated can effectively "draw a picture" of such stimuli on the surface of the receptor. In the visual system, however, some sensory elements are specifically adapted to handle such special problems in a more economical manner; i.e., they are specifically "tuned" to respond to movement or shape.

Finally, the neurons of the various sensory modalities share a number of functional features that seem to help code their input. First of all, there is a great deal of spontaneous activity in all systems; that is, neurons may be firing in the complete absence of stimulation.[2] The presence of spontaneous activity means that input may be coded either by increased or decreased firing in the neurons (Figure 4.1). This results in much greater flexibility in coding stimulus input than might otherwise be the case. In addition, individual receptor cells and neurons within each sensory system are interconnected. These connections allow mutual *inhibition* to occur between elements of the system, so that stimulation of one cell may result in the reduction of output from a neighboring cell (see Figure 4.14). Interactions of this sort permit the differences between stimuli or stimulus locations to be "sharpened."

All told, there seem to be three fundamental means for coding sensory input. The simplest, conceptually, involves the stimulation of specialized

[2]Recently, Siegel and McGinty (1976) published a report in which they found that the brainstem of cats contained neurons that show no spontaneous activity. Such neurons could be identified, however, by their discharge to specific stimuli. These neurons remained "silent" in the absense of sensory stimulation for as long as 40 minutes. About 30 percent of the cells sampled in this study were of this type. Siegel and McGinty suggest that cells which are not spontaneously active may be numerous throughout the brain and may play a special role in sensory reception. Such cells might be much less "ambiguous" in their coding than spontaneously active cells. It remains to be seen what modifications in our understanding of coding mechanisms are necessitated by this discovery. At the present time, our theories of coding and brain function generally are based on the notion that most cells are spontaneously active, and, though this may require revision, it certainly is not wrong in an absolute sense.

sensory units, each devoted to a particular sensory "quality." A second coding device preserves the spatial relations among the receptors being stimulated—anatomical layout is employed as the coding system. The third means of coding involves a variety of ways of modulating the firing patterns of individual neurons. Which particular coding mechanism is used is sometimes a matter of dispute. In fact, several may be employed simultaneously, but different sensory systems seem to emphasize one or another coding mechanism.

The material that follows will sketch the highlights of each sensory system and will stress the areas of agreement rather than their differences in detail. All sensory systems seem to share a number of organizational and functional features that should be borne in mind when examining the individual system. (For a more detailed account, see the excellent text by Uttal [1973]).

TASTE

Taste would appear to be a relatively undramatic sensory system with which to begin our discussion. However, the taste system clearly illustrates some of the principles of coding to which we have alluded. While usually not considered vital to the life of the organism, there are instances in which discriminations of harmful substances are made on the basis of taste. It has also been shown that taste sometimes may play an important role in the regulation of nutritional intake when the organism is deficient in hormonal or dietary substances (Overmann, 1976). For instance, rats fed diets that are deficient in certain vitamins will, when given the opportunity, self-select the appro-

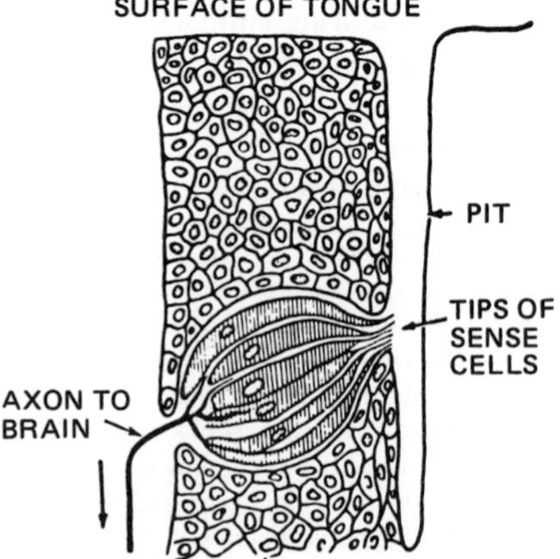

Figure 4.2. Sensory structures for taste. Taste bud with tips of the sense cells in the pit forming the "moat" of a papilla. (From Woodworth, R. S. and Marquis, D. G. *Psychology*, 5th ed. N.Y.: Holt, Rinehart & Winston, 1947.)

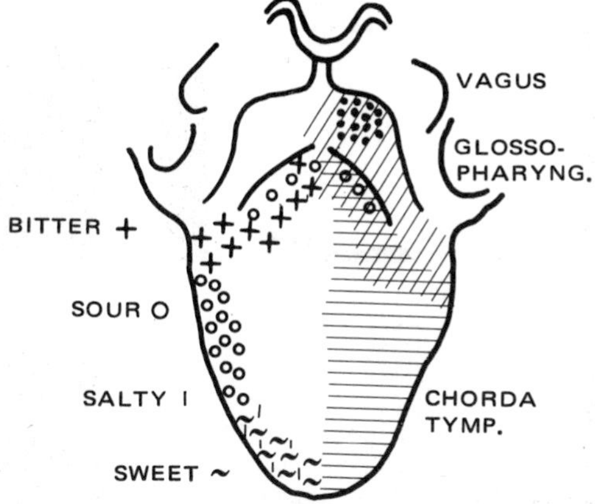

Figure 4.3. Sensitivity of the tongue in different areas for the four primary tastes and the nerve supply. (From Schneider, M. *Einfuhrung in die Physiologie des Menschen.* Berlin: Springer-Verlag, 1964.)

priate foods to compensate for the deficiency. Similarly, adrenalectomized or parathyroidectomized rats will balance their intake of saline and calcium solutions, respectively. Animals with sections of their peripheral taste nerves are not capable of making such selections. On the other hand, guinea pigs apparently like the taste of ascorbic acid and their need for Vitamin C does not appreciably modulate their intake; in fact, they will ingest many times the dose needed to meet nutritional requirements (Smith & Balagura, 1975).

It has long been known that psychologically there are four basic taste qualities: salt, sweet, bitter, and sour; that is, mixing appropriate proportions of stimuli with these qualities will reproduce any taste. This, then, suggests that there are receptors corresponding to these basic taste qualities and it is also well-known that taste sensitivity and receptors (*taste buds*) are differentially distributed on the top and sides of the tongue and in the palate and throat (see Figures 4.2 and 4.3). Not so well-understood, however, are the chemicals which elicit these particular responses. There is little doubt that the hydrogen ion (H+) in acids yields a sour taste, but the bases for the other taste qualities have not yet been identified.

Though psychologically there apparently exist basic taste qualities, at a neural level the individual taste qualities are not segregated, thus raising the important question of how the stimuli are coded.

Pattern Coding System

Electrical recordings from individual nerve fibers (Pfaffmann, 1955) or individual receptor cells (Kimura & Beidler, 1965) show the discharge patterns elicited by different taste substances. As can be seen in Figure 4.4, most units are *not* responsive to one taste substance exclusively; on the contrary,

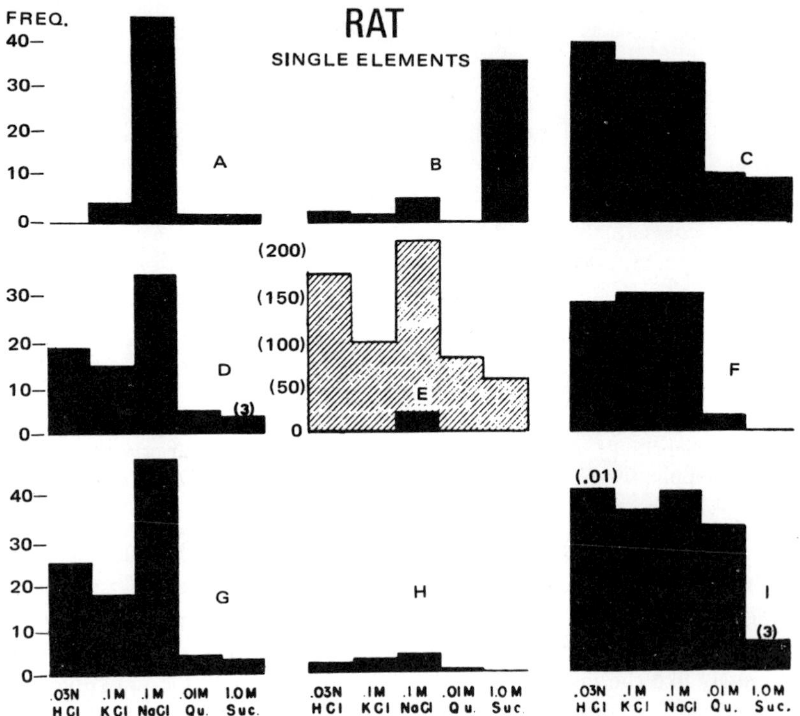

Figure 4.4. Bar graphs summarizing frequency of response during the first second to five standard taste solutions in nine different single fiber preparations in the rat. Sucrose of 0.3 M was used as test solution in elements D and I, 0.01 M HCL in element I. In all other cases concentrations are as shown on *abscissa. Cross-hatched bar graph* superimposed on figure for element E shows relative magnitude of total nerve response for test solutions. *Figures in parentheses* give magnitudes in arbitrary units. Note that only elements D and G resemble the response of the total nerve. (From Pfaffmann, C. Gustatory nerve impulses in rat, cat, and rabbit. *Journal of Neurophysiology,* 1955, *18*, 429–440.)

they show responsiveness to several substances, although generally in differing patterns. A change in the intensity of the stimulus will also change the response of the unit; that is, it will increase or decrease the discharge to that stimulus. Thus, any single unit cannot itself discriminate a given stimulus. However, while the total firing will be altered with changes in stimulus intensity, the *pattern* of firing across the many units activated will not change with stimulus intensity. Therefore, while any single unit cannot discriminate particular stimuli, the firing pattern of the many units activated is capable of such discrimination. In fact, such a system should be extremely sensitive because there would be as many across-unit patterns as there are stimuli. In this way, it is possible to encode more sensory messages than there are neural elements. Such a coding system is efficient. It has been suggested that it is representative for all sensory systems (Erickson, 1968).

Psychophysical investigations suggest that the same coding system operates in humans also (McCutcheon & Saunders, 1972; Bealer & Smith, 1975). And while it is well-known that there are cross-cultural differences in preferences for complex tastes such as foods, it is interesting to note that there apparently are also different preferences for the basic taste qualities. Thus, Indian laborers showed similar preference–aversion curves as Westerners for salty and sweet stimuli but markedly high preferences for sour and bitter. Dietary history probably accounts for this (Moskowitz, Kumaraiah, Sharma, Jacobs, & Sharma, 1975).

CNS Connections in Taste

Figure 4.5 is a highly schematic diagram of the CNS connections involved in taste. The taste buds deliver their information to the CNS through the branches of three cranial nerves; the VIIth (Facial), IXth (Glossopharyngeal), and Xth (Vagus). The fibers of these nerves form the solitary tract in the medulla and terminate in the *solitary nucleus*. Afferent messages then course through the *medial lemniscus* to the *lateral posteroventral* nucleus of the thalamus and thence to the cortex. This pathway parallels that of the Vth

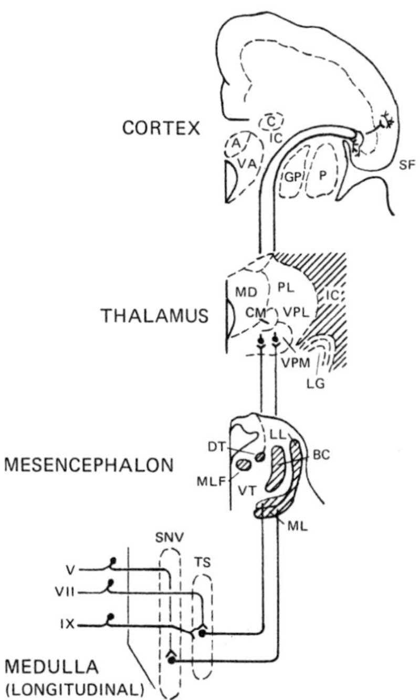

Figure 4.5. Summary diagram, highly schematic, representing taste and somatosensory pathways from face. A, Anterior thalamic nucleus; BC, brachium conjuctivum; C, caudate nucleus; CM, n. centrum medianum; DT, dorsal secondary trigeminal tract; GP, globus pallidus; IC, internal capsule; LG, lateral geniculate body; LL, lateral lemniscus; MD, n. medialis dorsalis; ML, medial lemniscus; MLF, medial longitudinal fasciculus; P, putamen; PL, n. lateralis posterior; SF, sylvian fissure; SNV, spinal nucleus of Vth nerve; TS, nucleus of tractus solitarius; VA, n. ventralis anterior; VPL, n. ventralis posterolateralis; VPM, n. ventralis posteromedialis (arcuate nucleus); VT, ventral secondary trigeminal tract. [From Patton, H. D., Taste, olfaction and visceral sensations. In T. C. Ruch et al (Eds.), *Neurophysiology*, 2nd ed. Philadelphia: W. B. Saunders Company, 1965.]

(Trigeminal) nerve mediating somatic sensibility of the face and tongue, and the cortical termination is also adjacent to the somatosensory receiving area for the face (see Figure 4.13). Therefore, to oversimplify, one can expect that CNS lesions or dysfunctions affecting facial sensitivity are likely also to involve taste mechanisms, and vice versa.

OLFACTION

Both taste and olfaction, or smell, are chemically mediated senses, but the search for the basic chemical stimuli involved in smell has been even more difficult and less successful. One reason for this is the relatively lesser control over the sensory stimuli of smell. Another reason, a major one, is the fact that there has been little agreement on the psychological qualities of the mechanisms being investigated. There is no definitive list of basic qualities for smell as there is for taste. Classically, the following six categories are considered basic (Henning, cited by Woodworth & Schlossberg, 1954): fragrant, ethereal, resinous, spicy, putrid, and burnt. Other workers have postulated from four to nine basic qualities.

Theories concerning the nature of the physical stimuli elicting olfactory sensations are also largely speculative at the present time. Some theories assume that smell depends on the presence of specific, active chemical constituents; other approaches deemphasize the specific chemicals and postulate that it is the overall size and shape of the molecule that is of importance. The latter "lock and key" type of theory holds that any molecule that happens to fit the receptor will elicit the sensation. Obviously, much work remains before this issue is resolved.

Taste and Smell

A number of sensory discriminations that we ordinarily attribute to taste are actually made on the basis of smell. For instance, onions and apples cannot be discriminated if the nose is kept closed. Conversely, conditioned responses to certain odorous substances, such as camphor, ether, and chloroform, persist, in the dog at least, after section of the olfactory nerve. Such a result would indicate that the discrimination of such substances is at least partially determined by tactile components as well as olfaction (Allen, 1937).

Structure of the Olfactory System

The receptors for smell are found in two small (2.5 cm^2) patches of yellow *olfactory epithelium* at the top of the nasal passages. They are actually out of the main airstream and protected from it by the structure of the passages and

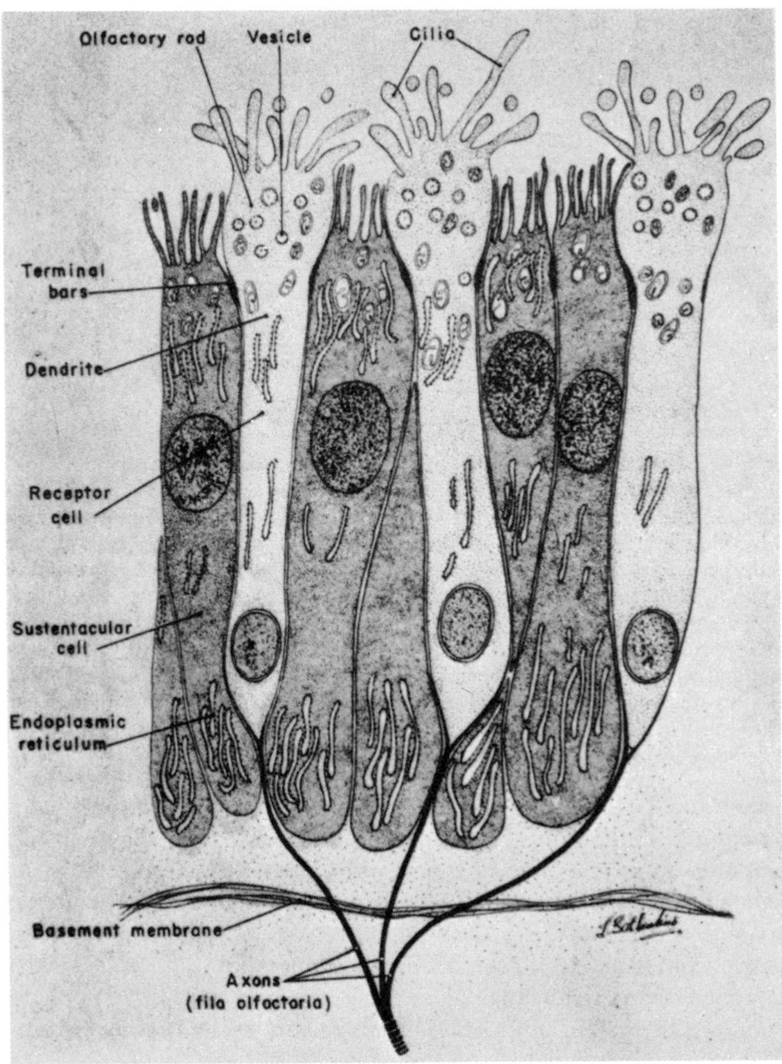

Figure 4.6. Receptors of the olfactory epithelium. [From DeLorenzo, A. J. D. Studies on ultrastructure and histophysiology of cell membranes, nerve fibers, and synaptic junctions in chemoreceptors. In Y. Zotterman (Ed.), *Olfaction and Taste.* Oxford: Pergamon, 1963, 5–17.]

a covering layer of mucosa. Figure 4.6 is a schematic of their structure—the hairlike structures are thought to be the actual receptor surface.

Unlike other systems, the receptor in olfaction is directly part of the primary sensory neuron. The axon of the neuron then courses to the *olfactory bulb* (Figure 4.7). Axons from many thousands of receptors converge in

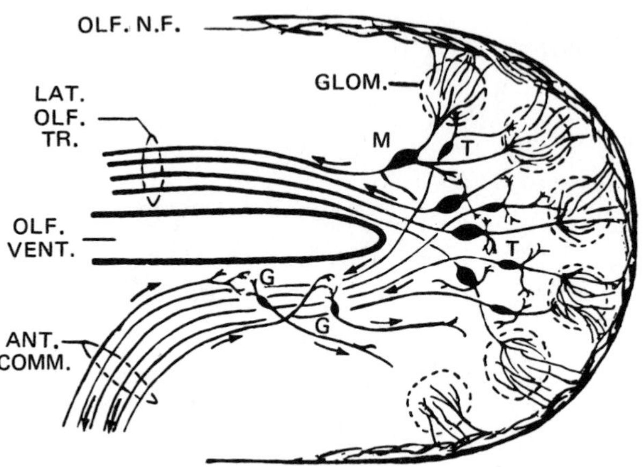

Figure 4.7. General arrangement of the neural paths in the olfactory bulb. Fibers from the receptor cells are collected on the surface of the bulb (OLF.N.F.) and participate in the formation of more deeply situated glomeruli (GLOM), which also receive the dendritic processes of the mitral cells (M) and the tufted cells (T). Axons of mitral cells are mainly collected into the lateral olfactory tract (LAT. OLF. TR.) and run to the primary olfactory cortex. The finer axons of tufted cells pass into the anterior limb of the anterior commissure, reaching the opposite bulb where they synapse with deeply situated granule cells (G). Axons of granule cells are directed peripherally at least as far as the fields of the mitral and tufted cells. OLF. VENT. represents the olfactory ventricle present in lower mammals and continuous with the cerebral ventricular system. (From Adey, W. R., The sense of smell. *Handbook of Physiology, Neurophysiology,* Sec. I, vol. 1, 1959, 535–548.)

the bulb into conglomerations of neurons (*glomeruli*). The *lateral olfactory tract* consists of the axons of cells that synapse with these glomeruli. Here again, numerous cells make such synapses with each glomerulus. The lateral olfactory tract terminates in the *olfactory tubercle, prepyriform cortex,* and parts of the *amygdaloid nuclei* of the limbic system at the base of the brain (Figure 1.8). It would appear to be an error to consider this system as primarily olfactory in function; more likely, olfaction contributes to the functioning of this system in emotion. The olfactory system is the only sense modality not represented in the thalamus.

The neural structure of the olfactory system suggests that it is well suited to the type of across-unit pattern discrimination coding system described for taste but, at this point, such an inference is speculative. However, there is also evidence that an interesting form of coding by topographical layout also may be employed to discriminate different odorants. Mozell and Jagodowicz (1973) presented evidence comparing the olfactory mucosa to the functioning of the detector system in a gas chromatograph. The chromatographic analysis of chemicals is based on the fact that different molecules have a differential attraction to the medium through which they pass. Mozell and Jagodowicz suggest that molecules of different odorants migrate at different rates across the olfactory mucosa, and they presented model experiments to support this notion. In effect, then, this mechanism would be involved in the initial detection of different odorants, and a pattern system for coding would be involved at subsequent neural levels.

THE SOMATIC SENSES

The layperson commonly refers to the sense of "touch." In reality, however, touch is but one of several somesthetic qualities. *Somesthesis* (or the body senses) refers to the various senses of the skin and of bodily movement.

Cutaneous Senses

Cutaneous senses are senses of the skin. In everyday experience we commonly distinguish among several cutaneous sensations or sensory qualities: touch, tickle, cold, warmth, itch, pricking pain, dull pain, and pressure. When the skin is examined or "mapped" for its sensitivity to a variety of stimuli, however, two facts emerge (Woodworth & Schlossberg, 1954): (1) The skin is not uniform in its sensitivity; in fact, some very sensitive spots are surrounded by areas of greatly decreased sensitivity, and the distribution of these sensitive areas varies over the skin. (2) Apparently four basic maps of the skin can be plotted—one each for touch, pain, cold, and warmth. Since the maps are not identical and the maps of other sensations, such as itch, may be superimposed on these, it seems logical to conclude that these four basic cutaneous sensations each have their own type of receptor in the skin. In fact, research has proceeded on this premise for some 100 years. However, it can be seen from Figure 4.8, which represents the variety of receptors identified in the skin, that there are more than the expected four. Furthermore, most studies correlating sensory quality with microscopic examination of the skin seem to agree that specialized, encapsulated end organs cannot be found in hairy skin (Kenshalo & Nafe, 1962); yet, hairy skin exhibits much the same sensitivity for touch, warmth, and cold as smooth skin. Thus, the evidence seems to be against theories requiring specialized end organs to code these qualities of cutaneous sensitivity.

The Quantitative Theory

If there are no specialized receptors for the various cutaneous sensations, then how are they mediated? One theory, the so-called quantitative theory (Kenshalo & Nafe, 1962), is representative of several pattern theories of cutaneous sensory coding (see Uttal, 1973). It holds that the qualities of cutaneous sensation are partly a function of the mechanical and thermal properties of the tissue in which the sensory nerves terminate and partly a

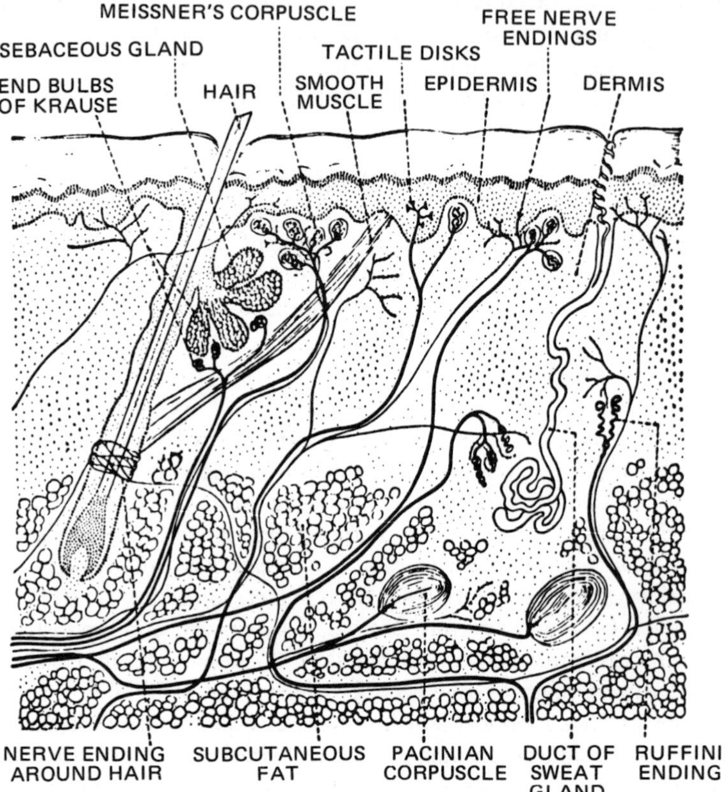

Figure 4.8. Schematic representation of the nerve supply of skin with sparse hair. Not all the endings shown are to be found in any one skin area. The heavy lines are myelinated fibers, the light lines, nonmyelinated fibers. (Modified after Gardner, E. *Fundamentals of Neurology*. Philadelphia: W. B. Saunders Company, 1968.)

function of variations in the temporal and spatial patterns of neural discharge of those nerves. Basically, sensations of pressure, warmth, and cold all share a common adequate stimulus—movement, either of the receptor or the tissue in which the nerve terminates. Warmth and cold are mediated through movement of the smooth muscles of the cutaneous vascular (blood) system—the smooth muscles relax when warmed and contract when cooled. Similarly, pressure sensations are derived from movement of the skin. Qualitative differences in sensations from various mechanical stimuli are thus thought to result from different patterns of neural excitation. In other words, depending on the nature of the mechanical stimulus, the deformations and movement of the skin will be different and will result in different patterns of neural discharge, yielding the touch, pressure, and tickle of everyday experience. The difference between thermal and tactile sensations depends on the central connections that the nerves make in the brain.

The pattern theories of somatosensory coding will require a great deal of experimental validation. However, they are plausible and in accord with what we know about the workings of other sense modalities.

Pain Sensitivity

Pain sensitivity is unique in that it exists in virtually all tissues of the body except the brain itself (the meninges, the membranes "wrapping" the brain, are pain-sensitive, however). A variety of clinical phenomena give rise to conditions of pathological pain, that is, pain apparently without adequate stimuli. In contrast, there are some individuals who are seemingly incapable of feeling pain. Dogs reared experimentally under conditions of restricted sensory input lack normal pain-avoidance responses; they seem actually to be impaired in their capacity to perceive pain (Melzack & Scott, 1957). Thus, pain perception is not simply a biological "given"; rather, it appears to be influenced by the experience one has with pain. The elucidation of these anomalies would, obviously, contribute a great deal to our knowledge of the physiological mechanisms of pain perception.

Pain Mechanisms

One of the controversies about Müller's doctrine of specific nerve energies centers around the problem of pain perception. It is obvious that excessive stimulation in any sense modality may be painful. Does this imply that pain is not a specific and separate sense system, and that Müller's doctrine is incorrect in that the several sense modalities may give rise to at least two sensations, e.g., touch *and* pain? The evidence seems to support Müller, however. It is possible to isolate neural fibers that respond to tactile sensations and not to pain, and vice versa. Also, certain lesions of the CNS show such dissociation of sensitivity between pain and other sensations.

Traditionally, it has been maintained that pain receptors are free nerve endings and that pain impulses are carried in small diameter sensory nerves; but the matter has been the subject of considerable controversy and this theory appears to be inadequate. More recent formulations (Melzack & Wall, 1965) have emphasized the relative *balance* of activity in more central locations. Figure 4.9 is a schematic of the system that Melzack and Wall suggest mediates pain. Briefly, the diagram suggests (1) that a system of inhibitory connections in the spinal cord, the *substantia gelatinosa*, modulates the synaptic transmission of impulses from peripheral nerves to the CNS; (2) the relative balance of activity in large and small diameter fibers determines the output through this controlling system; and (3) the control system also receives feedback information from the CNS. In sum, rather than depending on the activity of specialized receptors for pain, the theory suggests that it is the patterning of excitation in the afferent pathway that serves as the coding mechanism.

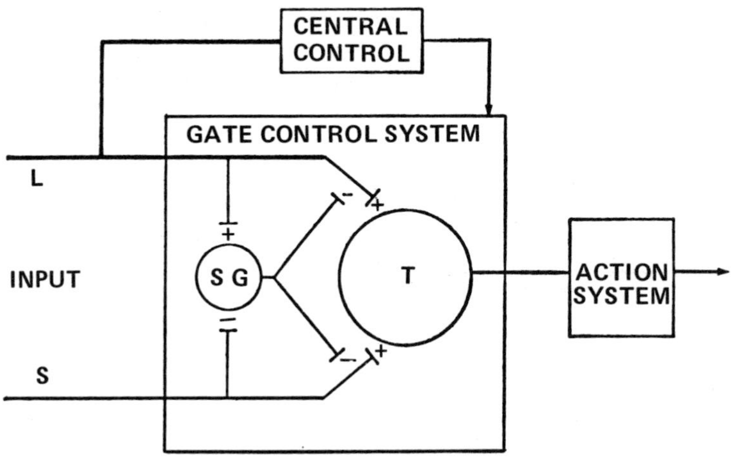

Figure 4.9. Schematic diagram of the gate control theory of pain mechanisms: L, the large-diameter fibers; S, the small-diameter fibers. The fibers project to the substantia gelatinosa (SG) of the spinal cord and first central transmission (T) cells. The inhibitory effect exerted by SG on the afferent fiber terminals is increased by activity in L fibers and decreased by activity in S fibers. The central control trigger is represented by a line running from the large-fiber system to the central control mechanisms. These mechanisms, in turn, project back to the gate control system. The T cells project to the entry cells of the action system. +, Excitation; −, Inhibition. (From Melzack, R. and Wall, P. D., Pain mechanisms: A new theory. *Science*, Nov. 1965, *150*, 971–979. Copyright 1965 by the American Association for the Advancement of Science.)

One implication of this theory is that concurrent, nonpainful stimulation should alter the response to painful stimulation. Several experiments (e.g., Higgins, Tursky, & Schwartz, 1971; Satran & Goldstein, 1973) seem to show that pain tolerance is increased by such extraneous stimulation. A second implication of this theory is that activation of some CNS locations should be effective in reducing pain—the theory calls for CNS mechanisms that feed back to the periphery and are capable of modifying the pain "gate." An experiment by Mayer, Wolfle, Akil, Carder, and Liebeskind (1971) appears to support this. Electrical stimulation of several discrete sites in the mesencephalon and diencephalon of the rat abolished responses to intense pain but did not appear to result in a general deficit in sensory, emotional, or attentional mechanisms. The response to pain was eliminated if the painful stimulus was applied to a restricted peripheral locus, but was present during electrical stimulation if the painful stimulus was applied outside this locus. Most animals also responded to visual, auditory, and tactile stimuli during brain stimulation. Mayer et al. suggest that their brain stimulation activated a system which has inhibitory action on sensory transmission in the spinal cord.

More recently, Akil, Mayer, and Liebeskind (1976) found that the pain tolerance resulting from such electrical stimulation can be partially reduced by administering a narcotic antagonist. This implies that the electrical stimulation may operate to release an endogenous substance that normally acts as a pain reducer. Such experiments give rise to the idea that it may be possible to develop analgesics (pain reducers) which are effective without leaving the complications of drugs such as morphine, which also produce euphoria and addiction.

Acupuncture

Acupuncture is a procedure for alleviating pain developed in China and only recently the subject of scientific investigation. The treatment may involve a variety of techniques but all center around the insertion and manipulation of needles in supposedly critical points in the body. The result is said to be reduction or elimination of pain, in some instances to the point of not requiring pharmacological anesthetics in order to perform otherwise painful surgery. Responses to painful stimuli are influenced by a variety of psychological factors, including hypnosis, placebos, cultural training, and anxiety. Whether acupuncture is another such psychologically mediated influence or if it has a direct physiological effect is a matter of current controversy. The matter is relevant here since the treatment does not employ any currently known neural mechanism though it might be relevant to the gating notions just discussed.

Recently, Clark and Yang (1974) applied a signal detection theory analysis to an experiment in which subjects were administered painful stimulation with and without acupuncture. Signal detection theory analyzes the subjective reports of the subjects into two components: One provides an index of sensory sensitivity and the other attempts to measure the subject's response bias or criteria for responding (see Swets, 1961). Clark and Yang (1974) reported that acupuncture did not affect sensitivity to the stimuli but did cause the subjects to raise their criterion for calling a given stimulus painful. They, therefore, concluded that the "subjects experienced equal amounts of 'physiological' pain" with and without acupuncture (p. 1097). These results are important but stating them this way opens a potential hazard. Clark and Yang's conclusion seems to fall back to a position of mind-body dualism which hardly answers the question of what mechanisms are involved in alleviating pain. Is alleviation of "psychological" pain any less real than aleviation of "physiological" pain? It would seem that Clark and

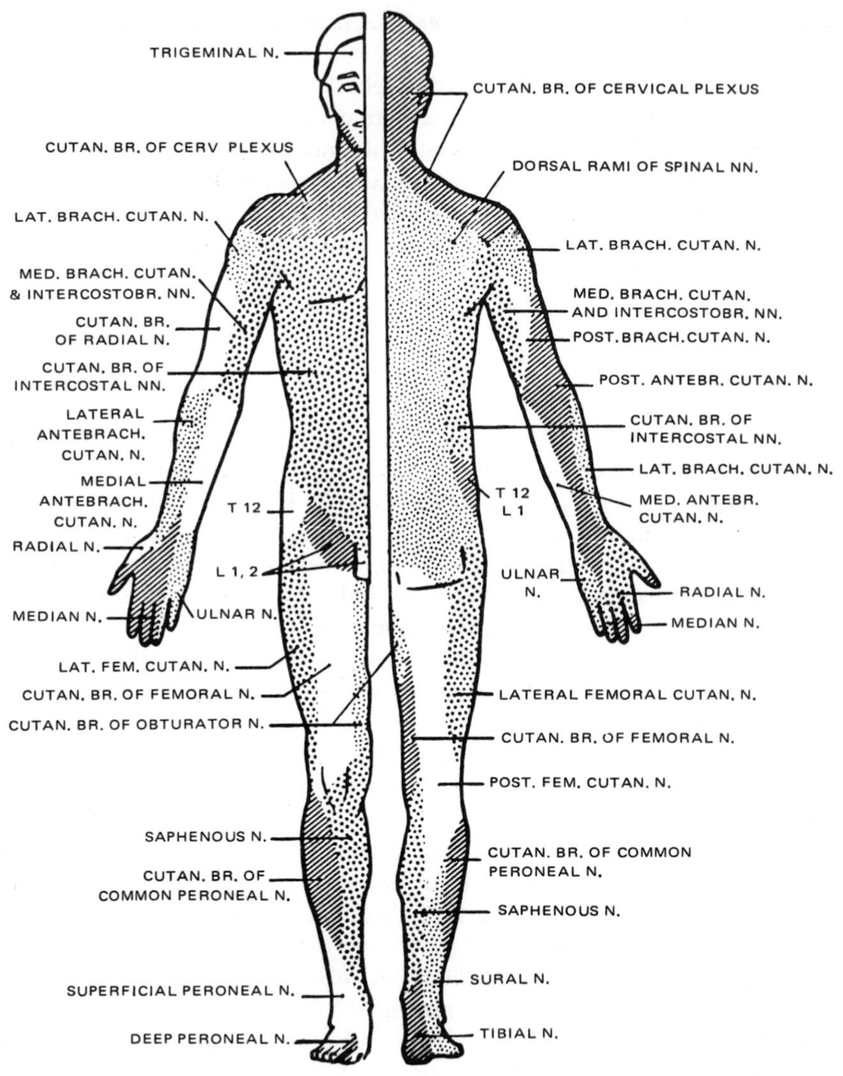

Figure 4.10. Diagram of the distribution of peripheral nerves to skin. The left half of the figure represents the anterior surface of the body, the right half the posterior. Note the differences between this type of distribution and that illustrated for spinal nerves in Figure 4.11. Only in the trunk are the patterns similar. The skin of the trunk is supplied segmentally by intercostal and subcostal nerves, by cutaneous branches of the lumbar plexus, and by dorsal rami of spinal nerves. (From Gardner, E. *Fundamentals of Neurology*. Philadelphia: W. B. Saunders Company, 1968.)

Yang have merely restated the problem that the physiological psychologist wants to solve!

Perception of Body Movement

Information associated with body movement arises from two general sources: (1) muscles, tendons, and joints, and (2) the vestibular system of the inner ear. Sensations arising from the first source are called *kinesthesia*, *proprioception*, or *position sense*. The second source is responsible for the sense of body balance.

Much more is known about kinesthesia than we are able to detail here (see Uttal, 1973). Suffice to say that there are special receptors within the muscles, tendons, and joints. Coding of different kinds of mechanical distortion is accomplished through these receptors: Some respond to active contraction of the musles, others to passive stretch (that is, fiber length per se), and still others to tension in the muscles. Similarly, the nonauditory, vestibular portions of the inner ear (note the semicircular canals in Figure 4.15) are specialized to respond to rotation in the three dimensions of space and contribute along with vision to our appreciation of body balance.

In general, these sensory activities are vital for the maintenance of posture, balance, movement, and coordination of the eyes during movement. Coordinated movement depends on the integrity of these systems, and there is constant interplay and feedback between the sensory and motor mechanisms involved in each phase of any movement. Most often, however, we are not immediately aware of this constant sensory activity. On the other hand, disturbance in such activity has profound effects behaviorally and poses a host of problems to the neurologist.

CNS Pathways

Figure 4.10 shows the distribution of peripheral nerves to the skin. Figure 4.11 shows that topographic coding of afferent messages from the skin is maintained into the spinal cord. Figure 4.12 is representative of several afferent pathways to the brain involved in the somatic senses; tactile afferents are diagrammed here.

Nerve impulses from touching the skin or hairs are carried by both myelinated and unmyelinated fibers to the spinal cord through the *dorsal roots*. Once sensory information reaches the cord, several alternate pathways are possible. Some establish reflex connections with ventral root fibers and lead directly to motor responses. Others synapse in the H-shaped gray mat-

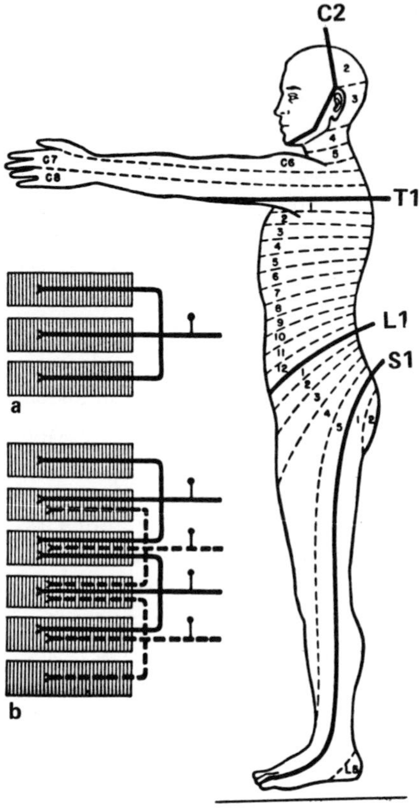

Figure 4.11. Schematic representation of the distribution of spinal nerves to skin. Each numbered zone refers to an area of skin supplied by the spinal nerve of the corresponding number. The letters refer to cervical, thoracic, lumbar, and sacral. Thus, the zones between C2 and T1 are supplied by cervical nerves. The first cervical nerve rarely gives any significant supply to skin. Skin above C2 is supplied by the trigeminal nerve. The diagram does not show variation or overlap. The latter is illustrated in *a* and *b*, showing, for example, that in the trunk region each spinal nerve sends branches to at least three segmental areas of skin (a), and each area has branches from at least three spinal nerves (b). Therefore, if a single spinal nerve is cut, the area it supplies will still receive fibers from adjacent nerves. Sensation will be diminished but not lost. (From Gardner, E. *Fundamentals of Neurology*. Philadelphia: W. B. Saunders Company, 1968).

ter (cell bodies) with cells whose axons cross the midline of the cord and proceed to the thalamus (*anterior spinothalamic tract*). Another path from the dorsal roots ascends on the side of entrance in the *posterior funiculus* to the medulla and ends in the *nucleus gracilis* or the *nucleus cuneatus*—the former receiving fibers from the lower limbs and trunk, the latter from the upper limbs and trunk. Axons arising from these nuclei cross the midline and ascend as the *medial lemniscus* to the thalamus. After a synapse in the thalamus, impulses ascend through the *internal capsule* to the *postcentral gyrus* of the cortex.

The cord, then, contains both pathways that cross to the opposite side of the body and uncrossed pathways, but the medula contains mainly pathways that are crossed. The medial lemniscus also contains fibers from the nucleus of the trigeminal nerve, which carries impulses from the head and face. The

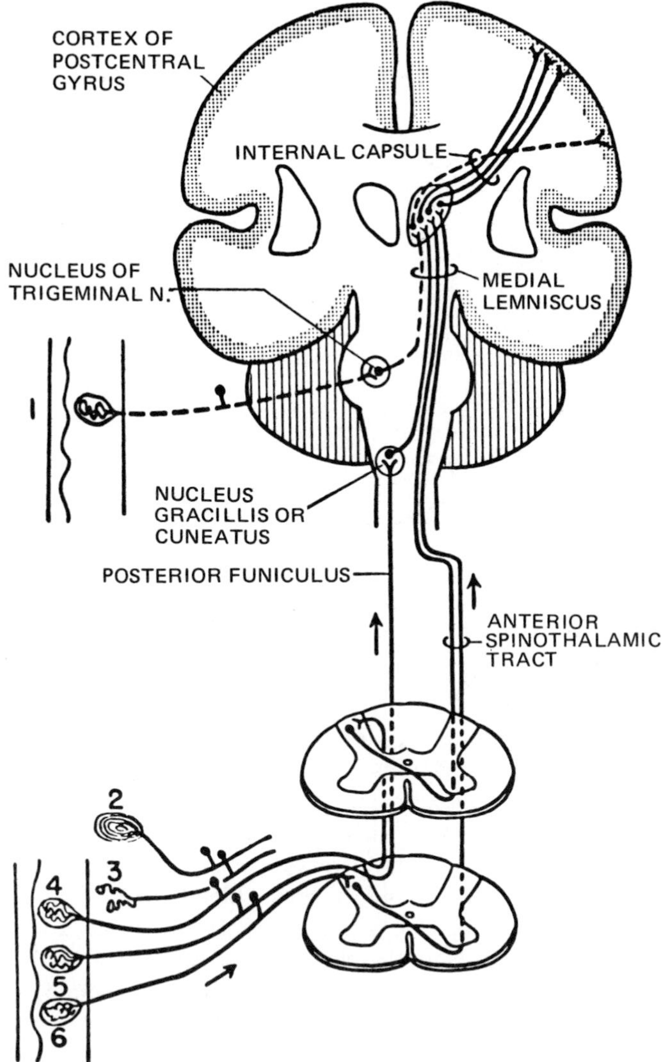

Figure 4.12. Composite diagram of several afferent paths to the cerebral cortex. Numbers 1, 4, 5, and 6 indicate Meissener's corpuscles. Note that tactile paths have several routes in the spinal cord and that 2 (pacinian corpuscle) and 3 (joint receptor) have paths which, in the spinal cord, are similar to the path taken by 5, but, for purposes of simplification, are not drawn. (From Gardner, E. *Fundamentals of Neurology*. Philadelphia: W. B. Saunders Company, 1968.)

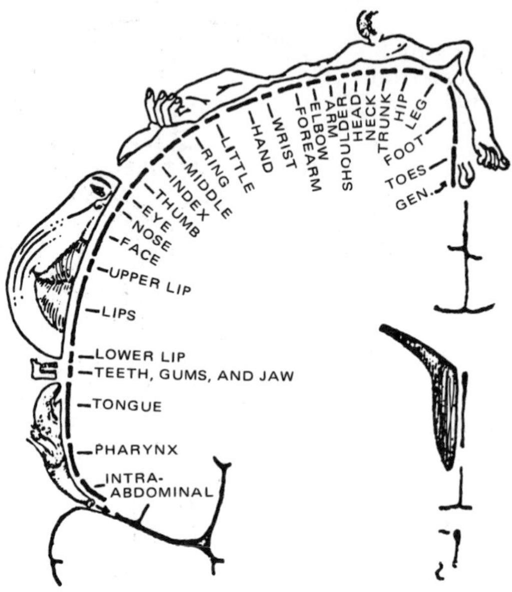

Figure 4.13. Homunculus for human somatosensory I cortex shown on a cross section through the hemisphere. The dimensions of the various bodily parts are in proportion to the cortical area devoted to them. (From Penfield, W., and Rasmussen, T. *The Cerebral Cortex of Man.* N.Y.: Macmillan, 1950.)

postcentral gyrus is the primary cortical receiving area (somatosensory I) for information from the contralateral (opposite) side of the body for the somatic senses, with the exception of pain. (It would be difficult to specify a "primary" area for pain because so many locations seem to be involved.) It is important to note that this contralateral system maintains topographic representation of the skin throughout its course. (See Figure 4.13 for the cortical representation.) These pathways provide rapid transmission to the cortex and precise localization. Note that there exists a somatosensory II—a second area which has inputs from both sides of the body in overlapping fashion. Somatosensory II inputs are at least partly independent of those for somatosensory I.

Variations on the above described pathways exist for the various other somatic senses and the bodily locations involved. For instance, pain and temperature sensations from the skin ascend through the cord in the *lateral* spinothalamic tract. These details are of great importance in the clinical treatment of a large variety of sensory disorders. Surgery may be necessary, and the precise location of the relevant tracts becomes of prime importance, although even severing the known, appropriate tracts often fails to relieve intractable pain. It is such results which, in part, suggest the more complicated patterning theories of pain mentioned earlier.

Finally, it should be obvious that the results of transection of neural pathways are very much dependent on the level at which the transection is made; that is, cutting the median nerve in the arm will have less widespread effect than will transection of the posterior funiculus in the cord. Conversely, the neurologist is often able to localize the level of the impairment from a knowledge of which sensory functions remain, which show a deficit, and the relative degree of deficit.

Contralateral Specificity

Although there is controversy about the specificity of the peripheral receptor mechanisms of the somatic senses, such specificity is fairly well established for more central neurons of the *contralateral system*, the system that conveys information from the opposite side of the body. Thus, a single cell in the thalamus or cortex will be responsive to only one type of somatic stimulus. The topographical organization of the contralateral system, however, does not imply a point-by-point representation of the skin on the cortex. Rather, a given peripheral spot will, when stimulated, maximally activate a given cortical spot, but will also activate the surrounding cortical area. Conversely, areas surrounding the peripheral spot will also activate the same cortical location but to a lesser extent. Thus, the skin area to which a given cortical spot responds may be quite large; in fact, it is generally much larger than the receptive area of individual peripheral receptors themselves. Despite this, we can still make quite sharp differentiations between spots close together on the skin.

Figure 4.14 illustrates how modulation of the spontaneous firing pattern of individual neurons probably contributes to making these discriminations. Here only the behavior of two cortical cells is graphed, but it is not hard to imagine large numbers of cells acting in reciprocal excitatory and inhibitory fashion. Thus, cortical cells excited by a given stimulus are surrounded by cells that are inhibited by the same stimulus; the cortical region responding is therefore limited. Stimulation of adjacent skin areas would tend to inhibit cortical cells previously responding and excite cortical cells previously inhibited. Differentiation of two different skin areas is, then, sharpened by this reciprocal mechanism.

Spinothalamic System

While the contralateral system (Mountcastle [1961] calls it the "lemniscal" system) conveys information from the opposite side of the body, the *spinothalamic system* carries ipsilateral information—that is, information from the same side of the body. To a considerable extent, though not exclusively, somatosensory areas I and II seem to be the cortical representations of the lemniscal and spinothalamic systems, respectively.

The most interesting features of the spinothalamic system are: The

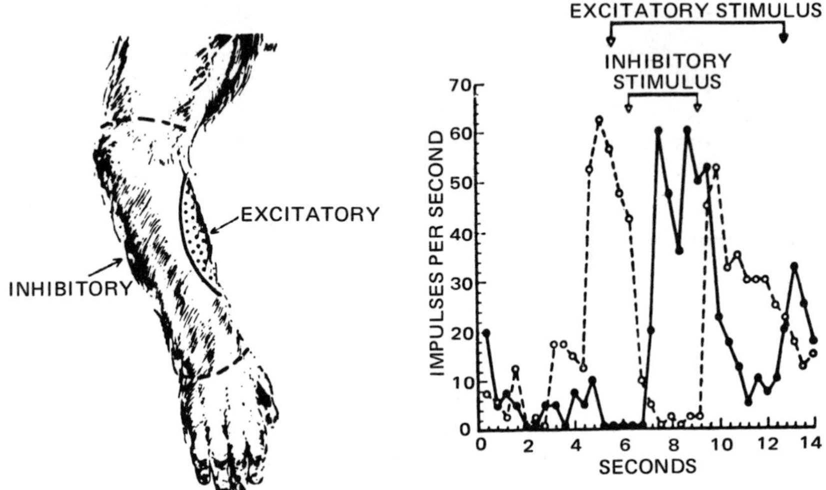

Figure 4.14. Afferent inhibition in the somatic system. A neuron of the postcentral gyrus of the macaque monkey was driven from the receptive field of the skin of the contralateral preaxial forearm, as shown in the drawing, and its discharge was inhibited by light mechanical stimulation within a much larger surrounding area, the inhibitory receptive field. This stimulation excited a second neuron whose discharges were also observed in the record, and the second neuron was inhibited by stimuli within the excitatory receptive field of the first. The reciprocal behavior of the two cells is indicated by the graph of impulse frequency versus time—the first cell by the dashed line, and the second by the solid line. (From Mountcastle, V. B. and Powell, T. P. S. Neural mechanisms subserving cutaneons sensibility, with special reference to the role of afferent inhibition in sensory perception and discrimination. *Bulletin of the Johns Hopkins Hospital,* 1959, *185*, 201–232. © The Johns Hopkins University Press.)

receptive fields show no topographical pattern; the receptive fields are much larger than in the contralateral system, encompassing in some instances virtually the entire body surface; and the different sensory qualities of the system are not separated spatially—that is, some cells are responsive to more than one kind of stimulation (Mountcastle, 1961). We see, then, that the precise coding systems that we have been emphasizing are not represented in the spinothalamic system. Or perhaps it is better to state that in contrast to the precise *discriminations* mediated in the contralateral system, the spinothalamic system seems coded to deal with more general aspects of sensation and to convey qualitative data about peripheral stimuli.

Cortical Changes With Sensory Injury

In keeping with the material presented in the previous chapter and the present concern with coding, it is pertinent to mention here that injury to peripheral receptors causes structural alterations in somatosensory cortical neurons. Van der Loos and Woolsey (1973) demonstrated that single whiskers and receptive units on the muzzle of mice are related to particular cortical units; destruction of a whisker apparatus at birth resulted in an absence of the cortical unit later. Thus, the structure of the cortex is determined, in part, by peripheral sensory conditions.

AUDITION

Great impetus has been given to the study of audition, or hearing, in the past few decades by electronic advances that have made it possible to measure more accurately both sound and the physical apparatus of hearing.

Sound

The physical stimuli for hearing are vibrations of the air caused by the movement of a physical object. These vibrations, or sound waves, may be described in terms of their frequency. Humans are not capable of hearing all sound frequencies. The human ear responds to a range of frequencies from about 20 to 20,000 *Hertz* (Hz = cycles/second). Other animals, including the dog, cat, bat, whale, and porpoise, have much higher upper limits to their frequency range. The human ear is most sensitive to frequencies between 1,000 and 4,000 Hz.

Structure of the Ear

Figure 4.15 is a diagram of the accessory apparatus of the auditory system. Air vibrations traveling in the ear canals are transmitted to the middle ear by the vibration of the *tympanic membrane*, which in turn moves three bones or *ossicles*—the *malleus*, *incus*, and *stapes*. The foot of the stapes transmits its vibrations to the fluid filling the canals of the *cochlea*. Thus, air vibrations are brought to the appropriate location and are transformed into fluid vibrations, which in turn are transformed into mechanical changes within the cochlea. Figure 4.16 shows the arrangement of the latter structure. Fluid movement in the cochlea causes the *basilar membrane* to move relative to the *tectorial membrane*, thus bending and distorting the *hair cells* between them, giving rise to nerve impulses in the cochlear branch of the VIIIth nerve.

Theories of Ear Function

Over the past century, many researchers have attempted to analyze the mechanical properties of the ear or, as we currently define the problem, the conversion of sound into a functional neural code. Two general lines of theorizing about the auditory apparatus have emerged—place theories and frequency theories. *Place theories*, in one form or another, can be traced at

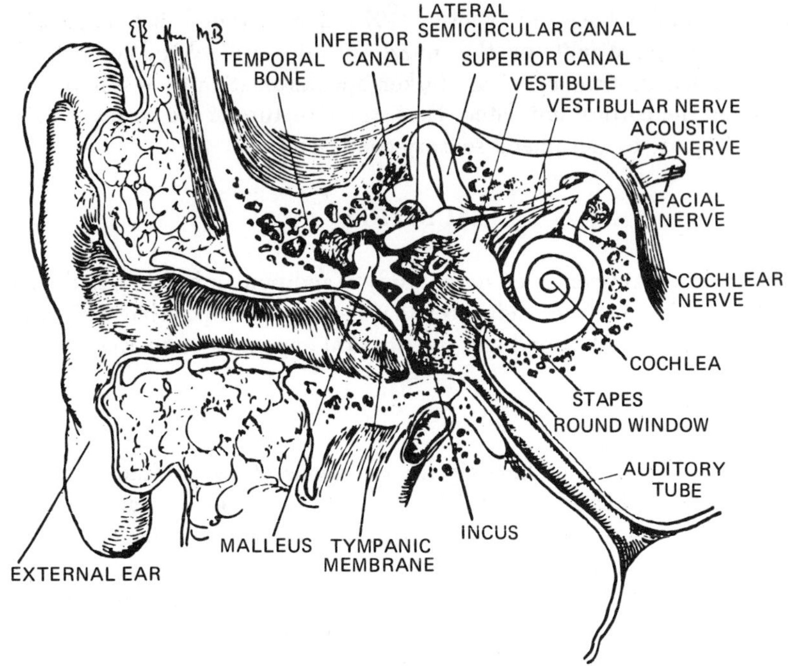

Figure 4.15. Semischematic drawing of the ear. Note the ossicles extending across the middle ear cavity. The greater part of the course of the facial nerve through the ear has been omitted. (Modified from Max Brodel by Gardner, E. *Fundamentals of Neurology.* Philadelphia: W. B. Saunders Company, 1968.)

least as far back as Helmholtz. Basically, they assume that the basilar membrane consists of a large number of elements that are specifically responsive to selected frequencies. Such elements are likened to piano or harp strings which vibrate in resonance to specific frequencies. *Frequency theories* propose the existence of neural impulses that are capable of responding at the same rate as the input stimulus. Recordings from the auditory nerve have shown such responses up to about 4000/sec. Although such measurements certainly do not cover the range of frequencies that can actually be discriminated, there is, in fact, a problem in explaining even that degree of frequency following. In other words, the fastest neural fibers cannot respond at a rate greater than about 1000/sec; how then does the auditory nerve follow frequencies to about four times that rate? The explanation has been in terms of a "volley" principle: Different sets of fibers within the auditory nerve fire alternately, so that while no one set fires faster than 1000/sec, by alternating they can, together, follow to about 4000/sec.

In 1962, Georg von Békésy was awarded the Nobel prize for his work on the peripheral auditory mechanisms. His findings seem to lend support to

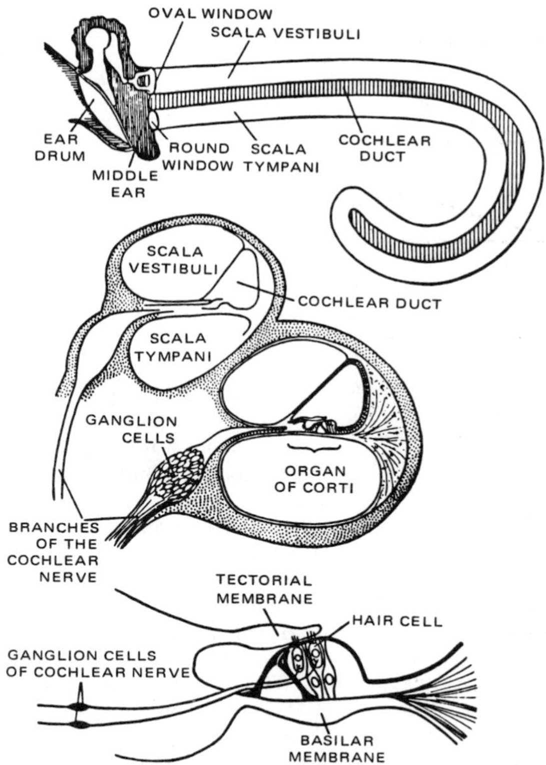

Figure 4.16. Various schema of the inner ear. The upper drawing represents the cochlea as if it were uncoiled. Note how the stapes fits into the oval window. The scala vestibuli communicates with the scala tympani, which terminates at the round window. Compare with Figure 4.15. The middle drawing represents the cochlea cut at a right angle to or across the first plane, indicating the shape and relationships of the cochlear duct. The peripheral processes of the bipolar ganglion cells extend to the spiral organ of Corti. The lower drawing is of the spiral organ of Corti. Most of the cells have been omitted, since all are either hair cells or supporting cells. (From Gardner, E. *Fundamentals of Neurology*. Philadelphia: W. B. Saunders Company, 1968.)

both the place and frequency theories. In very simplified form, von Békésy found that a tone will produce a traveling wave in the fluid of the cochlea that causes a zone of maximum displacement of the basilar membrane in a particular location (different tones will have their zones of maximum displacement in different locations). High-frequency tones maximally distort the basilar membrane close to the stapes; intermediate tones operate over the remainder of the membrane; and low-frequency tones tend to distort the entire membrane (Figure 4.17). Thus, it would appear that for high frequencies, the locus of displacement of the basilar membrane is of paramount

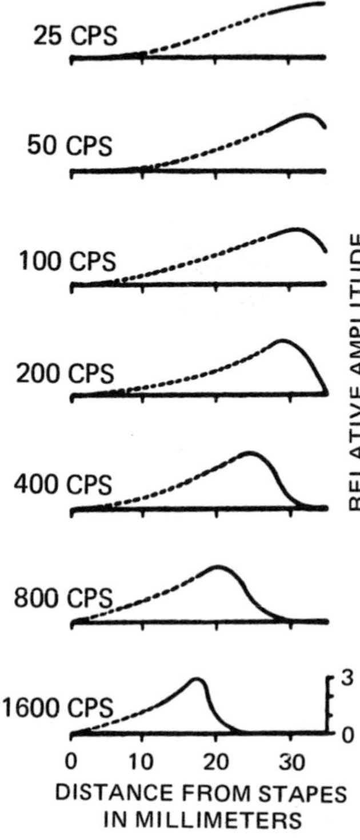

Figure 4.17. Displacement amplitudes along the cochlear partition for different frequencies. The stapes was driven at a constant amplitude, and the amplitude of vibration of the cochlear partition was measured. The maximum displacement amplitude moves toward the stapes as the frequency is increased. [From von Békésy, G. and Rosenblih, W. A., The mechanical properties of the ear. In S. S. Stevens (Ed.), *Handbook of Experimental Psychology*. N.Y.: John Wiley, 1951. Copyright © 1951, John Wiley & Sons. Reprinted by permission of John Wiley & Sons, Inc.]

importance in coding the stimulus, while for lower stimulus frequencies, the frequency of neural discharge is the coding mechanism.[3]

CNS Pathways

As Figure 4.18 indicates, the central nervous system connections for the auditory system are complex. The pathway is *bilateral*, each ear projecting to both sides of the brain. There are at least four synapses between the ear and the cortex. The major pathway, after the synapses in the medulla, involves the *lateral lemniscus*, *inferior colliculus*, and *medial geniculate* of the thalamus, and finally the cortex. Numerous alternative pathways appear to be possible, however, and there are extensive connections to other loci which probably participate in reflexive and orienting movements coordinating with visual and motor mechanisms.

Figure 4.19 shows one representation of the cortical areas in the cat that are responsive to auditory stimulation; it must be noted that researchers have not come to any precise agreement on the exact extent and location of

[3]For a more detailed description of von Békésy's findings and a discussion of the remaining uncertainites in the reception of auditory stimuli, see Utall (1973).

these areas. What is clear, however, is that there is extensive cortical involvement in auditory functions and that the interrelationships and functioning of these areas are complex. It should also be noted that the cochlea is spatially represented in the several auditory regions; that is, the topographic organization of the cochlea is preserved in each.

The coding functions carried out in the cochlea would appear to be limited, and they are augmented by more central processes. Katsuki (1961) has investigated the activity of single cells of the central auditory pathways.

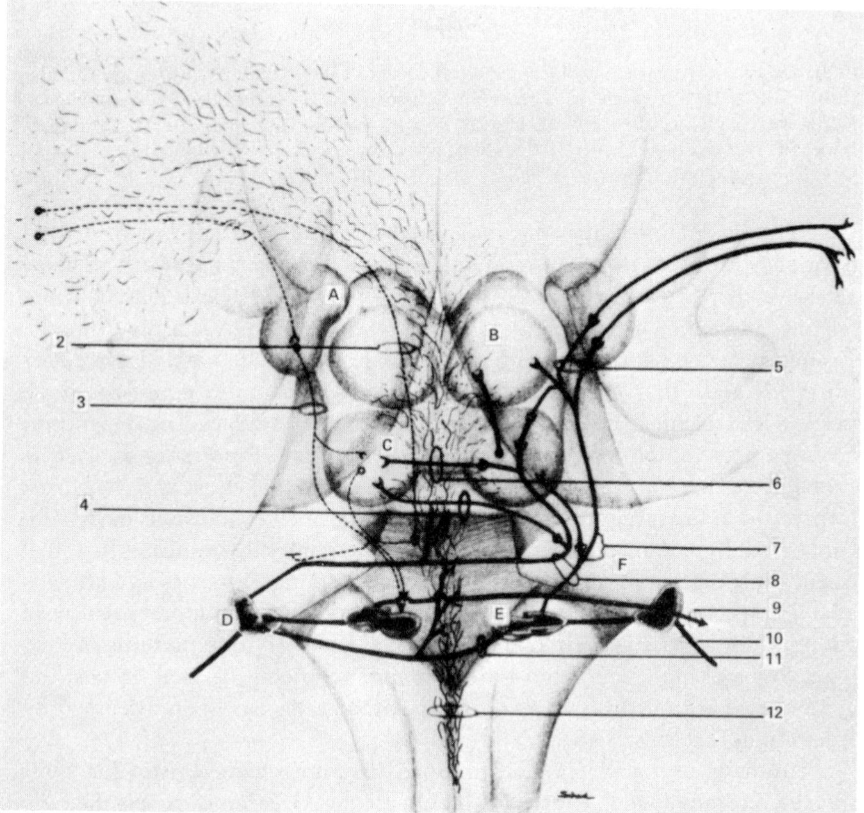

Figure 4.18. Main features of the known connections of the auditory pathways in the cat: A, medial geniculate body; B, superior colliculus; C, inferior colliculus; D, cochlear nucleus; E, superior olive; F, cut section of brachium pontis; 2, corticopontocerebellar pathway; 3, recurrent fibers throughout the auditory projection pathway; 4, commissure of inferior colliculus; 5, brachium of inferior colliculus; 6, commissure of inferior colliculus; 7, nucleus lateral lemniscus; 8, lateral lemniscus; 9, olive cochlear bundle; 10, cochlear nerve; 11, trapezoid body; 12, reticular system (diffuse projection to cerebral crotex). (From Ades, H. W., Central auditory mechanisms. *Handbook of Physiology, Neurophysiology,* Sec. I, vol. 1, 1959, 585–613.)

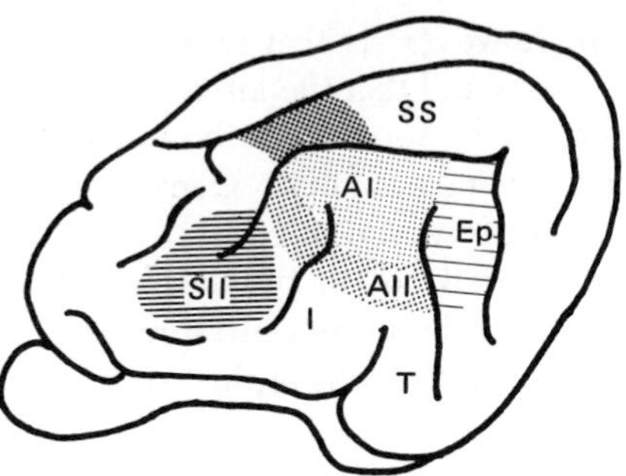

Figure 4.19. Auditory areas of the cerebral cortex of the cat: AI, auditory area I; AII, auditory area II; Ep, posterior ectosylvian; I, insular; T, temporal; SII, somatic area II; SS, suprasylvian. [From Neff, W. D., Neural mechanisms of auditory discrimination. In W. A. Rosenblith (Ed.), *Sensory Communication.* Cambridge, Mass.: M.I.T. Press, 1961. Reprinted by permission of The M.I.T. Press.]

Given sufficient intensity, the individual neurons will respond to a wide frequency range. With more moderate stimuli, however, neurons will show selective responses to restricted bands of frequencies. These may be quite narrow, indicating that individual neurons may be quite sharply "tuned." Examples of such tuning are presented in Figure 4.20. Katsuki concludes from this and other evidence that the coding of complex sounds is done partly at the cochlea and continues on into the CNS. Such coding depends in large part on inhibitory reactions between neurons. Frequency analysis is probably completed at the medial geniculate of the thalamus, and the cortex is involved in the integration of complex sounds. Such conclusions have been supported by numerous experiments which generally indicate that frequency discrimination can be maintained after animals are subjected to cortical lesions. However, more complex discriminations of temporal patterns of auditory stimulation—such as the difference between tone patterns of low, high, low and high, low, high—are lost after restricted cortical lesions (the general role of the cortex in auditory discriminations has been discussed by Elliott and Trahiotis. [1972]).

Animals emit calls or vocalizations that are characteristic for their species. In some instances at least, it appears that these species-specific calls have definite meaning for the animals. A study by Wollberg and Newman (1972) indicates that auditory neurons in the cortex of the monkey are selectively sensitive to different calls. Some cells showed complex firing patterns to many vocalizations, while other cells showed a simple response pattern to but one call; most cells were between these two extremes. Thus, in addition to simple frequency tuning, these neurons respond to specific *complex* sounds that seem to have utility for the animals. This suggests a rudimentary

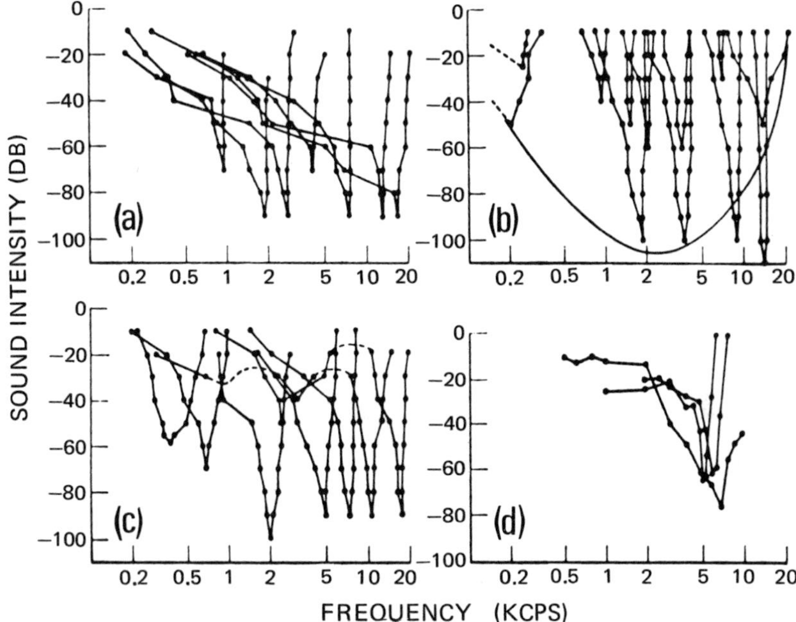

Figure 4.20. Response areas of single neurons obtained from (a) cochlear nerve, (b) inferior colliculus, (c) trapezoid body, and (d) medial geniculate body. [From Katsuki, Y., Neural mechanisms of auditory discrimination in the cat. In W. A. Rosenblith (Ed.), *Sensory Communication*. Cambridge, Mass.: M.I.T. Press, 1961. Reprinted by permission of The M.I.T. Press.]

basis for language. It also suggests that the nervous system need not build its responses to complex language stimuli from more elementary responses to simple sounds.

Finally, it should be noted that the presence of two ears and the bilateral central representation of each ear in the CNS facilitates a number of fine discriminations that help the organism locate sound in space. Human beings, for example, are capable of detecting a time difference in stimulation between the two ears of less than .5 msec. When two such tones are presented separately to the two ears, they appear to be localized in space in the direction of the first tone.

VISION

Vision has traditionally received the greatest amount of research attention and is probably the best understood of all the sensory systems. Even though

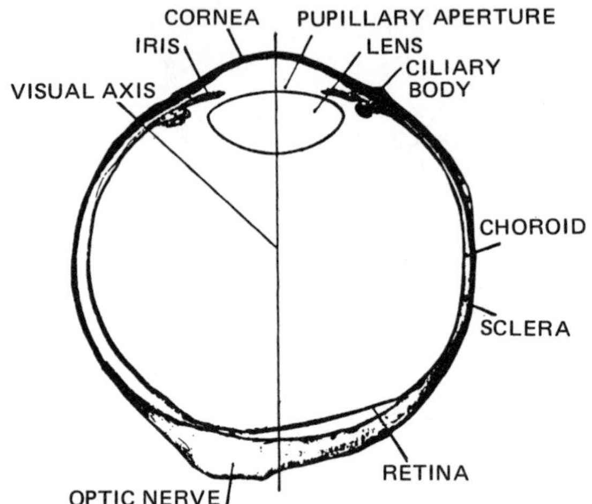

Figure 4.21. Horizontal section of a human eye. The lens, which was removed to facilitate making the section, has been drawn in its correct position, but the suspensory strands around it have been omitted. Note that the retina has partially separated from the other coats of the eyeball. The dark line in the posterior part of the iris is due to the presence of pigment. (From Gardner, E. *Fundamentals of Neurology*. Philadelphia: W. B. Saunders Company, 1968.)

much has been known about it for a long time, certain important facts have emerged only recently. These clarify some long-standing controversies about how coding is carried out in the visual system.

Structure of the Eye

Figure 4.21 illustrates the gross structure of the eye, which consists mainly of accessory apparatus concerned with the transmission and focusing of light on the retina. The retina contains the receptive elements of main interest to us here. The accessory structures permit the optical functioning of the eye in much the same manner as a camera—light is admitted through the *cornea*, passing through a regulatory opening (*the pupil*), and is focused by the *lens* on the photosensitive retina. The common visual defects that plague many of us are generally concerned with this accessory apparatus.

The retina contains elements that are actually part of the brain and, accordingly, presents the complex structure that would be expected of brain tissue (Figure 4.22). The basic photosensitive elements are the rods and cones. These are not always clearly distinguishable structurally, nor are they separated functionally; but, as we shall see, they do have different photoreactive properties. (Incidentally, for light to reach these receptive elements, it must pass through blood vessels, nerve fibers, and cell bodies—seemingly not a very efficient engineering design!) The next link in the chain

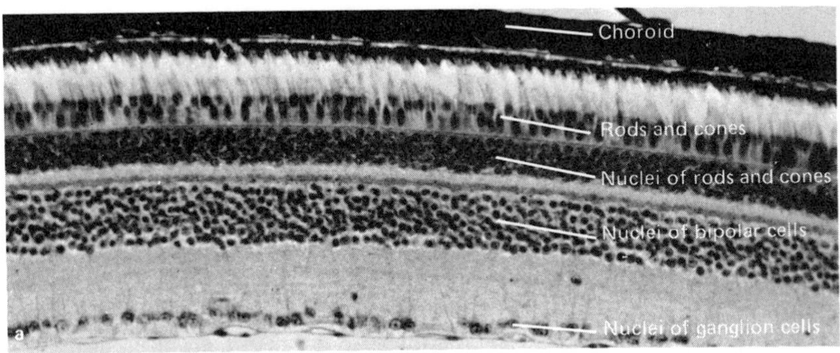

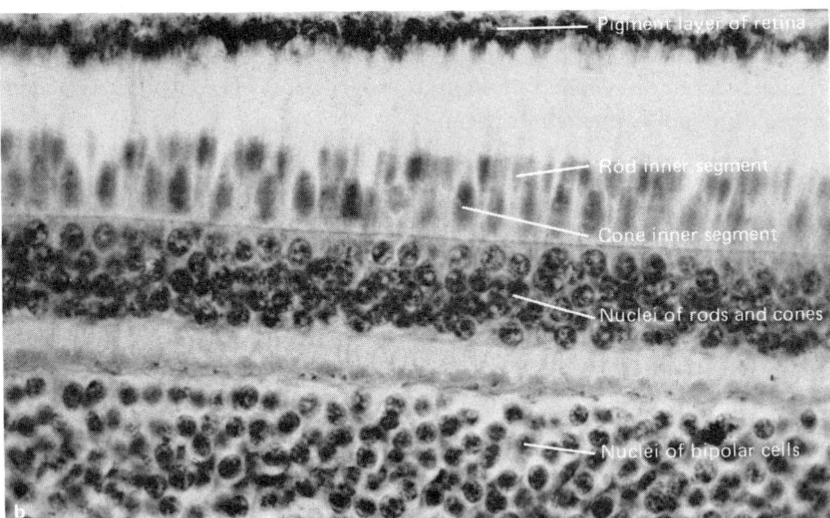

Figure 4.22. Photomicrographs of retina of copperhead snake (similar in many respects to human retina): (a) includes all the layers; (b) at a higher magnification, showing particularly the rods and cones. The staining method does not demonstrate neuronal processes. (These sections, made by Dr. Gordon Walls, are from Gardner, E. *Fundamentals of Neurology*. Philadelphia: W. B. Saunders Company, 1968.)

transmitting visual information consists of *bipolar* cells.[4] Most commonly these cells synapse with both rods and cones, sometimes in large numbers; alternatively, some bipolar cells link with cones only and, in the *fovea*, an area of the retina composed exclusively of cones, a single cone may synapse

[4]Sensory neurons frequently are bipolar in shape; that is, the cell body lies alongside a long fiber extending in one direction to form the dendrite and in the other to form the axon.

with a single bipolar cell. The next elements are *ganglion* cells, and these seem to be of two types: Those that connect with a great number of bipolar cells, and those that ultimately link with only one or two cones.

Thus, there are two basic systems in the retina. One of these, consisting solely of cones, is differentiated by the fact that it provides relatively direct lines to the optic nerve and more central neural structures. The other system is composed of both rods and cones and shows a great deal of convergence among elements. This structural convergence provides the substrate for interactions that result in facilitative and inhibitory changes in elements of the system in response to changes elsewhere. Additional neural elements seem to provide further for such interaction by establishing "horizontal," intraretinal connections—that is, connections not directed toward central transmission.

It should be noted that the distribution of rods and cones in the retina is not uniform. Thus, the fovea contains only cones, but the retinal periphery is extremely deficient in cones. Paralleling this difference is an increased convergence of peripheral elements on single ganglion cells. This convergence would seem to correspond to the loss of detailed discriminability associated with peripheral retinal stimulation.

CNS Connections

The ganglion cells of the retina give rise to fibers that converge to form the *optic* nerve. The place of their convergence produces the *blind spot* in the retina, because there are no photosensitive elements in this area. Figure 4.23 shows the course of the optic nerve through the *optic chiasma* to the *lateral geniculate body* of the thalamus where another synapse occurs; information is then passed on to the *occipital cortex.* Note that not all optic nerve fibers cross the midline in the chiasma of mammals (in nonmammalian species they all cross); fibers from the temporal side of the retina do not cross, while fibers from the nasal side of the retina cross to the opposite hemisphere. Fibers or collaterals also travel to the midbrain area, and many terminate in the *pretectal* area and/or *superior colliculus.* They may have other functions, but such connections mediate optic reflexes and orienting responses of the eyes. There are also other thalamic nuclei that receive visual information, but this seems to be secondary to the lateral geniculate input.

The lateral geniculate body is a multilayered structure, with the cells of each layer receiving input from specific portions of the retina of one or the other eye. Thus, the topographic arrangement of each retina is preserved. Similarly, the retina is represented topographically at the visual cortex. In fact, the retina may be said to be "amplified" in its cortical representation; that is, a single foveal cone may be represented cortically by as many as 100 cortical cells. It is speculated that this "fine grain" representation is the basis

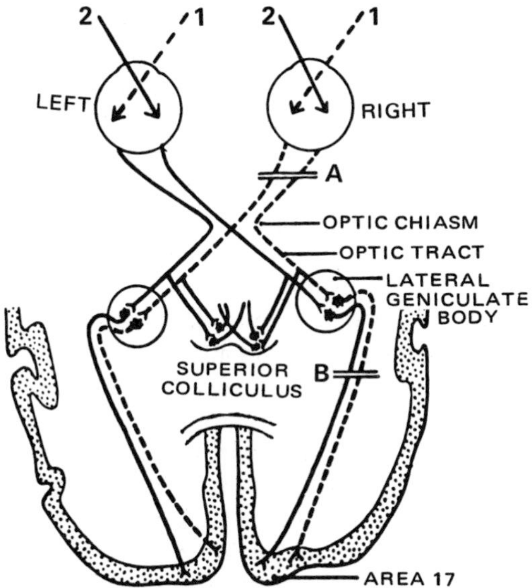

Figure 4.23. The visual pathways. Arrows numbered 1 indicate that light from objects in the right visual fields (when looking straight ahead) reaches the left halves of the retinae. The reverse is true for the opposite visual fields. The collaterals from the visual path (to the superior colliculi for reflexes) are really separate fibers and not branches of true visual fibers. Cutting the optic nerve at A causes complete blindness in that eye. A lesion at B, however, causes blindness in the left half of each field of vision (arrows numbered 2). (From Gardner, E. *Fundamentals of Neurology*. Philadelphia: W. B. Saunders Company, 1968.)

for the high degree of human visual acuity, a discriminability seemingly not possible from the structure of the retina alone. It should be noted that, in contrast to the geniculate, cortical cells receive binocular input.

Finally, like the other modalities, vision is represented in several cortical locations. Visual III is adjacent to Visual I in the occipital area; Visual II overlaps the auditory cortex in the cat; and, in the monkey, a fourth area, involved in visual discriminations, has been identified in the temporal lobe.

With this brief introduction to the structure of the visual system, we can now turn to the functional implications of this structure; that is, what are its consequences for the coding of visual information?

Duplicity Theory of Visual Functioning

Distinguishing the photoreceptors of the retina into rods and cones implies a functional difference between these elements. Such a functional difference is, indeed, the basis for the duplicity theory of visual functioning. It is assumed that these elements comprise two functional systems: One system consists of the rods, which function at low levels of illumination, as in night vision, and are insensitive to color; the other system consists of the cones, which require greater illumination levels for their functioning and are color responsive. As we have already mentioned, cones are more numerous in the central portions of the retina, and their connections are such as to allow for greater acuity of perception. Rods are more predominant in the retinal periphery, and their converging connections permit only the more gross discriminations but at the same time enhance sensitivity to weak stimuli. It should be noted that normally everyone is color blind in the retinal periphery. As a patch of light moves from the periphery toward the fovea, yellows and blues are perceived first, and it is only in the center of the retina that reds and greens are perceived. This zonal distribution of color receptivity is important in theoretical formulations about color vision.

Figure 4.24 shows how the rods and cones may be differentiated on the basis of their sensitivity to light after varying periods in the dark. The break in the curve after about 10 minutes in the dark indicates that the cones have reached their maximum sensitivity, but the rods continue to show further adaptation and a much lower final threshold. Note that the scale here is in log units of illumination, and a sensitivity change of over 4 log units occurs, or a factor of about 10,000!

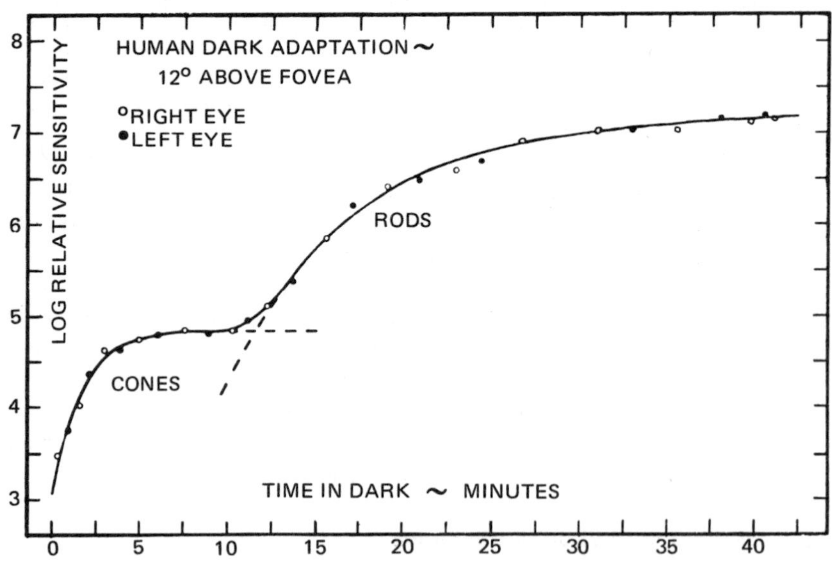

Figure 4.24. Dark-adaptation of the human eye measured in a peripheral area which contains both rods and cones. The dark adaptation of the cones is completed within about 5 min, that of the rods within about 45 min. (From Wald, G., Iodopsin. *Journal of General Physiology*, 1954–55, 38, 623–681.)

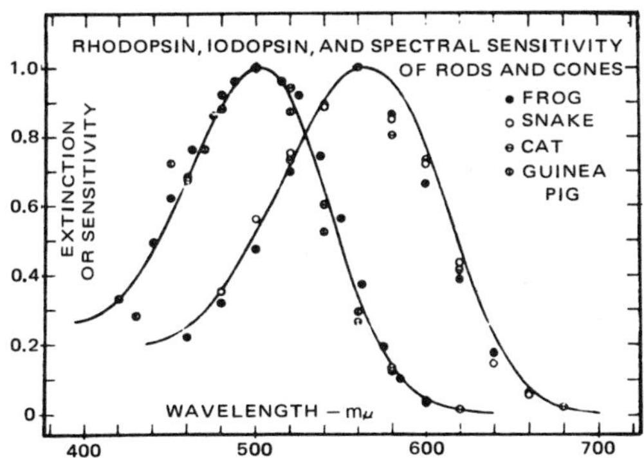

Figure 4.25. The absorption spectra of chicken rhodopsin and iodopsin compared with the scotopic and photopic sensitivities of various animals. The *lines* show the absorption spectra of the visual pigments, the *points* electrophysiological measurements of spectral sensitivity. (From Wald, G., Iodopsin. *Journal of General Physiology,* 1954–55, *38*, 623–681.)

Photochemistry

The process of reception of light is photochemical in nature; that is, it involves chemical reactions induced by light. In general, basic visual pigments are involved—*rhodopsin* in the rods and *iodopsin* in the cones. These consist of a variety of pigments that differ according to the species of animal and whether the receptors are rods or cones. However, these varieties are similar in that they are all composed of *retinene* and a particular variety of a protein material, *opsin*—it is the opsins that differ (Wald, 1959). A good bit of the chemistry concerned in the breakdown and resynthesis of these pigments is known.

Figure 4.25 shows that the rods and cones are differentiated in their sensitivity to light of different wavelengths by their respective pigments. Also shown is the almost perfect correspondence between sensitivity determined chemically and sensitivity determined by electrical recording from the neural elements in a variety of species. A similar correspondence can be demonstrated between the chemical processes and behavioral responses in humans.

Functional Characteristics of Visual Stimuli

Kuffler (1953) studied the "receptive fields" of individual cells in the cat retina; Figure 4.26 diagrams his results. Depending on the location of the stimulus light on the retina, the unit from which the recording was taken responded with one of three patterns of response—a discharge to the onset

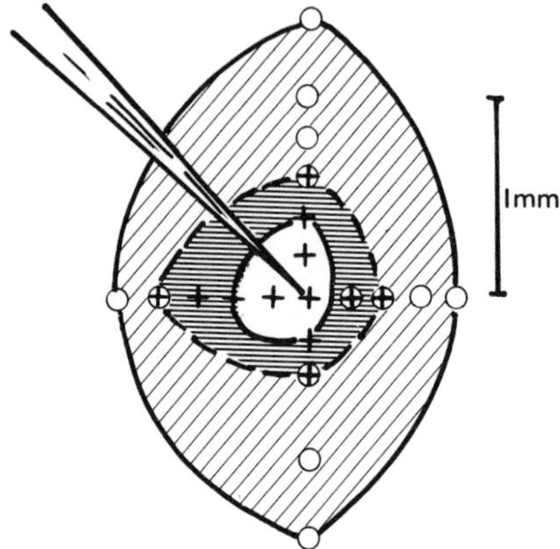

Figure 4.26. Distribution of discharge patterns within receptive field of ganglion cell (located at tip of electrode). Exploring spot was 0.2 mm in diameter, about 100 times threshold at center of field. Background illumination approximately 25 mc. In central region (crosses), "on" discharges were found, while in diagonally hatched part only "off" discharges occurred (circles). In the intermediary zone (horizontally hatched), discharges were "on-off." Note that change in conditions of illumination (background, etc.) also altered discharge pattern distribution. (From Kuffler, S. W., Discharge patterns and functional organization of the mammallian retina. *Journal of Neurophysiology,* 1953, *16,* 37–68.)

of the light in the central zone of receptivity, a discharge to the offset of the light in the outer zone, or both onset and offset discharges in an intermediate zone. Other cells showed the reverse pattern—offset discharge in the center and onset in the periphery. The distribution of the patterns could be altered by changing the illumination conditions. Figure 4.27 shows some of these patterns and also shows that onset and offset discharges are the result of mutually inhibiting processes. Thus, the pattern of response to light is not "fixed" even in response to a simple stimulus such as light onset, but involves complex excitatory and inhibitory interactions among the receptive elements of the retina.

In addition to such relatively complex responses to simple light stimuli, the retina of some species is capable of "analyzing" much more complicated stimuli. Experiments recording reponses from single optic nerve fibers in the frog (Maturana, Lettvin, Pitts, & McCulloch, 1960) used a variety of stimuli including lines, edges, dots, and checkered patterns. These were moved across the frog's visual field. Five categories of neural units or "detectors" were found, classifiable on the basis of the stimuli that evoked their responses: (1) Some cells respond to edges—the stimulus is the edge of an object that is lighter or darker than the background. The cells fire so long as the edge remains in the receptive field. (2) Some cells respond maximally to small dark objects with sharply contrasting edges that move within the receptive field, for example, moving insects in the frog's natural environment.

(3) Other units respond best to contrasting edges that move in *particular* directions across the receptive field. (4) Another category of cells shows discharge when the receptive field is dimmed. And finally (5) there are cells which fire continuously in inverse proportion to the light intensity. Each of these classes of response is independent of changes in the general level of illumination. It is thus possible to see that as objects pass through the visual field of the frog, their characteristics, in terms of movement, contrast with the background, edges, and the shadows they cast, are "analyzed" by different sets of responsive elements. In other words, it is not necessary to suppose that any sort of complex "interpretive" process is called for to understand "how the animal perceives" such characteristics—they are directly coded by the receptor system. It should also be noted that these separate types of detectors are kept segregated in their projections to the CNS; in the frog, the optic nerve projects to the superior colliculus, and each of the above detector types projects to a specific layer.

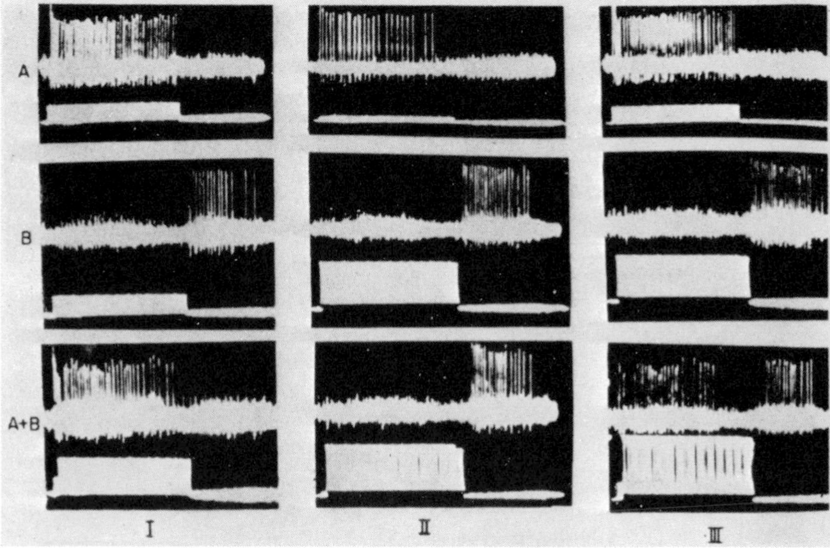

Figure 4.27. Interaction of two separate light spots. Single ganglion cell discharge during background illumination of 20 mc. Spot A, 0.1 mm in radius, was placed in center of receptive field at tip of recording electrode. Spot B, 0.2 mm in radius, was 0.6 mm away in surround. Flashed separately, they set up "on" (A) and "off" (B) responses. With a simultaneous flash, A + B in column I, "off" response was supressed and at same time, the number of "on" discharges in A + B is slightly reduced as compared with A. In II, intensity of spot A was reduced, while spot B was increased (note flash strength indication on second beam). As a consequence, B suppressed "on" discharge of A. In III, both spots were "strong." When flashed together (A + B), they reduced each other's discharges. Flash duration was 0.33 sec, potentials were 0.3 mV. (From Kuffler, S. W., Discharge patterns and functional organization of the mammallian retina. *Journal of Neurophysiology*, 1953, *16*, 37–68.)

Figure 4.28. Complex Responses of Single Cells in Cat Visual Cortex

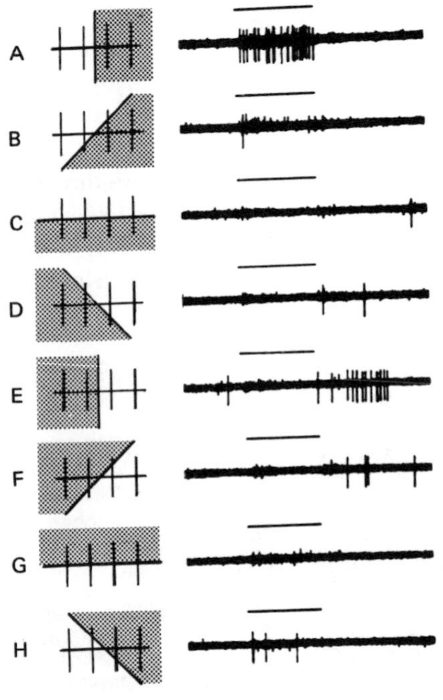

Figure 4.28a. Responses of a cell with a large (8 × 16°) complex receptive field to an edge projected on the ipsilateral retina so as to cross the receptive field in various directions. (The screen is illuminated by a diffuse background light, at 1.0 $\log_{10}$ cd/m^2. At the time of stimulus, shown by upper line of each record, half the screen, to one side of the variable boundary, is illuminated at 1.0 $\log_{10}$ cd/m^2, while the other half is kept constant.) A, vertical edge with light area to left, darker area to right. B-H, various other orientations of edge. Position of receptive field 20° below and to the left of the area centralis. Time, 1 sec.

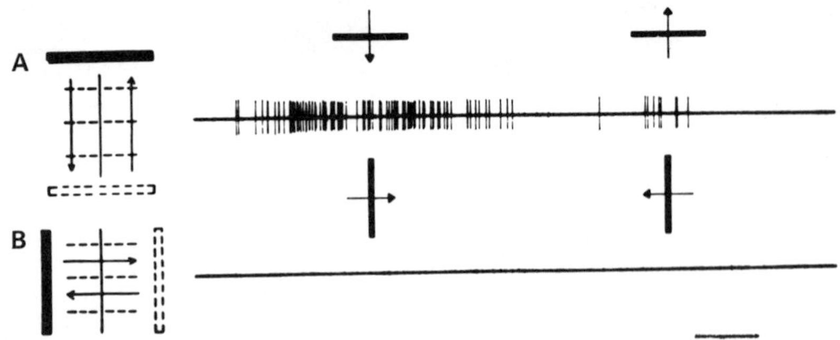

Figure 4.28c. (Same cell as in Figure 4.28b.) Movement of black rectangle 1/3 × 6° back and forth across the receptive field; A, horizontally oriented (parallel to receptive-field axis); B, vertically oriented. Time required to move across the field, 5 sec. Time, 1 sec.

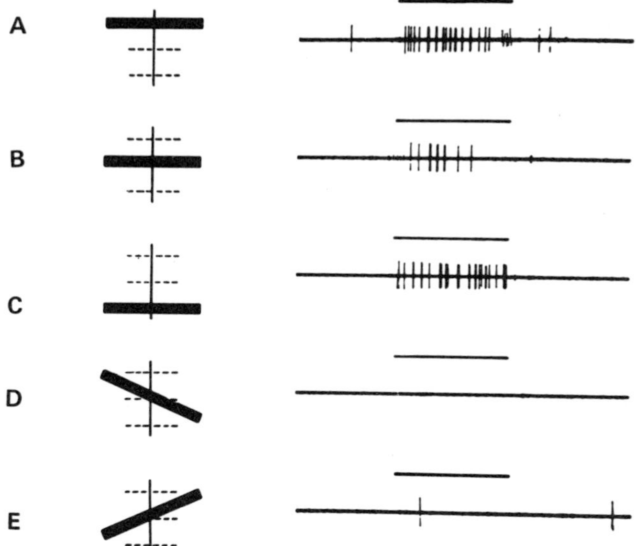

Figure 4.28b. Cell activated only by left (contralateral) eye over a field approximately 5 × 5°, situated 10° above and to the left of the area centralis. The cell responded best to a black horizontal rectangle, 1/3 × 6°, placed anywhere in the receptive field (A–C). Tilting the stimulus rendered it ineffective (D–E). The black bar was introduced against a light background during periods of 1 sec, indicated by the upper line in each record. Luminance of white background, 1.0 $\log_{10}$ cd/m^2; luminance of black part, 0.0 $\log_{10}$ cd/m^2. A lesion, made while recording from the cell, was found in layer 2 of apical segment of postlateral gyrus.

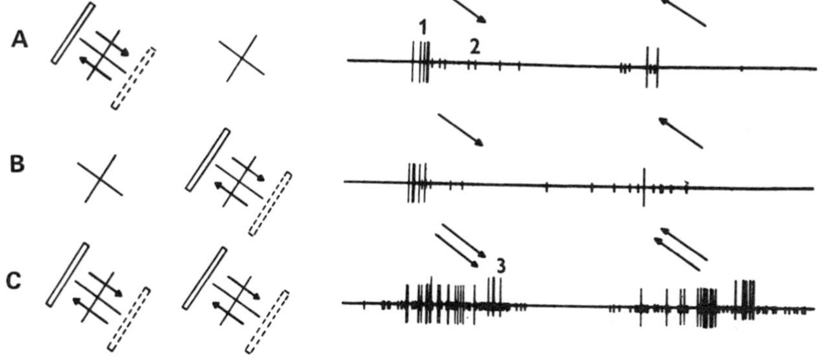

Figure 4.28d. Examples of binocular synergy in a simultaneous recording of three cells (spikes of the three cells are labeled 1–3). Each of the cells had receptive fields in the two eyes; in each eye the three fields overlapped and were situated 2° below and to the left of the area centralis. The crosses to the left of each record indicate the positions of the receptive fields in the two eyes. The stimulus was 1/8 × 2° slit-oriented obliquely and moved slowly across the receptive fields as shown—A, in the left eye; B, in the right eye; C, in the two eyes simultaneously. Time, 1 sec. (From Hubel, D. H. and Wiesel, T. N., Receptive fields, binocular interaction, and functional architecture in the cat's visual center. *Journal of Physiology*, 1961, *160*, 106–154. By permission of Cambridge University Press.)

The complexity of response exhibited in the retina of the frog, however, is not necessarily characteristic for all animals; in higher animals, such as the cat, these functions appear to be carried out at cortical rather than retinal levels. Examples of such responses from the cat's cortex are illustrated in Figure 4.28. It is probable that having such functions at the cortex, rather than at the retina, permits the cat to employ them in much more complex behavior than the frog can exhibit.

Color Vision

Historically, there have been two major theories about the mechanisms of color perception. Each is relatively old, but it is only quite recently that definitive evidence about either has been forthcoming. Both theories assume that the cones of the retina are the basic receptors; from this common start the theories diverge.

The *trichromatic* theory was proposed by Thomas Young at the beginning of the nineteenth century and was later elaborated by Helmholtz. Basically, it assumes that there are three kinds of cones. Each of these cone types is more sensitive than the other two in a restricted portion of the visual spectrum. Thus, one type is more sensitive in the red, one in the green, and one in the blue region of the spectrum. Combinations of output from these receptors determine the hue seen. When these outputs are about equal, the resulting sensation is white. There is no special luminosity (brightness) receptor in this system.

The *opponent process* theory is principally associated with Ewald Hering, whose work dates from the 1870s. A recent version of the theory suggested that there are four kinds of color receptors—red, green, blue, and yellow cone types. These were presumed to be linked in opposing pairs—yellow-blue and red-green. In addition, the theory assumed that there was a separate luminosity mechanism that mediates colorless (white, grey, and black) sensations. In this model, colorless sensations are not dependent on the mixing of colors as in the trichromatic model.

Each of these hypotheses has its strong and weak points. The main advantages of the trichromatic model would appear to be its simplicity and the straightforward predictions it makes, which are easily verifiable. Among its chief faults is its difficulty in accounting for the fact that totally color-blind persons have approximately normal sensitivity for brightness. This would be evidence against the trichromatic theory's assumption that the perception of white comes from the addition of activity in the three basic color receptors. The opponent process theory also seems better able to account for such phenomena as retinal color zones, complementary colors, contrast effects, and certain aspects of color-blindness. On the other hand, it is a more complex theory and its deductions are more intricate. As we shall see, however, recent research strongly suggests that both theories are correct!

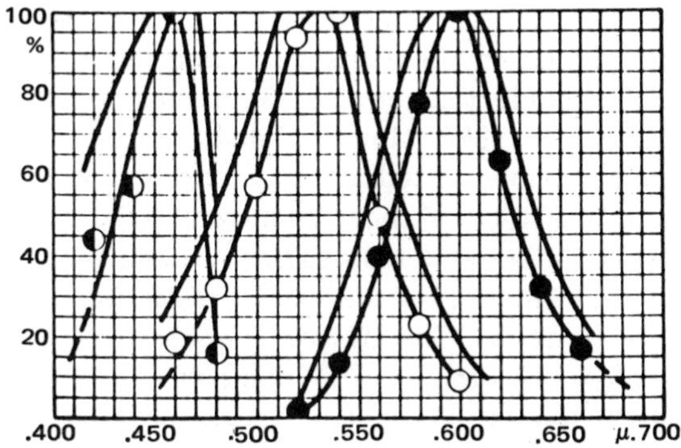

Figure 4.29. Averages of individual modulators as obtained by selective adaptation. *Filled circles:* red modulators; *open circles:* green modulators; *half-filled circles:* blue modulators. Outer contours indicate dispersion. (From Granit, R., The colour receptors of the mammallian retina. *Journal of Neurophysiology,* 1945, *8,* 195–210.)

Work on the electrophysiological responses of the eye and the biochemistry of retinal pigments is both extensive and complex. For this reason, we can cite only selected examples from the voluminous research literature.

Dominators and Modulators

Of major importance were Granit's studies of single unit responses from the eye (1955). With electrodes in retinal ganglion cells, Granit found that there were two types of recordable responses. The first of these were from units that he termed *dominators*. These were units that responded to a wide range of wavelengths and were similar in sensitivity characteristics to rhodopsin.

The second type of unit was termed *modulators* and showed a much more restricted response curve, such units showing peaks of sensitivity at different wavelengths. In other words, dominators tend to be unresponsive to color differences and responsive to light generally, while modulators show preferential peaks of sensitivity to different colors (compare Figure 4.29 with Figure 4.25). It must be remembered that the organization of the retina is such that responses from ganglion cells probably reflect a good deal of interaction between photoreceptive elements, so a simple correspondence between these results and rod and cone functioning cannot be made. However, Granit interpreted these results as indicative of the basic correctness of the Young-Helmholtz trichromatic theory of color perception.

Functional Characteristics of Pigment

To best substantiate the trichromatic model, one would like to show that three basic photosensitive pigments, each mediating a restricted band of wavelengths, can be isolated chemically from cones of the retina. Progress toward this goal, particularly in animals, is being made. Short of this goal, however, it is still possible to determine the functional characteristics of the presumed pigments. In 1964 (Marks, Dobelle, & MacNichol; Brown & Wald), it was finally demonstrated for the first time that the human retina contains the three basic types of cones predicted by the trichromatic model. The method employed for this demonstration essentially consists of passing a narrow beam of light into *single* cones in the retina and analyzing the light reflected back by the retina. The method is exceedingly more complicated than is indicated here, and there are refinements and corrections that need to be investigated. Nonetheless, it shows clearly that single cones differentially absorb light in three basic regions of the spectrum. Thus, after some 150 years, the basic notions of the Young-Helmholtz theory have been demonstrated to hold for human color vision, at least at the retina. That the trichromatic model holds for retinal processes leads to our next consideration.

Lateral Geniculate Responses to Light

A number of investigations of central nervous system activity indicate that a simple trichromatic model is not a sufficient mechanism to account for CNS responses to light stimuli. This work is probably best exemplified by DeValois and his co-workers (DeValois, Abramov, & Mead, 1967). They recorded single-cell responses to light of varying wavelengths in the lateral geniculate of the monkey (macaque).

Lateral geniculate cells generally are "spontaneously" active even when the animal is in the dark; thus it is against this background discharge level that the response to light must be evaluated. A variety of cell types were identified. Some cells responded to lights of all wavelengths with increased discharge (excitatory response); other cells responded by a decrease of discharge to the same light stimuli (inhibition). Together, these two cell types form a system that is extremely sensitive to changes in brightness; this particular system is, however, quite unresponsive to wavelength (color) differences. Another type of cell showed color responsiveness—excitation to certain wavelengths and inhibition to others. These cells have an *opponent* organization; that is, when adapted to light of some particular wavelength, they respond with an increased (+) firing rate to a shift in one direction from the adaptational wavelength, and with a decrease (−) when the shift is in the opposite direction. Such cells are most sensitive to wavelength changes in certain parts of the spectrum. They may, therefore, be characterized as responsive to red (R) and green (G), or to yellow (Y) and blue (B). The result is four subtypes of cells: R+G−, R−G+, Y+B−, and Y−B+.

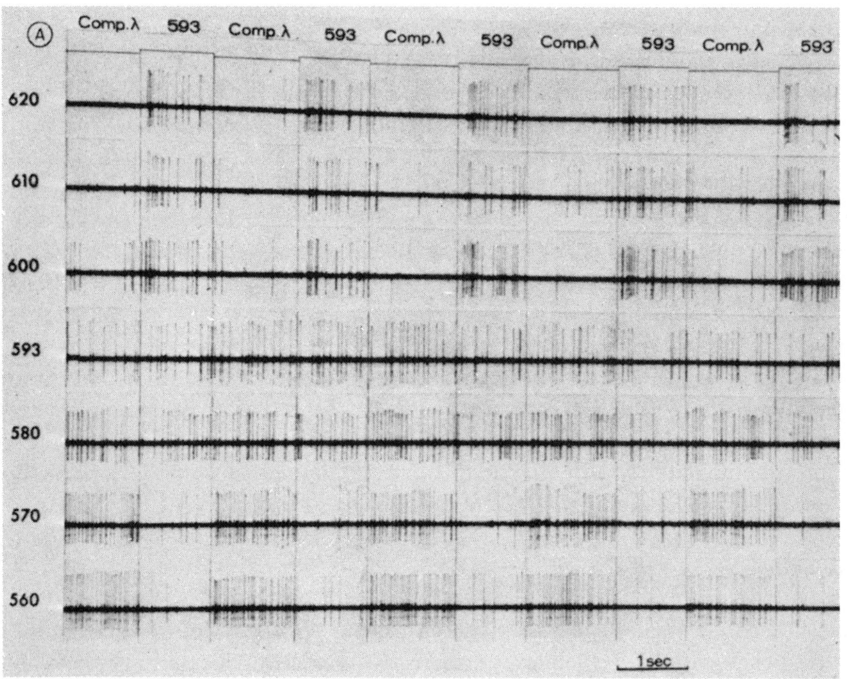

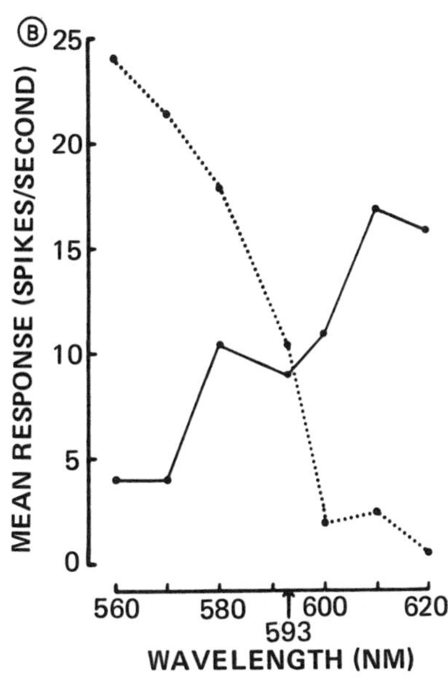

Figure 4.30. (A) Oscilloscope records of responses of a G + R–cell of the lateral geniculate nucleus to wavelength shifts between a 593 nm standard and various comparison wavelengths whose values are on the ordinate. All stimuli equated for luminance. Top line is the signal marker; upward deflection indicates standard wavelength, downward deflection comparison wavelength. (B) Plot of responses of cell in A. Responses to standard (solid line) were averaged over the five cycles at each wavelength as were the responses to comparison stimuli (dotted line). (From DeValois, R., Abramov, I., and Mead, W. R., Single cell analysis of wavelength discrimination at the lateral geniculate nucleus in the macaque. *Journal of Neurophysiology,* 1967, *30,* 415–433.)

The response of a G+R− cell is shown in Figure 4.30. Here recordings were made when the stimulus was switched back and forth between lights of 593 nm and each of the other indicated wavelengths.[5] When the switch was to a shorter wavelength, the cell responded with increased spike output; when the switch was to a longer wavelength, the cell responded with inhibition. Switching back to 593 nm produced a change dependent on the wavelength from which the switch was being made. In other words, the response of such cells is *not* fixed; it is the result of excitatory and inhibitory influences, and these influences change across the visual spectrum. These cells have also been shown to be relatively insensitive to changes in brightness. In fact, as their sensitivity to color changes in response to different wavelengths, their sensitivity to brightness changes in an inverse manner—where they are maximally sensitive to color they are minimally sensitive to brightness. As can be seen, then, the system that operates in the lateral geniculate is very similar to the opponent process model originally described by Hering almost 100 years ago.

Conclusions

Retinal color mechanisms, then, seem to consist of a system of three cone types, each with its particular photosensitive pigment. The neural responses to the actions of these pigments converge, probably before the level of the ganglion cells of the retina, for processing in the CNS. The basic organization of such a system is illustrated in Figure 4.31. Note that in this model, it is not the retinal receptors that provide the color coding; rather it is assumed that color coding results from neurophysiological events at the level of opponent organization. This organization into an opponent process system takes advantage of the sharpened discriminations possible through playing excitatory and inhibitory mechanisms against each other. Thus, while there are three distinct cone types, their absolute sensitivities cover a relatively broad range of the spectrum; their combination into an opponent form for processing probably maximizes the fine wavelength discriminations that we know the human organism actually does make.

SUMMARY

Our inquiry into the coding mechanisms employed in the nervous system started with the recognition that there are three fundamental means of accomplishing this function: (1) Stimulation of specialized receptor and CNS units; (2) topographical preservation of the location of the receptors stimulated; and (3) modulation of the discharge pattern of CNS units. That the

[5]nm = *nanometer*. An equivalent term, currently not in use, is *millimicron* (mμ): These units are one-thousandth of a millionth of a meter.

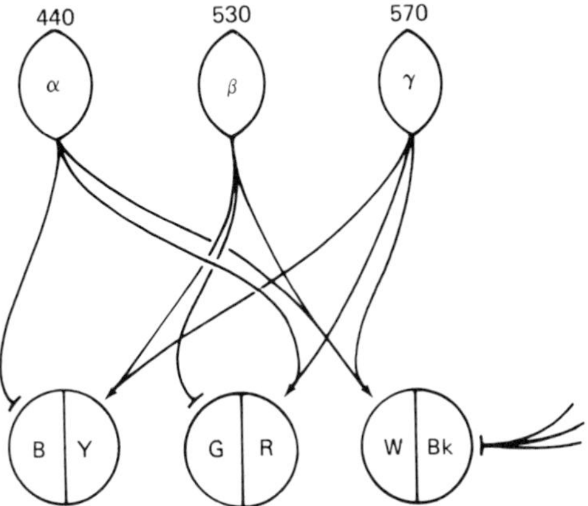

Figure 4.31. Schematic diagram of the organization of three retinal cone types into an opponent processing neural response system. The numbers above each cone type represents their optimal wavelength sensitivity. (From Hurvich, L. M., and Jameson, D. Opponent processes as a model of neural organization. *American Psychologist,* 1974, *29,* 88–102.)

CNS is, in general, topographically organized has been well recognized. Thus, research has concentrated on basic sensory qualities and the presumed specialized receptors that mediate them. This research has been particularly successful in the study of vision; three basic retinal cone types have been identified that mediate color vision. On the other hand, the search has been remarkably unsuccessful in the somesthetic systems, where probably only the vestibular receptors for bodily movement and the sensors of joint, tendon, and muscle activity go unchallenged. Receptors for touch, cold, warmth, and pain have yet to be positively identified. Moreover, even where such specialized receptors have been located, it is becoming increasingly obvious that there is no exclusive reliance on this type of coding. Thus, for instance, the special receptors of color vision, taste, and audition are all augmented by additional coding processes in the CNS that modulate the activity patterns evoked by these special receptors. The interplay of excitatory and inhibitory mechanisms allows for greater flexibility and complexity of the coding. It seems apparent that without this interplay, the coding of complex visual properties such as directionality of movement and angularity through single-cell activity would not be possible; many more cells would be necessary for such complex analyses. In any event, the efficiency of our information processing would be much reduced. Though speculative at this time, it seems probable that further research will see the extension of our understanding of such mechanisms into the less well-known sensory systems such as olfaction.

We have generally concerned ourselves in this chapter with the question of how the CNS codes the physical properties of environmental energy.

In the next chapter, we will concentrate on how we deal with the psychologically meaningful stimuli composed of such physical energy.

REFERENCES

ADES, H. W. Central auditory mechanisms. In J. Field, H. W. Magoun, & V. E. Hall (eds.), *Handbook of physiology, neurophysiology, I.* Washington, D. C.: American Physiological Society, 1959, pp. 585–613.

ADEY, W. R. The sense of smell. In J. Field, H. W. Magoun, & V. E. Hall (eds.), *Handbook of physiology, neurophysiology, I.* Washington, D. C.: American Physiological Society, 1959, pp. 535–547.

AKIL, H., MAYER, D. J., & LIEBESKIND, J. C. Antagonism of stimulation-produced analgesia by naloxone, a narcotic antagonist. *Science*, 1976, *191*, 961–962.

ALLEN, W. F. Olfactory and trigeminal conditioned reflexes in dogs. *American Journal of Physiology*, 1937, *118*, 532–540.

BEALER, S. L., & SMITH, D. V. Multiple sensitivity to chemical stimuli in single human taste papillae. *Physiology and Behavior*, 1975, *14*, 795–799.

BORING, E. G. *A history of experimental psychology.* New York: Appleton-Century-Crofts, 1929.

BROWN, P. K., & WALD, G. Visual pigments in single rods and cones of the human retina. *Science*, 1964, *144*, 45–52.

CLARK, W. C., & YANG, J. C. Acupunctural analgesia? Evaluation by signal detection theory. *Science*, 1974, *184*, 1096–1097.

DAVIS, H. Peripheral coding of auditory information. In W. A. Rosenblith (ed.), *Sensory communication.* New York: Wiley, 1961, pp. 119–142.

DELORENZO, A. J. D. Studies on the ultrastructure and histophysiology of cell membranes, nerve fibers, and synaptic junctions in chemoreceptors. In Y. Zotterman (ed.), *Olfaction and taste.* Oxford: Pergamon, 1963, pp. 5–17.

DEVALOIS, R., ABRAMOV, I., & MEAD, W. R. Single cell analysis of wavelength discrimination at the lateral geniculate nucleus in the macaque. *Journal of Neurophysiology*, 1967, *30*, 415–433.

ELLIOTT, D. N., & TRAHIOTIS, C. Cortical lesions and auditory discrimination. *Psychological Bulletin*, 1972, *77*, 198–222.

ERICKSON, R. P. Stimulus coding the topographic and nontopographic afferent modalities: On the significance of the activity of individual sensory neurons. *Psychological Review*, 1968, *75*, 447–465.

GARDNER, E. *Fundamentals of neurology*. Philadelphia: W. B. Saunders, 1968.

GRANIT, R. The color receptors of the mammalian retina. *Journal of Neurophysiology*, 1945, *8*, 195–210.

HIGGINS, J. D., TURSKY, B., & SCHWARTZ, G. E. Shock-elicited pain and its reduction by concurrent tactile stimulation. *Science*, 1971, *172*, 866–867.

HUBEL, D. H., & WIESEL, T. N. Receptive fields, binocular interaction and functional architecture in the cat's visual center. *Journal of Physiology*, 1962, *160*, 106–154.

HURVICH, L. M., & JAMESON, D. Opponent processes as a model of neural organization. *American Psychologist*, 1974, *29*, 88–102.

JONES, E. G., BURTON, H., & PORTER, R. Commissural and cortico-cortical "columns" in the somatic sensory cortex of primates. *Science*, 1975, *190*, 572–574.

KATSUKI, Y. Neural mechanism of auditory sensations in the cat. In W. A. Rosenblith (ed.), *Sensory communication*. New York: Wiley, 1961, pp. 561–585.

KENSHALO, D. R., & NAFE, J. P. A quantitative theory of feeling: 1960. *Psychological Review*, 1962, *69*, 17–33.

KIMURA, K., & BEIDLER, L. M. Microelectrode study of taste bud of the rat. *American Journal of Physiology*, 1956, *187*, 610.

KUFFLER, S. W. Discharge patterns and functional organization of mammalian retina. *Journal of Neurophysiology*, 1953, *16*, 37–68.

MARKS, W. B., DOBELLE, W. H., & MACNICHOL, E. F. Visual pigments of single primate cones. *Science*, 1964, *143*, 1181–1182.

MATURANA, H. R., LETTVIN, J. Y., PITTS, W. H., & MCCULLOCH, W. S. Anatomy and physiology of vision in the frog. *Journal of General Physiology*, 1960, *43*, Suppl. 2, 129–175.

MAYER, D. J., WOLFLE, T. L., AKIL, H., CARDER, B., & LIEBESKIND, J. C. Analgesia from electrical stimulation of the brainstem of the rat. *Science*, 1971, *174*, 1351–1354.

MCCUTCHEON, N. B., & SAUNDERS, J. Human taste papilla stimulation: Stability of quality judgments over time. *Science*, 1972, *175*, 214–216.

MELZACK, R., & SCOTT, T. H. The effects of early experience on the response to pain. *Journal of Comparative and Physiological Psychology*, 1957, *50*, 155–161.

MELZACK, R., & WALL, P. D. Pain mechanisms: A new theory. *Science*, 1965, *150*, 971–979.

MOSKOWITZ, H. W., KUMARAIAH, V., SHARMA, K. N., JACOBS, H. L., &

SHARMA, S. D. Cross-cultural differences in simple taste preferences. *Science*, 1975, *190*, 1217–1218.

MOUNTCASTLE, V. B. Some functional properties of the somatic afferent system. In W. A. Rosenblith (ed.), *Sensory communication.* New York: Wiley, 1961, pp. 403–436.

MOUNTCASTLE, V. B., & POWELL, T. P. S. Neural mechanisms subserving cutaneous sensibility, with special reference to the role of afferent inhibition in sensory perception and discrimination. *Bulletin of the Johns Hopkins Hospital,* 1959, *105*, 201–232.

MOZELL, M. M., & JAGODOWICZ, M. Chromatographic separation of odorants by the nose: Retention times measured across in vivo olfactory mucosa. *Science*, 1973, *181*, 1247–1249.

NEFF, W. D. Neural mechanisms of auditory discrimination. In W. A. Rosenblith (ed.), *Sensory communication.* New York: Wiley, 1961, pp. 259–278.

OVERMANN, S. R. Dietary self-selection by animals. *Psychological Bulletin,* 1976, *83*, 218–235.

PATTON, H. D. Taste, olfaction, and visceral sensations. In T. C. Ruch, H. D. Patton, J. W. Woodbury, & A. L. Towe (eds.), *Neurophysiology.* Philadelphia: W. B. Saunders, 1961, pp. 369–385.

PENFIELD, W., & RASMUSSEN, T. *The cerebral cortex of man.* New York: Macmillan, 1950.

PFAFFMANN, C. Gustatory nerve impulses in rat, cat and rabbit. *Neurophysiology,* 1955, *18*, 429–440.

SATRAN, R., & GOLDSTEIN, M. N. Pain perception: Modification of threshold of intolerance and cortical potentials by cutaneous stimulation. *Science*, 1973, *180*, 1201–1202.

SCHNEIDER, M. *Einführung in die Physiologie des Menschen.* Berlin: Springer, 1964.

SIEGEL, J. M., & MCGINTY, D. J. Brainstem neurons without spontaneous discharge. *Science*, 1976, *193*, 240–242.

SMITH, D. F., & BALAGURA, S. Taste and physiological need in Vitamin C intake by guinea pigs. *Physiology and Behavior, 1975, 14*, 545–549.

STARR, A. Suppression of single unit activity in cochlear nucleus of the cat following sound stimulation. *Journal of Neurophysiology,* 1965, *28*, 850–862.

SWETS, J. A. Is there a sensory threshold? *Science*, 1961, *134*, 168–177.

UTTAL, W. R. *The psychobiology of sensory coding.* New York: Harper & Row, 1973.

Van der Loos, H., & Wolsey, T. A. Somatosensory cortex: Structural alterations following early injury to sense organs. *Science*, 1973, *179*, 395–398.

von Békésy, G. On the resonance curve and the decay period at various points on the cochlear partition. *Journal of Acoustical Society of America*, 1949, *21*, 245–254.

von Békésy, G., & Rosenblith, W. A. In S. S. Stevens (ed.), *Handbook of experimental psychology*. New York: Wiley, 1951, pp. 1075–1115.

Wald, G. The photoreceptor process in vision. In J. Field, H. W. Magoun, & V. E. Hall (eds.), *Handbook of physiology, neurophysiology, I*. Washington, D. C.: American Physiological Society, 1959, pp. 671–691.

Wald, G., Brown, P. K., & Smith, P. H. Iodopsin. *Journal of General Physiology*, 1954–55, *38*, 623–681.

Wollberg, Z., & Newman, J. D. Auditory cortex of squirrel monkey: Response patterns of single cells to species-specific vocalizations. *Science*, 1972, *175*, 212–214.

Woodworth, R. S., & Marquis, D. G. *Psychology* (5th ed.). New York: Henry Holt, 1947.

Woodworth, R. S., & Schlossberg, H. *Experimental psychology*. New York: Henry Holt, 1954.

5

Attention and Perception

In the previous chapter we were concerned with the question of how information impinges upon the organism. Here our concern will shift to the processes involved in the utilization of that information. It should be obvious that these are closely related aspects of a total information processing problem, i.e., what information is available and how it is coded necessarily must influence the utilization of that information. We have seen that the receptive processes do not pass on completely unorganized, "raw" messages. Rather, considerable coding and organization of stimulus information is carried out in the initial sensory processes. The existence of neural elements directly responsive to this coding makes complex interpretive processes unnecessary—the brain does not somehow have to "reconstruct" the external world in order to deal with it.

It should be apparent then that sensory and cognitive processes are at least contiguous and interdependent. At the same time, however, we must acknowledge that the data we will consider here are relatively fragmentary and unconnected; that is, at the present time they form no unified body of information that could be termed a "physiology of perception." Rather, we shall have to look at relatively compartmentalized pieces of the total problem. One result of this is that the more complex theories of human perception and cognition are not yet amenable to neurophysiological test.

The kinds of issues with which we will be generally concerned are readily illustrated. For instance, we are not merely passive receivers of sensory information—we select from the environment what we attend to. Not only do we select between sensory modalities, but within those modalities as well. Thus, we can apparently choose to note or not to note what the individuals at a party are wearing, and we can usually listen to one or another of them despite the general sound level in the room. Our conversation with them is immediately intelligible—if not intelligent—despite the fact that we each may be uttering sentences that the speaker may never have said exactly this way before nor the listener heard before. When these well-organized processes break down, a variety of "explanations" may be offered. For example, at a party, or in an experiment, when someone does not respond to the stimulus information available, is it because there is a sensory deficit—i.e., the information was not received? Or was there a motivational change, for example, the person no longer wants to continue the conversation? Perhaps the person doesn't "understand" the messages or has "forgotten" the responses required to respond. Thus, learning, memory, motivation, etc., all contribute to the processes which we are attempting to deal with here, and there may be no easy way to separate their contribution.

RETICULAR THEORY OF PERCEPTION

As we saw in the previous chapter, much of our fundamental knowledge of the response of the CNS to sensory input comes from recording experiments carried out in animals. And it is to such experiments that we must first turn to provide the necessary background for a consideration of the mechanisms involved in the "higher" levels of information processing. In these experiments, simple stimuli such as brief, mild electric shocks, light flashes, and clicks are presented and the electrical responses of the CNS are recorded. The animal subjects in the initial experiments we will consider were only passively involved; that is, they were not required to make behavioral responses to the stimuli. Such experiments, then, do not directly involve issues concerning perception of stimuli. However, the results of such experiments provided suggestions that were subsequently tested in experiments designed to manipulate attention and perception.

Stability of Evoked Responses

In experiments employing acutely prepared, anesthetized animals, the electrical responses evoked from the CNS by sensory stimuli are characterized by a great deal of stability. When recording such responses between the peripheral receptors and the cortex, one finds that they are reliably recorded at each way station through the spinal cord, brainstem, thalamus, and on to the cortex. Such recordings were responsible for the initial delineation of the so-called primary receiving areas of the cortex and the classical sensory pathways. The responses are relatively invariant and stable in their amplitudes.

Such results fit well with a view that neural impulses are subject to psychological influences only when they reach the cortex and that it is to the cortex that we should look for such influences. This conclusion is drastically modified, however, when unanesthetized animals are employed; the high amplitude, stable responses of the specific sensory cortex are then greatly increased in variability and reduced in mean amplitude. Additionally, areas outside the specific sensory systems are now seen to respond also to these afferent messages. This is particularly true of the reticular system and the nonspecific, nonsensory portions of the thalamus.

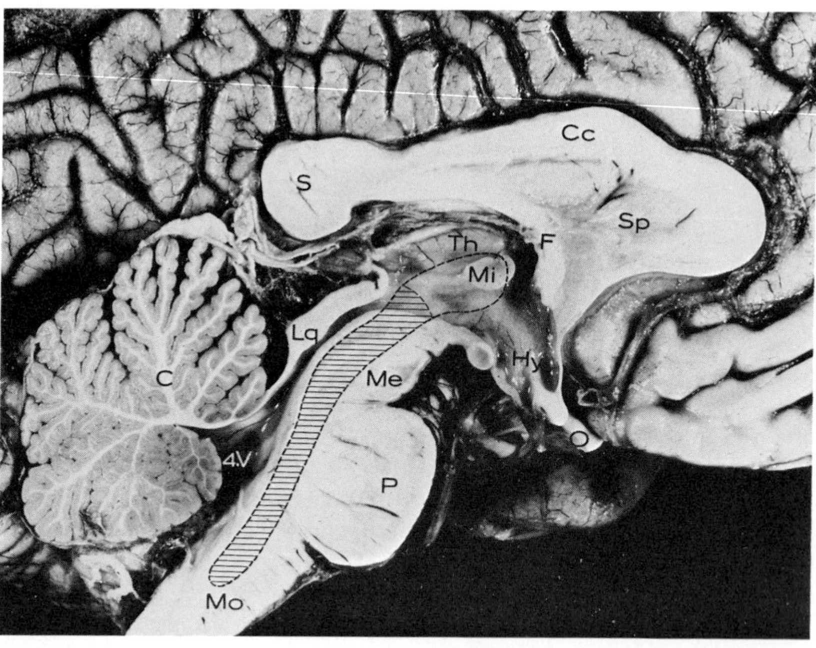

Figure 5.1. Rostrocaudal extent of the reticular formation in a median sagittal section through the human brain. The reticular formation of the medulla oblongata, pons, and midbrain is cross-hatched; the reticular formation of the diencephalon is unshaded. C, cerebellum; Cc, corpus callosum; F, fornix; Hy, hypothalamus; Lq, lamina quadrigemina; Me, midbrain; Mi, massa intermedia thalami; Mo, medulla oblongata; O, optic nerve; P, pons; S, splenium corporis callosi; Sp, septum pellucidum; Th, thalamus. (From Pilleri, Birkmayer, W. and Pilleri, G. *The Brainstem Reticular Formation and Its Significance for Autonomic and Affective Behavior.* Basle, Switzerland: Hoffman-LaRoche & Co., 1966.)

The Reticular System

The *reticular formation* is a "core" of neural tissue extending from the spinal cord through the brainstem and thalamus (Figure 5.1). It consists of an intermingling of cell bodies and fibers in a complex network or reticulum. Surrounding this core are the classical ascending sensory pathways and descending efferents. One important characteristic of this system is that it receives input from the sensory systems. The precise collateral inputs from the various sensory systems are still a matter of dispute but the important facts are that individual reticular neurons may receive input from two or more sensory systems and these show interactions.

The reticular system is intimately related to the processes involved in sleep and arousal, which form the subject of our inquiry in the next chapter. Here we will be primarily concerned with the possible role of the reticular system in attention. For the moment, then, it will be sufficient to indicate that electrical stimulation of the reticular system in an inattentive, drowsy animal causes the animal to become alert and orient to the environment. Accompanying the behavioral effect is a change in the electroencephalogram (EEG); the previously high voltage and slow wave EEG, indicative of a drowsy state, is replaced by a low voltage, fast frequency recording (see Figure 6.3). This type of behavioral arousal appears comparable to both spontaneous behavioral alerting and that produced when a novel environmental stimulus is presented. Of major interest then, is whether such behavioral effects have any relationship to the variability of the electrical responses that can be recorded in the CNS to environmental stimulation. In other words, is the reticular system a mediator of the psychological process we call attention?

Central Control of Afferent Messages

For a considerable time, anatomical evidence has been available to show that within, or associated with, the various sensory pathways there also exist *efferent* (descending) pathways. Beginning in the early 1950s, systematic investigation of a variety of sense modalities revealed that afferent messages may be inhibited—i.e., modulated or suppressed—through the action of these efferent pathways.

Inhibitory Influence

When reticular activation occurs, inhibitation of sensory input results. It is possible to find augmentation of input with reticular stimulation, but

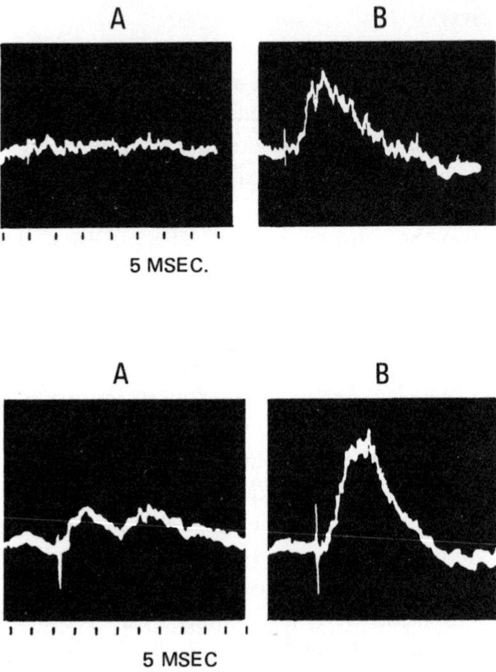

Figure 5.2. Release of tonic, descending inhibitory influences by anesthesia and by cord transection in curarized cats without central anesthesia. *Top row*: Left ventral column response to feeble dorsal root stimulation (a) before and (b) after injection of 45 mg chloralose per kg. *Bottom row*: Effect of high cord section on ventral column response (a) before and (b) one hour after transection. In each experiment the stimulus intensity and location were kept constant. (From Hagbarth, K. E. and Kerr, D. I. B., Central influences on spinal afferent conduction. *Journal of Neurophysiology*, 1954, *17*, 295–307.)

suppression is more usual. Evidence for such inhibitory effects is available from touch receptors, stretch receptors, the olfactory bulb, and throughout the auditory and visual systems (see Livingston, 1959; Granit, 1955; Hernández-Péon, 1961, 1966). We will illustrate the steps in arriving at this conclusion.

Figure 5.2 demonstrates the presence of *tonic* (sustained), descending inhibitory influences operating at the level of the spinal cord. When such influences are removed, either through the application of general anesthesia or through transection of the spinal cord above the locus of recording, there is a drastic increase in the amplitude of the potentials evoked by weak dorsal root stimuli. In other words, normally there is some strong inhibitory process serving to suppress input, and this process originates from mechanisms located more centrally than the spinal cord; in particular, the reticular system has been implicated.

In addition to this tonic control, the reticular system is capable of *phasic* (transitory) control. Figure 5.3 is representative of experiments showing this phasic influence of the reticular system in the modulation of sensory input. In this experiment, auditory potentials were recorded from the cochlear nucleus of the brainstem before and after stimulation of the midbrain reticular system (MRF). The reticular stimulation resulted in a reduction of amplitude of the cochlear nucleus potentials. Again, this result is typical of those obtainable at all levels of the nervous system, from receptor to cortex.

Polysensory Response in MRF

Another indicator of the role of the reticular system in stimulus reception is that excitation of the various sensory modalities results in evoked responses throughout that system. There does not seem to be any marked segregation of input within the system either; responses to two or more modalities are commonly recorded from the same electrode sites. The latter has been

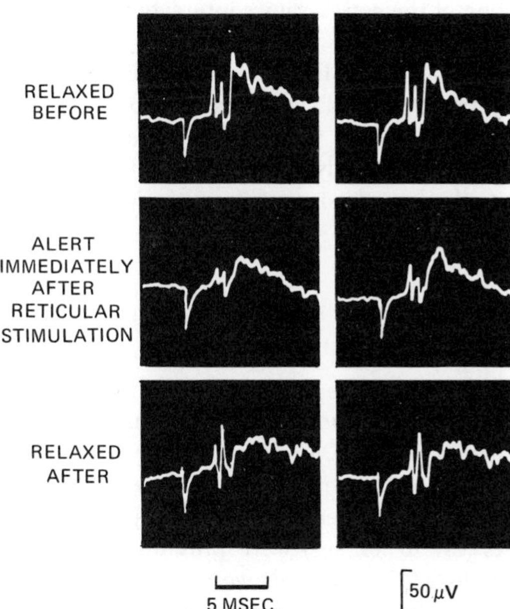

Figure 5.3. Effects of electrical stimulation of mesencephalic reticular formation upon the auditory potentials recorded from the dorsal cochlear nucleus in a cat with electrodes permanently implanted. The evoked potentials were reduced significantly during the alertness induced by brief reticular stimulation (2 sec). [From Hernández-Péon, R., Reticular mechanisms of sensory control. In W. A. Rosenblith (Ed.,) *Sensory Communication*. Cambridge, Mass.: M.I.T. Press, 1961. Reprinted by permission of The M.I.T. Press.]

demonstrated in recordings from both gross electrodes and from microelectrodes. Thus, many reticular units appear to be polysensory, or responsive to more than one sense modality.

Figure 5.4, an example of the interaction between afferent messages in the reticular formation, tends to prove that the same units are mediating responses to both modalities. With the appropriate timing of the interval between the stimuli, the second response is attenuated. It should also be noted that similar results have been obtained from the cortex. In the absence of anesthesia, cortical areas that were previously "silent" under anesthesia show widespread evoked responses. These areas are outside the primary receiving areas; they are the so-called association areas. They receive input from the various sense modalities and show interaction of the inputs. Responses in these areas are not dependent on the functional integrity of the primary areas; lesions of the primary receiving areas do not eliminate the association area responses to the respective stimuli (Buser, Borenstein, & Bruner, 1959).

And finally, the cortex also exerts descending effects on the reticular system. Stimulation of the cortex shows interaction with ascending afferent impulses in reticular neurons.

The picture that emerges from the above discussion is that stimulus reception involves a potential dynamic balance between afferent receptor activity and efferent influences from the cortex and the reticular system, which are themselves reciprocally related. These, then, are the basic considerations leading to the hypothesis that the reticular system is a mediator of perceptual processes.

Experimental Basis

Against this neurophysiological background, Hernández-Péon, Scherrer, and Jouvet (1956) performed the first experiment that directly attempted to show that differences in attention result in differential effects on the evoked responses recordable from the CNS. They employed electrodes chronically implanted in the cochlear nucleus of cats. On recovery from surgery, the animals were tested for the presence of evoked responses to auditory stimuli. Short tone bursts (.01 to .02 sec) were presented through a loudspeaker under two conditions: (1) The animals were simply sitting in the recording box; (2) one of three types of additional environmental stimulation was supplied in order to attract the cats' attention. One stimulation was visual—mice in a closed bottle were placed alongside the cats; another was olfactory—fish odor was passed through a tube into the enclosure; and the third was somatic—a noxious electric shock was administered to the forepaw. Figure 5.5 is representative of the results obtained. When the cat sat quietly in a relaxed manner, the responses evoked by the tone were relatively large. When the cat was attentive to the mice in the jar, the evoked responses were

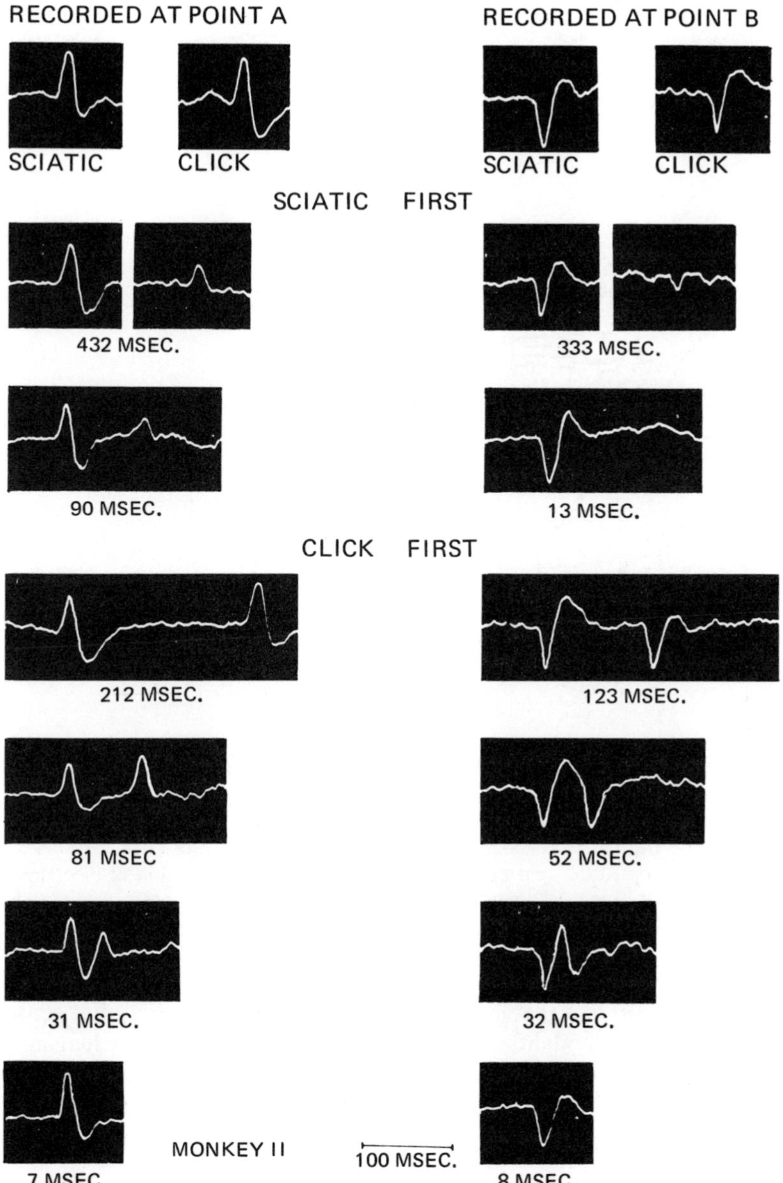

Figure 5.4. *Top row*: Records of potentials evoked at two points in the reticular formation of the monkey's brain by single sciatic and auditory stimuli. Point *B* was 2 mm below point *A*. *Lower records*: Interaction of the two modalities at different intervals of pairing evidenced by attenuation of second response. (From French, J. D., Verzeano, J., and Magoun, H. W., An extralemniscal sensory system in the brain. *Archives of Neurology and Psychiatry*, 1953, *69*, 505–581. Copyright 1953, American Medical Association.)

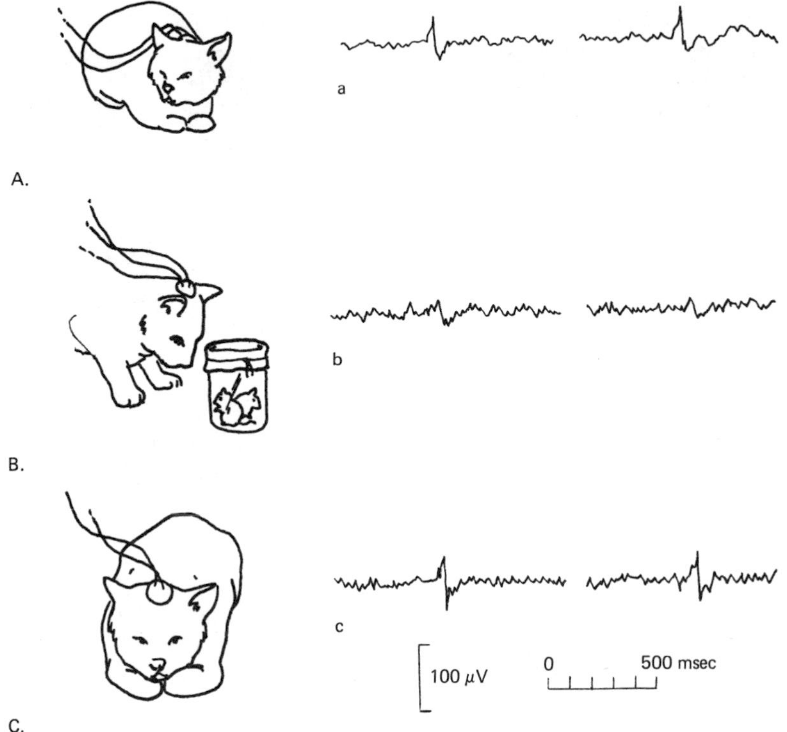

Figure 5.5. Direct recording of click responses in the cochlear nucleus during three periods; cat figures were traced from photographs taken simultaneously with the electrical recordings. *Top and bottom*: Cat is relaxed; the click responses are large. *Middle*: While the cat is visually attentive to mice in a jar, the click responses are diminished in amplitude. (From Hernández-Peón, R., Modification of electrical activity in cochlear nucleus during attention in unanesthetized cats. *Science,* Feb. 1956, *123,* 331–332.)

reduced in amplitude. These results were interpreted as suggesting that selective attention to a particular sense modality operates to inhibit sensory input in all other modalities and that this inhibition is a mechanism for achieving focused attention. Thus, incoming messages are screened and some are prevented from reaching higher levels of the nervous system; i.e., the mechanisms serving perception and consciousness. The results have been repeated in a variety of investigations in several different sense modalities (Hernández-Peón, 1961).

The above experiment manipulated the animal's attention; "perception" also implies something about the meaning of stimuli and that it is possible to change the meaning of a stimulus for an animal. Figure 5.6 (Galambos & Sheatz, 1962) illustrates two procedures that have been employed for that purpose—habituation and conditioning. With the introduction of a novel stimulus, the animal usually orients to the stimulus and shows the previously mentioned EEG changes indicative of arousal. If the stimulus is repeated, however, these changes drop out again—habituation has occurred and presumably the stimulus now lacks significance for the animal. The top three lines of Figure 5.6 show evoked potentials from the cortex of a monkey in response to clicks. In the first line is the initial response to clicks. (The figure presents the average response to a series of clicks.) Presentation of the clicks was continued for some time thereafter, following which the second and third lines were recorded. The evoked responses were considerably smaller after habituation than they had been on the initial presentation of the clicks. In an attempt to manipulate the significance of such environmental stimuli for the animal, several investigators have employed conditioning procedures. In the present instance, after the animal was habituated to the clicks, each click was followed by a puff of air to the face of the monkey; such a procedure restored the animal's interest in the stimuli. After this procedure, the evoked reponses were much larger than the responses either before or

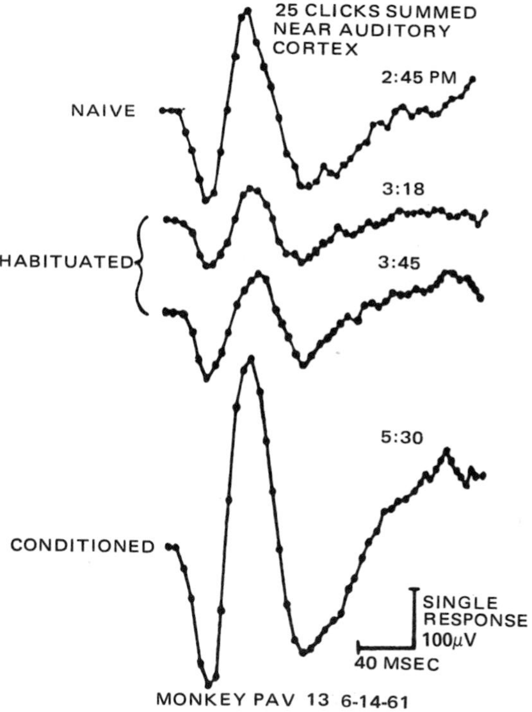

Figure 5.6. Click-evoked responses averaged by computer. Bipolar recording from cortex of inferior bank of superior temporal gyrus in monkey. (From Galambos, R. and Sheatz, G. G., An electroencephalograph study of classical conditioning. *American Journal of Physiology*, 1962, *203*, 173–184.)

after habituation. (The mechanisms of conditioning will be discussed in Chapter 12; for the moment we are interested only in the fact that the stimuli should have a changed meaning for the animal.)

Results such as these have been interpreted in the following way: After habituation, when stimuli no longer have any particular behavioral significance for the animal, they are subject to a filtering or modulating process that reduces the magnitude of their impact on the CNS; this reduced impact is demonstrated in the smaller evoked potential recorded, If behavioral significance is added or restored to the stimuli through conditioning, the evoked responses reflect this increased impact of the stimuli by demonstrating greatly increased size. This augmented size is reduced again by subsequent extinction. Again, these results have also been found to apply to other sensory modalities (see Hernández-Péon, 1961).

Reticular Hypothesis

As a result of experiments such as these, Hernández-Péon (1961) has suggested the hypothesis that the reticular system acts as an integrating mechanism regulating the activities of (1) a sensory amplifying system located in the specific sensory receiving areas of the cortex and (2) a filtering system operating at the brainstem and spinal cord levels. In this conception, the reticular system receives information from and transmits information to both of the latter systems and regulates their operation. Thus, through the action of the reticular system, "a filtering system is closely linked to those mechanisms that select the information to be amplified at higher levels of the brain" (Hernández-Péon, 1961, p. 517).

The above, then, outlines a basic theory of reticular activity in perception and the major types of evidence presented for the theory. This theory, however, has not received unequivocal support.

Criticisms of Reticular Theory

On the basis of these and other experiments, it appears inconceivable that the reticular system should have no role in attention and perceptual processes. On the other hand, the theory sketched above simply does not appear adequate from a conceptual standpoint, nor are the experiments cited in support of the theory adequate. We will briefly examine both deficiencies.

Conceptual Criticisms

Basically, the reticular theory outlined above rests on three assumptions:

1. The amplitude of an evoked response is indicative of how much information is transferred—the larger the amplitude, the more information.

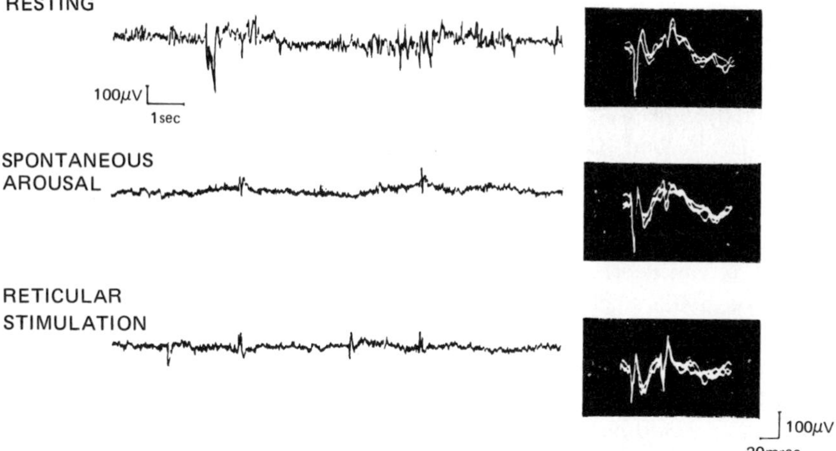

Figure 5.7. Paradoxical effects of reticular stimulation on somatosensory recovery function. Unanesthetized acute cat; pairs of electrical stimuli to the radial nerve with recording from somatosensory I. Note that during resting and spontaneous arousal, the response to the second stimulus is attenuated. Following reticular stimulation, the first response is attenuated and the second response is greatly augmented. (From Schwartz, M. and Shagass, C., Reticular modification of somatosensory cortical recovery function. *Electroencephalography and Clinical Neurophysiology*, 1963, *15*, 265–271.)

2. Reduction or augmentation of evoked response amplitude indicates the operation of inhibitory or excitatory influences, respectively.
3. The filtering of information at peripheral nervous system levels can account for the selectivity of attentional and perceptual processes.

None of the above assumptions seems to have any sound empirical support. For instance, it has been shown that when the gross evoked response is reduced in amplitude, the discharge rates of the contributing single cells may be unchanged, reduced, or even increased (Hagbarth & Fex, 1959). Thus, the simple amplitude change may reflect a very complex pattern of affairs at the single cell level and it is doubtful that an increase or decrease can be directly related to any concomitant change in the information transmitted across the synapses.

Figure 5.7 illustrates that the second assumption is also too simple. A common neurophysiological technique for determining the response capacities of a neural system is to test the *excitability cycle* or *recovery function*. In this technique, a standard stimulus is followed at varying time intervals by a second stimulus. By comparing the response elicited by the second stimulus to the response to the first stimulus, it is possible to see to what extent the system has recovered from the effects of the first stimulus. If there is less response to the second stimulus, it is concluded that there is some aftereffect of the first stimulus which depressed the reponse to the second stimulus. The top line of Figure 5.7 illustrates such a depression of amplitude of the second response. The stimuli were shocks to the radial nerve in the forepaw of the cat and the responses were recorded at the cortex. The second stimulus followed the first by some 40 msec, and the response to it was smaller—this would be considered an inhibitory effect. It has also been shown that reticular stimulation results in a reduction of the amplitude of peripherally elicited somatosensory cortical responses (Bremer, Stoupel, & Van Reeth, 1960; Gauthier, Parma, & Zanchetti, 1956; Schwartz & Shagass, 1962). Such a reduction might also be indicative of an inhibitory effect. The bottom line of Figure 5.7, however, shows that when the test of recovery is applied immediately after reticular stimulation, there is a seemingly paradoxical result: The response to the first stimulus of the pair is reduced, as would be expected, but the response to the second stimulus is greatly augmented. Such a result suggests the simultaneous presence of both excitatory and inhibitory effects. (Note that this occurs only with EEG arousal produced by reticular stimulation—spontaneous arousal does not have this effect.) It would certainly be possible to construct a theory to handle these findings but the point is that inferences based solely on evoked response amplitude are likely to be misleading or oversimplified.

That the third assumption is faulty has been amply demonstrated in the human literature. For example, subjects may be instructed to shadow (i.e., repeat back) information presented in one ear while they are simultaneously presented with information in both ears. Significant amounts of the information in the unattended ear can be retrieved (Triesman, 1960; Moray, 1959). This suggests that selective attention at least does not involve the complete filtering of information at the peripheral level—some information is cortically available. And perhaps more cogently, it suggests that some sort of preliminary higher level processing is carried out in order to accomplish the selectivity of attention. That is, rather than selective attention being the result of a filtering process, the information is at least partially processed, rejected, and then screened out. Generally, filtering conceptions of selective attention are not well-regarded by theorists of human information processing (Walley and Weiden, 1973).

Experimental Criticisms

The first criticism of the experiments by Hernández-Péon and others centers around their lack of control of the peripheral receptors. In brief, if the effects ascribed to control by the reticular system of afferent input can, in fact, be traced to such factors as receptor orientation, then there is no need to postulate any special effects of the reticular system. The most telling criticisms in this regard have been made by Worden and his colleagues (Worden & Marsh, 1963; Marsh, Worden, & Hicks, 1962; Worden, 1966).

During habituation and learning, and with shifts in attention, animals assume characteristic postures that alter the orientation of their sense receptors with respect to environmental stimuli. Marsh et al. (1962) studied the effects of such shifts in receptor position on cochlear nucleus potentials evoked by auditory stimuli. Sound stimuli delivered through a centrally located loudspeaker show complex acoustic fields in small test boxes such as those commonly used for electrophysiological recordings from animals. The variations in such fields may be detected with electronic recordings by simply moving a microphone around the test enclosure. Marsh et al. were able to demonstrate that such variations are closely correlated with variations in cochlear nucleus responses recorded from the cat. Even small shifts of head orientation can produce significant variation in the potentials. Such shifts are entirely compatible with those demonstrated by the cat shown in Figure 5.4 from the experiment by Hernández-Péon et al.

Worden, Abraham, Marsh, and Whittlesey (1964) developed earphones suitable for use in the unrestrained cat and showed that about 80 percent of the variability in cochlear potentials due to variations in head position could be eliminated by their use. In two experiments (Worden & Marsh, 1963; Worden et al., 1964), these investigators tried to replicate the finding of reduced amplitude of cochlear potentials as a result of habituation. In neither study could they find evidence for such an effect. With bilaterial electrode placements and with adjacent placements on the same side, amplitude changes in opposite directions were frequently recorded. For a given set of electrodes, amplitude changes were frequently different for two different habituation tests. "It seems unlikely that differential attentiveness between right and left inputs is a factor, since loss of attentiveness during habituation is assumed to reflect loss of stimulus novelty. There is little appeal in the notion that during acoustic habituation the animal becomes more attentive to the stimulus at one ear and less so at the other, especially since the direction of amplitude changes is not consistent at either ear" (Worden, 1966, p. 78).

Thus, the findings in animals of auditory evoked-response changes due to shifts in attention and habituation are compatible with a combination of (1) failure to adequately control for shifts in receptor orientation to the stimuli, (2) inadequate sampling within the cochlear nucleus, and (3) inadequate sampling over a period of time.

In addition, adjustments in peripheral accessory mechanisms, such as the pupil of the eye and the muscles of the middle ear, must also be considered. One function of such structures is apparently to protect the receptors from extremely high intensity stimuli; they do, however, show fluctuation in their operation at more moderate levels. It is also of interest that Hess and Polt (1960) report pupil diameter changes in both cats and humans as a function of the interest value of the stimulus; with interest-provoking stimuli, the pupil dilates.

In the case of the muscles of the ear, the effect of such activity on the amplitude of evoked responses is rather ambiguous. Hugelin, Dumont, and Paillas (1960) found that reticular stimulation in cats produced a reduction in cochlear nucleus responses to clicks, and that the reduction could be eliminated by cutting the middle ear muscles or paralyzing the animal with drugs. On the other hand, Moushegian, Rupert, Marsh, and Galambos (1961) found that cutting the middle ear muscles did not eliminate the habituation, distraction, and conditioning effects reported by Hernández-Péon. This discrepancy in results may be due to the fact that Hugelin et al. employed acute preparations, fixed in position in the stereotaxic instrument, while Moushegian et al. used freely moving, chronic preparations; that is, the contaminating effects of changes in receptor orientation may have again entered into the latter results as in the original experiment by Hernández-Péon et al.

Another major experimental criticism of Hernández-Péon's theory is that while the theory postulates that the reticular system *differentially* filters afferent information, the experiments failed to show that any filtering (if it does occur) is, in fact, differential. To do this, the experiments should show that relevant information in, say, the visual system is enhanced, or at least not reduced, while irrelevant information in, say, the auditory system is reduced. This aspect of the theory has been tested primarily in human subjects but the tests have not been particularly rigorous (see Näätänen, 1967, 1975). The experiments here have been numerous and complex—we will only summarize. Näätänen has emphasized that many of the experiments are suspect because the temporal patterning of presentation of the stimuli allows the subject to predict beyond chance levels the occurrence of the relevant and irrelevant stimuli. Such predictions allow the subjects to prepare for relevant stimuli and differentially relax before irrelevant stimuli. Thus, the very issue under test is vitiated by the experiments. Generally, those experiments which seem to avoid this problem have failed to show that differential attention exerts any selective effects on evoked potentials (the work of Hillyard, Hink, Schwent, and Picton [1973] may be a valid exception).

Conclusions

Anatomically and physiologically, it is clear that the reticular system is uniquely organized and situated so as to be potentially capable of a role in attention and perception. The reticular system does receive and send impulses concerned with stimulus processing and some filtering effects can be demonstrated. The question, then, seems to be not whether the reticular system is involved, but the level of involvement and the mechanisms in which it participates. For instance, Fuster and Uyeda (1962) reported that the performance of monkeys on a test involving tachistoscopic presentation of stimuli was improved by mild stimulation of the midbrain. But this does not necessarily support the Hernández-Péon theory as to the way in which the reticular system plays a role. Furthermore, even if some sort of filtering process is involved in attention, peripheral filtering does not appear to be sufficiently selective nor does it account for some of the evident behavioral capacities of differentially attentive human subjects.

A number of theorists have attempted alternative physiological constructions that might remedy the defects of simple reticular theory. Walley and Weiden (1973) have presented one that might be considered representative. Their theory depends on "feature analyzers" of the sort encounterd in our review of sensory processes, i.e., neurons that respond selectively to certain attributes of the stimulus, such as lines, orientation, movement, and so forth. It is argued that such stimulus processing extends from the sensory systems into the association cortex. Individual units of this type are combined through learning into pattern recognition circuits or *gnostic units*. Such units become hierarchically organized into interacting circuits. Lateral connections between such organizations allow for mutually inhibiting influences. The activation of one set of circuits inhibits others, accounting for the selectivity of attention at a much higher level of stimulus processing than simple reticular theory, and only after some preliminary processing of the information. Reticular activity is seen to influence these gnostic units through its effects on the inhibitory connections between them.

Walley and Weiden have presented some mathematical simulations of the properties of neurons in such units, and the tests that have been attempted seem to show reasonable approximations to the known properties of neurons. Such results suggest some general kinds of physiological research that might be attempted in order to validate the theory. However, more direct tests of the functional features of gnostic units, and the behavior to be predicted from any physiological manipulation, are not so obvious; for example, how do we experimentally manipulate gnostic units? The best that we can say is that the theory seems to be conceptually more in tune with known behavioral capacities but we do not seem capable of testing it very well. One possibility for investigation might be through EEG and evoked-response recording in an attempt to get at the functional properties of the gnostic units even if they cannot be directly manipulated. We shall return to this subject in a later section of this chapter. Now, however, we shall briefly discuss other, nonreticular CNS influences on attention and perception.

NONRETICULAR INFLUENCES

The purpose of this section is to broaden our perspective on the CNS structures and mechanisms influencing attentive and perceptual processes. Although categories such as "attention," "perception," "learning," and "motivation" have behavioral significance in the minds of psychologists, the brain is not organized physiologically into corresponding functional units.

The Effects of Lemniscal Lesions

The primacy of the reticular system in attention and perception has been challenged in a direct manner by comparing the effects of medial and laterally placed midbrain lesions in chronic cat preparations (Sprague, Chambers, & Stellar, 1961; Sprague, Levitt, Robson, Liu, Stellar, & Chambers, 1963). Lateral lesions were made in an effort to interrupt the classical, ascending sensory pathways while doing minimal damage to the more medially located reticular system. Extensive pre- and postoperative testing was carried out, permitting evaluation of long-term deficits as a result of lesions. (For a portrayal of the profound changes in behavior resulting from lateral lesion, see the description of individual animals in Sprague et al., 1963.)

In these experiments, animals with large bilateral lesions of the lateral lemniscal pathways showed the expected deficits in tactile, auditory, proprioceptive, nociceptive, and gustatory responses. In addition, however, they showed unexpected deficits in visual and olfactory activity. They were generally mute and exhibited an extreme deficit in affective behavior. Their aversive reaction to attack was minimal, and they showed no pleasure responses to petting or sexual stimulation. Aggressive and rage responses were extremely limited. Much of the waking behavior of these animals consisted of stereotyped, hyperactive, exploratory activity.

Animals with unilateral lesions provided interesting comparisons between the lesioned and unlesioned sides. It was possible to see marked sensory defects on the side contralateral to the lesion. Nonetheless, extensive testing and special training procedures seemed to indicate that the defect was not so much a simple sensory deficit as a failure to attend to relevant environmental stimulation and to use such information in making adaptive responses to the environment. "For example, the cat in pursuit of a mouse on the ipsilateral side would lose it and appear to forget it when it passed into the contralateral field. . . . Similarly, there was little or no response to threatening movements of the examiner's hand toward the contralateral eye; when the tail was pinched, the animals attacked objects held in the ipsilateral visual field like normal cats but ignored objects in the contralateral field" (Sprague et al., 1961, p. 168). Similarly, conditioned responses to tactile stimulation of the contralateral foreleg could be obtained only after extensive training which directed the animal's attention to that leg; thus, when oriented to the leg, conditioned responses would occur, while in the absence of overt orientation they would not.

Finally, the animals also demonstrated exaggerated oral activity. There was overeating, objects too large to swallow were firmly clamped in the mouth for long periods of time, small inedible objects were seized and swallowed, and the animals engaged in incessant licking and chewing of the hair and skin of the back and tail when confined in a cage.

All these changes occurred in animals that at the same time showed good behavioral and EEG arousal. Obviously, the lesions disrupted a wide variety of differing behaviors. In interpreting these results, Sprague et al. (1961) contended that the changes resulting from lateral lesions were mainly attributable to extensive sensory deprivation of the forebrain. They compared their results with the effects of sensory isolation on humans and animals, the behavior of autistic children, and the results of neocortical lesions. Their conclusion: "Without a patterned afferent input to the forebrain via the lemnisci, the remaining portions of the central nervous system, which include a virtually intact reticular formation, seem incapable of elaborating a large part of the animal's repertoire of adaptive behavior" (Sprague et al., 1961, p. 173).

Hippocampal Activity

In a resting, inattentive animal, the EEG is said to be *synchronized;* that is, it is characterized by generalized, high voltage, slow wave activity. In contrast, when a novel or meaningful stimulus is presented to such an animal, the EEG shows a change called *desynchronization*. No longer uniform, the EEG is now characterized by a much more irregular appearance, with lower voltages and faster frequencies. This EEG change, or *arousal* reaction, is accompanied by behavioral indications that the animal is attending to the stimulus. Typically, animal subjects turn the head toward the stimulus, prick up the ears, and may approach the locus of the stimulus, sniffing and investigating. This total response pattern is known as the "orienting reflex" in Pavlov's terminology or, more generally, as the *orienting response*. It is related to reticular functioning and probably is dependent also on hippocampal activity.

But EEG desynchronization is not a uniform characteristic observable from all brain locations during behavioral alerting. In point of fact, neocortical *desynchronization* is frequently accompanied by *synchronization* in the hippocampus, that is, relatively high-amplitude slow waves in the theta band (4 to 6 Hz). Conversely, synchronization of the cortex is accompanied by desynchronization in the hippocampus (Green & Arduini, 1954). Thus, hippocampal activity seems to show the inverse of the usual relationship between the EEG and behavioral activiation (see Figure 5.8). Grastyan, Lissak, Madarasz, and Donhoffer (1959) presented evidence that suggested, however, that hippocampal slow activity was associated with the animal's orienting responses to the source of the conditioned stimulus in a learning situation. This orientation to the conditioned stimulus appeared only after

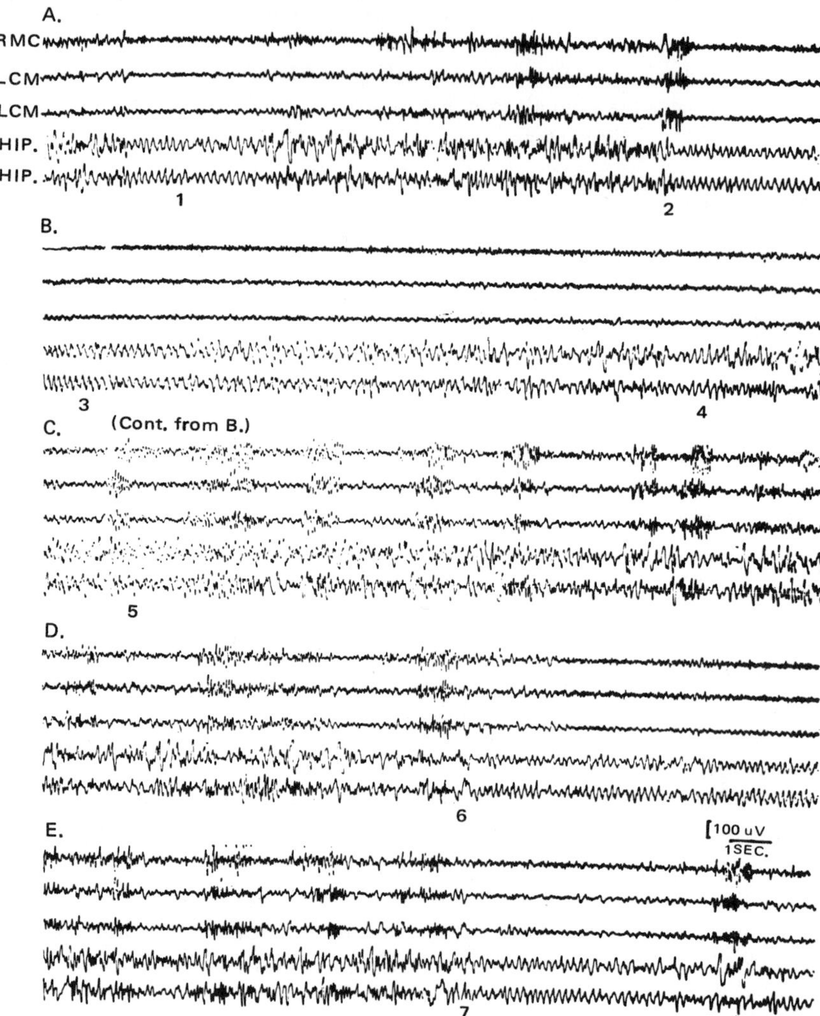

Figure 5.8. Cortical and hippocampal EEG activity during sleep and arousal in an anesthetized rabbit. RMC and LMC, right and left motor cortices; R. Hip. and L. Hip., right and left hippocampi. In (a), the animal is drowsy. A transition is seen between 1 and 2. At 2, the animal nodded and apparently woke up. In (b) and (c), the animal changed in behavior from alertness to drowsiness or light sleep. Note the gradual desynchronization of the hippocampus between 3 and 4 and the abrupt appearance of regular spindles in the cortical record at 5. In (d), while the animal was drowsing, a cat was brought into the room. Up to 6, the cat was on an EEG console out of sight of the rabbit. At 6, the cat placed its forepaws on the ledge of the cable input window and stared at the rabbit. The following arousal lasted for about 30 sec, although the cat immediately returned to the console. Record (e) shows a response in the same animal, three weeks later, to a similar exposure to a cat. Note the brevity in this case. The cat was in view at 7 and spindles returned at 8. (From Green, J. D. and Arduini, A., Hippocampal electrical activity in arousal. *Journal of Neurophysiology*, 1954, *17*, 533–557.)

some training; it diminished and disappeared as the conditioned response became established. Associated with the reduced orienting behavior was a loss in the hippocampal theta.

Hippocampal activity has been implicated in a variety of psychological functions ranging from orienting responses to learning and memory. Here the data seem to indicate a relation between focused attention and hippocampal mechanisms.

Frontal Lobe Mechanisms

Experiments have established that frontal lobe lesions affect delayed response performance. *Delayed response* tasks require the subject to use the memory of some prior aspect of the problem situation. Thus, for instance, delayed alternation in a maze requires that the subject remember which way it turned at the previous choice point; delayed reaction tasks require the subject to remember where the reward is after some delay. Tasks of this type have been regarded principally as tests of short-term memory, and a vast literature has evolved from the disturbances in this performance produced by frontal cortex lesions (see Warren & Akert, 1964).

One consideration in analyzing the deficits in delayed response performance obtained with frontal lesions has been attentional changes. The deficit in delayed reaction in monkeys can be at least partially overcome if the animal is allowed to obtain food from the correct receptacle before imposing the delay, or if the lights are turned off during the delay interval, or if training is conducted under light sedation. Each of these maneuvers appears to be a means of reducing the distractions impinging on the subject and helping to ensure attention to relevant aspects of the test situation. From research such as this comes the suggestion that frontal lobe mechanisms may be important in attention.

Autonomic Feedback to the CNS

Reflexive, homeostatic mechanisms for regulating blood pressure and heart rate exist in the aortic arch and carotid sinus[1]; these mechanisms have been shown to have afferent input to the lower brainstem and seem capable of exerting inhibitory control over CNS activity through the reticular system. Thus, stimulation of the carotid sinus has been shown to result in a marked reduction in frequency of the EEG; cardiovascular control over the duration of EEG arousal has been shown. Rage responses in cats with the cortex

[1]The aorta is the single large artery coming from the top of the heart; it runs in a relatively horizontal orientation, the *aortic arch*, giving off arteries to the head, and then turns downward, distributing blood to the trunk and lower parts of the body. A major artery to the head, supplying the brain, is the internal carotid; the *carotid sinus*, an enlargement in this artery, contains these receptors.

removed have been suppressed by stimulation of carotid and aortic afferents; reaction time studies in humans have shown differential effects associated with presentation of the stimuli in different phases of the cardiac cycle—faster reaction times occur during contraction of the heart with its increased pressure.

These and other results led Lacey (e.g., 1967) to suggest the hypothesis that situations characterized by pleasant stimuli, attention to the environment, and "environmental intake" are associated with depressor-decelerative responses in the cardiovascular system (lower pressure, slower heart rate), while situations characterized by noxious stimulation, rejection of the environment, and concentration on internal stimulation are accompanied by pressor-accelerative responses (higher pressure, faster rate). Only heart rate and blood pressure measures seem to differentiate between these two types of stimulus conditions; other conventional measures of autonomic arousal, such as respiration and skin conductance, do not.

In other words, Lacey's hypothesis suggests that cardiovascular influences feed back to the CNS and exert at least partial control over attentive processes.

Obrist (e.g., Obrist et al., 1974) has offered an alternative to the cardiovascular feedback model described by Lacey. He suggests that the cardiac changes are simply part of a larger, overall pattern of somatic response change. Thus, in stituations in which cardiac deceleration occurs, reduction in other somatic activity, such as eye movement or muscle activity in the limbs, should also occur. Conversely, other situations will elicit increases in somatic and cardiovascular activity. This position, unlike Lacey's, ascribes no special role to cardiovascular mechanisms in mediating attention. Finally, it should also be noted that cardiac and somatic effects on the CNS may both be the resultant of some prior CNS mechanism that takes precedence over both.

Differentiating these various models has not proven particularly successful to date—there is both positive and negative evidence for each. Edwards and Alsip (1969) tested for stimulus detection during spontaneous periods of high and low heart rate without finding any significant effects. They noted that Lacey's theory does not specify the origin of the heart rate and blood pressure changes. It may be that some unknown process affects both cardiovascular changes and stimulus reception. It may also be that only cardiovascular changes of a specific origin are effective in altering stimulus reception. In any case, their experiment suggests that heart rate changes per se are not a sufficient means of changing perceptual sensitivity. On the other hand, Spence, Lugo, and Youdin (1972) found support for Lacey's hypothesis in an analogous situation. Subjects were asked to listen to a 17-minute tape of a patient and to pay attention to the presence of references to a particular theme in that tape. Instances of that theme were better detected when associated with lower heart rates. However, in his review of the litarature, Hahn (1973) is skeptical of the theory, and more recent evidence contains some contradictions (Lang, Gatchel, & Simons, 1975; Velden & Juris, 1975).

On the other hand, Obrist (1976; Obrist et al., 1974) has pursued the relation between cardiac function and somatic activity. Generally, situations that lead to increases or decreases in somatic activity are also associated with metabolically appropriate changes in cardiac output. This leads Obrist to suggest that phasic cardiac activity per se (short-term activity) has relatively little effect on perceptual processes. Rather, he emphasizes that longer term responses of the subject, the coping mechanisms employed to deal with stress, become significant. For Obrist, then, the problem of interest becomes the association between coping mechanisms and the occurrence of heart disease. We shall return to this question in Chapter 7 when we discuss emotional response mechanisms.

CNS ELECTRICAL ACTIVITY AS AN INDICATOR OF COGNITIVE PROCESSES

We have previously discussed the use of evoked responses to evaluate the hypothesis that differential attention to stimuli is reflected in the amplitude of the evoked responses. Here we will be essentially asking whether CNS electrical recordings reflect any other perceptual or cognitive processes.

Most of the studies that we have previously dealt with were carried out in animal subjects. The primary advantage of such experiments is the possibility of testing neurophysiological formulations that depend on radical surgical techniques for verfication. But in animal experiments it may be difficult to find out if the subjects are indeed attending to the stimulus of interest—of interest, that is, to the psychologist. The development of computer techniques for the recording of CNS responses from the brains of intact human subjects has provided psychologists with a tool that has high face validity for the study of perceptual processes. Such techniques have two advantages: (1) brain responses may be recorded while taking advantage of the human subject's ability to follow specific instructions; and (2) they do not entail the prolonged training procedures required in animal experiments. Such recordings would seem to provide an opportunity to obtain some insight into how the CNS (even if only that part adjacent to scalp electrodes) processes sensory input.

Perceptual Threshold

Awareness

A variety of evoked response experiments have been concerned with the relationship between the ability to report the presence or nature of the stimulus and the occurrence of recordable evoked responses. Some of these results are not particularly clear, and further work will be necessary.

The fact that evoked responses are recordable from the brains of anesthetized subjects makes it obvious that the presence of evoked electrical activity doesn't necessarily mean that the subject is aware of the stimulus. However, it is also obvious that in both anesthetized and unanesthetized subjects, some minimum stimulus intensity is necessary for the evoked electrical activity to appear. Shagass and Schwartz (1961) systematically varied the intensity of stimulation of the ulnar nerve in the wrist in humans while recording somatosensory potentials from scalp electrodes. They found that the first appearance of recordable potentials was correlated with the ability to report the presence of the stimulus; stimuli too weak to be reported did not elicit any brain responses. Similar results have been reported in the auditory system (Geisler, Frishkopf, & Rosenblith, 1958).

These results were followed up by a study in cats designed to check whether weak stimuli might evoke responses that went undetected in the human experiments because the recording electrodes were placed on the scalp rather than directly on brain tissue (Schwartz & Shagass, 1961). In the cats, recordings were made from peripheral cutaneous nerves, the thalamic relay for somatosensory transmission, and somatosensory area I of the brain. In all instances, if the stimulus was of sufficient intensity to evoke a response from the peripheral nerve, transmission was complete throughout the system, and responses were also recorded at both the thalamic and cortical levels. Furthermore, Bourassa and Swett (1967) showed that stimuli minimal for eliciting responses in cutaneous nerves and the cortex were capable of mediating a discrimination controlling the occurrence of bar-pressing responses in cats.

Results such as these would seem to argue against any notions about "subliminal" perception—perception of stimuli too weak to enter consciousness. Schwartz and Shagass (1961) suggested that experiments reporting subliminal perception probably are really dealing with differential attention to strong and weak stimuli.

However, awareness of the stimuli need not invariably accompany the presence of evoked responses in conscious subjects. Indeed, strong stimulation of muscle afferents in cats did not mediate a discrimination even though nerve responses could be recorded (Swett & Bourassa, 1967). Moreover,

Libet, Alberts, Wright, and Feinstein (1967) claimed to find evoked responses to stimulation of the skin in the somatosensory cortex of unanesthetized patients during brain surgery, even though stimulation was not reported by the patients. When the median nerve was stimulated at the wrist, however, there was a correlation between the report of the stimulus and the appearance of evoked responses. Finally, thalamic stimulation evokes large responses in the cortex and is not accompanied by awareness (Bourassa & Swett, 1968; Libet et al., 1967).

About all that can be said at present is that under some circumstances, the report of the stimulus is correlated with the appearance of evoked responses in the brain, while under other circumstances evoked responses of considerable amplitude may be recorded, but the subjects are not capable of discriminating the stimuli. What differentiates these two situations is not clear. There is the suggestion (Donchin & Sutton, 1970) that some of the ambiguity here is due to faulty methodology. In order to compare behavioral and electrical measures, the responses should be obtained under similar conditions; Donchin and Sutton suggest that the behavioral thresholds were biased toward lesser sensitivity in some of the experiments reporting a lack of relationship between electrical and perceptual measures. In any event, it is clear that the presence of an evoked response is no guarantee that stimuli are perceived; determining that stimuli are perceived depends on behavioral tests, not neurophysiological recordings.

In the above experiments, the stimuli were varied on the intensity dimension; in other experiments, the reportability of the stimulus has been varied by employing the backward masking paradigm (Donchin, Wicke, & Lindsley, 1963; Schiller & Chorover, 1966; Vaughan & Silverstein, 1968). In the backward masking situation, if a target stimulus (typically visual) is followed within some 50 milliseconds by another stimulus in the same modality (a bright flash of light), subjects generally are unable to discriminate the target stimulus; this occurs even though the target comes first; hence the name "backward" masking. The first stimulus also varies in apparent brightness at interstimulus intervals shorter or longer than those leading to complete masking.

Several experiments have been performed to see what happens to brain responses evoked by these stimuli. Donchin et al. (1963) and Vaughan and Silverstein (1968) reported that perceptual masking and brightness changes correlate with evoked-response changes. Such results suggest that responses to the target stimulus are "displaced" or overridden by the responses to the masking stimulus. In contrast, Schiller and Chorover (1966) suggested that evoked-response amplitude and latency correlate with the actual physical intensity of the stimuli but not with their apparent brightness—i.e., the correlation is with the physical parameters of the stimulus, not with the psychological response. No two of these experiments employed the same stimulus conditions, however, and this may account for some of the discrepancies. But Schwartz, Whittier, and Schweitzer (1977) were able to demonstrate that small but substantial evoked responses to the target stimuli could be recorded during backward masking despite the inability of the subjects to discriminate them. Furthermore, masked targets can be made discriminable again if a second mask is added—the second mask blocks the effect of the first one. Though the targets are again discriminated, the evoked response appears exactly the same as when the targets were not discriminated. Thus the presence of an evoked response need not guarantee perception of the stimulus and where the test stimuli can be discriminated, the amplitude of the responses is not necessarily related to the accuracy of the discrimination.

Content Discrimination

Earlier we referred to neurophysiological theories of perception which postulate that the CNS employs hierarchically organized feature analyzers in perception—so-called gnostic units; we speculated that recording experiments might provide descriptions of the functional characteristics of such units. A number of experiments have been carried out that can be viewed as related to this general question. More specifically, the basic question asked in these experiments is whether the evoked response encodes the cognitive content of the eliciting stimulus? For example, does the word DOG elicit a different brain response from the word CAT and, if so, is it because the percepts are different?

For instance, John, Herrington, and Sutton (1967) presented their subjects with four sets of stimuli. The results from 12 of the 20 subjects suggested: (1) The response to a blank flash of light is altered by the presence of a geometric form in the visual field. (2) Different shapes of equal area evoke different responses. (3) Similar shapes of different area evoke similar responses. (4) Different words, equated for the area covered by the printed letters, elicit different responses. These results strongly suggest that different percepts are associated with the elicitation of different evoked responses.

Before we accept such a conclusion, however, it is necessary to show that the evoked-response differences are due to the percepts elicited and not simply to the physical differences between the stimuli. Thus, in the experiment by John et al., different stimuli, though equated for area, actually stimulated different retinal receptors. Do the evoked-response differences reflect the coding of stimulus input or the processing of that input which results in behavioral discrimination?

Schwartz has carried out several experiments devoted to this issue (Sandler & Schwartz, 1971; Schwartz & Rem, 1975; Rem & Schwartz, 1976);

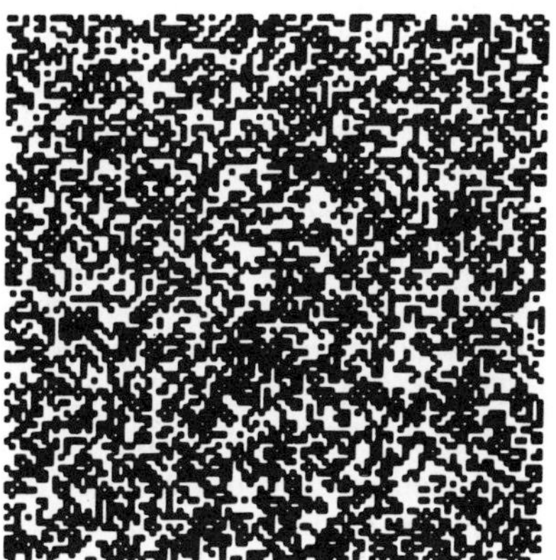

Figure 5.9. Random dot stereogram. When viewed stereoscopically a vivid three-dimensional figure can be seen. (From Julesz, 1971)

the experiment by Rem and Schwartz (1976) is particularly pertinent. In normal visual perception, stimuli are presented which evoke specific patterns of excitation on the retina; perception of stimulus content, then, is completely confounded with the particular pattern of retinal excitation. However, Julesz (1964, 1971) has developed a mode of stimulus presentation which avoids this confounding. Julesz's stimuli (Figure 5.9) are composed of two panels. Each panel consists of a matrix of randomly arranged dots; the two panels actually differ in that some of the dot elements of one are systematically displaced horizontally. When viewed stereoscopically, so that each panel is presented to one eye only, the two images can be fused, resulting in a vivid, three-dimensional figure. With such stimuli, perception of their figural content is a central process—content is not correlated with the retinal image. These stimuli, then, provide a unique method for testing the hypothesis of whether content perception is encoded in the evoked response.

The Rem and Schwartz experiment employed three of these stimuli in an anaglyph version; that is, the two panels were printed in different colors, one red and one green, and superimposed on each other; by viewing the stimuli through glasses containing one red and one green filter, the two panels were presented separately, one to each eye.

Basically, the experiment involved discriminating pairs of the three stimuli. One set of conditions varied the duration of stimulus exposure so as to alter the discriminability of stimulus content. A second set of manipulations used neutral density filters to prevent stimulus content from being perceived and colored filters to permit it. In summary form, the experiment indicated that color and the layout of the dot patterns altered the evoked-response waveform recorded, independent of the ability to perceive stimulus content. In addition, viewing three-dimensional stimuli, as opposed to contentless stimuli, also altered the evoked-response waveforms, again independent of the specific content of the stimuli. Finally, and most important, perception of stimulus content was not associated with any further evoked-response changes.

These results suggest that evoked responses primarily reflect the encoding of the physical features of the stimuli—variables of concern in the previous chapter. Such features are registered with the onset of a stimulus. However, perceiving, "understanding," or discriminating stimuli requires additional CNS processing time and it appears that such activities are not reflected in evoked responses that are recorded with current methods (see Schwartz [1976] for a more extensive critique of the relevant literature).

But even if the information content intrinsic to a stimulus is not encoded in the evoked response, a number of experiments suggest that more general informational functions are.

Information Delivery and Expectancy

The immediately preceding discussion indicated that information intrinsic to a stimulus is not encoded in the evoked response. Stimuli may, however, be employed in a more general, cuing manner; that is, in some situations the stimulus delivers information by its presence or absence. In those situations, expectancies can be met or not. Whether ambiguities are resolved, and what information is delivered depends on prior instructions or experience with the stimuli rather than any decoding of the stimuli themselves.

For instance, Sutton, Braren, Zubin, and John (1965) and Sutton, Tueting, Zubin, and John (1967) compared stimulus conditions that were predictable by the subjects with those that were unpredictable. Figure 5.10 illustrated the results of one of the simpler situations employed (Sutton et al., 1967). All the responses illustrated were evoked by single-click stimuli. On some trials (not shown) double clicks were presented; on such trials, the second click might occur either 180 or 580 msec after the first click. The top line of the figure illustrates the response obtained when the subject was informed that only one click would occur. The next three lines show that a large positive component appears in the response and that it shifts its latency to correspond in time with the resolution of the subject's uncertainty. In other words, if the subject could be sure that a second click would not occur after only 180 msec, the positive wave occurred at that point; if he could not be sure there would not be a second click until 580 msec had passed, the positive peak occurred at the later point.

These experimenters emphasize that their results cannot be attributed to nonspecific effects, but rather that they are selective effects and depend on how the stimuli are defined by the experimental situation. It should be noted, however, that these recordings were obtained from the vertex area of

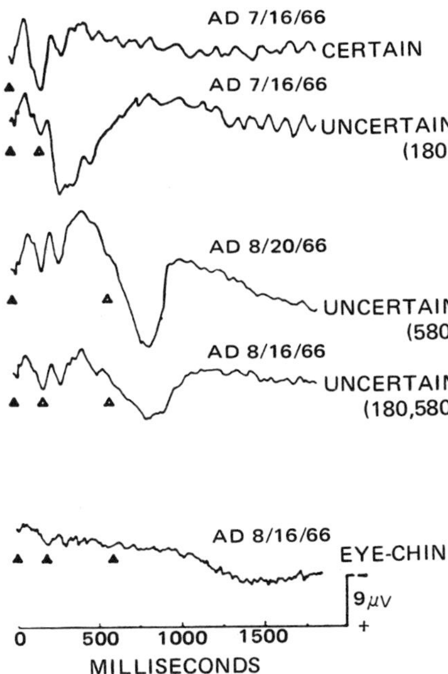

Figure 5.10. Average response waveforms to single clicks obtained for one subject under several experimental conditions. In the *certain* condition, the subject knew only single clicks would be delivered. In the *uncertain* conditions, some presentations contained double clicks; these might occur 180 or 580 msec after the first click or at either time after the first click. Solid triangles (▲) time when single click was delivered; open triangles (Δ) time when a second click might have been delivered but was not. (From Sutton, S., Tueting, P., Zubin, J., and John, E. R., Information delivery and the sensory evoked potential. *Science*, March 1967, *155*, 1436–1439. Copyright 1967 by the American Association for the Advancement of Science.)

the head; that is, they are not from primary receiving areas for sensory stimuli but from an area that is responsive to a variety of sensory inputs. Ritter and Vaughan (1969) demonstrated a similar positive potential in detection experiments; their potential was most prominent in difficult detection situations and appeared in response to both signal and nonsignal stimuli. As the complexity of the information processing demands on the subject are increased, the larger the late positive components of the evoked response (Poon, Thompson, & Marsh, 1976).

Many studies have been devoted to this evoked-response component (see, for instance, Ruchkin, Sutton, & Tueting, 1975). Generally, the component reflects the presence of a stimulus that provides significant information or is salient for the subject. Conversely, the component also seems to be "emitted" when such a stimulus is expected but does not occur. The component is larger for less frequent events and smaller for more frequent events.

Similarly, a number of studies (e.g., Porjesz & Begleiter, 1975) have shown that the nature of the subject's expectancies about a stimulus may determine its response characteristics, irrespective, of the actual stimulus parameters. Thus, a medium-intensity stimulus, which is either guessed beforehand or expected to be a high- or low-intensity stimulus, evokes a response in accord with the expectation rather than with the actual physical intensity.

The Contingent Negative Variation. There is a second type of potential that can also be recorded from the vertex or more frontal placements. *The contingent negative variation*, or *CNV* (Walter, Cooper, Aldridge, McCallum, & Winter, 1964), is a slow, negative change, recordable with DC amplifiers and electrodes. This occurs in the period between the evoked responses to paired stimuli where the first of the pair is a warning or preparatory stimulus and the second requires some sort of response or decision by the subject (Figure 5.11). The CNV is larger in situations requiring detection and discrimination of stimuli. In a review of the complex literature on the CNV, Tecce (1972) concluded that the CNV is chiefly related to attention and arousal. Generally, the CNV seems to be responsive to manipulations that might also be expected to affect evoked potentials (cf. review by Cohen, 1969).

Motor Potentials. A third type of potential is also a slow negative change that appears to be localized in frontal or vertex recordings and is associated with the readiness to make motor responses (Deeke, Scheid, & Kornhuber, 1969).

Relations Among Potentials. At the present time, the relationships among these various potentials is just beginning to be clarified. Karlin (1970), for instance, suggested that the various evoked-response changes may be due to differential attention to critical stimuli or relaxation from such attention following them. Relaxation from the attentive condition might be associated with a *positive* change in the CNV, which would contribute an enhanced appearance to the positive components of the evoked response seen in some of the experiments we have been discussing. Similarly, the motor potential could also contribute to apparent evoked-response changes. The problem, then, is to determine if these various potentials have similar mechanisms and functional characteristics or if they can be differentiated.

Without going into the technical details, a number of investigations indicate that the late positive components of evoked potentials and CNVs

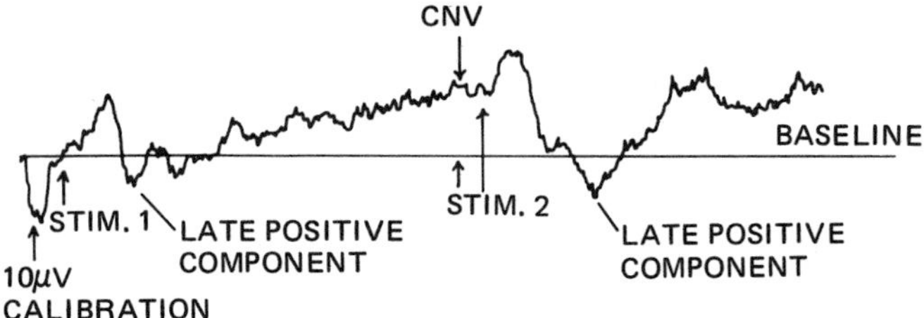

Figure 5.11. The Contingent Negative Variation (CNV). DC recording between an electrode on the vertex of the head and right mastoid. The first stimulus (Stim. 1) was a click. The second stimulus (Stim. 2) was a tone requiring a response from the subject. The CNV is the slow upward potential between the two stimuli and is measured from the base line. Also indicated are the late positive components of the evoked responses to the two stimuli. The tracing is the average response to 40 presentations of the paired stimuli, each recorded for 2 secs.

can be independently manipulated and have somewhat different cortical distributions (Donchin et al., 1975). Similarly, the CNV and the motor readiness potential can also be separated by their functional characteristics (Rohrbaugh, Syndulko & Lindsley, 1976). It thus appears that there are several electrical responses that may prove helpful in dissecting the neurophysiological mechanisms involved in perceptual processes.

Conclusions

In order for environmental stimuli to enter consciousness and perceptual processes, they must make an impact on the CNS. This impact is reflected in the evoked response that may be recorded; unless such responses can be recorded, we can assume that the stimuli will not be perceptible, consciously or otherwise. However, the fact that stimuli do gain access to the CNS is no guarantee that they will be perceived—other processes intervene, such as the selectivity of our perceptual mechanisms. It appears that this selectivity is a relatively subtle process; i.e., its manifestations have been extraordinarily difficult to demonstrate in a convincing fashion with current methods. Similarly, the processes by which the CNS handles the content of information are also subtle and, furthermore, do not seem to be available to conventional recording procedures. On the other hand, gross subject dispositions—for example, expectancies about stimuli or sets to process information in certain ways—are reflected in relatively large changes in electrical activity which can be recorded from nonspecific cortical locations that are apparently available to a variety of sensory inputs. It seems plausible to suggest that the failure to detect the more subtle changes results from two things: One is the fact that evoked responses primarily reflect information *transfer*, the arrival of information; the second is that information processing may be reflected in the activity of cellular organizations too small and discrete to be discernible against the background of the larger or more numerous cell masses normally recorded by conventional EEG techniques. Our present failures to find CNS correlates of subtle behavioral processes such as attention and perception should be taken as an opportunity to define more critically the experimental techniques used to search for them.

ARTIFICIAL SENSORY SYSTEMS

Many patients in neurology clinics present symptoms that would seem to bear on the issues under discussion here. For instance, as we shall discuss further in Chapter 13, language functioning is typically controlled by one hemisphere of the brain—usually the left hemisphere. Patients with parietal lobe damage in the right hemisphere often demonstrate abnormal concepts of body image, distortions in perception of the external environment, and an inability to reconstruct their environment through drawings. They frequently show a lack of awareness of the left side of the body, with a neglect of the left side in dressing, undressing, and washing (Marcus, 1972, p. 502). While extremely interesting, such observations require pursuit on a piecemeal basis, i.e., a case history approach, and such is not feasible here. But some clinical research on the development of artificial sensory systems, designed, for instance, to substitute for vision in the blind, does appear particularly pertinent.

It is obvious that one may be able to identify an object either through touch or through vision; and when the identification is through touching the object, there generally is no claim that the object has been "seen." But is there a sense in which it might be appropriate to argue that blind persons can "see" through the use of artificial sensory systems? In essence, if it can be shown that such persons behave in accord with the behavior of sighted individuals, this would seem adequate justification for assuming they have the *perceptual* capabilities for "vision."

There are two basic approaches that are currently being utilized to provide substitutes for vision in blind individuals: One employes alternate means of stimulating the remaining functional neural mechanisms of vision and the other attempts to employ an alternative sensory system.

Electrical Stimulation of the Visual Cortex

A number of laboratories (e.g., Dobelle, Mladejovsky, & Girvin, 1974) are experimenting with the implantation of matrices of electrodes on the visual cortex. Such electrodes could be coupled with a small television camera; the visual image picked up by the camera could control which points in the matrix are stimulated. In the tests that have been carried out, stimulation of individual electrodes results in discrete photic sensations or "phosphenes"—points of light in space. These may sometimes flicker and some have an orange hue. On repeated stimulation, the phosphenes appear to maintain a consistent location in space, and the stimulation of several electrodes simultaneously has led to the identification of simple patterns such as letters.

The apparent advantage of such an approach is that researchers can employ normally available neural mechanisms involved in vision. This might cut down on any extensive training that other approaches might require. One major disadvantage of this approach is the surgery required, with its attendant risks. More subtle, however, is the question of whether it will be possible to place enough electrodes suitably with respect to both neural locus and relationship to the environment so as actually to employ the normal neural mechanisms. Thus the current approach seems to employ the simple but perhaps very limited technique of topographically representing the visual stimulus on the cortex—drawing pictures on the cortex. Such an approach bypasses much of the organization that takes place in the more peripheral parts of the nervous system, with the possible result that "sophisticated" neural mechanisms are stimulated with too crude a visual stimulus. Obviously, judging this issue must await further refinements and tests.

Tactile Substitutes for Vision

In an alternative approach (e.g., Bach-y-Rita, 1972), a television camera is hooked to a matrix of vibrators that is placed against the skin. Here, pictures of the stimulus are drawn on the skin. The results with this approach are, at this time, very impressive in some respects. Simple objects and faces of people can be identified, relative position of objects can be discriminated, including the fact that one object may be between the observer and the second object, and motion of objects is interpretable. In the latter regard, it is particularly interesting that the position of the stimulation matrix on the skin is apparently of no consequence. That is, the vibrators may be attached to either the back or the chest; in either case, a sudden motion of the stimulus directly toward the observer's face (and the TV camera) produces a looming sensation, with a typical startle pattern of leaning backward and spreading the hands and arms—the subjects react as would a normally sighted individual.

The major disadvantage of this approach is the training that is required. The absence of operative procedures is an obvious advantage. In addition, putting the stimulus into the perceptual system "early" (at the receptor level) may prove advantageous in that it allows the system's organizing functions to operate normally. Indeed, it may be that this accounts for the relatively more sophisticated perceptual results that have been found thus far.

In any event, quite aside from the practical applications of these methods, both suggest that perceptual capabilities are not strictly "bound" to the sensory modalities employed. Perceptual functions normally considered visual can be carried out either by other modalities or when normal receptor processes are bypassed.

SUMMARY

That we are selective in our attention to some stimuli and not others and that such selectivity varies appropriately according to circumstances, is, of course, self-evident. That the CNS must be organized to accomplish this also is beyond question. The basic properties of the reticular system appear to be such that this system most likely plays a role in mediating these abilities. It is also clear, however, that the reticular system is not likely to be the only locus of such activity.

At the present time, the major impediment to progress toward development of a neurophysiology of perception and attention appears to be methodological. That is, our neurophysiological techniques, particularly those applicable to intact, active human subjects, appear to be adequate for analyzing neither the sophisticated perceptual capacities of humans nor the theoretical mechanisms postulated to account for the behavior. At the present time, such research in humans is largely limited to studies of gross evoked responses recorded from scalp electrodes. These studies have been valuable in showing some associations between electrical activity and gross behavioral capacities; however, they appear to be insensitive to more sophisticated mechanisms of selective attention and identification of different stimulus objects. Much effort has been expended in trying to develop sophisticated psychological theories based on physiological data, such as evoked responses, with relatively limited implications. The problem, then, for the future, will be to refine our physiological methods so as to make them more commensurate to the perceptual behavior we are trying to analyze.

REFERENCES

Bach-y-Rita, P. *Brain mechanisms in sensory substitution.* New York: Academic Press, 1972.

Bourassa, C. M., & Swett, J. E. Sensory discrimination thresholds with cutaneous nerve volleys in the cat. *Journal of Neurophysiology*, 1967, *30*, 515–529.

Bourassa, C. M., & Swett, J. E. Detection thresholds and evoked potentials to subcortical stimulation in the cat. *Proceedings of the American Psychological Association*, 1968, *3*, 311–312.

BREMER, F., STOUPEL, N., & VAN REETH, P. C. Nouvelles recherches sur la facilitation et l'inhibition des potentiele évoques corticaux dar.s l'éveil réticularie. *Archives Italiennes de Biologie*, 1960, *98*, 229–247.

BUSER, P., BORENSTEIN, P., & BRUNER, J. Étude des systèmes "associatifs" chez le chat anesthésie au chloralose. *Electroencephalography and Clinical Neurophysiology*, 1959, *11*, 305–324.

COHEN, J. Very slow brain potentials relative to expectancy: The CNV. In E. Donchin & D. B. Lindsley (eds.), *Average evoked potentials, methods, results, and evaluations.* Washington, D. C.: NASA, 1969, pp. 143–198.

DEEKE, L., SCHEID, P., & KORNHUBER, H. H. Distribution of readiness potential, pre-motion positivity, and motor potential of the human cerebral cortex preceding voluntary finger movement. *Experimental Brain Research (Berlin)*, 1969, *7*, 158–168.

DOBELLE, W. H., MLADEJOVSKY, M. G., & GIRVIN, J. P. Artificial vision for the blind: Electrical stimulation of visual cortex offers hope for a functional prosthesis. *Science*, 1974, *183*, 440–444.

DONCHIN, E., & SUTTON, S. The "psychological significance" of evoked responses: A comment on Clark, Butler, and Rosner. *Communications in Behavioral Biology*, 1970, *5*, 111–114.

DONCHIN, E., TUETING, P., RITTER, W., KUTAS, M., & HEFFLEY, E. On the independence of the CNV and P300 components of the human averaged evoked potential. *Electroencephalography and Clinical Neurophysiology*, 1975, *38*, 449–461.

DONCHIN, E., WICKE, J. D., & LINDSLEY, D. B. Cortical evoked potentials and perception of paired flashes. *Science*, 1963, *141*, 1285–1286.

EDWARDS, D. C., & ALSIP, J. E. Stimulus detection during periods of high and low heart rate. *Psychophysiology*, 1969, *5*, 431–434.

FRENCH, J. D., VERZEANO, J., & MAGOUN, H. W. An extralemniscal sensory system in the brain. *Archives of Neurology and Psychiatry*, 1953, *69*, 505–518.

FUSTER, J. M., & UYEDA, A. A. Facilitation of tachistoscopic performance by stimulation of midbrain tegmental points in the monkey. *Experimental Neurology*, 1962, *6*, 384–406.

GALAMBOS, R., & SHEATZ, G. G. An electroencephalograph study of classical conditioning. *American Journal of Physiology*, 1962, *203*, 173–184.

GAUTHIER, C., PARMA, M., & ZANCHETTI, A. Effect of electrocortical arousal upon development and configuration of specific evoked potentials. *Electroencephalography and Clinical Neurophysiology*, 1956, *8*, 237–243.

GEISLER, C. D., FRISHKOPF, L. S., & ROSENBLITH, W. A. Extracranial responses to acoustic clicks in man. *Science*, 1958, *128*, 1210–1211.

GRANIT, R. *Receptors and sensory perception.* New Haven, Conn.: Yale University Press, 1955.

GRASTYAN, E., LISSAK, K., MADARASZ, I., & DONHOFFER, H. Hippocampal electrical activity during the development of conditioned reflexes. *Electroencephalography and Clinical Neurophysiology,* 1959, *11*, 409–430.

GREEN, J. D., & ARDUINI, A. Hippocampal electrical activity in arousal. *Journal of Neurophysiology,* 1954, *17*, 533–537.

HAGBARTH, K. E., & FEX, J. Centrifugal influences on single unit activity in spinal sensory paths. *Journal of Neurophysiology,* 1959, *22*, 321–338.

HAGBARTH, K. E., & KERR, D. I. B. Central influences on spinal afferent conduction. *Journal of Neurophysiology,* 1954, *17*, 295–307.

HAHN, W. W. Attention and heart rate: A critical appraisal of the hypothesis of Lacey and Lacey. *Psychological Bulletin,* 1973, *79*, 59–70.

HERNÁNDEZ-PÉON, R. Reticular mechanisms of sensory control. In W. A. Rosenblith (ed.), *Sensory communication.* New York: Wiley, 1961, pp. 497–520.

HERNÁNDEZ-PÉON, R. Physiological mechanisms in attention. In R. W. Russell (ed.), *Frontiers in physiological psychology.* New York: Academic Press, 1966, pp. 121–147.

HERNÁNDEZ-PÉON, R., SCHERRER, H., & JOUVET, M. Modification of electrical activity in cochlear nucleus during "attention" in unanesthetized cats. *Science*, 1956, *123*, 331–332.

HESS, E. H., & POLT, J.M. Pupil size as related to interest value of visual stimuli. *Science*, 1960, *132*, 349–350.

HILLYARD, S. A., HINK, R. F., SCHWENT, V. L., & PICTON, T. W. Electrical signs of selective attention in the human brain. *Science*, 1973, *182*, 177–180.

HUGELIN, A., DUMONT, S., & PAILLAS, N. Formation reticulaire et transmission des information auditives au niveau de l'oreille moyenne et des voies acoustiques centrales. *Electroencephalography and Clinical Neurophysiology,* 1960, *12*, 797–818.

JOHN, E. R., HERRINGTON, R. N., & SUTTON, S. Effects of visual form on the evoked response. *Science*, 1967, *155*, 1439–1442.

JULESZ, B. Binocular depth perception without familiarity cues. *Science*, 1964, *145*, 356–362.

JULESZ, B. *Foundations of cyclopean perception.* Chicago: University of Chicago Press, 1971.

KARLIN, L. Cognition, preparation, and sensory-evoked potentials. *Psychological Bulletin*, 1970, *73*, 122–136.

LACEY, J. I. Somatic response patterning and stress: Some revisions of activation theory. In M. H. Appley and R. Trumbull (eds.), *Psychological stress: Issues in research.* New York: Appleton-Century-Crofts, 1967, pp. 14–37.

LANG, P. J., GATCHEL, R. J., & SIMONS, R. F. Electrocortical and cardiac rate correlates of psychophysical judgment. *Psychophysiology,* 1975, *12,* 649–655.

LIBET, B., ALBERTS, W. W., WRIGHT, E. W., JR., & FEINSTEIN, B. Responses of human somatosensory cortex to stimuli below threshold for conscious sensation. *Science,* 1967, *158,* 1597–1600.

LIVINGSTON, R. B. Central control of receptors and sensory transmission system. In J. Field, H. W. Magoun, & V. E. Hall (eds.), *Handbook of physiological, neurophysiology, I.* Washington, D.C.: American Physiological Society, 1959, pp. 741–760.

MARCUS, E. M. Cerebral cortex: Functional localization. In B. A. Curtis, S. Jacobson, & E. M. Marcus (eds.), *An introduction to the neurosciences.* Philadelphia: W. B. Saunders Company, 1972, pp. 483–535.

MARSH, J. T., WORDEN, F. G., & HICKS, L. Some effects of room acoustics on evoked auditory potentials. *Science,* 1962, *137,* 280–282.

MORAY, N. Attention in dichotic listening: Affective cues and the influences of instructions. *Quarterly Journal of Experimental Psychology,* 1959, *9,* 56–60.

MOUSHEGIAN, G., RUPERT, A., MARSH, J.T., & Galambos, R. Evoked cortical potentials in absence of middle ear muscles. *Science,* 1961, *133,* 582–583.

NÄÄTÄNEN, R. Selective attention and evoked potentials. *Annales Academiae Scientiarum Fennicae,* 1967, *151,* 1–226.

NÄÄTÄNEN, R. Selective attention and evoked potentials in humans—a critical review. *Biological Psychology,* 1975, *2,* 237–307.

OBRIST, P. A. The cardiovascular-behavorial interaction—as it appears today. *Psychophysiology,* 1976, *13,* 95–107.

OBRIST, P. A., HOWARD, J. A , LAWLER, J. E., GALOSY, R. A., MEYERS, K. A., & GAEBELEIN, C. J. The cardiac-somatic interaction. In P. A. Obrist, A. H. Black, J. Brener, & L. V. DiCara (eds.), *Cardiovascular psychophysiology.* Chicago: Aldine, 1974, pp. 136–162.

PILLERI, G. The anatomy, physiology, and pathology of the brainstem reticular formation. In W. Bockmayer & G. Pilleri (eds.), *The brainstem reticular formation and its significance for autonomic and affective behavior.* Basle: Hoffmann-LaRoche, 1966, pp. 9–78.

POON, W., THOMPSON, L. W., & MARSH, G. R. Average evoked potential changes as a function of processing complexity. *Psychophysiology,* 1976, *13,* 43–49.

Porjesz, B., & Begleiter, H. The effects of stimulus expectancy on evoked brain potentials. *Psychophysiology,* 1975, *12,* 152–157.

Rem, M. A., & Schwartz, M. Retinal vs. central processes in determining averaged evoked response waveforms. *Physiology and Behavior,* 1976, *16,* 705–709.

Ritter, W., & Vaughan, H. G., Jr. Averaged evoked responses in vigilance and discrimination: A reassessment. *Science,* 1969, *164,* 326–328.

Rohrbaugh, J. W., Syndulko, K., & Lindsley, D. B. Brain wave components of the contingent negative variation in humans. *Science,* 1976, *191,* 1055–1057.

Ruchkin, D. S., Sutton, S., & Tueting, P. Emitted and evoked $\overline{\text{P300}}$ potentials and variations in stimulus probability. *Psychophysiology,* 1975, *12,* 591–595.

Sandler, L., & Schwartz, M. Evoked responses and perception: Stimulus content versus stimulus structure. *Psychophysiology,* 1971, *8,* 727–739.

Schiller, P. H., & Chorover, S. L. Metacontrast: Its relation to evoked potentials. *Science,* 1966, *153,* 1398–1400.

Schwartz, M. Averaged evoked responses and the encoding of perception. *Psychophysiology,* 1976, *13,* 546–553.

Schwartz, M., & Rem, M. A. Does the averaged evoked response encode subliminal perception? *Psychophysiology,* 1975, *12,* 390–394.

Schwartz, M., & Shagass, C. Physiological limits for "subliminal" perception. *Science,* 1961, *133,* 1017–1018.

Schwartz, M., & Shagass, C. Effect of different states of alertness on somatosensory and auditory recovery cycles. *Electroencephalography and Clinical Neurophysiology,* 1962, *14,* 11–20.

Schwartz, M., & Shagass, C. Reticular modification of somatosensory recovery function. *Electroencephalography and Clinical Neurophysiology,* 1963, *15,* 265–271.

Schwartz, M., Whittier, O. M., & Schweitzer, P. R. AERs and perception: Implications of responses to retroactively masked stimuli. 1977, unpublished.

Shagass, C., & Schwartz, M. Evoked cortical potentials and sensation in man. *Journal of Neuropsychiatry,* 1961, *2,* 262–270.

Spence, D. P., Lugo, M., & Youdin, R. Cardiac changes as a function of attention to and awareness of continuous verbal text. *Science,* 1972, *176,* 1344–1346.

Sprague, J. M., Chambers, W. W., & Stellar, E. Attentive, affective, and adaptive behavior in the cat. *Science,* 1961, *133,* 165–173.

Sprague, J. M., Levitt, M., Robson, K., Liu, C. N., Stellar, E., & Chambers, W. W. A neuroanatomical and behavioral analysis of the syndromes resulting from midbrain lemniscal and reticular lesions in the cat. *Archives Italiennes de Biologie,* 1963, *101,* 225–295.

Sutton, S., Braren , M., Zubin, J., & John, E. R. Evoked-potential correlates of stimulus uncertainty. *Science,* 1965, *150,* 1187–1188.

Sutton, S., Tueting, P., Zubin, J., & John, E. R. Information delivery and the sensory evoked potential. *Science,* 1967, *155,* 1436–1439.

Swett, J. E., & Bourassa, C. M. Comparison of sensory discrimination thresholds with muscle and cutaneous nerve volleys in the cat. *Journal of Neurophysiology,* 1967, *30,* 530–545.

Tecce, J. J. Contingent negative variation (CNV) and psychological processes in man. *Psychological Bulletin,* 1972, *77,* 73–108.

Triesman, A. Contextual cues in selective listening. *Quarterly Journal of Experimental Psychology,* 1960, *12,* 242–248.

Vaughan, H. G., & Silverstein, L. Metacontrast and evoked potentials: A reappraisal. *Science,* 1968, *160,* 207–208.

Velden, M., & Juris, M. Perceptual performance as a function of intracycle cardiac activity. *Psychophysiology,* 1975, *12,* 685–692.

Walley, R. E., & Weiden, T. D. Lateral inhibition and cognitive masking: A neuropsychological theory of attention. *Psychological Review,* 1973, *80,* 284–302.

Walter, W. G., Cooper, R., Aldridge, V. J., McCallum, W. C., & Winter, A. L. Contingent negative variation: An electrical sign of sensorimotor association and expectancy in the human brain. *Nature,* 1964, *204,* 380–384.

Warren, J. M., & Akert, K. (eds.) *The frontal granular cortex and behavior.* New York: McGraw-Hill, 1964.

Worden, F. G. Attention and auditory electrophysiology. In E. Stellar & J. M. Sprague (eds.), *Progress in physiological psychology,* Vol. 1. New York: Academic Press, 1966, pp. 45–116.

Worden, F. G., & Marsh, J. T. Amplitude changes of auditory potentials evoked at cochlear nucleus during acoustic habituation. *Electroencephalography and Clinical Neurophysiology,* 1963, *15,* 866–881.

Worden, F. G., Marsh, J. T., Abraham, F. D., & Whittlesey, J. R. B. Variability of evoked auditory potentials and acoustic input control. *Electroencephalography and Clinical Neurophysiology,* 1964, *17,* 524–530.

6

Sleep and Wakefulness

Why do we sleep? In everyday language we say that we "feel tired" and therefore lie down and sleep; on arising, we "feel refreshed." We may also indicate that we "can't stay awake" or that something is "putting us to sleep." Such language would seem to imply something about the mechanisms that control sleep. Some of these phrases imply that sleep is a passive process; that is, we sleep because of a *failure* in certain mechanisms to keep us awake. Other ways of characterizing sleep seem to imply that something *actively* induces sleep. We talk about sleeping "peacefully" and about "fitful" sleep; at times we are aware of having dreams, and at other times we seem not to dream. Is sleep a unitary process or is there more than one kind of sleep? We generally feel "better" after a "good night's sleep," as though sleep has resulted in some sort of restorative process. Does this imply something about the function sleep serves? This chapter will examine the mechanisms that control the waking and sleep states and try to answer these questions.

The study of sleep and wakefulness also has relevance for a number of other topics of interest: We shall see that the mechanisms involved are related to those discussed in the previous chapter on mechanisms of perception; sleep mechanisms also seem to have relevance for our ability to learn; many psychiatric disorders involve disturbances of sleep. Finally, the study of sleep and wakefulness illustrates the full gamut of experimental procedures available to the physiological psychologist and their skillful combination in particular investigations is very well illustrated here.

CRITERIA OF SLEEP

Before investigating the mechanisms involved in sleep, it is necessary to consider the criteria by which the inference is made that an individual is asleep. In some experimental investigations this may be more than an academic question. This is particularly true in research with animal subjects after surgical intervention. In such instances, the subjects may be unable to display some of the criteria by which we ordinarily decide that the organism is asleep.

Sleep Concomitants

Under most circumstances, it is easy to judge whether an organism is awake or asleep. Sleeping individuals are generally characterized by a reduction in bodily activity, the assumption of characteristic postures, and a lack of responsiveness. In contrast to an individual in a pathological state such as coma, a sleeper may be aroused by strong environmental stimulation. But people may use these signs to feign sleep, and so they are not absolutely reliable indicators of the sleep state. Autonomic activity (for example, heart rate, blood pressure, respiration, and gastric activity) also changes at least somewhat during sleep, but these indications also may not be definitive—the same changes accompany prolonged rest.

The activity of the eye muscles and pupils are, however, reliable indicators of sleep. The eyelids are generally closed in sleep; more important, the eyes are usually in an outwardly divergent position in humans and in a downward position in the cat. Pupillary constriction (myosis) also occurs. In animal investigations, degrees of myosis, along with certain EEG conditions, are taken as signs of various stages of sleep, although in some instances even these criteria have required modification.

Generally, of course, the agreement among as many of the above concomitants of sleep as can be obtained leads to an inference that the subject is either awake or asleep (Kleitman, 1963).

EEG Activity

That the brain is continuously electrically active was first discovered by Richard Caton in 1875 in studies in animals. The first human EEG recordings were made in 1924 by Hans Berger. Berger's recordings, from widely

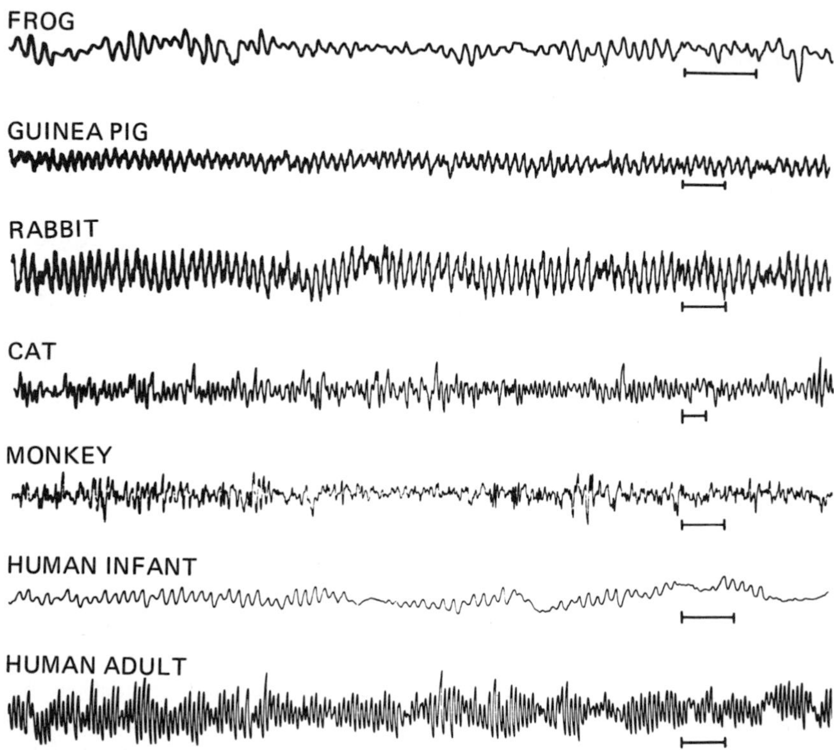

Figure 6.1. EEG tracings from various species as indicated. Calibration bar below each record equals 1 sec. The human infant and adult records were obtained with scalp electrodes; all others were derived from electrodes on the surface of cortex. [From Morrell, F., Electrical signs of sensory coding. In G. C. Quarton, T. Melnechuk, and F. O. Schmitt (Eds.), *The Neurosciences, A Study Program*. N.Y.: The Rockefeller University Press, 1967, 452–469.]

spaced electrodes on the scalp, showed that the EEG was dominated by a rhythmic activity of about 8 to 12 Hz, averaging around 10 Hz, called *alpha* activity. Another band of activity, the *beta* band, is low-voltage activity around 18 to 30 Hz. Finer localization shows that alpha activity predominates in the parietal-occipital area. Other frequency bands have been identified as well: *Delta* activity is in the range of 1 to 3 Hz, and *theta* ranges around 6 Hz. We would be getting far removed from our subject matter to pursue clinical electroencephalography in any depth here, but the occurrence of delta and theta activity in the awake, adult human subject may be indicative of pathology. On the other hand, as we shall see, low-frequency activity is a prominent feature of the normal EEG in the sleeping individual. Figure 6.1 shows some typical EEG patterns in various species. (Examples

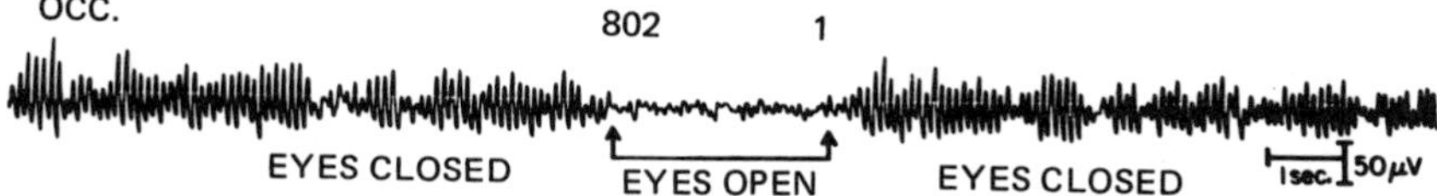

Figure 6.2. Activation pattern. Blocking of the human alpha rhythm is produced by eye opening in a normal human subject. Derivation is from right occipital electrode referred to linked ears. [From Morrell, F., Electrical signs of sensory coding. In G. C. Quarton, T. Melnechuk, and F. O. Schmitt (Eds.), *The Neurosciences, A Study Program.* N.Y.: The Rockefeller University Press, 1967, 452–469.]

of pathological EEGs can be found in the *Atlas of Electroencephalography* by Gibbs & Gibbs [1952].)

Alpha activity is most prominent in subjects resting with the eyes closed. As indicated in Figure 6.2, when the eyes are then opened, the alpha disappears and the record changes to a lower voltage, faster activity. This phenomenon, *alpha blocking*, is associated with attention to newly given stimulus input. In general, lower voltage, faster frequencies in the EEG are indicative of alerting or arousal of the subject; higher voltage, slower frequency EEGs, tend to indicate lessened arousal, sleep, or similar states. These relationships are depicted in Figure 6.3, which shows EEG tracings during different states of behavioral arousal. If an EEG shows higher voltage, lower frequency activity, it is described as a *synchronized* EEG; conversely, low voltage, fast activity is called *desynchronized.* The use of these terms stems from the early assumption that the wave activity of the EEG consists of the combined spike discharges of many single cells. If such discharges were relatively synchronous in occurrence, they would add to produce high voltage, slow waves; if such discharges were not well synchronized, the result would be low voltage, fast activity. It is now recognized that these assumptions are, at the least, not sufficient to explain the waveform activity seen in the EEG (see Andersen & Andersson, 1968); nonetheless, these terms persist as descriptive of the EEG activity, if not the mechanisms.

Various EEG classificatory systems have been formulated that generally attempt to scale the depth of sleep into about four stages, which, however, do not show sharp boundaries. The system of Dement and Kleitman (1957a) is widely accepted (Figure 6.4). In *stage 1,* when the subject becomes drowsy, the alpha activity becomes irregular and a bit slower than in the waking condition. In *stage 2*, spindle-shaped (waxing and waning) activity of about 14 Hz appears on a low-voltage background with added 3 to 6 Hz activity. In *stage 3,* delta activity appears along with spindling, and in *stage 4,* slow delta activity predominates. Stage 4 is, of course, the deepest stage of sleep in this classification scheme. During uninterrupted sleep through the

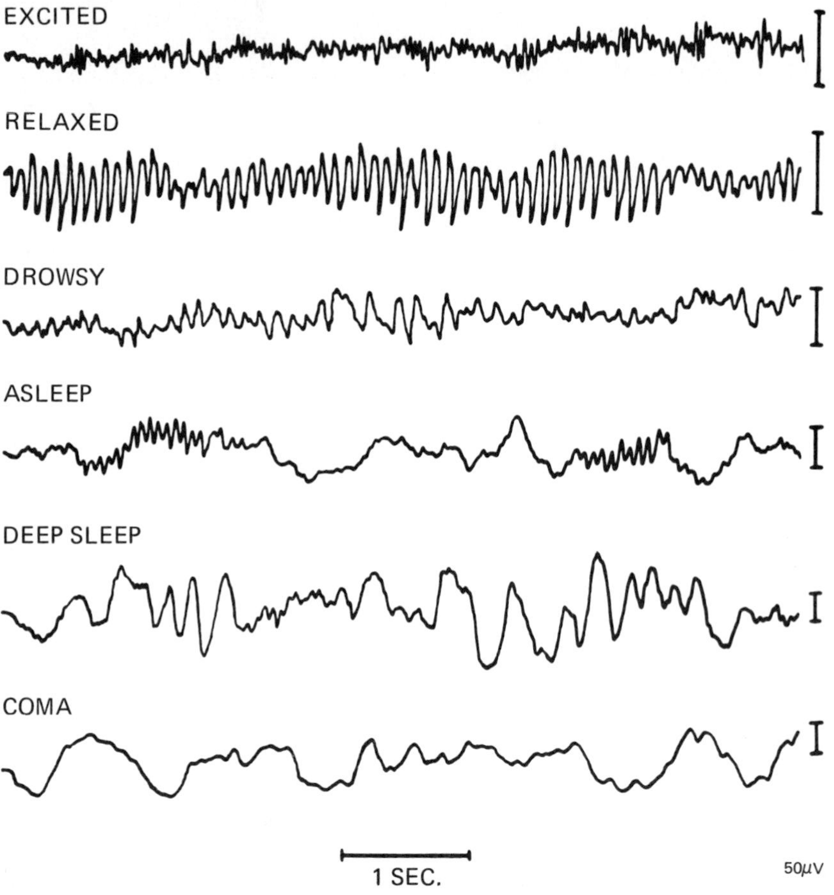

Figure 6.3. Typical EEG records from normal subjects in different states of arousal and from a comatose subject. (From Penfield, W. and Jasper, H. H. *Epilepsy and the Functional Anatomy of the Human Brain.* Boston: Little, Brown and Company, 1954.)

night, the individual shows a fairly regular cycling in the pattern of EEG exhibited, and the depth of sleep fluctuates in accordance with this (see Kleitman, 1963). These, then, comprise the essential facts that have been available since the 1930s. Figure 6.4 shows an additional sleep stage, *REM* sleep, which was discovered later. REM sleep will be discussed on p. 218.

NEURAL MECHANISMS OF SLEEP AND WAKEFULNESS

The following sections will take a chronological approach to the major discoveries about sleep and wakefulness.

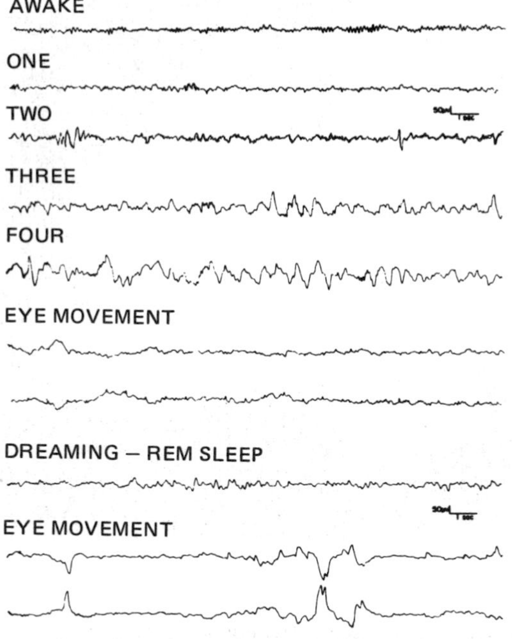

Figure 6.4. Human EEG illustrating Dement-Kleitman classification of EEG stages of sleep and eye movements. The eye movements at the bottom of the figure are the rapid eye movements seen only during REM sleep. (From Johnson, L. C., Sleep and sleep loss: Their effects on performance. *Research Reviews,* 1967.)

Early Formulations

The investigation of neural mechanisms of sleep began in earnest in the 1930s and 1940s. Bremer's (1935, 1954) experiments, in particular, have become classics in the field.

Cerveau Isolé and Encéphale Isolé

Bremer's experiments were performed with acutely prepared cats (Figure 6.5).[1] In one experiment, involving the *cerveau isolé,* the brainstem was transected between the superior and inferior colliculi of the midbrain, isolating the cerebral hemispheres from the brainstem. An animal thus prepared could not be aroused by sensory stimulation and showed the EEG and ocular signs of sleep. In the second procedure, the *encéphale isolé,* the whole brain and brainstem were isolated from the spinal cord by a transection at the top of the cord. In this preparation, the EEG and ocular signs of wakefulness and

[1]In contrast to animals prepared for long-term observation and allowed to recover from the operative procedures, acutely prepared animals are employed immediately after the operative procedure and are subsequently sacrificed. For many kinds of experiments this is a quite adequate procedure, but, as we shall see below, it has complicated the interpretation of studies of sleep mechanisms.

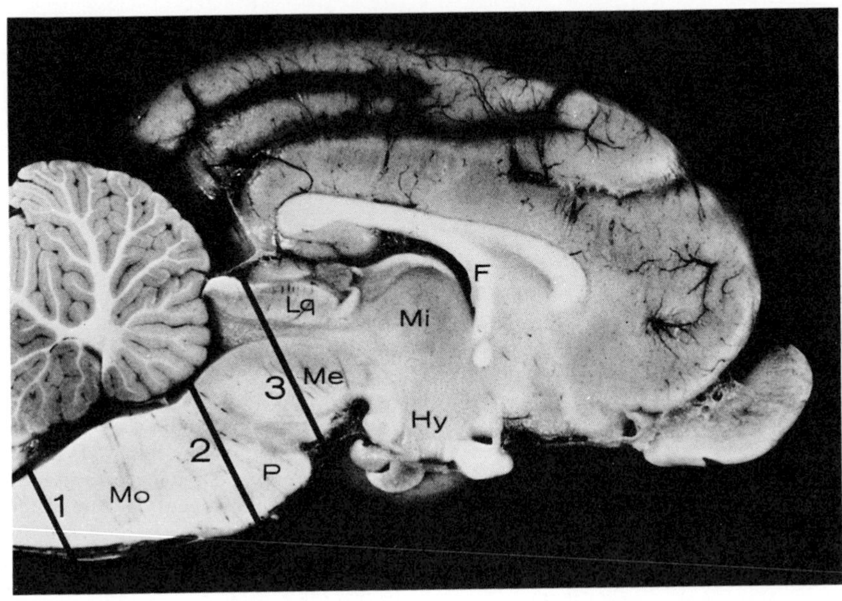

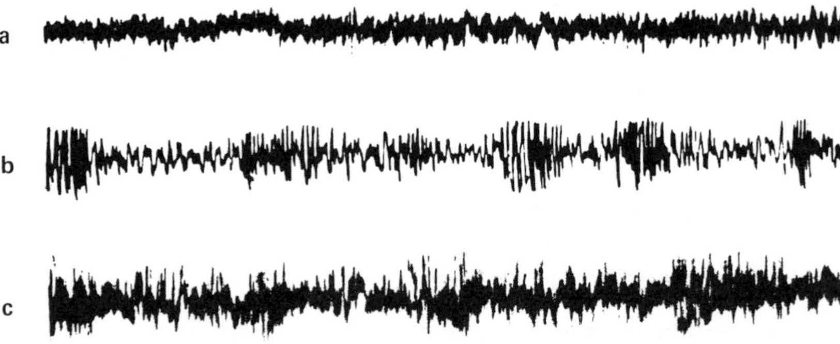

Figure 6.5. Sagittal section of the cat's brain showing the location of critical transections. *1* and *3* illustrate Bremer's experiments. In the *encéphale isolé* (*1*), a section is made at the spinal or bulbar level; the cat is capable of showing the normal waking EEG as in *a*. In the *cerveau isolé* (*3*), the section is made between the colliculi in the midbrain; the cat shows a predominant sleep pattern in the EEG as in *c*. *2* is a pontine transection, the effects of which depend on its precise location. Here the section is somewhat rostral and produces a sleep EEG as in *b*; a more caudal section produces an aroused EEG (see Figure 6.10). *F*, fornix; *Hy*, hypothalamus; *Lq*, lamina quadrigemina; *Me*, midbrain; *Mi*, massa intermedia thalami; *Mo*, medulla oblongata; *P*, pons. (From Birkmayer, W. and Pilleri, G. *The Brainstem Reticular Formation and Its Significance for Autonomic and Affective Behavior*. Basle, Switzerland: Hoffman-LaRoche & Co., 1966.)

sleep were both obtainable. Bremer concluded that the difference in results in the two preparations was due to the relative sensory influx available to the animals in the two instances. In the *cerveau isolé,* all sensory inflow except olfactory and visual was eliminated. Bremer reasoned that adequate afferent input was necessary for the maintenance of the waking state, and the reduced input in the *cerveau isolé* was insufficient for maintenance of wakefulness. In other words, sleep was seen as a *passive* phenomenon resulting from a functional deafferentation of the brain; reduction of input was thought to result in the loss of the awake condition.

Implication of the Thalamus

During the early 1940s, a number of experiments were carried out suggesting that thalamic mechanisms might be involved in sleep. Figure 6.6 illustrates the type of evidence by Dempsey and Morison (1942), Morison and Dempsey (1943), and Jasper (1961), implicating the medial thalamus in the process of synchronization of the cortical EEG. Trace *A* of the figure illustrates spontaneous spindle activity such as would occur in natural sleep. Trace *B* shows a spindlelike burst of activity triggered by a single shock to the *central medial nucleus* of the thalamus. Trace *C* shows the *recruiting response* elicited by reptitive stimulation of the same locus. The increasing voltage, or recruitment, that occurs with repetitive stimulation is characteristic of this response. The waxing and waning, which yield the spindle

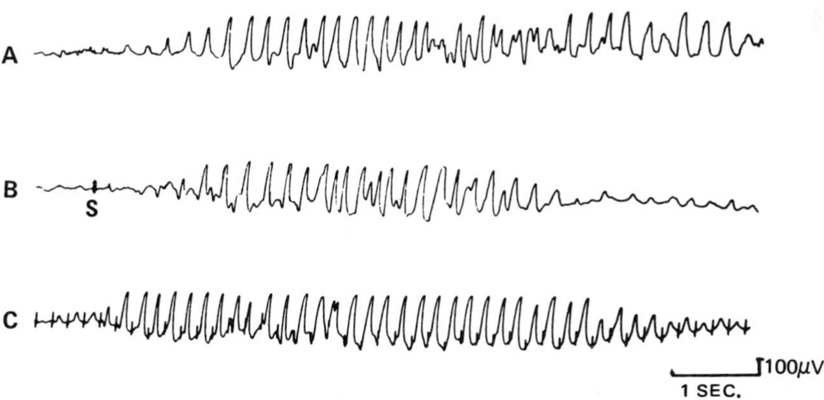

Figure 6.6. Ink-writer records of a spontaneous spindle burst (*A*); a burst triggered by a single shock to the central medial nucleus (*B*); and a typical recruiting response (*C*) from the suprasylvian gyrus of a cat anesthetized with Nembutal. See text for explanation. [From Jasper, H. H., Thalamic reticular system. In D. E. Sheer (Ed.), *Electrical Stimulation of the Brain.* Austin: The University of Texas Press, 1961, 275–287. Copyright 1961 by The University of Texas Press.]

shape of the response train, is also characteristic. The similarity among the spontaneous activity and the evoked activities in *B* and *C* is striking and is taken to indicate that the nonspecific thalamus (as distinguished from the more lateral areas involved in the specific sensory projection systems) contains mechanisms controlling synchronization of the spontaneous EEG.

That this synchronizing effect of thalamic stimulation is pertinent to the mechanisms of sleep is indicated by the experiments performed by W. R. Hess (in Akert, 1961). Low-voltage stimulation, at low repetition rates (less than 15 Hz) in similar locations, seems to induce sleep in the cat that is in every way comparable to natural sleep. Sleep resulted from two or three periods of stimulation of 30 to 60 seconds' duration at intervals up to 5 minutes.

These data are extremely suggestive, of course, in implicating these areas in induction of sleep; however, it is not clear that the stimulation indeed produced the sleep. Thus, laboratory cats, if left undisturbed, spend 60 to 70 percent of their time in sleep (Jouvet, 1967). It may be that what Hess observed was the fortuitous association of sleep periods with experimental stimulation.[2]

Implication of the Hypothalamus

A series of experiments by Ranson (1939) and Nauta (1946) implicate the hypothalamus (see Figure 6.5) in sleep regulation. Ranson, working with the monkey, showed that extensive destruction of the thalamus did not result in sleep or wakefulness disturbances, but lesions restricted to the posterior hypothalamus resulted in profound somnolence. Animals with such lesions could be roused by strong stimulation but fell back to sleep readily. Such results indicate the location of a "wakefulness center" in this region. Nauta, working with the rat, found similar results with posterior lesions, but he also found continuous wakefulness in animals with lesions in the preoptic nucleus of the anterior hypothalamus. Such animals were never observed to sleep until they were exhausted and fell into a coma and died. Thus, in addition to a wakefulness center, there was indication of a "sleep center."

[2]It should also be apparent that the elicitation of any behavior by electrical stimulation does not provide unequivocal evidence concerning the localization of the influencing mechanisms. With electrical stimulation we cannot selectively stimulate cell bodies located in the area in contrast to axons that may traverse the area but derive from distantly located nuclei. Chemical stimulation may offer the possibility of selective excitation of cells, but chemicals may spread from the presumed stimulation site. Neural degeneration resulting from discretely placed lesions offers the possibility of tracing circuits that may be involved. Obviously, the judicious use of a combination of methods is indicated. On the other hand, it should also be apparent that neither lesions nor stimulation can be expected to have isolated effects; that is, they probably affect dynamically balanced systems. Thus, a behavioral change after a lesion is not likely to be the simple result of the tissue removed but also of changes in the functioning of the remaining tissue.

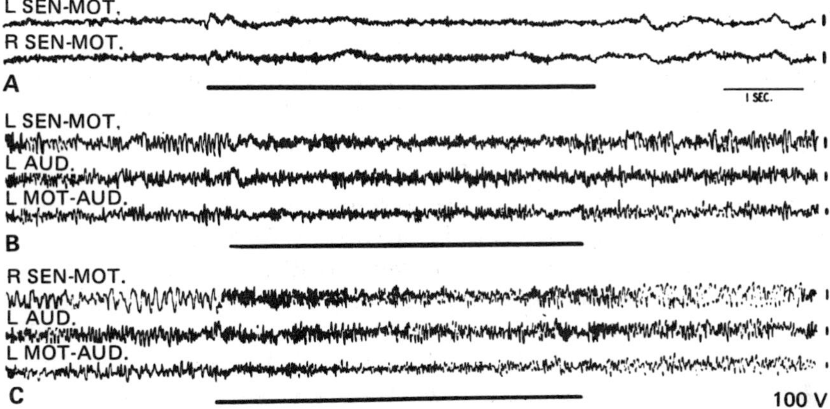

Figure 6.7. Effect of reticular stimulation on electrocortical activity in the unanesthetized encephale isolé. Left bulbo-reticular stimulation (3V, 300/sec) is without effect upon the fully activated cortex (*A*), but evokes characteristic low-voltage, fast activity when spontaneous synchrony is present (*B* and *C*). (From Moruzzi, G. and Magoun, H. W., Brainstem reticular formation and activation of the EEG. *Electroencephalography and Clinical Neurophysiology*, 1949, *1*, 455–473.)

These results, strongly indicating the existence of sleep-inducing mechanisms in the forebrain, formed the early basis for an *active* theory of sleep in contrast to a passive theory. In other words, the suggestion is that, rather than being attributable to reduction or failure of mechanisms acting to keep the organism awake, sleep is itself an actively induced process with mechanisms of its own. In fact, the suggestion of both sleep and wakefulness mechanisms leads directly to the inference that the two states are not necessarily reciprocally related at all.

This conceptualization of sleep and wakefulness mechanisms was more or less forgotten in the tremendous outpouring of research on the reticular system.

Reticular Theory

In 1949, Moruzzi and Magoun performed an experiment that started a flood of research on the reticular system. As indicated in Chapter 5, the *reticular system* is a complex network of cells, forming a "core" of tissue extending from the spinal cord through the brainstem and thalamus (Figure 5.1). The Moruzzi and Magoun experiment (1949) consisted of electrically stimulating this reticular substance at the mesencephalic level with high-frequency (100 to 300/sec) pulses. As seen in Figure 6.7, when such stimuli were delivered while the EEG showed sleep activity, an immediate transition to a low-voltage, desynchronized EEG occurred. Such desynchronization is characteristic of alertness and behavioral arousal (although in this case the animals were acutely operated upon and held in a stereotaxic instrument). Such a result, of course, suggests that the midbrain reticular formation (*MRF*) is at least part of a system reponsible for the awake, behaviorally alert condition. It also suggests that Bremer's experiments on the *cerveau isolé* require reinterpretation—the MRF, rather than the classical sensory pathways, is responsible for the maintenance of the alert condition. (Bremer's transection of the brainstem cut both the sensory pathways and MRF.) Note, however, that the theory of sleep here is still a passive one, holding that sleep occurs when the reticular production of the alert condition is lacking.

Lindsley, Schreiner, Knowles, and Magoun (1950) tested reticular involvement in sleep with both EEG and behavioral observations in cats with a variety of lesions and with chronically implanted electrodes. The cats were observed for a maximum of 2 months. Some cats had lesions restricted to portions of the reticular system, ranging (in different cats) from the hypothalamus caudally to the pons. In other animals, lesions were restricted to the more lateral sensory pathways surrounding the reticular system. Figures 6.8 and 6.9 illustrate some of the EEG results obtained. Where the lesions interrupted the reticular system, there was chronic somnolence and EEG synchrony. In such instances, activation of the EEG and behavioral arousal were still possible with strong sensory stimulation but were usually confined to the immediate stimulation period and disappeared in the absence of such stimulation. Conversely, lesions sparing the reticular system left the animals with the ability to remain awake much of the time, judging from both their behavior and the low-voltage, fast EEG. Thus, the integrity of the reticular system would appear to be necessary for maintenance of the waking condition.

Nonspecific Arousal Function

From about 1950 to 1958, research was basically built upon the above findings. The role of the reticular system in many diverse functions was investigated. The anatomical substrates of the system, its role in activation and inhibition of motor performance, attention, perception, and emotion, and its response to drugs were all intensively investigated (O'Leary & Coben, 1958). For our present purposes, only a few points need be noted. Despite the apparent complexity of its functions and the degree of organization revealed by these investigations, the general picture that emerged stressed the *nonspecific*, arousal functions of the reticular system. Alertness, both behaviorally and in the EEG, can be elicited by high-frequency stimulation anywhere within the confines of the system. The system was viewed as maintaining a "tonic" or sustained arousing influence on the cortex. It was also stressed that the cortex exerts a feedback influence on the reticular system. At the diencephalic end of the system, it was soon discovered that the areas responsible for spindling and recruiting responses can also produce

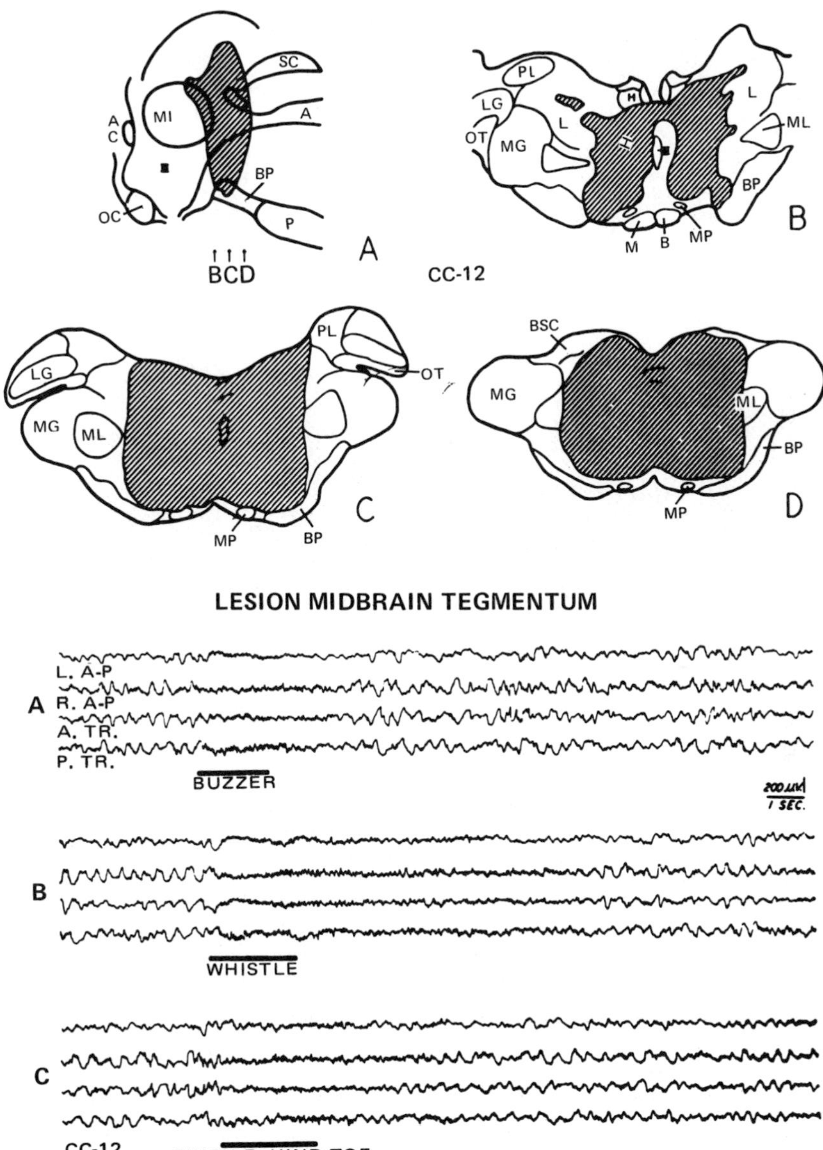

Figure 6.8. Top: Large lesion of anterior end of midbrain tegmentum. (*A*) sagittal plane; (*B–D*) transverse sections. Bottom: EEG of cat with this lesion. Arousing effects of buzzer (*A*), whistle (*B*), and pinch (*C*) on seventh postoperative day. Recordings from left anterior-posterior, right anterior-posterior, left-right anterior (transcortical), and left-right posterior regions of cortex. (From Lindsley, D. B., Schreiner, L. H., Knowles, W. B., and Magoun, H. W., Behavioral and EEG changes following chronic brainstem lesions in the cat. *Electroencephalography and Clinical Neurophysiology*, 1950, 2, 483–498.)

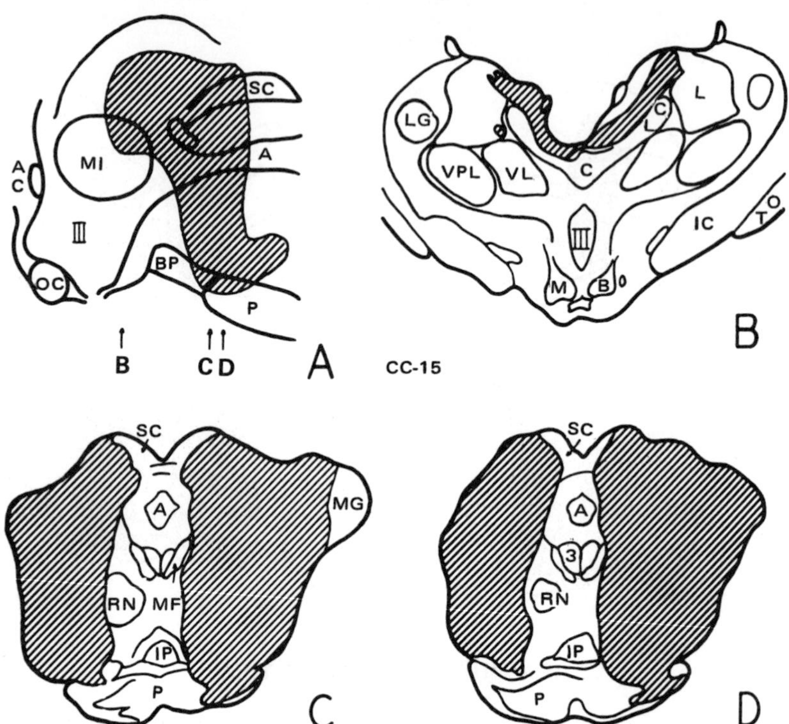

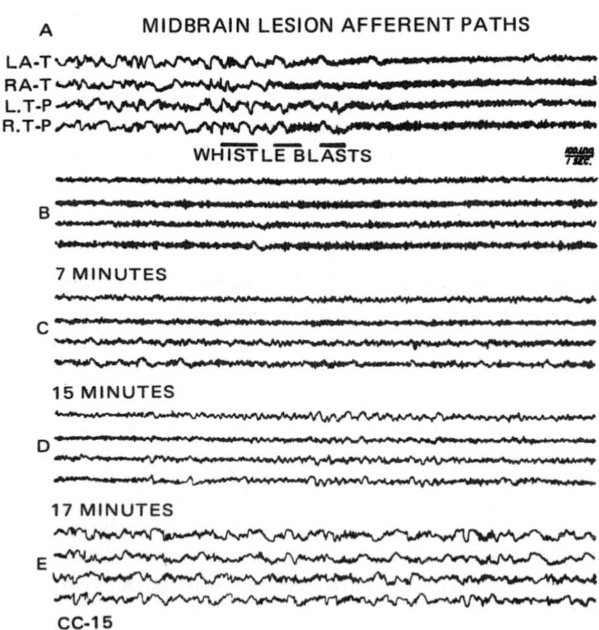

Figure 6.9. *Top:* Lesion of sensory paths in lateral midbrain. (*A* sagittal plane; (*B–D*) transverse sections. *Bottom:* EEG of cat with this lesion. Arousal by whistle blasts on twelfth postoperative day. Strips *A* and *B* are continuous; *C* is 7 min after *A*; *D*, 15 min after *A*; and *E*, 17 min after *A*. EEG between left anterior-temporal, right anterior-temporal, left temporal-posterior, and right temporal-posterior regions. (From Lindsley, D.B., Schreiner, L.H., Knowles, W.B., and Magoun, H.W., Behavioral and EEG changes following chronic brainstem lesions in the cat. *Electroencephalography and Clinical Neurophysiology*, 1950, 2, 483–498.)

a "phasic" or short-term arousal if stimulated at high frequency. Thus, either synchronizing or desynchronizing effects may be elicited from the so-called thalamic reticular system (Jasper, 1961). The synchronizing effects of thalamic stimulation could be blocked, however, with MRF or thalamic arousing stimulation.

It should be pointed out, however, that designation of the thalamic nonspecific areas as the rostral end of the reticular system has been questioned. Schlag, Chaillet, and Herzet (1961) demonstrated that the recruiting and desynchronizing effects of thalamic stimulation could be separated; in fact, appropriately placed lesions on the mesencephalic-diencephalic border eliminated the EEG alerting response to thalamic stimulation while the recruiting function was maintained. Furthermore, blockage of recruiting by simultaneous high-frequency stimulation on the contralateral side of the thalamus was no longer possible after such lesions. Generally, then, these authors concluded that the ability of the thalamic areas to show desynchronizing responses resulted from the mediation of "downstream" connections of the thalamus to the mesencephalon.

Questioning the Theory

There were only two disturbing notes in the picture of reticular function that was emerging. One arose from the study of drugs and their action on the CNS and the reticular system in particular. It was discovered that EEG and behavioral conditions could be dissociated. Thus, atropine injections resulted in slow-wave EEG activity similar to sleep, but the animals so treated remained behaviorally alert and active (Wikler, 1952; Bradley & Elkes, 1953). Similarly, physostigmine produced a desynchronized EEG without resulting in behavioral alerting (Bradley & Elkes, 1953). Both atropine and physostigmine act on cholinergic transmission. It was apparent, therefore, that whatever the mechanism of action of these drugs, the state of behavioral arousal of the organism cannot be inferred simply from the EEG.

The second source of difficulty in understanding the function of the reticular system came from lesion studies. A number of investigators (for example, Adametz, 1959) found that if lesions in the MRF were made in stages, with recovery allowed between successive stages, even animals with large final lesions could demonstrate alert behavior and learning. Thus, loss of the MRF was not critical to the maintenance of the awake state. Generally, neither of these complications was considered terribly serious for the general picture of the relation between midbrain reticular function and behavior. However, problems were due to come up again shortly.

In summary, then, during the time from Moruzzi and Magoun's first experiments to about 1958, there emerged a picture of reticular activity that conceptualized the problem of sleep and wakefulness as one of understand-

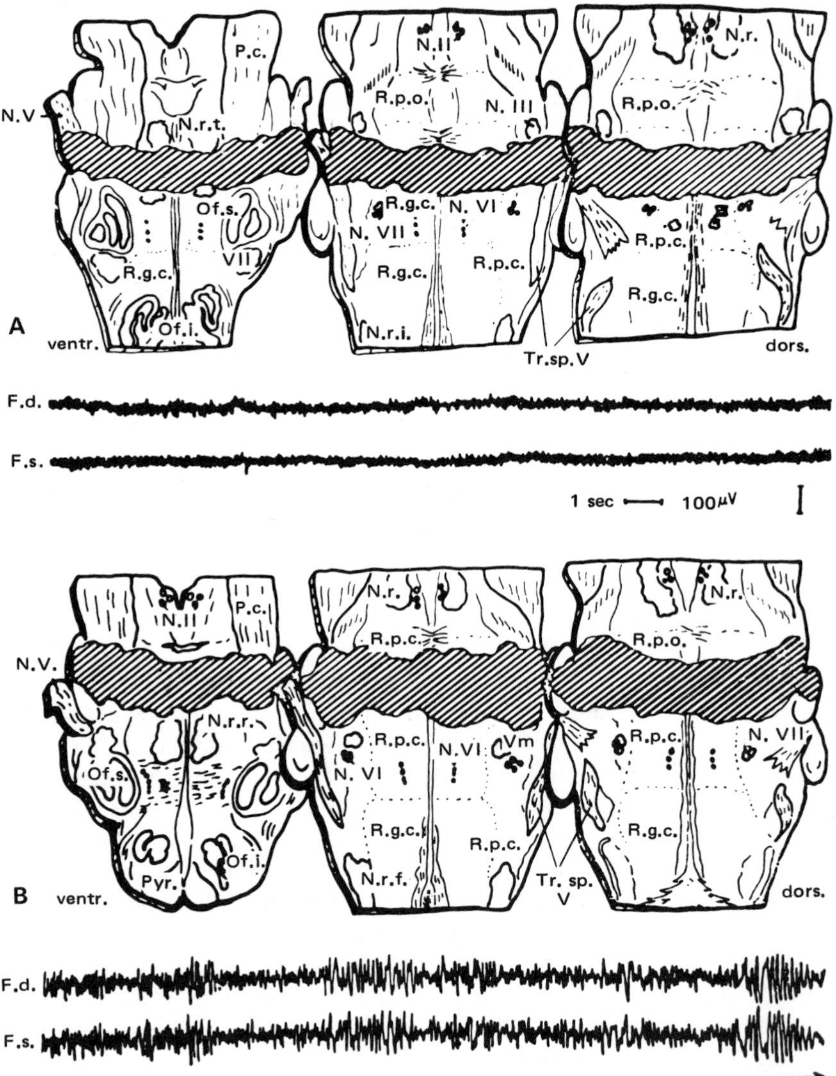

Figure 6.10. EEG pattern from right (F.d.) and left (F.s.) frontal cortex following (*A*) midpontine and (*B*) rostropontine transection. Horizontal sections of brainstem. (From Batini, C., Morussi, G., Palestini, M., Rossi, G. F., and Zanchetti, A., Effects of complete pontine transections on the sleep-wakefulness rhythm: The midpontine pretrigeminal preparation. *Archives Italiennes de Biologie*, 1959, 97, 1–12.)

ing the reticular mechanisms through which the organism maintained the waking state; that is, sleep was seen as the passive result of loss of the waking condition. However, several lines of evidence soon showed that this was an incomplete formulation.

Reticular Theory Revised

In 1959, another important experiment transecting the brainstem was reported—the midpontine pretrigeminal (premidbrain) preparation (Batini, Moruzzi, Palestini, Rossi, & Zanchetti, 1959). The experiments essentially repeated Bremer's *cerveau isolé* procedure but with the plane of transection shifted caudally in some instances (Figure 6.10). With rostral transection, Bremer's original results were confirmed—that is, sustained cortical synchronization was seen. When, however, more caudal, midpontine transections were made just in front of the entrance of the trigeminal nerve, the cortical EEG showed a strong predominance of desynchronized activity. That this desynchronization is indicative of the waking condition is implied by observations such as: (1) pupillary dilation occurs to significant visual stimuli; (2) following of visual stimuli, at least in the vertical plane, is possible; and (3) there is evidence that such animals are conditionable (Affanni, Marchiafava, & Zernicki, 1962).

These results—coupled with the fact that encéphale isolé preparations do show alternation of sleeping and waking EEGs—suggested the following conclusions: With rostral transections, the synchronized EEG of the cerveau isolé results from cutting off the isolated forebrain from activating structures in the rostral pons. The midpontine pretrigeminal preparation shows persistent cortical desynchronization because this preparation does contain the latter structures but is, in turn, itself cut off from more caudally situated synchronizing structures. These synchronizing structures lie in the caudal pons and possibly the medulla, since the encéphale isolé, with its even more caudal section, does show both types of EEG activity.

A variety of experiments, attempting to localize these effects more precisely by employing discrete lesions, have been carried out. Their details are complex and need not concern us here (see Jouvet, 1967, for references). Suffice it to say that they support the existence of separable mechanisms controlling the waking and sleeping conditions; the conceptualization of sleep as a passive result of the failure of activation processes is not tenable.

REM Sleep

Up to this point, we have uniformly followed the classical interpretation that high-voltage, slow frequencies in the EEG are generally indicative of sleep, and that a low-voltage, fast-frequency EEG indicates activation and behavioral arousal. We previously noted, however, that there are some pharmacologically induced exceptions to this behavior–EEG relationship. Around 1958, the systematic exploration of another exception was begun; it has led to the conceptualization that sleep is not a single uniform state but rather consists of two states that are qualitatively quite different.

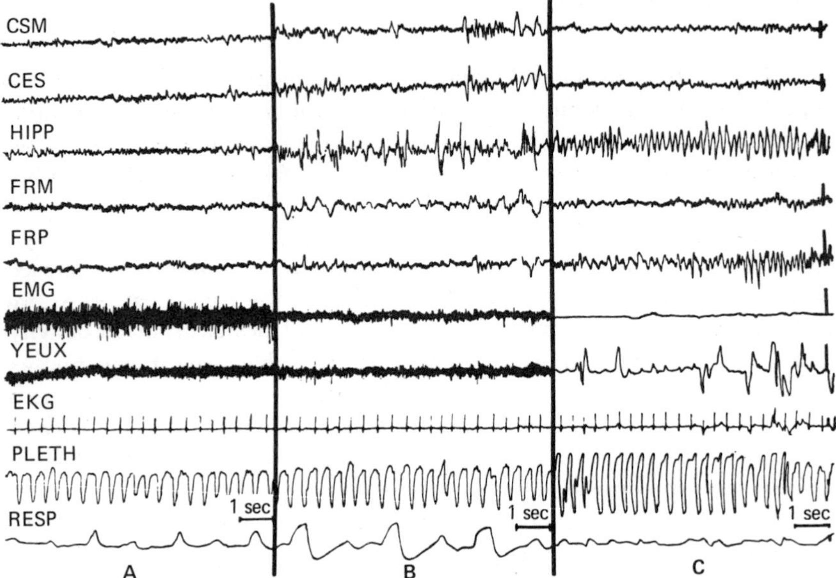

Figure 6.11. Polygraphic aspects of the two states of sleep in the cat. *A* (*wakefulness*): Fast cortical and subcortical activity; increased muscle (EMG) activity. *B* (*slow sleep*): Cortical spindles and slow waves; high-voltage spikes at ventral hippocampus (HIPP); slow waves in mesencephalic reticular formation (FRM); decrease in EMG activity of the neck. *C* (*paradoxical sleep*): Low-voltage, fast cortical activity similar to wakefulness; regular theta activity at the ventral hippocampus; phasic activity in pontine reticular formation (FRP); total disappearance of EMG activity of the neck; clusters of rapid eye movements (YEUX), change in respiratory activity (RESP), and plethysmographic index of the front leg (PLETH). CSM, sensorimotor cortex; CES, ectosylvian cortex. Scale: 1 sec, 50 μ v. (From Jouvet, M., Récherches sur les structures nerveuses et les mécanismes responsables des differentes phases du sommeil physiologique. *Archives Italiennes de Biologie*, 1962, *100*, 125–206.)

In a series of experiments in both cats and humans, Dement and Kleitman (Dement, 1958; Dement & Kleitman, 1957a, b) investigated the fact that low-voltage, fast-frequency EEGs are obtainable from normal subjects who are, by behavioral criteria, apparently asleep. During normal sleep there are recurring periods of low-voltage, fast EEGs accompanied by rapid movements of the eyes (REM) and extreme loss of tone in the antigravity muscles, particularly in the neck. Such periods are contrasted with waking and more classical sleep EEGs in Figure 6.11. In humans, such periods start about an hour after the onset of sleep, recur about every 80 to 90 minutes, last about 20 minutes, and comprise about 20 to 25 percent of the total sleeping time. About 80 percent of the time, subjects awakened during such periods report that they had been dreaming.

A variety of terms have been applied to this sleep condition, each descriptive of some aspect of the condition that might be deemed significant. Among many other names, it has generally been termed REM because of the rapid eye movements, *paradoxical* because of the desynchronized EEG, and *rhombencephalic* because of the brainstem location of the neural mechanisms controlling it. In distinguishing the two states of sleep, we will refer to *REM sleep* or to *slow sleep* (the classical, slow-frequency EEG condition).

Interest in REM sleep has grown tremendously since 1958. Here are some highlights of the research: A number of factors point to REM sleep as a deeper stage of sleep than slow sleep. Myosis is generally more extreme than in slow sleep, although there are sometimes sudden pupillary dilations accompanying bursts of REM activity. In the cat, arousal thresholds using MRF stimulation are greatly increased. Thresholds for environmental stimulation are also raised. If behavioral arousal does not occur by such manipulations, the EEG may revert to slow sleep. The further reduction in muscle tone during REM is also suggestive of a deeper sleep. Nonetheless, it has been argued, particularly in reference to humans, that REM sleep is a lighter sleep condition. For instance, it may be that the greater arousal thresholds are due essentially to the subject's distraction by dream activity. Jouvet (1967) suggests that the question of relative depth of sleep is ambiguous in view of the increasing evidence that slow sleep and REM sleep are *qualitatively* different states.

Without going into the anatomical details, here is a summary, condensed from Jouvet (1967), of some pertinent characteristics of REM sleep in the cat: The eye movements of REM sleep are governed by mechanisms different from those subserving eye movements in the waking condition and appear in animal preparations that are incapable of waking eye movements; newborn kittens, for instance, although blind at birth, show REM activity. In conjunction with the onset of REM sleep, there is the occurrence of 200 to 300 microvolt, monophasic spikes in the pons, lateral geniculate, and occipital cortex. Such activity precedes the loss of muscle tone, the EEG changes, and the eye movements, and it continues through the REM period. Similar activity may be evoked in the geniculate from pontine stimulation, but this is not possible during arousal or slow sleep. The indications are that such activity represents an extraretinal, pontine influence on the lateral geniculate and cortex. Generally speaking, it is clear that the structures responsible for REM sleep have a pontile location—the removal of all neural structures rostral to the pons does not prevent REM activity in the pons. On the other hand, the rostral structures through which the ascending influence of such activity is channeled have not yet been fully identified. Finally, there exists a sufficient number of experimental results to suggest that the neural activation occurring during REM sleep is different from that associated with awake, behavioral arousal, despite the EEG similarities in the two conditions.

Forebrain Mechanisms

From the preceding material, we can see that the late 1940s through the 1960s there was increasing attention paid to brainstem mechanisms influencing the sleep–wakefulness cycle. In fact, during this period the trend was toward more caudally directed investigation; that is, starting with midbrain experiments, the research has progressively moved "downstream" toward the spinal cord. In recent years, however, a number of investigators have reminded us of the probable influence of more rostrally located mechanisms. They have, once again, begun to look at the locations earlier investigated by Ranson, Nauta, and Hess.

Preoptic Stimulation

Hernández-Péon and Chavez-Ibarra (1963) were able to elicit sleep in cats by stimulating the preoptic region (rostral to the hypthalamus and just dorsal to the optic chiasma), either chemically, with cholinergic drugs, or electrically, with low-frequency stimulation. By itself, this result would be suggestive but still subject to the criticisms made earlier of stimulation studies. In conjunction with the work of Sterman and Clemente (1962) and McGinty and Sterman (1968), however, it takes on added significance. Unlike other studies of sleep induction with electrical stimulation, the study by Sterman and Clemente succeeded in inducing sleep with *high*-frequency stimulation (to 250 Hz). Normally such stimulation, when applied to awake animals, results in EEG and behavioral alerting; in the present instance it induced sleep. Furthermore, the onset of sleep appeared uniformly more rapidly than in other studies. Sleep induction with subcortical electrical stimulation has usually required as long as several minutes of repeated stimulation; but in these studies the average time was about 30 sec, with a range from 5 sec to 3 min. Lesions in the preoptic area of cats (McGinty & Sterman, 1968) confirmed Nauta's prior work in the rat. Large bilateral lesions of this area resulted in complete sleeplessness, followed by exhaustion and death in a few days. Smaller lesions resulted in a marked reduction of both slow sleep and REM sleep. Sleep suppression in animals with smaller lesions had a gradual onset, reaching a peak after 2 to 3 weeks, and was followed by a complete or partial recovery after 6 to 8 weeks.

Together, then, these results are strongly suggestive of sleep induction mechanisms located far anterior to the brainstem mechanisms that we have previously discussed. The following experiments by Villablanca confirm this inference.

Chronic Forebrain Lesions

Much of the material that we have so far considered comes from studies employing radical lesions, such as transections of the brainstem, where observations were made for only relatively short periods of time. There are at least two possible considerations that must be evaluated before it can be concluded that the lesions produced the observed behavior. Most obviously, such operations might produce a depressant effect. It may be difficult to distinguish between an animal that is comatose (with a chronically synchronized EEG) because it has failed to recover from the trauma of the operation and an animal that is simply chronically asleep. On the other hand, there is also the possibility that lesioning may leave the remaining tissue hypersensitive. Either possibility would be decreased by observing such animals over sustained periods that would permit EEG and behavioral changes to resume normal patterns.

Villablanca has carried out a series of experiments devoted to observing the long-term recovery of animals with various lesions implicating the forebrain in sleep. In the first of these experiments (Villablanca, 1966), long-term observations were made of cerveau isolé cats. In these experiments, transections were made at the midbrain level and the animals carried electrodes implanted in the cortex and in the brainstem below the transection. Thus, the electrical activity of both the isolated forebrain, or cerveau isolé, and the brainstem could be observed simultaneously and compared. During the first 10 to 15 postoperative days, these animals displayed little or no motor activity. But unquestionably, in the later stages of recovery they displayed waking behavior.

During later stages of recovery, they were seen crouching, sitting, attempting to walk, and making climbing movements if suddenly stopped by a wall. The eyelids were open with the pupils widely dilated; with sudden noises, the animals responded with a rotation of the head toward the source of the noise. They also displayed defensive reactions to noxious stimuli. If left undisturbed, the animals showed a decrease in motor activity; they would lie down, close the eyelids, and exhibit pupillary myosis. In short, these animals behaviorally exhibited alternation between apparent waking and sleeping behavior.

Figure 6.12 illustrates the main features of the results of EEG recording in these animals. Two animals are represented, one after 37 postoperative days and the other after 79 postoperative days. The cortical recordings (upper two traces) in part A of the figure show that the chronic *cerveau isolé* is capable of demonstrating both the synchronized EEG characteristic of slow sleep and the desynchronized EEG classically associated with the alert animal. The recordings from pons and midbrain show sustained desynchroniza-

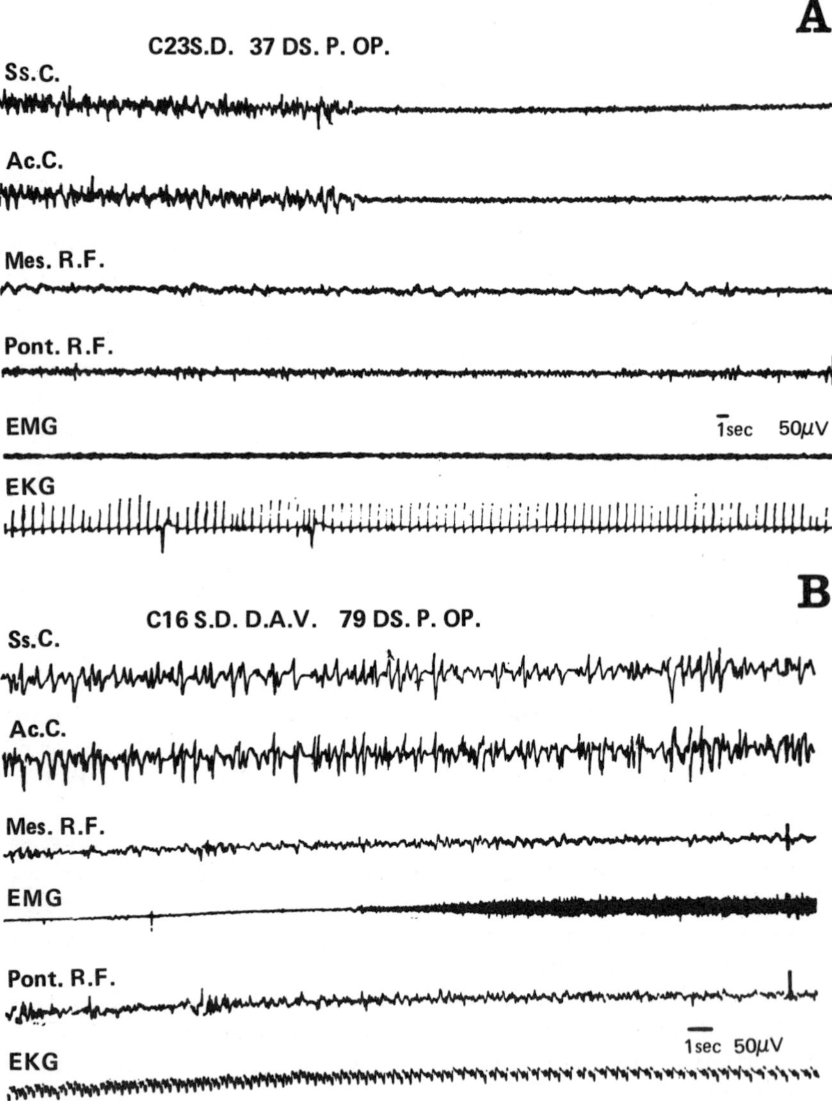

Figure 6.12. Dissociation between cortical and brainstem EEG in chronic cats with mesencephalic transection. *A*: The upper two leads show a spontaneous ending of a cortical synchronization period, while the recordings from mesencephalic and pontine reticular formation do not exhibit any change. *B*: Sudden ending of a period of extreme pupillary myosis as shown by activation of the silent EMG, ceasing of grouped waves at brainstem level, and slowing of heart rate; note that no concomitant change is seen at the cortex. Ss.C.: Primary somatosensory cortex; Ac.C.: primary acoustic cortex. (From Villablanca, J., Behavioral and polygraphic study of "sleep" and "wakefulness" in chronic decerebrate cats. *Electroencephalography and Neurophysiology*, 1966, *21*, 562–577.)

tion, a pattern that was invariant throughout for all such brainstem recordings. In other words, the electrical activity of the cortex showed alternate synchronization and desynchronization independent of the subcortical activity, which showed only sustained desynchronization. The records from the second animal (part *B*) illustrate that activity characteristic of REM sleep in the normal animal was seen in the brainstem portion of these animals. Periodically, the desynchronized pontine recording was accompanied by spiking and the extreme loss of muscle activity (EMG), which are normally characteristic of REM sleep. These signs appeared simultaneously with synchronization at the cortex. As in REM sleep, the animals concomitantly showed extreme pupillary myosis. Thus, these records illustrate the independence of cortical and brainstem electrical activities in the chronic midbrain preparation. They also illustrate that the brainstem counterparts of normal REM sleep still occur in these animals.

The above results seem to lead to the following conclusions: (1) Rostral forebrain structures are capable of independently controlling the sleep–wakefulness cycle of the cortex in the chronically maintained midbrain-transected animal. Sleep–wakefulness, then, in the cortex is not dependent on brainstem reticular mechanisms. (2) The data are, however, in agreement with earlier conclusions that structures controlling REM sleep are located in the pons; in the chronically transected animals, the rostral structures did not exhibit electrical activity correlated with the muscular and pupillary signs of REM sleep. (3) The independence of electrical activity above and below the transection tends to rule out any *integration* of rostral and caudal structures based on chemical mechanisms. This is not to say that chemical mechanisms do not influence the normal sleep–wakefulness cycle in the intact animal; it simply indicates that the coordination between the rostral and caudal structures that is seen in the normal, intact animal is achieved through neural mechanisms.

The role of rostral forebrain structures in the control of sleep has been delimited further by Villablanca in two other experiments. In the first of these (Villablanca & Marcus, 1972), the neocortex and parts of the limbic system were removed or separated from the remainder of the neural axis, leaving a "diencephalic" cat. Five animals were studied postsurgically for 2 to 6½ months. Behaviorally, these animals were generally characterized by motor hyperactivity and irritability; they were responsive to external stimuli, though they were severely limited in their responsiveness. All the animals displayed the ocular and pupillary signs characteristic of both slow and REM sleep. However, they exhibited a marked and persistent reduction in overall sleep. Less than 1 percent of all observation time consisted of REM sleep (versus some 14 percent in inact cats), and about 6 percent was devoted to slow sleep (versus 38 percent in intact cats. Recordings from the intact thalamic area indicated changes between slow wave and fast activity paralleling the ocular and muscular signs of wakefulness, slow, and REM sleep.

In the second study, Villablanca and Salinas-Zeballos (1972) conducted a complementary experiment, in which they removed the thalamic structures but left the remaining forebrain intact.[3] These athalamic cats were characterized by marked postural and locomotor difficulties and diminished sensitivity to stimuli, particulary blindness and loss of pupillary reflexes. Nonetheless, they still displayed ocular and pupillary signs characterstic of wakefulness, slow sleep, and REM sleep. Such a result emphasizes that the ocular and pupillary signs of sleep are independent of the mechanisms subserving normal visual perception. As with the diencephalic cats, both slow sleep and REM sleep were greatly diminished, though neither was reduced quite so drastically as in the diencephalic cat. Athalamic cats also showed a persistent disparity between EEG and behavior. That is, during the early recovery from the lesions, high-voltage slow waves dominated the EEG irrespective of the animals' behavior; toward the end of the experiment (as long as 6 months later) this dissociation was confined to the transition periods between waking and sleep or between REM and slow sleep.

Together, these last two studies suggest that there are both sleep-enhancing and sleep-suppressing mechanisms in the diencephalon. The two studies appear to have differentially affected the normal balance of activity between these mechanisms. Dissociations between EEG activity and behavior during transitions between sleep and waking and REM and slow sleep suggest that the thalamus must also participate in the "coupling" of anterior and caudal brainstem mechanisms.

Conclusions. Any conception of sleep as simply a passive loss of the waking condition is incomplete. Both the brainstem and the forebrain contain mechanisms that promote both waking and sleep. Furthermore, while these brainstem and forebrain mechanisms operate in concert in the normal animal, the experiments reviewed here indicate that they are capable of independent operation. It has also been suggested (Villablanca, 1966), that the independent operation of brainstem and forebrain mechanisms indicates the possibility that such dissociation might occur in some normal conditions: Somnambulism might be a condition in which there is a sleeping brain in a waking body; dreaming might represent a bodily sleep condition with the brain operating at a level almost, but not quite, that necessary for full awareness.

Finally, sleep itself must be redefined to recognize that it consists of a mixture of what are apparently two qualitatively different conditions, REM sleep and "slow" sleep.

[3]Note that removal of the thalamus affects only part of the total diencephalic area which was spared in the previous experiment.

CHEMICAL FACTORS IN SLEEP AND WAKEFULNESS

Thus far, we have been exclusively concerned with neural mechanisms that function to control sleep and wakefulness. In point of fact, however, neural investigations were actually preceded by a number of theories that regarded chemical conditions in the internal environment as causes of sleep. Such theories were largely displaced by neural studies, but interest is again reviving in chemical factors. Kleitman (1963) has summarized a great amount of research in this area.

Accumulation of Substances

The earliest theories of this type postulated that sleep is the result of the accumulation of certain substances, usually metabolic end products, that cause toxic-like depression of brain activity. The removal of these substances during sleep accounts for the return to the waking state. Carbon dioxide and lactic acid are two substances that feature prominently in these theories. A variation of this type of theory calls for cyclical activity in the various endocrine glands.

Injection of Chemicals

Much experimental work has been done with the injection of a variety of chemical substances as a means of inducing sleep. A typical example is the injection of calcium chloride intracerebrally, the rationale being a purported decrease in calcium during anesthesia and sleep. Early experiments suffered from the fact that control solutions, or the mere insertion of the needle into the brain, also produced sleep. In addition, some of the experimental effects that apparently had positive results also had confounding side effects. Thus, in experiments on the cerebrospinal fluid, it has been found that the injection procedure may result in a temperature elevation; sleep could be secondary to the temperature change.

More recently, Veale and Myers (1971) experimented with altering the ionic concentrations of the extracellular fluid of the hypothalamus. Increased sodium concentration led to agitation, hyperactivity, and defense reactions, while increased calcium concentrations led to sleep. Other ions, such as magnesium and potassium, were ineffective. These experiments suggest that balance between relative concentrations, rather than absolute level, is the critical variable.

Conditions of the Blood

Experiments attempting to establish the existence of some substance circulating in the blood have involved blood transfusions from sleep-deprived animals to other animals, establishment of crossed blood circulation between animals, and the observation of Siamese twins. Generally, such experiments must be considered inconclusive. The simultaneous observation of a waking and a sleeping member of a pair of animals with crossed circulation does not rule out the presence of additional factors operating to prevent the appearance of sleep in one of the animals and not in the other—differential hunger or attention to environmental stimuli might be simple examples of such extraneous factors.

An experiment by Monnier and Hösli (1964) is noteworthy in apparently avoiding some of these problems. These workers were able to produce either sleep or alertness with the same technical procedures; this makes the evaluation of controls much easier. Chemical extractions were made from the blood of individual donor rabbits with artificial kidneys. The question posed was whether such an extract contains active substances that differ, depending on the state of alertness of the donor. Three groups of animals served as donors. The first group consisted of animals in which sleep was induced by electrical stimulation of the nonspecific thalamus; the animals in the second group were stimulated in the MRF with high-frequency stimuli, producing behavioral arousal and EEG dysynchronization; the third group of animals were similarly implanted with thalamic or midbrain electrodes but were only shamstimulated. Extracts from individual donors were injected into the veins of individual, freely moving rabbits, which were then observed for behavioral and EEG changes. Extracts from sleeping donors induced behavioral sleep and increased delta and spindling activity in the EEG; extracts from alerted donors increased EEG desynchronization and motor activity from control, resting levels; injections from control donors only slightly activated the behavior and EEGs of the recipients.

These results strongly suggest that chemical conditions in the blood exert some influence on sleep and wakefulness mechanisms. In other words, it is probable that the activity of the neural mechanisms that we have been discussing throughout this chapter is sensitive to, or modulated by, some chemical constituents in the blood system. The nature of these chemical conditions is not yet known, however.

Effects of Drugs

Another kind of investigation concerns the effects of various drugs on sleep and wakefulness. The literature on the subject is voluminous but inconclusive (see Kleitman, 1963). As an example of the complexities inherent in this field, the experiments by Steiner, Pscheidt, and Himwich (1963) might be cited. These workers found that the drugs reserpine and etryptamine could each produce quite opposite EEG effects, depending on whether the drugs were administered prior to or after the surgery implanting the electrodes. While the nature of the interaction is not understood, it is obvious that at least some drug effects are a result of interaction with the state of the organism.

Differentiation in Synaptic Mechanisms

Thus far, this section has been concerned with the effects of chemicals circulating systemically in animals. Recent advances concerning chemical, synaptic transmitter substances allow us to focus on a somewhat different biochemical question: Are the neural mechanisms subserving sleep and wakefulness differentiated in their synaptic mechanisms?

During the 1960s, the development of new histological techniques enabled the localization of certain presumed synaptic transmitters within specific neural locations. Basically, the chemical procedures employed stain aminergic neurons in such a manner that they fluoresce with characteristic colors for norepinephrine, dopamine, and serotonin. It was discovered that these substances appear in neurons that exist in particular nuclei and tracts that are relatively isolated from each other. (Figures 8.13 and 8.14, presented in connection with the neural systems involved in the control of eating, illustrate the separate distributions of norepinephrine and dopamine.) There exists a variety of ways to interfere with these transmitters: specific neural pathways may be electrolytically lesioned; certain drugs interfere with the synthesis of these transmitters; other drugs selectively destroy the terminals receiving the transmitters. These and other techniques have all been employed in attempts to see if specific transmitters are involved in the mediation of different sleep phenomena. Jouvet (1969) has developed a model which proposes that slow sleep is principally serotonin-dependent while REM sleep depends on the combined actions of serotonin, norepinephrine, and acetylcholine.

Jouvet's Model

Serotonin-containing neurons are found particularly in the pons (raphe nuclei system along the midline). Lesions destroying 80 to 90 percent of these neurons resulted in profound insomnia, according to both behavioral and EEG criteria, with slow sleep never occurring more than 10 percent of the time. REM sleep was never observed in these animals. The volume of the lesions correlated well with the percentage of sleep demonstrated, with greater amounts of sleep occurring in animals with smaller lesions. REM sleep seems dependent on the prior occurrence of a minimum amount of slow sleep; thus REM occurred only in those animals demonstrating slow sleep at least for 15 percent of the time. Biochemical analysis indicated that animals with raphe lesions show no brain changes in noradrenaline, only significant decreases in serotonin. Injections of 5-hydroxytryptophan, the immediate biochemical precursor of serotonin, resulted in the restoration of normal amounts of slow sleep in lesioned animals.

REM sleep is a more complicated process: Basically, the slow sleep, serotogenic raphe system acts on cholinergic mechanisms which then trigger a final, noradrenergic mechanism located in the *locus coeruleus* of the pons. This sequence of activities is supported by the fact that slow sleep appears to be a necessary precondition for REM sleep; that destruction of the locus coeruleus selectively suppresses REM sleep, leaving slow sleep undisturbed; and that a variety of drugs intefering with serotonin, acetylcholine, and norepinephrine all produce changes in REM sleep. This conception, along with some of the supporting evidence, is diagrammed in Figure 6.13.

There are some problems with this model, however. Thus, Dement et al. (1969) found that chronic treatment with p-chlorophenylaline, which blocks serotonin synthesis, produced only a transient insomnia; within a week, both slow sleep and REM sleep had returned to near baseline quantities. The EEG spikes in the pons, lateral geniculate, and cortex that normally accompany REM were now also present throughout the 24-hour recording period, regardless of the EEG state. Dement et al. speculated on the possible relationship of this disturbance of REM spiking to hallucinogenic activity in schizophrenia; we shall return to this question later (Chapter 14). In humans, p-chlorophenylalanine has been used in the treatment of malignant tumors. Wyatt et al. (1969) showed that such treatment selectively reduced REM sleep; slow sleep was undisturbed. Results such as these might be indicative of species differences in the transmitters controlling sleep; alternatively, they might be indicative of inadequacies in the model (some other examples of problems may be found in Williams, Holloway, & Griffiths, 1973).

Generally, however, the studies that form the basis for the biochemical model strongly complement the studies on the neural mechanisms of REM and slow sleep discussed in earlier sections. They again indicate that the neural structures involved are differentially located and functionally separable to some degree. They also suggest differences in the biochemical transmitters controlling different sleep phenomena.

FUNCTIONAL CHARACTERISTICS OF REM AND SLOW SLEEP

Why do we sleep—that is, what function is accomplished by sleep? As long as sleep appeared to be a single process, it seemed obvious and sufficient to answer that sleep serves some restorative function, though the nature

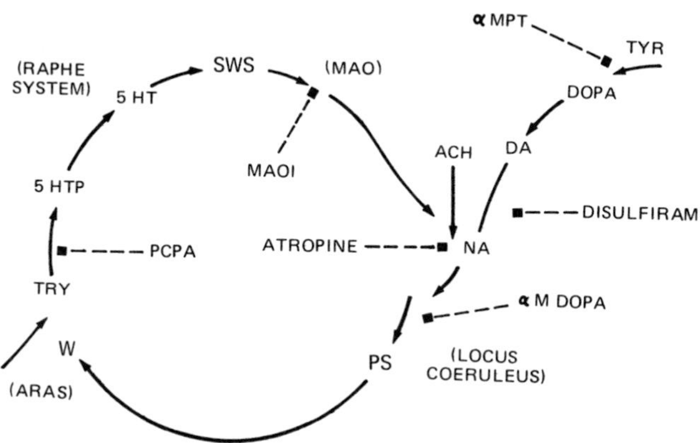

Figure 6.13. Schematic diagram representing possible monoaminergic mechanisms involved in the two states of sleep (in the cat). It is postulated that the mammallian brain undergoes cyclical biochemical changes from waking (W), which depends upon the ascending reticular activating system (ARAS), of which the neuromodulator is still unknown, to slow-wave sleep (SWS), which depends upon serotonin (5 HT)-containing neurons of the raphe system, and finally to paradoxical sleep (PS), which depends upon noradrenalin (NA)-containing neurons located in the nucleus locus coeruleus. In the normal adult cat, the first two steps of this cycle are reversible (W⇌SW⇌PS), whereas the final step from PS to W is never reversed. The actions of several drugs that may block certain steps of this cycle are represented. p-chlorophenylalanine (PCPA), which inhibits the enzyme tryptophan hydroxylase (TRY), decreases cerebral 5 HT by impairing its synthesis, and thereby leads to total insomnia, which is reversed by a secondary injection of 5 HTP, the immediate precursor of 5 HT. Monoamine oxidase inhibitors (MAOI), which prevent the catabolism of serotonin, lead to an increase in slow-wave sleep and to total suppression of paradoxical sleep. Thus, the action of a metabolite of 5 HT may possibly be involved in the triggering of paradoxical sleep mechanisms. Atropine, which suppresses the final steps of paradoxical sleep, and inhibition of muscle tonus may act upon a cholinergic mechanism that may be responsible for the triggering of noradrenergic mechanisms of paradoxical sleep. The latter mechanisms may be altered by numerous drugs, all of which may selectively suppress paradoxical sleep in the cat: α-methyl-p-tyrosine (α MPT), which impairs the synthesis of DOPA and NA at the level of tyrosine hydroxylase (TYR); disulfiram, which inhibits the action of the enzyme dopamine β-hydroxylase and thus prevents the synthesis of NA from DOPA; and, finally, α-methyldihydroxylalanine (α M DOPA), which may act as a false transmitter when it is converted to α-methylnoradrenalin. (From Jouvet, M., Biogenic amines and the state of sleep. *Science*, Jan. 1969, *163*, 32–41. Copyright 1969 by the American Association for the Advancement of Science.)

of what requires restoration and how it was restored remained unknown. With the discovery that sleep consists of an admixture of two separable processes—slow sleep and REM sleep—it became clear that the restorative assumption was merely a convenient label. The existence of two processes implies, at the very least, that they are functioning through different mechanisms or in different ways. As a consequence, studies began to investigate the functional differences between these two states. In the following pages, we shall examine some of the ways in which this research is currently being carried out and some of the speculations about its implications.

This problem has been attacked in a variety of ways and on different analytic levels. Some approaches stem from psychological theories about the function of different sleep states. Thus many of these studies employ deprivation techniques—selectively depriving subjects of one or another EEG-defined level of sleep—and the effects of such deprivation are sought in subsequent behavior. Other approaches emphasize the physiological mechanisms operating in different sleep conditions and attempt to manipulate them directly and then to assess subsequent behavioral changes. Much attention has been focused on REM sleep.

REM Sleep and Dreaming

Numerous studies have used the selective deprivation technique to examine the characteristics of both REM and slow sleep. This procedure was first used in a study by Dement (1960).

One characteristic of REM sleep that was obvious from the time of its discovery is its association with dreaming. (Although the association between REM sleep and dreaming is extremely strong, dreams do occur to some degree in slow sleep; the latter dreams, though, tend to be less vivid and have more poorly defined imagery than the dreams of REM sleep.)

Deprivation of REM Sleep

In Dement's study, subjects slept in the laboratory, with recording leads on for picking up EEG and eye movements. After an adaptation period, the subjects were awakened when the recordings showed REMs and desynchronized EEGs. Following several such nights of awakenings, the subjects were allowed to sleep undisturbed for several nights. Thus, the design was one of deprivation of REM sleep and dreaming, followed by a recovery period. Members of a control group were also awakened, as in the deprivation experiment, but only after the episode of REM sleep was complete. As with the REM-deprived group, the control group was also allowed several subsequent nights of uninterrupted sleep.

As REM deprivation increased, the number of awakenings the experimenter had to do because the onset of REM episodes increased; that is, with the deprivation of REM sleep, there seemed to be an increase in the subects' "attempts" at REM sleep. During the recovery period, the amount of time spent in REM sleep increased some 50 percent from the adaptation period. Thus, deprivation of REM sleep appeared to induce a need for REM sleep as manifested both by increasing attempts at REM sleep during deprivation and increased REM sleep during recovery. The control procedure of awakening the subjects after the completion of REM episodes indicated no significant effects—that is, the above results depended on awakening the subjects specifically during REM episodes.

Some interesting behavioral changes seemed to accompany the deprivation. With deprivation, the subjects became anxious, irritable, and had difficulty concentrating. One subject could not complete the study, and two subjects continued on the condition that the deprivation period was terminated. These psychological changes disappeared during recovery and were not present during the control awakenings (these psychological findings do need replication, however). These results were interpreted as indicating that a certain amount of dreaming is necessary each night. This conclusion is perhaps accurate, but it ignores the fact that some 20 percent of awakenings from REM sleep are not accompanied by dream reports. In other words, dreaming and REM sleep are partially confounded in the natural order of events. It therefore remains to be seen whether they can be adequately separated to determine if it is a need for dreams or a need for the physiological condition of REM sleep alone that was demonstrated.

Sleep Disturbances

Because of the association between dreaming and REM sleep, it is interesting to look at the sleep activity of individuals showing such sleep disturbances as somnambulism, enuresis (bed-wetting during sleep), and nightmares. It might be expected that such disturbances would occur predominantly or even exclusively during REM sleep; but Jacobson, Kales, Lehmann, and Zweizig (1965), in a study of EEG recordings from a group of somnambulists, found that episodes of sleep-walking occurred during slow-wave sleep. REM sleep occurred independently of these episodes and was not affected by them. Similarly, Broughton (1968) has summarized the data on enuresis and nightmares as well as somnambulism and finds that they are not associated with REM sleep. Rather, these sleep disorders occur during arousal from slow-wave sleep. Differences in autonomic measures between subjects experiencing these disorders and normal subjects are present throughout the sleep period but occur at a clinically overt level in slow-wave sleep. Such sleep disturbances cannot, therefore, be considered as REM sleep/dreem equivalents.

Excitation During REM Sleep

An essential characteristic of REM sleep that needs to be taken into account in any functional analysis of sleep mechanisms is that it is a time of considerable excitation within the brain. Numerous studies (see Roffwarg, Muzio, &

Dement, 1966, and Ephron & Carrington, 1966, for references) show, for instance, increases in spontaneous neural activity, elevation in blood flow, and facilitation of sensory transmission during REM sleep. In some cases, such activation exceeds that of the waking condition. As summarized by Roffwarg et al. (1966, p. 606), "During REM sleep, the brain appears to be 'in business for itself'." This "business" seems to be concerned with perception of and reaction to internally generated stimuli—the dream. What then is the functional significance of this activity?

Developmental Factors in REM Sleep

Roffwarg et al. (1966) have attacked the question of the functional significance of REM sleep from a developmental point of view. Because of its identification with dreaming, it was somewhat unexpected that greater amounts of REM sleep are found in infants than in adults. In addition, the patterning of sleep differs between infants and adults. As we have previously noted, REM sleep in adults is preceded by slow sleep; REM sleep seems to require prior slow sleep. In infants, however, there is an almost direct transition from wakefulness to REM sleep, and it is only after the initial REM episode that there is any protracted slow sleep. Figure 6.14 shows the differing amounts of REM and slow sleep exhibited by different age groups. It can be seen that, both absolutely and relatively, infants spend much more time in REM sleep than adults.

The role that sensory stimulation plays in the development of the organism has previously been noted (see Chapter 2); many studies indicate that structural development and functional capabilities are impaired in the absence of such stimulus input. Coupling these data with the apparent degree of brain excitation during REM sleep, Roffwarg et al. hypothesize that the function of REM sleep is to provide intense stimulation to the developing CNS during uterine development and postnatally, when stimulation from the environment is minimal. The subsequent diminution in REM sleep is postulated to indicate the lesser need that the mature brain has for such endogenously supplied stimulation. REM sleep is then seen as providing stimulus support for development of the CNS during its maximal growth period.

Cortical Homeostasis

Ephron and Carrington (1966) have attempted to construct a somewhat more general and more comprehensive theory of sleep than Roffwarg et al. They have proposed a concept of *cortical homeostasis* during sleep. We know the condition of slow sleep to be characterized by quiescence and loss of tonus and that of REM sleep to be characterized by excitation and heightened cortical tonus. The two conditions are thus seen as interacting to maintain a

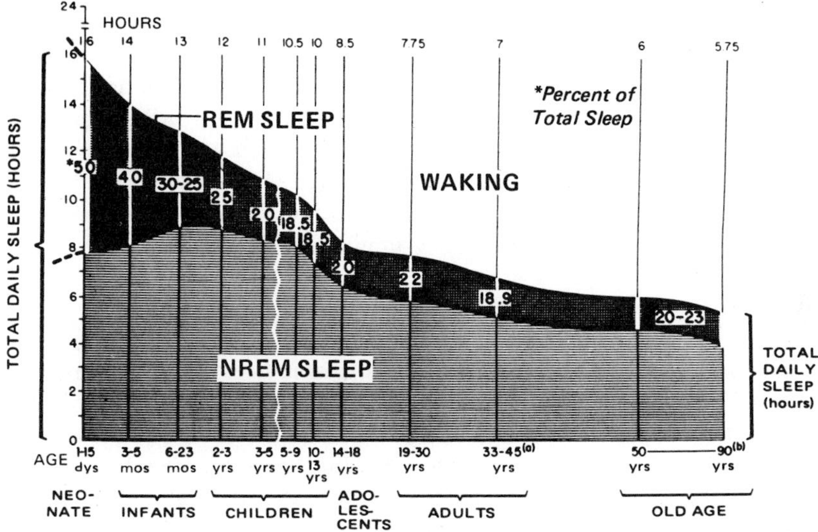

Figure 6.14. Graph showing changes (with age) in total amounts of daily sleep, daily REM sleep, and percentage of REM sleep. Note sharp dimunition of REM sleep in the early years. REM sleep falls from eight hours at birth to less than one hour in old age. The amount of slow sleep throughout life remains more constant, falling from eight hours to five hours. In contrast to the steep decline of REM sleep, the quantity of slow sleep is undiminished for many years. Although total daily REM sleep falls steadily during life, the percentage rises slightly in adolescence and early adulthood. This rise does not reflect an increase in amount; it is due to the fact that REM sleep does not diminish as quickly as total sleep. Work in several laboratories indicates that the percentage of REM sleep in the 50- to 85-year group may be somewhat higher than represented here. (From Roffwarg, H. P., Muzio, J. N., and Dement, W. C., Ontogenetic development of the human sleep-dream cycle. *Science,* April 1966, *152,* 604–619. Copyright 1966 by the American Association for the Advancement of Science.)

biologically appropriate state of cortical excitation. With the onset of sleep, there is a deepening of slow sleep and organismic rest, which, when it reaches a preset level, triggers the activation characteristic of REM sleep. REM sleep, as in the Roffwarg theory, serves as a source of endogenous excitation.

The major difference between these theories seems to be one of emphasis. Roffwarg et al. stress that REM sleep decreases during the course of development, but Ephron and Carrington note that REM sleep does, after all, continue to occur in the adult organism. The two approaches would seem to be complementary rather than in opposition.

Yet any conception of REM sleep that restricts it to the role of supplying endogenous stimulation to the brain seems to be incomplete. Studies of selective deprivation indicate that there is a physiological need for this activity, for which environmental stimulation cannot substitute. In fact, an experiment by Horne and Walmsley (1976) suggests that REM sleep is unaffected by prior visual stimulation. In this experiment, an attempt was made to "load" subjects with differential amounts of visual stimulation and to determine whether there were any effects on subsequent sleep. REM sleep was unaffected but slow sleep increased under the high load condition. REM sleep appears to be more than simply a source of stimulation. At the very least, REM sleep would seem to provide stimulation in conjunction with some other vital activity that occurs simultaneously.

Physiological Functions of REM Sleep

A large number of behavioral and physiological indices have been correlated with REM sleep in animals. Thus, for instance, depriving rats of REM sleep[4] lowers their thresholds for rewarding electrical stimulation of the brain and raises their response rates for such self-stimulation (see Chapter 11). Conversely, allowing rats to self-stimulate lowers the amount of REM during recovery following REM deprivation (Steiner & Ellman, 1972). REM deprivation lowers seizure thresholds in response to electroconvulsive shock (Cohen & Dement, 1965) and electroconvulsive seizures decrease REM sleep without a subsequent rebound or make-up effect (Cohen & Dement, 1966). REM sleep percentage also correlates with the learning of an avoidance task (Delacour & Brenot, 1975). The results of a large number of behavioral and pharmacological studies suggest that underlying these effects is a common dependence on catecholamine-containing neurons—neurons employing dopamine and norepinephrine. Stern and Morgane (1974) argue that one possible physiological function of REM sleep, then, is to maintain catecholamine functioning in the CNS: After REM deprivation the responsiveness of catecholamine systems is depressed; drugs which enhance catecholamine activity reverse these deficits. Conversely, it has also been found that agents which depress catecholamine availability increase REM, while catecholamine-enhancing agents decrease REM. Stern and Morgane also hypothesize that the function of REM in restoration of catecholamines may be indicative of its more general function in the modulation of protein synthesis in the brain.

In comparison to other hypotheses about REM sleep, Stern and Morgane's is attractive in its concentration on physiological mechanisms. By dealing with mechanisms, the generality of the hypothesis is likely to be

[4]If a rat is isolated on a small block set in water, it is possible for it to sleep and not get wet, so long as it does not relax its head and neck muscles. Under these conditions, rats display slow-wave sleep but not REM sleep.

greater and tests of the hypothesis would seem to be more direct and meaningful.

Slow Sleep and Total Sleep Deprivation

Agnew, Webb, and Williams (1964) carried out a study depriving subjects of stage 4, slow sleep. Rather than awakening the subjects, a tone was sounded that "moved" the subjects from stage 4 slow sleep into stages 1 to 3. During recovery from this deprivation, there was an increase in the proportion of time spent in stage 4 sleep. The deprivation produced no consistent change to another sleep stage nor was the time spent in REM sleep affected. Thus, although there appears to be a physiological "need" for stage 4 slow sleep as evidenced by the deprivation technique, Agnew et al. did not observe any consistent behavioral changes.

In another experiment, Webb and Agnew (1965) limited young male adults to only 3 hours of sleep a day for 8 consecutive days. EEG recordings during sleep revealed that the limited sleep periods were not simply a miniature of regular sleep periods; compared with either the full night's sleep or the first three hours of unrestricted sleep, sleep on the experimental nights showed a marked augmentation in the percent of time spent in stage 4 slow sleep. In absolute terms, almost as much time was spent in stage 4 sleep on experimental nights as occurred during unrestricted sleep. The increase in stage 4 sleep was largely at the expense of stage 3 sleep. During the recovery night, the early part of the sleep period was also dominated by stage 4 sleep, and it was not until stage 4 sleep had run its course that substantial amounts of REM sleep appeared.

This seems to support the previously mentioned idea that REM sleep is dependent on the prior occurrence of slow-wave sleep; that is, REM sleep is in some way triggered by slow sleep.

In a study of acute restriction of sleep, Webb and Agnew (1975) limited subjects to 2 or 4 hours of sleep on one night and studied the effects on the following night's sleep. Note that most sleep studies have generally limited the recovery period to 8 hours of sleep. In this study, the following night's sleep was unrestricted. Of interest is the fact that the first 8 hours of that sleep was not different in any significant way from baseline measures before the restricted night. However, the subjects subsequently slept longer and the increased sleep time was composed mainly of stage 2 and REM. Webb and Agnew raised two interesting questions: Why is it that the initial 8 hours of unrestricted sleep did not show the effects of the prior deprivation, and what happens to the sleep debt if subjects do not "sleep out" after restricted sleep regimes?

Generally, then, these studies point to the fact that there are "needs" for slow sleep as well as for REM sleep and that slow sleep does take precedence over REM sleep. What functions are served and the mechanisms operating in slow sleep deprivation effects are not clear, however.

SUMMARY

Research into the functions and mechanisms of sleep had a slow onset in the 1930s and 1940s but rapidly gained momentum ever since. Paralleling the pace of research, there has been an accompanying shift in our understanding of the mechanisms and our theories of sleep. Sleep used to be considered a simple state of quiescence, passively brought about. Now a picture has emerged of a complex state composed of at least two heterogeneous, active processes—slow sleep and REM sleep—existing in a dynamic state of delicate interaction.

It is clear that while quiescence and deafferentation of the brain may play a role in sleep, particularly in sleep onset, sleep is also characterized by periods of high excitability and activity. The mechanisms responsible for these processes appear to be discrete and localizable. Of particular importance are loci in the brainstem, especially the pons; however, more rostral forebrain mechanisms are also involved. Apparently, at least under extreme conditions, as in Villablanca's experiments, they are capable of independently controlling slow sleep and wakefulness. Nonetheless, there exist a number of gaps and inconsistencies in the information available.

The relationships between REM and slow sleep require further clarification and the functional "purpose" of the various sleep stages—particularly slow sleep—needs to be investigated. Similarly, the relationships between rostral and caudal neural structures, and their integration in producing the normal sleep pattern, needs to be clarified. Based on the productivity of recent years, future research into sleep mechanisms promises to be exciting.

REFERENCES

ADAMETZ, J. H. Rate of recovery of function in cats with rostral reticular lesions. *Journal of Neurosurgery*, 1959, *16*, 85–98.

AFFANNI, J., MARCHIAFAVA, P. L., & ZERNICKI, B. Higher nervous activity in cats with midpontine pretrigeminal transections. *Science*, 1962, *137*, 126–127.

AGNEW, H. W., JR., WEBB, W. B., & WILLIAMS, R. L. The effects of stage four sleep deprivation. *Electroencephalography and Clinical Neurophysiology*, 1964, *17*, 60–70.

AKERT, K. Diencephalon. In D. E. Sheer (ed.), *Electrical stimulation of the brain.* Austin, Texas: University of Texas Press, 1961, pp. 288–310.

ANDERSEN, P., & ANDERSSON, S. A. *Physiological basis of the alpha rhythm.* New York: Appleton-Century-Crofts, 1968.

BATINI, C., MORUZZI, G., PALESTINI, M., ROSSI, G. F., & ZANCHETTI, A. Effect of complete pontine transections on the sleep-wakefulness rhythm: The midpontine pretrigeminal preparation. *Archives Italiennes de Biologie,* 1959, *97,* 1–12.

BRADLEY, P. B., & ELKES, J. A. The effect of atropine, hyoscyamine, physostigmine and neostigmine on the electrical activity of the brain of the conscious cat. *Journal of Physiology,* 1953, *120,* 14–15.

BREMER, F. Cerveau isolé et physiologie du sommeil. *Compte Rendu de la Société de Biologie,* Paris, 1935, *118,* 1235–1241.

BREMER, F. The neurophysiological problem of sleep. In E. D. Adrian, F. Bremer, H. H. Jasper, & J. F. Delafresnaye (eds.), *Brain mechanisms and consciousness.* Oxford: Blackwell, 1954, pp. 137–162.

BROUGHTON, R. J. Sleep disorders: Disorders of arousal? *Science,* 1968, *159,* 1070–1078.

COHEN, H. B., & DEMENT, W. C. Sleep: Changes in threshold to electroconvulsive shock in rats after deprivation of paradoxical phase. *Science,* 1965, *150,* 1318–1319.

COHEN, H. E., & DEMENT, W. C. Sleep: Suppression of rapid eye movement phase in the cat after electroconvulsive shock. *Science,* 1966, *154,* 396–398.

DELACOUR, J., & BRENOT, J. Sleep patterns and avoidance conditioning in the rat. *Physiology and Behavior,* 1975, *14,* 329–335.

DEMENT, W. The effect of dream deprivation. *Science,* 1960, *131,* 1705–1707.

DEMENT, W. C. The occurrence of low voltage, fast electroencephalogram patterns during behavioral sleep in the cat. *Electroencephalography and Clinical Neurophysiology,* 1958, *10,* 291–296.

DEMENT, W. C., & KLEITMAN, N. Cyclical variations in EEG during sleep and their relation to eye movements, body mobility, and dreaming. *Electroencephalography and Clinical Neurophysiology,* 1957, *9,* 673–690. (a)

DEMENT, W. C. & KLEITMAN, N. The relation of eye movements during sleep to dream activity: An objective method for the study of dreaming. *Journal of Experimental Psychology,* 1957, *53,* 339–346. (b)

DEMENT, W., ZARCONE, V., FERGUSON, J., COHEN, H., PIVIK, T., & BARCHAS, J. Some parallel findings in schizophrenic patients and serotonin-depleted cats. In D. V. Siva Sanker (ed.), *Schizophrenia: Current concepts and research.* Hicksville, N. Y.: PJD Publications, 1969, pp. 775–811.

DEMPSEY, E. W., & MORISON, R. S. The production of rhythmically recurrent cortical potentials after localized thalamic stimulation. *American Journal of Physiology,* 1942, *135,* 293–300.

EPHRON, H. S., & CARRINGTON, P. Rapid eye movement sleep and cortical homeostasis. *Psychological Review,* 1966, *73,* 500–526.

GIBBS, F. A., & GIBBS, E. L. *Atlas of electroencephalography.* Cambridge, Mass.: Addison-Wesley, 1952.

HERNÁNDEZ-PEÓN, R., & CHAVEZ-IBARRA, G. Sleep induced by electrical or chemical stimulation of the forebrain. In R. Hernández-Peón (ed.), *The physiological basis of mental activity.* New York: American Elsevier, 1963, pp. 188–198.

HORNE, J. A., & WALMSLEY, B. Daytime visual load and the effects upon human sleep. *Psychophysiology,* 1976, *13,* 115–120.

JACOBSON, A., KALES, A., LEHMANN, D., & ZWEIZIG, J. R. Somnambulism: All night electroencephalographic studies. *Science,* 1965, *148,* 975–977.

JASPER, H. H. Thalamic reticular system. In D. E. Sheer (ed.), *Electrical stimulation of the brain.* Austin, Texas: University of Texas Press, 1961, pp. 277–287.

JOHNSON, L. C. Sleep and sleep loss: Their effects on performance. *Naval Research Reviews,* 1967, *20,* 16–22,.

JOUVET, M. Récherches sur les structures nerveuses et les mécanismes responsables des differentes phases du sommeil physiologique. *Archives Italiennes de Biologie,* 1962, *100,* 125–206.

JOUVET, M. Neurophysiology of the states of sleep. *Physiological Reviews,* 1967, *47,* 117–177.

JOUVET, M. Biogenic amines and the states of sleep. *Science,* 1969, *163,* 32–41.

KLEITMAN, N. *Sleep and wakefulness.* Chicago: University of Chicago Press, 1963.

LINDSLEY, D. B., SCHREINER, L. H., KNOWLES, W. B., & MAGOUN, H. W. Behavioral and EEG changes following chronic brainstem lesions in the cat. *Electroencephalography and Clinical Neurophysiology,* 1950, *2,* 483–498.

MCGINTY, D. J., & STERMAN, M. B. Sleep suppression after basal forebrain lesions in the cat. *Science,* 1968, *160,* 1253–1255.

MONNIER, M., & HÖSLI, L. Dialysis of sleep and waking factors in blood of the rabbit. *Science,* 1964, *146,* 796–798.

MORISON, R. S., & DEMPSEY, E. W. Mechanism of thalamocortical augmentation and repetition. *American Journal of Physiology,* 1943, *138,* 297–308.

MORRELL, F. Electrical signs of sensory coding. In G. C. Quarton, T. Melnechuk, & F. O. Schmitt (eds.), *The neurosciences, a study program.* New York: Rockefeller University Press, 1967, pp. 452–469.

MORUZZI, G., & MAGOUN, H. W. Brainstem reticular formation and activation of the EEG. *Electroencephalography and Clinical Neurophysiology,* 1949, *1,* 455–473.

NAUTA, W. J. H. Hypothalamic regulation of sleep in rats: An experimental study. *Journal of Neurophysiology,* 1946, *9,* 285–316.

O'LEARY, J. L., & COBEN, L. A. The reticular core—1957. *Physiological Reviews,* 1958, *38,* 243–276.

PENFIELD, W., & JASPER, H. H. *Epilepsy and the functional anatomy of the human brain.* Boston: Little, Brown, 1954.

PILLERI, G. The anatomy, physiology, and pathology of the brainstem reticular formation. In W. Birkmayer & G. Pilleri (eds.), *The brainstem reticular formation and its significance for autonomic and affective behavior.* Basle: Hoffman-La Roche, 1966, pp. 9–78.

RANSON, S. W. Somnolence caused by hypothalmic lesions in the monkey. *Archives of Neurology and Psychiatry,* 1939, *41,* 1–23.

ROFFWARG, H. P., MUZIO, J. N., & DEMENT, W. C. Ontogenetic development of the human sleep-dream cycle. *Science,* 1966, *152,* 604–619.

SCHLAG, J. D., CHAILLET, F., & HERZET, J. P. Thalamic reticular system and cortical arousal. *Science,* 1961, *134,* 1691–1692.

STEINER, S. S., & ELLMAN, S. J. Relation between REM sleep and intracranial self-stimulation. *Science,* 1972, *177,* 1122–1124.

STEINER, W. G., PSCHEIDT, G. R., HIMWICH, H. E. Influences of methodology on electroencephalographic sleep and arousal: Studies with reserpine and etryptamine in rabbits. *Science,* 1963, *141,* 53–55.

STERMAN, M. B., & CLEMENTE, C. D. Forebrain inhibitory mechanisms: Sleep patterns induced by basal forebrain stimulation in the cat. *Experimental Neurology,* 1962, *6,* 103–117.

STERN, W. C., & MORGANE, P. J. Theoretical view of REM sleep function: Maintenance of catecholamine systems in the central nervous system. *Behavioral Biology,* 1974, *11,* 1–32.

VEALE, W. L., & MYERS, R. D. Emotional behavior, arousal and sleep produced by sodium and calcium ions perfused within the hypothalamus of the cat. *Physiology and Behavior*, 1971, *7,* 601–607.

VILLABLANCA, J. Behavioral and polygraphic study of "sleep" and "wakefulness" in chronic decerebrate cats. *Electroencephalography and Clinical Neurophysiology*, 1966, *21*, 562–577.

Villablanca, J., & Marcus, R. Sleep-wakefulness, EEG and behavioral studies of chronic cats without neocortex and striatum: The 'diencephalic' cat. *Archives Italiennes de Biologie*, 1972, *110*, 348–382.

Villablanca, J., & Salinas-Zeballos, M. E. Sleep–wakefulness, EEG and behavioral studies of chronic cats without thalamus: The 'athalamic' cat. *Archives Italiennes de Biologie*, 1972, *110*, 383–411.

Webb, W. B., & Agnew, H. W., Jr. Sleep: Effects of a restricted regime. *Science*, 1965, *150*, 1745–1747.

Webb, W. B., & Agnew, H. W., Jr. The effects on subsequent sleep of an acute restriction of sleep length. *Psychophysiology*, 1975, *12*, 367–370.

Wikler, A. Pharmacological dissociation of behavior and EEG sleep patterns in dogs. *Proceedings of the Society for Experimental Biology and Medicine*, 1952, *79*, 261–265.

Williams, H. L., Holloway, F. A., & Griffiths, W. J. Physiological psychology: Sleep. *Annual Review of Psychology*, 1973, *24*, 279–316.

Wyatt, R. J., Engleman, K., Kupfer, D. J., Scott, J., Sjoerdsma, A., & Snyder, F. Effects of parachlorophenylalanine on sleep in man. *Electroencephalography and Clinical Neurophysiology*, 1969, *27*, 529–532.

7

Emotion

We all experience conditions that we label as emotional states. We can confidently distinguish times when we "feel" happy, sad, afraid, angry, and so on. We behave in ways that are considered appropriate to such feelings. There are also bodily signs that accompany these feelings and behaviors. Such signs are likely to include pronounced changes in sweating, trembling of the limbs, increases or decreases in heart rate, flushing or blanching of the skin, or changes in breathing. And, finally, we can identify, at least by example, the stimulus conditions that occasion these feelings and changes in bodily activity and overt behavior.

Given the relative ease with which these identifications are made by the layperson, the problem for the psychologist interested in studying emotions appears to be relatively simple: All that seems to be required is to tabulate which stimulus conditions, behaviors, bodily changes, and feelings converge to produce observable patterns. Unfortunately, no clear patterns have emerged from such analyses. That this is the case may not be so surprising if we consider that individuals may do different things when they are sad, for instance, or that two situations may require very different behaviors even though we are still feeling sad in each. Furthermore, we sometimes show mixed or inappropriate behaviors, as when we giggle despite the solemnity of the occasion. And finally, the bodily changes that accompany different emotional feelings have not been clearly differentiated. Nonetheless, our emotions are real—they have a major part in our everyday lives and may be of vast importance for our activities and even our continued healthy existence. How, then, to study the emotions?

The study of emotions and emotional behavior has historically provided one major context for pursuing the "mind–body problem." How do we account for psychological conditions such as "feelings" within a biological, physical organism? Several general approaches have emerged. Physiologically oriented theories attempt to relate specific patterns of either peripheral autonomic or central neural activity to various emotional states. Cognitively oriented theories recognize that a background of autonomic and central neural activity is present in all emotions but look to the learning history of the organism and the specific situation in which emotional arousal occurs in order to identify the specific emotion. Generally, cognitively oriented theories tend to emphasize central neural processes if they consider physiological processes at all, while some physiological theories have relied entirely on the concept of feelings as an accompaniment of certain patterns of peripheral activity. Based on the results to date, it has not been possible to produce a generally comprehensive theory for differentiating emotional states. As a result, many workers are taking a more modest approach to the problem. That is, they are looking at variables and parameters of variables as they operate in specific experimental contexts. By nibbling away at the edges of the total problem, it is hoped that eventually the total problem will disappear or turn out to be no problem at all (e.g., Mandler, 1975).

Our discussion will focus on two physiologically relevant considerations: the mechanisms operating in emotional states and physiologically related techniques for the control of emotions.

HISTORICAL APPROACHES TO EMOTION

Two theories that are historically prototypical of the physiological approach are the James-Lange and the Cannon-Bard theories. The James-Lange theory is a peripheral theory, the Cannon-Bard, a central one. The details of the factual accuracy of these formulations are not so important as are their respective orientations and the lines of research stemming from them.

The James-Lange Theory

Generally speaking, it is not difficult to recognize the occurrence of emotional behavior in others. When we see someone laugh or cry, we are quite confident that some emotion is represented. There sometimes may be doubt about the specific emotion (some people do cry with happiness), but gener-

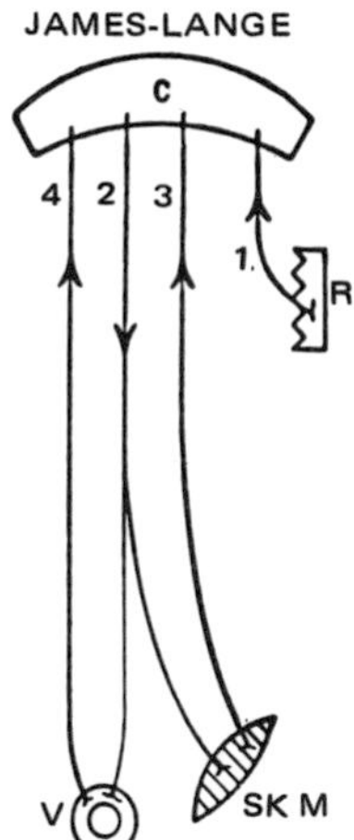

Figure 7.1. Diagram of the James-Lange theory of emotion. *R*, receptor; *C*, cerebral cortex; *V*, viscera; *Sk M*, skeletal muscle. The connecting lines represent nerve pathways; direction of impulses is indicated by arrows. (From Cannon, W. B., Again the James-Lange and the thalamic theories of emotion. *Psychological Review*, 1931, *31*, 281–295.)

ally our judgments are rather accurate. Thus, actors can perform successfully; the stuff of good acting seems to be the ability to appropriately and convincingly emulate the behavior of emotion.[1] The James-Lange theory of emotions implicitly recognizes the existence of such emotional behavior, but its concern is with the subjective experience, the feeling, of emotion.

The James-Lange theory attempts to account for emotional feelings on the basis of the activity of the peripheral autonomic and somatic response systems and their resulting sensory feedback. It is common to summarize the theory with an epigrammatic statement such as, "We do not run when we see the bear because we are afraid, but rather we see the bear and are afraid because we run." Such a statement is accurate as far as it goes, but it tends to overlook the major point, which is that there is no intervening cognition of emotion that precedes the physiological arousal—the arousal is the emotion. As James expressed it, "Bodily changes follow directly the perception of the exciting fact, and the feeling of the same changes as they occur IS the emotion" (James, 1890).

The James-Lange theory is characterized by the following major points: (1) It is a peripheral theory in that emotional experience is accounted for by activity of peripheral organs. (2) Both afferent and efferent connections between these peripheral organs and the cortex are seen as direct—there is no intervening mechanism. (3) It is a theory designed to account for emotional feeling or experience rather than emotional behavior.

Figure 7.1 is a diagrammatic representation of the theory.

[1]It is also of no little interest that actors report that the process of portraying emotional behavior induces *feeling* of the appropriate emotions. This would be predicted from the James-Lange theory.

Cannon's Objections to the James-Lange Theory

The Cannon-Bard theory is a central one, and it stands in opposition to the peripheral James-Lange position. Cannon's objections to the James-Lange formulation are listed under five separate headings (Cannon, 1929):

1. *Total separation of the viscera from the central nervous system does not impair emotional behavior.* Cannon quotes experiments of Sherrington in which high cervical transections of the spinal cord and vagus nerve in dogs were carried out, and experiments from his own lab in which the sympathetic division of the autonomic nervous system was sectioned in cats. (See Figure 1.12; the vagus is number X and has a distribution to most of the visceral organs.) In both sets of animals, all the behavioral signs of emotion possible to such animals could be elicited. That is, hissing, growling, retraction of the ears, baring of the teeth, and striking with the paw were all shown by the sympathectomized cats. While neither of these experiments completely removed all peripheral somatic and autonomic connections pertinent to the James-Lange formulation, it was expected that at least some emotional deficit would result from these procedures. That this was not the case was taken by Cannon to be evidence against the James-Lange theory.

It has been argued, however, that James' claim was that *experience* of emotional feeling rather than the ability to *express* emotion depended on these peripheral factors. Hebb (1949) contends that the Sherrington and Cannon arguments are irrelevant to the point made by the James-Lange theory and "would not be possible if there were not the immutable idea that *only* emotional awareness or feeling can produce emotional response. If the response is there, the feeling must be also. Such illogic, assuming James to be wrong first, in order to prove him wrong, is the clearest evidence of the hold traditional ideas have on psychological thought" (Hebb, 1949, p. 237).

Introspective reports from human clinical cases have also been cited as refutations of the James-Lange theory. But the fact that human quadriplegics with cervical sections have reported distinct and unchanged emotional feelings is not conclusive evidence, because such persons have had a long prior history of normal emotional mechanisms and appropriate conditioning of emotions. Animal experiments indicate that the absence of an intact sympathetic nervous system is detrimental to the *acquisition* of conditioned avoidance responses, but the continued performance of such response is possible if the surgical intervention follows acquisition (Wynne & Solomon, 1955). In any case, Hohmann (1966) reports there indeed are decreases in felt emotion after spinal cord injury in humans.

2. *The same visceral changes occur in very different emotional states and in nonemotional states.* Here Cannon argues that autonomic activation is

diffuse and general: "The responses in the viscera seem too uniform to offer a satisfactory means of distinguishing emotions which are very different in subjective quality. Furthermore, if the emotions were due to afferent impulses from the viscera, we should expect not only that fear and rage would feel alike but that chilliness, hypoglycemia, asphyxia, and fever should feel like them. Such is not the case" (Cannon, 1929).

This objection prejudges the issue. It is an empirical question which requires investigation to determine whether there are autonomic response differences in different emotional states, particularly differences in the patterning of such responses.

3. *The viscera are relatively insensitive structures.* Cannon points out that the visceral organs are poorly supplied with sensory nerves and that we are not aware of a great deal of normal activity. Again, the argument would not appear particularly damaging. The fact remains that we are aware of heart, blood circulation, temperature, and stomach sensations. Minimal as these are, they may be enough.

4. *Visceral changes are too slow to be a source of emotional feeling.* In essence, this criticism says that the latency of autonomic arousal is terribly long by comparison with somatic responses, and to this must be added the transmission time to and from the cortex. Hence, visceral changes could not occur soon enough to be responsible for affective changes. We all can probably cite incidents when we became afraid only after the danger was over; so this criticism would not appear to be damaging to the James-Lange theory. Also, since it would involve measuring the timing of introspective reports, verification of this point would seem to be an impossible task.

5. *Artificial induction of the visceral changes typical of strong emotions does not produce them.* Adrenergic substances apparently act as transmitters in the sympathetic nervous system. They also circulate freely in the bloodstream and are capable of direct excitation of certain smooth muscles. Injections of epinephrine would, therefore, be expected to mimic sympathetic arousal and, Cannon argues, result in emotional responses if the James-Lange theory were correct. He states that experimental injections of epinephrine produce the expected somatic sensations but only "an indefinite affective state coldly appreciated, and without real emotion." If there are any emotionally related feelings, they are expressed as, "I feel as if afraid," "as if they are about to do something to me," "as if I were going to weep without knowing why." Cannon did not regard such statements as representing true emotions. The validity of his criticism depends on the extent to which the response to epinephrine is comparable to the total response of the autonomic system in genuine emotion—and on whether one accepts Cannon's criteria of "true" emotions. If one doesn't, these results would be considered partial support for James' position!

Generally, then, it appears to be fair to conclude that Cannon's arguments did not really effectively discredit the James-Lange peripheral theory of emotion.

The Cannon-Bard Theory

Cannon went on to propose a centrally oriented theory, which was elaborated by Bard. This theory served as a starting point for later central formulations.

Cannon attributed emotional *experience* to thalamic functioning, and emotional *behavior* to hypothalamic functioning. Figure 7.2 diagrams the theory more completely. Normally, the thalamus is under the inhibitory control of the cortex (path 3). Generally, incoming stimuli pass through the thalamus without releasing this inhibition. If, however, the stimuli evoke conditioned responses of an appropriate nature in the cortex, the inhibition is released and results in hypothalamic discharge through paths 2 and 4. Other stimuli, such as those giving rise to startle responses or having properties for innately arousing emotional responses, may directly override the inhibition of the thalamus; in these cases; the thalamus discharges directly through paths 2 and 4. Note that it is the feedback to the cortex from the thalamus, along path 4, which produces the conscious experience of emotion and the caudal discharge of path 2 that produces the emotional behavior.

The details of this theory are perhaps only of pedagogic or historical interest. As we shall see, the contribution of the thalamus to emotion is not clear and is, most certainly, not exclusive. Nevertheless, this theory does serve as a model of those approaches that stress the interrelationship between cortex and subcortical emotional centers, and is a recurrent concept.

Relations to Present Research

Neither the James-Lange nor the Cannon-Bard theory is acceptable in unmodified form today. However, their respective orientations still are represented and they do serve to illustrate the general nature of the problems involved in attempting to explain emotions. One general line of research today is still concentrated on peripheral autonomic and skeletal correlates of emotion. A related question revolves around the possibility of distinguishing between different emotions on the basis of patterns of physiological arousal. This line of research is generally heir to the James-Lange concern with emotional experience. For the most part, such research has been carried out with human subjects. Another general line of research follows the Cannon-Bard model in its concern with CNS correlates of emotional behavior. For the most part, animals are the primary subjects. Recent research results seem to suggest that two things are happening: That emotional behavior and

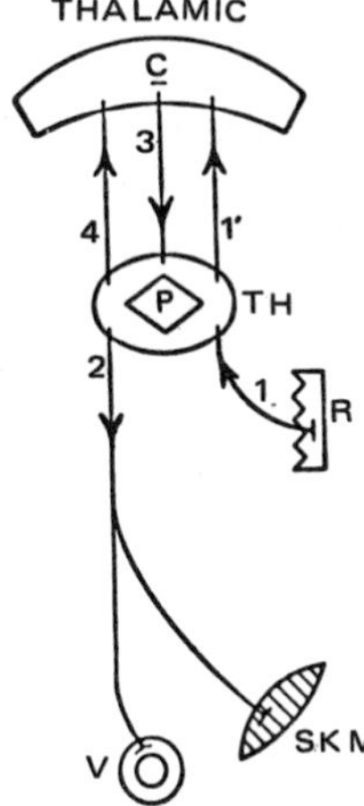

Figure 7.2. Diagram of Cannon's thalamic theory of emotion. *R*, receptor; *C*, cerebral cortex; *V*, viscera; *Sk M*, skeletal muscle; *Th*, thalamus; *P*, pattern. The connecting lines represent nerve pathways; the directions of impulses are indicated by arrows. Corticothalamic pathways 3 is inhibitory in function. (From Cannon, W. B., Again the James-Lange and the thalamic theories of emotion. *Psychological Review*, 1931, *31*, 281–295.)

emotional feeling can be independent is becoming clearer; at the same time, the nature of their obvious interaction is also being demonstrated for a wide variety of specific experimental circumstances.

PERIPHERAL MECHANISMS OF EMOTION

One major concern in our discussion of the peripheral mechanisms of emotion will be differentiating the various emotional states. A related task involves specifying procedures designed to gain control over peripheral mechanisms. Thus, our concentration will be on the autonomic and endocrine influences in emotion. The basic organization of these systems has been outlined in Chapter 1.

Stimulus Considerations

In order to show a physiological differentiation between emotions, one is seemingly required to elicit separate, pure emotions for study. "Any given stressful stimulus has a great likelihood of producing a variety of affective patterns within a subject group and mixtures of affective states within individuals. Not only can one not assume that a correctly chosen stimulus will produce a pure affect state but the evidence points to the contrary. . . . it may well be the crucial factor which makes it difficult for us to uncover specific response patterns" (Oken, 1967, p. 46). But this has not stopped researchers from trying!

In regard to stimulus conditions, the realism of laboratory situations must also be considered. It is at least open to question whether showing a film of gory automobile accidents elicits the same emotions, or the comparable degree of emotional arousal, as would actual involvement in such an accident. Investigators also must contend with the probable recognition on the part of their subjects that there are limits beyond which experiments in the lab will not go; implicitly, subjects are confident that they will not be harmed. Recognition of this fact has led some experimenters to elaborate devices that simulate the occurrence of accidents in the lab; actual data collection occurs during the "accident," while the ostensible experiment serves as the control period. Alternatively, it is sometimes possible to collect relevant data under naturally encountered conditions. For instance, astronauts have transmitted data about bodily activity during flight.[2]

Recent Theoretical Approaches

The Emergency Theory of Emotions

From our earlier discussion it might be assumed that Cannon's theoretical position resulted in his complete disregard of peripheral events in emotion. On the contrary, he did indicate a role for peripheral events which has modern counterparts. While changes in such peripheral systems were not considered necessary for the feeling or expression of emotions, and particular responses were not conceived to be related to particular emotional states, Cannon suggested a general role for peripheral events. His *emergency theory* suggests that this role is to prepare the body for the energy expenditure necessary in the various emotional states. Without detailing the particulars (some of Cannon's ideas are incorrect), Cannon proposed that adrenal epinephrine and the sympathetic nervous system cooperate to produce a condition of preparedness for either "fight or flight." Thus, there are such changes as redistribution of the blood from the viscera to the brain and muscles, increased availability of energy supplies for consumption by the muscles, and respiratory changes. Generally, there is a diffuse mobilization of the body to meet emergency.

Psychosomatic and Stress Reactions

Some aspects of psychosomatic medicine can be considered logical extensions of Cannon's position. It has long been recognized that the existence of strong and prolonged emotional states may lead to alteration in normal bodily functioning. A variety of disorders are known to be correlated with such emotional states. While the exact relationship to psychological factors is in

[2]It is of interest to note that the issues sketched here come up even in highly realistic situations. Thus, the question can be raised whether a rocket flight was, indeed, stressful for a Mercury astronaut! (Ruff & Korchin, 1967, discussion).

most instances a matter of conjecture, there is general acceptance that disorders such as ulcers, asthma, high blood pressure, and migraine headaches are, at least, exacerbated by emotional arousal. However, it has also been claimed that certain emotional states are specifically related to certain symptoms. Thus, Alexander (1950, p. 74) states, "For example, chronically sustained hostile impulses can be correlated with a chronic elevation of the blood pressure while dependent help-seeking trends go with increased gastric secretion."

While the above reactions are specific, the concept of undifferentiated stress has also received considerable attention, primarily as a result of the work of Selye (1950). Bodily changes similar to those occurring in emotion also occur in conditions of overwork, heat and cold exposure, tubercle bacilli, and X-ray exposure. In short, there is a stereotyped, nonspecific response which Selye characterized as the *stress response*, or "general adaptation syndrome." This syndrome is comprised of three stages: The first, or *alarm*, reaction consists of those bodily reactions normally associated with emotion. This stage is characterized by sympathetic arousal, epinephrine discharge, and the associated changes in heart rate, blood, and muscle tone. In the second, or *resistance*, stage the initial surge of emergency reaction is passed, and the organism makes a more enduring and maximal adaptation to the stressor. If the stressor continues or the adaptation in the second stage proves ineffective, a third, or *exhaustion*, stage is reached in which adaptation breaks down. Generally, the major impact of stressors is exerted on the pituitary-adrenal system. Secretion of adrenal cortical hormones is stimulated by adrenocorticotrophic hormone (ACTH) released by the anterior pituitary. Stress results in abnormal amounts of adrenal secretion, and animal experiments show that the adrenals are enlarged. Variation in adrenal output in the three stages of the adaptation syndrome (excess secretion in resistance and deficient secretion in exhaustion) have differential consequences. Thus cardiac and hypertensive disorders are exacerbated by excess adrenal output, and arthritic and rheumatic disorders are aggravated by decreased output.

The point to be made here is that the concept of stress emphasizes the common, *non*specific aspects of a large number of heterogeneous stimulus conditions. But as Oken notes, "Even if many affects are associated with the common features of a general stress response, the question remains as to what additional differences exist between affect states" (1967, p. 46).

A recent review by Stein, Schiavi, and Camerino (1976) reinforces the role that stress plays in disrupting general health. These workers have documented how psychosocial factors, such as crowded housing conditions and stress treatments, may either increase or decrease the susceptibility of animals to some infections, to some neoplastic processes (tumors and cancers), and to some immunity reactions. Their review of the mechanisms involved implicates the hypothalamus, autonomic nervous system, and neuroendocrine activity.

Activation Theory

The reticular system of the brainstem must be considered in connection with emotion, too. EEG and behavioral arousal parallel the changes we have been calling "emotional"; conversely, with waking, arousal, orienting responses, and so on, there are parallel sympathetic responses. There is a theory that these various EEG, skeletal motor, and autonomic changes are all indices of the more general property of "activation." A continuum is seen to exist from coma and sleep at the low end of the scale, through waking and attentive behavior, to extreme emotional arousal at the upper end. This continuum

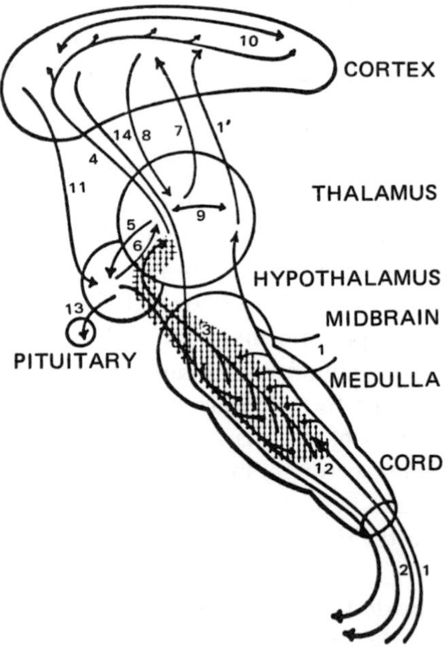

Figure 7.3. Schematic representation of principal CNS relations in emotion according to activation theory: 1—somatic and cranial afferents; 1′—direct thalamocortical projections; 2—visceral afferent pathways; 3—centripetal projections of reticular formation; 4—diffuse thalamocortical projections; 5 and 6—interconnections of hypothalamus and thalamus; 7 and 8—interconnections between thalamus and cortex; 9—intrathalamic connections; 10—intracortical connections; 11—corticohypothalamic pathways; 12—visceral efferent pathways; 13—hypothalamohypophyseal tract; 14—corticospinal pathways. The cross-hatched area represents the reticular formation. [From Lindsley, D. B., Emotion. In S. S. Stevens (Ed.), *Handbook of Experimental Psychology*. N.Y.: John Wiley, 1951. Copyright © 1951, John Wiley & Sons. Reprinted by permission of John Wiley & Sons, Inc.]

reflects the degree to which the organism is *activated,* or mobilized, for activity. Activation theory, then, attempts to encompass the problem of emotion within a broader, general context (see Lindsley, 1951). However, the specificity of the emotion seems to lose its intrinsic interest in such a theory.

It might appear paradoxical to consider EEG changes and reticular activity along with *peripheral* mechanisms of emotion. The basic justification for this is that activation theorists have employed the EEG in the same way that they have employed peripheral measures. They consider EEG changes as merely another, equivalent, indicator. In other words, the EEG is employed as though it were a peripheral measure. Also, activation theory is based on the convergence of visceral, somatic, and sensory afferent impulses in the reticular system. Thus, while workers who emphasize CNS mechanisms in emotion implicitly recognize the links between the brain areas under consideration and the peripheral mechanisms, activation theorists make this a cornerstone of their approach.

Basically, activation theory rests on the following main assumptions (Lindsley, 1951): (1) In emotion, the EEG shows the characteristic arousal response, i.e., low voltage, fast activity. (2) The arousal reaction can be elicited from stimulation of the reticular system of the brainstem and diencephalon. (3) Destruction of these areas abolishes the arousal reaction. (4) After such destruction, the behavioral picture is incompatible with emotional excitement or arousal; that is, apathy, somnolence, and catalepsy prevail. (5) Motor mechanisms of emotional expression either are identical with or overlap those of the EEG-activating mechanism. Figure 7.3 diagrams these essential relations of activation theory.

These, then, constitute the major theoretical points about peripheral mechanisms in emotion. The following sections will discuss the empirical findings bearing on the issues raised.

Attempts to Differentiate Emotions

Despite the volume of research on autonomic responses, there are actually relatively few studies directly devoted to the question of distinguishing, physiologically, between different emotions. Perhaps the most widely known study in this area is that of Ax (1953), in which he attempted to differentiate between fear and anger. Ax used each subject as his own control, thus eliminating differences among subjects in such factors as general emotionality.

Fear Versus Anger

Ax's study employed simulated situations. Paid volunteers were recruited ostensibly for a study of differences between people with and without hypertension; the subjects were to relax and listen to music while autonomic recordings were made. The fear stimulus was an unannounced, gradually increasing shock to the little finger. When the subject reported the shock, the experimenter expressed surprise, checked the apparatus, set off sparks near the subject, and reported a dangerous short-circuit. After muddling about for some time in confusion, the experimenter reported fixing the apparatus. The anger-provoking situation was generated by an arrogant, incompetent, surly technician who generally abused the subject for a period of time. The order of the two situations was counterbalanced across subjects. Remarks of the subjects during these situations and subsequent interviews were taken as indicating that the appropriate affects were indeed elicited.

Fourteen autonomic measures were taken. Seven showed significant differences between the fear and anger conditions: Anger was characterized by a rise in diastolic blood pressure, an increase in both the number of galvanic skin responses and in muscle tension, and a drop in the heart rate. Fear, on the other hand, was accompanied by increases in skin conductance, in the number of muscle tension peaks, and in respiration rate. In essence, then, these results indicate that different profiles of physiological response are elicited by situations leading to anger as against fear. Ax related these results to the effects produced by injections of epinephrine and norepinephrine. Thus the response pattern in anger is comparable to the physiological changes produced by combined injections of epinephrine and norepinephrine, while the changes in fear are similar to those produced by injections of epinephrine alone.

Ax also reported the correlations between the various autonomic measures that were recorded in this study. *Within* either stimulus condition—that is, the anger or fear situations—the correlations between the various measures were uniformly low, averaging .09 for fear and .16 for anger. In contrast, the correlations for each variable *between* the two conditions averaged .53. In other words, a given autonomic measure correlated better with itself across conditions than it did with other autonomic variables within the same condition. The implications of this type of finding will be discussed later.

Sadness Versus Mirth

In contrast to the above approach, where each subject was his own control, some experiments use the less satisfactory independent groups design. An attempt to differentiate between sadness and mirth used the latter plan (Averill, 1969). In this study, autonomic responses were recorded from three groups of subjects while they watched different films, one sad, one comic, and one control. The sad film was concerned with the assassination of President Kennedy; the comic film was an adaptation of a Mack Sennett comedy;

and the control film described a trip by two amateur ichthyologists. Prestimulus physiological levels were assessed in all groups during the showing of a short documentary film.

When compared with the control group, both the sadness and mirth groups showed increased sympathetic activation. Electrodermal responses (GSR and skin conductance) were prominent in both groups; but the sadness group was distinguished by cardiovascular changes, while the mirth group showed respiratory changes. As Averill himself noted, however, it is possible that the same emotion—sadness, for instance—evoked by two different stimulus conditions might also lead to differences as large as those seen in this study between mirth and sadness. Additionally, the correlations between the physiological measures taken and psychological indices of emotion, also taken during the experiment, were uniformly small.

Anxiety Versus Normalcy

Very common in the literature, though least satisfactory for answering the type of question that we are considering here, is the experimental design that compares some group with a control—for instance, an anxious group with a normal control group. Presumably, differences between such groups tell us something about the manifestations of anxiety. On the other hand, there are no assurances that the differences are indeed *specific* to anxiety; there may well be other differences between such groups that are uncontrolled. Generally, subjects (typically patients) who are more anxious are found to show greater sympathetic activity.

A variant on this type of study is the report of autonomic responses in a pair of identical schizophrenic twins (Levene, Engel, & Schulkin, 1967). The report is of interest since numerous studies indicate that autonomically mediated reponses of identical twins are highly similar. These particular twins, though both schizophrenic, showed marked behavioral differences. Clinically, one of the brothers was more blatantly psychotic and disorganized; he displayed more anxiety and seemed more concerned with his psychological difficulties. The other brother appeared passive, noncommunicative, and constricted, with little display of affect. In brief, the resting autonomic activity of the first brother was in keeping with the behavioral differences between them; he displayed higher systolic blood pressure, faster breathing rate, higher skin conductance, higher heart rate, and lower face and finger temperature, all of which generally indicate higher sympathetic activation. In response to the stress of listening to tape recordings of interviews between their family and their psychiatrist about themselves, the first twin was also more reactive, though both showed increased responses in comparison to changes produced by control tapes. Primarily, the difference between the twins was one of the *pattern* of reaction, the first twin responding with skin conductance changes and the second twin with vascular responses.

The above studies, while not exhaustive, constitute examples of the most direct evidence that can be brought to bear on the question of differentiating between emotions on the basis of peripheral, autonomic measures. The evidence is certainly not overwhelming. There is, however, the suggestion that the basic notion of differentiating emotions on the basis of *patterns* of autonomic activity is worthy of further investigation. It is indeed strange how few specific tests of this proposition have actually been made. This attests to the pervasive influence of considerations leading to alternate research questions and experimental designs. Some of these considerations will be examined below.

Autonomic Response Specificity

It was previously noted that although Ax found it possible to differentiate between fear and anger on the basis of the patterns of autonomic response recorded, he found only low, nonsignificant correlations between his various autonomic measures *within* each emotional situation; between conditions, the correlations were much higher. This is by far the common finding. On the basis of Cannon's emergency theory or on the basis of activation concepts, one would expect to find that both types of correlations would be uniformly high, if the autonomic nervous system responds as a whole. That the correlations are low within specific conditions is an indication that argues against these conceptions.

Lacey and his colleagues (see Lacey, 1950; Lacey, Bateman, & VanLehn, 1953; Lacey, 1967) have devoted considerable experimental effort to clarifying this situation. Lacey's hypothesis of "autonomic response specificity" derives from the following considerations; "The autonomic nervous system does indeed respond to experimentally imposed stress 'as a whole' in the sense that all autonomically innervated structures seem to be activated, usually in the direction of apparent sympathetic predominance. But it does not respond 'as a whole' in the sense that all autonomically innervated structures exhibit equal increments or decrements of function. Striking intra-individual differences in the degree of activation of different physiological functions are found when the different reactions are expressed in equivalent units" (Lacey et al., 1953, p. 8).

Basically, then, the notion of autonomic response specificity says that individuals may be differentiated on the basis of consistent, individual patterns of reaction to stressors. The evidence for this will be discussed below. Note, however, that while critical of activation theory and theories emphasizing general responses of the autonomic system, Lacey stays within those traditions in his choice of stressors for his test situations. But it is at

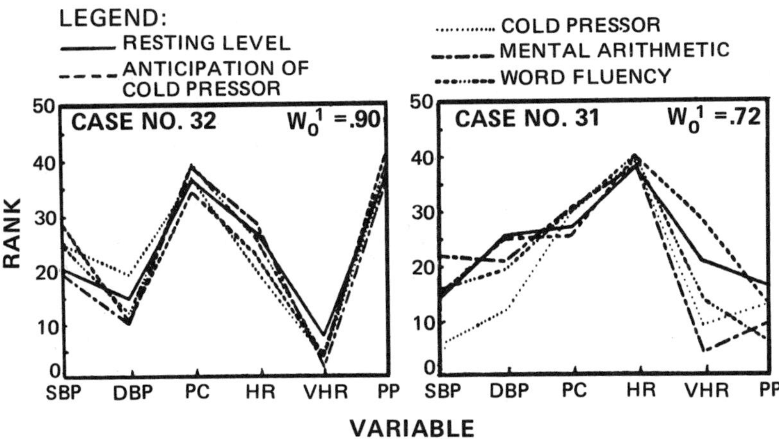

Figure 7.4. Two examples of idiosyncratic response-patterns (autonomic tension scores) reproduced over five occasions of measurement. Physiological variables (see footnote 3) are on the abscissae. The ordinates are ranks, showing the relative position of the S in the total group of 42 Ss. High ranks are given to high physiological levels of function. W_0^1 is the coefficient of pattern-concordance, corrected for continuity. (From Lacey, J. I. and Lacey, B. C., Verification and extension of the principle of autonomic response-stereotype. *The American Journal of Psychology*, 1958, *71*, 50–73. Copyright University of Illinois Press.)

least open to question whether the types of stress situations that are employed in these experiments are functionally equivalent to stituations which produce what both the layman and the clinical psychologist label with terms like "fear," "sadness," and "frustration."

Lacey's first experiments (see Lacey, 1950) were designed to show that (1) in response to a *given* stress situation, individuals do not show concordant changes in all autonomic measures, and (2) there are wide individual differences in the patterns of change that are obtained. Later experiments (Lacey et al., 1953; Lacey & Lacey, 1958) were designed to show that (3) in *different* stress situations, individuals showed common response patterns. Finally, it was shown (Lacey & Lacey, 1962) that (4) these patterns of response to stress are reliable for individuals across long time periods.

Figure 7.4 (Lacey & Lacey, 1958) is illustrative of the first three of these points. In this experiment, the subjects were exposed to four stresses: a word fluency test in which the subject was required to say aloud all the words she could think of beginning with the letter *W*; a mental arithmetic test in which the subject was required to multiply a two-digit number by a one-digit number and then add a one-digit number to the product; the cold pressor test; and the anticipation of the latter. (The cold pressor test requires the subject to immerse one foot in an ice-water bath and keep it there for a specified time period; it is a painful procedure.)

In response to any one of the stressors, for example, the cold pressor or the arithmetic test, individual subjects showed different degrees of arousal on the several autonomic measures taken.[3]

Thus, as illustrated, subject 32 ranked high for response on *PC* but was quite low in *VHR*, while placing around the middle of the distribution for *SBP*. That there are wide individual differences in patterns is illustrated by comparison of the profiles obtained from different subjects in response to any one stressor; in contrast to subject 32, subject 31 showed her highest relative scores on *HR* rather than *PC* and was relatively more responsive on *DBP* and less on *SBP*. Across stressors for a given subject, there is a decided similarity of response patterns; similar patterns were elicited regardless of the stressor employed.

Figure 7.5 is illustrative of the final point: Shown here are the responses to cold pressor tests administered four years apart. These response patterns tend to be stable for each individual over time.

In summary, then, Lacey has demonstrated that individuals reliably show differential autonomic responses to stress. In any response system, one may be markedly reactive, while in other systems he may be only average in response or less than average. The pattern of response that a given subject shows tends to be reproducible across stressors which seem to vary widely in psychological impact and in physiological demands placed on the organism. It is because of the relative *invariance* of the response pattern that Lacey tends to ignore the nature of the immediate affective response that a stressor has for the individual. While this response specificity cannot be denied, it is only appropriate to point out that Lacey has not actually attempted to test the effect of differences in affective response.

We have already (Chapter 5) had occasion to mention Lacey's proposals relating to autonomic responses and attentional mechanisms. That work follows from the contradictions between autonomic response specificity and activation theory. On the other hand, it also is related to work dealing with the ability of subjects to cope with stress, which we shall review in a later section. But first we shall prepare for that review by addressing the role of cognitive influences on emotion.

Cognitive Approaches to Emotions

As indicated earlier, cognitively oriented theorists suggest that homogeneous autonomic response patterns can be associated with differential emotions—the individual's learning experiences and evaluation of the stimulus situation provide the basis for associating different affective states

[3]Systolic blood pressure, *SBP*; diastolic blood pressure, *DBP*; palmar skin conductance, *PC*; heart rate, *HR*; heart rate variability, *VHR*; pulse pressure, *PP*.

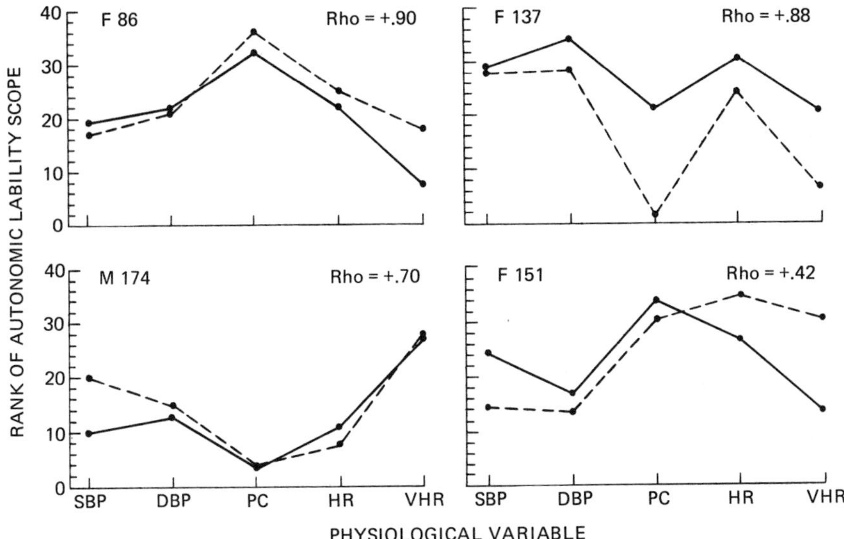

Figure 7.5. Four examples of profiles of autonomic response for individuals showing highly reproducible patterns over a four-year period. Physiological variables (see footnote 3) are shown on the abscissae, the relative standing of the individual in the group on the ordinates. The *solid line* represents the profile obtained by averaging the responses to two administrations of the cold pressor test in year 1; the *dashed line* was obtained by averaging the two responses in year 4. (From Lacey, J. I. and Lacey, B. C., The law of initial value in the longitudinal study of autonomic constitution: Reproducibility of autonomic responses and response patterns over a four-year interval. *Annals of the New York Academy of Sciences*, 1962, 98, 1257–1290.)

with those homogeneous autonomic changes. This approach is most strongly represented in an experiment reported by Schacter and Singer (1962).

The point of departure for Schacter and Singer is the relative failure of physiologically oriented theories of emotion to differentiate among specific emotional states. From this base, three propositions were developed: (1) Given a state of physiological arousal for which the individual has no immediate explanation, he will use the cognitions available to him in order to "label" this state of arousal. Thus, the same arousal state will receive different labels depending on the cognitions available. (2) Given a physiological arousal state for which the individual has an appropriate explanation (for example, "I feel this way because I have just been given an injection of a drug"), there will be no additional need for the individual to evaluate the aroused state. He will, therefore, be unlikely to label his feelings in terms of any alternatives supplied from the environment. (3) Given the appropriate cognitive circumstances, the individual will label his feelings as emotional only to the extent that he experiences a state of physiological arousal. Thus, if drugs or surgical intervention prevent the arousal, the cognitive circumstances would not be interpreted as emotional. These propositions were tested in the following experiment.

Subjects were asked to participate in an experiment ostensibly to evaluate the effects of a vitamin supplement on visual function. In reality, the injections they received were either epinephrine or a placebo. The injections, then, were designed to manipulate arousal of the sympathetic nervous system. Manipulation of the availability of an appropriate explanation for the subjective responses to epinephrine was achieved by the information given the subject: The *epinephrine-informed* group was told by the physician giving the injection that they would feel some side effects, including hand tremors, face-flushing, and pounding of the heart. The *epinephrine-ignorant* group was told that there would be no side effects of the injection. The *epinephrine-misinformed* group was told that the injection would make their feet feel numb, produce an itching sensation over parts of the body, and cause a slight headache. The placebo group was given the same information as the *epinephrine-ignorant* group. Generally, then, these instructions were designed to provide an explanation for the subjective responses to epinephrine that was more or less appropriate.

Cognitive factors were varied by manipulating the social conditions in which the subjects experienced their subjective responses to the injections. The attempt was to induce a state of euphoria or of anger. In one condition, subjects were placed within a situation with a stooge who was trained to act euphorically; in the other condition, the stooge was trained to act angrily. The stooges were ostensibly other subjects who were also waiting for the "vitamin" injections to take effect. A standard routine by the stooges was employed in each of the social situations. In the euphoria condition, the stooge played basketball with paper balls, flew airplanes, shot paper wads, and so on, accompanying his behavior with appropriate remarks. In the anger condition, the stooge expressed increasing hostility about the experimenter, the procedures, and the personal nature of the information asked of the subjects. His behavior was designed to start mildly and end by expressing rage.

The experiment thus manipulated physiological arousal (through injection of epinephrine or a placebo), appropriateness of explanation (through differential instructions about side effects), and cognitive input (through the actions of the stooges), and attempted to study the interactions among these variables.

The results of this experiment were evaluated in terms of self-ratings by the subjects of their mood following exposure to the stooges and the degree to which they overtly participated in activities initiated by the stooges. That physiological arousal was obtained was indicated by the fact that subjects receiving the epinephrine injections showed elevated pulse levels after exposure to the stooges, whereas the placebo subjects showed a decline in pulse rate. Self-ratings reflected this arousal in that the epinephrine groups all showed a higher incidence of palpitations and tremors than the placebo groups; the incidence of numbness, itching, and headache did not discriminate among the groups. The results of this experiment generally conformed to expectation: (1) Subjects correctly informed of the effects of epinephrine injections were, by behavioral measures and by self-report, less emotionally aroused than subjects ignorant or misinformed of the effects. (2) The emotional self-reports and the behavior were consistent with the cognitive, social circumstances; that is, euphoria or anger appeared, depending on the actions of the stooges. (3) Generally, placebo subjects showed less emotional behavior and fewer reports of emotion than epinephrine subjects.

"To the extent that Schachter and Singer maintain that unique autonomic response patterns are not required for each and every unique emotional experience, they tend toward agreement, in some respects, with the Cannon-Bard interpretation of emotion. However, to the extent that Schacter and Singer's model stipulates that autonomic nervous system arousal is a *necessary* albeit not sufficient component of emotional experience, they agree with the James-Lange approach to emotion" (Harris & Katkin, 1975, p. 906). Some researchers, however, have taken a further step and maintain that the subject need not even perceive his *actual* autonomic arousal; if it is the cognitive interpretation of internal events that determine emotional behavior, then even false information about the subject's autonomic arousal should effectively modify his emotional responses. Thus, if the subject can be made to think that his heart rate increased even if it did not, the emotional response should be changed. This point of view suggests, then, that actual autonomic arousal is not necessary for the attribution of affect to external stimuli. Experiments testing this proposition have had mixed results (see Harris & Katkin, 1975).

Since the Schacter and Singer experiment is so central to all these extensions of the cognitive approach, let us look more closely at that experiment. Schacter and Singer acknowledged that the results of their experiment do not rule out the possibility that there are physiological differences among different emotional states. Nonetheless, they interpreted these results as compatible with the assumption that such differences do not exist. Let us examine the merits of this implication.

The basic problem with this experiment is the fact that we have no way of determining whether different physiological conditions did in fact exist in the different cognitive conditions; the anger and euphoria conditions may indeed have resulted in different physiological responses. That uniformly elevated pulse rates existed in the various epinephrine groups does not allow the interpretation that the physiological response profiles of the subjects were indeed similar across conditions. From a single response measure, it would be hazardous to deduce this in view of what we know about autonomic response specificity. Further, it is entirely possible that epinephrine injections may have a "catalytic" effect on emotional responding. (A nonspecific effect of epinephrine may make the elicitation of *specific* physiological responses to appropriate stimuli easier.) To deny that cognitive factors play a role in the generation of emotional responses, both behavioral and physiological, would be ridiculous—emotions are not endogenously generated by autonomic neural centers operating independent of the environment. Demonstrating that cognitive factors play a role in emotional response is not, however, equivalent to showing that all emotional responses share a uniform, nondifferentiating state of physiological arousal.

THE INFLUENCE OF COPING MECHANISMS

To this point we have been careful to distinguish among emotional feelings, behaviors associated with emotion, and concomitantly occurring autonomic changes. But the relationships between these three aspects of emotion have been considered casually and unidirectionally; that is, we have considered whether the behavior resulted in the feelings and peripheral autonomic changes (James-Lange) or whether feelings resulted in behaviors and autonomic changes (Cannon-Bard). It is now time to consider more specifically the role of the accompanying behavior in these relationships. How the organism deals with a specific stimulus situation may modify both the affect and the peripheral autonomic responses.

Some few examples from a much larger literature (see, e.g., Levi, 1975, and Obrist, Black, Brener, & DiCara, 1974) may suffice to indicate that it is not possible to conceptualize simple relations between feelings and behavior, or between feelings and autonomic responses, or between behavior and autonomic responses.

CER Development

The first example (Brady, 1975) illustrates the relative independence of behavioral and autonomic variables in the course of conditioned emotional response (CER) training in the monkey. CER training involves the presentation of an external stimulus—in this case a 3-minute series of clicks—which is followed by a strong shock. When carried out in conjunction with performance on a concurrent lever-pressing task—for food, for instance—the presentation of the clicks disrupts the lever-pressing performance in the well-trained animal. Figure 7.6 shows the acquisition of such CER training. The lower panel of the figure shows that within three such presentations of clicks the lever-pressing response was disrupted completely. Heart rate and sys-

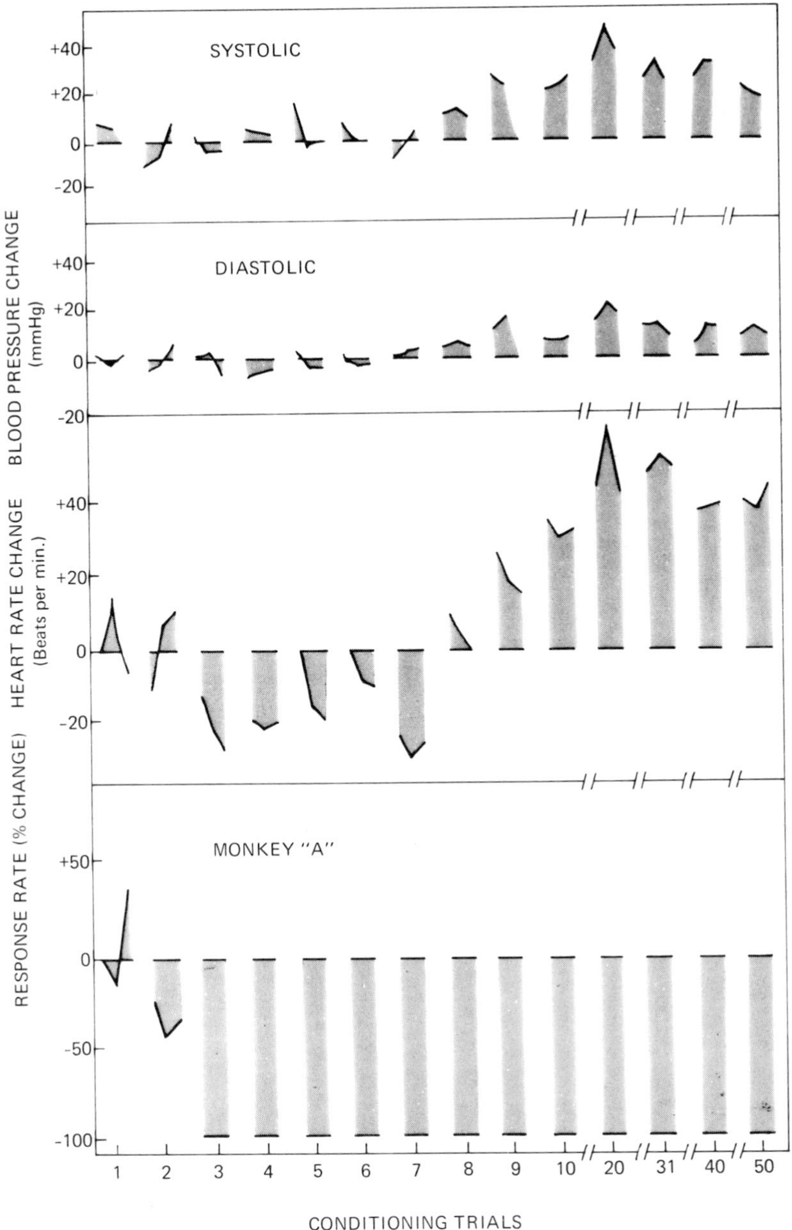

Figure 7.6. Minute-by-minute changes in blood pressure, heart rate, and lever-pressing response rate for monkey A on successive 3-min clicker-shock trials during acquisition of the conditioned emotional response. (From Brady, J. V. Toward a behavioral biology of emotion. In L. Levi (Ed.), *Emotions: Their parameters and measurement.* New York: Raven Press, 1975, 17–46.)

tolic and diastolic blood pressure changes continued over a much more protracted period. Thus, heart rate in the first two periods of click presentation showed a mixture of acceleration and deceleration; from the third through the seventh trials, heart rate showed a deceleration; finally, on subsequent trials there was an acceleration of heart rate that finally stabilized at some 40 beats/min above control levels. Diastolic and systolic blood pressure changes were minimal through the seventh trial, after which both increased. These autonomic changes, it must be noted, took place in the absence of variation in the external behavioral manifestations of the "emotional" response to the clicks.

Interaction of Stressors

Figure 7.7 is another example from the animal literature (Brady, 1975). Here, the changing nature of physiological responses to shock, as a function of ongoing behavior, are illustrated. Blood plasma concentrations of epinephrine and norepinephrine were measured. In the first panel, the effects of free, noncontingent shock are illustrated; there were minimal changes in epinephrine and norepinephrine. The second panel shows their concentrations in conjunction with an avoidance training procedure—the animal was required to press a lever periodically (2 sec) in order to avoid the occurrence of shock. A modest change in norepinephrine level and no change in epinephrine level occurred after training was completed. The third panel shows the hormonal concentrations when free shock was given during the avoidance performance. Norepinephrine levels were markedly increased and a sharp increase in epinephrine levels also occurred, despite the fact that neither free shock nor avoidance by themselves produced any observable epinephrine response.

Coping and Ulcers

A series of experiments by Weiss (1971a, b, c), provides an example of how reactions to stress can be modified by the consequences of the coping behavior. The basic experimental situation employed in these experiments involved rats turning a wheel in order to escape or avoid shock to the tail—wheel-turns postponed the next occurrence of shock for 200 secs. The various experiments involved manipulations of the stimulus conditions pertaining to this basic escape-avoidance arrangement. In each experiment, one group of animals served in the basic escape-avoidance arrangement; yoked with each of these animals were two other animals; one received the same stimulus conditions and the same shocks as the escape-avoidance animal but this animal's wheel-turning had no consequence for escape or avoidance of shock; the other yoked animal merely received the stimulus condi-

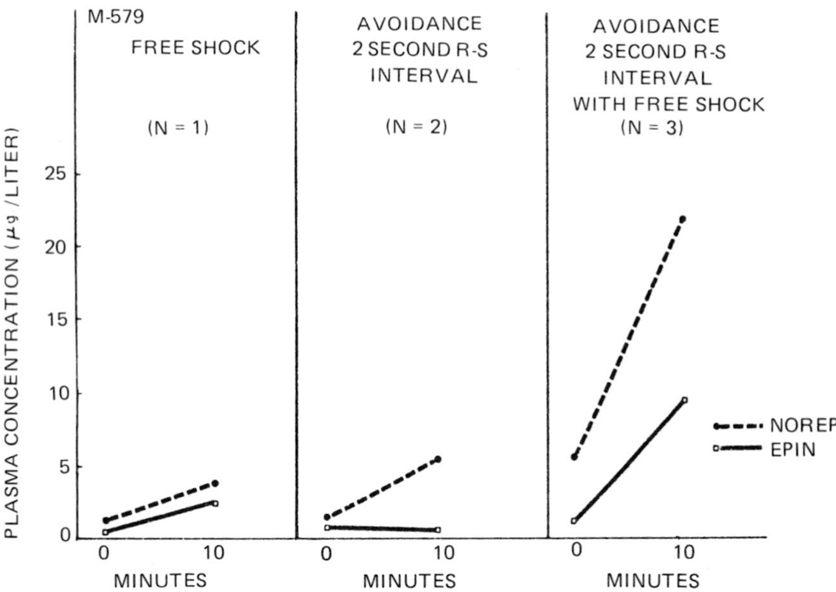

Figure 7.7. Plasma epinephrine and norepinephrine levels during a "free shock" session before avoidance training (left panel), during performance sessions without an external "warning" stimulus after avoidance training (middle panel), and during performance sessions with "free shock" after avoidance training (right panel). (From Brady, J. V. Toward a behavioral biology of emotion. In L. Levi (Ed.), *Emotions: Their parameters and measurement.* New York: Raven Press, 1975, 17–46.)

tions and did not receive shock. In addition to tabulating wheel-turning, these experiments examined the rats for gastric ulcers and for levels of corticosterone, an adrenal hormone.

In the first experiment (Weiss, 1971a), the effects of supplying warning signals was manipulated. In one condition, a warning signal preceded the occurrence of shock; in a second condition, a series of signals were presented which, in effect, provided an external clock measuring the time to the next shock; in the third condition, no signals were provided. In all conditions, those animals which could escape or avoid shock developed less ulceration than did the yoked, helpless animals that merely received the same shock patterns. The discrete warning signals also had an effect, however: Such warning signals reduced ulceration in both animals which could escape or avoid and in the yoked helpless subjects. Corticosterone levels were similarly reduced.

In the second experiment (Weiss, 1971b), the effects of introducing conflict were examined. Signaled avoidance produced minimal ulceration in the previous experiment. Here that condition was combined with a brief punishing shock for making the correct avoidance or escape response; the yoked animals received, in one case, the signals and the shock wihout being able to avoid or escape, and in the other, the signals alone. Thus, for the avoidance-escape animals, the situation became a conflict situation—they could avoid or escape a strong shock if they took a brief shock; the yoked helpless animals again received the same shocks. Here, the yoked helpless animals did not develop as much ulceration as did the avoidance-escape animals. Corticosterone levels paralleled the ulcer finding. Thus, coping behavior (escaping or avoiding) can be more ulcerogenic than helplessness.

In the first experiment, considerable ulceration occurred in animals performing the unsignaled avoidance task. The third experiment (Weiss, 1971c) tested the effects of providing a brief feedback signal after each appropriate response to emphasize that shock was terminated or delayed. This procedure reduced the ulceration in the escape-avoidance animals almost to that of the yoked unshocked animals; in fact, both yoked and avoidance-escape animals without the feedback signals and the yoked helpless animals had considerably greater ulceration.

These results emphasize that the consequences of shock (ulceration and hormone levels) are not fixed. Rather, they depend on the responses to that stress that the animals make. Weiss has developed a theory in which two factors interact to produce ulceration: Coping responses and the feedback from such responses. Generally, a high output of attempts to deal with stress *increases* ulceration; at the same time, the more adequate the feedback from such attempts, the *less* the ulceration. Thus, animals that frantically turned the wheel may have been successful in their avoidance, but such wheel-turning allows less adequate feedback—i.e., the fact that wheel-turning does avoid or escape shock is less apparent. Weiss (1971c) showed that such animals actually had greater ulceration than animals turning the wheel less in the avoidance-escape conditions of these experiments.

Task Engagement

Finally, from the human literature (Obrist, 1976) the following may be cited. In a vigilance task, subjects were given a shock for not responding fast enough to the critical signals. If the task was either too easy or too difficult, systolic blood pressure and heart rate tended to drop over the duration of the task; in conditions in which the task was difficult but possible, these parameters tended to remain high. Thus, providing conditions which make a task too easy *or* too difficult results in a greater dissipation of sympathetic nervous system effects, while keeping the subjects engaged perpetuates the effects.

Conclusions

The data reviewed in this section concentrate on the overt behavior and the physiological responses associated with stress situations. They are clear in showing that these may be quite independent, though interacting, variables in the total picture of the response to stress. It should be remarked that none of these experiments dealt with the experiential dimension of emotion. It does seem appropriate, however, to infer that the subjects felt differently depending on the coping behavior in which they engaged and its adequacy. To state the matter another way: Classically, experimenters have employed relatively standardized stimulus situations to induce different affects and have attempted to see if differential patterns of peripheral autonomic responses were elicited. This approach ignores the fact that subjects in such experiments are not passively engaged—they attempt to deal with the stresses and requirements of the experiments. Such coping attempts can also have differential adequacy. Depending on the experimental situation, the cognitive interpretation of it by the subjects, the responses possible in it, and the adequacy of such responses (and these may vary for different subjects in an experiment) different subjective responses should indeed by expected despite the standardization of the imposed stress condition.

Biofeedback

Before turning from the subject of peripheral mechanisms of emotion, we will take a look at the implications of biofeedback procedures for the control of physiological indices of emotionality. *Biofeedback* generally refers to techniques designed to gain control over internal responses such as heart rate, blood pressure, or the EEG through operant, instrumental conditioning procedures, i.e., in contrast to classical, or Pavlovian, conditioning procedures. More specifically, the use of operant techniques is predicated on the assumption that control over these internal responding systems is generally difficult or not ordinarily possible since we generally are not aware of them. By providing externalized and augmented information about such responses, however, it may be possible to gain such operant control.

There has generally been an assumption throughout the history of psychology that responses of the skeletal muscles are "voluntary" and subject to CNS control; responses of the viscera and autonomic nervous system, on the other hand, have been presumed to be "involuntary" and subject to automatic, homeostatic mechanisms. Correlated with these assumptions is the notion that skeletal-motor responses can be controlled through operant conditioning techniques while the only way to gain control over autonomic and visceral responses is through classical conditioning techniques (Kimmel, 1974). A number of investigators attempted to test whether visceral autonomic responses could be operantly conditioned but their reported successes were generally only skeptically received. This was so because visceral autonomic responses can be influenced by skeletal responses; i.e., exercise, breathing, tensing of the muscles, etc. can alter heart rate, blood pressure, and other autonomic responses. Thus, any apparent operant conditioning might have been mediated or indirectly obtained through unrecorded skeletal changes rather than from any direct effect of operant reinforcement contingencies.

Thus, the general area of biofeedback research contains two sets of issues. One set revolves around the theoretically important issue of whether autonomic and visceral responses are directly conditionable using operant techniques. If the autonomic system cannot be conditioned with instrumental procedures, this strengthens the belief that instrumental and classical procedures are somehow different in their mechanisms.

The second set of issues concerning biofeedback revolves around the therapeutic implications of being able to instrumentally condition autonomic responses: If they can be so conditioned, the possibility is opened for controlling emotional responses and disease processes such as hypertension without resorting to drugs and other medical treatments that may be both costly and potentially dangerous. As will be apparent, these two sets of issues are *not* necessarily related.

Theoretical Issues

Miller (1969) has outlined the results of an elaborate series of experiments designed to deal with the theoretical issue. Basically, these experiments attempted to instrumentally condition autonomic responses in animals that were incapable of overt skeletal responding; they had been paralyzed by drugs to prevent such skeletal-motor responding. Miller thus sought to answer the basic question, In the absence of possible skeletal mediation, can an animal, for instance, raise its blood pressure in order to obtain a reinforcement?

In one particularly striking report of success (DiCara & Miller, 1968), paralyzed and artificially respirated rats were rewarded by electrical stimulation of the brain for changing the balance of vasomotor activity in the two ears. The animals learned to produce relative vasodilation in one ear and vasoconstriction in the other (blushing in one ear and blanching in the other). These blood flow changes were independent of vasomotor responses in the forepaw or tail and also of heart rate or temperature changes. These results indicate not only that vasomotor responses can be instrumentally conditioned but that the sympathetic nervous system, which is largely responsible for these effects, is capable of showing a high degree of specificity of response, i.e., the vasomotor effects were not general effects of the vascular system but were specific to vasomotor changes in the ears.

In the course of pursuing and replicating findings such as these, not only have other investigators had difficulty in obtaining similar effects, but Miller too, after a great deal of initial success with such procedures, recently has had difficulty with instrumentally conditioning cardiovascular responses (Miller & Dworkin, 1974). This has raised the question of the validity of all the previous experiments. The issues here are complicated, but basically they involve variables such as the neuromuscular blocking agents used to produce muscular paralysis and the parameters of the artificial respiration employed to sustain the animals. These technical complications are being worked out (e.g., Middaugh, Eissenberg, & Brener, 1975; Hahn, Schwartz, & Sapper, 1975) and, at least under limited circumstances, such cardiovascular conditioning apparently can take place (Middaugh et al., 1975).[4]

From a theoretical standpoint, then, an important issue has been whether autonomic responses can be instrumentally conditioned. If you lie down in order to reduce your heart rate, the control manifested is theoretically trivial; however, if you have heart disease, whether such control is of a theoretically trivial sort or produced through operant conditioning is of much less consequence. The human literature does contain numerous instances of autonomic control through the application of conditioning procedures (see Kimmel [1974] for references). Not only is it irrelevant for the therapist and his patient if such control was achieved by instrumental conditioning or otherwise, but it might be possible to improve the technique if readily available mediators *could* be employed. Thus, from a therapeutic standpoint, the issues become the efficiacy of feedback procedures and their behavioral effects.

Therapeutic Issues

Blanchard and Young (1973, 1974) have surveyed much of the literature on conditioning of cardiovascular responses. The issues they raised have general applicability for conditioning of all autonomic responses.

The vast majority of studies that have been carried out have been con-

[4]But a whole set of conceptual issues concerning whether instrumental autonomic activity is mediated or directly reinforced and if it can be "voluntary" is being reappraised. Is the procedure of employing paralyzed animals even appropriate? Blocking overt motor responses doesn't prevent *central* neural activity; that is to say, "thinking about" movements is not blocked even if muscle movements are, and this central activity may be linked to autonomic changes. Furthermore, not only autonomic activity can be mediated—the learning of new skeletal-motor skills demonstrates that cognitive mediation is a factor here too. What constitutes "appropriate" and "inappropriate" mediation? What does "voluntary" mean, and what operational definition distinguishes it from "involuntary" activity? And, finally, yoga, meditation, and relaxation training are reported to result in profound abilities to control autonomic activity, often greater than those ascribed to conditioning. Are conditioning procedures then simply inefficient means of producing relaxation?

cerned with demonstrating that biofeedback procedures produce their desired effects. As such, these studies naturally have been concerned with demonstrating statistically significant effects. But statistical significance is not necessarily equivalent to practical or therapeutic significance. Most studies have demonstrated heart rate changes of a few beats per minute or blood pressure changes of a few millimeters of mercury—results that are hardly of consequence for patients with a disease condition. There are exceptions to be found in the literature, to be sure. For instance, Stephens, Harris, Brady, and Shaffer (1975) found some subjects capable of showing heart rate increases up to 46 beats per minute and heart rate decreases up to 14 beats per minute. Generally, however, such studies are still exceptional, and, for the most part, studies with well-controlled experimental procedures have employed normal subjects rather than patient populations. If biofeedback is to play a significant therapeutic role, control, however it is achieved, will have to produce clinically satisfactory and stable results.

Similarly, it remains to be seen how well any changes that are achieved are transferred beyond the clinician's office when the patient is no longer in touch with the biofeedback recording instruments. Are real, live patients, not healthy college students, able to achieve sufficient self-monitoring and self-control so as to employ any training to their advantage in their everyday lives? These questions are only beginning to be approached.

What are the *behavioral* effects of biofeedback training—that is, does alteration of a physiological function change any behavior? Obviously, if a patient has high blood pressure and biofeedback training can succeed in lowering that pressure, this achievement is an end in itself. But there are some situations—conditioning of changes in the alpha activity of the EEG, for instance—where this is not necessarily the case. In one study (Beatty, Greenberg, Deibler, & O'Hanlon, 1974), suppression of EEG theta (3 to 7 Hz) activity enhanced performance on a monitoring task while increasing theta degraded performance. On the other hand, depression of alpha activity (8 to 12 Hz) has often been associated with anxiety; but production of alpha in a feedback session was not prevented by the anxiety associated with the threat of shock; conversely, the presence of alpha did not prevent the anxiety (Orne & Paskewitz, 1974). Generally, we should not expect that control over a single physiological variable is likely to be an effective preventative for complex psychological states.

Finally, it might be remarked that biofeedback therapies are based on the rationale of eliciting responses that are incompatible with the undesirable symptoms that bring patients to therapy. For some patients, symptom elimination may be all that is needed; yet this technique raises the question of whether symptom elimination might result in the production of new symptoms.

Biofeedback has provided some data of great theoretical interest. It is causing us to reexamine some of our preconceptions about the interaction of emotional feelings, behavior, and physiological accompaniments. However, for use as a therapeutic tool, it requires a great deal more testing.

CENTRAL MECHANISMS OF EMOTION

Research on the central mechanisms of emotion has mainly involved animal studies, and, as a consequence, our emphasis will be on emotional *behavior* rather than emotional *feeling*. In addition, most of this material deals with negative emotions such as fear, rage, and aggression. Nonetheless, there has been little tendency in the animal literature to stray from the concept of differentiated emotions.

In effect, when we talk of central neural structures involved in emotion, we are including almost the entire CNS. Virtually every major area of the CNS has been implicated in one experiment or another in the mechanisms of emotion; the literature is vast. At the present time there is no completely satisfactory theory to integrate the empirical findings, but one set of concepts dominates this area and that is the role of the *limbic system* in emotional behavior. This system and its role will, therefore, be discussed first. We will then consider the empirical evidence concerning the remainder of the CNS.

The Limbic System and the Hypothalamus

The general shape and location of the limbic system was shown in Figure 1.8; Figure 7.8 diagrams some of the anatomic connections within the system. There is no precise, limited definition of the limbic system; different writers vary in exactly what they are willing to include under this term. This varying usage comes about because of the extensive nature of the connections of the parts of this system to other, functionally related areas, such as the hypothalamus. Basically, the term *limbic* (border) refers to cortex that is both phylogenetically older and less complex than the neocortex. The neocortex has six structural layers, while limbic cortex may have from three to five layers. As Figure 7.8 indicates, the limbic cortex is largely hidden from direct view by its medial location between the hemispheres. Cortical areas in the system include the *cingulate* gyrus on the medial surface of the hemispheres and the *pyriform* and *entorhinal* areas of the temporal lobe. Noncortical structures that all writers include as part of the limbic system are the *amygaloid complex* of nuclei, the nuclei of the *septal* area, and the *hippocampus*. A major fiber bundle associated with the limbic system and the hypothalamus is the *fornix*. Because these structures were once considered to be largely olfactory in function, a term still associated with this system is *rhinencephalon*, or "nose brain." Paul MacLean has suggested the term "visceral brain," in view of the association of this part of the brain with autonomic functioning.

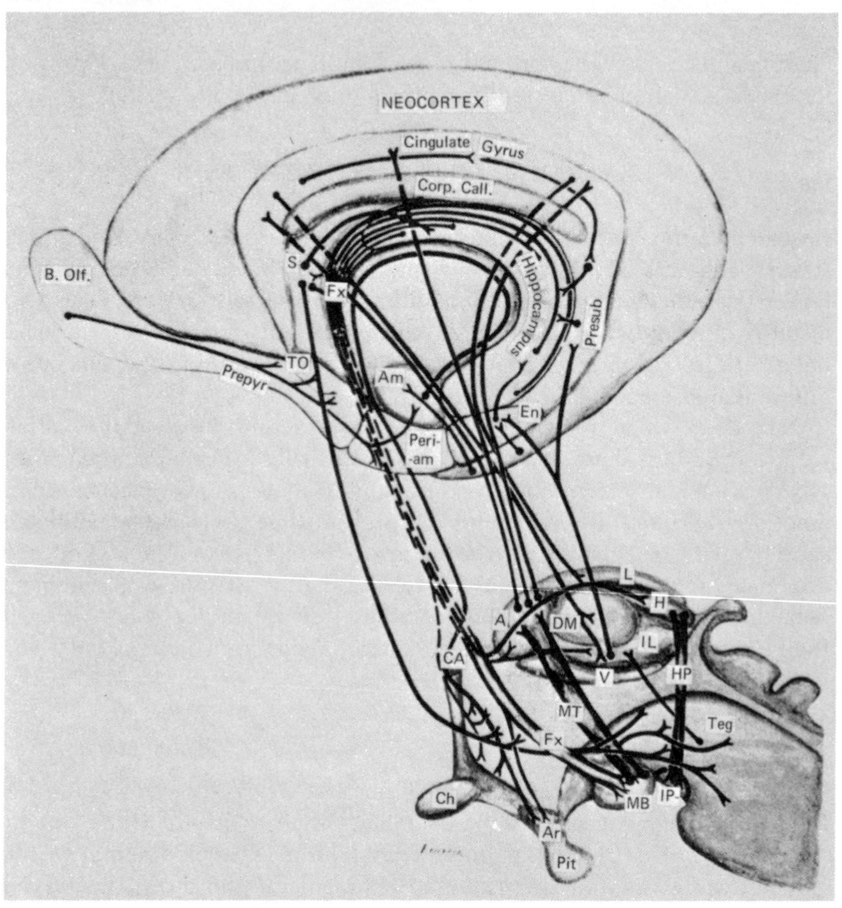

Figure 7.8. Schematic diagram of the principal anatomical relationships between the limbic cortex and several subcortical structures related to the limbic system. The brainstem portions of the system have been schematically displayed from the hemisphere and represented in the lower half of the illustration in order to facilitate visualization of the numerous anatomical interconnections involving these structures. Abbreviations: *A*, anterior nucleus of the thalamus; *Am*, amygdaloid complex; *Ar*, arcuate nucleus; *B. Olf.*, olfactory bulb; *CA*, anterior commissure; *Ch*, optic chiasm; *Corp. Call.*, corpous callosum; *DM*, medial dorsal nucleus of the thalamus; *En*, entorhinal area; *Fx*, fornix; *H*, habenular complex; *HP*, habenulo-interpeduncular tract; *IL*, intralaminar thalamic nuclei; *IP*, interpeduncular nucleus; *L*, lateral thalamic nucleus; *MB*, mammillary body; *MT*, mammillothalamic tract; *Periam*, periamygdaloid cortex; *Pit*, pituitary; *Prepyr*, prepyriform cortex; *Presub*, presubiculum; *S*, septal region; *Teg*, midbrain tegmentum; *TO*, olfactory tubercle; *V*, ventral nucleus of the thalamus. [From Brady, J. V., Motivational-emotional factors and intracranial self-stimulation. In D. E. Sheer (Ed.), *Electrical Stimulation of the Brain.* Austin: The University of Texas Press, 1961, 413–430. Copyright 1961 by The University of Texas Press.]

Attention to the limbic system in connection with emotional behavior was first drawn by the neurologist Papez in 1937, largely on the basis of the anatomical connections involved; MacLean (1958) is most responsible for the later development of the theory. In their view, the limbic system and the hypothalamus provide the substrate for emotional experience and behavior.

The hypothalamus (Figure 7.9) occupies only a few cubic millimeters at the base of the brain in the general region over the optic chiasm and the pituitary gland. It is only diffusely organized, both structurally and functionally. Many diverse functions, both behavioral and physiological, seem to be served from common areas; there is only poor correlation, at best, between structure and function. Additionally, many fiber tracts pass in, around, and through this area. Thus, experimental manipulations on discrete functions of the hypothalamus are largely impossible. From a physiological standpoint, the hypothalamus is known to exert considerable influence over autonomic functioning: stimulation of this area produces changes in blood pressure, pupillary dilation, sweating, and body temperature. Hypothalamic neurons also exert influence over pituitary activity through both neural mechanisms and their own secretory activity. The hypothalamus is also involved in sexual activity and is sensitive to sex hormones circulating in the blood. Finally,

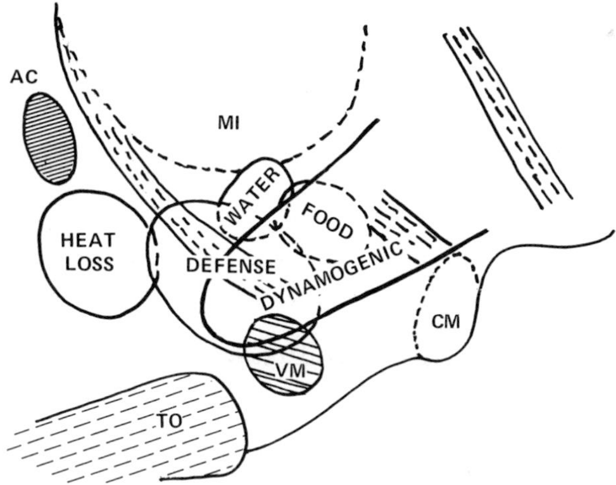

Figure 7.9. Localization and mutual relationships of hypothalamic areas for affective defense, heat loss, water intake, food intake, and dynamogenic activity (arousal, restlessness, locomotion, and flight). Dynamogenic reactions are localized more laterally than affective defense. None of these areas corresponds to a nucleus or a nuclear complex. *AC*, anterior commissure; *CM*, mammillary body; *MI*, massa intermedia; *TO*, optic tract; *VM*, ventromedial hypothalamic nucleus. [From Akert, K., Diencephalon. In D. E. Sheer (Ed.), *Electrical Stimulation of the Brain.* Austin: The University of Texas Press, 1961, 288–310. Copyright 1961 by The University of Texas Press.]

hypothalamic processes are involved in the body's basic metabolic activity; these have their counterparts in behavior related to food and water.

The above activities are mediated by complex anatomical pathways leading from the hypothalamus. These activities are influenced by the profuse afferent connections bringing information to this area. Afferents come to the hypothalamus from several limbic structures, the diffuse thalamic nuclei, the reticular system, and the neocortex, to name only some prominent sources of input. There is also physiological evidence that the hypothalamus receives information from all the peripheral sensory systems. The role of this area in sleep mechanisms has previously been noted. Behavioral consequences of hypothalamic activity will be discussed in several subsequent chapters as well as the present one.

Limbic Mechanisms in Emotion

That the limbic system is involved in emotions seems without question. On the other hand, to equate limbic functioning and emotional behavior would be a gross oversimplification and hardly merited from the evidence. The literature here is enormous and we shall, therefore, depend largely on review articles that summarize the outcome of many studies. But first, a few examples that seemingly do demonstrate a relationship between the limbic system and emotion.

Animal Studies

The attention of psychologists was drawn to the temporal lobe portions of the limbic system with the description of what has become known as the Klüver-Bucy syndrome (Klüver & Bucy, 1939). Normally, rhesus monkeys are aggressive and difficult to handle. With large temporal lobe lesions, the monkeys became tame and seemed to lose their fear of other species. In addition, they showed a psychic blindness, increased general activity, compulsive oral behavior, and hypersexuality. By "psychic blindness," Klüver and Bucy mean that the animal seems to be impelled to have contact with any visual object and seems to have lost any idea of the functional significance of visual objects. Oral manifestations included the mouthing of feces, nails, dirt, and cage parts. Hypersexuality was indicated by both an increase in the amount of sexual response and an increase in the range of objects eliciting sexual responses. Either sex was approached without apparent discrimination, masturbation was prominent, and attempts were made to copulate with other species, such as cats and dogs. Subsequent studies, designed to delimit the anatomical locus of these effects, have been directed to the amygdaloid complex (see Goddard, 1964).

Generally, amygdalectomy has resulted in taming, and this is especially prominent in naturally ferocious species. On the other hand, a significant number of studies do report that animals show increased rage responses after amygdalectomy. The seeming contradiction here may be largely due to differences in the functional role of the amygdala in different species. Pribram (1962) has attempted to account for the discrepancies by suggesting that amygdalectomy might interfere with the animal's ability to distinguish home and foreign territory, resulting in an anomalous display of sexual and aggressive responses.

A number of studies (Kling, Orbach, Schwartz, & Towne, 1960; King & Meyer, 1958) have shown that the amygdala interacts with the ventromedial hypothalamus and the septum to control rage responses. By themselves, septal lesions (Brady & Nauta, 1953) or ventromedial lesions (Wheatley, 1944) each produce savage behavior; the effects of such lesions are lessened, however, in combination with lesions in the amygdala. It appears, though, that the order in which the lesions are made may influence whether tameness or savageness will result. Septally lesioned rats lost their savageness with amygdalectomy, but amygdalectomized rats showed some increases in savageness with septal lesions (King & Meyer, 1958).

Evidence from Human Psychosurgery

In 1966, Charles Whitman went to the top of the clock tower at the University of Texas with a high powered rifle. Before he was killed by the police, Whitman killed 14 and wounded 31 passersby. The night before, he killed his wife and his mother. At autopsy, it was found that he had a tumor in one temporal lobe. Whitman is but one example of literally hundreds of cases of persons demonstrating violent, uncontrolled aggression and rage reactions where limbic system involvement is at least suspected.

In addition to demonstrable tumors, a variety of other clinical evidence suggests limbic involvement in human aggression and rage responses. Epilepsy involving the temporal lobe is often accompanied by personality changes ranging from irritability to violent aggressive outbursts. Surgery to the temporal lobe is often successful in controlling the seizures in such cases and is also effective in reducing the aggressive behavior and reversing personality changes. On the basis of the animal literature implicating the amygdaloid nuclei of the temporal lobe, stimulation or surgical removal of these nuclei has been carried out. Generally, amygdaloid stimulation in humans has been reported to promote or increase aggressive behavior and surgical removal has been reported to be effective in its reduction. Septal stimulation has been reported to be effective in blocking hostile reactions (Moyer, 1976).

The analysis of aggression is a complex topic about which several recent books have been written. Limbic system involvement is but one facet and should not be construed to be the only, or even the major, cause. One comprehensive book is that of Moyer (1976), who concentrates on the psychobiological foundations of aggression; but he emphasizes limbic system involvement and is generally sympathetic to surgical intervention as a last resort treatment. A balancing view, skeptical of surgical techniques, has been presented by Valenstein (1973). Valenstein questions the specificity of the neural tissue removed by such procedures and the adequacy of the evaluation procedures. In addition, important ethical questions are raised by the use of such techniques.

Theories of Limbic Function

The above examples are not exhaustive by any means; they are intended merely to illustrate reasonably clear examples in which emotional effects seem to have been obtained from limbic manipulations. But this picture requires modification. For instance, lesions throughout the limbic system have been shown to influence behavior based on fear motivation. Included here are lesions of the amygdala, hippocampus, cingulate cortex, and septum. But in one of the most widely cited animal studies, McCleary (1961) demonstrated that cingulate lesions produced a deficit in active, but not passive, avoidance.[5] Conversely, septal lesions produced a deficit in passive, but not active, avoidance. McCleary argues that such results contradict explanations based on simple changes in fear as a result of the lesions. He has suggested that the septum and cingulate cortex are involved in antagonistic ways in inhibition and facilitation of responses. This interpretation was the forerunner of several theories of limbic functioning that emphasize other than emotional aspects of limbic influence.

Hippocampus

An early review of hippocampal function by Douglas (1967) emphasized that hippocampal lesions do not result in any obvious emotional consequences, that animals with hippocampal lesions generally show greater resistance to extinction, less spontaneous alternation, and poor reversal learning. Douglas rejected hypotheses that the hippocampus functions as a center for olfaction, that it functions in emotional responsiveness, or that it is concerned with the registration of recent memory.

On a descriptive level, Douglas suggested that hippocampal lesions produce a deficit in the ability to inhibit or withhold prepotent responses. To account for this deficit, Douglas and Pribram (Douglas, 1967; Douglas & Pribram, 1966) suggested that the function of the hippocampus is the inhibition of attention to stimuli which initiate these responses. The hippocampus is hypothesized to exclude stimulus patterns from attention by exerting efferent control over the sensory systems. The theory is similar, then, to the reticular model of attention discussed in Chapter 5. In support of this

[5]"Active" avoidance requires the animal to respond in order to avoid shock, while "passive" avoidance requires the animal to withhold a response in order to avoid shock.

idea, there is, for instance, evidence of the suppression of input to the hypothalamus from sensory or lemniscal sources by hippocampal stimulation. The afferent input concerned here is input that is associated with *non*reinforcement. This mechanism is conceivably involved in habituation, extinction, passive avoidance, and reversal learning. The Douglas-Pribram model also suggests a role for the amygdala: It is seen as increasing the probability of attention to stimuli that are reinforced, either negatively or positively; amygdaloid activity would increase or facilitate the sensory input.

The Douglas-Pribram formulation emphasized inhibition of stimulus input; a similar inhibitory concept, suggested by Kimble (1968), emphasizes that responses, rather than the eliciting stimuli, are inhibited. Micco and Schwartz (1971) tested the effects of hippocampal lesions on inhibitory processes and concluded that such lesions disrupted response inhibition.

A more recent review by Jarrard (1973) emphasizes the diversity of the anatomic organization of the hippocampus and suggests that it has multiple influences. There is convincing evidence from the human literature that the hippocampus is involved in memory (Chapter 13); the animal literature generally fails to support this, suggesting a species difference in functioning. Jarrard also acknowledges hippocampal effects on response inhibition. But he stresses that the hippocampus also has a role in motivation. Specifically, the hippocampus serves as a negative feedback mechanism to dampen the activity of other structures concerned with the control of activation and incentive motivation.

Septum

As indicated above, one striking effect of septal lesions is the appearance of savageness. But recent reviews of septal functioning (Fried, 1972; Lubar & Numan, 1973) stress a multiplicity of effects. For example, lesions in different septal nuclei produce impaired ability to alter responses on the basis of proprioceptive cues; increased negative reactions to unpalatable solutions; increased intake of water; and over-responding to positively motivating stimuli. It is also suggested (Lubar & Numan, 1973) that avoidance-response changes as a result of septal lesions (McCleary, 1961) are indeed produced by reductions in fear per se; decreased fear (CER) would produce a deficit in passive avoidance but would facilitate active avoidance since the animal would be less likely to "freeze" (see Hedges, Van Atta, & Thomas, 1975).

Amygdala

Goddard (1964) concluded that while the amygdala is important in the regulation of emotions, especially fear, it is not essential to their elaboration. The amygdalectomized animal "overeats, responds sexually to all stimuli even remotely resembling a receptive female, approaches all stimuli whether dangerous or not with curiosity, and is unresponsive to variations in deprivation and food reward. In other words, it does not know when to stop." Goddard suggested that the amygdala is specifically concerned with "the inhibition of motivations and the satiation of drives" (Goddard, 1964, p. 102).

But that the amygdala is also not a homogeneous structure with respect to its effects is illustrated by two more recent studies. Miczek, Brykczynski, and Grossman (1974) found that small lesions in certain amygdaloid and associated structures reduced or eliminated attacks and dominance behavior in male rats. The same lesions had little or no effect on pain-induced fighting between rats, however, nor on mouse killing by the rats. Other lesions inhibited pain-induced aggression but did not modify attack or dominance behavior. Research by Grossman, Grossman, and Walsh (1975) produced differential inhibition and facilitation of active and passive avoidance learning dependent on the location of lesions in the amygdala.

Summary

The above constitute examples from a highly complex literature. They illustrate the changing nature of conceptions about the limbic system. It is clear that Papez's original conception of limbic function is both right and wrong. It is right in attributing a role for the limbic system in emotion but taken literally, it is wrong in being too simplistic. With the changes in conceptualization, however, one constancy does seem to remain: That is, that the limbic system generally seems to be concerned more with the modulation of responses than with their production. With respect to emotional behavior, the concept of the limbic system as a response-modulating system seems to fit within the general framework of the Cannon-Bard theory of emotion: As we shall see, the hypothalamus and other CNS locations may be effector mechanisms while the limbic system seems to serve as a controlling mechanism.

The Brainstem and Spinal Cord

The limbic system is not the sine qua non for all emotional behavior. A variety of experiments generally point to the conclusion that at least fragments of emotional responsiveness can be elicited from animals with transections at varying levels of the brainstem down to, and including, the spinal cord. Generally, the higher the level of transection, the more complete is the appearance of the response. Animals with brainstem transections do not, however, show the integration of responses characteristic of normal animals. Thus, they may show respiratory changes, growl, hiss or spit, and lash their tails; but these responses occur in relative isolation and are not combined into directed attack as they would be in the normal animal.

Responses such as these are forthcoming when the central gray area of the mesencephalon, between the cerebral aqueduct and the reticular core, is electrically stimulated. Lesions here reduce or eliminate such responses to stimulation of the hypothalamus or amygdala, while the converse is not true; that is, responses to central gray stimulation persist despite hypothalamic and amygdala lesions. Bilateral lesions of this midbrain area result in permanent impairment of aggressive responses in chronic cat preparations. These results would indicate a circuit for aggressive responses consisting of the amygdala, hypothalamus, and central gray, the central gray serving as more than simply an efferent relay, but rather as an important regulatory mechanism (Fernandez de Molina & Hunsperger, 1962).

Given brainstem and spinal preparations, such animals are emotionally responsive only to somesthetic stimuli. Additionally, as would also be expected, animals with brainstem lesions producing somnolence are also difficult to arouse emotionally. However, it will be well to recall from Chapter 5 the experiments of Sprague, Levitt, Robson, Lui, Stellar, and Chambers (1963). One of the main features of animals with bilateral lesions of the lemniscal pathways, sparing the reticular core, was an extreme deficit in affective response. The deficit in these animals was not limited to a particular emotional response, but cut across aggressive, rage reactions and pleasurable responses. Sprague et al. emphasized relative sensory isolation of the forebrain as a factor in these results. The results imply that more than intact neural centers for emotional behavior are required—that emotional behavior results from an integration of endogenous activity with appropriate environmental input.

Diencephalic Mechanisms

That the hypothalamus and thalamus play important roles in emotional behavior was indicated early by experiments on animals with the cortex removed (decortication) or cerebral hemispheres removed (decerebration) (Bard, 1928). Generally, such animals characteristically show much reduced thresholds for rage reactions; for example, violent rage responses can be triggered by stimulation that would be trivial and innocuous for the normal animal. Such rage differs from that in the normal animal only in that it is poorly directed in regard to the provoking stimuli. In view of the blindness of such animals, this is to be expected. That the hypothalamus is particularly involved is implied by the results of experiments in which successive lesions are made. Complete rage responses are elicitable in animals with all tissue above the hypothalamus removed; it is only with transections below the caudal hypothalamus that the total response pattern becomes fragmented as in the brainstem animal. These results imply a role for both the hypothalamus and the cortex in the control of emotional behavior, the hypothalamus as an integrating mechanism and the cortex as an inhibiting mechanism (Bard & Macht, 1958).

It would be expected that lesions of the hypothalamus would impair emotional responsiveness, and, generally, this seems to be the case. However, it is noteworthy that animals with lesions in the ventromedian area are *more* apt to be vicious (Wheatley, 1944).

These results with surgical procedures are supported by experiments in which the hypothalamus was stimulated. We have previously called attention (Chapter 3) to the experiments of W. R. Hess (Akert, 1961). Hess elicited full-blown, well-oriented rage and attack responses with electrical stimulation of the hypothalamus in the cat. More fragmentary responses, without directed attack, were elicited by Masserman (1941), but his electrode locations probably were not comparable to Hess'. More recently, Roberts (1958) and Miller (1961) have indicated that components of this total behavioral complex could be elicited separately from different electrodes. Thus, they distinguish three reactions to hypothalamic stimulation: alarm, flight, and rage.

Evidence specifically concerned with thalamic involvement in emotion is much less numerous and more equivocal than for the hypothalamus. "Anxious," "defensive," and "painlike" responses are elicitable from the posteroventral nucleus (somatosensory relay). Such responses might be expected, however, to be the equivalent of those elicited by peripheral, painful stimuli in view of the role of this nucleus in afferent, somatosensory transmission. Stimulation of the dorsomedial nucleus, however, evokes a "fearlike" crouching response in cats, and lesions of this area seem to reduce fearful behavior (Roberts, 1962). Because of the sensory and nonspecific alerting function of the thalamus, it would be difficult to ascribe exclusive emotional effects to thalamic areas. Thus, reduced emotionality as a result of lesions or increased emotionality as a result of stimulation may both be secondary to effects of changes in sensory functioning.

A number of workers have characterized the rage responses resulting from decerebration and stimulation of the hypothalamic area as "sham rage" or "pseudoaffective" responses. At issue here is whether such responses are real in the sense of having accompanying subjective responses or feelings. One way to try to answer this question is to attempt to condition the behavior. Masserman (1941) was not successful in conditioning responses to hypothalamic stimulation and this suggested to him that these responses merely respresent motor manifestations. Similarly, Roberts (1958) demonstrated rapid escape learning but no learning to avoid stimulation of the hypothalamus evoking the flight response. It should also be noted that at least one study with monkeys (Delgado, Rosvold, & Looney, 1956) suggests that, unlike hypothalamic stimulation, stimulation of restricted limbic loci, notably certain amygdaloid nuclei, results in fear responses that can be conditioned. This is also true of dorsomedial thalamic stimulation in the cat (Roberts, 1962).

On the other hand, there is evidence that hypothalamic stimulation is not devoid of affective consequences for the animal. Roberts and Kiess (1964) elicited attack on rats by stimulating the hypothalamus of cats. Such attack behavior was not itself conditionable but did have reinforcing properties in that the cats learned an instrumental response which allowed them the opportunity to attack the rats. In the absence of the goal object, the rat, the electrical stimulation alone was ineffective in producing the learning. We have previously noted the similarity of behaviors elicited through hypothalamic stimulation and the fixed action patterns of the ethologists (Chapter 3). It is probable that further analysis along these lines may clarify the affective reality of these responses.

Biochemical Mechanisms

Both the human and the animal literature suggest that different synaptic transmitter systems are involved in different emotions. Some findings implicate the behavioral aspect of emotion while other findings relate to the peripheral autonomic aspect. For instance, Bernard, Berchek, and Yutzey (1975) have demonstrated alterations in hypothalamic levels of norepinephrine and dopamine and in limbic levels of dopamine as a result of septal lesions that produced increased savageness. In humans, high blood levels of dopamine β-hydroxylase, the enzyme that converts dopamine to norepinephrine, have been implicated in hypertension (Schanberg, Stone, Kirschner, Gunnells, & Robinson, 1974). On the other hand, low levels of dopamine β-hydroxylase have been found in the locus coeruleus of rats bred for spontaneous hypertension (Nagatsu et al., 1976).

However, it is unlikely that simple relations between transmitters and emotions can be found. In a review devoted to avoidance behavior, Anisman (1975) has emphasized that such behavior shows time-dependent cyclical variations and these variations may be related to variations in the balance between excitatory catecholamine and inhibitory cholinergic systems. In addition, there is evidence that these systems may be mutually regulatory—that is, excessive stimulation in one system may cause a compensatory rebound in the other.

SUMMARY

Are different emotional states characterized by distinguishable physiological responses? This is the question with which we began our discussions, and it appears that we have now come full circle. On one hand, logic would seem to demand a positive answer: Any behavior, or any conscious content (affect), must have its physiological representation in the organism, and, if the behavior or feeling *is* different from some other, there must ultimately be some difference in the physiological processes. Thus, even starting from a cognitive view of emotion, somewhere in the organism a distinctive physiological response must occur in order to "label" the specific emotion. If one looks at the literature concerning peripheral autonomic responses, there is some limited evidence that differential responses can be recorded in situations arousing different affects. Similarly, if one looks at the literature concerning central neural mechanisms in emotion, particularly in regard to the limbic system, there is at least the suggestion that different emotions have different controlling mechanisms. But limbic mechanisms are probably not purely emotional—they seem to have other regulating functions as well.

That the evidence for specificity of emotions is relatively weak suggests that we may have been approaching the question improperly. Historically, both laypersons and psychologists have treated emotions as though they were relatively fixed "things" to be located within the organism. But our overview of the research suggests that this is not appropriate. "Emotions" are a complex amalgam of behavior, cognitions, physiological changes, and feeling. Any one element, by itself, does not cause the others—feelings do not uniformly lead to specific behaviors (Cannon-Bard), nor do behaviors necessarily entail constant physiological changes (James-Lange). "Emotions," then, rather than being "things," may represent processes, processes of adaptation to changes in our environment and our attempts to cope with those changes. Not only are "happiness" and "anger" different, but so too are the "angers" we experience in different circumstances; we do different things, have different physiological changes and, probably, feel somewhat differently. Seeking to identify "anger," as a "thing" in the CNS, then, becomes somewhat beside the point. We may be able to find some communalities among a great variety of circumstances all of which we may label "anger," but we shall have overlooked the very processes that make these different.

REFERENCES

AKERT, K. Diencephalon. In D. E. Sheer (ed.), *Electrical stimulation of the brain*. Austin, Texas: University of Texas Press, 1961, pp. 288–310.

ALEXANDER, F. *Psychosomatic medicine*. New York: Norton, 1950.

ANISMAN, H. Time-dependent variations in aversively motivated behaviors: Nonassociative effects of cholinergic and catecholaminergic activity. *Psychological Review*, 1975, 82, 359–385.

AVERILL, J. R. Autonomic response patterns during sadness and mirth. *Psychophysiology*, 1969, *5*, 399–414.

AX, A. F. The physiological differentiation between fear and anger in humans. *Psychosomatic Medicine*, 1953, *15*, 433–442.

BARD, P. A diencephalic mechanism for the expression of rage with special reference to the sympathetic nervous system. *American Journal of Physiology*, 1928, *84*, 490–515.

BARD, P., & MACHT, M. B. The behavior of chronically decerebrate cats. In *Ciba Foundation Symposium, Neurological basis of behavior*. London: Churchill, 1958, pp. 55–71.

BEATTY, J., GREENBERG, A., DEIBLER, W. P., & O'HANLON, J. F. Operant control of occipital theta rhythm affects performance in a radar monitoring task. *Science*, 1974, *183*, 871–873.

BERNARD, B. K., BERCHEK, J. R., & YUTZEY, D. A. Alterations in brain monoaminergic functioning associated with septal lesion induced hyperactivity. *Pharmacology, Biochemistry and Behavior*, 1975, *3*, 121–126.

BLANCHARD, E. B., & YOUNG, L. B. Self-control of cardiac functioning: A promise as yet unfulfilled. *Psychological Bulletin*, 1973, *79*, 145–163.

BLANCHARD, E. B., & YOUNG, L. D. Of promises and evidence: A reply to Engel. *Psychological Bulletin*, 1974, *81*, 44–46.

BRADY, J. V. Motivational-emotional factors and intracranial self-stimulation. In D. E. Sheer (ed.), *Electrical stimulation of the brain*. Austin, Texas: University of Texas Press, 1961, pp. 413–430.

BRADY, J. V. Toward a behavioral biology of emotion. In L. Levi (ed.), *Emotions: Their parameters and measurement*. New York: Raven Press, 1975, pp. 17–46.

BRADY, J. V., & NAUTA, W. J. H. Subcortical mechanisms in emotional behavior: Affective changes following septal forebrain lesions in the albino rat. *Journal of Comparative and Physiological Psychology*, 1953, *46*, 339–346.

CANNON, W. B. *Bodily changes in pain, hunger, fear and rage* (2nd ed.). New York: Appleton-Century-Crofts, 1929.

CANNON, W. B. Again the James-Lange and the thalamic theories of emotion. *Psychological Review*, 1931, *31*, 281–295.

DELGADO, J. M. R., ROSVOLD, H. E., & LOONEY, E. Conditioned fear by electrical stimulation of the monkey brain. *Journal of Comparative and Physiological Psychology*, 1956, *49*, 373–380.

DICARA, L. V., & MILLER, N. E. Instrumental learning of vasomotor responses by rats: Learning to respond differentially in the two ears. *Science*, 1968, *159*, 1485–1486.

Douglas, R. J. The hippocampus and behavior. *Psychological Bulletin*, 1967, *67*, 416–442.

Douglas, R. J., & Pribram, K. H. Learning and limbic lesions. *Neuropsychologia*, 1966, *4*, 197–220.

Fernandez de Molina, A., & Hunsperger, R. W. Organization of the subcortical system governing defense and flight reactions in the cat. *Journal of Physiology*, 1962, *160*, 200–213.

Fried, P. A. Septum and behavior: A review. *Psychological Bulletin*, 1972, *78*, 292–310.

Goddard, G. V. Functions of the amygdala. *Psychological Bulletin*, 1964, *62*, 89–109.

Grossman, S. P., Grossman, L., & Walsh, L. Functional organization of the rat amygdala with respect to avoidance behavior. *Journal of Comparative and Physiological Psychology*, 1975, *88*, 829–850.

Hahn, W. H., Schwartz, M. L., & Sapper, H. V. The effects of d-tubocurarine chloride and respiratory settings on heart rate and blood gas composition in the albino rat. *Psychophysiology*, 1975, *12*, 331–338.

Harris, V. A., & Katkin, E. S. Primary and secondary emotional behavior: An analysis of the role of autonomic feedback on affect, arousal, and attribution. *Psychological Bulletin*, 1975, *82*, 904–916.

Hebb, D. O. *Organization of behavior*. New York: Wiley, 1949.

Hedges, A. S., Van Atta, L., & Thomas, J. B. Septal lesions facilitate in shift from conditioned escape to conditioned avoidance behavior in the rat. *Physiology and Behavior*, 1975, *14*, 25–30.

Hohmann, G. W. Some effects of spinal cord lesions on experienced emotional feelings. *Psychophysiology*, 1966, *3*, 143–156.

James, W. *The principles of psychology*. New York: Holt, 1890.

Jarrard, L. E. The hippocampus and motivation. *Psychological Bulletin*, 1973, *79*, 1–12.

Kimble, D. P. Hippocampus and internal inhibition. *Psychological Bulletin*, 1968, *70*, 285–295.

Kimmel, H. D. Instrumental conditioning of autonomically mediated responses in human beings. *American Psychologist*, 1974, *29*, 325–335.

King, F. A., & Meyer, P. M. Effects of amygdaloid lesions upon septal hyperemotionality in the rat. *Science*, 1958, *128*, 655–656.

Kling, A., Orbach, J., Schwartz, N. B., & Towne, J. C. Injury to the limbic system and associated structures in cats. *Archives of General Psychiatry*, 1960, *3*, 391–420.

Klüver, H., & Bucy, P. C. Preliminary analysis of functions of the temporal lobes in monkeys. *Archives of Neurology and Psychiatry*, 1939, *42*, 979–1000.

LACEY, J. I. Individual differences in somatic response patterns. *Journal of Comparative and Physiological Psychology*, 1950, *43*, 338–350.

LACEY, J. I. Somatic response patterning and stress: Some revisions of activation theory. In M. H. Appley & R. Trumbell (eds.), *Psychological stress*. New York: Appleton-Century-Crofts, 1967, pp. 14–37.

LACEY, J. I., BATEMAN, D. E., & VANLEHN, R. Autonomic response specificity: An experimental study. *Psychosomatic Medicine*, 1953, *15*, 8–21.

LACEY, J. I., & LACEY, B. C. Verification and extension of the principle of autonomic response-stereotypy. *American Journal of Psychology*, 1958, *71*, 50–73.

LACEY, J. I., & LACEY, B. C. The law of initial value in the longitudinal study of autonomic constitution: Reproducibility of autonomic responses and response patterns over a four-year interval. *Annals of the New York Academy of Sciences*, 1962, *98*, 1257–1290.

LEVENE, H. I., ENGEL, B. T., & SCHULKIN, F. R. Patterns of autonomic responsivity in identical schizophrenic twins. *Psychophysiology*, 1967, *3*, 363–370.

LEVI, L. (ed.), *Emotions: Their parameters and measurement*. New York: Raven Press, 1975.

LINDSLEY, D. B. Emotion. In S. S. Stevens (ed.), *Handbook of experimental psychology*. New York: Wiley, 1951, pp. 473–516.

LUBAR, J. F., & NUMAN, R. Behavioral and physiological studies of septal function and related medial cortical structures. *Behavioral Biology*, 1973, *8*, 1–26.

MACLEAN, P. D. The limbic system with respect to self-preservation and preservation of the species. *Journal of Nervous and Mental Disease*, 1958, *127*, 1–11.

MANDLER, G. The search for emotion. In L. Levi (ed.), *Emotions: Their parameters and measurement*. New York: Raven Press, 1975, pp. 1–16.

MASSERMAN, J. H. Is the hypothalamus a center of emotion? *Psychosomatic Medicine*, 1941, *5*, 3–25.

MCCLEARY, R. A. Response specificity in the behavioral effects of limbic system lesions in the cat. *Journal of Comparative and Physiological Psychology*, 1961, *54*, 605–613.

MICCO, D. J., & SCHWARTZ, M. Effects of hippocampal lesions upon the development of Pavlovian internal inhibition in rats. *Journal of Comparative and Physiological Psychology*, 1971, *76*, 371–377.

MICZEK, K. A., BRYKCZYNSKI, T., & GROSSMAN, S. P. Differential effects of lesions in the amygdala, periamygdaloid cortex, and stria terminalis on aggressive behavior in rats. *Journal of Comparative and Physiological Psychology*, 1974, *87*, 760–771.

Middaugh, S., Eissenberg, E., & Brener, J. The effect of artificial ventilation on cardiovascular status and heart rate conditioning in the curarized rat. *Psychophysiology,* 1975, *12,* 520–526.

Miller, N. E. Learning and performance motivated by direct stimulation of the brain. In D. E. Sheer (ed.), *Electrical stimulation of the brain.* Austin, Texas: University of Texas Press, 1961, pp. 387–396.

Miller, N. E. Learning of visceral and glandular responses. *Science,* 1969, *163,* 434–445.

Miller, N. E., & Dworkin, B. R. Visceral learning: Recent difficulties with curarized rats and significant problems for human research. In P. A. Obrist, A. H. Black, J. Brener, & L. V. DiCara (eds.), *Cardiovascular psychophysiology: Current issues in response mechanisms, biofeedback, and methodology.* Chicago: Aldine, 1974, pp. 312–331.

Moyer, K. E. *The psychobiology of aggression.* New York: Harper & Row, 1976.

Nagatsu, T., Ikuta, K., Numata (Sudo), Y., Kato, T., Sano, M., Nagutsu, I., Umezawa, H., Matsuzaki, M., & Takeuchi, T. Vascular and brain dopamine β-hydroxylase activity in young spontaneously hypertensive rats. *Science,* 1976, *191,* 290–291.

Obrist, P. A. The cardiovascular-behavioral interaction—as it appears today. *Psychophysiology,* 1976, *13,* 95–108.

Obrist, P. A., Black, A. H., Brener, J., & DiCara, L. V. (eds.). *Cardiovascular psychophysiology: Current issues in response mechanisms, biofeedback, and methodology.* Chicago: Aldine, 1974.

Oken, D. The psychophysiology and psychoendocrinology of stress and emotion. In M. H. Appley & R. Trumbull (eds.), *Psychological stress.* New York: Appleton-Century-Crofts, 1967, pp. 43–62.

Orne, M. T., & Paskewitz, D. A. Aversive situational effects on alpha feedback training. *Science,* 1974, *186,* 458–460.

Pribram, K. H. Interrelations of psychology and the neurological disciplines. In S. Koch (ed.), *Psychology: A study of a science,* Vol. 4. New York: McGraw-Hill, 1962, pp. 119–157.

Roberts, W. W. Rapid escape learning without avoidance learning motivated by hypothalamic stimulation in cats. *Journal of Comparative and Physiological Psychology,* 1958, *51,* 391–399.

Roberts, W. W. Fear-like behavior elicited from dorsomedial thalamus of the cat. *Journal of Comparative and Physiological Psychology,* 1962, *55,* 191–198.

Roberts, W. W., & Kiess, H. O. Motivational properties of hypothalamic aggression in cats. *Journal of Comparative and Physiological Psychology,* 1964, *58,* 187–193.

RUFF, G. E., & KORCHIN, S. J. Adaptive stress behavior. In M. H. Appley & R. Trumbull (eds.), *Psychological stress*. New York:Appleton-Century-Crofts, 1967, pp. 297–323.

SCHACHTER, S., & SINGER, J. E. Cognitive, social, and physiological determinants of emotional state. *Psychological Review*, 1962, *69*, 379–399.

SCHANBERG, S. M., STONE, R. A., KIRSCHNER, N., GUNNELLS, J. C., & ROBINSON, R. R. Plasma dopamine β-hydroxylase: A possible aid in the study and evaluation of hypertension. *Science*, 1974, *183*, 523–524.

SELYE, H. *The physiology and pathology of exposure to stress*. Montreal: Acta, 1950.

SPRAGUE, J. J., LEVITT, M., ROBSON, K., LUI, C. H., STELLAR, E., & CHAMBERS, W. W. A neuroanatomical and behavioral analysis of the syndromes resulting from midbrain lemniscal and reticular lesions in the cat. *Archives Italiennes de Biologie*, 1963, *101*, 225–295.

STEIN, M., SCHIAVI, R. C., & CAMERINO, M. Influence of brain and behavior on the immune system. *Science*, 1976, *191*, 435–440.

STEPHENS, J. H., HARRIS, A. H., BRADY, J. V., & SHAFFER, J. W. Psychological and physiological variables associated with large magnitude voluntary heart rate changes. *Psychophysiology*, 1975, *12*, 381–387.

VALENSTEIN, E. S. *Brain control*. New York: Wiley, 1973.

8

Hunger and the Regulation of Food Intake

In order to function, animal organisms must fulfill certain bodily needs. These include needs for food and water, regulation of body temperature, elimination of waste materials, and breathing oxygen. To some extent at least, these needs are interdependent—for example, our ability to utilize food substances requires oxygen for metabolism. This chapter and the next will discuss the needs for food and water, respectively, as prototypes of the general question of need regulation.

As will be evident, there is considerable overlap between the CNS mechanisms concerned with hunger and thirst; in fact, evaluating that overlap is itself an important question. As a consequence, it will be necessary at times to indicate some things about the mechanisms subserving thirst here, even though the major discussion of that system will be deferred until the next chapter.

Superficially, our needs for food seem unspecific. Unlike the need for oxygen, which is highly specific (there is no substitute for oxygen), a variety of foodstuffs are interchangeable; thus, we can eat broccoli instead of asparagus. Nonetheless there are specific needs for salts, proteins, carbohydrates, and vitamins. In certain instances, deficiencies in one of these nutrient categories can result in specific behaviors. There have been a number of classical experiments in which subjects have even self-selected the appropriate salt or vitamin that compensated for their particular need. Having recognized this factor, we shall be more concerned here with the factors involved in the control of the amount of food ingested.

The general question of how an organism regulates its requirements for food and water can be broken down into a number of subsidiary questions. What initiates the desire to eat or drink? What determines how much is eaten or drunk? What stops the eating and drinking? It is obvious that learned habits play a role in the answers to these questions: Three meals a day is not a uniform human practice, nor are chocolate-covered ants a general dietary staple.

Historically, the study of food and water regulation has been approached from a physiological standpoint. As might be expected, theories of hunger and thirst have drawn either on peripheral or central mechanisms. A few peripheral theories have been "general" in the sense that they ascribe hunger and thirst to mechanisms dispersed throughout the body; each cell has its metabolic requirements and these, together, contribute to hunger and thirst motivations. Most peripheral theories, however, have been "local" in that they assign paramount importance to specific organs or regions of the body. Most prominent in the case of hunger are stomach mechanisms; in thirst it is postulated that mechanisms are activated by a dry mouth and throat. Central theories, of course, account for hunger and thirst on the basis of brain mechanisms. Today, central theories have largely come to mean hypothalamic and associated subcortical mechanisms.

Relative emphasis on peripheral and central mechanisms has shifted from time to time, in large part depending on available research methods. But no exclusive priority can be ascribed to either type of mechanism.

PERIPHERAL MECHANISMS OF HUNGER

In this section we will enumerate a number of peripheral factors that influence our food intake, factors that modulate the quantity of food ingested without being the sole determinants of hunger.

Local theories of hunger have tended to emphasize the stomach as the source of the hunger drive. Taste factors have also been assigned a role in mediating the amount and type of food ingested. Of course, food entering the stomach normally comes through the mouth, but the connection between mouth and stomach may be experimentally separated and this has contributed greatly to the understanding of these two factors.

The Stomach

The stomach has long been considered important in regulating hunger and its importance was corroborated in the late nineteenth century by direct observation. In 1882, a hunter on the American frontier was injured by a

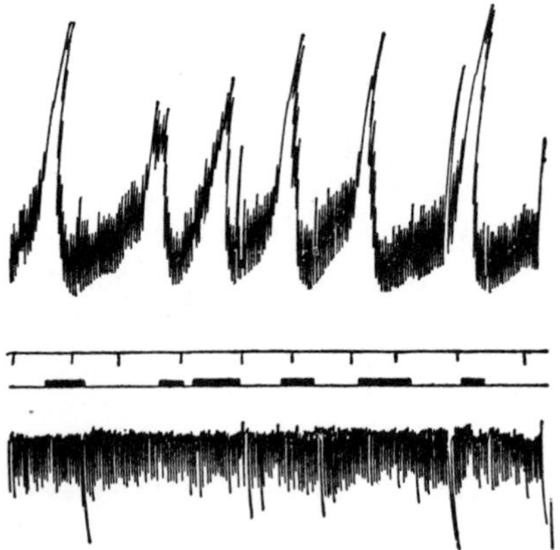

Figure 8.1. The top record represents intragastric pressure (the small oscillations due to respiration, the large to contractions of the stomach); the second record is the time in minutes (10 min); the third record is W's report of hunger pangs; the lowest record is respiration registered by means of a pneumograph about the abdomen. (From Cannon, W. B. and Washburn, A. L., An explanation of hunger. *American Journal of Physiology*, 1912, *29*, 441–454.)

gunshot wound that left an opening in his side (a *fistula*) all the way through the stomach. His stomach activity was subsequently observed under a variety of conditions by the physician William Beaumont (see Rosenzweig, 1962). Beaumont observed the secretion of the stomach and also made the important observation that putting food directly into the stomach alleviated the sensation of hunger.

Hunger Pangs

An experiment influential in bolstering the role of the stomach in hunger regulation concerned the sensation of "hunger pangs." Before this experiment, physiologists disagreed over the question of whether the stomach actually contracted during hunger. Cannon and Washburn's (1912) experiment thus attempted to correlate the occurrence of stomach contractions with the phenomenal report of hunger. Figure 8.1 shows the simultaneous records obtained from a balloon swallowed by Washburn, and inflated in his stomach, and his subjective report of hunger. The coincidence of hunger reports with contractions, and the absence of reports when contractions ceased, were taken as evidence that the contractions give rise to the sensation of hunger.

Although the existence of hunger contractions in the stomach was confirmed, there is evidence that they were in fact an artifact of placing a balloon in the stomach. R. C. Davis, Garafalo, & Kveim (1959) used abdominal electrodes to record stomach motility. They found that stomach activity is lowest when the stomach is empty. They also could not confirm the correlation of stomach contractions and the sensation of hunger. Furthermore, introducing a balloon into the stomach increased the electrical activity, causing Davis et al. to suggest that Cannon's results were an artifact of placing the balloon into the stomach.

Distension

Among the gastric factors that can influence food intake is stomach distension. Everything else being equal, it is clear that the larger the volume of food in the stomach, the less the subsequent intake. An experiment by Schwartzbaum and Ward (1958) suggests that osmotic[1] pressure of substances in the stomach may also be a factor in inhibiting eating, independent of the nature of the substance.

Schwartzbaum and Ward loaded rats by stomach intubation with glucose, sodium chloride, or sodium saccharin, all at the same osmotic concentration; these substances were all tested over a range of osmotic concentration for their effects on subsequent food intake. This study indicates that hypertonic preloads reduced food intake, while hypotonic and isotonic loads tended to increase the intake of dry food. Food consumption did not differ between glucose and sodium choride preloads, suggesting that the caloric properties of the substances are not a factor in short-term regulation of intake.

Caloric Regulation

However, a number of studies have shown that over a longer period (several days) food intake is well regulated by caloric content. For instance, Carlisle and Stellar (1969) fed rats lab chow mixed with oil. In one preparation, increasing the added oil increased the caloric content of the diet; in another preparation, increasing the oil decreased the caloric content per unit volume of the diet; in the control preparation, the oil did not affect the caloric content. Thus, in this experiment there was simultaneous variation of the caloric content and the oily taste of the diet. Briefly, the animals tended to adjust their intake so as to maintain a consistent caloric level. There was also evidence that palatability of the diet was an important factor in determining intake but palatability could not account for the caloric regulation that was also occurring. Thus the finding was that normal rats maintain a relatively constant caloric intake over a wide range of variation in dietary caloric density and texture.

Intragastrically preloaded monkeys (McHugh, Moran, & Barton, 1975) also provide evidence of caloric regulation. Since food was placed directly

[1]For a definition of osmosis, see Chapter 9, p. 337. For definitions of the terms iso-, hypo- and hypertonic, see footnote 2, p. 335.

into the stomach, taste factors were controlled and the volume, caloric density, and the nature of the nutrient preloaded, were varied. The animals ate subsequent standard meals so as to regulate accurately their total caloric intake.

Intragastric Regulation

Finally, Epstein and Teitelbaum (1962) showed that total food regulation in rats could be achieved solely through intragastric regulation. In their experiment, rats self-injected liquid food directly into their stomachs by pressing a bar. Oropharyngeal (mouth and throat) influences were completely bypassed by this technique, and the rats obtained all their food in this manner. They appropriately varied their bar pressing to compensate for the experimenter's manipulation of the concentration of the injected food and the schedule of reinforcement in order to maintain normal weight. But Snowdon (1969) found some limitations on this result: Eliminating oropharyngeal sensations does produce a decrement in motivation to work for food. As Epstein and Teitelbaum indicate, the fact that oropharyngeal stimulation is not necessary for food regulation does not mean that it normally does not contribute to such regulation. Certainly taste mediates normal selection of the type of food, and in an animal searching for food in the environment, taste and smell aid the search. When such detection and discrimination are not required, however—as in this experiment—regulation of the amount consumed can still occur.

OROPHARYNGEAL FACTORS

Several lines of evidence militate against any exclusive dependence of hunger on stomach activity. Surgical patients whose entire stomach has been removed report a normal desire for food and normal regulation. Animals with similar operations or with denervation of the stomach also show normal food regulation.

Hunger Reduction

Experiments on the rat from Miller's laboratory (Kohn, 1951; Berkun, Kessen, & Miller, 1952) indicate that both oropharyngeal and stomach factors play a role in the reduction of hunger motivation. In these experiments, hunger drive was measured by both instrumental (rate of response for food) and consummatory measures (amounts ingested). Prefeeding the rats with food injected directly into the stomach significantly reduced hunger by these measures, but less so than food taken orally. These results are commensurate with those obtained by Beaumont.

Also pertinent is an experiment by Miller and Kessen (1952) which indicated that with injection of food directly into the stomach as the reward, rats could learn to choose the correct side of a maze; again, food by mouth was a superior reinforcement. These results indicate that decrements in consummatory and instrumental behavior with injected food were produced by decrements in hunger rather than aversive factors such as nausea. Thus, although food directly in the stomach is effective in reducing hunger, food by mouth is more so and indicates that some oral factor is also involved in cessation of hunger. There is the suggestion (Nicolaïdis, 1969) that oral stimulation with sweet solutions will cause early, "preadaptive" bodily responses, which are anticipatory of later metabolic modifications resulting from food absorportion; some of these might be conditioned responses while others could be unconditioned. They might account for the rapidity of the effects of food by mouth.

An interesting series of experiments on intragastric feeding with human subjects was reported by Jordan (1969). The results emphasize the motivational strength of oral stimulation. In this experiment, volunteers fed themselves either orally or intragastrically, but in both instances the food (Metrecal) was delivered by pump. With pump rates kept constant, intragastric intake was comparable to oral intake; variation in pump rates generally resulted in increased intake. With simultaneous oral and intragastric intake, the subjects overate and did not respond to the total caloric intake. Most striking in this respect is the fact that when intragastric intake was of a 90 percent diluted solution, the volume of intake increased only slightly and did not compensate for the caloric dilution.

Short-term regulation during intragastric feeding is, then, based on volume rather than the caloric value of the food, and oral factors tend to override gastric factors in this regulation (as indicated by the overeating during simultaneous oral and intragastric feeding). Finally, intragastric feeding appears to be less satisfying in that the subjects reported strong cravings for chewing, tasting, and swallowing following intragastric meals.

Up to this point, the results of intragastric feeding seem clear: Intragastric feeding is a relatively satisfactory means of regulating food intake and will support the learning of some instrumental responses in order to receive such injections. An experiment by Holman (1969) complicates this conclusion, however. In a lever-pressing task, Holman found that rats would press for intragastric injections of food only if there was an accompanying oral stimulus—weak saccharin solutions, temperature changes in the nasopharynx, or licking and chewing of the lever seemed to be a necessary mediator for the lever pressing. The rats did not press for either oral stimulation or intragastric feeding alone. Another interesting finding was that the choice between two oral stimuli was affected by intragastric injection of food; that is, taste stimuli which had been reinforced with intragastric food were preferred. Here, intragastric injections had the power to enhance the value of oral stimuli but not to reinforce operant behavior directly. Such results suggest two relatively weak reinforcing effects; apparently neither oral nor intragastric effects were sufficient by themselves but could summate to reinforce operant behavior.

Taste and Flavor of Food

In their natural habitats, animals learn to avoid ingesting foods that cause illness, even though in some instances the illness may develop only after considerable delay. In the laboratory, comparable results have been produced with a variety of techniques. Thus, rats learn to avoid preferred saccharin solutions which are followed as much as hours later by illness-producing doses of X-radiation (Garcia, Kimeldorf, & Hunt, 1961). Alternatively, as has been mentioned, rats apparently learn to self-select those diets that make up for nutritional deficiencies. These effects seem to be mediated on the basis of taste mechanisms (see Rozin, 1969; Rozin & Kalat, 1971).

In a related approach, Le Magnen (1969) has shown that animals relate the flavor (smell) of a food substance to its subsequent effects. In a training period, alternate presentations of two flavors were made; rats eating one of the flavors received intravenous administrations of a dietary supplement, while those eating the other flavor received isotonic saline. After the training period, the free choice of the food with the supplemented flavor was reduced. A reduced choice of the supplemented food occurred only in intact rats exposed to both a flavor and the supplement: Control experiments indicated that (1) supplements are ineffective in producing a differential choice if the distinctive flavor is omitted; (2) the flavors by themselves do not produce differential choice in the absence of the supplement; and (3) anosmic rats, who cannot distinguish the flavors, do not show the differential choice despite the presence of both the flavors and the supplement. The results, therefore, present evidence for a learned discrimination based on smell.

While these effects stress learning influences on dietary selection, Morrison (1974) has presented evidence that palatability of food changes simply as a function of prior tasting of food. That is, simply tasting a food substance lowers its future desirability for rats. The effect is short lasting, recovery occurring within 30 minutes, and independent of nutritional effects per se. Most of us do seem to grow tired of large quantities of any single food substance in a meal, but, on the other hand, there is also the almost insatiable desire to continue eating salty peanuts once started—the mechanisms producing such fluctuations in palatability are presently unknown.

Hunger Stimuli

The preceding discussion indicates that purely local gastric and oral factors cannot adequately account for hunger and the satiation of hunger. Since feeding stops long before absorption of nutrients by bodily tissues can be completed, a logical conclusion is that some message is transmitted centrally. Several theories postulate the existence of central receptors sensitive to peripherally determined chemical or physiological conditions. Neural transmission of messages about these conditions may be of some consequence, but the fact that normal food regulation goes on despite the lack of a stomach or neural afferents from the stomach suggests nonneural mechanisms. A likely candidate for this role is blood sugar. Glucose is a prime source of energy, and its cycles of availability seem rapid enough to account for hunger and satiation cycles. These and other considerations have led to the suggestion of a *glucostatic* theory of hunger (Mayer, 1953).

Glucostatic Theory

The simplest version of a glucostatic hypothesis would relate the absolute levels of blood sugar to the rise and fall of hunger. That such is not the case, however, has been amply documented; for instance, diabetes is characterized by abnormally high blood sugar levels, but hunger is far from minimized (see M. I. Grossman, 1955). As a consequence, this simple theory has been revised to take into account the utilization of glucose. In short, the glucostatic theory suggests that "glucoreceptors" in the CNS are sensitive to the rate of glucose utilization. Low rates of utilization lead to hunger and food intake, while high rates of utilization lead to feelings of satiety and the cessation of feeding. To verify this theory, Mayer and his colleagues have attempted to use arterial-venous glucose differences (Δ-glucose) as an index of utilization. Figure 8.2 summarizes experiments in which reports of hunger were correlated with Δ-glucose in human subjects. The parameter of importance here is the *difference* between the curves. Though both curves may rise or fall together, hunger was absent only when a substantial (10 mg/100 cc) Δ-glucose was obtained; conversely, lower values were correlated with hunger.

A number of lines of evidence tend to support a glucostatic theory and these will be discussed in considering CNS mechanisms. Nonetheless, the glucostatic hypothesis would seem to be only the leading one of several possibilities. But, note again, we are primarily concerned here with total food regulation; while a glucostatic theory would be useful in this respect, it probably could not account for specific hungers without appropriate modification.

Other hypothesized peripheral stimuli for hunger are fat storage, body temperature, and hormonal factors.

Lipostatic Theory

Kennedy (1953) suggested that animals regulate their food intake to maintain a fixed level of fat deposits within the body. Such a lipostatic theory seems best suited to account for the long-term weight regulation observed in ani-

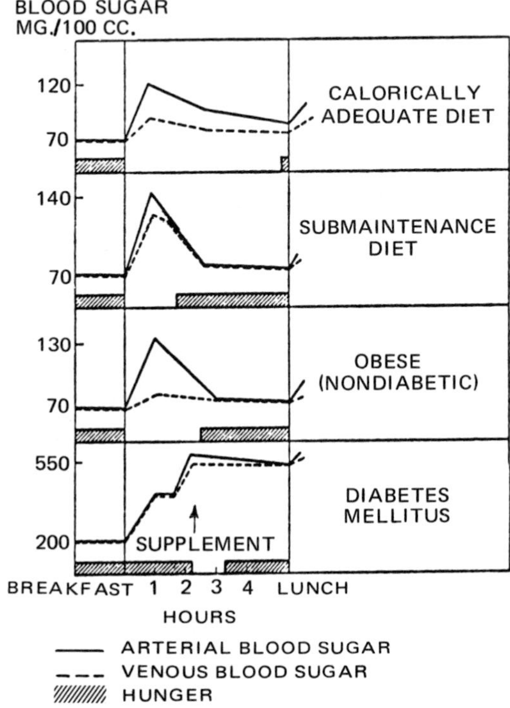

Figure 8.2. Typical morning correlations of Δ-glucose and hunger feeling. The size of the Δ-glucose (peripheral glucose arterio-venous difference) correlates with hunger feelings. No hunger feeling appears if the Δ-glucose is greater than 10 mg per 100 cc. [From Mayer, J., Glucostatic mechanism of regulation of food intake. Reprinted by permission from *The New England Journal of Medicine* (249; 13–16, 1953).]

mal subjects, but evidence also points to involvement in the short-term regulation of daily meals. Again, we shall return to lipostatic theory when we discuss the operation of central mechanisms in eating behavior.

Thermostatic Theory

The thermostatic theory (Brobeck, 1948) proposes that animals eat to maintain their body temperature and stop eating to prevent hyperthermia. Alterations in feeding and drinking with temperature changes of the body or hypothalamus have been reported (Andersson & Larsson, 1961; Sundsten, 1969; Stevenson, 1969). In fact, Stevenson reports a high correlation between body temperature and blood sugar after insulin injections, indicating that these factors may be part of an overall mechanism. However, while environmental temperature does affect food and water regulation, there is no evidence that internal temperature changes are responsible for normal food and water regulation (Friedman & Stricker, 1976).

Hormonal Theory

Experiments by J. D. Davis, Gallagher, Ladove, and Turausky (1969) do provide strong evidence for a hormonal inhibition of eating which is mediated through the blood supply. These experiments employed rats chronically prepared for blood transfusion in such a manner as to allow the blood of two rats to be completely intermixed—that is, half the blood of each of a pair of animals was its own and half was from the other rat.

In the first experiment, the blood of satiated and deprived rats was mixed and the animals were then allowed to feed. The deprived rats showed a 50 percent depression in food intake. The satiated rats did not show any appreciable intake. The second experiment evaluated the possibility that these results could in some way be attributed to the mechanical properties of the transfusion process rather than the actual transfusion of a satiety factor in the blood of the satiated animals. For this purpose, transfusions were made between pairs of rats both of which were deprived. The fact that eating was not inhibited demonstrates clearly that the prior results are not such an artifact. The third experiment involved transfusions between paired rats, one of which had been allowed ad-lib access to food, and the other of which obtained his total daily food ration in a 30-minute bar-pressing session. Transfusion was carried out just prior to the bar-pressing session, resulting in a bar-pressing reduction of 59 percent.

This experiment also replicated the second experiment by transfusing blood to the bar-pressing rats after the ad-lib rats had been deprived of food for 24 hours. Bar pressing was not affected in this instance. These bar-pressing results were obtained with continuous reinforcement; when the experiment was repeated using variable interval reinforcement, the response rate was not reduced. This result suggests that the blood factor responsible for prior results does not act by modifying the effort expended to obtain food.

While these results are extremely suggestive of a blood-borne satiety factor, they must not be accepted without reservation. Walike and Smith (1972), for example, were unable to demonstrate either a satiety factor or a hunger-stimulating factor. Their procedures were, however, markedly different from those of Davis et al., involving chronic cross-circulation between monkeys. Thus, it is not clear what effect species differences might generally have, and whether species-specific immunity reactions might have precluded obtaining a positive result.

More recently, positive results from a satiety factor were again obtained

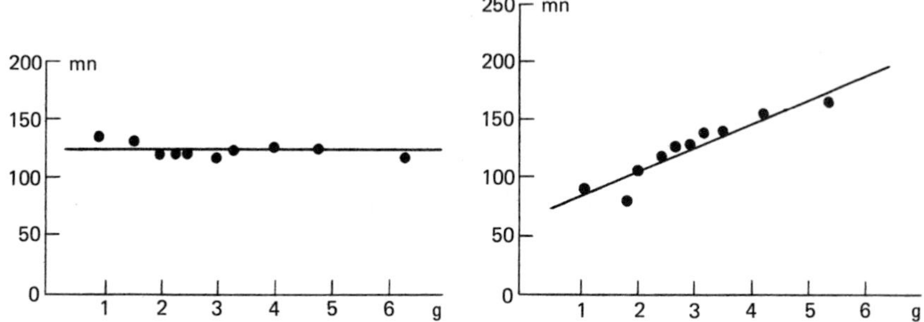

Figure 8.3. Relationships between meal size and length of the preceding and subsequent intervals. Meal length is unrelated to the preceding interval but positively related to the subsequent interval. (From LeMagnen, J., Peripheral and systematic actions of food in the caloric regulation of intake. *Annals of the New York Academy of Sciences*, 1963, *157*, 1126–1157.)

in experiments with rats. Cholecystokinin is a hormone released from the duodenum (small intestine) as a result of ingesting food; by injecting this hormone, Gibbs, Young, and Smith (1973) obtained direct evidence that it may qualify as a blood-borne satiety factor. Naturally, the hormone appears rapidly following food ingestion, and injected in physiologically appropriate doses, it inhibits further eating for a period of some 30 minutes; it is selective in that drinking is not inhibited and it does not appear to operate by making the animals sick.

In general, then, the research has suggested that eating may be controlled by inhibitory feedback from satiety signals, and this is accomplished through a blood factor(s). Such a suggestion is compatible with the correlation between meal size and the time to the next meal, as illustrated in Figure 8.3. It can be seen that meal size is not correlated with the time since the previous meal, but with the time to the next meal. These results indicate the operation of postprandial (after eating) inhibitory factors—that is, meal size determines the subsequent duration of satiation. This correlation has also been confirmed by Snowdon (1969) for intragastrically fed rats. It has been postulated, however, that instead of directly controlling the length of intermeal intervals, recently ingested food actually produces "error" signals with respect to which subsequent feeding behavior is adjusted (Panksepp, 1973), i.e., by indicating deficiencies.

Finally, Panksepp (1973) points out that feeding can become "uncoupled" from any underlying physiological determinants. For instance, changing to a highly palatable food can produce gross overeating in both humans and animals; the problem is to determine for how long and to what extent the uncoupling can continue and to identify those mechanisms that restore the coupled state.

Summary

Peripheral theories of hunger point to a variety of oropharyngeal and post-ingestional, gastric and humoral, factors in hunger. Each of these undoubtedly plays some role in the regulation of food intake in the normal animal. None of these, however, can be considered critical. In fact, experimental subjects, both human and animal, have been shown to be capable of relatively normal food regulation in the absence of most of these signals. Thus, these peripheral factors normally *help* determine what foods will be ingested, when ingestion will occur, and how much will be taken, but they cannot be considered to be sole determinants.

CENTRAL MECHANISMS: THE HYPOTHALAMUS

For over a century now it has been suspected, on the basis of clinical observation, that central mechanisms are involved in the regulation of food intake. Only recently, however, have these speculations been supported by the results of scientific experimentation. The structure most frequently mentioned as influencing food and water regulation is the hypothalamus. Much research indicates a need to distinguish between the ventromedial and lateral aspects of the hypothalamus.

Ventromedial Effects

It had long been noticed that, among other symptoms, certain patients with tumors at the base of the brain also showed extreme obesity, but it was not known whether the obesity was caused by hypothalamic or pituitary damage. Hetherington and Ranson (1942) demonstrated that obesity could be produced in animals solely through hypothalamic lesions in the ventromedial nuclei. Figure 8.4 illustrates the comparison between a control and an experimental mouse with ventromedial lesions (the effects have also been produced in rats, monkeys, cats, and dogs).

It has been maintained that such animals become fat because they overeat (thus the term *hypothalamic hyperphagia*), not because of some defect in their metabolism (Brobeck, Tepperman, & Long, 1943; Teitelbaum, 1961). Figure 8.5 illustrates this overeating and shows that there are essentially two phases to this hypothalamic obesity: (1) a dynamic phase, during which the animals overeat and gain weight, and (2) a later, static phase, during which food intake may actually drop but the animal maintains a new, high weight level. Note that these animals do, however, show an

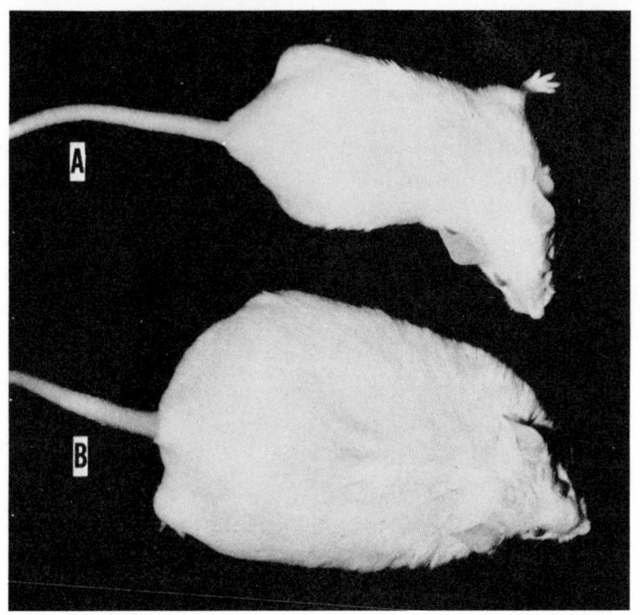

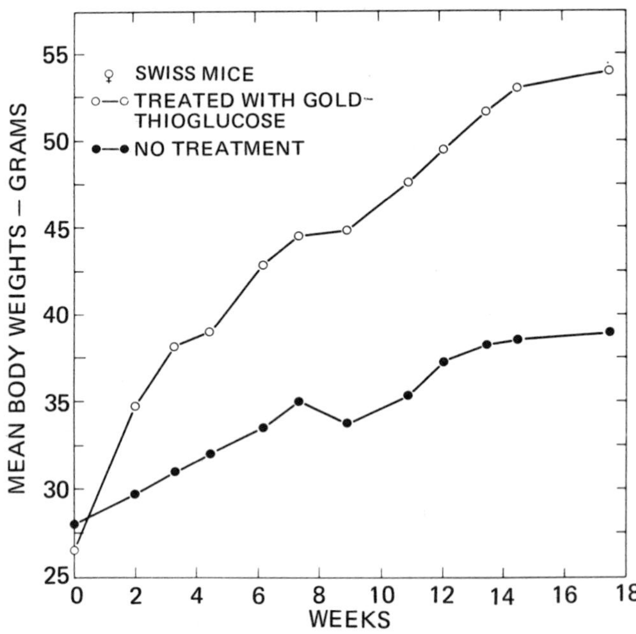

Figure 8.4. Average weights of two groups of mice observed for 18 weeks. *A*, untreated (control) group; *B*, each animal in this group received a single intraperitoneal injection of 0.5 gm of goldthioglucose per gram of body weight. A typical member of each group is shown above. (From Schwartz, I.L., Cronkite, E.P., Johnson, H.A., Silver, L., Tenzer, D., and Debons, A.F., Radioautographic localization of the "satiety center." *Transactions of the Association of American Physicians*, 1961, *74*, 300–317.)

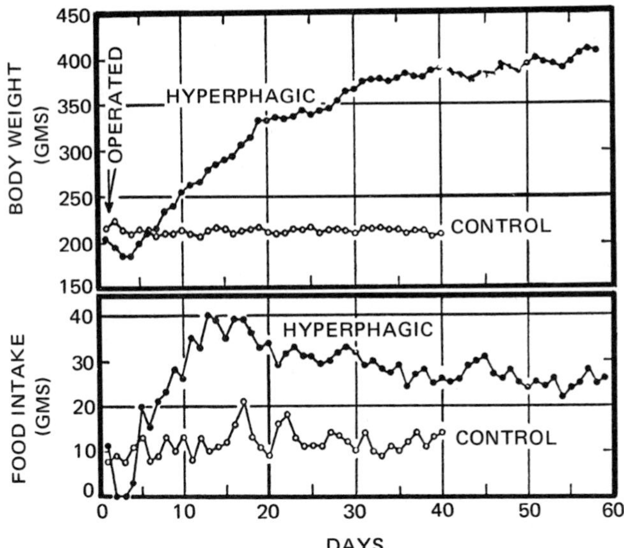

Figure 8.5. Postoperative body weight and daily food intake of a hyperphagic animal compared to that of a normal unoperated control animal. [From Teitelbaum, 1961. Reprinted from *Nebraska Symposium on Motivation* by Jones (Ed.), by permission of University of Nebraska Press. Copyright 1961, University of Nebraska Press.]

adjustment; they do not eat themselves to death but rather maintain their weight at the new altered level.

That the disorder in these animals concerns weight regulation is indicated by data illustrated in Figure 8.6. Thus, an animal which overeats under the influence of insulin injections does not show a large additional weight increment after ventromedial lesions. Note also that an animal suffering from hypothalamic hyperphagia can be starved back to a normal weight; however, when it is allowed back on ad-lib feeding, it returns to an obese level. In addition, it has been shown that in the absence of the hypothalamic lesions, animals do not maintain their overeating when insulin injections are stopped (Teitelbaum, 1961).

These results lend support to Kennedy's lipostatic theory (1953) and suggest that the ventromedial hypothalamus contains receptors sensitive to a circulating metabolite related to the animal's fat deposits.

Glucose

Generally, the ventromedial lesions we have been discussing have been produced electrolytically, that is, by passing an electric current through the tissue. In the case of the mouse in Figure 8.4 the lesion actually was produced in a very different manner. Gold is an element that is toxic to neural

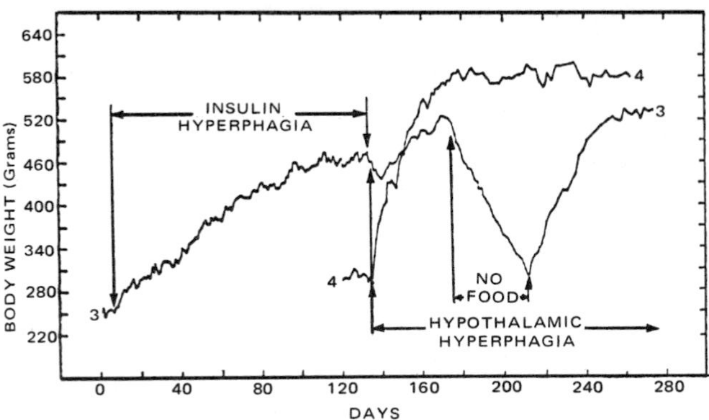

Figure 8.6. Rate of weight gain in hypothalamic hyperphagia if the animal (No. 3) is previously made to overeat and become obese by protamine zinc insulin injections. This is compared with the rate of weight gain in animal No. 4, which starts from a normal weight, and with animal No. 4's own weight gain after it has been starved back to its normal weight level. [From Teitelbaum, 1961. Reprinted from *Nebraska Symposium on Motivation* by Jones (Ed.), by permission of University of Nebraska Press. Copyright 1961, University of Nebraska Press.]

cells. A variety of organic compounds may be prepared which have a gold moiety attached to them. One such compound is goldthioglucose. When injected into mice, goldthioglucose results in hyperphagic animals with lesions of the ventromedial hypothalamus, as illustrated in Figure 8.7.

After the appearance of the hyperphagic symptoms, mice injected with goldthioglucose were sacrified and prepared for histological examination. The brain tissue was then subjected to neutron bombardment, causing the gold to become radioactive. The tissue could then be assayed for localized radioactivity. The detection of radioactivity in the ventromedial hypothalamus, as seen in Figure 8.7, indicates a selective affinity of the goldthioglucose for this location. Presumably this is due to the affinity of the glucose part of the compound for the ventromedial nuclei. Control experiments revealed that animals injected with a different gold-treated compound, goldthiomalate, did not demonstrate concentrated radioactivity in the ventromedial area nor did they demonstrate hyperphagia. This experiment (I. L. Schwartz, Cronkite, Johnson, Silver, Tenzer, & Debons, 1961) provides a strong indication of support for Mayer's glucostatic theory of hunger regulation. Thus, the ventromedial hypothalamic area contains receptors sensitive to circulating glucose, and lesions of this area disrupt normal food and weight regulation.

It should also be noted that in addition to the hypothalamus, three other sites showed some significant radioactivity (Figure 8.8): (a) a small midline area between the optic chiasm and the anterior commissure; (b) the septum and ventral hippocampal commissure; and (c) the midline of the brainstem in

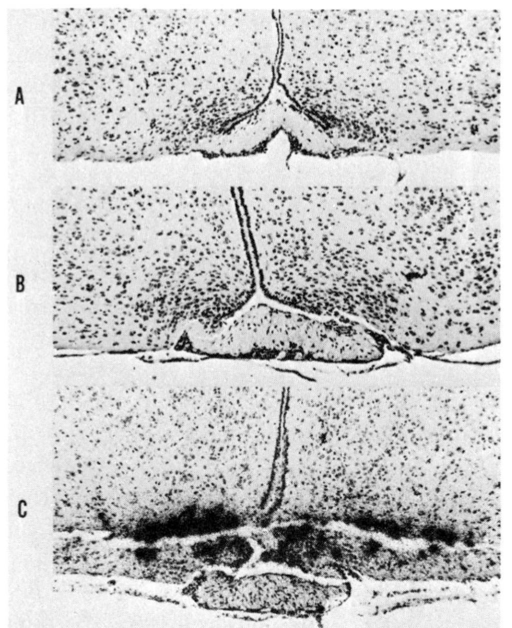

Figure 8.7. Radioautographs of sections through the hypothalamus of mice. *A*, untreated. *B*, treated with a single intraperitoneal injection of 0.5 gm of goldthiomalate per gram of body weight. *C*, treated with a single intraperitoneal injection of 0.5 gm of goldthioglucose per gram of body weight. Only *C* developed hyperphagia and obesity. (From Schwartz, I. L., Cronkite, E. P., Johnson, H. A., Silver, L., Tenzer, D., and Debons, A. F., Radioautographic localization of the "satiety center." *Transactions of the Association of American Physicians*, 1961, *74*, 300–317.)

the floor of the fourth ventricle. Schwartz et al. suggest that these areas may also participate in appetite regulation or other functions sensitive to circulating glucose. (Though not considered likely, all the results could, alternatively, be due to "leakage" in the blood-brain barrier.)

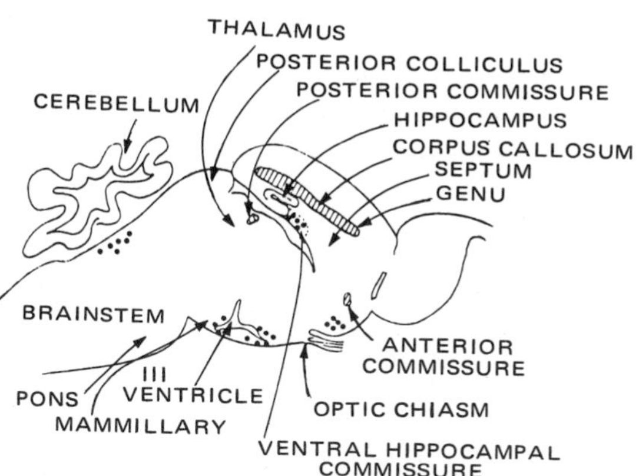

Figure 8.8. Sketch of a parasagittal section through the mouse brain. The small darkened circles indicate foci of gold accumulation. (From Schwartz, I. L., Cronkite, E. P., Johnson, H. A., Silver, L., Tenzer, D., and Debons, A. F., Radioautographic localization of the "satiety center." *Transactions of the Association of American Physicians*, 1961, *74*, 300–317.)

In sum, ventromedial hypothalamic lesions produce a condition of hyperphagia that appears to be a consequence of impaired weight regulation. The ventromedial area also appears to be selectively sensitive to glucose. Thus, these data lend support for both the glucostatic and lipostatic theories of hunger regulation.

Lateral Lesions

That electrical stimulation of the lateral hypothalamus may evoke stimulus-bound eating and drinking (Chapter 3) certainly suggests a role for this area in the normal regulation of these behaviors. Experiments placing lesions in this area confirm this role.

If, instead of ventromedial lesions, lesions are placed in the lateral hypothalamus, the behavioral effect is opposite to that which we have been discussing—the animals die because they fail to eat or drink (Anand & Brobeck, 1951). Teitelbaum and Epstein (1962) have shown, however, that with intensive care and appropriate attention to the water requirements of such animals, they may be kept alive and show a characteristic recovery pattern. Lateral hypothalamic lesions produce a complex syndrome of deficits, and deficits in drinking are at least as prominent as losses in feeding behavior.

The following paragraphs describe symptoms characteristic of rats with large bilateral lesions of the lateral hypothalamus.

Stage I: Aphagia and Adipsia. The animals refuse to eat (aphagia) and do not drink water (adipsia). During this stage animals will die unless kept alive by tube feeding. Generally, the animals actively resist contact, by mouth, with food or water—such contact seems aversive.

Stage II: Anorexia and Adipsia. Animals will eat wet, palatable foods, such as tasty liquid diets, chocolate, and cookies. They refuse dry food and do not drink water. Supplementation of their intake by tube feeding is still necessary; the animal is anorexic—that is, it does not eat enough to keep itself alive and well.

Stage III: Adipsia and Dehydration Aphagia. Animals will regulate their caloric intake with wet foods but still refuse to drink water. The palatability of the food is no longer of such importance as indicated by the fact that animals will regulate their intake if it is available intragastrically. While they will still not drink water, they can be trained to take sweet, nonnutritive solutions such as saccharin. Hydration, either through the ingestion of such sweet solutions or intragastrically, is necessary if the animals are to continue to eat dry food; in the absence of appropriate hydration, the animals will starve. Analysis of the behavior of these rats in response to saccharin solutions indicates that, in effect, they are "eating" the sweet solution rather than engaging in "drinking." Thus, the adipsia is still present.

Stage IV: Recovery. Most rats can be brought to a condition in which they will drink water and maintain their weight with water as the only fluid. However, water regulation is only superficially normal. Two facts indicate this: One is that when injected with hypertonic salt solutions, the animals do not drink water as normal animals do; the second is that the animals drink only while they are eating. Thus, these animals seem to be drinking in order to maintain a wet mouth which enables them to eat, and drinking apparently remains secondary to eating. This phenomenon has been termed "prandial drinking." Such rats, in contrast to normal ones, will also reject water that is only slightly adulterated with quinine. Food intake is also not completely normal in that it too may be disrupted by small amounts of quinine.

Summary of Syndrome

The above stages are summarized in Figure 8.9. The figure does not indicate variations in the severity of the deficits nor the progression of recovery, both of which seem related to the size and location of the lesions.

It is clear that lateral hypothalamic lesions result in deficits in both eating and drinking. Aphagia always seems to be transient, while adipsia can be permanent. Teitelbaum and Epstein (1962) emphasize that they have never seen a case of pure aphagia without adipsia. It is also clear that feeding recovers before drinking, if drinking recovers at all. It thus appears that the lesions affect drinking more heavily than feeding.

It is also worth noting that it is possible, with large lesions covering both ventromedial and lateral areas, to have an animal capable of showing both

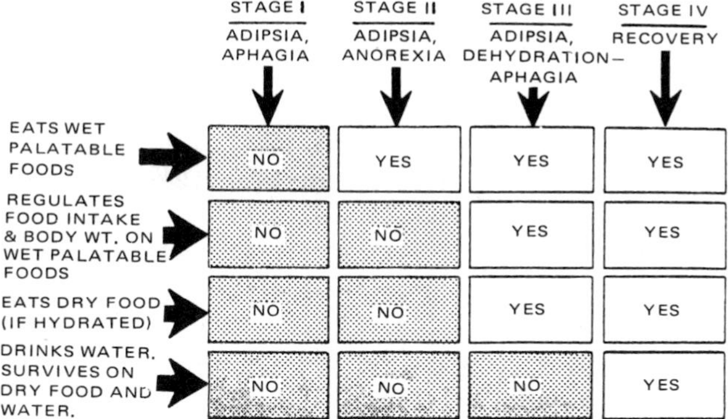

Figure 8.9. Stages of recovery seen in the lateral hypothalamic syndrome. (The critical behavioral events which define the stages are listed on the left.) (From Teitelbaum, P. and Epstein, A. N., The lateral hypothalamic syndrome: Recovery feeding and drinking after lateral hypothalamic lesions. *Psychological Review*, 1962, 69, 74–90. Copyright 1962 by the American Psychological Association. Reprinted by permission.)

hypothalamic hyperphagia and the lateral hypothalamic syndrome. Such an animal is initially aphagic and adipsic, in accord with the lateral syndrome, but when caloric regulation is reestablished in stage III, the animal will become hyperphagic if adequately hydrated. This is important in that it indicates that the presence of intact lateral mechanisms is not necessary for the production of hyperphagia.

Hypothalamic Lesions and Hunger

The preceding sections provide a basic outline of the effects of hypothalamic damage on eating. The material in these sections indicates dual control over hunger: Lateral hypothalamus mechanisms seem to be involved in the initiating of eating (a feeding center), and ventromedial mechanisms seen to be involved in the cessation of eating and long-term weight regulation (a satiety center). We shall have to make a more detailed examination of the anatomy and chemistry involved in order to identify exact physiological mechanisms that produce the symptoms observed when these systems suffer damage. However, before doing so, it will be worthwhile to pay more critical attention to the symptoms themselves. For instance, can we say that animals with ventromedial hypothalamic damage are hungrier than normals or that animals with lateral damage are less hungry?

Hunger Drive

Hypothalamic hyperphagic rats, as the name implies, eat voraciously, at least during the dynamic phase of the disorder. Such increased eating implies a concomitant increase in hunger drive. The literature examining this question has become somewhat confused over the last several years. To begin with, an early experiment by Miller, Bailey, and Stevenson (1950) suggested that this increased eating did not agree with other possible measures of hunger. Thus, if there were an increase in hunger, such animals would be expected to work harder for food and to overcome interposed obstacles to eating more readily than normal animals. But animals with ventromedial lesions actually demonstrated less work than normals: They pressed a bar less often on a 5-minute fixed interval schedule during all deprivation intervals up to 96 hours; they also ran slower to get food in alley tests and pulled less against a restraining harness than normals. In addition, they ate less when required to move weighted lids off food cups and tolerated less quinine adulteration of their food than normal animals. These results actually suggest a reduction in hunger, which has led researchers to hypothesize that ventromedial lesions may interfere more with the mechanisms of stopping eating than with hunger.

Teitelbaum (1955) extended these studies by showing that ventromedial animals are more sensitive to the stimulus qualities of their diet than normal

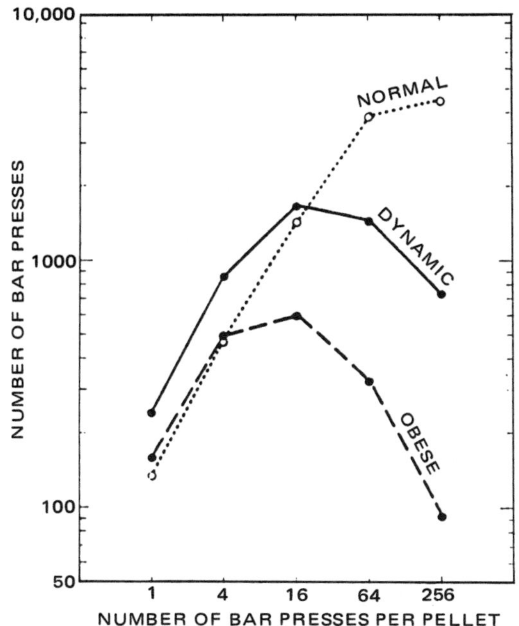

Figure 8.10. Mean number of bar-presses (per 12-hour period) of normal, obese hyperphagic, and dynamic (nonobese) hyperphagic animals, as a function of the number of bar-presses required to obtain each pellet. (From Teitelbaum, P., Random and food-directed activity in hyperphagic and normal rats. *Journal of Comparative and Physiological Psychology*, 1957, *50*, 486–490. Copyright 1957 by the American Psychological Association. Reprinted by permission.)

animals. Three groups of rats were used: Normals, obese ventromedial animals, and dynamic hyperphagics. This latter group consisted of hyperphagics maintained on restricted amounts of food so that they did not become obese. Both obese and dynamic hyperphagics failed to regulate their caloric intake as well as normals when nonnutritive cellulose was added to the diet in increasing proportions; they consistently decreased their intake, while normals compensated for about 75 percent of the diluted nutritive value. Obese animals also decreased their food intake when the diet was changed to powdered food rather than pellets, ate less food when it was adulterated with quinine, and ate more food when dextrose was added. In contrast, normal animals tended to compensate for these changes in order to maintain an appropriate caloric intake. Dynamic hyperphagics differed from the obese animals in that they were not affected by these manipulations and seemed to overeat heedlessly.

Teitelbaum suggested that these differences were due to changes in the internal environment of the obese animals produced by their excessive fat deposits. Both dynamic and obese ventromedial animals show less random activity than normals in response to food deprivation and less food-directed activity (Figure 8.10). Again, the fact that dynamic animals are more like normals than obese animals suggests a role for stored fat deposits in the regulation of these activities. Generally, these results are characterized as paradoxical—ventromedial animals eat more but are less hungry and they are also more finicky about what they eat.

In opposition to Miller et al. (1950) and Teitelbaum (1957), Falk (1961) found a high correlation between bar-pressing rate increases (on a variable interval schedule) and weight gain after ventromedial lesions. His results indicate that the increased consummatory activity of ventromedial animals *is* accompanied by increased motivation. Singh (1972) has also presented evidence indicating that ventromedial lesions do not result in lowered food motivation. Given a choice between obtaining freely available food and food from pressing a bar, it has been reported that normal animals prefer to work for the food. Similarly, Singh reported that rats with ventromedial lesions also preferred working to "freeloading." In addition, if the bar pressing was rewarded with adulterated pellets while the free food continued to be regular pellets, the lesioned animals continued their work preference to a greater extent than did the control animals.

In a second study, Singh (1973) tested the idea that the ventromedial animals' poorer performance on fixed ratio schedules (Teitelbaum, 1957) might be a result of their increased emotionality. Such a hypothesis was based on the observation that ventromedial animals were more jumpy and resistant to handling and that over-responsiveness to the generally aversive characteristics of fixed ratio schedules may have produced the decrement. Consequently, Singh attempted to adapt the animals to the schedule prior to making the lesions. Post-lesion performance was no longer deficient.

Pursuing a different approach, Kent and Peters (1973) tested both control and lesioned animals at the same percentage of *preoperative* body weight: "when these comparisons are made at levels approaching satiety for the control rats, VMH [ventromedial hypothalamic] rats are much more willing to work to obtain food. . . . The present data suggest that VMH lesioned rats overeat and become obese when given free access to food because they are 'more hungry' than normal rats" (p. 96). Wampler (1973) reached similar conclusions in yet another experiment. Intuitively, these later results seem more comprehensible; it is difficult to see how destruction of a satiety center would result in decreased motiviation.

A recent study by Devenport and Balagura (1971) suggests that it also would be a mistake to consider the feeding deficit in the lateral hypothalamic syndrome as due to a lack of hunger. Recovered lateral hypothalamic rats were some five to six times faster in initiating eating in either familiar or novel environments than were normal controls—or animals with septal or ventromedial hypothalamic lesions. They were also significantly faster in acquisition of a food-rewarded maze response. Devenport and Balagura suggest that rather than being less hungry, lateral hypothalamic animals are in a chronic state of deprivation that actually produces high hunger levels. Their eating deficit and weight loss, however, stem from an inability to consume sufficient amounts of food and to metabolize it efficiently.

Support for this position is provided by Lindholm, Shumway, Grijalva, Schallert, and Ruppel (1975). They found that lateral hypothalamic lesions were followed within 24 hours by the development of gastric lesions. Such lesions were more extensive than those produced by food or water deprivation or by operative trauma alone. In further studies (Grijalva, Lindholm, Schallert, & Bicknell, 1976), it has been found that reducing the animals to 80 percent of normal body weight prior to the lesion lessens the post-lesion aphagic period and the incidence of gastric pathology; slow reduction of weight, by "dieting" the rats, was also more beneficial than a rapid reduction by starving the animals. Thus, gastric pathology, rather than motivational changes, may be a primary factor in the aphagia produced by lateral hypothalamic lesions.

Finickiness

Ventromedial animals probably are hungrier than normals under approriate conditions of comparison and they also appear more finicky about what they will eat; that is, they respond more to the taste qualities of their food than to its caloric value. Many studies have shown that ventromedial animals do show exaggerated responses under a variety of manipulations of the taste qualities of the food—dry, diluted foods are underconsumed and oily, tasty, or sweet diets are overconsumed. But ventromedial animals do track the caloric value of their food even if such tracking is less well performed than in normal animals (Carlisle & Stellar, 1969; Levison, Frommer, & Vance, 1973). "The ability to modulate caloric intake accurately is severely constrained by the palatability (taste and texture) of various diets" (Carlisle & Stellar, 1969, p. 114). With a highly palatable diet, Smutz, Hirsch, and Jacobs (1975) found that ventromedial rats in the static (obese) stage compensated for caloric dilution as well as normal rats.

Jacobs and Sharma (1969) have presented a series of experiments in rats and dogs which suggest an interesting hypothesis that applies to normal as well as ventromedial animals. They suggest that "eating for calories" is limited to ad-lib feeding schedules, and that hunger increases the importance of taste cues. This hypothesis may be illustrated by the data of Figure 8.11. Here we see, contrary to what common sense might indicate, that normal hungry dogs decreased their intake when the diet offered was diluted by 25 percent cellulose. Other experiments support these results (see Valenstein, 1967). "Common sense assumes that hungry animals are *less* discriminating about taste in their excited search for calories, and that one has time to be a gourmet only under conditions of relative surfeit. What we are saying . . . is that the animal eats for calories when he does not need them, and eats for taste when he needs calories. Thus, for us, the hungry animal is *more*, rather than *less*, discriminating, much like the 'finicky' hypothalamic hyperphagic rat. The hypothalamic hyperphagic is merely a pathological caricature of the normal animal in severe energy deficit, with the important difference that

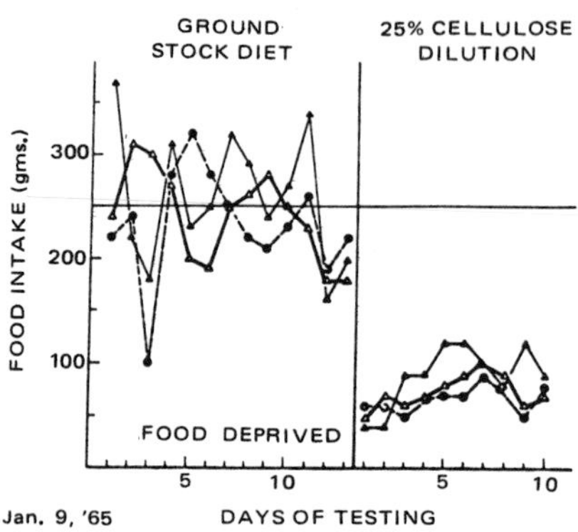

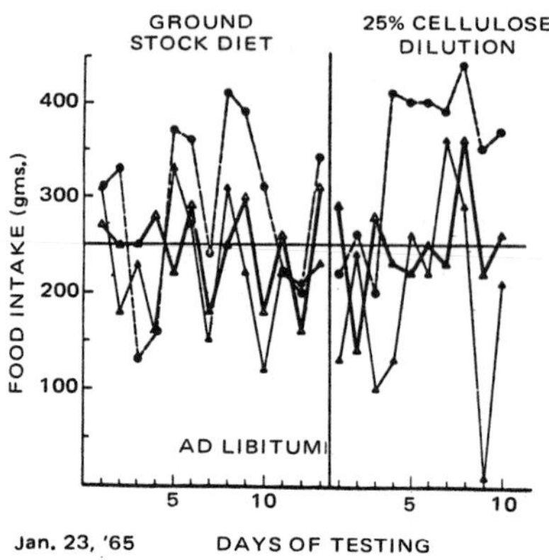

Figure 8.11. Effect of cellulose dilution on the intake of stock diet in ad-lib (N = 3) or food-deprived (N = 3) beagle dogs. (From Jacobs, H. L. and Sharma, K. N., Taste versus calories: Sensory and metabolic signals in the control of food intake. *Annals of the New York Academy of Sciences,* 1969, *157,* 1084–1125.)

the normal animal is in energy deficit, while the obese animal is being fooled by misinformation, signaling a nonexistent deficit" (Jacobs & Sharma, 1969, p. 1089). This hypothesis merits further consideration.

Set-Point for Weight

Although ventromedial rats may be finicky about the palatability of their diets, we may have to modify that conclusion somewhat.

Part of Kennedy's (1953) lipostatic theory maintains that the increased food intake of these rats reflects a change in the metabolic systems of the animals which leads to the development of obesity—these animals are not fat because they overeat but rather are fat independent of their eating. This position is in contrast to that cited earlier (Brobeck, Tepperman, & Long, 1943), which denied any metabolic change. Some evidence is available for this part of Kennedy's theory: Rabin (1974) showed that some rats with ventromedial lesions demonstrated increased body fat despite the fact that they did not eat more than control rats. Be that as it may, the second part of Kennedy's theory asserts that the effect of ventromedial lesions is to elevate a regulatory mechanism that determines the upper limit of body fat or weight. Thus, the resulting hyperphagia is the means of achieving this greater body fat. It will be recalled that the data of Figure 8.6 suggest just this—the animals appear to be operating at a new baseline for weight after the lesions.

Ferguson and Keesey (1975) have presented evidence that the defense of this new set-point or baseline level is the primary symptom in the syndrome produced by ventromedial lesions, *not* the finickiness of the animals.

Their experiments were based on the idea that the ventromedial lesion disrupts the upper but not the lower limit for body weight. Thus, they argue, if finickiness is primary, ventromedial animals given food adulterated with quinine immediately after surgery should eat even less than controls. Similarly, if a control rat is reduced in weight below the level that it would maintain on the quinine-adulterated diet, it should become hyperphagic until it reached that weight level; on the other hand, a finicky, lesioned animal might be expected to lose even more weight.

Predictions about finickiness proved untrue—ventromedial rats were able to defend the lower limit of their weight levels quite as well as control animals. "Thus, ventromedial hypothalamic animals overeat and become obese on palatable diets, but defend the same lower weight level as controls when challenged with unpalatable diets" (Ferguson & Keesey, 1975, p. 478).

Ferguson and Keesey suggest that ". . . a stable body weight is maintained because food remains appetizing as long as the individual's body weight is below his 'set point,' but it becomes unappealing when his weight is raised to or above this level. . . . it is proposed that the primary consequence of VMH lesions is to weaken this weight-dependent control over the organism's reactivity to palatable diets; that is, VMH lesions decrease the sensitivity of those mechanisms normally attenuating an animal's attraction to palatable diets at a particular body weight. As a result, a substantially higher level of body weight must be achieved before this palatable diet loses its positive effect" (p. 487).

Similarly, it has been suggested that lateral hypothalamic animals show reduced weight levels because they reduce their food intake in accord with their symptoms of adipsia and finickiness in response to unpalatable diets (Mufson & Wampler, 1972). Alternatively, the reduced weight level might be better ascribed to an alteration in the lower limit of their set-point for regulation of body weight (Boyle & Keesey, 1975). Boyle and Keesey found that the weight of lateral animals remained at reduced levels, relative to control animals, regardless of diet and under conditions of high fluid intake induced by offering highly palatable drinking solutions. They concluded that a primary shift in set-point for body weight, rather than finickiness, accounts for the reduced intake of food in lateral hypothalamic animals.

Summary and Conclusions

The material that we have reviewed in the preceding section suggests that we are in the midst of changing conceptions of the notion of "hunger." Over the past 25 or more years, the basic facts have remained relatively clear: Generally, animals with ventromedial hypothalamic lesions eat large quantities of food and gain weight rapidly; they then stabilize at a high weight level and their eating tapers off to relatively normal quantities. Conversely, animals with lateral hypothalamic lesions show reduced food intake, a severe adipsia, and, if care is taken to maintain their hydration, they recover while maintaining a reduced level of body weight. What has required clarification are the fine-grain details of the functional behavior and the underlying mechanisms resulting in these eating and weight changes. Finickiness, responsiveness to the taste of food, changes in drive level, and alteration of biological mechanisms setting weight levels have been variously proposed as explanations.

First, it should be clear that in some sense all these interpretations are true, i.e., under certain test conditions each of these interpretations is supported by the resulting behavior. Second, that this is so certainly indicates that the system we are considering does not operate as if a single factor, "hunger," were operating. Thus, on some measures, animals with either of these lesions appear less hungry than controls, while on other measures they appear more hungry. The data necessary to a complete interpretation are probably not yet available, but finickiness and motivation to eat seem to be influenced by the body's set-points for weight regulation; all these factors together, then, seem to influence what we subjectively call "hunger."

IS THE HYPOTHALAMUS PRIMARY IN THE CONTROL OF FEEDING?

To this point, the evidence presented here has indicated a dual control over hunger: Lateral hypothalamic mechanisms seem to be involved in setting lower weight limits and initiating eating, and ventromedial mechanisms seem to be involved in setting upper weight limits and the cessation of eating. This simple, dual control over feeding behavior was considered well established for a relatively long time. Recently, however, much evidence has accumulated to challenge this notion. These challenges do not question the results of placing lesions in the hypothalamus; rather they question the precise location of the mechanisms involved and their modes of action. They take several diverse forms.

Intrahypothalamic Relations

Ventromedial-Lateral Connections

Intrahypothalamic relationships are not as simple as we have indicated up to this point. We have referred to the ventromedial area and the lateral area; these designations have been used more in a descriptive sense than in an anatomically precise sense; actually the hypothalamus is organized diffusely from a structural standpoint. The simple attribution of satiety control mechanisms to the ventromedial "area" and feeding control mechanisms to the "lateral" hypothalamus is probably too simple. While lesions of the ventromedial nuclei have been shown to produce hyperphagia, it is not clear that these nuclei are the only neural elements involved. In fact, hyperphagia has been produced in some instances by lesions sparing these nuclei. Albert and Storlein (1969) produced hyperphagia most reliably with stereotaxically placed, bilateral knife cuts when both cuts were between the ventromedial and lateral areas. When one of the cuts entered the ventromedial hypothalamus, hyperphagia was less reliably produced; with cuts touching on the lateral area, hyperphagia was infrequently produced. These results are compatible with the idea that *connections* between the ventromedial and lateral areas are involved in producing hyperphagia but do not require that either area is specifically the origin or termination of the fibers. In a similar study with comparable results, Gold (1970) did not find any neural degeneration in the ventromedial nuclei as would be expected if the knife cuts severed direct connections from this location to the lateral hypothalamus. Several possibilities exist for explaining this lack of degeneration, not the least of which is that the system is a multisynaptic one; but the fact remains that destruction of the ventromedial area per se is not critical for producing hyperphagia.

A number of more recent studies have pursued this matter (e.g., Storlien & Albert, 1972; Sclafani, Berner, & Maul, 1973, 1975). The anatomical

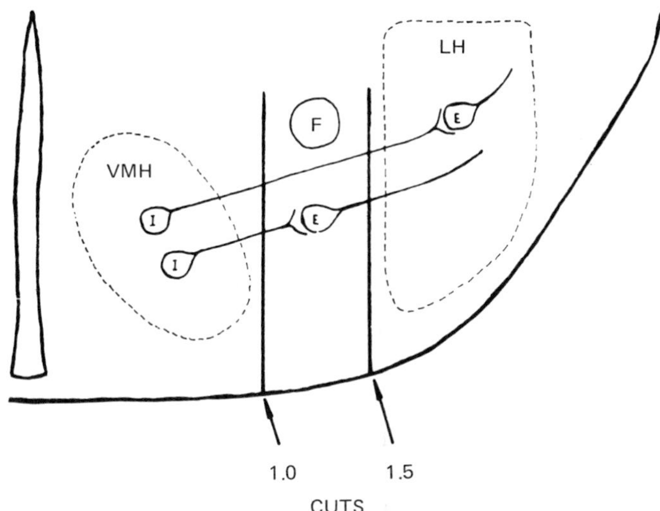

Figure 8.12. Schematic of knife-cut experiments and possible neural circuitry connecting ventromedial and lateral hypothalamic areas. VMH = ventromedial hypothalamus; LH = lateral hypothalamus; I = feeding inhibitory neuron; E = feeding excitatory neuron; F = fornix; 1 (and 1.5) refer to distances lateral to midline. (From Sclafani, A., Berner, C. N., and Maul, G. Multiple knife cuts between the medial and lateral hypothalamus in the rat. *Journal of Comparative and Physiological Psychology*, 1975, *88*, 210–217.)

issues involved go beyond the complexity suitable for discussion here but we can generally indicate the trend that such studies show. The general procedure involves placing very fine cuts, parasagittally, at various rostral-caudal levels, between the ventromedial and lateral hypothalamic areas. The results of such cuts frequently differ, depending on their exact location. For instance, though at the same rostral-caudal location and similar in extent of cutting, cuts just lateral to the ventromedial nucleus produced greater hyperphagia and obesity than cuts placed medial to the lateral hypothalamic area (see Figure 8.12). It is often possible to obtain restricted manifestations of the total ventromedial syndrome, depending on the location of the cuts. Sequential combinations of cuts, spread over time, often produce asymmetric results, i.e., their result may depend on which cut is first in the sequence. Though there is evidence that there are reciprocal connections between the ventromedial and external areas, such results generally seem to indicate that many of the effects of large lesions in these areas may result from lesioning of tracts which pass through these areas or terminate in them while originating elsewhere.

Mid-Lateral and Far-Lateral Regions

There are also problems with respect to the lateral hypothalamic syndrome. Morgane (1961) distinguished between a mid-lateral and a far-lateral hypothalamic area. Electrical stimulation of both areas results in feeding responses in satiated animals, but only stimulation of the far-lateral area caused satiated animals to cross an electrified grid in order to bar-press for food. Lesions of the medial forebrain bundle[2] anterior and posterior to the classic feeding and satiety areas did not affect normal feeding but resulted in failure of the animals to cross the grid; these results imply a separation between "feeding" and "hunger." Thus, basic feeding can occur in the absence of the medial forebrain bundle, but hunger motivation, as indicated by willingness to overcome obstacles to get to food, seems dependent on the medial forebrain bundle. Finally, simultaneous stimulation of ventromedial and far-lateral areas resulted in feeding in satiated animals but failure to cross the grid to bar-press for food. This seems to indicate that the ventromedial "satiety" area acts on the medial forebrain bundle, the "hunger" system, rather than the far-lateral "feeding" system.

In other studies, Morgane found that mid-lateral and far-lateral lesions produce somewhat different effects: In keeping with the previous study, mid-lateral lesions are less severe in effect and seem to be related to the

[2]The medial forebrain bundle is a multineuronal fiber pathway extending from the septal area of the forebrain to the brainstem. It courses through the lateral hypothalamus and features prominently in the mechanisms of self-stimulation (Chapter 11).

motivation to feed, while far-lateral lesions seem to produce a more fundamental and less easily reversed aphagia (cf. Morgane & Jacobs, 1969).

EXTRAHYPOTHALAMIC INVOLVEMENT

That areas of the brain other than the hypothalamus are also involved in feeding behavior has been known for some time. A study by Robinson and Mishkin (1962) may be taken as illustrative of the possible extent of such extrahypothalamic influence. This study examined the effects of electrically stimulating hypothalamic and extrahypothalamic sites on the intake and ejection of food and water and vomiting in monkeys. Food and water intake were elicited in 13 satiated animals from 62 hypothalamic sites and 94 extrahypothalamic locations. Food ejection (the cessation of chewing and expulsion of the food with the tongue) was evoked from 12 hypothalamic and 110 extrahypothalamic placements in 10 monkeys. Ejection was not accompanied by signs of emotional disturbance, and preliminary work indicated that the monkeys would work for stimulation of the majority of points eliciting ejection. Gagging and vomiting were elicited from 166 placements in 11 animals. While these figures are highly dependent on the sampling procedures employed, they do illustrate substantial extrahypothalamic involvement in food-related behavior and give some indication of its prevalence. The loci implicated by this study cover portions of the frontal lobe, temporal lobe, cingulate gyrus, septum, and the thalamus in addition to the expected hypothalamic locations.

Morgane (1969) has particularly stressed the role of the limbic system in food regulation. A number of studies have reported hyperphagia after amygdalectomy. In fact, Morgane and Kosman (1960) found that amygdalectomy combined with ventromedial lesions seemed to intensify the effects of either operation alone. On the other hand, studies may also be cited which show aphagia after amygdaloid lesions. Caudally, in the midbrain, periaqueductal gray lesions also produce hyperphagia (Skultety, 1969). Rostrally, neocortical involvement is implicated by Teitelbaum and Cytawa's (1965) report that depression of cortical function with potassium chloride will reinstate the lateral hypothalamic syndrome in recovered animals. These results amply illustrate a large literature documenting the anatomical extent of the systems involved.

Most recently, however, a great deal of attention has been focused on fiber tracts that originate in the midbrain and brainstem and project rostrally, through the hypothalamus, to a number of forebrain locations. Figures 8.13 and 8.14 schematically illustrate the tracts involved. As indicated earlier in Chapter 6, these tracts were identified on the basis of fluorescence techniques—they fluoresce with different characteristic colors for norepinephrine, dopamine, and serotonin. In the hypothalamus, the

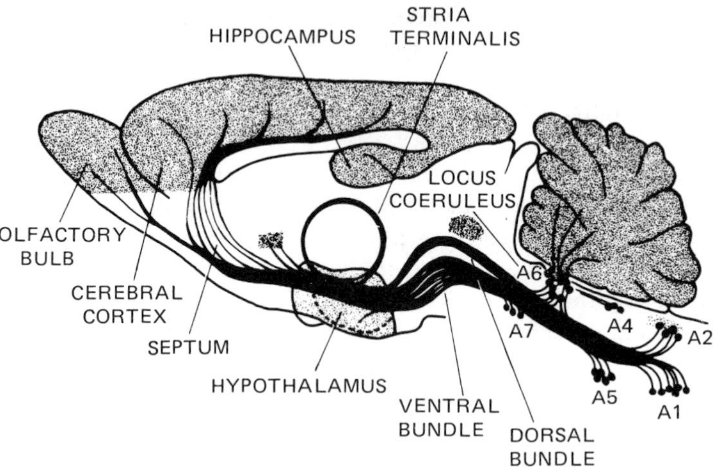

Figure 8.13. Schematic diagram illustrating the distribution of the main ascending central neuronal pathways containing norepinephrine. The stippled regions indicate the major nerve terminal areas. (From Ungerstedt, U. Stereotaxic mapping of the monoamine pathways in the rat brain. *Acta Physiologica Scandinavica,* 1971, Supplement 367, 1–48.)

ventral noradrenergic bundle (Figure 8.13) occupies a position in the vicinity of the ventromedial nuclei. A dopamine system (Figure 8.14) on the other hand, courses rostrally through the far-lateral hypothalamus in its route to the basal ganglia (also see Figures 1.7 and 14.8). These locations, coupled with the results of the lesion studies employing restricted knife cuts in the hypothalamus, suggest that the ventromedial hypothalamic syndrome might actually be caused by damage to the ventral noradrenergic bundle and the lateral syndrome might result from damage to the dopamine system, i.e., destruction of hypothalamic neurons might not actually be critical. We shall examine some representative examples of research directed toward this question.

Gold (1973) compared the weights of rats with restricted medial hypothalamic lesions. Some of these destroyed the ventral noradrenergic bundle without impinging on the ventromedial nucleus. Other lesions spared the ventral noradrenergic bundle. Generally, Gold concluded that the greatest weight gains were associated with lesions of the ventral bundle. Apparently the previous implication of the ventromedial nucleus resulted from the fact that it is merely a prominent landmark in the vicinity of the effective mechanism.

In another approach, Ahlskog and Hoebel (1973) destroyed the ventral noradrenergic bundle in the midbrain area, i.e., not directly impinging on the hypothalamus at all. In their experiment, the bundle was destroyed by either electrolytic lesions or the injection of 6-hydroxydopamine, which appears to destroy catecholaminergic neurons selectively. Note in Figure 8.13 that the norepinephrine system also contains a dorsal bundle that is physically separate for part of its pathway; this portion of the system was selectively injected with 6-hydroxydopamine also. Either electrolytic lesions or 6-hydroxydopamine lesions of the ventral bundle produced hyperphagia and obesity. Dorsal bundle injections were no more effective than control procedures. The hyperphagic animals showed an almost complete loss of noradrenergic fluorescence in the hypothalamus and forebrain.

These studies, then, suggest that norepinephrine is the transmitter in a satiety mechanism and the anatomical pathway involved is the ventral noradrenergic bundle.

More recently, two papers (Breisch, Zemlan, & Hoebel, 1976; Saller & Stricker, 1976) have indicated a role for serotonin in the regulation of food intake. Two types of drugs were used in this research: one, *p*-chlorophenylalanine is a drug that depletes serotonin by inhibiting enzyme activity involved in the production of serotonin; the second type depletes serotonin by damaging the serotonin-containing neurons. Both of these treatments resulted in hyperphagia in rats. It is possible that serotonin is specifically involved in the regulation of food intake, as part of a satiety mechanism. Alternatively, serotonin has been shown to have influences suggestive of a general inhibitory role, of which the inhibition of food intake may be only one instance. In either event, the relative roles of serotonin and norepinephrine in any satiety mechanism will have to be explicated.

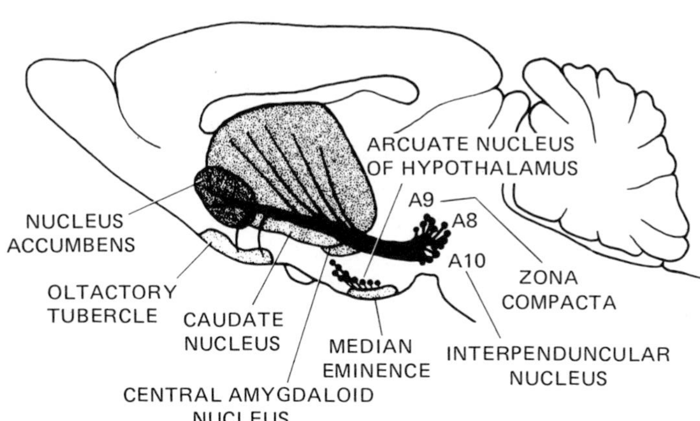

Figure 8.14. Schematic diagram indicating the distribution of the main central neuronal pathways containing dopamine. The stippled regions indicate the major nerve terminal areas. (From Ungerstedt, U. Stereotaxic mapping of the monoamine pathways in the rat brain. *Acta Physiologica Scandinavica*, 1971, Supplement 367, 1–48.)

Zigmond and Stricker (1972, 1973) used chemical injections to destroy the dopamine-containing neurons. Briefly, the essentials of the lateral hypothalamic syndrome were reproduced by these procedures. Just as lateral hypothalamic animals show recovery of some minimal control of feeding, so too do chemically treated animals. Subsequent to that recovery, electrolytically lesioned and chemically treated animals were both subjected to injections of an inhibitor of catecholamine synthesis; both such groups were more sensitive to the inhibitor than control animals and showed a transient return of aphagia and adipsia. Thus, it was concluded that both the loss and the recovery of feeding and drinking depend on catecholamine-containing neurons.

Neill and Linn (1975) investigated the effects of lesions in the anterior terminations of the dopamine system, i.e., well rostral to the hypothalamus. Again, in brief, aspects of the lateral syndrome were found in different animals and the specific symptom manifested seemed to be dependent on the exact location of the lesion.

The above results certainly suggest that phenomena previously attributed to the destruction of hypothalamic tissue per se, in reality, result from destruction of tracts passing through the hypothalamus. However, before uncritically accepting this conclusion, a note of caution should be added. Ahlskog, Randall, and Hoebel (1975) have reported that there are some marked differences in eating habits between rats with classical hypothalamic hyperphagia and animals made hyperphagic by destruction of the ventral noradrenergic bundle. In comparing such animals, they found that (1) norepinephrine loss caused hyperphagia only at night (classical lesions result in a loss of diurnal eating patterns, with hyperphagia throughout the 24-hour day); (2) norepinphrine loss caused less hyperphagia overall; (3) hypothalamic lesions caused overeating without a depletion in norepinephrine; and (4) the two forms of hyperphagia can be combined in one animal to produce a degree of hyperphagia not seen with either lesion alone. Thus, they concluded that classical leisons produce hyperphagia by disrupting systems other than those involved in satiety mechanisms dependent on the ventral nordrenergic bundle.

Similarly, Stricker and Zigmond (1974) have stressed that while there are parallels between the effects of lateral hypothalamic lesions and destruction of the dopamine system, there are also some important differences. In addition, drugs used to destroy the dopamine system may not be any more selective for dopamine than are electrolytic lesions (Evans, Armstrong, Singer, Cook, & Burnstock, 1975). All these issues are currently under investigation.

Finally, Zeigler and Karten (1974) suggest that part of the classical lateral hypothalamus syndrome may actually be attributable to sensory effects resulting from incidental damage to sensory fibers (trigeminal nerve from the face) located adjacent to the lateral hypothalamus. Lesions there produced a syndrome of aphagia, adipsia, and finickiness of shorter duration.

Summary and Conclusions

The material we have just reviewed illustrates a common historical trend observable in all scientific research. The dramatic changes in eating and weight regulation that resulted from placing lesions in the ventromedial and lateral areas of the hypothalamus tended to foster a view that hypothalamic mechanisms were at least paramount, if not the sole mechanisms, in the control of feeding. With refinement of the experimental questions, however, it has become obvious that this view is simplistic. All the evidence is certainly not in as yet, but it appears safe to say that what at first appeared to be relatively unitary syndromes can be fractionated on the basis of a complex of diverse physiological mechanisms, each with, perhaps, relatively localizable anatomic substrates. Thus, although it is probably not incorrect to speak of ventromedial hypothalamic hyperphagia or a lateral hypothalamic syndrome, such designations obscure the fact that systems ranging from the brainstem to the cortex—including a variety of subcortical forebrain locations—contribute to normal food regulations. An important concentration of such systems happens to occur in the hypothalamus but this can no longer be considered primary.

CHEMICAL STIMULATION OF THE BRAIN

Thus far, we have concentrated on anatomic structures and their relationships to food regulation. But as the preceding section has indicated, analysis from the standpoint of the transmitter systems involved in such relations can also prove valuable. We will now address that issue from the standpoint of chemical stimulation.

Electrical stimulation of the brain is a simple and productive research technique, but it suffers from two major disadvantages. One of these is the fact that it indiscriminately activates both synaptic junctions and fibers passing through the region. Thus, the locus of its effects cannot be precisely delimited. A second disadvantage is that where two or more neural mechanisms exist in close proximity, electrical stimulation will indiscriminately excite all such circuits. If, however, different neural circuits are coded by the fact that they employ different synaptic transmitters, chemical stimulation offers the possibility of (1) stimulating only at the synapse and (2) selectively stimulating, depending on the chemicals applied. Nonetheless, chemical stimulation techniques must cope with the problem of restricting the area over which the chemicals diffuse.

Food and Water Intake

Direct chemical stimulation of the brain was first used in the study of hunger and thirst mechanisms by S. P. Grossman (1960). Grossman's technique involved the chronic implantation of a double-walled cannula system into the hypothalamus of rats. This system was constructed from two syringe needles—an inner and an outer tube. The outer tube served as a guide and the inner tube carried crystalline chemicals, allowing for multiple placements over a period of time and the use of several chemicals (liquid chemicals may be similarly injected, through the inner tube).

Grossman's initial experiments involved the measurement of food and water intake of satiated rats following the injection of a variety of chemicals into the lateral hypothalamus. The injection of epinephrine or norepinephrine (adrenergic stimulation) resulted in highly reliable increases in food consumption beginning 5 to 10 minutes after injection. The effect persisted for 20 to 40 minutes. Carbachol or acetylcholine injections (cholinergic stimulation) in the same animals at the identical loci produced highly reliable increases in water consumption with latencies and durations comparable to the food intake after adrenergic stimulation. Cholinergic stimulation did not result in food consumption, while the water consumed after adrenergic stimulation appeared to be secondary to the consumption of the dry food. In the presence of water only, food- and water-satiated rats did not drink measurable amounts in response to adrenergic stimulation. As a control, comparable amounts of sodium chloride were injected; no significant food or water consumption occurred. Another control was the utilization of strychnine (a CNS exciter) in comparable amounts; again the results were negative.

Thus, food and water regulation would appear to be under control of separate neural circuits which, however, are spatially proximate. Feeding mechanisms may be selectively activated by adrenergic stimulation, and drinking mechanisms may be activated by cholinergic stimulation.

The results of cholinergic stimulation on water intake were quickly extended by Fisher and Coury (1962). Briefly, these authors showed that cholinergic stimulation throughout the general confines of the limbic system was effective in inducing drinking behavior. These results indicate, of course, that drinking mechanisms are not confined to the hypothalamus. Coury (1967) has since reported that adrenergic stimulation of the limbic system is also effective in eliciting eating. It is noteworthy that all of these studies emphasize the fact that small (on the order of .25 mm) displacements of the cannulae can result in the acquisition or loss of a locus showing a positive effect of stimulation. In his study, Coury stimulated the same sites with both adrenergic and cholinergic chemicals; the effective loci could be classified as either dual or single response types—that is, responding to one or the other chemical, or both. Only 15 percent of the limbic locations tested were dual response sites.

An experiment by S. P. Grossman (1964) is suggestive of a possible mode of action of limbic mechanisms in controlling natural drive states. He found that neither adrenergic nor cholinergic stimulation of the amygdala had any significant effect on food or water consumption, respectively, in satiated rats. In deprived animals, however, adrenergic stimulation increased food intake, and cholinergic stimulation increased water intake. These results suggest that while the amygdala may participate in the modulation of hunger and thirst, it does not participate in the onset of eating and drinking.

Alpha and Beta Adrenergic Mechanisms

The data we have thus far reviewed have stressed a relationship between cholingeric stimulation and drinking, and adrenergic stimulation and eating. Accumulating evidence seems to suggest a more complex relationship, however.

The response to adrenergic substances in the peripheral nervous system has been differentiated into *alpha* and *beta* subcategories. These subcategories have been predicated on the observation that certain sites predominantly respond to one or another of the adrenergic agents, and different agents predominantly stimulate different peripheral responses. It has been suggested that the brain may also contain receptors that are differentially responsive to alpha and beta substances.

One set of studies (Leibowitz, 1970, 1971, 1975a, b) has suggested that eating is mediated by alpha mechanisms while drinking is the result of mutually reinforcing alpha and beta mechanisms. Another set of studies (Margules, 1970a, b) suggests that alpha receptors mediate satiety.

This conflict has not yet been resolved. Research has been complicated by the fact that different experiments test different implications of these theories in different species or inject chemical stimuli into different loci. These studies to which we have just referred, for example, have been done in the rat. Simpson, Baile, and Krabill (1975), however, found alpha adrenergic feeding in sheep and alpha adrenergic satiety in steers.[3]

[3]The effect of adrenergic stimulation apparently depends also on the portion of the light-dark cycle in which the injection is made. Margules, Lewis, Dragovich, and Margules (1972) found that norepinephrine suppressed feeding in the dark portion of the cycle and facilitiated feeding in the light portion of the cycle. But Armstrong and Singer (1974) also controlled the relative hunger levels during the two portions of the cycle and found the opposite: Norepinephrine increased eating in the dark and depressed eating in the light. They interpreted their result as a failure to support an adrenergic satiety theory.

Perhaps of greater importance than the resolution of this conflict is the resolution of the apparent contradiction between the facts that lesions of an ascending adrenergic system produce hyperphagia while stimulation with adrenergics in the same general area may produce eating. These results are not necessarily incompatible but demonstrating that they are not, and the mechanisms of why not, may prove to be the most interesting problem.

RECENT THEORETICAL APPROACHES TO THE STIMULUS FOR HUNGER

As we have indicated, over approximately the last quarter century, the stimuli considered responsible for hunger motivation have mainly been attributed to two peripheral factors, fat storage (and/or body weight) and glucose utilization. Generally, it has been proposed that lipostatic factors control long-term regulation and glucostatic factors, short-term regulation. More recently, lipostatic mechanisms have received greater attention. For instance, LeMagnen, Devos, Gaudillière, Louis-Sylvestre, and Tallon (1973) stress that there is diurnal variation in fat storage and utilization and these are relevant for short-term regulation. However, at the present time, increasing emphasis is being placed on several other peripheral considerations.

Fatty acids injected into the hypothalamus reduce food intake in sheep (Baile, Simpson, Bean, McLaughlin, & Jacobs, 1973) and modify the electrical activity of hypothalamic neurons (Oomura, Takamura, Sugimori, & Yamada, 1975). But alterations in the ionic environment, through the infusion of solutions containing excess ions into the ventricular system, have produced changes in feeding, drinking, and temperature regulation (Meyers & Bender, 1973; Seoane & Baile, 1973); in particular, excess calcium ions induced eating. Calcium ions might induce feeding through the release of norepinephrine in a neural feeding system. It is also well-known that female sex hormones play a role in modulating feeding (e.g., Simpson & Dicara, 1973). The point, then, is that there may be a whole range of substances, making up a chemical "profile" reflecting the metabolic condition of the body, which affect brain mechanisms controlling feeding and hunger (Myers, 1975).

Chemical Profile Theory

Figure 8.15 illustrates the experimental set-up which is generally basic to Myers' formulation. This set-up permits a liquid to be perfused through the brain of an animal where it can pick up locally present chemicals; the solution is then pumped to a second animal where the effects of these chemicals on the animal's behavior can be assessed. In experiments such as these, it

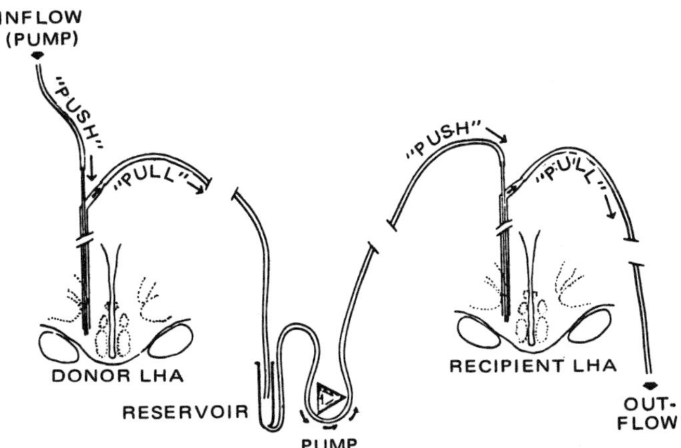

Figure 8.15. Schematic representation of transfusion of hypothalamic chemical factors between conscious monkeys. Saline or cerebrospinal fluid is pumped via "push" cannula through the donor monkey's lateral hypothalamus (LHA) and by gravity withdrawn via "pull" cannula into reservoir. Effluent is then taken by triangular peristaltic pump via "push" cannula into recipient monkey's lateral hypothalamus, then withdrawn via "pull" cannula through outflow tube. (From Myers, R. D., Chemical mechanisms in the hypothalamus mediating eating and drinking in the monkey. *Annals of the New York Academy of Sciences*, 1969, *157*, 918–933.)

was found that solutions taken from fasted monkeys and introduced into sated monkeys resulted in the recipients feeding voraciously. Conversely, when the solution was drawn from sated donors, the eating of fasted monkeys was reduced. In both instances, no single chemical substance can be substituted for the endogenous material so as to duplicate completely its effects, even though many single substances can be applied, as we have indicated earlier, that initiate feeding or reduce food intake.

Basically, then, Myers' theory is that there are two chemical "profiles" for the regulation of feeding. One profile, a peripheral one, reflects the chemical state of the bloodstream of the animal and pertains to its current state of metabolism, nutrient status, etc.; this profile acts as a stimulus. The other profile, a central one, concerns the neurochemical activity of the brain mechanisms devoted to the maintenance and behavior of the animal. As a result of continuous monitoring of the peripheral profile, changes occur in the CNS and these are reflected in the constituents of the central profile. The peripheral profile probably contains glucose, insulin, amino acids, and satiety-signalling factors, such as cholecystokinin for short-term regulation, and fatty acids and gonadal hormones for long-term regulation. It is not clear whether vitamins and minerals are included in the peripheral profile—they may not exert a direct CNS effect.

The peripheral profile, together with sensory input from olfaction, taste, and the alimentary system, activates the central feeding circuitry and general activating mechanisms. The operation of this system is reflected in the central profile that can be extracted. Thus, it would contain acetylcholine, norepinephrine, dopamine, calcium, etc. ". . . the actual behavior of consuming food is determined ultimately by the profile of substances, in terms of the ratio of one to another, that are released from neurons . . ." (p. 77).

Energy Metabolism Theory

Earlier formulations, which concentrated on glucostatic and lipostatic stimuli for hunger, and Myers' formulation, which emphasizes the diversity of substances responsible for hunger, all attribute hunger to *specific* chemical substances. A somewhat different emphasis is represented by a recent formulation by Friedman and Stricker (1976). They suggest "that the stimulus for hunger should be sought among changes that occur in the supply of metabolic fuels rather than in the utilization of specific nutrients or in levels of fuel reserves" (p. 409).

Friedman and Stricker start from a review of the peripheral physiological mechanisms devoted to energy metabolism. Of major concern in this review is that the body employs a variety of energy sources at different times and circumstances, including fats, carbohydrates, and proteins, as well as glucose. The liver plays a central role in orchestrating the efficient storage and utilization of these energy sources. Friedman and Stricker propose that the stimulus for hunger may result from changes in the oxidation processes within the liver associated with the use of these fuels. Basically, such a proposal is tantamount to concentrating on the management of caloric status as the stimulus for hunger. In this view, traditional concepts like hunger and satiety centers in the brain, glucostatic and lipostatic brain receptors, and set-points for body weight, are considered unnecessary. Ventromedial hypothalamic lesions produce a disruption in metabolic processes and such an animal increases its food intake *because* it is gaining weight rather than *in order* to gain weight. Lateral lesions probably affect all motivated behaviors, not just feeding, though they may alter metabolism too, in ways opposite to ventromedial lesions.

"In other words, it is the liver that may integrate information about caloric homeostasis and provide the specific stimulus to the brain, and it is the liver whose function appears to be most affected by feeding and thus allow rapid feedback for the termination of hunger" (p. 424).

Summary

Historically, glucose utilization and fat stores have been emphasized as the stimuli for hunger. Two more recent approaches emphasize that there is greater diversity of peripheral substances involved in hunger. One of these

(Myers), suggests that a large number of peripheral chemicals, together, contribute to hunger. The other (Friedman and Stricker) suggests that while there is diversity in the metabolic fuels to obtain the body's energy, the basic consideration in determining hunger lies in the metabolic processes employed to extract that energy; thus, changes in these processes, in the liver, are the stimulus for hunger. As is evident, we are in the midst of an era of research devoted to reevaluating previously accepted concepts of brain function and their relation to psychological constructs like hunger and drive.

SUMMARY

The analysis of hunger and feeding mechanisms is undergoing rapid change. In the mid-1950s, what seemed to be a clear view of the regulation of eating behavior began to emerge. This view recognized that peripheral, oropharyngeal, and gastric factors play a role in the initiation and cessation of eating but emphasized that this role is primarily one of monitoring intake. It appeared that short-term, meal-length regulation of how much and what substances were ingested could be ascribed to such peripheral influences, but more fundamental regulation was sought in the CNS—in particular, in the hypothalamus.

The emerging picture was simple and elegant. In this conception, the hypothalamus contains two mechanisms controlling food intake: a ventromedially located "satiety" center and a laterally located "feeding" center. Activity of the feeding center initiates eating, and activity in the satiety center inhibits eating. Thus, there is a dual, excitatory and inhibitory, control of food intake. These neural centers were also assumed to respond to changes in their chemical milieu. Glucoreceptors acting in one or both of these areas seemed to be the most likely candidate for chemical control, but lipostatic mechanisms also received major attention.

In fact, this scheme was so clear that it was proposed as a model both for other motivational systems and for general hypothalamic functioning (see Stellar, 1954). Evidence was marshaled for the propositions that (1) damage to restricted hypothalamic loci results in motivational changes; (2) different parts of the hypothalamus are specifically critical to different motivational systems; and (3) in general, motivational systems are under dual, excitatory and inhibitory, control. It was acknowledged that hypothalamic activity was also modulated by events in the internal environment, by sensory stimuli, and by cortical and thalamic centers, but primacy was accorded to the hypothalamus. Early results with both electrical and chemical stimulation of the hypothalamus appeared to support strongly such a conception. But this primacy of the hypothalamus has recently come under strong attack as researchers became aware that hypothalamic functioning had been considered in isolation from the rest of the brain.

We have previously seen that the systems involved in sleep, arousal, attention, and emotional responding all range rostrally in anatomic extent from the brainstem to the thalamus, through the hypothalamus, and into the limbic system. The same appears to be true of the mechanisms controlling food and water regulation. Anatomically, the hypothalamus serves as a "bridge," linking the limbic forebrain with the mesencephalon. And like a bridge, its apparent importance is due to the funneling and concentration of traffic that occurs there.

Integration is achieved in this system through multiple, reciprocally related, and reentering circuits. "Downstream" effects of limbic and hypothalamic activity are fed to the mesencephalon and, in turn, can be fed back, rostrally, through ascending reticular pathways. Thus, alerting and EEG arousal can be elicited from hypothalamic and limbic stimulation as well as from reticular stimulation; sleep can be induced from cholinergic stimulation of forebrain locations; hyperphagia can be seen as the result of lesions appropriately placed in the amygdala, the hypothalamus, and the midbrain.

This new conception emphasizes that any motivated behavior requires a state of minimal arousal and alerting—i.e., reticular mechanisms. This arousal is general and nonspecific in that it probably has access to all basic response systems, the "instinctual core" of behavior. The hypothalamus may contain receptor mechanisms responsive to fluctuations in the nutritional status of the organism. But the nature and origin of such stimuli is presently being reevaluated. Any specialized hypothalamic receptors probably achieve their specific functions by feeding into the common instinctual core.

Obviously, the analysis of hunger is far from complete; what has been presented here is a status report that will require revision.

REFERENCES

AHLSKOG, J. E., & HOEBEL, B. G. Overeating and obesity from damage to a noradrenergic system in the brain. *Science,* 1973, *182,* 166–169.

AHLSKOG, J. E., RANDALL, P. K., & HOEBEL, B. G. Hypothalamic hyperphagia: Dissociation from hyperphagia following destruction of noradrenergic neurons. *Science*, 1975, *190*, 399–401.

ALBERT, D. J., & STORLIEN, L. H. Hyperphagia in rats with cuts between the ventromedial and lateral hypothalamus. *Science,* 1969, *165*, 599–600.

ANAND, B. K., & BROBECK, J. R. Hypothalamic control of food intake. *Yale Journal of Biology and Medicine,* 1951, *24,* 123–140.

ANDERSSON, B., & LARSSON, B. Influence of local temperature changes in the preoptic area and rostral hypothalamus on the regulation of food and water intake. *Acta Physiologica Scandinavica,* 1961, *52,* 75–89.

ARMSTRONG, S., & SINGER, G. Effects of intrahypothalamic administration of norepinephrine on the feeding response of the rat under conditions of light and darkness. *Pharmacology, Biochemistry and Behavior*, 1974, *2*, 811–815.

BAILE, C. A., SIMPSON, C. W., BEAN, S. M., MCLAUGHLIN, C. L., & JACOBS, H. L. Prostaglandins and food intake of rats: A component of energy balance regulation? *Physiology and Behavior*, 1973, *10*, 1077–1085.

BERKUN, M. M., KESSEN, M. L., & MILLER, N. E. Hunger-reducing effects of food by stomach fistula versus food by mouth measured by a consummatory response. *Journal of Comparative and Physiological Psychology*, 1952, *45*, 550–554.

BOYLE, P. C., & KEESEY, R. E. Chronically reduced body weight in rats sustaining lesions of the lateral hypothalamus and maintained on palatable diets and drinking solutions. *Journal of Comparative and Physiological Psychology*, 1975, *88*, 218–223.

BREISCH, S. J., ZEMLAN, F. P., & HOEBEL, B. G. Hyperphagia and obesity following serotonin depletion by intraventricular *p*-chlorophenylalanine. *Science*, 1976, *192*, 382–385.

BROBECK, J. R. Food intake as a mechanism of temperature regulation in rats. *Federation Proceedings, American Physiological Society*, 1948, *7*, 13.

BROBECK, J. R., TEPPERMAN, J., & LONG, C. N. H. Experimental hypothalamic hyperphagia in the albino rat. *Yale Journal of Biology and Medicine*, 1943, *15*, 831–853.

CANNON, W. B., & WASHBURN, A. L. An explanation of hunger. *American Journal of Physiology*, 1912, *29*, 441–454.

CARLISLE, H. J., & STELLAR, E. Caloric regulation and food preference in normal, hyperphagic, and aphagic rats. *Journal of Comparative and Physiological Psychology*, 1969, *69*, 107–114.

COURY, J. N. Neural correlates of food and water intake in the rat. *Science*, 1967, *156*, 1763–1765.

DAVIS, J. D., GALLAGHER, R. J., LADOVE, R. F., & TURAUSKY, A. J. Inhibition of food intake by a humoral factor. *Journal of Comparative and Physiological Psychology*, 1969, *67*, 407–414.

DAVIS, R. C., GARAFALO, L., & KVEIM, K. Conditions associated with gastrointestinal activity. *Journal of Comparative and Physiological Psychology*, 1959, *52*, 466–475.

DEVENPORT, L. D., & BALAGURA, S. Lateral hypothalamus: Reevaluation of function in motivated feeding behavior. *Science*, 1971, *172*, 744–746.

EPSTEIN, A. N., & TEITELBAUM, P. Regulation of food intake in the absence of taste, smell, and other oropharynegeal sensations. *Journal of Comparative and Physiological Psychology*, 1962, *55*, 753–759.

Evans, B. K., Armstrong, S., Singer, G., Cook, R. D., & Burnstock, G. Intracranial injection of drugs: Comparison of diffusion of 6-OHDA and guanethidine. *Pharmacology, Biochemistry and Behavior*, 1975, *3*, 205–217.

Falk, J. L. Comments on Dr. Teitelbaum's paper. In M. R. Jones (ed.), *Nebraska Symposium on Motivation*, 1961. Lincoln: University of Nebraska Press, 1961, pp. 65–68.

Ferguson, N. B. L., & Keesey, R. E. Effect of a quinine-adulterated diet upon body weight maintenance in male rats with ventromedial hypothalamic lesions. *Journal of Comparative and Physiological Psychology*, 1975, *89*, 478–488.

Fisher, A. E., & Coury, J. N. Cholinergic tracing of a central neural circuit underlying the thirst drive. *Science*, 1962, *138*, 691–693.

Friedman, M. I., & Stricker, E. M. The physiological psychology of hunger: A physiological perspective. *Psychological Review*, 1976, *83*, 409–431.

Garcia, J., Kimeldorf, D. J., & Hunt, E. L. The use of ionizing radiation as a motivating stimulus. *Psychological Review*, 1961, *68*, 383–395.

Gibbs, J., Young, R. C., & Smith, G. P. Cholecystokinin decreases food intake in rats. *Journal of Comparative and Physiological Psychology*, 1973, *84*, 488–495.

Gold, R. M. Hypothalamic hyperphagia produced by parasagittal knife cuts. *Physiology and Behavior*, 1970, *5*, 23–26.

Gold, R. M. Hypothalamic obesity: The myth of the ventromedial nucleus, *Science*, 1973, *182*, 488–490.

Grijalva, C. V., Lindholm, E., Schallert, T., & Bicknell, E. J. Gastric pathology and aphagia following lateral hypothalamic lesions in rats: Effects of preoperative weight reduction. *Journal of Comparative and Physiological Psychology*, 1976, *90*, 505–519.

Grossman, M. I. Integration of current views on the regulation of hunger and appetite. *Annals of the New York Academy of Science*, 1955, *63*, 76–89.

Grossman, S. P. Eating or drinking elicited by direct adrenergic or cholinergic stimulation of hypothalamus. *Science*, 1960, *132*, 301–302.

Grossman, S. P. Behavioral effects of chemical stimulation of the ventral amygdala. *Journal of Comparative and Physiological Psychology*, 1964, *57*, 29–36.

Hetherington, A. W., & Ranson, S. W. The spontaneous activity and food intake of rats with hypothalamic lesions. *American Journal of Physiology*, 1942, *136*, 609–617.

Holman, G. L. Intragastric reinforcement effect. *Journal of Comparative and Physiological Psychology*, 1969, *69*, 432–441.

Jacobs, H. L., & Sharma, K. N. Taste versus calories: Sensory and metabolic signals in the control of food intake. *Annals of the New York Academy of Sciences*, 1969, *157*, 1084–1125.

Jordan, H. A. Voluntary intragastric feeding: Oral and gastric contributions to food intake and hunger in man. *Journal of Comparative and Physiological Psychology*, 1969, *68*, 498–506.

Kennedy, G. C. The role of depot fat in the hypothalamic control of food intake in the rat. *Proceedings of the Royal Society*, Series B, 1953, *140*, 578–592.

Kent, M., & Peters, R. H. Effects of ventromedial hypothalamic lesions on hunger-motivated behavior in rats. *Journal of Comparative and Physiological Psychology*, 1973, *83*, 92–97.

Kohn, M. Satiation of hunger from food injected directly into the stomach versus food ingested by mouth. *Journal of Comparative and Physiological Psychology*, 1951, *44*, 412–422.

Leibowitz, S. F. Reciprocal hunger-regulating circuits involving alpha-and beta-adrenergic receptors located, respectively, in the ventromedial and lateral hypothalamus. *Proceedings of the National Academy of Sciences*, 1970, *67*, 1063–1070

Leibowitz, S. F. Hypothalamic alpha- and beta-adrenergic systems regulate both thirst and hunger in the rat. *Proceedings of the National Academy of Science*, 1971, *68*, 332–334.

Leibowitz, S. F. Patterns of drinking and feeding produced by hypothalamic norepinephrine injection in the satiated rat. *Physiology and Behavior*, 1975, *14*, 731–742. (a)

Leibowitz, S. F. Ingestion in the satiated rat: Role of alpha and beta receptors in mediating effects of hypothalamic adrenergic stimulation. *Physiology and Behavior*, 1975, *14*, 743–757. (b)

LeMagnen, J. Peripheral and systematic actions of food in the caloric regulation of intake. *Annals of the New York Academy of Sciences*, 1969, *157*, 1126–1157.

LeMagnen, J., Devos, M., Gaudilliere, J. P., Louis-Sylvestre, J., & Tallon, S. Role of lipostatic mechanism in regulation by feeding of energy balance in rats. *Journal of Comparative and Physiological Psychology*, 1973, *84*, 1–23.

Levison, M. J., Frommer, G. P., & Vance, W. B. Palatability and caloric density as determinants of food intake in hyperphagic and normal rats. *Physiology and Behavior*, 1973, *10*, 455–462.

Levitt, R. A., & Fisher, A. E. Anticholinergic blockade of centrally induced thirst. *Science*, 1966, *154*, 520–522.

Lindholm, E., Shumway, G. S., Grijalva, C. V., Schallert, T., & Ruppel,

M. Gastric pathology produced by hypothalamic lesions in rats. *Physiology and Behavior*, 1975, *14*, 165–169.

Margules, D. L. Alpha-adrenergic receptors in hypothalamus for the suppression of feeding behavior by satiety. *Journal of Comparative and Physiological Psychology*, 1970, *73*, 1–12. (a)

Margules, D. L. Beta-adrenergic receptors in the hypothalamus for learned and unlearned taste aversions. *Journal of Comparative and Physiological Psychology*, 1970, *73*, 13–21. (b)

Margules, D. L., Lewis, M. J., Dragovich, J. A., & Margules, A. S. Hypothalamic norepinephrine: Circadian rhythms and the control of feeding behavior. *Science*, 1972, *178*, 640–643.

Mayer, J. Glucostatic mechanism of regulation of food intake. *New England Journal of Medicine*, 1953, *249*, 13–16.

McHugh, P. R., Moran, T. A., & Barton, G. N. Satiety: A graded behavioral phenomenon regulating caloric intake. *Science*, 1975, *190*, 167–169.

Miller, N. E., Bailey, C. J., & Stevenson, J. A. Decreased "hunger" but increased food intake resulting from hypothalamic lesions. *Science*, 1950, *112*, 256–259.

Miller, N. E., & Kessen, M. L. Reward effects of food via stomach fistula compared with those of food via mouth. *Journal of Comparative and Physiological Psychology*, 1952, *45*, 555–564.

Morgane, P. J. Distinct "feeding" and "hunger motivating" systems in the lateral hypothalamus of the rat. *Science*, 1961, *133*, 887–888.

Morgane, P. J. The function of the limbic and rhinic forebrain-limbic midbrain systems and reticular formation in the regulation of food and water intake. *Annals of the New York Academy of Sciences*, 1969, *157*, 806–848,

Morgane, P. J., & Jacobs, H. L. Hunger and satiety. In G. H. Bourne (ed.), *World review of nutrition and dietetics*. Basel, Switzerland: Karger, 1969, pp. 100–213.

Morgane, P. J., & Kosman, A. J. Relationship of the middle hypothalamus to amygdalar hyperphagia. *American Journal of Physiology*, 1960, *198*, 1315–1318.

Morrison, G. R. Alterations in palatability of nutrients for the rat as a result of prior tasting. *Journal of Comparative and Physiological Psychology*, 1974, *86*, 56–61.

Mufson, E. J., & Wampler, R. S. Weight regulation with palatable food and liquids in rats with lateral hypothalamic lesions. *Journal of Comparative and Physiological Psychology*, 1972, *80*, 382–392.

MYERS, R. D. Chemical mechanisms in the hypothalamus mediating eating and drinking in the monkey. *Annals of the New York Academy of Sciences*, 1969, *157*, 918–933.

MYERS, R. D. Brain mechanisms in the control of feeding: A new neurochemical profile theory. *Pharmacology, Biochemistry and Behavior*, 1975, *3*, Supplement 1, 75–83.

MYERS, R. D., & BENDER, S. A. Action of excess calcium ions in the brain on motivated feeding in the rat: Attenuation by pharmarcological antagonists. *Pharmacology, Biochemistry and Behavior*, 1973, *1*, 569–580.

NEILL, D. B., & LINN, C. L. Deficits in consummatory responses to regulatory challenges following basal ganglia lesions in rats. *Physiology and Behavior*, 1975, *14*, 617–624.

NICOLAÏDIS, S. Early systemic responses to orogastric stimulation in the regulation of food and water balance: Functional and electrophysiological data. *Annals of the New York Academy of Sciences*, 1969, *157*, 1176–1203.

NISBETT, R. E. Hunger, obesity, and the ventromedial hypothalamus. *Psychological Review*, 1972, *79*, 433–453.

OOMURA, Y., TAKAMURA, T., SUGIMORI, M., & YAMADA, Y. Effect of free fatty acid on the rat lateral hypothalamic neurons. *Physiology and Behavior*, 1975, *14*, 483–486.

PANKSEPP, J. Reanalysis of feeding patterns in the rat. *Journal of Comparative and Physiological Psychology*, 1973, *82*, 78–94.

RABIN, B. M. Independence of food intake and obesity following ventromedial hypothalamic lesions in the rat. *Physiology and Behavior*, 1974, *13*, 769–772.

ROBINSON, B. W., & MISHKIN, M. Alimentary responses evoked from forebrain structures in Macaca mulatta. *Science*, 1962, *136*, 260–262.

ROSENZWEIG, M. R. The mechanisms of hunger and thirst. In L. Postman (ed.), *Psychology in the making*. New York: Knopf, 1962, pp. 73–143.

ROZIN, P. Adaptive food sampling patterns in vitamin deficient rats. *Journal of Comparative and Physiological Psychology*, 1969, *69*, 126–132.

ROZIN, P., & KALAT, J. W. Specific hungers and poison avoidance as adaptive specializations of learning. *Psychological Review*, 1971, *78*, 459–486.

SALLER, C. F., & STRICKER, E. M. Hyperphagia and increased growth in rats after intraventricular injection of 5,7-dihydroxytryptamine. *Science*, 1976, *192*, 385–387.

SCHWARTZ, I. L., CRONKITE, E. P., JOHNSON, H. A., SILVER, L., TENZER, D., & DEBONS, A. F. Radioautographic localization of the "satiety center."

Transactions of the Association of American Physicians, 1961, *74*, 300–317.

Schwartzbaum, J. S., & Ward, H. P. An osmotic factor in the regulation of food intake in the rat. *Journal of Comparative and Physiological Psychology*, 1958, *51*, 555–560.

Sclafani, A., Berner, C. H., & Maul, G. Feeding and drinking pathways between medial and lateral hypothalamus in the rat. *Journal of Comparative and Physiological Psychology*, 1973, *85*, 29–51.

Sclafani, A., Berner, C. N., & Maul, G. Multiple knife cuts between the medial and lateral hypothalamus in the rat: A reevaluation of hypothalamic feeding circuitry. *Journal of Comparative and Physiological Psychology*, 1975, *88*, 210–217.

Simpson, C. W., Baile, C. A., & Krabill, F. F. Neurochemical coding for feeding in sheep and steers. *Journal of Comparative and Physiological Psychology*, 1975, *88*, 176–182.

Simpson, C. W., & DiCara, L. V. Estradiol inhibition of catecholamine elicited eating in the female rat. *Pharmacology, Biochemistry and Behavior*, 1973, *1*, 413–419.

Singh, D. Preference for mode of obtaining reinforcement in rats with lesions in septal or ventromedial hypothalamic area. *Journal of Comparative and Physiological Psychology*, 1972, *80*, 259–268.

Singh, D. Effects of preoperative training on food-motivated behavior of hypothalamic hyperphagic rats. *Journal of Comparative and Physiological Psychology*, 1973, *84*, 47–52.

Skultety, F. M. Alterations of caloric intake in cats following lesions of the hypothalamus and midbrain. *Annals of the New York Academy of Sciences*, 1969, *157*, 861–874.

Slangen, J. L., & Miller, N. E. Pharmacological tests for the function of hypothalamic norepinephrine in eating behavior. *Physiology and Behavior*, 1969, *4*, 543–552.

Sloane, J. R., & Baile, A. Ionic changes in cerebrospinal fluid and feeding, drinking and temperature of sheep. *Physiology and Behavior*, 1973, *10*, 915–923.

Smutz, E. R., Hirsch, E., & Jacobs, H. L. Caloric compensation in hypothalamic obese rats. *Physiology and Behavior*, 1975, *14*, 305–309.

Snowdon, C. T. Motivation, regulation, and the control of meal parameters with oral and intragastric feeding. *Journal of Comparative and Physiological Psychology*, *1969*, *69*, 91–100.

Stellar, E. The physiology of motivation. *Psychological Review*, 1954, *61*, 5–22.

Stevenson, J. A. F. Mechanisms in the control of food and water intake. *Annals of the New York Academy of Sciences*, 1969, *157*, 1069–1083.

STORLIEN, L. H., & ALBERT, D. J. The effect of VMH lesions, lateral cuts, and anterior cuts on food intake, activity level, food motivation, and reactivity to taste. *Physiology and Behavior*, 1972, *9*, 191–197.

STRICKER, E. M., & ZIGMOND, M. J. Effects on homeostasis of intraventricular injections of 6-hydroxydopamine in rats. *Journal of Comparative and Physiological Psychology*, 1974, *86*, 973–994.

SUNDSTEN, J. W. Alterations in water intake and core temperature in baboons during hypothalamic thermal stimulation. *Annals of the New York Academy of Sciences*, 1969, *157*, 1018–1029.

TEITELBAUM, P. Sensory control of hypothalamic hyperphagia. *Journal of Comparative and Physiological Psychology*, 1955, *48*, 156–163.

TEITELBAUM, P. Random and food-directed activity in hyperphagic and normal rats. *Journal of Comparative and Physiological Psychology*, 1957, *50*, 486–490.

TEITELBAUM, P. Disturbances in feeding and drinking behavior after hypothalamic lesions. In M. R. Jones (ed.), *Nebraska Symposium on Motivation*, 1961. Lincoln: University of Nebraska Press, 1961, pp. 39–65.

TEITELBAUM, P., & CYTAWA, J. Spreading depression and recovery from lateral hypothalamic damage. *Science*, 1965, *147*, 61–63.

TEITELBAUM, P., & EPSTEIN, A. N. The lateral hypothalamic syndrome: Recovery of feeding and drinking after lateral hypothalamic lesions. *Psychological Review*, 1962, *69*, 74–90.

UNGERSTEDT, U. Stereotaxic mapping of the monoamine pathways in the rat brain. *Acta Physiologica Scandinavica*, 1971, Supplement 367, 1–48.

VALENSTEIN, E. S. Selection of nutritive and nonnutritive solutions under different conditions of need. *Journal of Comparative and Physiological Psychology*, 1967, *63*, 429–433.

WALIKE, B. C., & SMITH, O. A. Regulation of food intake during intermittent and continuous cross circulation in monkeys (*Macaca mulatta*). *Journal of Comparative and Physiological Psychology*, 1972, *80*, 372–381.

WAMPLER, R. S. Increased motivation in rats with ventromedial hypothalamic lesions. *Journal of Comparative and Physiological Psychology*, 1973, *84*, 275–285.

ZEIGLER, H. P., & KARTEN, H. N. Central trigeminal structures and the lateral hypothalamic syndrome in the rat. *Science*, 1974, *186*, 636–638.

ZIGMOND, M. J., & STRICKER, E. M. Deficits in feeding behavior after intraventricular injection of 6-hydroxydopamine in rats. *Science*, 1972, *177*, 1211–1214.

ZIGMOND, M. J., & STRICKER, E. M. Recovery of feeding and drinking after intraventricular 6-hydroxydopamine or lateral hypothalamic lesions. *Science*, 1973, *182*, 717–720.

9

Thirst and the Regulation of Water Intake

Living organisms require water. Our observations of ourselves and others also make it clear that this need for water is expressed in a potentially strong drive—thirst. As with food, deprivation would seem to be the basic operation in initiating the drive for water. However, in at least one respect, water regulation is more complicated than food regulation. While water deprivation is an effective means of producing thirst, it turns out not to be the only means.[1] Water regulation is also concerned with the *distribution* of water in the body. As we shall see, there are both naturally occurring and experimental conditions which alter that distribution but leave the total amount of water constant. If an animal drinks under rather diverse conditions of water distribution and water deficit, are the drives similar? In other words, is there more than one kind of thirst?

Historically, there have been three basic notions in contention to account for thirst (Fitzsimons, 1973):

[1]In this chapter we deal with homeostatic or regulatory mechanisms that are concerned with actual deficits in body water. However, there also exists a variety of conditions that lead to drinking even though the organism has no water deficit. These would be instances of *nonhomeostatic* drinking. Prominent here is so-called *psychogenic polydipsia*—excessive drinking associated with receiving a food award on an intermittent schedule (Falk, 1961). Kissileff (1973) has provided an excellent review of these conditions.

1. Thirst is a general sensation arising from the loss of body water.
2. Thirst is a sensation of local origin, specifically arising in the mouth and throat.
3. Thirst results from stimulation of receptors in the brain.

These theories are not necessarily incompatible and have not proven individually adequate to account for all phenomena of thirst. Most recently, it has been necessary to incorporate an important qualifying hypothesis, the so-called "double depletion" hypothesis, to take account of the factor of water distribution.

PERIPHERAL FACTORS IN THIRST

Our review of the mechanisms controlling food intake (Chapter 8) has already indicated the futility of pitting central against peripheral mechanisms for an exclusive account of intake regulation. Furthermore, as will be evident shortly, thirst particularly exemplifies the interaction of central and peripheral mechanisms in regulation. However, as Fitzsimons (1973) has documented, the notion that thirst is of local origin, arising from sensations in the mouth and throat, exerted a heavily disproportionate influence on the research into thirst, especially when espoused by Cannon: "In advocating the dry-mouth theory in such strong terms, Cannon had performed a disservice because he deflected interest from the more important questions of the nature of the changes in body fluids that underlie thirst and the neurological mechanisms activated by these changes. He had focused attention on one aspect only of the sensation and had put out of court consideration of other possible mechanisms" (p. 17–18). Nonetheless, this theory, which focuses on the role of the salivary glands in keeping the mucosa of the mouth and throat moist, is worth a brief examination.

Salivary Glands

Two experiments by Montgomery have a direct bearing on the role played by the salivary glands in thirst. In the first experiment (Montgomery, 1931a), total extirpation of the salivary glands of dogs was carried out, and observations of water intake were made over a protracted period. Removal of the salivary glands was without effect on total water intake—the animals drink small amounts more often, apparently because they had dry mouths, but their total intake was not altered. In the second experiment (Montgomery, 1931b), the effects of atropine and pilocarpine were studied on intact dogs and dogs with their salivary glands removed. Among their other effects, atropine and pilocarpine, respectively, inhibit and stimulate salivary secretion. These experiments were undertaken, despite the negative effects of the prior experiment, to check if the reported effects of the drugs on water intake might stem from action on locations other than the salivary glands. Repeated injections of small doses of atropine over a 3-day period were not effective in altering water intake in either dogs with or without salivary glands. Large doses of atropine were similarly ineffective in short-term (2-hour) tests. Pilocarpine, injected after 2 days of water deprivation, also did not alter water intake.

More recently, Falk and Bryant (1973) studied the effect of salivarectomy on drinking elicited by agents known to be *dipsogenic* (drink inducing). We will discuss the actions of such substances in greater detail later. Suffice it to say that isoproteronol and diazoxide are potent dipsogens whose actions are dependent on renin, a substance significantly involved in water intake; the salivary glands are one significant source of renin. Generally, rats given these drugs drank excess quantities of water but salivarectomized animals did so to a lesser degree. In contrast, animals given sodium chloride loads, which produce drinking through a different mechanism, were unaffected by salivarectomy when the sodium chloride was placed into the abdominal cavity. However, when it was given intragastrically, sodium chloride produced less drinking in desalivated rats. It is not clear from these experiments whether salivary secretions are simply altering the stimulus environment or whether some endocrine output from these glands is acting centrally. In either event, the salivary glands modulate the normal response to dipsogenic stimuli.

The above results may be taken as descriptive of the more general conclusion of peripheral research. As in the case of food regulation, no one peripheral factor is sufficient, of itself, to account completely for the control of water intake. Salivary secretion does play a role in the modulation of drinking, but it acts in concert with other factors, both peripheral and central. Thus, for instance, dogs drink in proportion to their water deficit and about equal to the deficit, but they stop drinking before the water can be absorbed by the bodily tissues. Dogs with esophageal fistulas also drink in proportion to their deficit but take about twice as much as intact dogs before temporarily stopping. Distension of the stomach can also inhibit water intake. Thus, oropharyngeal factors and gastric factors both play a role in monitoring water intake. Evidently, water intake is under multiple influences, both peripheral and central (Adolph, 1964).

Comparison of Oral and Gastric Factors

An example of the operation of oral and gastric factors on water intake in water-deprived rats is provided by Mook (1963, 1969). In this experiment, rats were prepared with an esophageal fistula and a gastric cannula (Figure 9.1) that permitted the rat to drink one solution orally while, at the same time, the same or a different solution—or no solution—was entering the

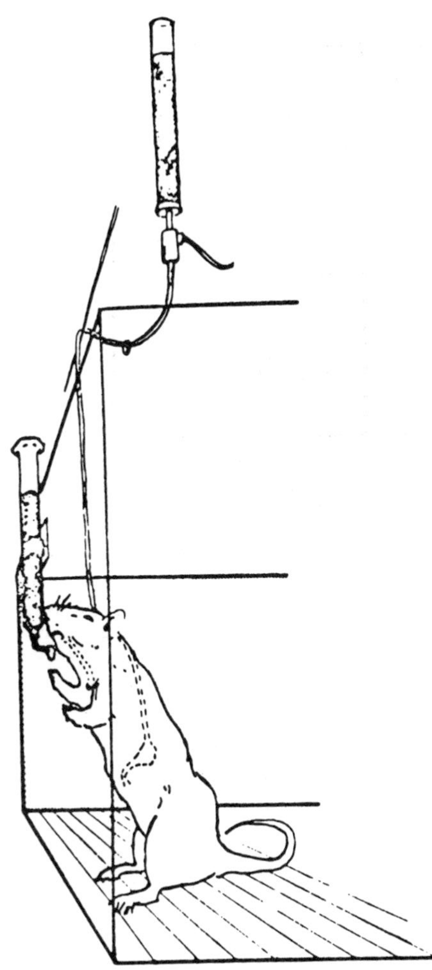

Figure 9.1. Rat with esophageal fistula and gastric cannula, operating the "electronic esophagus." (From Mook, D. G., Oral and postingestional determinants of the intake of various solutions in rats with esophageal fistulas. *Journal of Comparative and Physiological Psychology,* 1963, *56*, 645–659. Copyright 1963 by the American Psychological Association. Reprinted by permission.)

stomach. An "electronic esophagus," a device that monitored the licking behavior and controlled the flow of solution to the stomach, permitted the behavior to proceed as if the drinking situation were normal.

Figure 9.2 indicates what happened when the animal tasted different concentrations of sodium chloride solution (saline) while water, isotonic[2] sodium chloride, or hypertonic sodium chloride entered the stomach. First, with hypertonic saline entering the stomach, the drinking of water was elevated. Note that the system does not run away with itself—that is, the rat

[2]Under normal circumstances, the body's fluids contain about .9 percent sodium chloride. Solutions that contain that same ratio of dissolved substance to solvent are called *isotonic*. When the ratio is increased, the solution is called *hypertonic*. Finally, lesser ratios are called *hypotonic*.

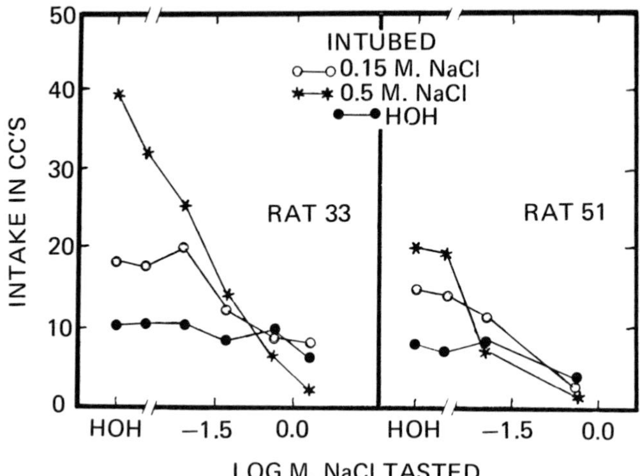

Figure 9.2. Intake as a function of sodium chloride concentration tasted, when water, isotonic (0.15 M) NaCl, and hypertonic (0.5 M) NaCl enter the stomach during drinking. (From Mook, D. G., Some determinants of preference and aversion in the rat. *Annals of the New York Academy of Sciences*, 1969, *157*, 1158–1175.)

does not drink or receive saline intragastrically, stimulating still more saline drinking. The amounts of water drunk were actually less than the rat demonstrated in sham drinking. Gastric distension is one obvious brake on this effect. Second, across each curve postingestional effects are constant; in other words, the same solution is being tubed intragastrically, regardless of the solution tasted. Thus the decline in intake with increasing salt concentration represents the operation of taste factors rather than postingestional factors. Normal animals drink more isotonic saline than water in preference tests. But the failure of these curves to rise over low salt concentrations suggests that this is because of postingestional factors; i.e., the reduced effectiveness of saline in meeting the animal's water requirements.[3]

THE DOUBLE DEPLETION HYPOTHESIS

As indicated earlier, water regulation is concerned with the distribution of water in the body as well as with the total water content. Water is distributed between intracellular and extracellular locations. And that distribution, in

[3]The explanation of why rats prefer hypotonic saline to water has been the subject of controversy. Deutsch and Jones (1960) and Deutsch and Deutsch (1966) suggest that it can be accounted for on the basis of taste factors rather than postingestinal factors. Regardless of the explanation, Mook's data are illustrative of a technique for separating oral and gastric influences.

turn, is affected by the relative concentrations of the fluid solutions in the intra- and extracellular spaces.

Osmosis

The body's cells are enclosed by membranes. These membranes permit some substances to pass through into the cells but other substancies are excluded. Therefore, there may be an unequal distribution of materials in solution (solutes) on the two sides of the membrane. *Osmosis*, the movement of water through membranes, results from such an unequal distribution of solutes. Different substances, or the same substance in different concentrations, produce different *osmotic pressures* or tendencies for water to cross cellular membranes. Water flows from the side with the lesser concentration of solutes to the side in which the concentration is higher, until the concentrations are equalized. Thus, thirst can be elicited in situations in which the total body content of water is not deficient, but the distribution of that water is out of balance. One effective means for demonstrating this is with salt solutions: Intravenous, intragastric, or subcutaneous injection of hypertonic salt results in the induction of drinking in previously water-sated animals. What happens is that the saline solution initiates a move toward osmotic equilibrium, and water moves from intracellular to extracellular locations, resulting in a relative dehydration of the cells. When allowed access to water, these experimental animals drink, demonstrating the effectiveness of cellular dehydration as a stimulus for thirst.

Conversely, if the extracellular fluid becomes depleted of sodium, there will be a movement of water into the cells to restore the transmembrane balance. Such a condition also leads to water intake. Here, the effective stimulus to thirst seems to be the decreased volume of the extracellular fluid, primarily the intravascular (blood) volume.

The double depletion hypothesis maintains, then, that there are two types of thirst. One, *cellular dehydration thirst*, is caused by loss of water intracellularly. The other is due to loss of volume in the intravascular fluid and is termed *hypovolemia*.

But, it might be maintained, drinking is drinking whatever the immediate cause, and, if animals drink water, why distinguish "thirsts"? An experiment by Stricker and Wolf (1967) makes it clear that the two types of thirst are not equivalent. If hypertonic saline injection produces thirst by decreasing intracellular fluids, it should be more effectively reduced by water than by isotonic saline; that is, the water would more effectively dilute the extracellular fluid and promote movement of water intracellularly. Conversely, if hypovolemic thirst results from decreased intravascular fluid volume, isotonic saline should more effectively reduce the thirst than water—

the saline would not cause a loss of water to the cellular fluid through osmosis.

Stricker and Wolf made rats thirsty by two different means: To produce cellular dehydration thirst, they were injected with hypertonic saline; to produce hypovolemic thirst, they were injected with polyethylene glycol. Polyethylene glycol induces *edema* (collection and isolation of fluid) at the injection site; the collected fluid comes from the intravascular volume and contains the appropriate solutes so the osmotic balance is not disturbed. Under the two types of thirst induction, the rats were pre-loaded, intragastrically, with either saline or water and then were tested for the amount of water that they freely ingested. As predicted, hypovolemic rats drink significantly less water after pre-loading with saline, while cellular dehydration rats drink significantly less water after water pre-loads. Thus, saline is a more efficient reducer of hypovolemic thirst, and water is a more efficient reducer of cellular dehydration thirst.

However, it should be noted that when given a free choice between saline and water, rats with both types of thirst chose to drink more saline. Thus, the preference data indicated that fluid intake is not solely a function of bodily requirements but may also be influenced by the palatability of the fluid. This might seem contrary to Mook's data cited earlier, which failed to show saline preferences because of the postingestional characteristics of saline. The contradiction is possibly resolved, however, by the fact that Mook employed tap water while Stricker and Wolf used distilled water, which is not as palatable.

In summary, then, there are at least two types of thirst. One is caused by depleting the body's cells of water and the other is caused by a loss of water from the intravascular volume. We shall now look more specifically at the mechanisms that mediate each type of thirst.

CELLULAR DEHYDRATION THIRST

Animals given injections of hypertonic sodium chloride drink water despite the fact that they were initially satiated for water. We ascribed the drinking to cellular dehydration, but let us take a look at how that conclusion can be substantiated. Blass (1973) has reviewed the details of this question; we will merely summarize them here.

The Adequate Stimulus

The simple operation of loading the animal with sodium chloride doesn't prove that cellular dehydration is the actual stimulus initiating drinking. Perhaps the excess sodium or chloride ions are the cause. Furthermore, the excess sodium chloride also initiates renal (kidney) defenses against the excess, resulting in changes in urine concentration and production. And, finally, some animals drink relatively small amounts of water after sodium chloride injections while others drink more copious amounts; this variation suggests that other factors may be operating to influence drinking.

Sorting out these problems was finally completed by an elegant series of experiments conducted by Fitzsimons (see Blass, 1973). In these experiments, nephrectomized (kidneys removed) rats were administered intravenous infusions of hypertonic solutions. Nephrectomizing the rats prevented any influence of urinary excretion on restoring appropriate osmotic balance. When the rats were given hypertonic sodium chloride and other substances that the cell membranes exclude, drinking ensued. Other substances, such as fructose and glucose, do pass through the cell walls; when they were infused, even in hypertonic concentrations, drinking did not occur. Fitzsimons showed that quite precise relations between increases in osmotic pressures, produced by the infusion, and changes in body weight, could be obtained for substances that do not pass through cell membranes. Note that body weight, not drinking per se, was the dependent measure, thus allowing the experimenter to control for water losses from the lungs, gastrointestinal tract, and the skin. These results, therefore, show that simply increasing the initial concentration of the solutes is not sufficient to produce drinking. If the substances do pass the cell membrane, dehydration of the cells does not occur and drinking does not occur. It is also clear that when the various losses are controlled, animals drink in quite precise amounts so as to offset cellular dehydration.

It should be noted, however, that the thirst produced by salt injection is not necessarily equivalent to that produced by water deprivation (Wayner & Kahan, 1969; Wayner & Petraitis, 1967). Thus, for instance, while water deprivation increased the wheel-turning activity of rats, sodium chloride injection did not affect wheel turning.

HYPOVOLEMIC THIRST

The body contains an elaborate set of mechanisms devoted to the conservation of its fluid levels (see Fitzsimons, 1971; Stricker, 1973). Central to these mechanisms is the kidney. When there is too much water in the body, the kidney secretes large volumes of dilute urine; when the water level is low, the kidney conserves water by secreting less of it and by increasing the concentration of the urine. The conservation of water by the kidney is under the control of *antidiuretic hormone* (ADH) released from the pituitary as a result of neural control in the hypothalamus. In addition, the kidney reponds to blood pressure changes. Low water levels lead to a reduction in blood volume and lowered blood volume results in reduced pressure. Blood pressure reductions in the venous system and in the kidney itself cause the kidney to secrete a substance called *renin.* Renin acts as an enzyme in the conversion of a substance in the blood to *angiotensin I*, which is then transformed to *angiotensin II*. This renin-angiotensin system has potent vasoconstrictive effects but it now seems clear that it also has a role in the initiation of thirst and drinking.

Multiple Factors in Hypovolemic Thirst

This simplified sketch enables us to infer that there are several ways in which blood volume losses can occur naturally or experimentally and lead to thirst and drinking. In passing, we have already mentioned some and we will now specifically enumerate them and some others.

The loss of blood through hemorrhage is one obvious hypovolemic condition that leads to thirst and drinking. Damage to the ADH system of the hypothalamus and pituitary (the disorder is called *diabetes insipidus*) can lead to excessive urine production and severe thirst. Excessive production of renin in the kidney is another natural condition leading to severe thirst. We have previously indicated that loss of sodium from the blood results in an osmotic change, the shift of water from blood plasma to intracellular locations, resulting in drinking. We have also noted earlier that if water is isolated from the system, as results when edema is produced by polyethylene glycol injection, drinking is stimulated. Another effective experimental technique for the production of thirst is to tie off the major abdominal vein (inferior vena cava), reducing the blood supply to the kidney; this results in copious drinking.

Note also that there is interaction among these various factors. Thus, for instance, polyethylene glycol injection results in an isosmolar loss of fluid; that is, the osmotic pressure balance of the remaining body fluids is not disrupted. However, when the animal drinks water as a result of the induced thirst, insufficient sodium is ingested and, over the longer run, there will be an increasing sodium depletion. The relations between thirst and appetite for sodium thus produce complicated effects on the quantities and types of fluids ingested (see Stricker, 1973).

And, finally, the following facts must be noted. Plasma renin activity is elevated with hypovolemia produced by polyethylene glycol injections and is comparable to that produced by tying off the vena cava. Yet, drinking persists in animals given polyethylene glycol after nephrectomy; in contrast, the vena cava preparation substantially reduces its water intake after nephrectomy. Thus, the deficits in extracellular fluid volume following polyethylene glycol must produce a stimulus to thirst in addition to that of the kidney's renin-angiotensin system; afferent stimulation from the pressure sensing systems is indicated (Stricker, 1973).[4]

INTERACTION OF THIRSTS

Given the complexity of the two thirst systems, it might be expected that actual drinking behavior will be a complicated function of the specific thirst-producing conditions that prevail and the fluids available for ingestion. Intracellular dehydration activates a neural system leading to drinking. If water is ingested, it rehydrates the cells and removes the stimulus for drinking, i.e., no inhibitory system appears necessary to stop the drinking. In contrast, in hypovolemic thirst a more complex condition prevails. About two-thirds of the body's total water resides in the intracellular component. When there is a large volumetric deficit, and a large ingestion of water, the blood plasma will be diluted by that water, resulting in movement of the water through the cell membranes to restore osmotic equilibrium. The result will be *overhydration* of the cells, with the larger portion of the water ingested going to the cells and only a limited restoration of the volumetric deficit. There appears to be some inhibitory mechanism that shuts down drinking despite a continuing volumetric deficit in order to prevent damage from overhydration of the cells. If, on the other hand, hypertonic salt solutions are ingested, volumetric deficit is better controlled, but this results in cellular dehydration. (It should now be clear why drinking seawater is hardly recommended!) In short, then, maximum restoration of volumetric deficits requires the ingestion of both water and salt in appropriate amounts. When both are available, it is possible to balance their intake so as to permit restoration of the plasma volume.

And, finally, the modulating effects of the kidneys and endocrine systems devoted to the conservation of water and minerals must be considered. In an experiment where diuresis (excess urinary flow) was induced pharmacologically, Rabe (1975) found that rats given both hypertonic saline and water to drink did not ingest enough fluids in the short run to make up for

[4]Some research by Almli (1971) and Weiss and Almli (1975) suggests that these results must definitely be qualified. In Almli's experiments, the onset of drinking induced by polyethylene glycol was actually associated with *hyper*volemia, not *hypo*volemia, which did not occur until an hour after the onset of drinking. Weiss and Almli presented evidence that the initial stimulus in hypovolemic thirst produced by polyethylene glycol may, in fact, be cellular dehydration and/or cellular volume decrease. However, it is not clear whether the same conclusion might be drawn about drinking induced by sodium depletion, vena cava ligation, or stimulation of the renin-angiotensin system. And, in addition, Lehr, Goldman, and Casner (1973) presented evidence that caval ligation may not have its dipsogenic effect through the renin-angiotensin system but rather through some other kidney mechanisms.

their hypovolemic loss; they did make up their intracellular deficit. Over a 24-hour period, however, both losses were apparently compensated. Rabe suggested potassium depletion, caused by the diuretic agent, might have played a role in this result. Be that as it may, he also suggested that volumetric deficits may be only poorly regulated by drinking, the primary regulation occurring through renal adjustment of water and salt excretion. On the other hand, cellular water deficits are well regulated by drinking, as was discussed earlier.

In summary, then, we see that the regulation of body water involves an exquisite interaction between physiological and behavioral mechanisms. The physiological mechanisms are devoted to monitoring of water content and the conservation of water and minerals. Many of them are initiated peripherally and produce afferent stimulation that activates central drive and response-producing mechanisms. The consequent behaviors complement the peripheral physiological mechanisms by culminating in the acquisition and ingestion of water and minerals. We will now look at the central mechanisms that mediate that behavior.

CENTRAL THIRST MECHANISMS

Our survey of mechanisms devoted to hunger and food regulation (Chapter 8) has already indicated much about the location of CNS mechanisms devoted to thirst and drinking. We shall not detail that material here. But recall that the lateral hypothalamic syndrome, which entails a profound depression of food regulation, also carries with it a severe deficit in the animal's drinking. In fact, while there appears to be recovery from the lesion in terms of the ability to regulate body weight, the only water intake seems to be in facilitation of eating—normal water intake seems to be permanently lost. Also recall that drinking may be elicited by chemical stimulation of the lateral hypothalamus and widespread locations in the limbic system. While much of that literature concerns a demonstrable involvement of cholinergic mechanisms in the mediation of drinking, there remains the controversial question of whether alpha and beta adrenergic mechanisms also exert an influence. We shall also have to examine what role peripherally and centrally produced renin and angiotensin play in the chemical mediation of drinking and thirst.

Thirst Receptors

The double depletion hypothesis of thirst has also received support from some CNS investigations. Specifically, such support comes from studies showing that the two types of thirst can be "uncoupled" by CNS manipulations, i.e., CNS modifications that affect one thirst mechanism are independent of the other mechanisms. The first such data were reported by Blass

(1968). In this experiment, rats with extensive damage to the frontal area of the brain did not drink, or drank considerably less water than normal rats, following cellular dehydration; in response to an isosmotic reduction in blood plasma, they drank normally. These results suggest that the brain mechanisms subserving drinking in response to the two types of water deficit are different.

Blass and Epstein (1971) followed up these results by attempting more specifically to localize receptors for cellular dehydration (osmoreceptors). A number of earlier studies, reviewed in Blass and Epstein's report, suggested that such osmoreceptors might be found in the lateral preoptic area, rostral to the hypothalamus. For instance, Andersson and Larson (1956) found that dogs with preoptic lesions did not drink following intravenous infusion of hypertonic saline but drank near normal quantities after water deprivation, which dehydrates both intracellular and extracellular water compartments.

Blass and Epstein's report can be taken as a model for a successful approach to the documentation of a brain mechanism. First, through the use of lesions, they determined the anatomic area involved. Lesions were placed in and around the lateral preoptic (LPO) and adjacent areas. The rats were then tested for drinking in response to systemic cellular dehydration and extracellular volemic depletion. On the basis of the animals' drinking responses, they could be segregated into three groups: One group consisted of rats whose lesions were ineffective in altering drinking in response to either thirst condition; a second group of rats was deficient in drinking in response to cellular dehydrational stimuli but was unaffected in response to volemic depletion; a third group of rats showed deficits in response to both dehydrational and volemic stimuli (Figure 9.3). Examination of the lesions indicated that only rats with lesions in the anteriomedial part of the LPO showed a deficit specific to and restricted to cellular dehydration.

Next, the problem was approached through chemical stimulation of the LPO. Four criteria were employed to show that the LPO is specifically responsive to dehydrational stimuli: (a) sensitivity—drinking had to be elicited by stimulation of the LPO zone by solutions whose osmotic characteristics approached the normal physiological range; (b) selectivity—drinking had to be elicited only by solutions excluded from cells (so that they would cause dehydration by osmotic shifts in water content, as in Fitzsimons' research cited earlier); (c) inhibition of drinking by local rehydration—removing the dehydrational stress by *local* injections of distilled water into the LPO had to inhibit drinking to *systemic* dehydrational stimuli but not to extracellular stimuli nor could it inhibit feeding; (d) anatomic specificity—chemical manipulation of hydrational conditions had to be limited to LPO and not effective in adjacent structures such as the lateral hypothalamus.

On all counts, Blass and Epstein were successful: Cellular dehydration of LPO by hypertonic solutions of sodium chloride or sucrose elicited long lasting drinking in water-sated rats, while injections of urea in LPO (urea

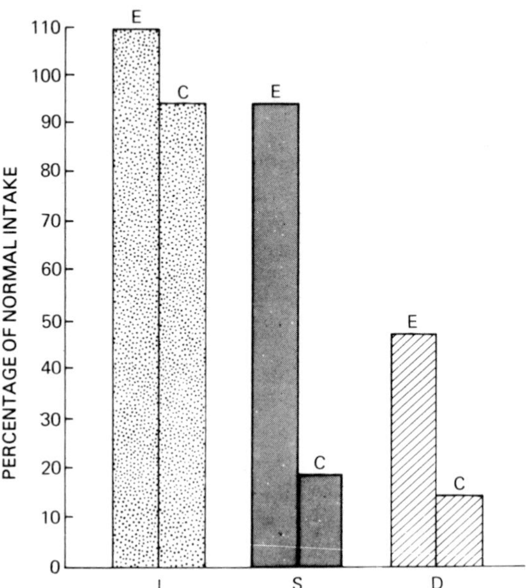

Figure 9.3. Drinking to extracellular hypovolemia (E) and to cellular dehydration (C) as percentage of normal response of (a) rats with ineffective lesions (Group I), (b) rats with lesions which cause a separation of controls of regulatory drinking (Group S), and (c) rats with lesions which produced a double deficit (Group D). (From Blass, E. M., and Epstein, A. N. A lateral preoptic osmosensitive zone for thirst in the rat. *Journal of Comparative and Physiological Psychology*, 1971, *76*, 378–394.)

does cross the cellular membrane) did not result in drinking. Cellular dehydration was effective in the LPO but ineffective in the lateral hypothalamus. Also, distilled water injections into the LPO severely reduced drinking induced by systemic cellular dehydration but did not inhibit drinking produced by the extracellular dipsogen renin. Similar injections in the lateral hypothalamus did not influence drinking to systemic cellular dehydration. Generally, then, these data fit all the criteria necessary for concluding that the LPO contains receptors that are specific to the mediation of an osmosensitive drinking mechanism. In addition, these data are complemented by very similar findings by Peck and Novin (1971) in the rabbit and by electrophysiological recording from LPO neurons in the rat by Malmo and Mundl (1975).[5]

[5]But note should be taken of Andersson's hypothesis that thirst is dependent on receptors that are responsive to sodium ions rather than being osmosensitive. He suggests that such receptors are located in the ventricular system. He further argues that LPO lesions have their effects because they impair the vascular supply to the relevant receptors, causing a delay in transfer of sodium ions (see the exchange between Peck, 1973, and Andersson, 1973).

These data also suggest that no special mechanism is required to terminate drinking induced by cellular dehydration; apparently drinking is continued until enough is ingested to restore cellular water, particularly in the LPO. This does not preclude peripheral factors, such as stomach distension, from playing a modulating role, but implies that long-term satiety is the simple result of removing the dehydrational stimuli.

Finally, the rats showing deficits to both cellular dehydration and volemic stimulation had lesions generally posterior to the critical zone for osmoreception but rostral to the lateral hypothalamic area. Their drinking deficit was described as similar to that of recovered lateral hypothalamic animals; the time for them to reach that degree of recovery differed, however, in that it took only 3 to 4 days. Though the data are scanty, these lesions suggest a convergence of several inputs which then feed through the lateral hypothalamus.

With respect to receptors for hypovolemia, it can only be stated that, thus far, none have been found, though the attempt has been made (see Stricker's review, 1973). Generally, the evidence seems to point toward afferent stimulation arising from peripheral pressure receptors, rather than specific receptors in the brain. However, as we shall presently see, the brain has proven responsive to local renin-angiotensin stimulation and the implications of this are not clear.

Chemical Stimulation of the Brain and Drinking

Grossman's (1960) finding that cholinergic stimulation of the rat brain selectively elicited drinking was quickly extended by Fisher and Coury (1962). As we have indicated previously, these investigators found that sites responsive to such cholinergic stimulation were diffusely located throughout the limbic system. The next major extension of this work was done by Levitt and Fisher (1966).

Levitt and Fisher noted the fact that lesions in many of the structures responsive to cholinergic stimulation do not disrupt normal drinking behavior. If the neural mechanisms controlling thirst consist of complex, redundant pathways working together, such results might be reasonable. It would be expected, however, that blockage of cholinergic drinking with the use of anticholinergic drugs should be similarly ineffective.

Levitt and Fisher's experiment consisted of locating pairs of cannulae in each animal, each of which yielded drinking with carbachol stimulation, and then testing for mutual blocking effects with the anticholinergic drug atropine. Thus, carbachol was introduced through one cannula and atropine through the other; drug sites were then reversed. In all instances, atropine blocked cholinergic drinking—blockage was bidirectional in each animal. When atropine was introduced at a site not responding to cholinergic stimulation, it was not effective in blocking the drinking. These results would seem to indicate that for cholinergically elicited drinking to occur, all of the components of the hypothetical drinking circuit of the limbic system must be functional.

Levitt and Fisher suggested that a major difference between water deprivation and cholinergically induced drinking may involve feedback from peripheral mechanisms. Thus, sustained input from these peripheral sources may permit the system to function, though some of its components are inoperative, while cholinergic stimulation alone is not sufficient to accomplish this. In any event, the fact that atropine does block the effect of carbachol lent additional support to the concept of cholinergic mediation of thirst.

But these results cannot be taken as evidence for a cholinergic system as *the* underlying mechanism in thirst. There are marked species differences in responses to cholinergic stimulation i.e., the rat may be the exception rather than the rule—and other possible chemical mediators have also been implicated. Thus, there is evidence that the cat does not respond to adrenergic and cholinergic stimulation by eating or drinking; rather the cat shows autonomic and emotional changes (Myers, 1964). In the monkey, a generalized cholinergic stimulation of the lateral hypothalamus seems to depress ingestive behavior in deprived animals, while adrenergic stimulation elicits both eating and drinking in sated animals (Myers, 1969). Finally, the rabbit seems to respond to cholinergic stimulation with food intake rather than drinking (Sommer, Novin, & LeVine, 1967). Each species, then, may be specifically adapted to different synaptic transmitters. Thus, it has been shown that gerbils drink to stimulation of the brain with norepinephrine (Block, Vallier, & Glickman, 1974) and monkeys (Myers, Hall, & Rudy, 1973) and rats (Stein & Seifter, 1962) drink to different varieties of cholinergic substances—nicotine and muscarine, respectively. On the other hand, there is commonality across species in that rats, gerbils, monkeys, goats, and cats all respond by drinking to intracerebral injections of angiotensin.

CNS Transmitters in Thirst

Research on the possible synaptic transmitters involved in the control of thirst and drinking has proliferated to such a degree that it is becoming difficult to see the forest for the trees. It may, therefore, be desirable to present one major, unified approach to the problem rather than many disparate findings. Fisher (1973) has presented what amounts to a "status report," and an organizing schema, which we shall generally follow. Obviously, what is presented is subject to continued revision and is not intended to be a final statement. And, it must be cautioned, despite the species differences indicated above, these data are based on experiments with the rat.

In accord with the material developed thus far, there are two basic questions regarding CNS transmitters that must be answered: (1)Which CNS transmitters can be identified as participating in the regulation of drinking? (2) Can different transmitters be implicated in control of the different types of thirst?

Before trying to answer these questions, we shall have to add one detail to the information presented thus far. We have previously indicated the role of the kidney's renin-angiotensin system in hypovolemic thirst. It is now necessary to indicate that the brain also seems to have a comparable renin-angiotensin system and this system seems to be involved in the control of drinking. This is indicated by the fact that angiotensin stimulation applied intracerebrally produces copious drinking. In fact, angiotensin appears to be the most potent dipsogen applied to the brain in that it elicits copious drinking with short latencies and with the smallest effective doses (Simpson & Routtenberg, 1973). These findings raise an interesting subsidiary problem. We know that epinephrine and norepinephrine are hormones produced by the adrenal gland and that they are also strongly implicated in the process of synaptic transmission. Does angiotensin operate similarly—that is, as a peripherally produced hormone, also found in the CNS, with possible transmitter functions?

The fact that rats will drink in response to either cholinergic or angiotensin stimulation of the brain suggests an obvious hypothesis: Cholinergic stimulation operates in a system mediating dehydrational thirst and angiotensin stimulation operates in a system mediating hypovolemic thirst. In fact (Fisher, 1973), has presented some preliminary evidence in support of this notion. In studying the fluid preferences of rats stimulated with each substance, he found that cholinergic stimulation resulted in a shift toward increased water consumption and angiotensin stimulation was followed by increased saline ingestion. But, as Fisher points out, angiotensin stimulation does produce copious drinking even when only water is available—in quantities that seemingly make it unlikely that even larger volumes of isotonic saline would be ingested. He, therefore, suggests that angiotensin may "act as an emergency signal to further sensitize several different functional systems in the brain, and that the *outcome* of its actions is only predictable in reference to the animal's physiological state at the time" (p. 252). In accord with this suggestion is that made by Block, Vallier, and Glickman (1974) in their study of drinking in the gerbil. That animal drinks to both angiotensin and norepinephrine stimulation. They indicated that the dipsogenic characteristics of angiotensin across a wide variety of species suggests a primitive, phylogentically old, brain mechanism dealing with water economy, while the organization and utilization of other CNS neurochemicals in thirst-related systems may vary among species.

Whatever the validity of the above speculations, Fisher's approach to analyzing the neurochemicals involved in thirst consists of employing pharmacological agents in an attempt to block the drinking elicited by different means of inducing thirst. As we have seen previously, drinking can be elicited by cholinergic brain stimulation and that same drinking can be prevented by simultaneously applying the anticholinergic drug atropine. But such an experiment does not differentiate whether the induced drinking is related to dehydrational or hypovolemic conditions, or possibly to both. In Fisher's studies, however, specific thirst induction procedures were employed and the aim was to block thirst selectively. In the ideal case, if, for instance, cellular dehydrational drinking can be blocked by application of an anticholinergic, and hypovolemic drinking cannot, we could infer a specificity of cholinergic synaptic transmission for cellular dehydrational thirst. As we shall see, that ideal is not realistic.

The general plan, then, of a recent series of experiments by Block and Fisher (1975) involved induction of thirst by a variety of specific means; blocking each such induction was attempted by applying varying doses of a variety of centrally active drugs known to affect different transmitter systems. In the first experiment, for instance, hypovolemic thirst was aroused by polyethylene glygol (PG) administration. Three dose levels of scopolamine hydrochloride were also injected (scopolamine is a blocker of muscarinic cholinergic transmission). Similarly, three dose levels of the drug haloperidol were also employed in an attempt to block dopaminergic transmission. (Note that a relationship between angiotensin and dopamine has been reported by others.) Finally, combinations of haloperidol and scopolamine were injected. Meanwhile, placebos were employed as a control. Mean water intake was the dependent measure after each of these treatments.

Scopolamine reduced water intake after PG by some 40 to 45 percent; interestingly, there was a limit to that effect, i.e., increasing the dose did not further limit the intake. Haloperidol produced a dose-dependent decrease in water intake after PG. But since the selectivity of the haloperidol in higher doses is suspect, the effect on dopamine with higher doses is open to some question. At the lowest dose, haloperidol produced a 35 percent decrement in intake. A combination of scopolamine and haloperidol, in amounts that separately produced 45 and 35 percent reductions in drinking, respectively, completely blocked water intake after PG administration. Thus, the blockage of drinking in hypovolemically induced thirst appears to be dependent on both cholinergic and catecholaminergic mechanisms.

In the second experiment, Block and Fisher produced cellular dehydration thirst by injecting hypertonic sodium chloride. Drug administration was similar to that in the first experiment. Again, drinking could be partially blocked by either the anticholinergic or the antidopaminergic but the combined injection did not completely eliminate drinking.

Isoproterenol is a beta-adrenergic substance that produces hypotension, elevated plasma renin levels, and increased water intake; this drug was employed as a dipsogenic stimulus in the third experiment. Both haloperidol and scopolamine produced dose-dependent reductions in drinking to isoproterenol, and a combination of the two completely blocked the drinking. Thus, both instances of hypovolemic thirst induction, PG and isoproterenol, seem dependent on the integrity of both cholinergic and catecholaminergic systems.

The fourth experiment tested for the blocking effects of haloperidol and scopolamine on thirst produced by 11- or 22-hour water deprivation. Generally, each drug partially blocked drinking and in combination they only partially blocked drinking also.

Two additional experiments essentially addressed the question of whether the blocking agents might have achieved their effects by generally debilitating the animals. Such apparently was not the case, since the animals did respond appropriately to manipulations affecting their food intake while under the influence of the thirst-blocking treatments.

Summary

These results, then, emphasize the pervasive involvement of both cholinergic and catecholaminergic (specifically dopamine?) systems in the mediation of thirst. They also suggest that hypovolemic thirst is principally dependent on these two systems alone, since blockage of these alone was sufficient to eliminate drinking induced by hypovolemia. On the other hand, dehydrational and deprivation thirst were not completely blocked by similar procedures, suggesting that other neurohumors are involved. Here it is pertinent to mention that DeWied (1966) failed to block dehydrational drinking with a serotonin blocker. Stated negatively, these results suggest that *no* major component of thirst is dependent on a single transmitter system.

Block and Fisher (1975) also emphasize that the anticholinergic blockade of drinking is not only partial but relatively constant across the thirst inducers they presented. Thus, they suggest that the cholinergic contribution to the maintenance or facilitation of differently derived thirsts is quite fixed. In other words, the cholinergic system may impinge on a number of neural systems involved in mediating specific forms of thirst, in equal measure, but not be crucial to any one of them. This view suggests a facilitative role for the cholinergic system in both dehydrational and volemic thirsts.

Angiotensin

Block and Fisher (1975) did not directly assess the role of angiotensin in their experiments. At the present time, the relevant data are fragmentary and certainly do not lend themselves to any precise conclusions.

As we have indicated, the existence of a renin-angiotensin system in the brain has been shown, and it is also clear that intracerebral stimulation with angiotensin is an extremely potent dipsogen. What is not clear are the details about the locus of action of angiotensin and its mode of action and specificity with respect to different means of inducing thirst.

A number of studies agree in showing that angiotensin is a potent dipsogen and in demonstrating that drinking can be elicited from widespread brain sites. For instance, Brophy and Levitt (1974) found dose-response relationships in the cat between angiotensin and drinking that did not differ across septal region, caudate nucleus, preoptic area, lateral hypothalamus, and lateral ventricle. A number of experiments (see Peres, Gentil, Graeff, & Covian, 1974, for a review) suggest that a dopaminergic system underlies the sensitivity of the brain to such angiotensin stimulation. However, Peres et al. found that a specific antagonist of angiotensin reliably blocked drinking to such stimulation but that dopamine blockers produce only inconsistent or partial blocking. Together, these results suggest the existence of widespread receptors specific to angiotensin.

An early study by Wolf and Miller (1964) suggested that the integrity of the lateral hypothalamus was essential for carbachol-induced drinking. Carbachol-induced drinking, elicited from preoptic and posterior hypothalamic sites, was severely reduced by lateral hypothalamic lesions. On the other hand, lesions of the preoptic area and posterior hypothalamus did not materially disturb drinking to lateral hypothalamic carbachol. More recently, Black, Kucharczyk, and Mogenson (1974) reached a similar conclusion with regard to angiotensin; again, lateral hypothalamic lesions disrupted drinking to angiotensin stimulation of the preoptic area. However, these findings have been subject to considerable controversy in that chemicals applied to specific brain locations may possibly have their effects through diffusion to other sites (see Routtenberg, 1967; Fisher & Levitt, 1967). Recently, Routtenberg (1972) suggested that the actual site of action for carbachol might be the subfornical organ, a highly vascularized structure which is located at the confluence of the lateral and third ventricles (Figure 1.8). Routtenberg's hypothesis is that carbachol and other chemical dipsogens might be reaching the subfornical organ through the vascular or ventricular systems rather than operating on their immediate sites of implantation. Routtenberg reported that subfornical lesions eliminated drinking to carbachol applied intraventricularly. Similarly, Simpson and Routtenberg (1973) reported that subfornical lesions eliminated the dipsogenic effects of angiotensin applied to the preoptic area. Yet Buggy, Fisher, Hoffman, Johnson, and Phillips (1975) have presented evidence that the subfornical organ is *not* the exclusive receptor site for angiotensin. They found that drinking to angiotensin recovered after subfornical lesions and that drinking could be produced after subfornical lesions by injecting angiotensin into the third ventricle. They suggested that a temporary obstruction, by edema or lesion debris, at the interventricular foramen might be produced by subfornical lesions, and this might block access of cerebrospinal fluid-borne angiotensin to third ventricle receptor sites. These sites are adjacent to hypothalamus and preoptic areas and injections here could be diffusing into the ventricles.[6]

These varying results only emphasize the multiplicity of problems with regard to the role of angiotensin: What is its role in the total picture of water economy? Where are the brain sites involved? Is it acting as an independent synaptic transmitter or is its action mediated, perhaps through one or more of the catecholamines? Obviously, much work will be required to pin down the action of angiotensin.

SUMMARY

In a general sense, the double depletion hypothesis has provided a schema for understanding the nature of the deficits involved in thirst. In a more particular sense, it has consummately guided and developed from the research into the peripheral physiological mechanisms concerned with the body's water economy. It does remain to be seen, however, if that hypothesis can be maintained when it comes to a functional description of the operation of the brain mechanisms involved in thirst and drinking. Thus, while there is strong evidence that brain receptors for osmosentive mechanisms are located in the preoptic area, that evidence has not gone completely without challenge, nor has it been possible to differentiate any brain mechanisms specifically related to hypovolemic thirst.

Several theoretical constructions can be put on the available evidence and, at present, it is not possible to discriminate among them. First, it is possible to construe the evidence to indicate that osmosensitive receptors exist in LPO; that the lateral hypothalamus may represent an important zone of convergence and/or transmission of osmosensitive and volemic information; and that no specific receptors exist in the brain for volemic deficits. Second, it is possible to speculate that the brain's angiotensin system is somehow involved in volemic control and that it, and some unknown receptor sites, possibly ventricular, exist alongside specific osmosensitive mechanisms as the complementary brain system suggested by the double depletion hypothesis. Finally, it is also possible to speculate that the brain

[6]Here we have been primarily concerned with diffusion of substances within the brain and the possible access of peripheral substances to the brain. However, Fisher (1973) has also demonstrated that the reverse process must also be considered as a possible artifact in this research area. For example, isoproterenol is a beta adrenergic compound known to be dipsogenic when applied to the brain. But Fisher has presented strong evidence that this dipsogenic effect is dependent on leakage to the periphery; thus kidney-related factors are probably responsible for increased drinking to either central or peripheral isoproterenol.

systems involved are *not* differentiated as suggested by the double depletion hypothesis—perhaps that hypothesis applies only to peripheral mechanisms.

This view finds suggestive support from several findings. A number of researchers have emphasized that ventricular sites, rather than hypothalamic or preoptic sites, are most sensitive to a variety of dipsogenic manipulations. Carbachol stimulation could be an exception to this, since it is seemingly more potent within brain tissue. But it is possible that it may not be acting within the primary receptor mechanism, that it is only involved in a second-step link in the system. In any event, Routtenberg's hypothesis of diffusion of applied chemicals to the ventricular system will be a difficult one to prove or disprove. Similarly, the ambiguous role of the brain's angiotensin system might be interpreted as in line with an hypothesis that the two peripheral thirst systems are not differentiated in the brain. This line of reasoning might suggest that the primary mediator of all thirst is the angiotensin system and that other neurochemicals perform their functions in later links in the system. There may be present reasons for emphasizing one or another of these (or other) possibilities, but there are no certain bases for unequivocally rejecting any of them.

The above lines of argument raise a corollary question: If there are differentiable bodily signals that indicate a specific type of thirst deficit, but no central differentiation of the mechanisms, how is it that animals respond to the different deficits by drinking different mixes of fluids? In fact, assuming that there are differentiable brain mechanisms for the different thirsts, we must still account for these same *behavioral* differences. As yet we have no satisfactory answer to this question. And, as Epstein (1973) has forcefully pointed out, when we have completely defined all the physiological controls of thirst and the brain mechanisms involved, we will still have to account for the anticipatory and affective aspects of drinking. We do not drink reflexively—rather we anticipate the need, and associated with the behavior are strong affective components. Simply ascribing these psychological functions to "memory" or "arousal systems" will not clarify their mechanisms.

REFERENCES

Adolph, E. F. Regulation of body water content through water ingestion. In M. J. Wayner (ed.), *Thirst.* New York: Macmillan, 1964, pp. 5–14.

Almli, C. R. Hypervolemia at the polyethylene glycol induced onset of drinking. *Physiology and Behavior,* 1971, 7, 369–373.

Andersson, B. Invited comment: Osmoreceptors versus sodium receptors. In A. N. Epstein, H. R. Kissileff, & E. Stellar (eds.), *The neuropsychology of thirst: New findings and advances in concepts.* Washington, D.C.: V. H. Winston and Sons, 1973, pp. 113–116.

ANDERSSON, B., & LARSON, S. Water and food intake and the inhibitory effect of amphetamine on drinking and eating before and after "prefrontal lobotomy" in dogs. *Acta Physiologica Scandinavica,* 1956, *38,* 22–30.

BLACK, S. L., KUCHARCYZK, J., & MORGENSON, G. J. Disruption of drinking to intracranial angiotensin by lateral hypothalamic lesion. *Pharmacology, Biochemistry and Behavior,* 1974, *2,* 515–522.

BLASS, E. M. Separation of cellular from extracellular controls of drinking in rats by frontal brain damage. *Science,* 1968, *162,* 1501–1503.

BLASS, E. M. Cellular-dehydration thirst: Physiological, neurological, and behavioral correlates. In A. N. Epstein, H. R. Kissileff, & E. Stellar (eds.), *The neuropsychology of thirst: New findings and advances in concepts.* Washington, D.C.: V. H. Winston and Sons, 1973, pp. 37–72.

BLASS, E. M., & Epstein, A. N. A lateral preoptic osmosensitive zone for thirst in the rat. *Journal of Comparative and Physiological Psychology,* 1971, *76,* 378–394.

BLOCK, M. L., & FISHER, A. E. Cholinergic and dopaminergic blocking agents modulate water intake elicited by deprivation, hypovolemia, hypertonicity, and isoproterenol. *Pharmacology, Biochemistry and Behavior,* 1975, *3,* 251–262.

BLOCK, M. L., VALLIER, G. H., & GLICKMAN, S. E. Elicitation of water ingestion in the Mongolian gerbil (*Meriones unguiculatus*) by intracranial injection of angiotensin II and 1-norepinephrine. *Pharmacology, Biochemistry and Behavior,* 1974, *2,* 235–242.

BROPHY, P. D., & LEVITT, R. A. Dose-response analysis of angiotensin- and renin-induced drinking in the cat. *Pharmacology, Biochemistry and Behavior,* 1974, *2,* 509–514.

BUGGY, J., FISHER, A. E., HOFFMAN, W. E., JOHNSON, A. K., & PHILLIPS, M. I. Ventricular obstruction: Effect on drinking induced by intracranial injection of angiotensin. *Science,* 1975, *190,* 72–74.

DEUTSCH, J. A., & DEUTSCH, D. *Physiological psychology,* Homewood, Ill.: Dorsey, 1966.

DEUTSCH, J. A., & JONES, A. D. Diluted water: An explanation of the rat's preference for saline. *Journal of Comparative and Physiological Psychology,* 1960, *53,* 122–127.

DEWIED, D. Effect of autonomic blocking agents and structurally related substances on "salt arousal of drinking." *Physiology and Behavior,* 1966, *1,* 193–197.

EPSTEIN, A. N. Epilogue: Retrospect and prognosis. In A. N. Epstein, H. R. Kissileff, & E. Stellar (eds.), *The neuropsychology of thirst: New findings and advances in concepts.* Washington, D.C.: V. H. Winston and Sons, 1973, pp. 315–332.

FALK, J. L. The behavioral regulation of water and electrolyte balance. *Nebraska Symposium on Motivation, 1961*. 9, Lincoln: University of Nebraska Press, 1961, pp. 1–33.

FALK, J. L., & BRYANT, R. W. Salivarectomy: Effect on drinking produced by isoproterenol, diazoxide and NaCl loads. *Pharmacology, Biochemistry and Behavior*, 1973, *1*, 207–210.

FISHER, A. E. Relationships between cholinergic and other dipsogens in the central mediation of thirst. In A. N. Epstein, H. R. Kissileff, & E. Stellar (eds.), *The neuropsychology of thirst: New findings and advances in concepts*. Washington, D.C.: V. H. Winston and Sons, 1973, pp. 243–278.

FISHER, A. E., & COURY, J. N. Cholinergic tracing of a central neural circuit underlying the thirst drive. *Science*, 1962, *138*, 691–693.

FISHER, A. E., & LEVITT, R. A. Drinking induced by carbachol: Thirst circuit or ventricular modification? *Science*, 1967, *157*, 839–841.

FITZSIMONS, J. T. The physiology of thirst: A review of the extraneural aspects of the mechanisms of drinking. In E. Steller & J. M. Sprague (eds.), *Progress in physiological psychology*, Vol. 4. New York: Academic Press, 1971, pp. 119–201.

FITZSIMONS, J. T. Some historical perspectives in the physiology of thirst. In A. N. Epstein, H. R. Kissileff, & E. Stellar (eds.), *The neuropsychology of thirst: New findings and advances in concepts*. Washington, D.C.: V. H. Winston and Sons, 1973, pp. 3–33.

GROSSMAN, S. P. Eating or drinking elicited by direct adrenergic or cholinergic stimulation of hypothalamus. *Science*, 1960, *132*, 301–302.

KISSILEFF, H. R. Nonhomeostatic controls of drinking. In A. N. Epstein, H. R. Kissileff, & E. Stellar (eds.), *The neuropsychology of thirst: New findings and advances in concepts*. Washington, D.C.: V. H. Winston and Sons, 1973, pp. 163–198.

LEHR, D., GOLDMAN, H. W., & CASNER, P. Renin-angiotensin role in thirst: Paradoxical enhancement of drinking by angiotensin converting enzyme inhibitor. *Science*, 1973, *182*, 1031–1034.

LEVITT, R. A., & FISHER, A. E. Anticholinergic blockade of centrally induced thirst. *Science*, 1966, *154*, 520–522

MALMO, R. B., & MUNDL, W. J. Osmosensitive neurons in the rat's preoptic area. *Journal of Comparative and Physiological Psychology*, 1975, *88*, 161–175.

MONTGOMERY, M. F. The role of the salivary glands in the thirst mechanism. *American Journal of Physiology*, 1931, *96*, 221–227. (a)

MONTGOMERY, M. F. The influence of atropine and pilocarpine on thirst (voluntary ingestion of water). *American Journal of Physiology*, 1931, *98*, 35–41. (b)

Mook, D. G. Oral and postingestional determinants of the intake of various solutions in rats with esophageal fistulas. *Journal of Comparative and Physiological Psychology*, 1963, *56*, 645–659.

Mook, D. G. Some determinants of preference and aversion in the rat. *Annals of the New York Academy of Sciences*, 1969, *157*, 1158–1175.

Myers, R. D. Emotional and autonomic responses following hypothalamic chemical stimulation. *Canadian Journal of Psychology*, 1964, *18*, 6–14.

Myers, R. D. Chemical mechanisms in the hypothalamus mediating eating and drinking in the monkey. *Annals of the New York Academy of Sciences*, 1969, *157*, 918–933.

Myers, R. D., Hall, G. H., & Rudy, T. A. Drinking in the monkey evoked by nicotine or angiotensin II microinjected in hypothalamus and mesencephalic sites. *Pharmacology, Biochemistry and Behavior*, 1973, *1*, 15–22.

Peck, J. W. Discussion: Thirst(s) resulting from bodily water imbalances. In A. N. Epstein, H. R. Kissileff, & E. Stellar (eds.), *The neuropsychology of thirst: New findings and advances in concepts.* Washington, D.C.: V. H. Winston and Sons, 1973, pp. 99–112.

Peck, J. W., & Novin, D. Evidence that osmoreceptors mediating drinking in rabbits are in the lateral preoptic area. *Journal of Comparative and Physiological Psychology*, 1971, *74*, 134–147.

Peres, V. L., Gentil, C. G, Graeff, F. G., & Covian, M. R. Antagonism of the dipsogenic action of intraseptal angiotensin II in the rat. *Pharmacology, Biochemistry and Behavior*, 1974, *2*, 597–602.

Rabe, E. F. Relationship between absolute body-fluid deficits and fluid intake in the rat. *Journal of Comparative and Physiological Psychology*, 1975, *89*, 468–477.

Routtenberg, A. Drinking induced by carbachol: Thirst circuit or ventricular modification? *Science*, 1967, *157*, 838–839.

Routtenberg, A. Intracranial chemical injection and behavior: A critical review. *Behavioral Biology*, 1972, *7*, 601–641.

Simpson, J. B., & Routtenberg, A. Subfornical organ: Site of drinking elicitation by angiotensin II. *Science*, 1973, *181*, 1172–1174.

Snyder, J. J., & Levitt, R. A. Neural activity changes with central anticholinergic blockade of cholinergically-induced drinking. *Pharmacology, Biochemistry and Behavior*, 1975, *3*, 75–79.

Sommer, S. R., Novin, D., & LeVine, M. Food and water intake after intrahypothalamic injections of carbachol in the rabbit. *Science*, 1967, *156*, 983–984.

Stein, L., & Seifter, J. Muscarinic synapses in the hypothalamus. *American Journal of Physiology*, 1962, *202*, 751–756.

Stricker, E. M. Thirst, sodium appetite, and complementary physiological contributions to the regulation of intravascular fluid volume. In A. N. Epstein, H. R. Kissileff, & E. Stellar (eds.), *The neuropsychology of thirst: New findings and advances in concepts.* Washington D.C.: V. H. Winston and Sons, 1973, pp. 73–98.

Stricker, E. M., & Wolf, G. Hypovolemic thirst in comparison with thirst induced by hyperosmolarity. *Physiology and Behavior,* 1967, *2,* 33–38.

Wayner, M. J., & Kahan, S. A. Central pathways in the salt arousal of drinking. *Annals of the New York Academy of Sciences,* 1969, *157,* 701–722.

Wayner, M. J., & Petraitis, J. Effects of water deprivation and salt arousal of drinking on wheel-turning activity of rats. *Physiology and Behavior,* 1967, *2,* 273–276.

Weiss, C. S., & Almli, C. R. Polyethylene glycol induced thirst: A dual stimulatory mechanism? *Physiology and Behavior,* 1975, *14,* 477–481.

Wolf, G., & Miller, N. E. Lateral hypothalamic lesions: Effects on drinking elicited by carbachol in preoptic area and posterior hypothalamus. *Science,* 1964, *143,* 585–587.

10

Sexual Behavior and Endocrine Functions

Physiological psychology is generally concerned with how factors internal to the organism interact with environmental events to modify behavior. Figure 10.1 schematically represents this situation. The loops on the left of the figure, including the external environment, receptors, CNS, and behavior, generally show where much of our emphasis has been placed in previous chapters—interrelations between the environment and the CNS. We have seen that these are dynamic relationships in that nervous system activity, resulting in behavior, modifies the environment, which, in turn, modifies the nervous system. But the nervous system also participates in another interaction, a dynamic relationship with its own chemical environment. The endocrine system, made up of those glands that secrete hormones into the blood supply, is a major factor in this internal interaction. Schematically, this is diagrammed on the right of Figure 10.1.[1] In discussing sexual and reproductive behavior, we will be emphasizing the right side of Figure 10.1.

[1]The diagram is oversimplifed in that it overlooks the fact that not all hormones are secreted in response to trophic hormones from the pituitary. Epinephrine and norepinephrine are adrenal hormones which are not so secreted, for instance. Then, too, not all hormones exert feedback on the pituitary.

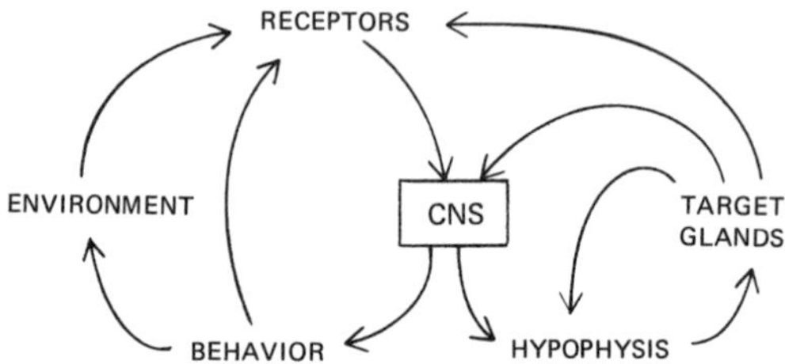

Figure 10.1. Relationships among behavior, CNS, and hormones. See text for details. (Modified from *Hormones and Behavior* by Whalen. 1967 by Litton Educational Publishing, Inc. Reprinted by permission of Van Nostrand Company.)

Hormonal functioning is crucial to sexual activity, particularly in lower animals. One question of concern will be the extent of that dependence for the human animal.

Figure 10.1. is meant merely to suggest the kinds of relationships that we will encounter. Thus, either directly or through mediation of the pituitary, we will find that CNS activity modifies hormonal secretion and that, conversely, hormonal secretion modifies CNS activity. Not only does hormonal activity influence behavior, but behavior influences hormonal activity. Similarly, sensory stimuli modify hormonal conditions and hormonal output modifies stimulus reception through its effects on receptors.

It should be noted that we will be concerned here specifically with copulatory activity. That is, we are abstracting from a total context which includes behaviors related to courtship, nesting, care of the young, aggressive, and migratory behaviors. The reader is referred to such texts as that by Marler and Hamilton (1967), Hinde (1970), and Eibl-Eibesfeldt (1970) for information relevant to these topics.

HORMONES AND SEXUAL PHYSIOLOGY

The hormones of most immediate concern to us here are those secreted by the gonads (sex glands)—estrogen and progesterone are secreted by the female *ovary* and androgen by the male *testis*. These glands and their hormones each serve several functions. The female ovary also produces the eggs necessary for sexual reproduction and the testes produce the sperm. These hormones play a role in the physical development of the oganism as well, since they are responsible for the final development of the genitalia and secondary sexual characteristics such as voice timbre, body hair, and fat distribution. And, as we shall see, their role in behavior is also crucial.

As indicated earlier (Chapter 1), the activity of the gonads is regulated by their reciprocal relationship to the anterior pituitary, or adenohypophysis. The gonadotrophic hormones secreted by the adenohypophysis include FSH (follicle stimulating hormone) and LH (luteinizing hormone). In the female, the secretion of these hormones is on a cyclical basis and, in cooperation with the brain and ovaries, they control the physiological condition of the reproductive apparatus. While the male generally does not show cyclical sexual changes, FSH and LH are important for sperm and androgen production.

In the female, FSH and LH promote the development of the ovarian follicle, from which the egg arises, and the secretion of estrogen. When blood levels of estrogen reach critical levels, they influence the pituitary to decrease FSH and increase LH output, which in turn results in ovulation. At this time, a third pituitary hormone, *prolactin,* results in the development of the *corpus luteum* in the ovary. The corpus luteum is essentially a temporary endocrine gland that secretes estrogen and progesterone. Progesterone is responsible for the preparation of the reproductive system so that a fertilized egg may be implanted and develop further. In the absence of fertilization, the corpus luteum degenerates, and all these preparatory changes are sloughed off and the cycle starts again. It might be noted that birth control pills usually contain both progesterone and estrogen in amounts that prevent the repetition of this cycle.

SEXUAL CYCLES

Reproductive activity is basically cyclical in its occurrence. In mammals, cycles appear mostly in the female, who is receptive to sexual activity only at certain times. The female rat, for instance, is receptive for only 6 hours in a cycle that repeats itself every 4 to 5 days, unless pregnancy occurs. Such short cycles are called *estrous cycles*, while the peak period of sexual activity is called *estrus*.

In different species, sexual cycles may vary greatly in regularity, frequency of occurrence, and duration. They also vary in their dependence on endogenous and external stimuli for their triggering. Human reproduction, for example, is limited by the female's approximately 28-day menstrual and 270-day pregnancy cycles, but it is not characterized by seasonal receptivity patterns.

On the basis of comparisons of the sexual behavior in different species, Beach (1947) suggested that animals with larger forebrains, and consequent greater cognitive abilities, are less dependent on hormonal mechanisms for the regulation of their sexual behavior. We shall refer to this hypothesis again later. Here, however, we might note that logically it would be expected that mating in higher mammals would be less related to the female's hormonal condition. Nadler (1975), however, has reported that lowland gorillas mate in a manner that is closely related to the female's cycle of sexual receptivity, while chimpanzees do not. Thus, two animals with comparable brain development differ in the extent to which their mating behavior is regulated by sexual cycles.

HORMONAL ACTIVITY AND STIMULUS RECEPTION

Sexual cycles are endogenous, but such cycles may depend on the reception of specific environmental stimuli. With certain birds, for example, reproductive activity seems to be triggered by the appearance of rain; if these birds live in an arid area, breeding may be quite erratic (Marler & Hamilton, 1967). Here, then, is an example of behavioral and hormonal changes which are triggered by a specific environmental stimulus.

Light-Dark Cycles

Light-dark cycles are another example of physical factors in the environment which may influence hormonal functioning. Male hamsters who were subjected to a regime of 1 hour of light and 23 hours of darkness provide a good illustration of this: Their gonads atrophied. A cycle of 16 hours of light and 8 hours of darkness prevented atrophy. Atrophy was also present in animals whose eyes had been enucleated. But when the pineal gland was removed, gonadal atrophy did not occur in animals subjected to either of these unfavorable lighting conditions (Hoffman & Reiter, 1965). Thus, the pineal gland plays a role in regulating gonadal activity so that it is compatible with changing environmental conditions.

The inhibitory effects of the pineal gland have also been demonstrated behaviorally, as indicated by a study by Baum (1968). Dark-reared male rats subjected to *pinealectomy* (removal of the pineal gland) showed earlier and more frequent mounting and pelvic thrusting than control animals, although other features of the complete male sexual pattern—that is, intromission and ejaculation—were not achieved at an earlier age. The pineal gland apparently influences only part of the entire pattern needed for reproduction.

Finally, it might be noted that the hamster's response to light prevents gonadal atrophy only if light is presented during an appropriate phase of an endogenous rhythm, which is approximately 24 hours in duration (Elliott, Stetson, & Menaker, 1972).

Odor

Hormonal Changes

As pet owners have long assumed, odor plays a role in the initiation of sexual activity in animals. Animals often respond to the odors of sexually active members of the opposite sex. For instance, sexually active male rats prefer the odors of receptive females to the odors of nonreceptive females; castrated and inactive males showed no such differentiation. Female rats that are receptive, whether sexually experienced or not, also show preferences for normal male odors (Carr, Loeb, & Dissinger, 1965; Carr, Loeb, & Wylie, 1966). More to the present point, however, is the fact that odor and visual stimuli may be more than discriminative; they actually may serve to initiate hormonal and other physiological changes important in the reproductive process. In ring doves, stimuli provided by the male promote endocrine changes in the female, and these initiate nest building, ovulation, and eventually incubation of the eggs (Lehrman, 1964). Erickson (1970) was able to demonstrate that castrated males exhibited various degrees of courtship behavior according to the amounts of hormones with which they had been injected, and that changes in the female's hormonal condition could be related to the degree of courtship behavior—in other words, the female's physiological condition was a function of the hormone given the male!

Parkes and Bruce (1961) have reviewed a number of studies demonstrating the effect of odor on the reproductive activities of mice. The estrous cycle of the mouse would appear to be under endogenous control, but a number of studies have shown that it may be influenced externally. Female mice showed an increase in *pseudopregnancies* (behavioral and hormonal changes characteristic of pregnancy without the actual presence of an embryo) when housed together in groups of four to a cage. Removal of the olfactory bulbs (Figure 7.8) prevented this effect. When housed in groups of 30 to a cage, the estrous cycle became highly irregular, with the majority of mice becoming sexually unreceptive for prolonged periods. When these mice were subsequently paired with a stud male, the effect was readily reversible, and mating occurred within 5 days. The presence of a separately caged male among females synchronized the females' cycles so that an abnormally high percentage of females mated on the same test day. That these effects are dependent on the odor of the males rather than their physical presence or behavior was demonstrated in control experiments.

Figure 10.2 illustrates that pregnancy, as well as sexual receptivity, is affected by odor in the mouse. If a newly mated female is removed from the stud male and exposed to other males of the same strain or, more effectively, to alien males (males of a different strain), pregnancy may be blocked, although the females subsequently return to an estrous condition and later have fertile matings with the new male. But if the original stud male is removed and then put back again, pregnancy will not be blocked. The sexual vigor of the alien male does not seem to play a part in this phenomenon, because sexually inactive males and castrates are also capable of inducing a pregnancy block. The effect is apparently attributable to the different odor of the alien male. Male-induced pregnancy termination occurs in other species as well, but there are also some interesting species-specific differences (see Stehn & Richmond, 1975).

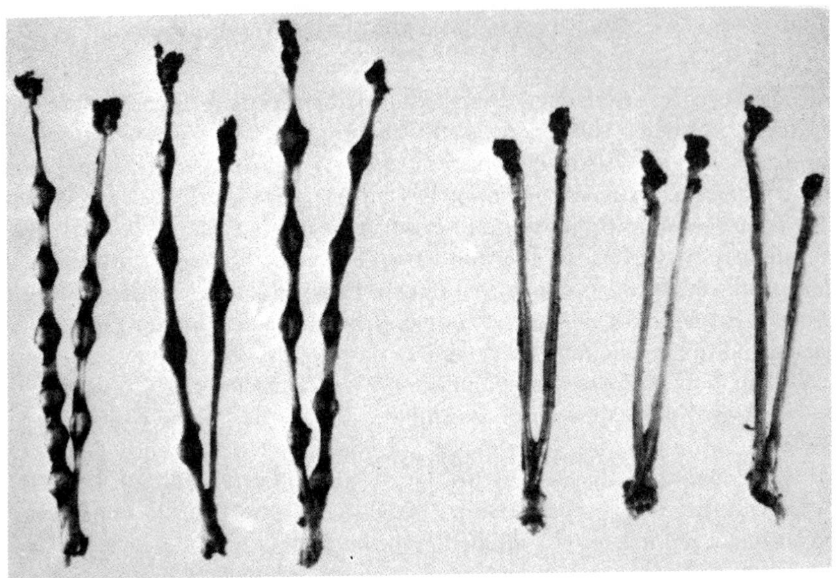

Figure 10.2. Effect on pregnancy of exposure to strange male, as seen in mouse uteri 7 days after mating with stud male. Group at left: Normal pregnancy. Group at right: Pregnancy blocked by presence of a strange male 24 hours after stud mating. (From Parkes, A. S. and Bruce, H. M., Olfactory stimuli in mammalian reproduction. *Science*, Oct. 1961, *134*, 1049–1054. Copyright 1961 by the American Association for the Advancement of Science.)

Behavioral Changes

In early reviews of the effects of sensory input on mating, Beach (1947) inferred that no sense modality is essential to the maintenance of sexual activity in the male mammal; sensory input serves an activating function and sensory deprivation simply raises the threshold for arousing the behavior. More recently, the situation has appeared more complex. In the sexually experienced cat (Aronson & Cooper, 1974), olfactory bulb removal did not produce any decrement. But in the male hamster olfaction has a critical role. Murphy and Schneider (1970) showed that male hamsters completely cease sexual activity after bilateral olfactory bulb removal, and Powers and Winans (1975) followed up by demonstrating that this is the result of elimination of olfactory stimuli, not some non-olfactory sexual involvement of the bulbs.

In the rat, Larsson (1975) found the effect of olfactory bulb removal to be dependent on the prior social experience of the males. The rats were bulbectomized either at 30 days or at 80 days of age. The rats bulbectomized at 30 days of age subsequently lived in isolation from other animals. The animals operated on at 80 days of age were divided into three groups: those that had lived in isolation from 30 to 80 days of age, those that had lived with other males, and those that had lived with females during this period. Bulbectomized rats with prior heterosexual social experience were not different from normal animals in copulatory ability; males living with other males prior to operation showed only minor deficits; males living without social contact after 30 days of age, however, were severely deficient whether operated on at 30 or 80 days of age (postpuberal). These data were interpreted to indicate that olfactory input is necessary for the initiation of sexual activity but not its maintenance. But appropriate controls appear to be missing in this experiment, since Pollack and Sachs (1975) found no deficits in the initiation of copulatory activity in males who had been bulbectomized at 6 days of age! Since Pollack and Sachs' animals were not socially restricted, social rather than odor variables may be the important factor. In male mice (Rowe & Smith, 1973), on the other hand, the olfactory bulbs seem to have a role in sexual activity independent of social experience.

Obviously, there are species differences in the role that olfactory stimuli play in the initiation and maintenance of sexual activity in the male animal. In the human, on the other hand, the role of specifically sexual olfactory stimuli is probably minimal or nonexistent (see e.g., Doty, Ford, Preti, & Huggins, 1975).

Intromission Factors

The copulatory act of the male rat consists of a series of mountings. Intromission occurs on some of these mountings. A series of 8 to 10 intromissions concludes with ejaculation occurring during the final intromission. Following a refractory period of some 5 minutes, a new series of mounts and intromissions may start. Adler (1969) demonstrated that a minimal number of intromissions prior to ejaculation is necessary for successful pregnancy. The general plan of his experiments involved allowing some males to copulate and ejaculate normally, while other males were first allowed to copulate with "teaser" females, animals that were removed after a number of intromissions. In this manner, ejaculations with the experimental females could be obtained after only a few intromissions. But with this minimum number of intromissions, pregnancy was unsuccessful.

Two major conditions must be satisfied for successful pregnancy in the female rat: (1) fertilization of the ova, and (2) the secretion of hormones, such as progesterone, which permit the fertilized eggs to become implanted in the uterus. Presumably the latter condition was not fulfilled when only a few intromissions occurred. Adler, Resko, and Goy (1970) provided direct evidence that intromission stimulates the hormonal process. They also showed that without at least one intromission prior to ejaculation, sperm did not reach the uterus.

Adler's laboratory (Adler & Zoloth, 1970) has also reported that copulatory behavior following too soon after a prior ejaculation could inhibit pregnancy in the rat. Unlike the prior results, this seems to be a mechanical effect—intromission causes the expulsion of sperm from the reproductive tract. This is indicated by the following experiment: Females were allowed two copulatory series, one with each of two genetically differentiable males (pigmented and unpigmented), so that it would be easy to identify the fathers of any offspring. In instances where the second series came within minutes after the first series, the resulting litters were usually produced by the second mating; with longer intervals, the offspring could more often be attributed to the first mating. Thus, hormonal effects are not implicated here.

But there are species differences in these effects. In contrast to the laboratory rat, post-ejaculatory copulation is necessary for pregnancy in cactus mice (Dewsbury & Estep, 1975). Estrous cycles were unaltered in about 90 percent of female cactus mice if sexual activity was terminated after a single ejaculation by the male. In those instances where further copulations were permitted, pregnancy or pseudopregnancy occurred in about 80 percent of the cases; in the latter instance, pregnancy (rather than psuedopregnancy) occurred with larger numbers of post-ejaculatory copulations. It must be emphasized that these post-ejaculatory copulations do not result in

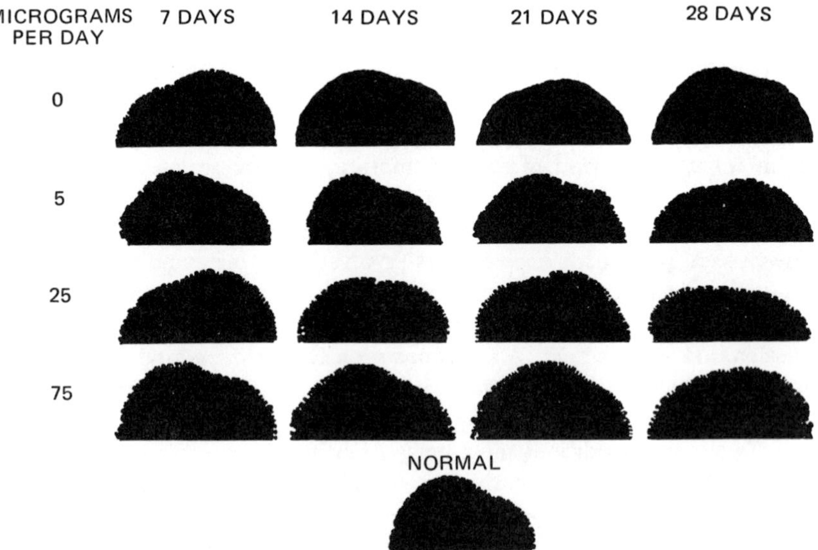

Figure 10.3. Silhouettes of one-half of cross sections from the glans penis of castrated rats treated with different amounts of androgen. The drawings represent actual tracings of projected images of histological sections. (From Beach, F. A. and Levinson, G., Effects of androgen on the glans penis and mating behavior of castrated male rats. *Journal of Experimental Zoology*, 1950, *114*, 159–171.)

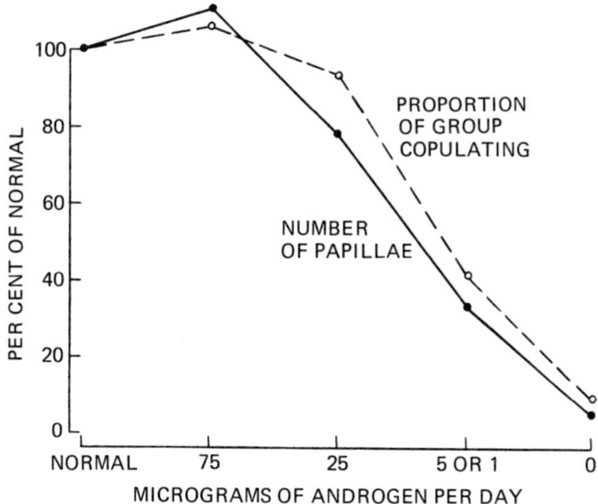

Figure 10.4. Effects of castration and androgen treatment upon the number of genital papillae and the number of animals continuing to copulate 4 weeks after operation. All scores are expressed as percentages of the averages for normal rats. (From Beach, F. A. and Levinson, G., Effects of androgen on the glans penis and mating behavior of castrated male rate. *Journal of Experimental Zoology,* 1950, *114,* 159-171.)

further ejaculations. Many species continue to copulate after attaining ejaculation. These results suggest that such post-ejaculatory copulations, without additional sperm transfer, are critical for the neuroendocrine changes necessary to halt estral cycling and for the initiation of pregnancy.

Hormonal Changes Inducing Sensory Changes

The data we have been considering demonstrate that stimuli from the external environment may induce hormonal changes. Figure 10.1 suggests, however, that the converse process may also be possible—hormonal activity may produce changes in sensory receptor systems so as to alter the response to the external environment. For instance, in the female rat, estrogen-treated ovariectomized animals showed larger sensory receptive fields in the genital area than untreated controls (Komisaruk, Adler, & Hutchison, 1972).

The glans penis of a normal male rat is characterized by deep folds and papillae that mediate tactile sensitivity; castration of the adult rat produced regressive changes, resulting in the loss of these characteristics (Figure 10.3). Beach and Levinson (1950) demonstrated that different amounts of replacement hormone were differentially effective in counteracting these effects and thereby restoring the tacile sensitivity of the penis. Figure 10.4 shows that there is a strong parallel between estimates of the number of papillae remaining four weeks after castration and the number of animals continuing to copulate. (Note that these measures were derived from different groups of animals, however.) Beach and Levinson therefore suggest that part of the loss in sexual performance after castration is due to a loss in tactile sensitivity.[2]

Sensory Control Over Sexual Responses

More direct evidence for the role of sensory input from the penis in the maintenance of copulatory activity in the male has been obtained in experiments in the rat, cat, and monkey. In the rat (Adler & Bermant, 1966), topically applied anesthesia temporarily eliminated intromissions though the rats continued to mount. Surgical section of the dorsal nerves of the penis does not interfere with erection but does desensitize the penis. In the rat (Larsson & Södersten, 1973), this operation did not interfere with attaining intromission; in fact, intromissions increased, but ejaculatory performance was impaired. In the monkey (Herbert, 1973), the same operation impaired ejaculation but initially had no effect on mounting; mounts subsequently declined with further testing. On the other hand, in the cat (Aronson & Cooper, 1966), this operation resulted in such disorientation of mounting that the cats could not achieve intromission; they did continue to mount, however.

Generally, the above results suggest that motivation was not directly impaired in these animals. The decline in mounting by the monkey appears to be a secondary effect because it could be temporarily increased by pairing the male with a strange female (perhaps mounting becomes unrewarding?). In any case, ejaculation is highly dependent on stimulation from the penis in the otherwise intact animal. However, it must not be assumed that peripheral sensory changes are paramount in the loss of sexual activity in castrated animals; these changes may be reversed by limited hormonal treatments, but sexual functioning apparently does not regain normalcy. Such findings emphasize that more central neural mechanisms are also affected by hormone losses (see Hart, 1974).

In the female, the species studied are more limited. However, the sexual performance of female rats is also controlled, in part, by sensory factors. Females regulate their contacts with males depending on whether the previous contact was a mount, an intromission, or an ejaculation (Bermant & Westbrook, 1966). However, such stimuli are not essential for the

[2]The role of gonadal hormones in sensory processes is not limited to sensations within the sexual context. It has been shown, for instance, that female rats consume more glucose or saccharin than males in preference tests where these substances are tested against water. This has been attributed to the effects of ovarian hormones. Ovariectomized females show lowered saccharin preference, and estrogen and progesterone injections reversed this. Testicular hormones have, at best, a mild suppressive effect on saccharin preference. Gonadal hormones also influence food intake and body weight (see Zucker, 1969, for details).

female rat's sexual activity; female rats surgically deprived of sensory stimuli from the genitalia and reproductive tracts continue to copulate (Kaufman, 1953).

EXPERIENTIAL DETERMINANTS OF SEXUAL BEHAVIOR

In Chapter 3, where we were concerned with the influence of early development on behavior, we took specific note of the impaired sexual activity of monkeys given abnormal rearing experience (Harlow, 1962). Here we shall enlarge on some of this material. In addition, we shall consider some effects of experiential variables on the individual's hormonal condition. Finally, we shall briefly survey some data that suggests parallels between behavior in animals and in humans.

THE EFFECTS OF REARING AND HOUSING

Imprinting-like Effects

Beauchamp and Hess (1973) studied the sexual courtship behavior of male guinea pigs reared in a variety of abnormal circumstances. Normally reared guinea pigs usually do not court members of other species. In general, these experiments found that males weaned during the first week after birth were more likely to direct sexual responses to other species than animals weaned later. Among early-weaned animals, some social experience (cohabitation) with other species was necessary for that species to elicit sexual responses, but the length of this experience and its timing appeared to be flexible. Early-weaned male guinea pigs appear to be left with a potential for responding to a wider range of sexual stimuli than normally reared animals.

In natural rodent populations, the breeding unit is small and social and geographic arrangements tend to promote inbreeding.[3] Inbreeding can have deleterious effects and many species seem to have mechanisms to reduce the probability of such inbreeding. The previously mentioned blockage of pregnancy by strange males may be one such mechanism; thus the blockage of pregnancy from familiar males (who have a high probability of being genetically related to the female) would favor outbreeding with the strange males.

Hill (1974) studied another behavioral mechanism in prairie deer mice. He formed four groups of animals: Two groups of bisexual pairs that had lived together starting at 21 days of age and two other groups that began living together at 50 days of age. Each of these groups was subdivided into

[3]Barash (1974) has provided an interesting description of the differing reproductive patterns and social behavior of marmot species as they relate to the quality of the physical environment that the different species occupy. Such data argue for the evolutionary development of social systems among different animal species.

groups consisting of sibling and nonsibling pairs. Litters from sibling parents were fewer in number and lighter in weight, illustrating the deleterious effects of inbreeding. But more importantly, from a behavioral standpoint, siblings paired early (21 days of age) had fewer litters. In addition, the proportion of litters in which at least one pup survived to weaning age was significantly lower in the two sibling groups. Although siblings paired later (50 days of age) produced more litters than early sibling pairs, they reared only about the same number of litters to wearning. Early pairing also delayed the onset of breeding; and this occurred both among siblings and nonsiblings. Thus a behavioral mechanism, rather than a genetic mechanism, seems to be involved. One explanation of the delayed reproduction might be that an extensive repertoire of play behavior between pairs living together from an early age interfered with their copulatory behavior as adults. Delayed reproduction, fewer litters, and poorer survival of offspring, however, would all contribute to a decreasing proportion of genetic inbreeding in the surviving population and to regulating population size.

Social Variables

Several studies have attempted to evaluate the effects of rearing rats in social isolation (see Spevak, Quadagno, Knoeppel, & Poggio, 1973). Generally, the specific results of these experiments are in conflict; thus some studies show that isolation inhibits adult sexual performance while others indicate that cohabitation inhibits such performance. What is clear, however, is that the male rat, even if isolated very early after birth, can perform sexually (irrespective of whether there are quantitative differences in comparison to rats raised normally or with other forms of social restriction). Furthermore, the performance of normally raised naive animals on initial copulatory tests differs little from that of the experienced animal (Rabedeau & Whalen, 1959). And while prepuberal experience can modify the quantiative characteristics of the male's copulatory performance, it does not produce qualitatively aberrant behavior (Kagan & Beach, 1953). Male rats are also not insensitive to their sexual consort—presumably sexually exhausted males may be stirred to renewed efforts if a new female partner is made available (Wilson, Kuehn, & Beach, 1963). Like humans, males and females of other species show preferences among potential sex partners (see Beach, 1976).

Not only do social variables produce alterations in behavior, recent work demonstrates that they also result in alterations in hormonal levels. In the monkey, Rose, Gordon, and Bernstein (1972) showed that plasma testosterone levels increased two to three times in males given access to receptive females. When the males were then subjected to sudden and decisive defeats in fights for dominance in an all-male group, testosterone levels fell to below pre-experimental baselines; however, reintroduction to the females resulted in a rapid rise to the previously elevated testosterone levels. It is probable that most changes in hormone levels are a direct effect of these experiences. Alternatively, the lowered hormonal levels could be an adaptive response; that is, punishment of aggressive behavior may result in a secondary, adaptive alteration in testosterone. Similarly, higher levels of testosterone on exposure to the females may support increased sexual activity rather than lead to it. The latter interpretations appear less likely, however.

Complementing the effects of strange males on estrus and pregnancy in the female mouse is a study showing alterations in plasma testosterone in males exposed to strange female mice (Macrides, Bartke, & Dalterio, 1975). In this study, males paired with a female for 1 week did not have higher testosterone levels than males remaining in all-male groups, but paired males showed a rise in testosterone within 30 to 60 minutes after a strange female was substituted for the resident female. Isolated males showed a comparable rise when paired with a female. Copulation with the female was not a necessary precondition for the testosterone rise. Similarly, substituting a male for the resident female did not produce the change. The changes, then, appear to be specific to the encounter with a strange female. At least one report suggests comparable results in human males (see Macrides et al., 1975).

On the other hand, long-term isolation in rats seems to effect a general increase in androgens in both sexes. In the female, this is accompanied by a lower synthesis of estrogens. Such long-term isolation was related to increased aggressiveness in both sexes (Dessi-Fulgheri, Lupo di Prisco, & Verdarelli, 1975).

Population Density

Animal Studies

Since Malthus, it has been believed that population size is limited by the available food supply and space. But observations of animals, both in the wild and in the laboratory, indicate that this is not true. In fact, it appears that populations of animals reach constant levels in the wild long before there is a shortage of food or space. Christian and Davis (1964) suggested that this regulation is accomplished on a hormonal basis. As population size increases, there are increased social and aggressive interactions among individuals. These interactions cause adrenal and gonadal hormonal changes, as a result of which matings are reduced and there is increased susceptibility to disease.

For instance, Ratcliffe and Snyder (1964) reported that the incidence of myocardial infarction (heart disease) increases in chickens in social and sexual groupings in comparison to isolated animals. Long-term isolation disrupts the social structuring of subsequently formed mice colonies; males are hyperaggressive and fail to establish stable hierarchies while females have fewer pregnancies and increased litter mortality (Ely & Henry, 1974). Mice that had previously experienced defeat showed greater adrenal responses than a control group when exposed to a trained fighter mouse. In fact, there was little difference in adrenal responses between previously defeated mice that were placed in the presence of the fighter and mice that were actually attacked by the fighter (Bronson & Eleftheriou, 1965). Similarly, Christian (1955) found that both adrenal gland increases and gonadal decreases were attributable to suppression of pituitary gonadotrophic activity as a result of adrenal changes.

Generally, then, a large number of findings suggest that manipulation of the living conditions of animals can result in profound changes in their hormonal status. Associated with such changes are likely to be behavioral changes that contribute to the regulation of population size so as to avoid the deleterious effects of overpopulation and outstripping of resources (see Wynne-Edwards, 1965). In the laboratory, however, it is possible to maintain such dense populations and such studies have called attention to profound behavioral disturbances that can occur when population regulation is lacking. Calhoun (1962) has reported a classic series of such studies.

Calhoun housed 80 rats in living space designed to accommodate 48 animals. There was plentiful food and water, however. The rats lived in four pens arranged to allow access between the pens in a limited, linear fashion, i.e., to go between pen 1 and pen 4, 2 and 3 had to be traversed.

Male rats fought and established dominance hierarchies; additionally, in the end pens, 1 and 4, it was possible for a dominant male to gain territorial control. Dominant males excluded subordinates from their territory and access to a hierarchy of females living in these pens. These territorial males maintained a perpetual vigil, sleeping during the wanderings of their harems, but awakening to repel the approach of any aggressive males. Dominant males did, however, tolerate the presence of subordinates within the territory provided they did not interfere with his sovereignty. Such subordinates did not attempt sexual activity with the females. Dominant males might inspect the nesting sites but rarely did so to ferret out females for sexual activity. In these pens, population density was lowest, mortality among offspring was least, and the harem females were the best mothers. Pregnancy rates in the two middle pens were about equal to those of pens 1 and 2 but mortality among infants ran upwards of 80 percent in the several experiments.

Females living in the middle pens became indifferent nest builders and care of pups was neglectful. Females in heat were pursued relentlessly by packs of males, some males pursuing females into the nests. Males in the middle pens continually ousted each other from dominance positions but more than half simply gave up partaking in these struggles. Aggressive, dominant males in these pens were the most nearly normal, seldom bothering females and juveniles. Below them were a group of pansexuals—animals indiscriminate in sexual advances to males, females not in estrus, and juveniles. Pansexuals rarely contended for status.

Two other groups of animals also withdrew from the dominance struggle. One group was completely passive, ignoring all other animals and in turn being ignored by them, not even being attacked. Interestingly, they appeared to be the healthiest physically but the most socially disrupted animals. Calhoun labeled the other withdrawn group the "probers." They lived in the middle pens, were hyperactive, hypersexual, and frequently became cannibalistic. Probers mated without the typical rat courtship behaviors, pursued females into the nests, and eventually ate any dead young found on these forays.

At the conclusion of one of these experiments, the four healthiest males and the four healthiest females were removed from the situation and allowed to survive. They were all six months old at the time. Despite the fact that they were no longer in an overcrowded environment, they produced fewer litters in the next six months than would normally be expected and none of the offspring survived to maturity. Clearly the detrimental effects of these experiments were persistent beyond the actual overcrowding.

Human Studies

It is all too easy to make the analogy between studies such as these in animals and the apparent behavioral pathology manifesting itself in some of our crowded cities. There is, however, very little direct evidence that the analogy is accurate. One study suggesting that it *is* accurate was reported by Galle, Gove, and McPherson (1972). This was a statistical study, relating population density in 75 community areas of Chicago to (1) fertility, (2) mortality, (3) ineffectual care of the young, (4) asocial, aggressive behavior, and (5) psychiatric disorder. Variables of social class and ethnicity were also examined to see if they modified the effects of density alone.

Simple measures of density, such as persons per acre, were not significantly related to social pathology if ethnicity and social class were taken into account. In other words, any effects of density were accounted for by ethnicity and social class *if density is considered simply on the basis of people and geographic area.* If density was viewed from a more personal standpoint, however, such as the number of persons per room, the number of rooms per housing unit, the number of housing units per structure, and the number of residential structures per acre, the picture changed.

If density was considered as a composite measure formed from these separate indices, density was significantly releated to each of the pathologies examined. Furthermore, the relationships held true even after social class and ethnicity were controlled. Indeed, simple relationships between pathology and social class or ethnicity were markedly reduced if the composite density factor was controlled. In other words, class and ethnic relationships to the pathologies examined seemed to operate through the density variable.

The general finding was that density increased the incidence of pathology; and a breakdown of the effects of density suggested that for mortality, fertility, care of the young, and antisocial behavior, the most important component of density is *number of persons per room.*

In this study, fertility increased as the population became more dense; this is directly contrary to the findings of animal studies such as Calhoun's. Several factors could contribute to this anomaly. A frequent finding of the animal studies has been the development of hypersexuality; an increase in sexuality among humans is likely to lead to increases in births provided the effects of hormonal conditions, territoriality, social competition for intercourse, etc., are weaker in humans, as might be assumed. Furthermore, overcrowding is likely to be a situation in which planning ahead is less probable, the ability to follow through on plans is lessened, and the practice of birth control may be ineffectual. However, regardless of the reasons for the anomaly, it is obvious that an increase in births in an already overcrowded situation is particularly destructive in that it compounds the problem.

Admission for psychiatric disorder was the only behavioral variable *not* strongly related to the density measures. In fact, psychiatric admissions were better correlated with the percentage of persons living alone. It could be, however, that overcrowding and alienation from social contact intitiate a disturbance that in turn leads to living alone.

Generally, overcrowding would seem to have its effects on humans by first increasing the number of social contacts and obligations, and the need to subordinate individual desires. Second, overcrowding would increase the occurrence of stimuli that are difficult to ignore. In reacting to these external demands, one would expect increased social conflict, irritability, withdrawal, and alienation.

On the other hand, before uncritically assuming that increased population density always leads to human behavioral pathology, we will need to examine the generality of these effects. For instance, social history and cultural differences may very well play a role: Are similar results found in India or Hong Kong and other high-density settings? A study of African bushmen (Draper, 1973) indicates they might not be—extreme residential crowding apparently does not produce stress in these people. Thus, we need to examine the role of concepts such as personal space and privacy which may differ significantly cross-culturally. Also, population density would seem to have its effects through emotional response changes similar to those that we have reviewed in animals; but it will be necessary to ascertain that the mechanisms that operate in animals are, in fact, comparable for human beings.

Conclusions

The material reviewed in this section indicates that gonadal function in lower animals may be facilitated or disrupted by a variety of physical and psychosocial stimuli. Some of these stimuli exert direct effects on the gonads, while other effects require mediation by other glands, particularly the adrenals. In either case, resulting gonadal changes are reflected in behavior changes. There is the suggestion that human behavior may, at least under some circumstances, be subject to similar influences.

HORMONAL ACTIVITY AND SEXUAL BEHAVIOR

The previous section emphasized the mutual interactions between environmental physical and psychosocial variables and the internal, hormonal condition of the organism. Behavioral changes as a result of this interaction were generally indicated. Here, we will more specifically examine the relationship between hormonal condition and sexual behavior. Of particular interest will be the degree to which the sexual behavior of different species appears to be dependent on hormones.[4]

A practical knowledge of the functions of the male gonads has been demonstrated by the age-old castration practices of farmers and kings. But the precise role of specific hormones can be shown only through experiments controlling the nature and dosage of replacement hormones. Because of the problems of isolation and synthesis of the hormones, such experiments are all of recent date. Many experiments with lower animals, such as the rat, have demonstrated that (1) castration reduces sexual behavior to near zero levels and (2) massive replacement doses of hormones may bring sexual behavior in castrates to normal levels. Hormone injections may also prematurely elicit sexual responses in juvenile animals (Noble & Zitrin, 1942).

On the other hand, limited clinical data obtained from adult castrated men indicate considerable variance; some are reported to show no decreases in sexual capacity and others to show decreases or total losses (Money, 1961). Recall from Chapter 2, however, that genetic and hormonal conditions have

[4]Again, it must be emphasized that we are focusing on but one behavior dependent upon sex hormones; dominance-aggressive, maternal, nesting, and other behaviors also show relationships to these hormones. Hart, (1974), for instance, has written about some of the other effects of male hormones.

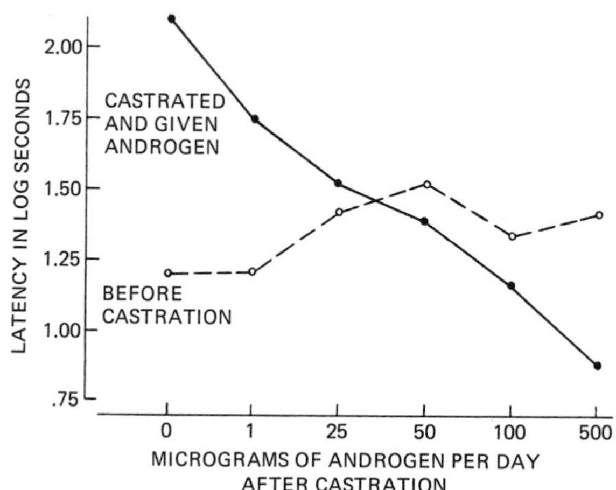

Figure 10.5. Average delay preceding the first sexual mount in preoperative tests and after castration and testosterone replacement in the male rat. (From Beach, F. A. and Holz-Tucker, A. M., Effects of different concentrations of androgen upon sexual behavior in castrated male rats. *Journal of Comparative and Physiological Psychology*, 1949, *42*, 433–453. Copyright 1949 by the American Psychological Association. Reprinted by permission.)

been considered to play only a minimal role in the development of sex role identification among humans. One question that must be examined, however, is whether sex role *identification* and sexual *motivation* or drive are similarly controlled. In looking at this question, we will begin by examining the role of hormonal conditions in the sexual performance of three animal species, rat, dog, and monkey. As will be apparent, "sexual performance" in each of these species can be fractionated into several components; the effects of hormonal conditions are not the same for all components.

The Rat

Female rats immediately lose all signs of sexual receptivity with ovariectomy. However, they can be rapidly restored to receptive status with injections of estrogens and progesterone. Male rats, on the other hand, show considerable retention of sexual capacity for some time following castration. On the average, male rats will retain the ejaculatory response for about 2 to 4 weeks. Beach and Holz-Tucker (1949) studied the effects of different amounts of hormone in daily replacement injections on the retention of sexual responses in the male rat. Figure 10.5 shows the average delay to the first sexual mount of different groups of rats before and after castration. With high doses of testosterone replacement, particularly with 500 micrograms per day, the delay was less than before castration.

Figure 10.6 shows the results for ejaculatory responses. Without hormone replacement, ejaculations rapidly dropped to near zero. Twenty-five micrograms of testosterone per day maintained ejaculation in 60 to 70 percent of the animals, and 500 micrograms resulted in 90 percent or better responding. Intermediate doses produced intermediate response rates and are not shown. Note that these data do not reflect any uniformity of response in individual animals; that is, on any given test a given animal might not ejaculate, but with increasing hormone dose the probability of his doing so was increased. Note also that a switch to 1 microgram after receiving no hormone did produce a slight increase in probability of ejaculation, whereas a switch to 5 micrograms after receiving 100 per day was ineffective. This indicates that high doses result in some later insensitivity to replacement. The results for intromission frequency paralleled those for ejaculation except that less hormone was required to maintain the behavior. From 50 to 70 micrograms per day seemed sufficient to maintain approximately normal total sexual capacity in the strain of animals employed.

In summary, Beach and Holz-Tucker reported that animals receiving low doses of testosterone were slow to initiate sexual contact, and mounting was sporadic and preceded by protracted periods of inattention to or mere investigation of the female. Copulatory attempts failed because of a lack of intromission, and successful intromissions were widely spaced. Ejaculations tended to occur with fewer intromissions and were followed by longer periods of sexual inactivity. But the sexual behavior of castrates receiving 100 or 500 micrograms of testosterone was equal or superior to their preopera-

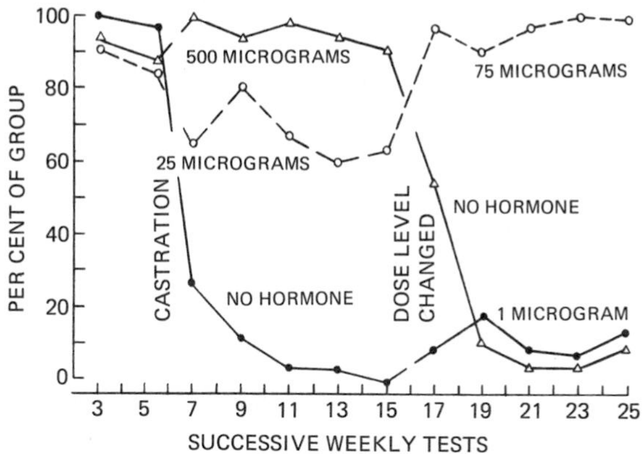

Figure 10.6. Proportions of three experimental groups of male rats ejaculating at least once during tests preoperatively and after castration and testosterone replacement. (From Beach, F. A. and Holz-Tucker, A. M., Effects of different concentrations of androgen upon sexual behavior in castrated male rats. *Journal of Comparative and Physiological Psychology*, 1949, *42*, 433–453. Copyright 1949 by the American Psychological Association. Reprinted by permission.)

tive performance; they were more likely to copulate in every test, and multiple ejaculations occurred more frequently. Note that no one measure, by itself, adequately defines the results—"sex drive" cannot be inferred from a single response measure.

The results of the above experiment do not indicate that individual performance differences among rats prior to castration can be attributed to differing amounts of precastration androgens. But Beach and Fowler (1959) investigated this problem. Here pre- and postoperative comparisons were made between animals receiving equal amounts of postcastration androgen. Each rat received 100 micrograms of testosterone per day after the operation; because of weight differences in the animals, this produced a dose range of .171 to .265 micrograms/gm of body weight. If individual differences are due to factors other than hormone levels, correlations between pre- and postoperative scores should be high; but if individual differences reflect hormone level, postoperative performance should be correlated with body weight. It was found that pre- and postoperative correlations of mounts, intromissions, and ejaculations ranged from +.60 to +.75. However, postoperative latency to first intromission, number of ejaculations, and intercopulatory intervals were also significantly correlated with body weight, although preoperative scores had not correlated significantly with body weight. The results, then, indicate that (1) individual differences in sexual activity after castration are not solely due to differences in effective hormone dosage, but (2) differences in effective hormone dosage do produce differences in some aspects of sexual behavior in the rat. Thus, both hormonal and nonhormonal factors contribute to individual differences in sexual activity. What these nonhormonal factors are remains to be discovered. They might include sensitivity differences in tissues affected by the hormones.[5]

The Dog

In addition to initial investigatory, arousing behavior and mounting, the male copulatory pattern in dogs is generally characterized by a single intromission and a subsequent "locking" period and ejaculation. The locking of the male and female occurs because, after insertion, the *bulbus glandis* at the base of the penis swells within the vagina and becomes considerably larger than the vaginal opening; the two animals may thus remain tied together for as long as an hour or more; ejaculation presumably occurs more or

[5]Such differences could be genetically or environmentally influenced. McGill and Haynes (1973) showed in mice that there are both strong genetic and unknown environmental sources of variance in the retention of ejaculatory response after castration. In mice that were presumably 100 percent heterozygous, the mean time to loss of the ejaculatory response was 68 days; in mice that were presumably homozygous, the mean time was about 7.5 days; one heterozygous mouse showed ejaculation 14 months after castration.

less continuously throughout this period. The effects of testicular hormones can be studied for each part of the total pattern of sexual activity.

The data reported by Beach (1970) are characterized by considerable individual variability—some dogs were severely disturbed in their sexual behavior after castration, while others were only minimally affected, if at all, by the loss of testicular hormones. Generally, in sexually mature, experienced males, complete copulatory activity can persist for more than 3 years after castration without any replacement hormones whatsoever. The adrenals secrete hormones which, it has been thought, may conceivably substitute for testicular hormones. Yet the persistence of sexual behavior in castrated dogs cannot be attributed to adrenal activity; adrenalectomy of two animals that had engaged in copulatory activity for more than 3 years after castration did not prevent copulation.

If latency to the first mount is taken as a measure of initial sexual arousal, the canine castrates performed as well as the control animals. The principal decrements that did occur were in the percentage of tests in which the animals locked, the duration of the locks when they occurred, and the greater number of mounts necessary to achieve intromission. In lock percentage, castrates performed at 83 percent of preoperative levels, but in lock duration their performance was only about 40 percent of preoperative levels. But one dog of the seven castrates showed no decrement at all in these activities, and only one dog showed complete cessation of locking behavior—and this did not happen until 14 months after castration. Castrates showed decreased penis and bulb measurements compared to controls, and bulb diameter seemed to correlate with lock duration. In animals that received replacement hormones, lock duration and percentage were increased.

Two dogs that had been subjected to prepuberal castration were also tested. The ability to achieve intromission was markedly impaired, and, although one of these animals did intromit, he never showed any locking behavior, probably because of deficient bulb size. Both animals were capable of reflexive erection and ejaculatory behavior (with the exception of the actual emission of semen) in responses to manual stimulation. Generally, however, the performance of the prepuberal castrates was inferior to that of the older castrates.

Finally, tests were performed on three dogs that were sexually naive, though castrated postpuberally; their behavior was compared to that of two naive but intact controls. (This experiment was complicated by the fact that all the dogs showed fright on introduction to the testing environment; none of them had ever been out of the colony room for their entire 3 years of life.) In their first postoperative tests, none of the castrates showed intromission, but the naive controls averaged only 20 percent. Testosterone treatment of the castrates improved their performance and locks were achieved; on 2.5

mg/kgm/day of testosterone, their behavior was equal or superior to that of the intact controls. Subsequent withdrawal of the testosterone and cessation of testing for 3 months seemed to reinstate the fear responses. However, one castrate and one control each achieved locks.

Obviously, the most significant result of these experiments is the fact that complete mating patterns may persist indefinitely in sexually experienced castrates without any replacement hormone therapy. In terms of average performance, the decrements that did occur were apparent within 6 months after operation, and no further deterioration occurred over the remaining time of observation (approximately 3 years). That prepuberal castrates exhibited mounting, thrust, and genital reflexes and seemed primarily deficient from a structural standpoint suggests that postpuberal hormones are not involved in the basic organization of the male coital pattern in the dog. But this does not apply to ovariectomized female dogs; they are sexually unresponsive.

The Monkey

In tests with 10 male monkeys, Phoenix, Slob, and Goy (1973) also found considerable individual variation in sexual behavior following castration. Prior to castration all of the monkeys ejaculated at least once in five tests. Within the first 5 weeks after castration, the frequency of intromissions and ejaculations both dropped significantly. By 1 year after castration, half the animals could still achieve intromission, and three ejaculated at least once in a five-test series. Pre-castration performance was not a good predictor of post-castration performance of individual animals. Two animals persisted in showing ejaculations in about half their tests 1 year after castration; two other animals failed to ejaculate at all after castration and their tests with intromission were drastically reduced. Replacement injections quickly restored complete sexual performance. Three years after castration (Phoenix, 1974), three animals were still showing ejaculatory responses, six achieved intromission, and all were still mounting.

Conclusions

In conclusion, several points need to be made. Foremost, perhaps, is that in no case can it be said that the adult sexual behavior of any species is completely independent of gonadal hormones. Thus, sexually immature female rodents and carnivores show none of the various responses characteristic of adult female estrus behavior, but immature males of these species do show portions of the adult patterns, albeit in weak and infrequent form. Also, prepuberal or adult ovariectomy immediately and permanently abolishes sexual heat in females of these species, while, after castration, the male may continue to show elements of the sexual response—for example, mounting

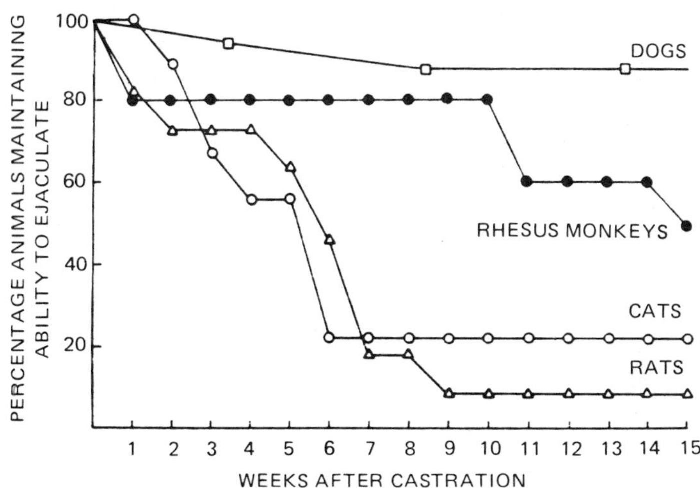

Figure 10.7. Species comparison of the percentage of animals maintaining the ability to ejaculate after castration. (From Hart, B. L., Gonadal androgen and sociosexual behavior of male mammals: A comparative analysis. *Psychological Bulletin*, 1974, *81*, 383–400.)

—indefinitely. The loss of functioning, when it occurs, tends to be much more gradual. In higher mammalian forms, dependence on gonadal hormones for the display of female receptivity or male copulatory behavior is lessened. Sexually mature male dogs and primates may show complete copulatory activity indefinitely after castration. In monkeys, chimps, and humans although the female goes through well-defined ovarian cycles, matings throughout the entire cycle are common. (But recall that this is not true of gorillas.)

The hypothesis that the degree of dependence on hormonal mechanisms for the maintenance of sexual activity is inversely related to the development of the higher cortical structures (Beach, 1974) seems to be only roughly true at best. Figure 10.7 was compiled by Hart (1974). If the hypothesis were completely accurate, one would expect monkeys to maintain a higher level of performance after castration than dogs, and cats might also be expected to surpass dogs.

At the human level, it is often said that adult sexual behavior and sex role identification is independent of gonadal hormones. The major evidence for such an assertion comes from the type of material reviewed in Chapter 2, showing that genetic and hormonal conditions do not necessarily determine sex role identification (also see Hardy, 1964; Hampson, 1965). However, it may be asked whether sex role identification and motivation for the engagement in sexual activity are similarly influenced by hormones. Whalen (1966), for instance, distinguishes between "arousal"—the current level of sexual excitation—and "arousability," the propensity for arousal. He argues that arousability is influenced by hormones in the adult human. Whalen also is careful to distinguish between the state of sexual motivation and the expression of that motivation. That sexual identification and object choice are learned does not imply that hormones do not affect arousability. Human castrates often do show lessened sexual activity. The data that exist seem to suggest that there may be libidinal deficits following castration even though qualitatively normal sexual behavior can persist after castration. Perhaps of greater interest is that all species seem to display large individual differences in their dependence on and response to hormones. The mechanisms mediating these differences are largely unknown.

HORMONAL SPECIFICITY

Thus far we have employed the general terms *estrogens* and *androgens* as though they referred to single compounds and as if estrogens exclusively mediated female sexual responses and androgens, exclusively male sex responses. In fact, however, this is not quite the case.

Androgen is a generic term for several hormones produced in the testes and adrenal glands, of which testosterone is one example. Estrogen is a generic term for several hormones produced in the ovaries and placenta—for example, estradiol. Moreover, the two groups of hormones are biochemically related. For instance, testosterone may be converted to estrogens, and there is evidence that some effects of testosterone in male sexual performance may require this conversion. Other androgens do not show this conversion and the several androgens have different behavioral and physiological effects. In addition, it is well-known that estrogens can facilitate male sexual performance and that testosterone can facilitate female sexual performance; furthermore, both sexes can show opposite sex-appropriate behavior and responses to hormone treatment. Current research is actively involved in pursuing these effects; some few illustrations follow.

High doses of testosterone can elicit feminine sexual responses in ovariectomized female animals. In addition, testosterone has been shown to increase the motivation of ovariectomized female rats to seek contact with males; dihydrotestosterone did not have this effect and the effect was inhibited by anti-estrogenic treatments. In the human female, androgens appear to be a more potent factor in restoring libidinal feelings than estrogens (McDonald & Myerson, 1973).

Several androgenic and estrogenic hormones may result in the display of male and female copulatory responses in both sexes in rats and hamsters (e.g., Coniglio, Paup, & Clemens, 1973; Noble & Alsum, 1975; Södersten & Larsson, 1975). Of interest is the fact that Luttge (Luttge, 1975; Luttge, Hall, Wallis, & Campbell, 1975) stimulated male and female sexual responses in gonadectomized rats with estrogen and androgen treatments and that such treatments were inhibited by anti-estrogens.

Estrogen treatment of castrated male rats can maintain ejaculatory responses; however, adrenalectomy eliminated this effect but failed to eliminate the ejaculatory response of those castrates treated with testosterone. Both estrogen and testosterone maintained mounting behavior in the adrenalectomized castrates, but testosterone was more potent than estrogen in maintaining intromission in these animals. These results illustrate how specific segments of the total copulatory behavior of an animal may be differentially affected by various hormones. They also suggest that adrenal androgens may mediate the effect of estrogens on ejaculatory behavior (Gorzalka, Rezek, & Whalen, 1975).

In the next section, we shall see how the CNS reveals these same interrelationships between masculine and feminine response capabilities.

HORMONAL ACTIVITY AND THE CNS

The hormonal effects that we have been reviewing are mediated through the central nervous system. How does this occur? We are actually seeking the answers to two questions: (1) the effects of gonadal hormones on the developing nervous system and (2) their effects on the more mature CNS. In recent years it has become apparent that the presence of gonadal hormones during early development shapes the later response potentials of the CNS. We shall, therefore, start by reviewing some of these findings.

THE DEVELOPING CNS

Changes in the developing CNS have been, for the most part, merely inferred from behavioral differences; actual anatomical and physiological differences have, as yet, rarely been observed.

The developing CNS of mammals is sensitive to circulating gonadal hormones at certain critical periods. In some animals, these critical periods occur prenatally, as in the guinea pig and monkey; in other animals, as in the rat, the first few days of postnatal life are critical. The experiments in this field have generally involved either castration and/or administration of gonadal hormones during these critical developmental periods. The findings seem to suggest enduring changes in the organization of the CNS, as demonstrated in the modified behavior of mature animals.

The effects that concern us may be illustrated by experiments reported by Feder and Whalen (1965) and Whalen and Nadler (1963). The general plan of the Feder and Whalen experiment was to test male rats for feminine sexual responses in adulthood. A group of males castrated within 4 days after birth was compared with a control group. Some members of both groups were given estradiol injections during this time. The control group was castrated when they reached adulthood. Finally, all the animals, when adults, were given estradiol and progesterone injections in an attempt to induce the responses of *lordosis* (arching of the back with elevation of the pelvis, exposing the perineum) and ear-wiggling, characteristics of behavioral receptivity in the female rat. Generally, males castrated during the first 4 days after birth showed the feminine responses to a greater degree than did the other groups. Female responses were suppressed in neonatally intact or castrated animals receiving estradiol during this same period. Thus, feminization was induced by the *lack* of androgens rather than by the presence of estrogens. In fact, as in a similar experiment with female rats (Whalen & Nadler, 1963), neonatal estrogen *suppressed* development of adult female sexual responses.

In Chapter 2 we mentioned the occurrence of fetally androgenized genetic females; similar conditions have been experimentally produced in animals. Phoenix, Goy, Gerall, and Young (1959) treated pregnant female guinea pigs with testosterone injections at various times during gestation. Generally, there were two dose groups, a low and a higher group. The low-dose group produced female offspring that appeared normal; the higher-dose group produced animals whose internal organs identified them as genetically female but whose external genitalia were indistinguishable with the naked eye from those of their male siblings and untreated males. These animals were designated as *hermaphrodites*. The responses in adulthood of both the unmodified females and the hermaphrodites to male and female hormones were tested. Their male siblings and males and females from untreated mothers were used as controls. All subjects were gonadectomized prior to the hormone tests. Some of the results of these experiments follow.

Prenatal administration of testosterone suppressed the capacity for adult females to respond to estradiol and progesterone injections with lordosis; this suppression was noted in unmodified females as well as in hermaphrodites. Testosterone given postnatally did not produce this effect. Adult hermaphrodites were more responsive to testosterone injections than gonadectomized normal females; that is, they showed more mounting behavior. Male siblings of these experimental animals did not differ from normal males in sexual performance.

In a similar experiment, Young, Goy, and Phoenix (1964) produced morphologically abnormal female monkeys (Figure 10.8). Of interest here is the fact that in these animals sexually differentiated social behavior, though not directly related to mating behavior, was also modified. Thus, threatening facial expressions and rough-and-tumble play, both characteristic of males

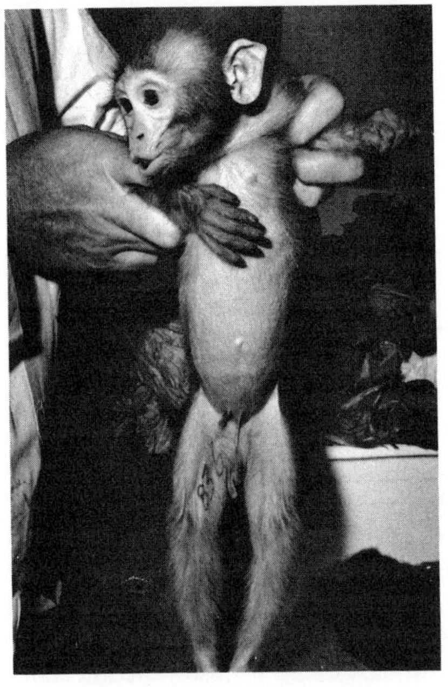

Figure 10.8. Female pseudohermaphrodite produced by injecting testosterone proprionate into the mother during pregnancy. A prominent, well-formed phallus is visible to the right of the empty scrotal fold. The surgical scar in the right inguinal region resulted from a laporotomy which showed that there was no testis. (From Young, W. C., Goy, R. W., and Phoenix, C. H., Hormones and sexual behavior. *Science*, Jan. 1964, *143*, 212–218. Copyright 1964 by the American Association for the Advancement of Science.)

rather than females, were greatly augmented by the prenatal testosterone. Similarly, Edwards (1968) showed that fighting behavior was augmented in neonatally androgenized female mice. Such results seem to be in accord with the tomboy behavior of androgenized girls.

Experiments such as these seem to justify the hypothesis that sex hormones serve a dual function: In the developing organism they serve an "organizing" or "differentiating" function, while in adulthood they are "activating." Note also that there is a common thread running through these studies: Either testosterone or estrogen injections at critical times produce masculinization of females, while lack of testosterone produces feminization of males. To put it another way, the *absence* of testosterone at the critical time leaves both males and females sensitive to the effects of female hormones and apt to display feminine behavior. Furthermore, the *presence* of either testosterone or estrogen desensitizes both sexes to the effects of estrogens. This suggests that animals are, in a sense, basically female early in development and that it is the presence of testosterone at the critical time which differentiates the males (Levine & Mullins, 1966).

It has been shown for rats and other rodents that the above description of the male organization is effected through hypothalamic control over the pituitary function. That is, a basically cylical pattern of hypothalamic activity becomes acyclical, leaving the pituitary function acyclical. But Karsch,

Dierschke, and Knobil (1973) showed that in the rhesus monkey pituitary responses comparable to those of the normal female could be obtained in the male. Since males are exposed to normally circulating androgens, these results might suggest that CNS involvement in sexual differentiation is different for rodents and primates, including human. Alternatively, perhaps the potential for cycling is eliminated from the hypothalamus in both instances, but retained by the pituitary.

Testosterone and androstenedione are two androgens, the former secreted primarily by the testes, the latter by the adrenals. Testosterone is also the much stronger androgen. Several experiments have indicated that the availability of one or the other of these androgens can produce lasting behavioral effects. For instance, Goldfoot, Feder, and Goy (1969) showed that androstenedione is not primarily responsible for the normal sexual development of the male rat. Male rats were castrated on the first or twentieth postnatal day; some of the first-day animals also received androstenedione injections. All the animals were subsequently tested for the display of feminine mating responses after estradiol and progesterone injections; some animals were also tested for masculine responses after testosterone injection. Basically, androstenedione-treated animals displayed a marked capacity for bisexual behavior—lordosis in response to estrogens, and mounting and intromission in response to testosterone. Twenty-day old castrates untreated with androstenedione generally failed to respond to testosterone but showed lordosis in response to estrogens. Thus, androstenedione differs from both neonatal testosterone and estrogen in that both of the latter eliminate the capacity for *bisexual* response, while androstenedione apparently permits it.

Increasing the ratio of androstenedione to testosterone in normal rats has similar effects. This was accomplished by Ward (1972) by stressing pregnant female rats—stress increases adrenal secretion and reduces gonadal output. In adulthood, male offspring of these stressed females showed lowered levels of male copulatory behavior and increased lordosis in response to estrogens after castration. Postnatal stress did not have such effects, indicating again that a critical period of development is involved. This mechanism could operate in reducing population density under stress.

An experiment by Nadler (1968) indicates that the thresholds for the effects of hormones may be different for behavioral and peripheral physiological indices of female sexual receptivity. Five-day-old female rats were implanted with different doses of testosterone in the brain. Higher doses of testosterone suppressed mating and ovulation and augmented male patterns of sexual response; lower doses inhibited ovulation and produced a persistent pattern of vaginal estrus and continuous behavioral receptivity. Thus, small amounts of testosterone may produce an acyclical pattern in the female rat but be insufficient to masculinize the behavior.

The Adult CNS

The role of the hypothalamus and other CNS areas in sexual behavior will be considered in the following section. Here we are simply concerned with the more specific question of the sensitivity of the CNS to gonadal hormones.

The most direct evidence of hormone sensitivity is probably found in experiments employing hypothalamic implants of hormones. When specific behavioral effects are elicited in this fashion from a given locus, and not from other loci, the existence of cells specifically responsive to the hormones is strongly suggested. An early indication of such effects was provided by Fisher (1956, 1967). Testosterone was implanted through cannulae into the brains of male and female rats. Anterior hypothalamic implants, just over the optic tracts, resulted in two kinds of behavior in the male: male sexual responses and maternal behavior (retrieving of young and nest-building). Male copulatory responses were also elicited in females. In the male, medially placed hormones evoked maternal behavior, and lateral placements evoked the copulatory pattern. These data seem to indicate that the brains of both males and females contain hormone-sensitive neurons mediating behaviors generally considered appropriate for the opposite sex. In addition, there seems to be some lack of specificity in these cells in that maternal behavior, which can normally be elicited by progesterone in the female, was elicited by testosterone in the male.

In a similar experiment, Lisk (1962) made hypothalamic implants of estradiol in ovariectomized female rats. The animals were tested for behavioral receptivity to sexually vigorous males; physiological receptivity was determined from vaginal smears. Behavioral receptivity resulted only from implants in the preoptic region or anterior hypothalamus. These responses occurred in as little as 3 days after implantation and continued for as many as 25 days in some experiments. Implants of these small amounts of hormone in other brain regions and in peripheral tissues, failed to evoke receptivity. Vaginal smears indicated a nonreceptive physiological condition throughout most of the time that behavioral responses were obtained. Similarly, Michael (1962) reported prolonged sexual receptivity in female ovariectomized cats with estrogen implantations in the hypothalamus. The implants were radioactively tagged, and certain neurons seemed to have a selective affinity for the labeled estrogen. Also, the influence of the hypothalamus in the release of pituitary gonadotrophins was indicated by the fact that estrogen implants in some hypothalamus locations resulted in atrophy of the ovaries and uterus, similar to the results of removal of the pituitary (Lisk & Newlon, 1962).

Several studies have used the detection of radioactivity from systemically injected hormones to determine the targets of such hormones (e.g., Sar

& Stumpf, 1973). Generally, such studies show concentrations of radioactivity in cells of the hypothalamus and the adjacent preoptic area. This is true of testosterone, estradiol, and progesterone.

A number of studies have shown that localized changes in the electrical activity of the hypothalamus and preoptic area can be recorded as a result of stimulation of the genitals of animals (e.g., Porter, Cavanaugh, Critchlow, & Sawyer, 1957). Furthermore, such recordings show an interaction between the stimulation and the hormonal condition of the animal; for example, immature male monkeys required both genital stimulation and testosterone injections to obtain the electrical recording changes (Chhina, Chakrabarty, Kaur, & Anand, 1968). The specificity of the recording site again suggests that these are target sites for the hormones. However, Sutin and Michael (1970) have questioned the behavioral significance of such recordings, since their experiments revealed no relationship between the recordings and behavioral receptivity of their female subjects.

Conclusions

Genetic "blueprints" determine the initial development of the nervous system. However, the material reviewed here indicates that the experimental introduction of hormones at appropriate times during that development alters the normal pattern of species-specific male and female sexual responding in adult animals. The data also suggest that the developing CNS of mammals is basically feminine in its organization, i.e., it is capable of mediating cyclical activity in the pituitary-gonadal system. Generally, it appears that if androgens are present at a critical time, this cycling is lost, at least in part, and the later capacity for feminine responses is curtailed. If androgens are absent at this critical time, the basically feminine response capacity is retained. In the adult organism, hormones have a further function of sensitizing or activating this previously organized neural substrate.

The above description characterizes the results of investigation in lower mammals. The degree to which it holds for humans is still unclear. As was indicated in Chapter 2, it is possible that in humans sexual identification and object choice are greatly influenced by sexual assignment and rearing conditions.[6]

However, there is evidence that suggests that such flexibility may be characteristic only of genetic females—recall that the presence of testosterone in genetic males may be far more limiting of adult sex role. While this

[6]Homosexuality appears in physiologically normal animals as well as in humans. Whether learning plays a role in its development is not clear. What is clear is that in humans no simple hormonal treatment alters the behavior. On the other hand, several hypotheses concerning hormonal involvement could be developed from some of the material presented here. These issues are still open.

is an entirely untested hypothesis, it is at least compatible with the data in lower mammals. Thus, a basically feminine CNS initially has the potential for either sex role; androgens in genetic females bias their responses away from the feminine; androgens in genetic males bias their responses even further toward the masculine; lack of androgens in both genetic females and males favors retention of the feminine CNS organization.

THE CNS AND REPRODUCTIVE BEHAVIOR

Both spinal and cerebral mechanisms influence sexual behavior. Beach (1967) has reviewed their relative contributions to copulatory responses. His review is based on the following propositions: (1) Species-specific copulatory patterns in vertebrates consist, in part, of reflexive responses mediated by the spinal cord and lower brainstem, which are capable of functioning independently from more anterior portions of the CNS. (2) In the intact adult organism, these spinal and lower brainstem mechanisms are subject to varying degrees of inhibitory control by the more anterior cerebral mechanisms. (3) Gonadal hormones probably have little direct effect on the more caudal, reflexive centers. (4) Copulatory behavior is influenced by gonadal hormones through their action on cerebral mechanisms controlling the lower, reflexive mechanisms.

Spinal Versus Cerebral Mechanisms

Proposition 1 above is demonstrated by many experiments showing genital reflexes in *spinal animals*, animals whose spinal cords have been severed from the remainder of the neural axis. Thus, erection and genital responses analogous to intromission and ejaculation were obtained in the spinal rat (Hart, 1968a) and dog (Hart, 1967a). In the intact dog, manual stimulation failed to produce ejaculatory responses of the intensity elicitable in spinal animals. This suggests, as proposition 2 says, that the spinal mechanisms are normally inhibited, and when this inhibition is removed, a fully intense reaction can occur. Experiments with rats also bear out this conclusion; spinal rats showed more genital reflex activity than normal rats similarly stimulated. That proposition 3 is only partly correct is indicated by the fact that while genital reflexes were elicitable in the spinal, castrated dog (Hart, 1968b) and rat (Hart, 1967b), some of their quantitative characteristics were sharply augmented by the administration of testosterone. Furthermore, Hart (1968c) showed that adult male rats castrated at 4 days of age showed deficient genital reflexes in tests after spinal transection and testosterone injection; similarly treated 12-day castrates were normal in their responses. These data indicate, then, that neonatal androgen does have an organizational effect on the spinal mechanisms mediating genital reflexes. Evidence for proposition 4, that gonadal hormones influence copulatory behavior through their effects on cerebral mechanisms, was reviewed above in discussing the effects of hormone implants.

The Role of the Neocortex

Beach (1947) has summarized evidence dealing with the effects of neocortical damage on sexual behavior. In the female guinea pig, rat, rabbit, and cat, decortication does not interfere with coital activity. But decortication does eliminate male-like mounting behavior in the female. There is some indication that the cortex exerts an inhibitory effect on feminine behavior—the thresholds for estrus responses appear lower after decortication.

In the male animal, cortical lesions are debilitating for sexual performance. Such lesions may contribute to sensory and motor impairments producing disoriented responses and may also limit general arousal, but there is also evidence that some small lesions have specific effects (Zitrin, Jaynes, & Beach, 1956; Larsson, 1964). Generally, then the evidence suggests that males and females of the same species are differentially affected by cortical lesions, with males being more dependent on intact cortical mechanisms.

The Role of the Limbic System

We have previously (Chapter 7) noted that the so-called Klüver-Bucy syndrome resulting from temporal lobectomy in male monkeys includes hypersexuality. A study of J. D. Green, Clements, and deGroot (1957) attempted more particularly to localize the effects of limbic lesions on sexual responding in the cat. This study is important also in that it included detailed preoperative observation of the animals; some so-called hypersexual responses have been observed also in neurologically normal animals (Michael, 1961). In the male cat, the occurrence of sexual and aggressive responses differs markedly depending on whether the animal is within or outside its home territory; that is, males must become adapted to a territory before engaging in either copulation or aggression.

Table 10.1 (from Green et al., 1957) lists the range of sexual activities displayed by these male cats and the changes in response before, during, and after adaptation to a territory. Also shown are response changes after hormone administration and after limbic lesions. In regard to hormonal changes, while Green et al. indicate that the response range may be drastically widened in the intact male cat given additional testosterone, they emphasize that the incidence of these behaviors is still quite small. Limbic lesions produced a similar widening of the response range, but the incidence was very much higher and carried over to behavior outside the home territory. These changes in sexual responding were produced by lesions of the pyriform cortex (Figure 10.9) underlying the amygdala: animals with lesions restricted to the amygdala, without pyriform involvement, did not show the sexual changes. No female animals showed any signs of altered sexual response as a result of limbic lesions; this may be a manifestation of the female's greater dependence on hormonal rather than neural mechanisms.

Table 10.1 The effects of territorial adaptation, hormones, and lesions on the observation of different sexual activities in the male cat

	NORMALS			*HORMONES*		*LESIONS*	
	Un-adapted	*Adapt-ing*	*Adapted*	*Un-adapted*	*Adapted*	*Un-adapted*	*Adapted*
Heterosexuality	–	–	+	–	+	+	+
Homosexuality	–	±	+	–	+	+	+
Pederasty	–	±	–	–	+	+	+
Plural coitus	–	–	+	–	+	+	+
Other species	–	–	–	–	+	+	+
Anesthetized animals	–	–	–	–	+	+	+
Inanimate objects	–	–	–	–	+	+	+
Masturbation	–	–	–	–	+	+	+

Note: + indicates the behavior was observed.

(From J. D. Green, C. D. Clements, & J. deGroot. Rhinencephalic lesions and behavior in cats. An analysis of the Klüver-Bucy syndrome with particular reference to normal and abnormal sexual behavior. *Journal of Comparative Neurology*, 1957, *108*, 505–545.)

These data are subject to several possible interpretations, including the possibility that pyriform lesions exert a specific effect on male sexual responding. Alternatively, however, the data appear to be compatible with our previous speculations about the role of the limbic system in response modulation and the role of rostral CNS structures in the inhibition of sexual responding. Thus, one interpretation of these data is that territorial considerations serve to inhibit the display of sexual responses, while hormones tend to have a disinhibiting function on CNS tissue. Thus, animals with pyriform lesions are disinhibited sexually because they fail to discriminate home territory from foreign territory. The progression in sexuality seen as one moves from left to right across Table 10.1 would then be seen as a result of alternative and differentially effective means of reducing the inhibition exerted on the intact substrate for sexual responses.

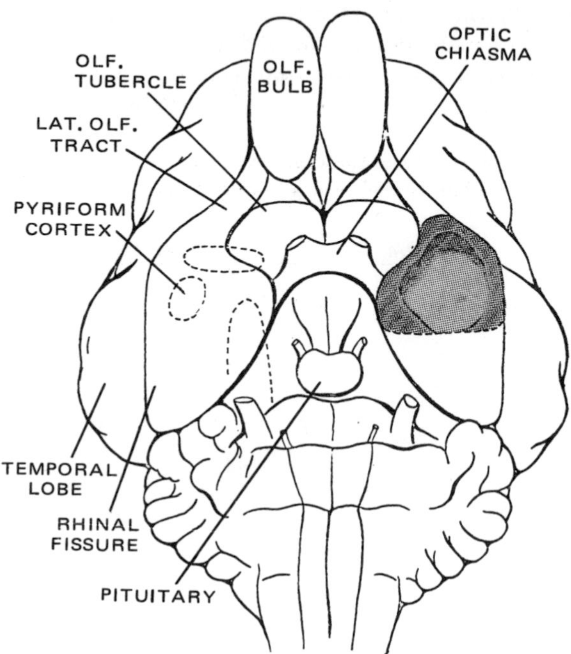

Figure 10.9. Ventral aspect of cat brain with projection onto surface of areas involved in animals showing various behavior patterns. At right, quartile distribution of incidence of involvement of both pyriform areas in male animals with hypersexuality. Areas behind dotted line not explored. On left, the three dotted zones indicate schematically that (rostral zone) lesions near anterior amygdala (branches of the middle cerebral artery) produce catelepsy. Lesions at the junction of basal and lateral amygdaloid nuclei produce hyperphagia and lesions in the hippocampus (caudal dotted zone) are followed by seizures. (From Green, J. D., Clements, C. D., and deGroot, J., Rhinencephalic lesions and behavior in cats: An analysis of the Klüver-Bucy syndrome with particular reference to normal and abnormal sexual behavior. *Journal of Comparative Neurology*, 1957, *108*, 505–545.)

A variety of other limbic locations have also been studied. Kimble, Rogers, and Hendrickson (1967) found little noticeable effect of dorsal hippocampal lesions on copulatory behavior in either males or females; the lesions appeared primarily to impair maternal behavior. Dewsbury, Goodman, Salis, and Bunnell (1968) found that mount and intromission latencies were increased in male rats with total hippocampal lesions; dorsal hippocampal lesions alone produced no effects. On the other hand, Bermant, Glickman, and Davidson (1968) found that dorsal lesions decreased intercopulatory and postejaculatory intervals in the male, while ventral lesions had little effect. It is probable that methodological differences account for some of the differing outcomes among these studies. Generally, though, any changes appear to be of a modulatory nature, affecting latency or rate of performance.

In a similar vein, Kurtz and Adler (1973) reported changes in electrical recordings from the hippocampus during copulatory behavior in the male rat. Hippocampal theta activity accompanied appetitive behaviors such as watching, sniffing, approaching, and mounting the female; intromission or ejaculation were followed by slowing and desynchronization of the hippocampal recordings. These data were interpreted within a general model of hippocampal action in appetitive and consummatory behavior.

Maclean and Ploog (1962) elicited penile erection in monkeys from stimulation of a variety of limbic structures. Since these studies did not test for actual copulatory behavior, an unambiguous interpretation of the result is not possible.

In the female, we have previously noted that Green et al. found no effects of pyriform lesions in the cat. Peretz (1967) suggested that hippocampal lesions reduced the vigor and incidence of lordosis to artificial stimulation of the vagina in the cat. But this study did not control the hormonal condition of the animals, and estradiol injections were able to reverse the effects of the lesions. Rodgers and Law (1968) found that lordosis could be elicited from widespread limbic locations by a variety of chemical agents. Note that the occurrence of lordosis, however, does not imply that the animals were behaviorally receptive—full receptivity cannot be inferred from a single response measure. More recently, Zasorin, Malsbury, and Pfaff (1975) inhibited lordosis and copulatory activity in fully receptive female hamsters by electrical stimulation of the septal area. The septal area also shows concentrations of radioactive estradiol.

Generally the most accurate summary seems to be that while sexual responding is influenced by limbic mechanisms, no limbic site appears critical; limbic mechanisms appear merely to modulate the occurrence of the responses.

The Role of the Hypothalamus and Preoptic Area

Our earlier discussion of the effects of implanted hormones has certainly indicated hypothalamic-preoptic involvement in sexual responding. As we shall see, this role appears to be crucial.

Elicitation of sexual responding by electrical stimulation of these areas corroborates their role. One of the earliest reports was that of Vaughn and Fisher (1962). In 3 of 30 male rats that had been implanted, these investigators found that electrical stimulation of the anterior dorsolateral hypothalamus markedly increased sexual capacity. Mounting was promptly initiated and continued at a high rate; intromissions were not followed by the usual grooming behavior; penile erection was constant during stimulation;

postejaculatory delays before initiating another copulatory series tended to be shortened. One rat showed as many as four ejaculations within a 5-minute stimulation period. The results of this experiment strongly suggest that hypothalamic stimulation reduced inhibitory processes.

More caudal stimulation, in the posterior hypothalamus, also affects male sexual performance (Caggiula & Hoebel, 1966) but the effect is somewhat different. With stimulus trains on for 3 minutes and then off for the same period, copulation became "stimulus bound"—i.e., copulation occurred during stimulation but not in its absence. However, sexual capacity was not altered as in Vaughn and Fisher's experiment.

Stimulation rostral to the hypothalamus, in the preoptic area, has been shown to have effects on responses of both males and females. In the opossum, Roberts, Steinberg, and Means (1967) elicited male mating responses in both males and females with equal facility by electrically stimulating the medial preoptic area. In a follow-up study, Berquist (1970) found that electrically elicited responses in the opossum, including male sexual behavior, were substantially raised in threshold only by posterior hypothalamic lesions; anterior and lateral lesions were without effect. The results are generally compatible with the hypothesis that hypothalamic influences act caudally, through the medial forebrain bundle, on mesencephalic or lower brainstem sensory-motor mechanisms. Finally, Malsbury (1971) found that electrical stimulation of the preoptic area facilitated male copulatory responses.

Generally, then, these stimulation results are consistent with the suggestion that a preoptic-hypothalamic pathway is important for sexual responding. Studies of lesions in these areas have not been entirely consistent but they generally indicate that this pathway is critical for the maintenance of sexual behavior.

Hypothalamic lesions have been reported to have a variety of effects. Rogers (1954) found that sexual functioning was impaired in male rats with posterior lesions but the effect could be reversed with gonadal hormone injections; more anterior lesions produced a decrement that could not be reversed. Lisk (1966) found that posterior lesions *augmented* copulatory behavior in male rats. He attributed the difference to the fact that he used a lesion method designed to produce less residual, irritative damage. Law and Meagher (1958) also found augmentation as a result of some hypothalamic lesions in the female rat. These animals mated during *diestrus* (vaginal nonreceptivity), indicating that there is a system exerting inhibitory control over mating in the female.

The results of preoptic lesions have not been entirely consistent either. Lott (1966), for instance, found no change in copulatory performance of male rats as a result of such lesions. He attributed prior findings of deficits in copulation to short-term testing and debilitation from the operation. Subsequently, however, several studies reported such deficits. Hendricks and Scheetz (1973) conducted a series of experiments in rats whose findings they interpreted as confirming the critical nature of a preoptic-hypothalamic pathway extending caudally for male copulatory activity. Hart (1974) found a similar result for male dogs. Preoptic lesions immediately stopped or curtailed copulatory behavior. Mounting and thrusting, as well as intromission and locking were reduced. The deficit was not an indirect result of disturbance in the hormonal condition of the animals. The immediate loss of copulatory behavior in this study is in contrast to the results of castration, where the loss, if any, is much more gradual. Hart suggested that this indicates a neural role for the preoptic area beyond any function it may serve as a target area for the mediation of hormonal effects.

In the female rat, Singer (1968) found a failure to display masculine copulatory behavior after preoptic lesions; feminine receptive behavior in response to gonadal hormones remained intact. Anterior hypothalamic lesions resulted in the loss of female sex responses and only partially affected male responses. These results imply at least partial separation of the mechanisms for male and female behaviors in the rat hypothalamus. Powers and Valenstein (1972) found that sexual receptivity was facilitated by medial preoptic lesions in females. Ovariectomized animals required reduced quanitites of estrogen to induce receptivity, suggesting that estrogen acts to reduce an inhibitory effect of this area. Finally, in an anatomic study, Raisman and Field (1971) found that axon terminations in the preoptic area were structurally different between the sexes.

Generally, then, the above results strongly implicate a pathway from the preoptic area, through the hypothalamus, to the midbrain, in control of sexual responding. This involvement is probably twofold in that it involves control of both endocrine and neural mechanisms. In addition, this pathway is probably sensitive to the effects of circulating gonadal hormones. There are also indications that this pathway partakes in both excitatory and inhibitory functions.

Midbrain and Neurochemical Mechanisms

After a series of intromissions, the male rat ejaculates; subsequent to that ejaculation, a 5- to 6-minute "refractory" period occurs, during which the animal is generally inactive. This refractory period is generally considered to be the result of inhibitory processes. Two recent studies of lesions in midbrain areas lend credence to this supposition.

The lesions in these studies were placed differently, though their results appear similar. In one study (Clark, Caggiula, McConnell, & Antelman, 1975), the lesions were placed so as to disrupt the dorsal norepinephrine bundle which courses through the midbrain to the hypothalamus (see Figure 8.13). In the other study (Barfield, Wilson, & McDonald, 1975), the lesions were placed more ventrally so as to interrupt the course of the dopaminergic system as it goes to the hypothalamus (see Figure 8.14). The major finding of both studies was a marked drop in the postejaculatory refractory period and a pronounced increase in the number of ejaculations per test session. Both studies raise the general question of the role of the transmitter systems involved; at this time, however, no coherent picture emerges.

Accumulating evidence suggests that serotonin serves an inhibiting function on copulatory activity in the male rat, and dopamine serves a facilitating function (see Malmnäs, 1976), although the results here are contradictory. In an attempt to pursue these contradictions with respect to the role of dopamine, Malmnäs (1976) tested the effects of injection of a wide dose range of L-dopa. L-dopa is a precursor of catecholamines in the CNS and, in combination with the injection of inhibitors of norepinephrine, the injections were designed to alter dopamine levels. The injections were made in castrated male rats given small doses of testosterone, designed to produce a submaximal amount of mounting behavior in the castrates. The intention, then, was to determine if alterations in dopamine levels would facilitate the effects of the minimal testosterone dose. In small doses, L-dopa produced such facilitation but higher doses resulted in an inhibitory effect. The facilitation was manifested in increases in ejaculation, as well as in attention to the females and intromission. The effects of L-dopa could be blocked by a dopamine receptor blocker. However, the results also suggested that epinephrine or norepinephrine also play a role, perhaps in controlling mounting. Thus, L-dopa can have either facilitating or inhibitory effects.

While serotonin systems seem to have an inhibiting function, different means of modifying serotonin have had contradictory results. Zemlan, Ward, Crowley, and Margules (1973) found that several serotonin antagonists, including parachlorophenylalanine (PCPA), induced lordosis in estrogen-primed ovariectomized, adrenalectomized, female rats. On the other hand, Gorzalka and Whalen (1975), in similar preparations, found no facilitation of lordosis. When the animals were given additional progesterone injections, PCPA inhibited lordosis somewhat rather than facilitating it. But Espina, Sano, and Wade (1975) found that, in females receiving estradiol and progesterone, a drug (alpha-methyltryptamine) which stimulates serotonin receptors inhibited lordosis. In the absence of progesterone the drug had no effect. These data were interpreted to indicate that progesterone acts to inhibit a serotonin-inhibiting system. The contradictions here may ultimately prove to be a function of dose levels of the drug and hormone combinations. In any event, it does seem clear that some relationships exists between serotonin and lordosis.

SUMMARY

In this chapter, we have explored the reciprocal relationships between the CNS and gonadal hormones in eliciting sexual behavior. Gonadal hormones seem to have two principal functions. Early in development they serve an organzing function, determining later response characteristics. Later in life, in the mature nervous system, gonadal hormones, serve a sensitizing function, arousing the developed response characteristics. Hormones share the latter function with other factors, such as environmental stimuli and past experience. Along with the greater development of the nervous system in higher mammals, the strict dependence on gonadal hormones for the ability to carry out the copulatory act has decreased; thus, the relative burden of the sensitizing function has shifted to other factors. But it is also unlikely that the sensitizing function of hormones is completely replaced, even in humans. In fact, individual differences in dependence on hormones within a given species are quite marked.

Generally, the evidence suggests that primitive sexual responses are organized at the brainstem and spinal levels of the CNS and that more rostral CNS mechanisms may serve to inhibit or modulate these primitive responses. Gonadal hormones generally seem to achieve their effects through reduction in neural inhibition.

There are sex differences within species in the relative dependence on neural and hormonal mechanisms for copulatory responding. In lower mammals, the female appears to be relatively more dependent on intact hormonal mechanisms and less dependent on intact neural mechanisms. But mammalian development generally seems to start from a base of bisexual capability in the CNS, with differentiation of the male normally occurring as a result of circulating androgens. Even so, considerable bisexual capacity is retained by the mature CNS. The hypothalamic-preoptic area of the brain seems to be particularly crucial as both a site for interaction between neural and hormonal systems and as a necessary neural substrate in mediating sexual behavior.

Finally, the gonadal hormonal system is subject to alteration from environmental and autonomic sources. In animals, such changes in gonadal function appear to be related to important changes in behavior regulating the social and sexual interactions among members of the species. It remains to be seen if comparable mechanisms can be demonstrated in humans.

REFERENCES

ADLER, N. T. Effects of the male's copulatory behavior on successful pregnancy in the female rat. *Journal of Comparative and Physiological Psychology,* 1969, *69,* 613–623.

ADLER, N., & BERMANT, G. Sexual behavior of male rats: Effects of reduced sensory feedback. *Journal of Comparative and Physiological Psychology,* 1966, *61,* 240–243.

ADLER, N. T., RESKO, J. A., & GOY, R. W. The effect of copulatory behavior on hormonal change in the female rat prior to implantation. *Physiology and Behavior,* 1970, *5,* 1003–1006.

ADLER, N. T., & ZOLOTH, S. R. Copulatory behavior can inhibit pregnancy in female rats. *Science,* 1970, *168,* 1480–1482.

ARONSON, L. R., & COOPER, M. L. Seasonal variation in mating in cats after desensitization of glans penis. *Science,* 1966, *152,* 226–230.

ARONSON, L. R., & COOPER, M. L. Olfactory deprivation and mating behavior in sexually experienced male cats. *Behavioral Biology,* 1974, *11,* 459–480.

BARASH, D. P. The evolution of marmot societies: A general theory. *Science,* 1974, *185,* 415–420.

BARFIELD, R. J., WILSON, C., & MCDONALD, P. G. Sexual behavior: Extreme reduction of postejaculatory refractory period by midbrain lesions in male rats. *Science,* 1975, *189,* 147–149.

BAUM, M. J. Pineal gland: Influence on development of copulation in male rats. *Science,* 1968, *162,* 586–587.

BEACH, F. A. Evolutionary changes in the physiological control of mating behavior in mammals. *Psychological Review,* 1947, *54,* 297–315.

BEACH, F. A. *Hormones and behavior.* New York: Paul B. Hoeber, 1948.

BEACH, F. A. Evolutionary aspects of psychoendocrinology. In A. Roe and G. G. Simpson (eds.), *Behavior and evolution.* New Haven, Conn.: Yale University Press, 1958, pp. 81–102.

BEACH, F. A. Cerebral and hormonal control of reflexive mechanisms involved in copulatory behavior. *Physiological Review,* 1967, *47,* 289–316.

BEACH, F. A. Coital behavior in dogs: VI. Long-term effects of castration upon mating behavior in the male. *Journal of Comparative and Physiological Psychology,* 1970, *70,* No. 3, Part 2, 1–32.

BEACH, F. A. Sexual attractivity, proceptivity, and receptivity in female mammals. *Hormones and Behavior*, 1976, *7*, 105–138.

BEACH, F. A., & FOWLER, H. Individual differences in the response of male rats to androgen. *Journal of Comparative and Physiological Psychology*, 1959, *52*, 50–52.

BEACH, F. A., & HOLZ-TUCKER, A. M. Effects of different concentrations of androgen upon sexual behavior in castrated male rats. *Journal of Comparative and Physiological Psychology*, 1949, *42*, 433–453.

BEACH, F. A., & LEVINSON, G. Effects of androgen on the glans penis and mating behavior of castrated male rats. *Journal of Experimental Zoology*, 1950, *114*, 159–171.

BEAUCHAMP, G. K., & HESS, E. H. Abnormal early rearing and sexual responsiveness in male guinea pigs. *Journal of Comparative and Physiological Psychology*, 1973, *85*, 383–396.

BERMANT, G., GLICKMAN, S. E., & DAVIDSON, J. M. Effects of limbic lesions on copulatory behavior of male rats. *Journal of Comparative and Physiological Psychology*, 1968, *65*, 118–125.

BERMANT, G., & TAYLOR, L. Interactive effects of experience and olfactory bulb lesions in male rat copulation. *Physiology and Behavior*, 1969, *4*, 13–17.

BERMANT, G., & WESTBROOK, W. H. Peripheral factors in the regulation of sexual contact by female rats. *Journal of Comparative and Physiological Psychology*, 1966, *61*, 244–250.

BERQUIST, E. H. Output pathways of hypothalamic mechanisms for sexual, aggressive, and other motivated behaviors in opossum. *Journal of Comparative and Physiological Psychology*, 1970, *70*, 389–398.

BRONSON, F. H., & ELEFTHERIOU, B. E. Adrenal response to fighting in mice: Separation of physical and psychological causes. *Science*, 1965, *147*, 627–628.

CAGGIULA, A. R., & HOEBEL, B. G. "Copulation-reward site" in the posterior hypothalamus. *Science*, 1966, *153*, 1284–1285.

CALHOUN, J. B. Population density and social pathology. *Scientific American*, 1962, *206*, 139–148.

CARR, W. J., LOEB, L. S., & DISSINGER, M. L. Reponses of rats to sex odors. *Journal of Comparative and Physiological Psychology*, 1965, *59*, 370–377.

CARR, W. J., LOEB, L. S., & WYLIE, N. R. Responses to feminine odors in normal and castrated male rats. *Journal of Comparative and Physiological Psychology*, 1966, *62*, 336–338.

CHHINA, G. S., CHAKRABARTY, A. S., KAUR, K., & ANAND, B. K. Electroencephalographic responses produced by genital stimulation and hormone administration in sexually immature rhesus monkeys. *Physiology and Behavior,* 1968, *3,* 579–584.

CHRISTIAN, J. J. Effect of population size on the adrenal glands and reproductive organs of male mice in populations of fixed size. *American Journal of Physiology,* 1955, *182,* 292–300.

CHRISTIAN, J. J., & DAVIS, D. E. Endocrines, behavior, and population. *Science,* 1964, *146,* 1550–1560.

CLARK, T. K., CAGGIULA, A. R., MCCONNELL, R. A., & ANTELMAN, S. M. Sexual inhibition is reduced by rostral midbrain lesions in the male rat. *Science,* 1975, *190,* 169–171.

CLEMENS, L. G., WALLEN, K., & GORSKI, R. A. Mating behavior: Facilitation in the female rat after application of potassium chloride. *Science,* 1967, *157,* 1208–1209.

CONIGLIO, L. P., PAUP, D. L., & CLEMENS, L. G. Hormonal factors controlling the development of sexual behavior in the male golden hamster. *Physiology and Behavior,* 1973, *10,* 1087–1094.

DESSI-FULGHERI, F., LUPO DIPRISCO, L., & VERDARELLI, P. Influence of long-term isolation on the production and metabolism of gonadal sex steroids in male and female rats. *Physiology and Behavior,* 1975, *14,* 495–499.

DEWSBURY, D. A., & ESTEP, D. Q. Pregnancy in cactus mice: Effects of prolonged copulation. *Science,* 1975, *187,* 552–553.

DEWSBURY, D. A., GOODMAN, E. D., SALIS, P. J., & BUNELL, B. N. Effects of hippocampal lesions on the copulatory behavior of male rats. *Physiology and Behavior,* 1968, *3,* 651–656.

DOTY, R. L., FORD, M., PRETI, G., & HUGGINS, G. R. Changes in the intensity and pleasantness of human vaginal odors during the menstrual cycle. *Science,* 1975, *190,* B16–B18.

DRAPER, P. Crowding among hunter-gatherers: The !Kung bushmen. *Science,* 1973, *182,* 301–303.

EDWARDS, D. A. Mice: Fighting by neonatally androgenized females. *Science,* 1968, *161,* 1027–1028.

EIBL-EIBESFELDT, I. *Ethology, the biology of behavior.* New York: Holt, Rinehart & Winston, 1970.

ELLIOTT, J. A., STETSON, M. H., & MENAKER, M. Regulation of testis function in golden hamsters: A circadian clock measures photoperiodic time. *Science,* 1972, *178,* 771–773.

ELY, D. L., & HENRY, J. P. Effects of prolonged social deprivation on murine behavior patterns, blood pressure, and adrenal weight. *Journal of Comparative and Physiological Psychology,* 1974, *87,* 733–740.

ERICKSON, C. J. Induction of ovarian activity in female ring doves by androgen treatment of castrated males. *Journal of Comparative and Physiological Psychology*, 1970, *71*, 210–215.

ESPINO, C., SANO, M., & WADE, G. N. Alpha-methyltryptamine blocks facilitation of lordosis by progesterone in spayed, estrogen-primed rats. *Pharmacology, Biochemistry and Behavior, 1975, 3*, 557–559.

FEDER, H. H., & WHALEN, R. E. Feminine behavior in neonatally castrated and estrogen-treated male rats. *Science*, 1965, *147*, 306–307.

FISHER, A. E. Maternal and sexual behavior induced by intracranial chemical stimulation. *Science*, 1956, *124*, 228–229.

FISHER, A. E. Chemical stimulation of the brain. In J. L. McGaugh, N. M. Weinberger, and R. E. Whalen (eds.), *Psychobiology, The biological bases of behavior*. San Francisco: Freeman, 1967, pp. 66–74.

GALLE, O. R.,GOVE, W. R., & MCPHERSON, J. M. Population and social pathology: What are the relations for man? *Science*, 1972, *176*, 23–30.

GOLDFOOT, D. A., FEDER, H. H., & GOY, R. W. Development of bisexuality in the male rat treated neonatally with androstenedione. *Journal of Comparative and Physiological Psychology*, 1969, *67*, 41–45.

GORZALKA, B. B., REZEK, D. L., & WHALEN, R. E. Adrenal mediation of estrogen-induced ejaculatory behavior in the male rat. *Physiology and Behavior*, 1975, *14*, 373–376.

GORZALKA, B. B. & WHALEN, R. E. Inhibition not facilitation of sexual behavior by PCPA. *Pharmacology, Biochemistry and Behavior*, 1975, *3*, 511–513.

GREEN, J. D., CLEMENTS, C. D., & DEGROOT, J. Rhinencephalic lesions and behavior in cats. An analysis of the Klüver-Bucy syndrome with particular reference to normal and abnormal sexual behavior. *Journal of Comparative Neurology*, 1957, *108*, 505–545.

HAMPSON, J. L. Determinants of psychosexual orientation. In F. A. Beach (ed.), *Sex and behavior*. New York: Wiley, 1965, pp. 108–132.

HARDY, K. R. An appetitional theory of sexual motivation. *Psychological Review*, 1964, *71*, 1–18.

HARLOW, H. F. The heterosexual affectional system in monkeys. *American Psychologist*, 1962, *17*, 1–9.

HART, B. L. Sexual reflexes and mating behavior in the male dog. *Journal of Comparative and Physiological Psychology*, 1967, *64*, 388–399. (a)

HART, B. L. Testosterone regulation of sexual reflexes in spinal male rats. *Science*, 1967, *155*, 1283–1284. (b)

HART, B. L. Sexual reflexes and mating behavior in the male rat. *Journal of Comparative and Physiological Psychology*, 1968, *65*, 453–460. (a)

HART, B. L. Alteration of quantitative aspects of sexual reflexes in spinal male dogs by testosterone. *Journal of Comparative and Physiological Psychology*, 1968, *66*, 726–730. (b)

HART, B. L. Neonatal castration: Influence on neural organization of sexual reflexes in male rats. *Science*, 1968, *160*, 1135–1136. (c)

HART, B. L. Gonadal androgen and sociosexual behavior of male mammals: A comparative analysis. *Psychological Bulletin*, 1974, *81*, 383–400.

HART, B. L. Medial preoptic-anterior hypothalamic area and sociosexual behavior of male dogs: A comparative neuropsychological analysis. *Journal of Comparative and Physiological Psychology*, 1974, *86*, 328–349.

HENDRICKS, S. E., & SCHEETZ, H. A. Interaction of hypothalamic structures in the mediation of male sexual behavior. *Physiology and Behavior*, 1973, *10*, 711–716.

HERBERT, J. The role of the dorsal nerves of the penis in the sexual behavior of the male rhesus monkey. *Physiology and Behavior*, 1973, *10*, 293–300.

HILL, J. L. *Peromyscus:* Effect of early pairing on reproduction. *Science*, 1974, *186*, 1042–1044.

HINDE, R. A.. *Animal behavior* (2nd ed.). New York: McGraw-Hill, 1970.

HOFFMAN, R. A., & REITER, R. J. Pineal gland: Influence on gonads of male hamsters. *Science*, 1965, *148*, 1609–1610.

KAGEN, J., & BEACH, F. A. Effects of early experience on mating behavior in male rats. *Journal of Comparative and Physiological Psychology*, 1953, *46*, 204–209.

KARSCH, F. J., DIERSCHKE, D. J., & KNOBIL, E. Sexual differentiation of pituitary function: Apparent difference between primates and rodents. *Science*, 1973, *179*, 484–486.

KAUFMAN, R. S. Effects of preventing intromission upon sexual behavior of rats. *Journal of Comparative and Physiological Psychology*, 1953, *46*, 209–212.

KIMBLE, D. P., ROGERS, L., & HENDRICKSON, C. W. Hippocampal lesions disrupt maternal, not sexual, behavior in the albino rat. *Journal of Comparative and Physiological Psychology*, 1967, *63*, 401–407.

KOMISARUK, B. R., ADLER, N. T., & HUTCHISON, J. Genital sensory field: Enlargement by estrogen treatment in female rats. *Science*, 1972, *178*, 1295–1298.

KURTZ, R. G., & ADLER, N. T. Electrophysiological correlates of copulatory behavior in the male rat: Evidence for a sexual inhibitory process. *Journal of Comparative and Physiological Psychology*, 1973, *84*, 225–240.

LARSSON, K. Mating behavior in male rats after cerebral ablation. II. Effects of lesions in the frontal lobes compared to lesions in the posterior half of the hemispheres. *Journal of Experimental Zoology*, 1964, *155*, 203–214.

Larsson, K. Sexual impairment of inexperienced male rats following pre- and postpuberal olfactory bulbectomy. *Physiology and Behavior*, 1975, *14*, 195–199.

Larsson, K., & Södersten, P. Mating in male rats after section of the dorsal penile nerve. *Physiology and Behavior*, 1973, *10*, 567–571.

Law, T., & Meagher, W. Hypothalamic lesions and sexual behavior in the female rat. *Science*, 1958, *128*, 1626–1627.

Lehrman, D. S. Control of behavior cycles in reproduction. In W. Etkin (ed.), *Social behavior and organization among vertebrates*. Chicago: University of Chicago Press, 1964, pp. 143–166.

Levine, S., & Mullins, R. F., Jr. Hormonal influences on brain organization in infant rats. *Science*, 1966, *152*, 1585–1592.

Lisk, R. D. Diencephalic placement of estradiol and sexual receptivity in the female rat. *American Journal of Physiology*, 1962, *203*, 493–496.

Lisk, R. D. Inhibitory centers in sexual behavior in male rat. *Science*, 1966, *152*, 669–670.

Lisk, R. D., & Newlon, M. Estradiol: Evidence for its direct effect on hypothalamic neurons. *Science*, 1963, *139*, 223–224.

Lott, D. F. Effects of preoptic lesions on the sexual behavior of male rats. *Journal of Comparative and Physiological Psychology*, 1966, *61*, 284–288.

Luttge, W. G. Effects of anti-estrogens on testosterone stimulated male sexual behavior and peripheral target tissues in the castrate male rat. *Physiology and Behavior*, 1975, *14*, 839–846.

Luttge, W. G., Hall, N. R., Wallis, C. J., & Campbell, J. C. Stimulation of male and female sexual behavior in gonadectomized rats with estrogen and androgen therapy and its inhibition with concurrent antihormone therapy. *Physiology and Behavior*, 1975, *14*, 65–73.

MacLean, P. D., & Ploog, D. W. Cerebral representation of penile erection. *Journal of Neurophysiology*, 1962, *25*, 30–55.

Macrides, F., Bartke, A., & Dalterio, S. Strange females increase plasma testosterone levels in male mice. *Science*, 1975, *189*, 1104–1105.

Malmnäs, C. O. The significance of dopamine, versus other catecholamines, for L-dopa induced facilitation of sexual behavior in the castrated male rat. *Pharmacology, Biochemistry and Behavior*, 1976, *4*, 521–526.

Malsbury, C. W. Facilitation of male copulatory behavior by electrical stimulation of the medial preoptic area. *Physiology and Behavior*, 1971, *7*, 797–805.

Marler, P. R., & Hamilton, W. J., III. *Mechanisms of animal behavior*.

New York: Wiley, 1967.

McDonald, P. G., & Meyerson, B. J. The effect of oestradiol, testosterone and dihydrotestosterone on sexual motivation in the ovariectomized female rat. *Physiology and Behavior*, 1973, *11*, 515–521.

McGill, T. E., & Haynes, C. M. Heterozygosity and retention of ejaculatory reflex after castration in male mice. *Journal of Comparative and Physiological Psychology*, 1973, *84*, 423–429.

Michael, R. P. "Hypersexuality" in male cats without brain damage. *Science*, 1961, *134*, 533–554.

Michael, R. P. Estrogen-sensitive neurons and sexual behavior in female cats. *Science*, 1962, *136*, 322–323.

Money, J. Sex hormones and other variables in human eroticism. In W. C. Young (ed.), *Sex and internal secretions* (3rd ed.). Baltimore: Williams and Wilkins, 1961.

Murphy, M. R., & Schneider, G. E. Olfactory bulb removal eliminates mating behavior in the male golden hamster. *Science*, 1970, *167*, 302–304.

Nadler, R. D. Masculinization of female rats by intracranial implantation of androgen in infancy. *Journal of Comparative and Physiological Psychology*, 1968, *66*, 157–167.

Nadler, R. D. Sexual cyclicity in captive lowland gorillas. *Science*, 1975, *189*, 813–814.

Noble, G. K., & Zitrin, A. Induction of mating behavior in male and female chicks following injection of sex hormones. *Endocrinology*, 1942, *30*, 327–334.

Noble, R. G., & Alsum, P. B. Hormone dependent sex dimorphisms in the golden hamster (*Mesocricetus auratus*). *Physiology and Behavior*, 1975, *14*, 567–574.

Parkes, A. S., & Bruce, H. M. Olfactory stimuli in mammalian reproduction. *Science*, 1961, *134*, 1049–1054.

Peretz, E. Effects of limbic cortex ablation on estrous response strength in cats. *Journal of Comparative and Physiological Psychology*, 1967, *63*, 220–222.

Phoenix, C. H. Effects of dihydrotestosterone on sexual behavior of castrated male rhesus monkeys. *Physiology and Behavior*, 1974, *12*, 1045–1055.

Phoenix, C. H., Goy, R. W., Gerall, A. A., & Young, W. C. Organizing action of prenatally administered testosterone propionate on the tissues mediating mating behavior in the female guinea pig. *Endocrinology*, 1959, *65*, 369–382.

Phoenix, C. H., Slob, A. K., & Goy, R. W. Effects of castration and replacement therapy on sexual behavior of adult male rhesuses. *Journal of Comparative and Physiological Psychology*, 1973, *84*, 472–481.

Pollack, E. I., & Sachs, B. O. Male copulatory behavior and female maternal behavior in neonatally bulbectomized rats. *Physiology and Behavior*, 1975, *14*, 337–343.

Porter, R. W., Cavanaugh, E. B., Critchlow, B. V., & Sawyer, C. H. Localized changes in electrical activity, following vaginal stimulation. *American Journal of Physiology*, 1957, *189*, 145–151.

Powers, B., & Valenstein, E. S. Sexual receptivity: Facilitation by medial preoptic lesions in female rats. *Science*, 1972, *175*, 1003–1005.

Powers, J. B., & Winans, S. S. Vomeronasal organ: Critical role in mediating sexual behavior of the male hamster. *Science*, 1975, *187*, 961–963.

Rabedeau, R. G., & Whalen, R. E. Effects of copulatory experience on mating behavior in the male rat. *Journal of Comparative and Physiological Psychology*, 1959, *52*, 482–484.

Raisman, G., & Field, P. M. Sexual dimorphism in the preoptic area of the rat. *Science*, 1971, *173*, 731–733.

Ratcliffe, H. L., & Snyder, R. L. Myocardial infarction: A response to social interaction among chickens. *Science*, 1964, *144*, 425–426.

Roberts, W. W., Steinberg, M. L., & Means, L. W. Hypothalamic mechanisms for sexual, aggressive, and other motivational behaviors in the opossum, *Didelphis virginiana*. *Journal of Comparative and Physiological Psychology*, 1967, *64*, 1–15.

Rodgers, C. H., & Law, O. T. Effects of chemical stimulation of the "limbic system" on lordosis in female rats. *Physiology and Behavior*, 1968, *3*, 241–246.

Rogers, C. M. Hypothalamic mediation of sex behavior in the male rat. Doctoral dissertation, Yale University, 1954.

Rose, R. M., Gordon, T. P., & Bernstein, I. S. Plasma testosterone levels in the male rhesus: Influences of sexual and social stimuli. *Science*, 1972, *178*, 643–645.

Rowe, F. A., & Smith, W. E. Simultaneous and successive olfactory bulb removal: Influence on the mating behavior of male mice. *Physiology and Behavior*, 1973, *10*, 443–449.

Sar, M., & Stumpf, W. E. Neurons of the hypothalamus concentrate [^{3}H] progesterone or its metabolites. *Science*, 1973, *182*, 1266—1268.

Singer, J. J. Hypothalamic control of male and female sexual behavior in female rats. *Journal of Comparative and Physiological Psychology*, 1968, *66*, 738–742.

Södersten, P., & Larsson, K. Lordosis behavior and mounting behavior in male rats: Effects of castration and treatment with estrodiol benzoate or testosterone propionate. *Physiology and Behavior*, 1975, *14*, 159–164.

Spevak, A. M., Quadagno, D. M., Knoeppel, D., & Poggio, J. P. Effects of isolation on sexual and social behavior in the rat. *Behavioral Biology*, 1973, *8*, 63–72.

Stehn, R. A., & Richmond, M. E. Male-induced pregnancy termination in the prairie mole, *Microtus ochrogaster*. *Science*, 1975, *187*, 1211–1213.

Sutin, J., & Michael, R. P. Changes in brain electrical activity following vaginal stimulation in estrous and anestrous cats. *Physiology and Behavior*, 1970, *5*, 1043–1051.

Vaughn, E., & Fisher, A. E. Male sexual behavior induced by intracranial electrical stimulation. *Science*, 1962, *137*, 758–760.

Ward, I. L. Prenatal stress feminizes and demasculinizes the behavior of males. *Science*, 1972, *175*, 82–84.

Whalen, R. E. Sexual motivation. *Psychological Review*, 1966, *73*, 151–163.

Whalen, R. E. (ed.). *Hormones and behavior*. New York: Van Nostrand Reinhold, 1967.

Whalen, R. E., & Nadler, R. D. Suppression of the development of female mating behavior by estrogen administered in infancy. *Science*, 1963, *141*, 273–274.

Wilson, J. R., Kuehn, R. E., & Beach, F. A. Modification in the sexual behavior of male rats produced by changing the stimulus female. *Journal of Comparative and Physiological Psychology*, 1963, *56*, 636–644.

Wynne–Edwards, V. C. Self–regulating systems in populations of animals. *Science*, 1965, *147*, 1543–1548.

Young, W. C., Goy, R. W., & Phoenix, C. H. Hormones and sexual behavoir. *Science*, 1964, *143*, 212–218.

Zasorin, N. L., Malsbury, C. W., & Pfaff, D. W. Suppression of lordosis in the hormone-primed female hamster by electrical stimulation of the septal area. *Physiology and Behavior*, 1975, *14*, 595–599.

Zemlan, F. P., Ward, I. L., Crowley, W. R., & Margules, D. L. Activation of lordotic dependency in female rats by suppression of seratogenic activity. *Science*, 1973, *179*, 1010–1011.

Zitrin, A., Jaynes, J., & Beach, F. A. Neural mediation of mating in male cats: III. Contributions of occipital, parietal and temporal cortex. *Journal of Comparative Neurology*, 1956, *105*, 111–125.

Zucker, I. Hormonal determinants of sex differences in saccharin preference, food intake, and body weight. *Physiology and Behavior*, 1969, *4*, 595–602.

11

Motivation: Implications of Brain Stimulation

For both the psychologist and the layperson, motivation is a key concept in understanding behavior. Behavior, whether of humans or animals, rarely seems aimless or random. The casual observer asks "why" or what is the "purpose" of a particular behavior? The psychologist is interested in the fact that behavior generally has apparent direction and goal orientation, as well as strength or force that energizes it. Each of the preceding chapters, piecemeal, has been concerned with factors that contribute to the apparent motivation of selected behaviors. In the present chapter, our concern will be with integrating these separate discussions and trying to arrive at a general statement about the concept of motivation based on current knowledge of physiological mechanisms.

In reviewing the material already presented, we see many instances of behavior that appear to result from the fact that the organism is simply "built" that way, i.e., genetic and instinctive mechanisms seem to guide or energize the behavior. In other instances, certain behaviors seem to be carried out because they result in the organism "enjoying" them—foods taste good, irrespective of their nutritional value, sex feels good, and exposure to a changing stimulus environment is somehow satisfying. In still other instances, behaviors appear to be designed to meet certain needs—deficits in essential materials are avoided or replenished. In a general way, then, the concept of motivation contains at least four considerations that require analysis:

1. The fact that behavior appears purposive and anticipatory
2. The pleasurable or hedonic aspects of motivation
3. The generality of the assumption that all motivations stem from bodily deficits
4. The physiological mechanisms that mediate motivation

Integrating these four considerations appeared to be possible with the discovery that electrical stimulation of selected areas of the brain could serve either as an aversive motivator (Delgado, Roberts, & Miller, 1954) or as a positive motivator (Olds & Milner, 1954) for the learning of responses. In the first instance, electrical stimulation could be substituted for painful, peripheral stimulation to produce learning; in the second instance, animals sought the opportunity to perform responses that resulted in electrical stimulation of the brain. We have also previously noted that electrical stimulation of the brain may elicit a variety of stimulus-bound behaviors, such as the complex motor patterns of eating, drinking, copulating, attacking, and gnawing, and that such behaviors seem to have motivational significance. Thus animals will perform a variety of instrumental behaviors, such as maze-running, in order to obtain an opportunity to perform these stimulus-bound acts. Electrical stimulation of selected brain areas can have either of two effects: It can motivate the performance of complex instrumental behavior or it can produce complex, species-typical behavior. In effect, it appears as if the stimulation activates essential neural mechanisms involved in the motivation and reinforcement of behavior. The properties of these mechanisms now can be more directly studied.

In addition, the material we have reviewed in the preceding chapters suggests a remarkable convergence on certain key structures and mechanisms. Hypothalamic, limbic, and brainstem mechanisms appeared again and again and certain transmitter systems were repeatedly implicated in the synaptic mechanisms employed in these structures. What does this convergence imply? That is, to what extent are there separate motivational systems and to what extent are they part of a unitary mechanism?

Our examination of the issues indicated above will start with a survey of the basic facts about the effects of electrical stimulation of the brain (ESB). The general focus of most of this research is concerned with the positive rewarding effects of ESB. We will then look at attempts to "dissect" the physiological substrate responsible for this rewarding effect. Finally, we shall examine the current status of theories designed to explain ESB reward.

What are the basic facts about the effects of electrical stimulation of the brain? Many issues require clarification: From which areas of the brain can these various effects be elicited? If ESB can act as a positive or negative reinforcer, what are its properties in these respects, i.e., are they the same or different from the more usual motivational and reinforcement manipulations of the experimental psychologist? What are the mechanisms through which ESB has these effects, i.e., are these mechanisms related to those of the more usual motivators and reinforcers? Basically, we will be asking whether ESB produces its effects because it stimulates the neural substrates for normal motivational and reward effects?

BASIC EFFECTS OF ESB

Description

Negative Reinforcement

Electrical stimulation of certain brain areas evokes a variety of pain and fearlike responses and flight reactions (see Chapter 7). Pain and fear elicited by external stimuli—electric shock to the feet, for example—can be used to motivate the learning and performance of specific responses. Such pain and fear can also be used to establish conditioned avoidance responses to specific stimuli or situations. They can be used to punish; and they can establish avoidance of food in hungry animals. The pain–fear (or alarm) responses elicited by diencephalic electrical stimulation are functionally equivalent in their effects to such responses elicited peripherally; i.e., the alarm reaction can be used in exactly the same manner as peripherally elicited pain and fear (Delgado et al., 1954; Miller, 1961). But stimulation of a limited area of the posterior hypothalamus elciting the flight response shows somewhat different properties.

Flight or escape motivation is similar to peripherally elicited pain and fear in that it will support the learning of responses instrumental in escape from the stimulation. Unlike peripherally elicited pain and fear, and unlike the alarm response, flight motivation does not support the learning of avoidance responses. Thus, cats stimulated in flight loci will not avoid such stimulation, although they will learn responses to escape it (Roberts, 1958a). That flight motivation supports escape but not avoidance learning is a paradoxical finding—other motivators that support escape learning, such as electric shock to the feet, generally will produce avoidance, too. Roberts (1958b) investigated this paradoxical effect by testing to see whether stimulation of such loci has both aversive and rewarding properties. He found that cats would indeed learn both to turn on and turn off such stimulation. He concluded that the onset of such stimulation was rewarding, and that it is only after this initial rewarding effect that the stimulation becomes aversive.

Recall also (Chapter 7) that a fearlike crouching response can be elicited from the dorsomedial thalamus and stimulation here will support both escape and avoidance learning (Roberts, 1962). There are, then, three kinds of responses elicitable with aversive brain stimulation: (1) a conditionable alarm reaction that probably involves stimulation of central pathways concerned with pain; (2) a fear reaction from the dorsomedial thalamus, also conditionable; and (3) a mixed type of response from the posterior hypothalamus which has both rewarding and punishing properties.

Positive Reinforcement

The basic findings of the Olds & Milner study (1954) can be summarized briefly: Rats with electrodes implanted in a variety of subcortical loci, but particularly in the septal area, worked at a bar-pressing task which resulted in electrical stimulation of these loci in much the same manner as animals work for conventional primary reinforcers like food and water. Such stimulation appeared to be rewarding in the sense that the rats actively sought the opportunity to produce the electrical stimulation.

This basic finding has been shown to hold for a range of animals, including the goldfish, rabbit, cat, monkey, and porpoise, as well as in humans. The effects of ESB on human subjects (Heath, 1963) have been observed exclusively in patients being operated on for a variety of physical or psychiatric disorders, which, of course, complicates the interpretation of the experimental results. Nonetheless stimulation in the septal area is reported as generally pleasurable and sexual in nature; it serves to arouse otherwise uncommunicative, catatonic patients, or to calm agitated, psychotic behavior. Stimulation in other areas is also generally pleasurable, although aversive and anxious feelings may be elicited in some locations.

Locus

Figure 11.1 is an early mapping of the locations from which ESB effects may be obtained. As can be seen, the areas center around the limbic, hypothalamic, and midbrain structures that we have found to be involved in the various separate motivational systems. And just as these separate systems have recently been shown to be related to catecholamine systems arising more caudally, in a like manner recent investigations have demonstrated that rewarding ESB effects can be obtained from these more caudal locations. Generally, the trend of research has been to follow the pathways depicted in Figures 8.13 and 8.14. An issue to which we will return later is whether rewarding ESB effects are dependent on the integrity of these pathways.

Figure 11.1 is a gross mapping in that it does not indicate the variability in strength of the rewarding effects that can be obtained throughout the areas involved. A rough index of the strength of reward is provided by the rate of response the animal uses to obtain the reward.

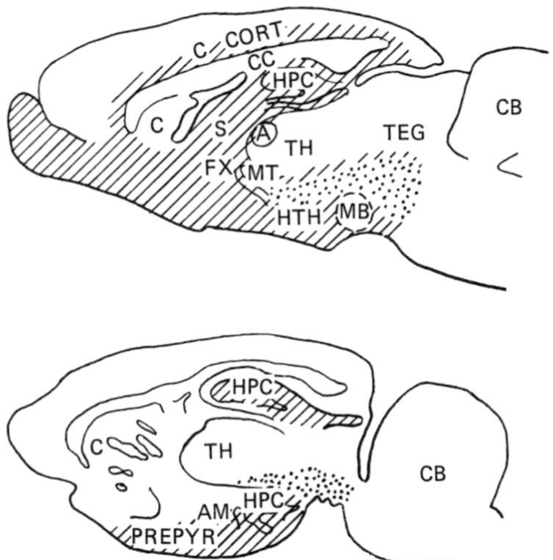

Figure 11.1. Medial and lateral sagittal sections of the rat brain showing, by cross-hatching, the areas where electric stimulation causes approach behavior and, by stippling, the areas where electric stimulation causes avoidance. *A*, anterior thalamus; *AM*, amygdala; *C*, caudate nucleus; *CB*, cerebellum; *CC*, corpus callosum; *C CORT*, cingulate cortex; *FX*, fornix; *HPC*, hippocampus; *HTH*, hypothalamus; *MB*, mammillary bodies; *MT*, mammillothalamic tract; *PREPYR*, prepyriform cortex; *S*, septal area; *TEG*, tegmentum; *TH*, thalamus. (From Olds, J., Self-stimulation of the brain. *Science*, Feb. 1958, *127*, 315–324.)

Rate of Response

In rats bar-pressing for ESB, the response rate may be as high as 7,000 responses per hour with electrodes in the medial forebrain bundle; rates of 300 to 1,000 responses per hour are usual with electrodes in the septal area. Such differences in the rate of response have been interpreted as an indicator that the medial forebrain bundle, particularly in its course through the hypothalamus, is a critical structure in producing the rewarding ESB effects.

Comparisons to Conventional Rewards

Consistency of Performance

Animals working for conventional reinforcers, such as food, demonstrate satiety with continued consummatory responses. Such satiation takes place relatively rapidly, particularly with regular reinforcement of instrumental responses. In contrast, animals with hypothalamic electrodes may bar-press for over 24 hours without showing any tendency to satiate. When exhausted, such animals sleep and then resume responding at the same high rate of response output. Animals with telencephalic electrodes, on the other hand, do show satiation effects; they reduce their response output after 4 to 6 hours (Olds, 1958a).

Early reports of ESB effects emphasized that while bar-pressing rates might be quite high compared to those obtained with conventional reinforcers, extinction was much more rapid. Furthermore, performance under partial reinforcement, as with ratio or interval schedules, was poorer; similarly, secondary reinforcement effects seemed more difficult to obtain, and maze performance under distributed practice was poorer. These early reports tended to emphasize differences between ESB and conventional reinforcers. However, later studies have tended to emphasize a more consistent performance under ESB reinforcement. Obviously, there exists considerable variation in performance, dependent on a multiplicity of factors.

For instance, a series of studies dealt with the effects of spaced versus massed trials. Seward, Uyeda, and Olds (1960) found that runway performance of rats receiving ESB in well-spaced trials did not improve within sessions but did if stimulation trials were closely massed. On the other hand, Scott (1967) found that with hypothalamic stimulation, rats ran well with spaced trials and there was no overnight performance decrement; but this was not true of rats given septal ESB.

Results with intermittent ESB were contrasted to the effects of conventional reinforcers on intermittent schedules. Within the same experiment, fixed ratio performance of different monkeys was limited to a low of 10 responses per reinforcement and to a high of 150 (Brodie, Moreno, Malis, & Boren, 1960). Conventional reinforcers show greater uniformity of results and generally higher performance levels. Extinction performance with ESB was similarly variable—some monkeys ceased responding after less than 100 responses while one gave over 9,000 responses. On the other hand, Keesey (1964) demonstrated that delay of reinforcement resulted in a performance gradient quite comparable to that generated under delay of food reinforcement.

We have noted that while responding for ESB may be quite strong, extinction is comparatively rapid. After such extinction, however, responding may be rapidly reinstated by "priming" the animal. That is, upon one or more ESBs delivered "for free" (noncontingently), the animal will generally start bar pressing again. Such noncontingent reinforcements seem to have a motivating effect whose theoretical significance will be discussed later.

Strength of Reward

The high response rates that are obtainable with ESB reward suggest that such rewards are strong. This is also indicated by tests pitting ESB against conventional reinforcers. For instance, rats were trained to obtain their entire ration of food in a limited session. When allowed a limited period in which to choose between ESB and food, these rats often chose ESB and neglected the food to the extent of starving (Spies, 1965; Routtenberg & Lindy, 1965). But note that animals given long-term access to both food and ESB can regulate their behavior so as to maintain appropriate food intake; in the short term, then, rats apparently do not have sufficient foresight to be able to do this.

In a provocative experiment, Gibson, Reid, Sakai, and Porter (1965) compared the inherent delay involved in obtaining conventional reinforcement (e.g., bar pressing for food) with the immediacy of ESB reinforcement. Gibson and his colleagues attempted to eliminate these differences. Two kinds of reinforcement groups were established—ESB and sugar water. These groups were further subdivided into direct and contingent response groups: Direct groups received immediate ESB or sugar water for simply contacting a dipper mechanism; contingent groups were required first to press a bar in order to activate the dipper mechanism. Comparisons were made between the groups for their response rate under regular reinforcement and under fixed ratio performance; they were also tested for resistance to extinction. In no case did performance differ as a function of the type of reinforcement. On the other hand, results typically attributed to differences between ESB and conventional rewards were produced here as a function of response type; that is, contingent responses resulted in slower response rates and greater resistance to extinction than direct responses. Thus, immediacy of reward, rather than the nature of the reward, appears to account for some differences between conventional reinforcers and ESB.

Interaction of ESB With Drive States

We have noted on several occasions that stimulation of hypothalamic loci may result in the elicitation of stimulus-bound behavior. Furthermore, Margules and Olds (1962) found that all hypothalamic placements that elicited eating behavior in their rats also supported high rates of self-stimulation. Conversely, only 4 of 18 rats that did not eat in response to stimulation engaged in self-stimulation. These effects, coupled with the known involvement of the hypothalamus in control of the various motivational systems, suggest that ESB reward effects are somehow related to the control of naturally occurring motivational states. If ESB involves neural mechanisms concerned with the control of hunger, variations in hunger should affect performance for ESB reward. Similarly, variations in hormonal levels should affect performance if ESB involves mechanisms mediating sexual responses. And, finally, if hunger and sexual motivation are independent of each other, the effects of manipulation of these systems should show independent effects on the performance for ESB. Considerations such as these have been important for those who maintain that ESB operates through the arousal of normal motivational mechanisms.

An early test of these predictions was carried out by Olds (1958c). Male rats were tested for bar pressing with ESB reward under alternate hunger and satiation and high and low androgen levels. Electrodes positively sensitive to androgen levels tended to be insensitive or inversely sensitive to hunger manipulations and vice versa. On the basis of these findings, Olds suggested that there are anatomically distinct hunger-reward and sexual-reward systems.

Hoebel has been particularly concerned with experiments that demonstrate a relationship between manipulations affecting normal motivational mechanisms and changes in instrumental responding for ESB (Hoebel, 1975). For example, a number of factors that increase eating behavior also increase self-stimulation for ESB, among others food deprivation, insulin diabetes, sweet tastes, and isotonic or hypotonic solutions. Conversely, factors that decrease food consumption, including stomach distension, glucose, antidiabetics, and excess body weight, reduce such self-stimulation. In addition, lesions affecting food intake show at least limited equivalent effects on stimulation for ESB. These results have encouraged Hoebel to propose a feeding reward–aversion theory, which maintains that hypothalamic reward (similar to the ESB effect) is involved in the reward of eating when the animal requires food, and hypothalamic aversion (similar to the ESB effect) results from satiation.

It should also be noted that those ESB parameters which elicit either self-stimulation or eating may be different. Ball (1969) found that longer durations of ESB were required for eating to occur and, when allowed to express a preference, rats chose short-duration ESB that supported bar pressing. Ball interpreted the results to indicate that the reinforcing effect of ESB is short-lived, decaying with continued stimulation, while longer duration ESB arouses the hunger drive.

Generally, results such as these are interpreted to indicate that the reward effects of ESB operate on mechanisms that control naturally occurring motivational states. There is also the suggestion that these naturally occurring states are controlled by systems that are separate and distinct from each other. We shall return to this issue again, but now we will examine some problems in interpreting the results of ESB.

PROBLEMS IN ESB INTERPRETATION

Mixed Positive-Negative Effects

That an animal turns on ESB certainly suggests that the ESB has positive rewarding effects. Does turning off the ESB necessarily indicate that the stimulation is aversive? A number of studies (Roberts, 1958; Bower & Miller,

1958; Brown & Cohen, 1959) have found that animals will both turn on and turn off ESB in specific electrode locations. Bower and Miller, as well as Stein (1962), have shown that in such situations animals will regulate the duration of ESB. Thus, if current levels are manipulated, rats will turn off the ESB sooner at higher current levels. Generally, it appeared that the tendency both to turn on and to turn off ESB was dependent on a mixture of rewarding and aversive effects.

But this interpretation has been challenged by other experiments. Valenstein and Valenstein (1964) found that repetitive turning on and off of rewarding ESB is not a special property of restricted stimulation sites, nor was it associated with sites implicated in aversive effects. Most importantly, they found that while ESB was more readily terminated when its intensity was higher, it was also more readily *turned on again* with these higher intensities. This behavior would not be expected if shutoff was produced by aversive effects of the stimulation. Similar repetitive turning on and off of environmental stimuli is characteristic of animals when the stimuli are under their control.

Steiner, Beer, and Shaffer (1969) suggested that the subject's opportunity to control its own rate of stimulation may be an important factor in these results. In their experiment, rats were first allowed to demonstrate stable self-stimulation. The exact temporal patterning of such self-stimulation was then recorded on tape, and the tape was subsequently used to initiate ESB. Under this tape-initiated stimulation, the rats readily learned to terminate ESB. They also learned to terminate ESB delivered in a regular pattern at the same average rate as their recorded, irregular pattern of self-stimulation. Termination latency was shorter under these conditions. Termination was not maintained for experimenter-initiated ESB presented at one-half the self-stimulation rate, but it was maintained with shorter latencies when ESB was presented at twice the self-stimulation rate. Since ESB may induce both overt and covert seizure activity (Porter, Conrad, & Brady, 1959), Steiner et al. suggested that the temporal patterning at which subjects self-stimulate may reflect the self-regulation of subconvulsive electrical discharge.

But the above should not be interpreted to indicate that there are not aversive systems. There are both positive and negative systems within the brain and these can exhibit interactions. Valenstein (1965) showed that an animal's response to overlapping stimulation of an aversive and a positive location depended on which stimulus was initiated first; thus the first stimulus determined whether the animal behaved as if the combination were either entirely positive or entirely aversive.

We can be sure that self-stimulatory behavior indicates that the stimulus is reinforcing, but termination of ESB does not necessarily indicate that the stimulation is aversive.

Response Rate

Research on ESB effects has overwhelmingly employed the operant techniques of the Skinner box, and rate of response has been the primary measure for the assessment of reinforcement with ESB. However, response rate may be a misleading index of reinforcement value; animals will often select ESB intensities or electrode placements that support lower response rates (Hodos & Valenstein, 1962). Competition tests, pitting ESB against other reinforcers, such as water or shock avoidance, indicate that rats will frequently continue to choose higher intensities of ESB over the competitor, even though such intensities support lower response rates (Valenstein & Beer, 1962).

Results such as these suggest that the drop in response rate commonly observed with higher intensities of ESB is not due to a lesser reinforcement value but rather to side effects, such as the elicitation of motor responses incompatible with continued high rates of response output. Another factor here is the possible persistence of effects from one ESB to the next. Thus, there may be carry-over effects with high-intensity ESB, and these may lead to a lower response output. Similarly, in regard to apparently mixed positive and negative effects of ESB, it may be that stimulation at these loci is not intrinsically aversive; rather, it is only stimulation at high rates that is avoided. Without a more complete understanding of these effects, interpretation on the basis of the rate of response is quite dubious. Generally, choice measures would seem preferable to rate measures as they allow assessment of *relative* strength.

PHYSIOLOGICAL SUBSTRATES OF POSITIVE REINFORCEMENT

Figure 11.1 generally indicates the loci from which ESB effects can be obtained. Can we more precisely delimit nuclear groups or pathways within these loci that are essential for the effects?

Primacy of the Medial Forebrain Bundle

We have previously mentioned that the highest sustained rates of self-stimulatory responses for ESB are obtained from electrodes in and around the medial forebrain bundle. This suggests that it may be critical to the ESB effect. It should be noted that the medial forebrain bundle is a heterogeneous collection of fibers coursing through the lateral hypothalamus; ascending and descending connections between the mid- and forebrain are represented here; its fibers contain both dopaminergic and adrenergic transmitters. Thus, the first attempts at localization of the rewarding ESB effect were gross in that they simply interrupted this total complex.

In a study by Olds and Olds (1965), electrodes were placed in both anterior and posterior portions of the medial forebrain bundle in the hypothalamus of rats. Both electrodes yielded self-stimulation behavior in each animal. Following tests for self-stimulation, bilateral lesions were placed at either the anterior or posterior site, and tests were continued for self-stimulation at the other site. Anterior lesions produced only a temporary loss of self-stimulation which subsequently recovered to approximately preoperative levels. Posterior lesions, on the other hand, resulted in a sustained decrement in self-stimulation. These results suggest that caudal conduction through the medial forebrain bundle is necessary to obtain self-stimulation.

Two other extensive studies, however, have failed to confirm this finding that the medial forebrain bundle is essential for self-stimulation. Valenstein (1966) studied the effects of medial forebrain bundle lesions through the anterior-posterior extent of the hypothalamus on septal self-stimulation. Given appropriate recovery from surgery, which often was markedly debilitating, these animals performed comparably to control animals receiving septal ESB. Lorens (1966) presented complementary findings for self-stimulation based on lateral hypothalamic electrodes. Both of these studies and the study of Keesey and Powley (1968) indicate, however, that while self-stimulation may not be abolished by lesions, there may be changes in the characteristics of the behavior. Thus, Keesey and Powley found that the thresholds for lateral hypothalamic reward were lowered by septal lesions in the rat. Lesions at other locations (see Asdourian, Stutz, & Rocklin, 1966; Valenstein, 1966) have similarly failed to locate any site that could be considered critical to the maintenance of self-stimulatory behavior. These results would seem consistent with the notion that such behavior is dependent on one or more diffusely located systems.

More recently, however, Szabó (1973 has suggested that these lesion studies may not be definitive. If the medial forebrain bundle were simply a bundle of long fibers, transecting it would be a legitimate test of its role in self-stimulation. But Szabó, arguing from anatomical and electrophysiological evidence, suggests that it consists of fibers with reverberatory connections (circular and recurrent) in the hypothalamus; he hypothesizes that it is just these characteristics that may be required for the rewarding effects of ESB. If such is the case, transecting the pathway would not affect the reward system in an appreciable manner.

Norepinephrine Theory of ESB Reward

Biochemical approaches may also have something to offer in disentangling the complex anatomy of the reward substrate. A large number of studies have shown that the rewarding effects of ESB can be modified by drugs that affect catecholamines. For some time there was the widespread assumption that the relevant amine is norepinephrine. Stein (1975) has reviewed much of this work.

Generally, drugs that cause the release of catecholamines from functional storage facilitate self-stimulation. Drugs that deplete catecholamine stores or inhibit its synthesis or those that block catecholamine receptors suppress self-stimulation. More specifically, however, drugs that block the synthesis of norepinephrine from dopamine have been shown to abolish self-stimulation. Intraventricular injection of norepinephrine after such blockage restored self-stimulation. Also, recall that norepinephrine has alpha and beta type receptors; the reward effects appear to depend on the presence of alpha receptors, because blockers of alpha activity reduce self-stimulation but blockers of beta action do not. Good self-stimulatory behavior has also been found in the caudal sites of origin of the norepinephrine-containing neurons (see Figure 8.13).

One of the problems associated with a norepinephrine theory of reward is the relative nonspecificity of the experimental manipulations. For instance, drugs that interfere with norepinephrine may have side effects on arousal. Rolls, Kelly, and Shaw (1974) showed that a blocker of norepinephrine receptors and a blocker of norepinephrine synthesis both produced sedative effects. On the other hand, self-stimulation was attenuated by a blocker of dopamine receptors that produced only minor sedation. Such results certainly suggest that dopamine plays a role in self-stimulation. These data should not be construed, however, to mean that norepinephrine has no direct effect.

A second problem associated with the norepinephrine theory is that drugs which affect norepinephrine generally have relatedly low pharmacological specificity. That is, dopamine may also be affected to at least some degree. A number of studies suggest that dopamine is actually very important in the ESB reward effect.

Dopamine Theory of ESB Reward

Lippa, Antelman, Fisher, and Canfield (1973) provided one example of the attempts to separate norepinephrine and dopamine effects on ESB. 6-Hydroxydopamine (6-OHDA) is a drug which, when injected intraventricularly, depletes the brain of catecholamines. The effect is more severe on norepinphrine than dopamine, however. Lippa et al. used this drug in combination with other, presumably more selective drugs. Thus, animals were first given 6-OHDA injections; bar-pressing for ESB was initially markedly impaired but the animals subsequently showed recovery of self-stimulation. After recovery, additional attempts to block norepinephrine were made by administering an alpha adrenergic blocker. The additional treatment did not appreciably affect the animals' self-stimulation. In normal animals, injection of the alpha blocker did not impair self-stimulation, while injection of a dopamine receptor blocker reduced self-stimulation by more than 50 percent.

Neill, Parker, and Gold (1975) attempted to interfere with the anterior projections of the dopamine system by local placements of 6-OHDA. The animals were tested for lateral hypothalamic self-stimulation and showed marked decrements. Animals with 6-OHDA placed in the septum did not show a deficit. Injection of crystalline dopamine into the sites previously showing the effects of 6-OHDA restored self-stimulation.

Though not a study of ESB reward, we might also note an interesting approach to the dopamine theory employed by Yokel and Wise (1975). Rats will press a bar in order to obtain intravenous injections of amphetamines. If the dose per injection is reduced, however, the bar-pressing rate increases—analogous to the effect of increasing the number of responses required in a fixed ratio schedule. This suggests that nonspecific deficits in bar pressing can be dissociated from any changes in the rewarding properties of amphetamine. Nonspecific changes would normally be expected to reduce bar pressing while reductions in reward value should increase bar pressing. Generally interfering with catecholamine synthesis causes an increase in bar pressing for amphetamine. In this experiment, specifically blocking dopamine receptors produced marked elevations in bar pressing for amphetamine while alpha and beta noradrenaline blockers produced some depression of bar pressing, implicating dopamine in the reward effect.

Norepinephrine Reward and Dopamine Motivation?

The above evidence suggests that both norepinephrine and dopamine are involved in the ESB self-stimulation effect. Can their respective roles be resolved? As we shall presently see, several theorists have suggested that ESB self-stimulation elicits two separable processes. One of these mediates the rewarding aspect of the stimulation while the other mediates a motivational effect. Thus, ESB is conceived both to arouse the animal and to reinforce prior responses. On the assumption that both norepinephrine and dopamine are required for ESB effects, Herberg, Stephens, and Franklin (1976) hypothesized that drugs most effective in influencing stimulation at a particular brain site would be those acting on receptors of the transmitter system *less* strongly stimulated by the ESB. Thus, self-stimulation from a noradrenergic locus should be particularly sensitive to drug-induced manipulation of the dopamine system and vice versa. Figure 11.2 illustrates their model for this process. In part (a) of the figure, an electrode is situated in a hypothetical pure adrenergic structure. Adequate response-contingent reinforcement is generated by the ESB but the response rate is dependent on the level of dopaminergic activity resulting from the ESB via efferent, tran-

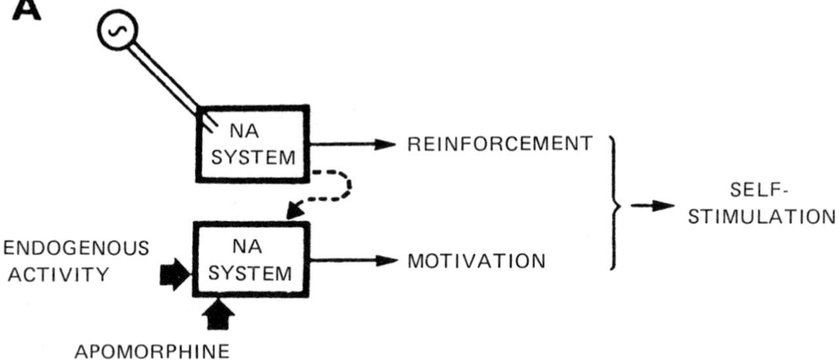

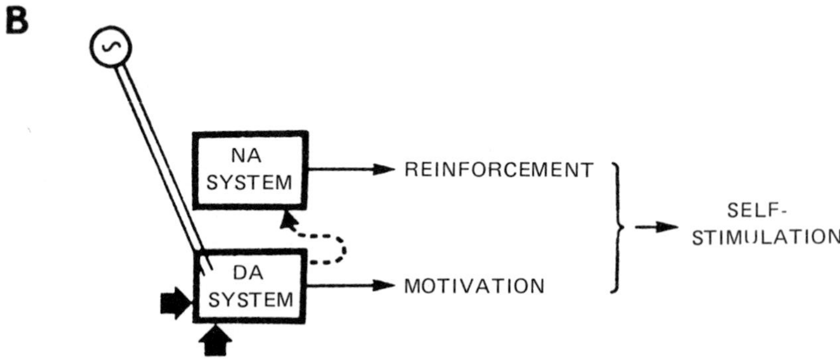

Figure 11.2. (a) Self-stimulation of a pure noradrenergic structure. Adequate response-contingent reinforcement is generated by the electrodes, and the rate-limiting factor is thus level of dopaminergic activity derived either from the stimulating electrodes via a transynaptic NA-to-DA route (broken line), or from endogenous motivational processes, and augmented in the present instance by apomorphine. (b) Self-stimulation of a purely dopaminergic structure. Adequate dopaminergic activity is elicited by the stimulating current, and the rate-limiting factor is thus the level of noradrenergic response-contingent reinforcement, derived transynaptically from dopaminergic pathways. Randomization of dopaminergic activity by apomorphine would disrupt the response contingency of the reinforcing signals and suppress self-stimulation. (From Herberg, L. J., Stephens, D. N., Franklin, K. B. J. Catecholamines and self-stimulation: Evidence suggesting a reinforcing role for noradrenaline and a motivating role for dopamine. *Pharmacology, Biochemistry and Behavior,* 1976, *4,* 575–582.)

synaptic pathways. The application of drugs (here, apomorphine) that stimulate the dopaminergic system, or endogenous drive processes (such as hunger), add to the motivational component. In part (b) of the figure, an electrode is situated in a hypothetical pure dopaminergic locus. Adequate motivation results from the ESB but the response is dependent on the level of noradrenergic response-contingent reinforcement derived transynaptically. Note that increasing the output of the dopamine system with apomorphine results in randomization of such transynaptic activity with respect to the instrumental responses, and should disrupt self-stimulation. This is exactly what Herberg et al. observed. On the other hand, drugs that either directly stimulated or blocked alpha adrenergic receptors generally depressed self-stimulation but had greater effects on electrodes located in predominantly dopaminergic loci, again, as expected if output of the dopamine system depends on activity in the norepinephrine system for reinforcement.

This model, then, assumes that both dopamine and norepinephrine are involved in the ESB effect and equates norepinephrine with a rewarding component and dopamine with drive or motivational component.[1] Electrodes in areas such as the medial forebrain bundle would probably stimulate both components and, therefore, would give results intermediate between the extremes of the model. The model appears worthy of consideration.

THEORIES OF ESB EFFECTS

Many researchers have attempted to formulate a theoretical basis for the effects of ESB. Some of these have aimed at a comprehensive theory but all generally focus on particular aspects of the ESB phenomenon. A major consideration is the fact that ESB can serve as a reinforcer and can also elicit stimulus-bound behavior.

Hedonistic Dual Mechanism

Olds' (1961, 1969; Olds and Olds, 1965) approach tends to be largely descriptive. He interprets the ESB results to indicate that there are two separate systems in the brain that can be activated by ESB. One of these gives rise to pleasurable sensations that experimental animals learn to maximize; the other gives rise to aversive sensations which animals learn to minimize. From a less descriptive and more theoretical standpoint, Olds (1969) has indicated how these two systems might be arranged so as to give either pleasurable, aversive, or mixed effects. Figure 11.3 diagrams the basic conception. The hypothalamus serves as the integration center for three systems: (1) Fibers originating in the limbic cortex, the medial forebrain bundle, yield pure positive reinforcement when stimulated. (2) Fibers of a periventricular system, originating in the hypothalamus, yield pure negative reinforcement when stimulated; periventricular fibers are inhibited by the medial forebrain bundle. (3) Another set of fibers originates in the hypothalamus and yields positive reinforcement; it, in turn, is inhibited by the periventricular system. This third set of fibers appears to be a final

[1]In regard to aversive effects of ESB, a number of experiments suggest that acetylcholine and serotonin may be involved. Serotonin seems to act in a system that mitigates the effects of aversive stimulation (see Leroux & Myers, 1975).

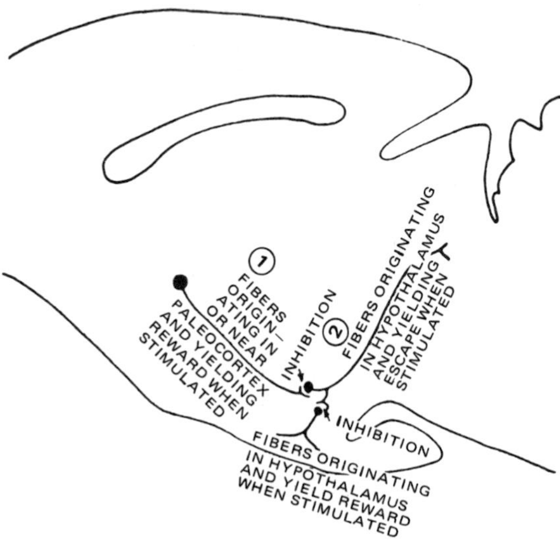

Figure 11.3. Hypothalamic reward system according to Olds. Fibers of the medial forebrain dundle, *1,* from the paleocortex, inhibit neurons of the periventricular system, *2,* which project toward the reticular system, *2* gives off collaterals which inhibit a group of neurons originating in the hypothalamus, whose axons travel in the medial forebrain bundle, side by side with those coming down from the paleocortex. These axons might carry integrated motivational messages—with positive reinforcements added and negative reinforcements subtracted—toward behavioral control mechanisms. (From Olds, J., The central nervous system and the reinforcement of behavior. *American Psychologist,* 1969, *24,* 114–132. Copyright by the American Psychological Association. Reprinted by permission.)

common pathway for both reward and punishment, reward being an active excitatory process and punishment an inhibitory process. Stimulation of hypothalamic areas where the reward and punishment systems meet yields the mixed positive-negative effects that have been of so much concern.

Simultaneous Motivation and Reinforcement

Like Olds, Deutsch advocates a dual mechanism model of ESB effects (e.g., Deutsch & Howarth, 1963). However, instead of pleasure and aversion, Deutsch argues that the two mechanisms are motivation and reward mechanisms. In the absence of ESB, motivational levels are low; each response resulting in ESB both reinforces that response and adds an increment to the motivational system. Thus, ESB simultaneously rewards the preceding response and raises the motivation for the next response. The peculiarly rapid extinction of self-stimulatory behavior results, then, from the decay of drive with the absence of ESB. Similarly, performance under massed and spaced trials favors massed procedures because of the lessened drive decay between trials.

Deutsch and Howarth (1963) presented the results of a series of experiments testing various deductions from this theory. In one such experiment (Howarth & Deutsch, 1962), it was hypothesized that extinction should be a function of the time since withdrawal of ESB rather than the number of responses. To test the hypothesis, during extinction the response lever was withdrawn from the Skinner box for varying time periods, then replaced so that normal extinction could continue. It was found that trials to extinction was a decreasing function of the period of time the lever was unavailable; if the lever was withdrawn for a longer period, fewer responses were made before the criterion of extinction was reached, suggesting that the passage of time allowed the motivation to dissipate.

Since response measures, such as rate of response and numbers of responses to extinction, are potentially confounded with the general activity level of the animal, it would be desirable to have a test of the drive decay hypothesis which is independent of such activity effects. Figure 11.4 presents the results of an experiment attempting to do this (Deutsch & Howarth, 1963). Rats were trained to find water on one side of a T-maze and ESB on the other. They were then given the opportunity to choose between these reinforcers under varying degrees of water deprivation and time since last ESB. It can be seen that the probability of choosing ESB decreased as a function of both the conflicting thirst and the time since last ESB.

Deutsch's notion of drive decay has not received unequivocal support. A number of experiments (see Stutz, Lewin, & Rocklin, 1965; Herberg,

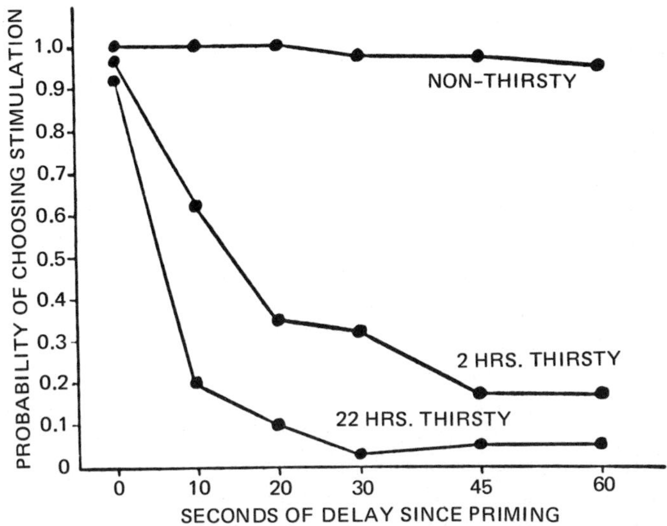

Figure 11.4. Probability of choice of brain stimulation as a function of delay since the last brain stimulus and competing drive. (From Deutsch, J. A. and Howorth, C. I., Some tests of theory of intracranial self-stimulation. *Psychological Review*, 1963, *70*, 444–460. Copyright 1963 by the American Psychological Association. Reprinted by permission.)

1963; Pliskoff & Hawkins, 1963) suggest that while drive decay may be of some consequence, its adequacy as a sole explanatory principle is suspect. Thus, Pliskoff and Hawkins replicated the Howarth and Deutsch (1962) experiment on lever withdrawal in extinction with one group of animals, but they found that a second group which had had training experience with periodic lever withdrawal showed increased resistance to extinction. Similarly, Stutz et al. showed that rats could be trained to wait for periods up to 20 minutes between short bouts of self-stimulation without showing any decrement in initiating their responses. Herberg's results suggest that training procedures with ESB that involve multiple experiences of training and extinction cycles facilitate the formation of a discrimination between training and extinction and thus give rise to the rapid extinction. Thus, these studies point to the importance of the conditions of training, as well as any possible effects of drive decay in producing rapid extinction.

It is also of interest that in an experiment purporting to support the drive decay hypothesis, Quartermain and Webster (1968) found results suggesting "that resistance to extinction after intracranial reinforcement is primarily a function of activity level." The Deutsch and Howarth experiment (1963) discussed above and presented in Figure 11.4 was designed to avoid such a conclusion!

Deutsch's hypothesis—that ESB reward functions by stimulating both motivational and reinforcement mechanisms simultaneously—was designed to explain two ways in which ESB supposedly differs from conventional reinforcers. Reinforcement with ESB shows little tendency to satiation, and instrumental responses show rapid extinction after ESB reinforcement. Neither Deutsch's experiments nor those cited in opposition have any bearing on the satiation issue. ESB probably does stimulate both reward and drive mechanisms, but it is doubtful, in view of the immediately preceding discussion and our prior survey of the differences between ESB and conventional reinforcers, that drive decay is the sole factor accounting for extinction differences. It is much more likely that the effects that have been reported also involve a complex function of differences in electrode placement (and consequent differences in strength of reward), training procedures, and relative delays of reward.

Deutsch's theory suggests that ESB stimulates two different neural systems. Another test of that theory, then, would be to demonstrate that the characteristics of the two neural substrates are in fact different. Gallistel (1975) has summarized a series of experiments devoted to this question. Some of these experiments have been designed to provide behavioral tests of the absolute refractory periods (see Chapter 1) of the neurons in the two systems. For example, if ESB is given with a certain set of stimulus parameters, adding extra stimulus pulses very shortly after each pulse in the ESB train should not be effective in changing the animal's responses *if* the additional pulses fall within the absolute refractory period produced by the individual pulses of the basic ESB train. On the other hand, if the additional pulses fall outside the absolute refractory period, they could be expected to add either to the reward or to the motivational properties of the ESB. Generally, experiments designed to test these notions (see Gallistel, 1975), have confirmed such hypotheses. The animals are tested in a situation in which they receive an initial priming stimulus following which they may bar-press for additional ESB. Either the priming ESB or the ESB resulting from bar-pressing is manipulated. The changes resulting from manipulation of the priming ESB are considered motivational and those resulting from manipulation of bar-pressing ESB are considered reinforcement effects. Neurons mediating the motivational effect of ESB seem to have an absolute refractory period of about 1.0 msec, while neurons mediating the rewarding effects of ESB seem to have a refractory period of about .5 msec. Thus, different populations of neurons are inferred to underlie the two effects of ESB.

Previously mentioned experiments on the transmitter systems involved in the ESB effect might also be in accord with Deutsch's theory. Recall that Herberg et al. (1976) equated dopamine with the motivational system and norepinephrine with the reward system. In addition, it might be noted that self-stimulation has been described as difficult to obtain or as "unenthusiastic" from electrodes in the locus coeruleus, one origin of norepinephrine fibers. This would be compatible with the assumption that ESB here principally has reward and not motivational effects. Strong ESB effects would be expected from mixed loci, such as the medial forebrain bundle–lateral hypothalamic area.

Drive-Reduction Theory

At first blush, the empirical facts about ESB would seem to discredit any hypothesis that reinforcement depends on the reduction of drive or need: Electrical stimulation can hardly be considered to satisfy any biological needs; it is the onset, not the offset, of positively reinforcing ESB which appears to be rewarding. Then, too, electrodes yielding positive reinforcement effects may also elicit stimulus-bound behavior; that is, seem to make the animal hungry or thirsty. However, it is conceivable that ESB operates in part to activate neural mechanisms that are normally active during drive reduction. Thus a number of theories are based on the assumption that ESB could activate inhibitory circuits to reduce drives.

Both Routtenberg and Lindy (1965) and Spies (1965) suggested that one interpretation of the self-starvation produced in rats working for ESB is that ESB operates through normal food regulating mechanisms, in effect, to produce an artificial drive reduction. Stutz, Rossi, and Bowring (1971) and

Rossi (1969) tested some implications of this hypothesis. If ESB serves as a substitute for food, ESB administered *noncontingently* by the experimenter should also serve to reduce food intake in self-depriving animals working for food. Also, food and water intake might be expected to be differentially affected by different electrode placements. These investigators found that animals would self-deprive themselves of food or water if either were placed in competition with responding for ESB. Animals self-depriving for water also self-deprived for food. Noncontingent ESB did not reduce either food or water intake, and the self-deprivation effect was not limited to ESB delivered to sites known to be involved in food and water regulation. Whether self-deprivation occurred seemed to be related to the strength of reward elicited by the ESB; that is, self-deprivers showed higher bar-pressing rates than nondeprivers. Generally, then, these results were interpreted as supporting a hedonistic rather than a drive-reduction theory; i.e., animals self-deprive because they prefer ESB to other rewards.

While experiments such as these would seem to rule out a strict drive-reduction interpretation of rewarding ESB effects, it is not clear what their implications are for some of the modified forms of the hypothesis that have been proposed. Without pursuing the details, a number of workers have presented modifications of the drive-reduction hypothesis (e.g., Miller, 1963; Grastyán, Karmos, Vereczkey, & Kellenyi, 1966). Szabó (1973) has suggested that the reverberatory possibilities of medial forebrain bundle anatomy are such that they could support such reinterpretations. At this point, one would have to conclude that while drive-reduction interpretations of the ESB effect seem less plausible, the evidence available does not seem to rule them out completely.

Incentive Theory

Historically, psychological theories of motivation have depended heavily of the notion of "drive," which views motivation as a response to signals deriving from deficit states in the organism. Our reviews of hunger and thirst mechanisms were also similarly oriented. However, it is also apparent that much of the behavior of animals, particularly those with more highly developed brains, does not depend on biological deficits. Such animals show play, curiosity, exploratory behavior, strong manipulatory needs, and a requirement for varied sensory input. Thus, much motivated behavior is initiated by external stimuli and cognitive processes. As a result, the concept of incentive motivation—responses energized by the "pull" or anticipation of stimuli rather than the "push" of internal, deficit signals—has become prominent. In addition, incentive motivation emphasizes the anticipatory and purposive aspects of biological needs. One approach to the effects of ESB has thus been to suggest that ESB operates on incentive mechanisms (e.g., Trowill, Panksepp, & Gandelman, 1969).

The fact that ESB is both reinforcing and capable of eliciting eating or drinking is paradoxical to drive theorists. But feeding or drinking elicited by ESB may result from activation of neural systems involved in the transmission of incentive stimuli—"appetite-whetting" stimuli. Incentive approaches to ESB suggest that apparent differences between normal motivational mechanisms and ESB, such as rapid extinction and difficulties with partial reinforcement and secondary reinforcement, can be attributed to variation in the relative delays of reinforcement and the deprivation state of the animal. Under low deficit conditions, as usually pertain in ESB experiments, ESB and conventional reinforcers show similar rather than different effects (Trowill et al., 1969).

Incentive stimuli acquire their properties through association with biologically significant stimuli—e.g., environmental cues associated with food. Thus, the concept of incentive motivation depends heavily on learning and memory. We will discuss the mechanisms of learning and memory later (Chapter 12) but here we might note that a number of experiments allude to the critical nature of the neural mechanisms mediating ESB effects for memory (see Routtenberg, 1975, for a review). The link between the norepinephrine and dopamine systems indicated in Figure 11.2 might be crucial to such learning and to incentive formulations of the ESB effect.

Preformed Motor Patterns Theory

The fact the ESB can produce stimulus-bound behavior is a cardinal feature of another approach to explaining ESB effects. Glickman and Schiff (1967) reviewed a large body of material and developed the view that complex species-typical motor patterns, including their sequential characteristics, are organized in a preformed state within the brainstem. Reinforcement consists of activation of these brainstem mechanisms for species-typical behavior.

Glickman and Schiff suggest an evolutionary development of the reinforcement mechanism. In primitive vertebrates, a reinforcing stimulus, such as food, served to initiate, guide, and maintain consummatory activity rather than to reinforce any prior chain of operant behavior. The subsequent evolution of the mammalian brain involved the development of pathways permitting those parts of the brain providing greater behavioral plasticity to interact with the more primitive motor mechanisms. "We visualize sets of parallel neural pathways regulating species-typical response patterns. It is the activation of these independent paths, by whatever means, which constitutes what is conventionally described as reinforcement. Those stimuli which are uniquely capable of reliably activating primitive approach or withdrawal sequences would be especially potent reinforcing agents. The learning of new responses would take place by contiguity" (Glickman & Schiff, 1967, p. 85).

This theory is very similar to the fixed action pattern of the ethologists and also to Roberts' work on attack and gnawing elicited by hypothalamic stimulation (see Chapter 3). In fact, Glickman and Schiff draw heavily on two experimental facts: (1) that the opportunity to engage in stimulus-bound behavior is reinforcing (as demonstrated by Roberts [Roberts & Carey, 1965; Roberts & Kiess, 1964]) and (2) that stimulus-bound behavior is elicited from areas supporting self-stimulation behavior. The paradox that stimulation which elicits eating (and arouses hunger?) also is *reinforcing* is avoided if activation of the neural mechanisms controlling responses constitutes reinforcement.

Summary

The several theories of the operation of ESB reinforcement effects that we have reviewed are not necessarily mutually exclusive. In fact, one of the problems here is that the empirical facts about ESB seem to be largely compatible, at least in large part, with all of them. In addition, the known physiological substrate mediating the ESB effect does not seem to preclude the possibility of any of these theories. Thus, for the moment at least, we cannot draw any definitive conclusions about the probable mechanisms of ESB reinforcement. Generally, however, it is the case that all of these theories assume that the ESB reinforcement effect operates through normal motivational mechanisms. Questioning this assumption provides an alternative approach to the analysis of the ESB effect. That is, does ESB evoke (a) specific and (b) normal motivational states?

ESB AND SPECIFIC MOTIVATIONAL STATES

The Specificity of the ESB Effect

How specific are the motivational effects of ESB? This question really contains two parts which are not necessarily related. One of these focuses on the properties of ESB and the other on the mechanisms. That is, if ESB reward is elicited from two different brain locations, are they perceptually different? And, are there discrete, genetically fixed, neural circuits which mediate ESB effects?

Discriminability of ESB Rewards

Animals readily discriminate naturally occurring motivational states by performing different responses in order to obtain different reinforcements. If ESB operates through normal motivational mechanisms, it would be expected that animals can discriminate ESB in different rewarding sites. Several experiments have been directed at this issue. Stutz (1968; Stutz,

Butcher, & Rossi, 1969) found that rats easily discriminate two ESB loci if the stimulations differ in reinforcing properties. However, when both sites yielded neutral reinforcing effects or both yielded positively reinforcing effects, the animals had difficulty in employing the ESBs as differential cues. This result suggests that ESB generally operates through a diffuse rewarding mechanism rather than specific mechanisms associated with different motivational states. On the other hand, Butcher and Stutz (1969) trained rats in discrimination tasks using ESB to two sites as discriminative cues where intensity and rewardability of the ESB cues were equated. Thus, anatomic locus of the ESB reward can be a perceptually salient property of ESB. But this result does not preclude the possibility that ESB operates through a diffuse rewarding mechanism. A rather crude analogy might be liking both cake and ice cream yet being able to distinguish between them.

Fixed Neural Circuits

In the presence of appropriate goal objects—food, water, blocks of wood, estrus females—a variety of stimulus-bound behaviors may be elicitable with ESB. The loci for such stimulus-bound behavior often coincide with those for the maintenance of self-stimulation. It has been suggested, therefore, that in self-stimulation experiments we are tapping the neural substrates of conventional motivational systems. However, recent work has challenged the validity of this conception and has also raised the issue of whether stimulus-bound behavior results from activation of circuits *specific* to the various drive states.

The original report dealing with this issue (Valenstein, Cox, & Kakolewski, 1968a) demonstrated that the behavior elicted by hypothalamic stimulation was subject to modification depite unchanged stimulus parameters. Thus, if a rat ate in response to hypothalamic stimulation, removal of the food and continued ESB (sometimes over a period of hours) might result in drinking, or gnawing of wood. On reintroduction of food, the new behavior generally continued just about as often as eating. Valenstein et al. concluded that hypothalmic circuits are not fixed in the behavior that they mediate.

Valenstein et al. also surveyed the anatomic data to support their conclusions. Earlier reports generally suggested a specificity in the hypothalamic areas from which stimulus-bound behavior may be elicited. Comparison of the implicated sites, however, indicates a tremendous overlap between them and a relative lack of restriction. These data, then, also suggest that stimulus-bound behavior is not mediated by discrete, motivationally relevant hypothalamic circuits.

A number of other investigators have replicated Valenstein's basic finding but disagree on its interpretation. Wise (1968) has suggested that there are genetically fixed circuits and the plasticity that is seen can be attributed to changes in threshold for the activation of these separate circuits. Cain, Skriver, and Carlson (1971) and Milgram, Devor, and Server (1971) have suggested that adaptational and habituation changes could produce variance in the behaviors elicited although the same specific neural elements are stimulated. On the other hand, Cox and Valenstein (1969) did not find any behavior changes that accompanied increases in stimulation current as might be expected from Wise's hypothesis about thresholds for the activation of different stimulus-bound behaviors.

Summary

ESB-induced reinforcement is apparently easily discriminable from nonrewarding stimulations. However, although animals can learn to discriminate two rewarding sites, perceptual generalization seems to be common. Stimulus-bound behavior shows considerable plasticity in that different behaviors can be evoked from the same electrode site. However, stimulation in conjunction with the relevant goal object, rather than simply stimulation alone, is necessary for the animal to show such variability. Thus, both the reinforcing and stimulus-bound effects of ESB are ambiguous with respect to their specificity. In other words, both effects show some properties that might be interpreted as resulting from a generalized, nonspecific mechanism while other properties are seemingly more compatible with the view that discrete, separable systems are stimulated. In the absence of more definitive experiments, the specificity issue must remain open. However, the significance of this issue is minimal in comparison to the question of whether the systems stimulated produce behavior representative of normal motivational mechanisms.

Stimulus-Bound Behavior and Normal Motivation

Does stimulus-bound behavior reflect normal motivational mechanisms? If, for instance, stimulus-bound eating does represent the elicitation of normal hunger motivation, it would be expected that animals eating in response to ESB should readily switch to eating other foods, or the same food in different form, when the original food substance is removed. But Valenstein et al. (1968b) reported that many animals that eat in response to ESB switch to drinking rather than to eating the same food in another form (for example, ground pellets) when the food pellets are removed. Familiarity with the food is probably not a major factor, for rats raised completely on a liquid diet ate food pellets in response to ESB and, further, when deprived of pellets did not eat the familiar liquid diet in response to the stimulation. Similarly, animals drinking in response to ESB do not continue to drink from a different, though familiar, type of container (Valenstein et al., 1970). Also, animals displaying stimulus-bound drinking show taste preferences different from animals drinking in response to water deprivation. Water-deprived animals prefer water to glucose solutions, but the converse is true of animals drinking in response to ESB (Valenstein, Kakolewski, & Cox, 1968). In addition, attempts to manipulate stimulus-bound behavior by interacting ESB with food and water deprivation failed to alter the stimulus-bound behavior (Valenstein et al., 1969). Finally, Valenstein et al. (1970) reported that stimulus-bound eating and drinking are stopped by discrete midbrain lesions, but such lesions do not interfere with normal food or water intake.

Such divergences between normal motivational states and the behavior induced by ESB suggest that it is unlikely that ESB arouses normal, need-determined behaviors. Furthermore, Phillips, Cox, Kakolewski, and Valenstein (1969) have demonstrated a stimulus-bound behavior which does not seem to satisfy the usual criteria for a "drive" or "need".

Rats were allowed to turn ESB on and off by shuttling between the ends of a box. When this behavior was established, a variety of edible and inedible objects were placed on the floor of the "on" side. The rats regularly picked up edible and inedible objects and carried them to the "off" side where they were dropped when the stimulus terminated. Objects were carried only during periods in which stimulation was on. Hunger increased the shuttling and carrying behavior but did not affect the choice of edible versus inedible objects. Most important, when ESB was delivered noncontingently, without regard to the animal's location within the shuttle box, object-carrying quickly ceased. Animals previously showing stimulus-bound eating or gnawing reverted to those behaviors. In other words, there had to be a regular spatial relation between stimulus onsets and offsets and the arrangement of the environment for object-carrying to be manifested.

Phillips et al. suggested that object-carrying is related to the normal hoarding, nest-building, and retrieval of young that is observed when rats establish a nesting territory; but since stimulation of specific neural sites, even in the presence of appropriate goal objects, is not sufficient to evoke the behavior, it is unlikely that a specific need was aroused by the ESB.

On the basis of these results, Valenstein et al. (1970) advanced a conception of ESB effects that is similar to that of Glickman and Schiff (1967) and Roberts and Carey (1965). Hypothalamic stimulation does not elicit specific hunger, thirst, and gnawing drives "but seems to create conditions which excite the neural substrate underlying well-established response patterns ['fixed action patterns']. Discharging this sensitized or excited substrate is reinforcing, and it can provide the motivation to engage in instrumental behavior which is rewarded by the opportunity to make the response. . . . Hypothalamic stimulation does not activate only one specific behavior pattern. The stimulation seems to excite the substrate for a group of responses that in a given species are related to a common state. . . . The states induced by hypothalamic stimulation are not sufficiently specified to exclude the possibility of response substitution. . . . The response that is elicited first appears to reflect a prepotency characteristic of the individual animal and species. . . . The association between the stimulation and the response may be strengthened as a by-product of repetition" (Valenstein et al., 1970, pp. 29–30).

A key point in Valenstein's analysis of stimulus-bound behavior is that the goal-object preferences of normally hungry and thirsty animals differ from those of brain-stimulated animals. Just how different are these goal-object preferences? Wise and Erdmann (1973) suggest that the differences may be the result of the relative emotionality of brain-stimulated animals.

The rats employed in Wise and Erdmann's experiment were not given ESB. They showed that deprived rats, indeed, were less reluctant than ESB animals to switch from one food to another and showed food preferences different from those reported for brain-stimulated animals. But emotional and unemotional rats differed in this regard: As reported for brain-stimulated rats, emotional, food-deprived rats were more reluctant to switch from a preferred to a nonpreferred food and were more likely to switch to drinking; they preferred a novel solid food to a familiar and preferred liquid diet. Thus, this experiment reproduced some of the peculiarities exhibited by brain-stimulated animals in unstimulated, emotional animals. Wise and Erdmann suggest, then, that ESB induces emotionality as well as making the animal hungry.

SUMMARY

Behavior generally seems goal directed and purposive; it is influenced by its hedonic consequences. Thus, psychologists have traditionally viewed behavior as stemming from a need to reduce or avoid basic bodily deficits. These observable attributes form the psychological concept of motivation. A physiological analysis is designed to (1) show mechanisms which mediate these attributes and (2) clarify any ambiguities in the behavioral construct. ESB has provided a tool which has been remarkably productive in that analysis.

Perhaps the most salient characteristic of ESB is that it apparently enables direct manipulation of the hedonic characteristics of motivation—that is, it can serve as a powerful positive or negative reward. But ESB research is helping to suggest a basically new conception of hypothalamic function and this new conception promises to clarify the relations between the psychological constructs of motivation and reinforcement. Traditionally, the hypothalamus has been viewed as related to phenomena covered by the behaviorist's term "drive." The reviews provided in previous chapters document how consummatory behavior can be elicited or influenced by manipulations of the hypothalamus; i.e., manipulation of specific circuits involved in the control of "drive."

There is much to support this view, as we have seen. ESB research, however, suggests the notion that the hypothalamus may be a site influencing the emission of prepotent, "fundamental" responses. Thus, perhaps the hypothalamus is involved in "drive" to the extent that such responses, though probably organized in the brainstem, are "sensitized" by hypothalamic activity. That the execution of prepotent responses seems to be reinforcing would account for the rewarding properties of hypothalamic ESB—that is, hypothalamic reward would be a by-product of the discharge of relevant brainstem circuits. ESB research has generally suggested that motivational and reinforcement mechanisms are, to a degree, separable. Furthermore, whether considered in terms of "incentive," or "drive," the "sensitizing" components of this system also seem to integrate with learning and memory mechanisms so as to attach significance to environmental stimuli and to provide the guiding and anticipatory aspects required of a motivational construct. Future research is likely to focus on the physiological substrate mediating this tie between the motivational system and learning and memory.

Two issues that have received a great deal of recent discussion concern the physiological substrate for ESB effects: To what extent are these genetically determined, fixed circuits and to what extent is the result of ESB-induced motivation comparable to naturally occurring motivation? In regard to the first question, proponents of both sides of this issue are in agreement on the fundamental empirical facts: ESB produces responses that may be quite variable and that variability depends on environmental constraints. In other words, ESB does not automatically result in a mechanical elicitation of set behavior patterns. This variability could result from the plastic properties of a diffusely organized system common to the several motivations; alternatively, it could result from changes in the response characteristics of closely packed, but separate, neural circuits. We simply have not had any experiments that critically test these alternatives.

In regard to the second issue, the comparison of ESB and naturally occurring motivation, the preceding chapters have emphasized the extent of both CNS and peripheral involvement in all the naturally occurring motivations. In view of that extent, it hardly seems likely that stimulating a selected, small site of the hypothalamus reproduces the full manifestations of an entire system. Thus, the differences between natural and ESB-induced motivations may have been overemphasized. In fact, the degree to which ESB can mimic natural motivation seems remarkable and suggests, then, that ESB is activating structures that are indeed focal and critical in those natural motivations.

Only a relatively brief period has elapsed since the initial discovery of the positive and negative reward effects of ESB, but the impact of this research area has been marked. The material reviewed here indicates the beginning of a redefinition of behaviorally derived concepts of "drive," "motivation," and "reinforcement," founded on a physiologically meaningful base. Reinforcement deriving from the discharge of a neural substrate for motor responses, which is sensitized by hypothalamic and limbic activity, appears conceptually quite different from a reinforcement concept emphasizing the decrease of hypothalamic "drive" states.

REFERENCES

Asdourian, D., Stutz, R. M., & Rocklin, K. W. The effects of thalamic and limbic system lesions on self-stimulation. *Journal of Comparative and Physiological Psychology,* 1966, *61,* 468–472.

Ball, G. G. Separation of electrical self-stimulation and electrically elicited eating in the hypothalamus. *Communications in Behavioral Biology,* 1969, *3A,* 5–10.

Bower, G. H., & Miller, N. E. Rewarding and punishing effects from stimulating the same place in the rat's brain. *Journal of Comparative and Physiological Psychology,* 1958, *51,* 669–674.

Brodie, D. A., Moreno, O. M., Malis, J. L., & Boren, J. J. Rewarding properties of intracranial stimulation. *Science,* 1960, *131,* 929–930.

Brown, G. W., & Cohen, B. D. Avoidance and approach learning motivated by stimulation of identical hypothalamic loci. *American Journal of Physiology,* 1959, *197,* 153–157.

Butcher, R. E., & Stutz, R. M. Discriminability of rewarding subcortical brain shock. *Physiology and Behavior,* 1969, *4,* 885–887.

Cain, R. E., Skriver, C. P., & Carlson, R. H. Habituation of electrically induced readiness to gnaw. *Science,* 1971, *173,* 262–264.

Cox, V. C., & Valenstein, E. S. Effects of stimulation intensity on behavior elicited by hypothalamic stimulation. *Journal of Comparative and Physiological Psychology,* 1969, *69,* 730–735.

Delgado, J. M. R., Roberts, W. W., & Miller, N. E. Learning motivated by electrical stimulation of the brain. *American Journal of Physiology,* 1954, *179,* 587–593.

Deutsch, J. A., & Howarth, C. I. Some tests of a theory of intracranial self-stimulation. *Psychological Review,* 1963, *70,* 444–460.

Gallistel, C. R. Motivation as central organizing process: The psychophysical approach to its functional and neurophysiological analysis. In J. K. Cole and T. B. Sonderegger (eds.), *1974 Nebraska Symposium on Motivation.* Lincoln, Nebraska: University of Nebraska Press, 1975, pp. 183–250.

Gibson, W. E., Reid, L. D., Sakai, M., & Porter, P. B. Intracranial reinforcement compared with sugar-water reinforcement. *Science*, 1965, *148*, 1357–1359.

Glickman, S. E., & Schiff, B. B. A biological theory of reinforcement. *Psychological Review*, 1967, *74*, 81–109.

Grastyán, E., Karmos, G. Vereczkey, L., & Kellenyi, L. The hippocampal electrical correlates of the homeostatic regulation of motivation. *Electroencephalography and Clinical Neurophysiology*, 1966, *21*, 34–53.

Heath, R. G. Electrical self-stimulation of the brain in man. *American Journal of Psychiatry*, 1963, *129*, 511–577.

Herberg, L. J. Determinants of extinction in electrical self-stimulation. *Journal of Comparative and Physiological Psychology*, 1963, *56*, 686–690.

Herberg, L. J., Stephens, D. N., Franklin, K. B. J. Catecholamines and self-stimulation: Evidence suggesting a reinforcing role for noradrenaline and a motivating role for dopamine. *Pharmacology, Biochemistry and Behavior*, 1976, *4*, 575–582.

Hodos, W., & Valenstein, E. S. An evaluation of response rate as a measure of rewarding intracranial stimulation. *Journal of Comparative and Physiological Psychology*, 1962, *55*, 80–84.

Hoebel, B. G. Brain reward and aversion systems in the control of feeding and sexual behavior. In J. K. Cole and T. B. Sonderegger (eds.), *1974 Nebraska Symposium on Motivation*. Lincoln, Nebraska: Universityof Nebraska Press, 1975, pp. 49–112.

Howarth, C. I., & Deutsch, J. A. Drive decay: The cause of fast "extinction" of habits learned for brain stimulation. *Science*, 1962, *137*, 35–36.

Keesey, R. E. Intracranial reward delay and the acquisition rate of a brightness discrimination. *Science*, 1964, *143*, 702–703.

Keesey, E., & Powley, T. L. Enhanced lateral hypothalamic reward sensitivity following septal lesions in the rat. *Physiology and Behavior*, 1968, *3*, 557–562.

Leroux, A. G., & Myers, R. D. Action of serotonin microinjected into hypothalamic sites at which electrical stimulation produced aversive responses in the rat. *Physiology and Behavior*, 1975, *14*, 501–505.

Lippa, A. S., Antelman, S. M., Fisher, A. E., & Canfield, D. R. Neurochemical mediation of reward: A significant role for dopamine? *Pharmacology, Biochemistry and Behavior*, 1973, *1*, 23–28.

Lorens, S. A. Effect of lesions in the central nervous system on lateral hypothalamic self-stimulation in the rat. *Journal of Comparative and Physiological Psychology*, 1966, *62*, 256–262.

Margules, D., & Olds, J. Identical "feeding" and "rewarding" systems in the lateral hypothalamus of rats. *Science*, 1962, *135*, 374–375.

MILGRAM, N. W., DEVOR, M., SERVER, A. C. Spontaneous changes in behaviors induced by electrical stimulation of the lateral hypothalamus in rats. *Journal of Comparative and Physiological Psychology*, 1971, *75*, 491–499.

MILLER, N. E. Learning and performance motivated by direct stimulation of the brain. In D. E. Sheer (ed.), *Electrical stimulation of the brain*. Austin, Texas: University of Texas Press, 1961, pp. 387–396.

MILLER, N. E. Some reflections on the law of effect produce a new alternative to drive reduction. In M. R. Jones (ed.), *Nebraska Symposium on Motivation*. Lincoln: University of Nebraska Press, 1963, pp. 65–112.

NEILL, D. B., PARKER, S. D., & GOLD, M. S. Striatal dopaminergic modulation of lateral hypothalamic self-stimulation. *Pharmacology, Biochemistry and Behavior*, 1975, *3*, 485–491.

OLDS, J. Satiation effects in self-stimulation of the brain. *Journal of Comparative and Physiological Psychology*, 1958, *51*, 675–678. (a)

OLDS, J. Self-stimulation of the brain. *Science*, 1958, *127*, 315–324. (b)

OLDS, J. Effects of hunger and male sex hormone on self-stimulation of the brain. *Journal of Comparative and Physiological Psychology*, 1958, *51*, 320–324. (c)

OLDS, J. Differential effects of drives and drugs on self-stimulation at different brain sites. In D. E. Sheer (ed.), *Electrical stimulation of the brain*. Austin, Texas: University of Texas Press, 1961, pp. 350–366.

OLDS, J. The central nervous system and the reinforcement of behavior. *American Psychologist*, 1969, *24*, 114–132.

OLDS, J., & MILNER, P. Positive reinforcement produced by electrical stimulation of septal area and other regions of rat brain. *Journal of Comparative and Physiological Psychology*, 1954, *47*, 419–427.

OLDS, J., & OLDS, M. Drives, rewards and the brain. In *New directions in psychology, II*. New York: Holt, Rinehart & Winston, 1965, pp. 327–410.

PHILLIPS, A. G., COX, V. C., KAKOLEWSKI, J. W., & VALENSTEIN, E. S. Object carrying by rats: An approach to the behavior produced by stimulation. *Science*, 1969, *166*, 903–905.

PLISKOFF, S. S., & HAWKINS, T. D. Test of Deutsch's drive-decay theory of rewarding self-stimulation of the brain. *Science*, 1963, *141*, 823–824.

PORTER, R. W., CONRAD, D. G., & BRADY, J. V. Some neural and behavioral correlates of electrical self-stimulation of the limbic system. *Journal of the Experimental Analysis of Behavior*, 1959, *2*, 43–55.

QUARTERMAIN, D., & WEBSTER, D. Extinction following intracranial reward: The effect of delay between acquisition and extinction. *Science*, 1968, *159*, 1259–1260.

ROBERTS, W. W. Rapid escape learning without avoidance learning motivated by hypothalamic stimulation in cats. *Journal of Comparative and Physiological Psychology,* 1958, *51*, 391–399. (a)

ROBERTS, W. W. Both rewarding and punishing effects from stimulation of posterior hypothalamus of cat with same electrode at same intensity. *Journal of Comparative and Physiological Psychology*, 1958, *51*, 400–407. (b)

ROBERTS, W. W. Fear-like behavior elicited from dorsomedial thalamus of cat. *Journal of Comparative and Physiological Psychology*, 1962, *55*, 191–197.

ROBERTS, W. W., & CAREY, R. J. Rewarding effect of performance of gnawing aroused by hypothalamic stimulation in the rat. *Journal of Comparative and Physiological Psychology*, 1965, *59*, 317–324.

ROBERTS, W. W., & KIESS, H. O. Motivational properties of hypothalamic aggression in cats. *Journal of Comparative and Physiological Psychology*, 1964, *58*, 187–193.

ROLLS, E. T., KELLY, P. H., & SHAW, S. G. Noradrenaline, dopamine and brain-stimulation reward. *Pharmacology, Biochemistry and Behavior*, 1974, *2*, 735–740.

ROSSI, R. R. The effects of competition between electrical stimulation of the brain and food or water in a choice situation. Master's Thesis, University of Cincinnati, 1969.

ROUTTENBERG, A. Intracranial self-stimulation pathways as a substrate for memory consolidation. In J. K. Cole and T. B. Sonderegger (eds.), *1974 Nebraska Symposium on Motivation.* Lincoln, Nebraska: University of Nebraska Press, 1975, pp. 161–182.

ROUTTENBERG, A., & LINDY, J. Effects of the availability of rewarding septal and hypothalamic stimulation on bar-pressing for food under conditions of deprivation. *Journal of Comparative and Physiological Psychology*, 1965, *60*, 158–161.

SCOTT, J. W. Brain stimulation reinforcement with distributed practice: Effects of electrode locus, previous experience, and stimulus intensity. *Journal of Comparative and Physiological Psychology*, 1967, *63*, 175–183.

SEWARD, J. P., UYEDA, A. A., & OLDS, J. Reinforcing effect of brain stimulation on runway performance as a function of interval between trials. *Journal of Comparative and Physiological Psychology*, 1960, *53*, 224–228.

SPIES, G. Food versus intracranial self-stimulation reinforcement in food-deprived rats. *Journal of Comparative and Physiological Psychology*, 1965, *60*, 153–157.

STEIN, L. An analysis of stimulus-duration preference in self-stimulation of the brain. *Journal of Comparative and Physiological Psychology*, 1962, *55*, 405–415.

STEIN, L. Norepinephrine reward pathways: Role in self-stimulation, memory consolidation, and schizophrenia. In J.K. Cole and T. B. Sonderegger (eds.), *1974 Nebraska Symposium on Motivation.* Lincoln, Nebraska: University of Nebraska Press, 1975, pp. 112–159.

STEINER, S. S., BEER, B., & SHAFFER, M. M. Escape from self-produced rates of brain stimulation. *Science*, 1969, *168*, 90–91.

STUTZ, R. M. Stimulus generalization within the limbic system. *Journal of Comparative and Physiological Psychology*, 1968, *65*, 79–82.

STUTZ, R. M., BUTCHER, R. E., & ROSSI, R. Stimulus properties of rewarding brain shock. *Science*, 1969, *163*, 1081–1082.

STUTZ, R. M., LEWIN, I., & ROCKLIN, K. W. Generality of "drive-decay" as an explanatory concept. *Psychonomic Science*, 1965, *2*, 127–128.

STUTZ, R. M., ROSSI, R. R., & BOWRING, A. M. Competition between food and rewarding brain shock. *Physiology and Behavior*, 1971, *7*, 753–757.

SZABÓ, I. Path neuron system of medial forebrain bundle as a possible substrate for hypothalamic self-stimulation. *Physiology and Behavior*, 1973, *10*, 315–328.

TROWILL, J. A., PANKSEPP, J., & GANDELMAN, R. An incentive model of rewarding brain stimulation. *Psychological Review*, 1969, *76*, 264–281.

VALENSTEIN, E. S. Independence of approach and escape reactions to electrical stimulation of the brain. *Journal of Comparative and Physiological Psychology*, 1965, *60*, 20–30.

VALENSTEIN, E. S. The anatomical locus of reinforcement. In E. Stellar and J. M. Sprague (eds.), *Progress in physiological psychology*, Vol. 1. New York: Academic Press, 1966, pp. 149–190.

VALENSTEIN, E. S., & BEER, B. Reinforcing brain stimulation in competition with water reward and shock avoidance. *Science*, 1962, *137*, 1052–1054.

VALENSTEIN, E. S., COX, V. C., & KAKOLEWSKI, J. W. Modification of motivated behavior elicited by electrical stimulation of the hypothalamus. *Science*, 1968, *159*, 1119–1121. (a)

VALENSTEIN, E. S., COX, V. C., & KAKOLEWSKI, J. W. The motivation underlying eating elicited by lateral hypothalamic stimulation. *Physiology and Behavior*, 1968, *3*, 969–971. (b)

VALENSTEIN, E. S., COX, V. C., & KAKOLEWSKI, J. W. The hypothalamus and motivated behavior. In J. T. Tapp (ed.), *Reinforcement and behavior.* New York: Academic Press, 1969, pp. 242–285.

Valenstein, E. S., Cox, V. C., & Kakolewski, J. W. Reexamination of the role of the hypothalamus in motivation. *Psychological Review*, 1970, *77*, 16–31.

Valenstein, E. S., Kakolewski, J. W., & Cox, V. C. A comparison of stimulus-bound drinking and drinking induced by water deprivation. *Communications in Behavioral Biology*, 1968, *2*, 227–233.

Valenstein, E. S., & Valenstein, T. Interaction of positive and negative reinforcing neural systems. *Science*, 1964, *145*, 1456–1458.

Wise, R. A. Hypothalamic motivational system: Fixed or plastic neural circuits? *Science*, 1968, *162*, 377–379.

Wise, R. A. Plasticity of hypothalamic motivational systems. *Science*, 1969, *165*, 929–930.

Wise, R. A., & Erdmann. Emotionality, hunger, and normal eating: Implications for interpretation of electrically induced behavior. *Behavioral Biology*, 1973, *8*, 519–532.

Yokel, R. A., & Wise, R. A. Increased lever pressing for amphetamine after pimozide in rats: Implications for a dopamine theory of reward. *Science*, 1975, *187*, 547–549.

12

Learning and Memory

Most, if not all, animals show modifications in their behavior that we call "learned," but no other animal shows the capacity for learning that humans do. Language, culture, technology, the organization of societies, these are all products of the human being's ability to learn. It is no wonder that learning, as a process, is a topic of such importance in psychology. It is interesting, then, that we have so much difficulty in defining the term precisely. At best, we characterize learning by its extrinsic characteristics. Thus, we say that learning is a process of behavior modification that requires practice and it is a relatively permanent change in behavior. We try to distinguish maturational processes from learning, motivational and sensitization changes from learning, and performance changes from the capacity for learning. But we have no intrinsic defintion of learning and, therefore, psychological theory is vague about a number of issues: Does all learning represent the operation of a single process—i.e., are classical conditioning, instrumental learning, and problem solving basically similar? We saw in the preceding chapter that we are not clear about the nature of the reinforcement process; however, is reinforcement necessary for learning to occur? Indeed, what is learned—S-R connection, S-S connections, cognitive maps, or something else?

A physiological approach may answer these questions by elucidating the intrinsic mechanisms of learning. If, for instance, it could be shown that for learning to occur, certain modifications of synaptic activity must take place, there would no longer be a need to ask questions about S-R versus S-S connections. Instead, we would be asking questions about the locus and characteristics of synaptic changes. A physiological approach, then, may clarify these behavioral questions.

We must also remain aware that learning is a *behavioral* process. In the material to follow, we shall encounter instances where measures are taken during learning or manipulations of neural systems are made in an attempt to demonstrate correlates or models of the learning process. By themselves, such correlates or models may be interesting but they must be validated against changes in overt behavior. For instance, suppose that a certain neural change is recorded during the learning of a specific behavioral response. The fact that the neural change is recorded simultaneously with the behavioral response does not guarantee that it is a result of the learning. Just as certain controls for pseudoconditioning, sensitization, etc., are applied by behavioral psychologists to ensure that the behavior is the product of learning, the same controls must be applied to neural correlates to ensure that they are genuinely the product of the learning. In other words, the neural change must be shown to occur only when there is overt behavioral learning. We will encounter experiments where such niceties have not or cannot yet be observed; under these circumstances, the results can only be considered suggestive.

However learning is defined, for a behavioral change to qualify as learned, a minimal feature it must show is persistence. That is, learned changes in behavior must be demonstrated to occur again at a later time, thus involving the phenomenon of memory. The study of learning concentrates on the acquisition of the behavioral change while the study of memory concentrates on the storage and retention of that change—these are complementary aspects of the same total process. In keeping with this division, the material in this chapter will be organized into two major sections. The emphasis in the first section will be on the acquisition process and the second will emphasize storage.

LEARNING

A variety of approaches has been taken to the study of the physiological substrates of learning. Historically, great emphasis has been placed on finding loci in the CNS which might be critical for learning to occur. In the absence of an unequivocal answer to this question, alternative strategies have been developed. One alternative has been to look for correlates of learning—that is, are there changes in the CNS that occur concomitant with the development of behavioral expressions of the learning process? Another alternative has been to attempt to develop "models" of the learning process. Modeling involves the development of simple procedures or animal preparations that might be considered representative of the more general process; analysis of the simpler situation should give insights into more complex learning processes. Some modeling experiments have attempted to use "simple" behavioral situations and/or primitive organisms whose CNS is readily analyzed. Other attempts have employed more artificial conditions, such as attempting to produce "conditioned" CNS changes directly, recording neural responses only, rather than behavior. We shall examine some examples of each of these approaches.

The Locus of Learning

Are there any loci in the CNS that can be considered critical for learning to occur? Obviously we must be wary of the trivial sense in which this might be true: A massive lesion of the reticular system, which resulted in a comatose animal, would not mean that the reticular system is necessary for learning, except in the sense that learning requires an awake, attentive organism. The search for loci of importance to learning, particularly in studies employing lesions, must cope with changes in motivation, sensory and motor capacity, and operative trauma. Lesions also involve more subtle, long-term effects on functioning (see Chapter 3 for details). Then, too, the age of the subject at the time of operation may be a significant variable. For instance, large bilateral lesions of the auditory cortex in adult cats result in the inability to learn a discrimination between two different sound patterns; similar lesions placed in infant cats had no effect on the learning of such discriminations (Scharlock, Tucker, & Strominger, 1963).

Spinal Cord

One approach to the neural mechanisms of learning is to attempt to determine the minimal neural unit necessary for learning to occur. If such a minimum functional unit could be isolated, it might then be employed as a model system for the learning process. A number of experiments have attempted to determine whether the spinal cord, isolated from the rest of the CNS, can serve as such a neural minimum.

Successful classical conditioning of the spinal cord was first reported by Shurrager and Culler (1940). A weak shock to the tail was used as the conditioned stimulus (CS) and a stronger shock to the hindpaw was used as the unconditioned stimulus (US). Since that time, a number of experiments (see Paterson, Cegavske, & Thompson, 1973) have been performed which have reported both success and failure with attempts at classical and instrumental conditioning of the cord. A variety of problems may be involved in whether success or failure was obtained, however. Some of these concern the conditioned stimulus (CS). In the Shurrager and Culler experiment, the CS may have elicited unconditioned muscle twitches that were mistakenly called conditioned responses, while in other experiments the CS may have acted to inhibit performance of the response. Other considerations include the time after spinal transection at which conditioning is carried out; for example, too soon after transection might produce an unstable preparation demonstrating pseudoconditioning.

More recently, several carefully controlled experiments have been performed which report successful training of the isolated spinal cord. Paterson et al. tested for classical conditioning using shock to a sensory nerve as the CS and shock to a motor nerve as the US. Controls for pseudoconditioning and sensitization were also carried out and proved negative. The response measured was response of the motor nerve to the CS. In these experiments, the CS, before conditioning, elicted a small response in the motor nerve, and this was augmented by the conditioning process. It is commonly assumed that conditioning involves new connections between the CS and US. This experiment suggests that existing, unused connections may be augmented, rather than new connections being formed. Durkovic (1975) has obtained very similar results.

Successful instrumental conditioning of the cord also has been reported (Chopin & Buerger, 1976). In these experiments, the hindlimb of the experimental animal was suspended over an aqueous solution; whenever an electrode attached to the limb contacted the solution, a shock was received. Thus, shock could be avoided by maintaining the leg in a flexed position. A control animal, similarly prepared with a spinal transection, was paired with the experimental animal; the control animal received shock, regardless of the position of its hindlimb, whenever the experimental animal was shocked. Generally, experimental animals showed flexion of the leg while control animals maintained the leg in an extended position.

Thus, the more recent experiments tend to be more uniformly positive about the occurrence of spinal conditioning. On the other hand, the conditioning that is obtained is not particularly robust and there does appear to be a great deal of variability between animals in conditionability. The spinal cord, then, seems to be less amenable to learned modifications than the more rostral CNS. On the other hand, further studies of the cord might open

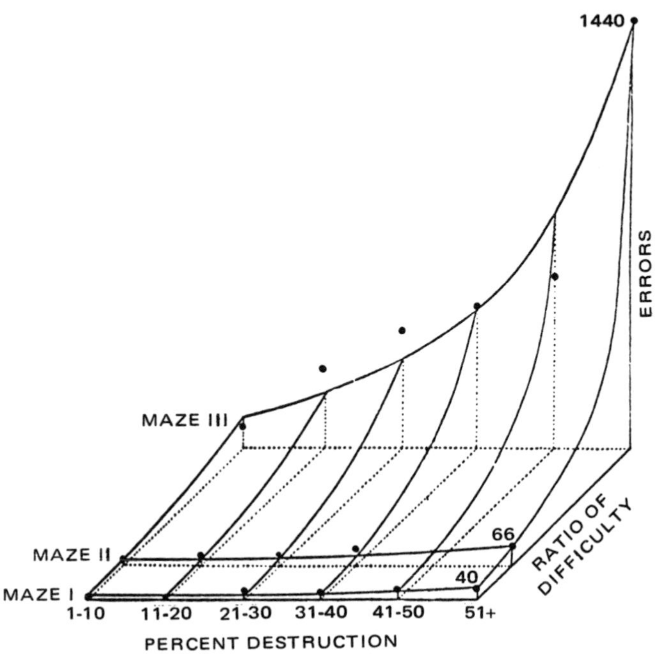

Figure 12.1. The relation between the extent of cerebral lesion, difficulty of the problem to be learned (maze learning), and the degree of retardation. The separation of the curves represents the relative difficulty of the problems for normal animals; the abscissae of the curves, the percentage of destruction; and the ordinates, the number of errors made during training. (From K. S. Lashley, *Brain Mechanisms and Intelligence.* Chicago: The University of Chicago Press, 1929. Copyright 1929 by The University of Chicago Press.)

the way to using it as a simplified model for the study of the basic processes involved in learning.

Cortex

Structurally, the brains of the higher mammallian species differ from those of lower forms in their very obvious increased development of the neocortex. It is natural to presume that this development is critical to the increased learning capacity displayed by the higher mammals. The search for cortical effects on learning processes has markedly influenced physiological theorizing about learning and memory.

Pavlov's early experiments and theorizing led him to the conclusion (Pavlov, 1928) that while no part of the cortex was specifically concerned with the formation of conditioned reflexes, the cortical area involved in the reception of the particular CS was necessary. A number of experiments (see Bromiley, 1948) have since shown that this is not the case. In a dog almost completely devoid of a neocortex, Bromiley successfully obtained discriminated avoidance conditioning, that is, avoidance responses to a light but not to a whistle.

Maze Learning. Some of the most extensive work on the role of the cortex in learning are Lashley's (1929) investigations of maze learning in the rat. Generally, these studies involved the placement of cortical lesions before and after the learning of mazes to assess the lesions' influence on acquisition and retention. Figure 12.1 depicts the major findings for acquisition. Here three mazes were employed, differing in degree of difficulty (number of blind alleys). In all three mazes, the number of errors during acquisition correlated with the percentage of the cortex destroyed; the size of these correlations increased with maze difficulty, going from .20 in Maze I to .58 in Maze II and .75 in Maze III. The more difficult the maze, the more deleterious was a given degree of cortical destruction. In no case was the location of the lesion critical—its effect depended only on its size. Thus, the rat's ability to learn mazes is not dependent on any particular cortical area but is dependent on the amount of cortical tissue left intact. Findings in regard to the retention of maze performance were similar: The degree of retention was dependent on the size of the lesion, i.e., there was less retention with larger lesions, but retention was not dependent on the location of the lesion. The more difficult the maze, the less the retention with a given size lesion.

Lashley generally interpreted the results of experiments such as this in terms of two complementary concepts: mass action and equipotentiality. The *mass action* principle is that the effect of cortical lesions is dependent on their size (mass), and it is the total volume of the available cortex which affects the performance. The *equipotentiality* principle is that the lesions have nonspecific effects; maze learning can be equally well mediated by any cortical area. Again, the two concepts are complementary and have similar implications.

On the basis of these results alone, an alternate interpretation is possible: The results could stem from the fact that maze learning is a multisensory task. In other words, when increasingly large lesions of the cortex are made, there is increasing interference with sensory functions. Thus, the mass action principle might result from the fact that a larger number of sensory modalities are subject to dysfunction when larger lesions are made. The equipotentiality principle might be due to the fact that different rats tend to employ different sense modalities for solving the mazes; thus with larger lesions there is a greater probability of affecting the relevant modalities. A number of experiments have shown that depriving rats of sensory information can essentially simulate Lashley's results with cortical lesions.

There have been several attempts to deal with this problem (see Lashley, 1943). Conceptually, the experiments are easy to design: Does peripheral blinding of the rat cause as great a deficit as the placement of visual cortical lesions? Or, alternatively, does the addition of visual cortical lesions in peripherally blinded animals add to their deficit? In practice, the experiments are somewhat ambiguous because of technical difficulties in placing the lesions—for example, lesioning all, but not more than, the visual cortex. Generally, such experiments seem to indicate that lesions of the visual cortex produce a greater deficit than that produced by peripheral blinding. Furthermore, undercutting the visual cortex by severing the thalamic input does not enhance the deficit produced by peripheral blinding. The results thus seem to support the notion that cortical lesions interfere with maze learning in a way that is in addition to any specific sensory loss; that is, the visual cortex is important to maze learning even in the absence of visual sensory information.

Lashley also introduced another concept—"vicarious functioning." Not infrequently, a specific habit may be lost after a lesion but the animal shows relearning; Lashley assumed that some of the functions of the lesioned area were "taken over" by an area unaffected by the lesion. In Chapter 3 we discussed some recent research dealing with recovery of functioning after lesions. The findings discussed there are pertinent here and may help explain some aspects of relearning after lesions.

Discrimination Learning. The above results apply to maze learning, but what of other learning tasks, such as discrimination problems? Obviously it would be expected that lesions which invade the specific sensory areas will have greater effects on sensory discrimination than those which do not. Generally, this is the case, but the results are more complicated. We have seen that cortical lesions do not affect the ability of the dog to make a conditioned response in the presence of a light. But suppose the problem is made more difficult by requiring the animal to discriminate between a lighter and a darker stimulus? Lashley (1929, 1935) also investigated this problem. Complete destruction of the visual cortex caused the loss of previously learned light-dark discriminations, but the animals were able to relearn the task. However, even small cortical remnants remaining after lesions could mediate complete retention of the discrimination. Thus, these results indicate that while the cortex is somehow involved in the discrimination learning in the normal animal, discrimination also may be learned in the absence of the cortex. Such results are often seen in lesion studies: There is a postoperative loss of the habit, but relearning is possible and often is as efficient as the original learning.

The results for visual discrimination are not unique. In the auditory modality, for instance, sound localization and the discrimination of temporal patterns of tones and tone duration are all lost after cortical lesions, while tone onset and intensity and frequency discrimination may still serve as a basis for learned responses (Neff, 1961).

Summary

Some implications of the effects of cortical lesions on learning seem clear:

1. The cortex cannot be said to be critical for learning generally; certain learned responses survive cortical ablation while others do not. Furthermore, in some instances, there may be no evidence of retention following cortical lesions, but the response may be relearned. This indicates that while the cortex may normally be involved in such tasks, it is not essential.
2. There seems to be a general relationship between task difficulty and cortical involvement, with only the simpler tasks surviving extensive cortical injury. Pattern detection requires more complex processing, which occurs at the cortex; detection of stimulation per se does not require the cortex.
3. Lashley's studies of maze learning do suggest, however, that the cortex does participate in some learning functions in a manner over and above its purely sensory functions.

Subcortical Mechanisms

There have been literally hundreds of experiments concerned with the effects of subcortical lesions on a variety of learning problems. Generally, the strategy of such experiments has been to place relatively delimited lesions in specific structures and to determine if such lesions result in learning deficits. The logic of such experiments requires that we search for specific loci involved in associative effects in order to assure ourselves that such lesions do not produce effects attributable to losses in motivation, sensory or motor capacity, attention, and so on. Without reviewing this voluminous literature, by and large, it has not proven possible to locate any single structure that could be characterized as functionally responsible for associative processes. Let us examine just one example.

We have previously seen that removal of the visual cortex disrupts brightness discrimination in the rat, but the animal can relearn the problem (Lashley, 1929, 1935). This result suggests that subcortical structures are mediating the habit in the absence of the cortex. It is not surprising, then, that destruction of the superior colliculi and pretectal regions prevented relearning of the discrimination in animals with visual cortical lesions (Lashley, 1935). These midbrain lesions would be expected to produce visual deficits. Note, however, that cortically intact rats are not disrupted in such discriminations by lesions of the superior colliculus (Ghiselli, 1938; Thompson, 1969). Rather than concerning ourselves with the presumed sensory losses that result from these lesions, investigation of the peculiar way in which this system functions would seem to be more in order. The discrimination seems to be mediated by the cortex normally, as indicated by its loss after cortical lesions, but it can be mediated subcortically in the absence of the visual cortex.

Locating structures responsible for learning must also take into account another factor—the variability of learned responses. An early experiment by Liddell (1942) clearly makes the relevant point. After a sheep was trained to flex its leg to avoid shock at the sound of a bell, the sheep was turned over onto its back. The sheep's head was now resting on the shock electrode. The bell was rung and, instead of flexing its leg as it had been trained, the sheep stretched all four legs and lifted its head from the electrode. Learning rarely, if ever, involves only discrete relationships between specific stimuli and responses. A neuropsychology of learning must be able to account for the generalizability of learning as has been illustrated in Liddell's experiment. This suggests that the learning process cannot be confined to single specific neural loci. The ubiquitous finding of relearning after lesions have impaired the retention of previously learned responses also suggests that learning cannot be confined to specific neural areas.

These and other arguments have been used by many theorists in favor of a conception of the *engram* (memory trace) that is diffuse. In other words, the engram is spread over most, if not all, of the brain whenever learning occurs. Lashley (1950), in summarizing his extensive research into this problem, concluded that all of the brain's cells are constantly active and participate in every activity—there are no cells reserved for special memories. He suggested that an alternative to specifically localized memory is that the neurons are sensitive to patterns or combinations of excitation. Such a conception permits the same neurons to participate in many engrams, and it is the *pattern of excitation* which determines the response obtained. (Similar conceptions have been offered by a number of other theorists; see John, 1967.)

Thus, the search for discrete localized structures responsible for learning has, for the most part, given way to a more diffuse conception, suggesting that the brain generally is involved. More recently, however, a number of lines of research seem to suggest that another alternative may exist. Though speculative at this point, these experiments present the possibility that certain discrete neural systems, albeit extensive in their anatomical extent, may be critical to the learning process.

One line of evidence follows in the tradition of Lashley and elaborates his work on visual discrimination learning. R. Thompson (1969) trained rats in three different visual discrimination problems: a brightness discrimination (white versus gray), a discrimination between horizontal versus vertical black-and-white stripes, and discrimination of a white cross on a black

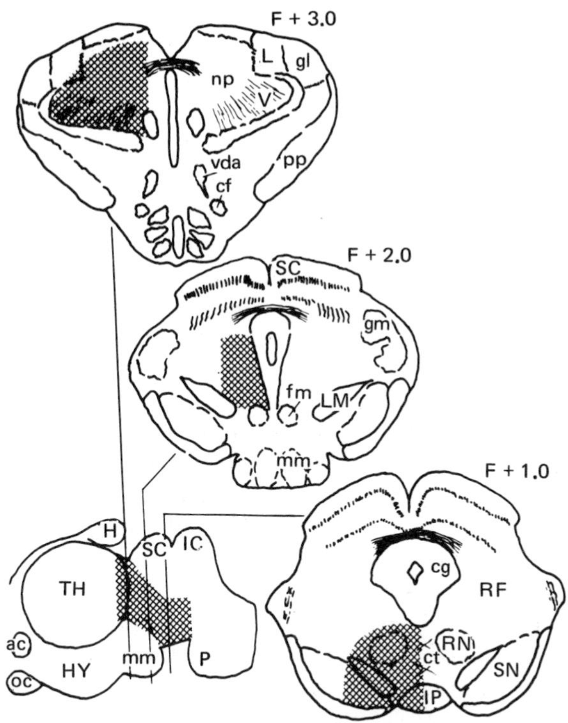

Figure 12.2. Schematic diagram of parasagittal section of brainstem (lower left) and three frontal sections showing critical subcortical areas (crosshatched) for normal performance of visual discrimination habits. (ac, anterior commissure; cf, column of fornix; cg, central gray; ct, central tegmentum; fm, habenulo-peduncular tract; gl, lateral geniculate nucleus; gm, geniculate nucleus; H, habenula; HY, hypothalamus; IC, inferior colliculus; IP, interpeduncular nucleus; L, lateral posterior thalamic nucleus; LM, medial lemniscus; MM, mammillary bodies; np, nucleus posterior; oc, optic chiasma; P, pons; PP, cerebral peduncle; RF, reticular formation; RN, red nucleus; SC, superior colliculus; SN, substantia nigra; TH, thalamus; V, ventral thalamic nucleus; vda, mammillo-thalamic tract.) (From Thompson, R., Localization of the "visual memory system" in the white rat. *Journal of Comparative and Physiological Psychology*, 1969, *69*(4), Part 2, 1–29. Copyright 1969 by the American Psychological Association. Reprinted by permission.)

background from a white disc on a black background. All problems were presented in a two-choice box, with escape from foot shock as the motivation. Retention was tested after brain lesions. Lesions were placed in 84 rats, and their loci varied over almost the entire extent of the brain rostral to, and including, the inferior colliculus. The only lesions that significantly disrupted performance on *all* of the discrimination problems were located in the occipital cortex, posterior thalamus, and ventral mesencephalon. Figure 12.2 is a diagram of the circuit involved in these lesions. Thompson (1969, p.

26) emphasizes that "the occipital cortex, posterior diencephalon, and ventral mesencephalon comprise the core of a neural system mediating storage, retrieval, and utilization of all visual engrams formed in the albino rat." He suggests that the visual circuit of Figure 12.2 may be prototypical of other specific memory systems as well; each modality may have a circumscribed, critical CNS circuit which mediates the learning of responses appropriate for that sensory system. Two or more of these circuits could overlap to comprise loci for the elaboration of complex memories and the integration of the several modalities. One such potential area of overlap is the ventral mesencephalon, because of its involvement in species-typical response sequences (see our discussion in Chapter 11; also Glickman & Schiff, 1967).

Thompson recognized that his particular experiments and their consequent results are limited by the methods and the particular learning tasks employed. He acknowledges that if he employed, for instance, positive reinforcement instead of escape from foot shock, and successive instead of simultaneous discrimination, the results would in all probability differ in detail from those he did obtain. Nonetheless, he suggests that any discrepancies would be due only to the extent to which other cortical and subcortical structures would be involved; the circuit between the occipital cortex, posterior diencephalon, and ventral mesencephalon is critical and would be at the central core of any visual engram.

The dorsal medial thalamus may also be part of an extensive system concerned with learning. A number of studies (see Means, Huntley, Anderson, & Harrell, 1973) have found learning deficits associated with lesions in this area. Means et al. found both an inability to acquire a visual-tactile discrimination after lesions here and severely deficient retention of a preoperatively acquired discrimination. Within the training period allotted, these deficits appeared to be permanent. Tests for food motivation, sensory deficits, and general activity did not produce any observable differences between the operated animals and controls.

The motivation and reward mechanisms discussed in the preceding chapter seem to be implicated by several recent lines of research. In one of these, Kent and Grossman (1973) placed thin cuts along the lateral borders of the hypothalamus designed to sever brainstem connections with the forebrain. These lesions produced aphagia and adipsia (see Chapter 8) but in addition resulted in severe learning impairments. Learning was tested using ESB, food motivation, and escape from foot shock; all were impaired. Both acquisition of new responses and retention of previously learned responses were deficient. Complex but presumably unlearned behavior, such as swimming and grooming, were unaffected. Simple sensory, motor, location, and exploratory functions were also unimpaired.

In a similar vein, Fibiger, Phillips, and Zis (1974) selectively lesioned the dopamine system arising in the brainstem. Rats with these lesions were deficient in the acquisition of both an avoidance response and an approach response for food. Animals overtrained on the avoidance response and then subjected to the lesions were essentially unimpaired in their retention, suggesting that the lesions affect learning only—i.e., they may impair the ability to be reinforced for correct responses.

Summary. The history of the search for CNS loci involved in learning shows several trends. Initially, research designs concentrated mainly on finding single, discrete, "critical" structures. When this strategy resulted in essential failure to localize the engram, theoretical models based on the assumption that learning and memory involved the entire brain became popular. It would be premature to dispute this notion unequivocally but recent results offer another possible model. It seems plausible to suggest that learning requires the concurrent operation of several systems or subsystems that are discretely organized but extend over considerable portions of the brain. Part of this network may be concerned with response mechanisms; another part of this network may be concerned with response mechanisms; a third part may involve mechanisms specifically concerned with specific sensory systems and/or reinforcement mechanisms. Interference with parts of these systems may thus produce temporary deficits but relearning might still be possible because the remainder of the system is intact. On the other hand, extensive interference with major systems, as with gross interference in the reward mechanisms, may prevent learning altogether. This model, then, is somewhere between conceptions that looked for discrete localization of the engram and conceptions that say that localization is impossible.

CNS Stimulation Experiments

Another approach to the locus of learning question utilizes the classical conditioning model and asks what neural elements in the linkage between CS and response are necessary. In the typical classical conditioning procedure, the subject is presented with a neutral environmental stimulus (CS), and this is followed by another environmental stimulus (US)—food, for example—which innately elicits some response—salivation, for example. Conditioning is then demonstrated when the CS elicits salivation. The studies to be considered here are based on a conception of conditioning as some sort of linkage or connection between the CS and the response. Researchers have thus sought to answer the question, What neural elements in this linkage are dispensable? The general plan of the experiments has been to inquire whether the usual environmental stimuli can be replaced by stimulation of the CNS.

It is clear that stimulation of the brain can serve as a substitute for environmental stimulation as the CS. Thus, when Loucks (1938) used electrical stimulation of the cortex as the CS, he was able to obtain evidence of both conditioned salivary responses and leg flexion. These results indicate that the peripheral sensory pathways associated with the CS can be eliminated—they do not contain elements necessary to the conditioning process.

Much more ambiguity surrounds the question of whether the peripheral pathways associated with the US can be eliminated. In an early study, Loucks (1935) stimulated motor cortex to elicit limb movements. A buzzer preceded cortical stimulation in an attempt to condition the limb movements. Loucks was unable to demonstrate that conditioning occurs when the unconditioned response is "forced" by stimulating the cortex. In another study Loucks and Gantt (1938) used electrical stimulation of the spinal cord for the US. When the US apparently did not stimulate pain pathways, conditioning was unsuccessful; when the US spread to or involved pain pathways, conditioning was successful. Reinforcement theorists have taken the results of these two studies to indicate that some reinforcement process is necessary for conditioning to occur.

More recently, Doty and Giurgea (1961) apparently were successful in employing shock to the cortex as the US in a classical conditioning situation. Such a result is important for its implication that conditioning can take place in the absence of any motivational involvement of the US. But the matter does not appear to have been settled by these findings. Figure 12.3 illustrates some of the issues that have become involved. The top part of the figure shows an unconditioned response (UR) to motor cortex stimulation; the bottom part of the figure shows a presumed CR early in training. The comparison illustrates one finding that is common in such experiments: The presumed CR and UR may differ from each other in the form of the movement. In fact, the UR may itself show variability—a not infrequent finding is that head and neck movements may predominate after a while though the stimulus was designed to produce leg movements. In addition, unsignaled presentations of the US seem to provoke particularly vigorous and abrupt URs which may even cause the animal to lose its balance. Considerations such as these have prompted additional experiments.

Doty and Giurgea attributed their success in obtaining conditioning with cortical stimulation as the US to their use of intertrial intervals on the order of 3 to 5 minutes; Loucks spaced his trials 30 to 60 seconds apart. It is not clear just why such a change might make a difference. On the other hand, Wagner, Thomas and Norton (1967) suggested that such conditioning is not devoid of motivational significance for the animal. They reasoned that while the US may not be inherently noxious, the UR may cause the animal to make preparatory postural adjustments to compensate for the loss of balance. By this line of reasoning, the fact that the CR often is not similar to the UR may reflect the fact that the optimal anticipatory adjustment need not be one that mimics the CR; in effect, the CR is considered here to be an instrumen-

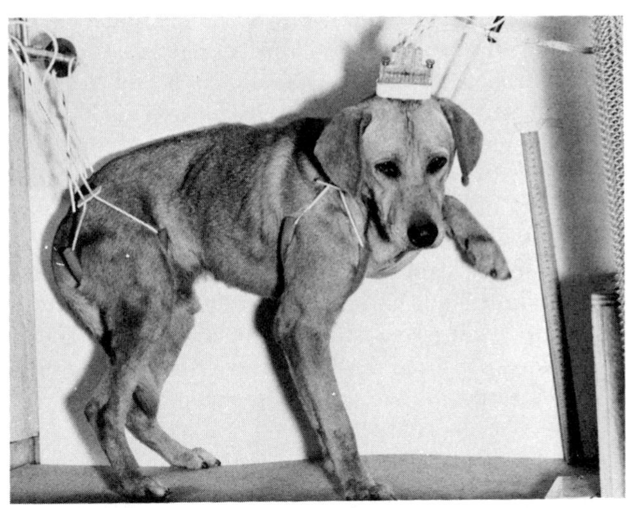

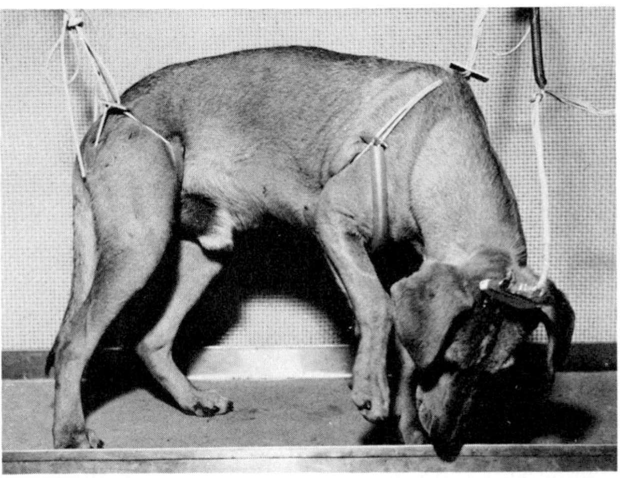

Figure 12.3. *Top*: Unconditioned motor response to stimulation of motor cortex. *Bottom*: One of the first CRs after pairing of visual cortical (CS) with motor cortex stimulation (US). [From Doty, R. W. Conditioned reflexes formed and evoked by brain stimulation. In D. E. Sheer (Ed.), *Electrical Stimulation of the Brain.* Austin: The University of Texas Press, 1961, 397–412. Copyright 1961 by The University of Texas Press.]

tal response, not a classically conditioned response, to avoid aversive effects of the UR. Wagner et al. conducted an experiment which provides indirect support for their position. Dogs were trained to press either of two panels for food. After such training, panel pressing also resulted in cortical stimulation which produced a hindleg UR. The two panels differed only in the fact that for one of them the UR was signaled by a prior one-second CS while the UR was unsignaled for the other panel. The dogs preferred to press the panel paired with the signaled URs, suggesting that the URs did have motivational significance. On the basis of this evidence, Wagner et al. suggested that the relevant difference between Loucks and Doty and Giurgea might not be the intertrial interval but rather the fact that Loucks suspended his animals in a hammock for training, while Doty and Giurgea required their animals to stand. Suspension in the hammock obviated the necessity for making preparatory postural adjustments and hence no conditioning occurred. Kandel and Benevento (1973) suggested still another alternative. They suggested that head and neck responses to the US reflexively inhibit leg responses and that head and neck responses are classically conditioned.

Summary. These experiments raise issues that seem to be central to understanding the conditioning process and its physiological substrate. What are the essential pathways involved in classical conditioning? Can classical conditioning occur in the absence of reinforcement? Answers to these questions must await experiments that more adequately control the nature of the UR and provide a rationale for responses to be scored as CRs. It is clear that only when a broad definition of acceptable CRs is employed is such conditioning particularly robust (Kandel & Benevento, 1973). On the other hand, it is clear that cortical stimulation can substitute for the CS and this result has been replicated many times. It is also clear that the animal need not actually make the UR for conditioning to be successful. Light and Gantt (1936) prevented UR occurrence by crushing the motor nerves leading to the appropriate muscles. Conditioning training was carried out during the ensuing muscular paralysis. After training, when the motor nerves had regenerated, flexion CRs were obtained despite the fact that they had never occurred during training.

Conditioning is not critically dependent on the peripheral receptors for the CS or on muscular effectors for the UR; each can be bypassed and successful conditioning can still occur. Between these extremes, perhaps in the central pathways connecting CS and UR, there may be a locus which cannot be bypassed such that mere continguity of CS and UR may not be sufficient.

Split-Brain Preparations

The neural locus of a training procedure can be roughly restricted if the learning is confined to one hemisphere of the brain; this would enable comparison of trained and untrained sides of the same brain. It may be accomplished by cutting the optic chiasm and the corpus callosum connecting the two hemispheres (see Figure 13.2). These operations restrict the visual input, and visually based learning, to one hemisphere. Thus, animals trained to perform visual pattern discriminations with one eye cannot perform them with the other if the operations are performed prior to training. Different, and even conflicting, tasks may be trained in the two hemispheres after such operations. (Corpus callosum transection also has profound effects on the integration of verbal and nonverbal functioning in humans, topics we shall discuss in the next chapter.)

Functional and reversible separation of the two hemispheres has been claimed through the use of chemicals such as potassium chloride. Experiments have been carried out suggesting that application of the drug to one hemisphere depresses the electrical activity of that portion of the cortex only and confines the training to the functionally active hemisphere. This interpretation is the subject of some controversy, however (see Schneider, 1967, 1968; Squire & Liss, 1968). We can only conclude here that the analytic tool used to study learning is itself in need of analysis before firm conclusions about learning can be drawn.

Autonomic Versus Skeletal Nervous System

In Chapter 7 we looked extensively at the issues raised by the application of biofeedback procedures to the training of autonomic responses. We will not repeat that material here. However, resolution of some of those issues may allow further investigation of any functional learning differences between the autonomic and skeletal motor systems. For instance, DiCara, Braun, and Pappas (1970) reported that removal of about 90 percent of the neocortex of the rat resulted in failure to acquire instrumental cardiac and gastrointestinal responses; the same responses could still be conditioned with classical techniques.

Electrophysiological Indices of Learning

Recordings of the electrical activity of the brain have been used in two ways to study the learning process. One group of studies has recorded changes in electrical activity as they occur in the course of the application of some training procedure. In these studies, the electrical changes are treated simply as "correlates" of the learning. Another approach has attempted to influence the electrical activity itself; that is, the electrical activity is subjected to the training routine instead of some overt motor response. The latter type of study attempts to build an electrophysiological model of the learning process based on electrical events in the CNS that might be occurring as an organism learns. We shall examine some examples of each approach.

Correlates of Learning

In the studies to be considered here, electrical activity of the brain is passively recorded while subjects are in the process of learning some overt motor response. The attempt is to seek correlations between the behavioral changes and the accompanying electrical records. Obviously, however, correlation does not necessarily imply any causal link between the two.

EEG During Conditioning. A number of studies have summarized the EEG changes observed during classical conditioning (see Yoshii & Maeno, 1958; Yoshii, Matsumoto, Ogura, Shimokochi, Yamaguchi, & Yamasaki, 1960; Sakhiulina, 1960). The precise details presented by different authors vary, at least in part because of the variety of techniques and conditioning paradigms employed.

The data can be generally described as follows: Prior to conditioning, the CS-to-be elicits an orienting reaction which is seen in the EEG as generalized cortical arousal and evoked potentials, with subcortical theta activity in the hippocampal-amygdala-reticular areas. Repeated unreinforced presentations of the stimulus result in habituation and loss of such reactions. These reactions are reinstated with the start of reinforced presentations of the CS and become stronger with continued reinforcement. These "conditoned" EEG reactions occur before any behavioral CRs appear and outlast the behavioral CR during extinction. If discrimination procedures are employed, the negative stimulus will at first elicit EEG reactions similar to those evoked by the CS, but with continued nonreinforcement the negative stimulus elicits slow-wave activity. Similarly, delay or trace conditioning procedures are characterized by slow-wave activity during the early portions of the CS-US interval; such slow activity is taken as characteristic of inhibitory processes. It should be clear that whether these EEG changes are in any way intrinsically related to the formation of the conditioned behavioral reaction is a moot point. Nonetheless, these EEG reactions and the general properties of the reticular system have led theorists (see Gastaut, 1958) to speculate about the primacy of the reticular system and hippocampus in the formation of conditioned reflexes. Important here is the convergence of sensory input that is seen in the reticular system (Chapter 5). We have also noted that hippocampal theta activity is a frequent accompaniment of cortical arousal.

The exact signifiance of the hippocampal activity is a matter of some debate. It has been argued that hippocampal activity is related to orienting responses, or to conditioned reflex formation, or to different patterns of

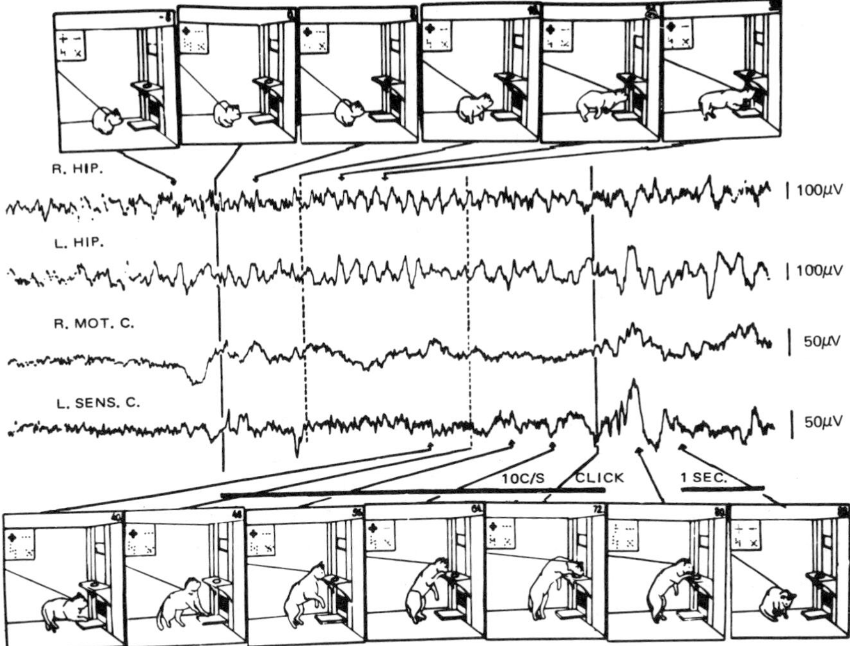

Figure 12.4. Demonstration of the simultaneous appearance of the rhythmic slow response and the orienting reaction. Recordings of the motor reaction (motion pictures) and the electrical activity were obtained synchronously. The motion pictures were taken at a rate of 16 pictures/sec. (Every eighth picture was projected and copied graphically.) The solid vertical lines indicate the duration of the conditioned stimulus, the dotted vertical lines that of the orientative reaction. The conditioned stimulus is also shown by the box flashing the symbol +. The source of the conditioned stimulus (loudspeaker) is indicated by a black box under the feeding device, toward which the orientation reflex is directed. As can be seen, the rhythmic slow activity and the orientative reaction coincide. (From Grastyán, E., Lissak, K., Madarasz, I., and Donhoffer, H., Hippocampal electrical activity during the development of conditioned reflexes. *Electroencephalography and Clinical Neurophysiology*, 1959, *11*, 409–430.)

motor performance. In any event, whatever the exact interpretation, a number of studies agree that early in training the hippocampus does show major modifications of its electrical activity. One example of such changes during instrumental conditioning is illustrated in Figure 12.4. But even if hippocampal changes are closely correlated with learning, it may still be asked whether such changes are necessary. Bennett (1973) tested cats for learning and retention of a discrimination task in which hippocampal theta activity accompanies responses on 90 to 95 percent of the trials. Some cats had theta activity blocked by central administration of scopolamine during training trials while other cats received the drug during retention trials. Under the drug, theta occurred on about 5 percent of the trials. Neither original learning nor retention of the task were affected by the drug administrations. Thus, hippocampal theta is not a necessary condition for learning to occur in this task. It also bears restating that even if the hippocampus may be normally involved, it is not critical for learning to occur—animals with hippocampal lesions do learn even if they are retarded in learning some responses.

Evoked Potentials and Learning. More recently, experimental emphasis has shifted from studies of gross EEG changes during learning to studies of what are hoped to be more specific mechanisms. For this purpose, evoked potential studies have been emphasized. This work has gone through several phases.

In the first phases of this research, many investigators reported that conditioning procedures resulted in augmentation of the amplitude of the evoked responses to the CS. Figure 12.5 is an early example of one such report. Here, a monkey was first habituated to tone beeps, and the beeps were then "reinforced" by the presentation of sugar. Note that no specific behavioral response was required and the experiment was assumed to involve conditioning only because the stimuli were presented in a manner similar to a conditioning paradigm (presumably the significance of the tones

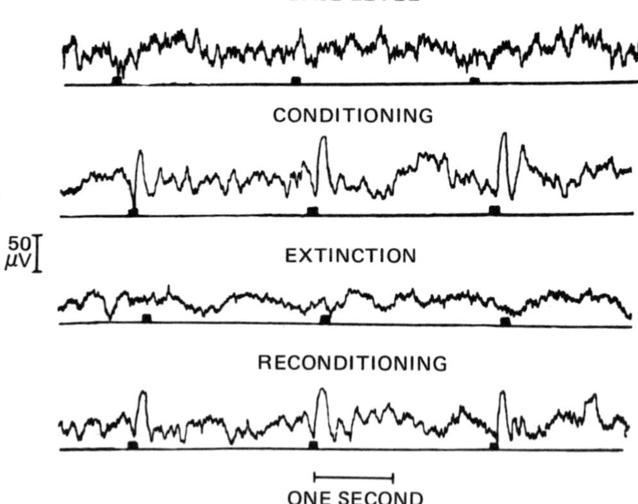

Figure 12.5. Sample hippocampal EEG records in one monkey. The small black squares beneath each record indicate onset and duration of the tone stimuli. During conditioning and reconditioning phases, a sugar pellet reward was delivered following each sequence of 10 tones. Tone periods were separated by silent periods averaging 3 min in duration. (From Hearst, E., Beer, B., Sheatz, G., and Galambos, R., Some electrophysiological correlates of conditioning in the monkey. *Electroencephalography and Clinical Neurophysiology*, 1960, *12*, 137–152.)

changed). Experiments such as this found that the amplitudes of evoked responses throughout the limbic and diencephalic areas were drastically augmented by "conditioning" procedures. But are these changes intrinsically related to the learning process?

Generally, a number of studies (Gerken & Neff, 1963; Hall & Mark, 1967; Mark & Hall, 1967) have all concluded that such changes are a transient result of emotional arousal rather than anything intrinsic to the learning process per se. They are most likely to occur in aversive, fear-producing training paradigms. In addition, Schwartz, Stewart, and Sunenshine (1969) attempted to relate evoked response amplitude to behavioral performance in a classical conditioning situation. Evoked responses to a light (CS) were recorded during habituation, conditioning, and extinction of eyeblink CRs. Several analyses indicated that there were no relationships between performance of the conditioned response and the evoked responses.

More recently, John (e.g., 1972) has suggested that evoked potential wave-shapes may represent the operation of two factors. One of these reflects the physical features of the evoking stimuli and the other is an endogenous process concerned with the meaning of the stimulus—a neural "readout" from memory. Evidence for the latter comes from the following type of experiment. Cats are first trained to make two different responses, one to each of two light flash stimuli differing in frequency, e.g., one flash sequence at 1/sec and one at 4/sec. When these performances are well established, testing with light flashes at 2/sec is begun, i.e., testing for generalization. It is claimed that the evoked responses to the 2/sec flashes resemble those produced to the 1/sec flash sequence when the animal makes the behavioral response appropriate to that frequency. Similarly, the evoked responses resemble those to the other frequency when the animal makes the behavioral response appropriate for that frequency. Generally, evoked response waveform differences occur in the later portions of the response.

The evoked responses that we have been discussing represent the activity of large numbers of neural cells. John's group (Ramos, Schwartz, & John, 1976) has also investigated the activity of single cells using the same procedures. Figure 12.6 is illustrative of their findings in the lateral geniculate nucleus and visual cortex. Each day's recordings are represented by two evoked responses (top line) and two histograms (bottom line) of the frequency of spike discharge of a single cell during the first 200 msec following each light flash. The columns of the figure indicate which of the two behavioral responses was made to the 2/sec generalization stimulus. The histograms differed according to which of the two responses the cat made to the generalization stimulus. In this instance, the evoked responses were not different for the two responses, so that cellular discharge is regarded as a more reliable discriminator. Figure 12.6 is illustrative of one type of cell found in this study—other cells were stable in their discharge characteristics

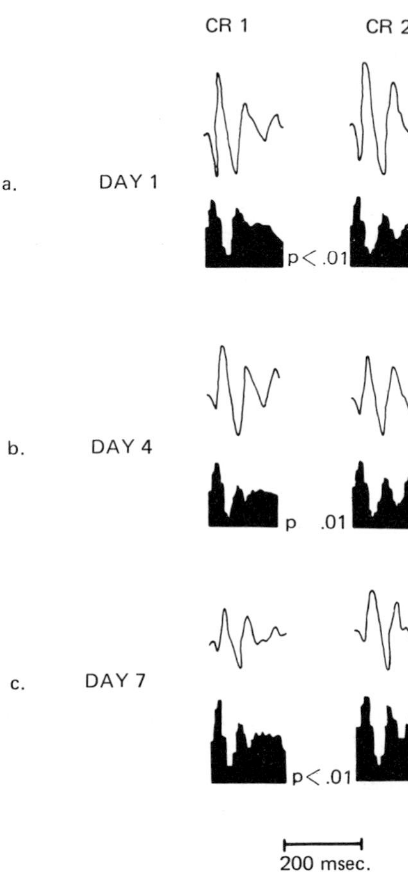

Figure 12.6. Evoked responses and histograms of cell discharge during tests of generalization. Note the consistent shape of the histograms in each column (same behavioral outcome on different days) and the significant difference between histograms on any row (different behavioral outcome on same day). The evoked responses were markedly less consistent day to day and did not differ according to behavioral outcome. (From Ramos, A., Schwartz, E., and John, E. R. An examination of the participation of neurons in readout from memory. *Brain Research Bulletin*, 1976, *1*, 77–86.)

and were unaffected by the response of the animal. Such stable response patterns were found in about 70 percent of the cells investigated; plastic patterns, reflecting the animal's responses, were found in about 30 percent of the cells. These results suggest that different cells mediate processing of exogenous stimulus features and endogenous memory processes.

Figure 12.7 (Berger, Alger, & Thompson 1976) shows another kind of evoked activity, this one again suggesting hippocampal involvement in learning. Histograms of spike activity in several hippocampal units (CA1 in the figure) revealed activity in conjunction with the nicitating membrane[1] response of the rabbit only when the CS and US were explicitly paired to produce conditioning. In control conditions, where CS and US were each presented but not paired, the hippocampal activity was absent even though the nicitating membrane responded to the US. In addition, it was shown that the hippocampal activity appeared very quickly, becoming manifest within

[1]The nicitating membrane is a second, inner "eyelid" possessed by some animals.

the first few conditioning trials. These data suggest that such hippocampal activity might be the earliest indication that learning is occurring.

Summary. The studies reviewed here generally suggest that certain electrophysiological changes occur in conjunction with training procedures. Whether any of these changes are a necessary concomitant of learning re-

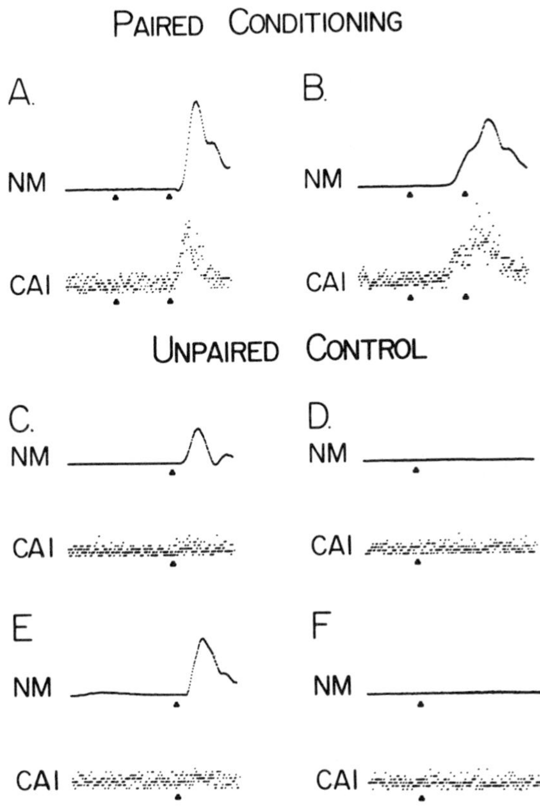

Figure 12.7. *Upper Trace*: Average nicitating membrane (*NM*) response for one block of eight trials. *Lower trace*: Hippocampal unit post-stimulus histogram for one block of eight trials. (a) First block of eight paired conditioning trials, day 1. (b) Last block of eight paired conditioning trials, day 1, after conditioning has occurred. First cursor indicates tone onset; second cursor indicates air puff onset. (c) First block of eight unpaired UCS-alone trials, day 1. (e) Last block of eight unpaired UCS-alone trials, day 2. Cursor indicates air puff onset. (d) First block of eight unpaired CS-alone trials, day 1. (f) Last block of eight unpaired CS-alone trials, day 2. Cursor indicates tone onset. Total trace length is 750 msec. Height of vertical bar to right of CA1 unit post-stimulus histogram in (a) is equivalent to 13 neural spike events. (From Berger, T. W., Alger, G., and Thompson, R. F. Neuronal substrate of classical conditioning in the hippocampus. *Science*, 1976, *192*, 483–485.)

mains to be demonstrated. These experiments have tended to look for learning changes in the activities of individual brain cells, a trend that is also evident in the studies to be considered next.

Conditioning of Neural Activity

Almost since the very beginning of EEG recording, attempts have been made to manipulate neural activity directly through the application of conditioning procedures; i.e., to build neural models of the conditioning process. Figure 12.8 shows one such experimental result that used light, generally a blocker of alpha activity in the EEG, as the US and a tone as the CS. The two were paired in a series of trials. A test with tone alone resulted in alpha blocking (CR). In their study, Jasper and Shagass (1941) claimed to be able to reproduce a variety of results appropriate to different Pavlovian conditioning

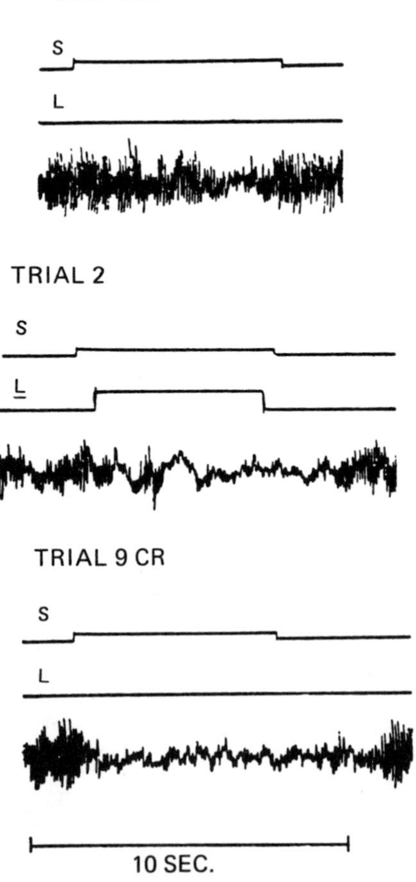

Figure 12.8. Simple CR in alpha block conditioning. Control shows sounds (S) without light (L) had no effect on alpha waves. Trial 2 was second conditioning trial. Trial 9 shows blocking of alpha rhythm as CR to sound. (From Jasper, H., and Shagass, C., Conditioning the occipital alpha rhythm in man. *Journal of Comparative and Physiological Psychology*, 1941, *28*, 373–388. Copyright 1941 by the American Psychological Association. Reprinted by permission.)

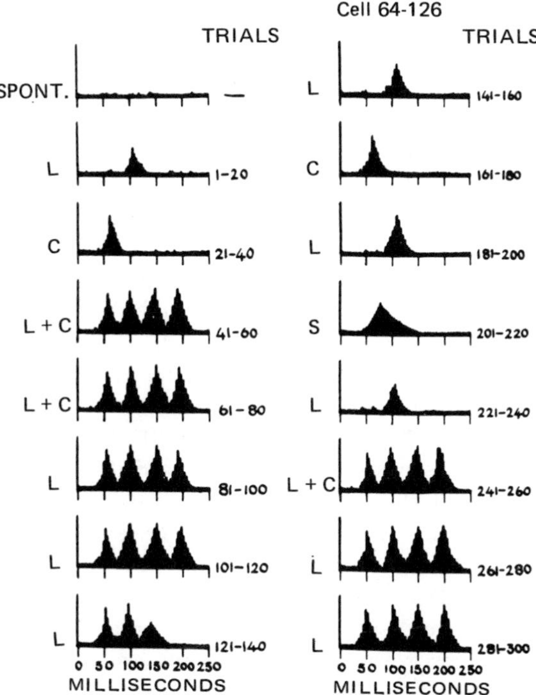

Figure 12.9. Cell was responsive to visual (L), acoustic (C), and tactile (S) stimulation. Illustrates PST histograms over the duration of experiment. Electric shock was used late in experiment as a "novel" stimulus and did not result either in "dishabituation" or response restoration. Note that each of the three modalities of stimulation produced a different histogram. Pairing of L+C results in a different response to L alone. [From Morrell, F., Electrical signs of sensory coding. In G. C. Quarton, T. Melnechuk, and F. O. Schmitt (Eds.). *The Neurosciences, A Study Program.* N.Y.: The Rockefeller University Press, 1967, 452–469.]

paradigms—trace, delay, backward, etc. A number of objections to the validity of such results has been raised, however (see Knott, 1941; Milstein, 1965), to the effect that they may represent sensitization and artifacts of motor responding rather than direct conditioning of the EEG.

Figure 12.9 illustrates a result highly suggestive of classical conditioning of single-cell discharges (Morrell, 1967). The cell represented here was from the visual cortex; however, in addition to responding to the light flash (L), it also fired in response to clicks (C) and shock (S). In the upper left of the figure is the histogram of the spontaneous discharge of this cell; it is flat, that is, spikes occurred at essentially random intervals.

Next, the cell was tested for response to light; spikes predominated some 100 msec after the flashes in a series of 20 responses to light. In response to single clicks, the spikes predominantly occurred earlier. Combined light and clicks, simultaneously presented (L + C), produced a pattern that was unlike either of the separate response patterns—that is, the histogram showed four modes, with the cell discharging cyclically over the 200 msec following the stimuli. After 40 such pairings, the response to light alone was tested again, and the response now resembled that to the combined stimuli; this continued to be the case for more than 40 trials. This "conditioned" response finally extinguished, and the response patterns to both light and click again resembled their original form. The response to shock was different from either of these patterns, and the subsequent response to light apparently was not affected by the prior run of 20 shock trials.

Finally, "reconditioning" was demonstrated. About 13 percent (102) of all cells sampled showed this type of plasticity.

A change in response characteristics of some lateral geniculate cells as a result of pairing of auditory and light stimuli has also been recently demonstrated (Chalupa, Macadar, & Lindsley, 1975). In this study, pairings resulted in a decrease in the discharge of the cells and, again, it was the response to light that showed the change. Interestingly, the cells never showed response to the tone itself. Pairings were effective with a CS-US interval of 0 or 100 msec but not with 500 msec.

Whether these studies represent neural models of behavioral conditioning is problematic since several dissimilarities from behavioral results and conditions optimal for behavioral conditioning are evident. For example, optimal behavioral conditioning occurs with about a 500 msec CS-US interval; then, too, behavioral classical conditioning results in the transfer to an ineffective stimulus (CS) the property of eliciting a response to an effective stimulus (US). Here, it is not even clear which stimulus was CS and which US. In any event, even if these results are not directly comparable to behavioral conditioning, they do represent a plasticity in cellular responsiveness that is likely to be of interest for the conditioning process.

Finally, several investigators (Olds & Olds, 1961; Olds, 1965; Fetz, 1969) have reported instrumental conditioning of neural responses, in which spontaneous changes in the firing rate were reinforced by rewarding ESB or food. In all these experiments, the animals were free to move; it is ambiguous then whether such conditioning is a direct consequence of reinforcement or an indirect consequence of "superstitious" movements that resulted in the recordable neural activity.

The same question can also be raised in regard to a number of reports of control over the amplitude of gross EEG activity. In fact, a report by Wyrwicka and Sterman (1968) indicates that such conditioning is accompanied by stereotyped postural adjustments. Wyrwicka and Sterman argue that these postures represent a state of central inhibition rather than functioning as a cause of the EEG changes, but at this point this appears to be a chicken-

and-egg problem. However, Miller (1969), in a review of the research, reported that Carmona was able to instrumentally condition EEG amplitude in curarized (paralyzed) rats.

Summary. The principal lesson to be learned from experiments attempting to condition neural activity directly is that they indicate the plasticity of the units concerned. Perhaps this phenomenon will prove unrelated to learning but during the course of research it will undoubtedly lead to much that might be relevant.

SIMPLER MODELS

Many nonmammalian animals have nervous systems whose simplicity and regularity allow us to identify the same specific neural cells in each experimental animal. These animals also show a primitive behavioral plasticity, habituation, also found in mammals. Habituation, or the decrease in response to a behaviorally irrelevant stimulus, is considered to be a primitive example of the learning process. For these two reasons, the presumed simpler process and the simplicity of the nervous system, the study of habituation in nonmammalian species may provide a useful model for the neural substrates of learning. Much of the work in this area has been reviewed in two volumes edited by Peeke and Herz (1973). We shall consider briefly some particularly relevant examples.

A series of experiments has attempted to pursue the habituation model in the marine mollusc *Aplysia* (Figure 12.10). The first experiment (Pinsker, Kupfermann, Castellucci, & Kandel, 1970) simply showed that *Aplysia* is capable of demonstrating the essential characteristics of behavioral habituation and dishabituation. Figure 12.10 illustrates the general experimental setup employed in these experiments. The response measured in these experiments was the gill-withdrawal reflex, which is part of a larger defensive response to potentially noxious tactile stimuli. When gill withdrawal was repeatedly evoked by a tactile stimulus to the siphon or mantle, the amplitude of the response showed a marked decrement; after rest, it exhibited spontaneous recovery. The habituated response appeared with renewed vigor in response to a strong tactile stimulus (dishabituation) to some other part of the body. Other characteristics included habituation of the disinhibiting stimulus, greater habituation with shorter interstimulus intervals, and greater habituation with weaker stimuli.

In the second experiment (Kupfermann, Castellucci, Pinsker, & Kandel, 1970), intracellular recordings were obtained from specific, identifiable gill motor neurons in the abdominal ganglion of *Aplysia* during the observation of behavioral habituation. It was first shown that gill contraction was

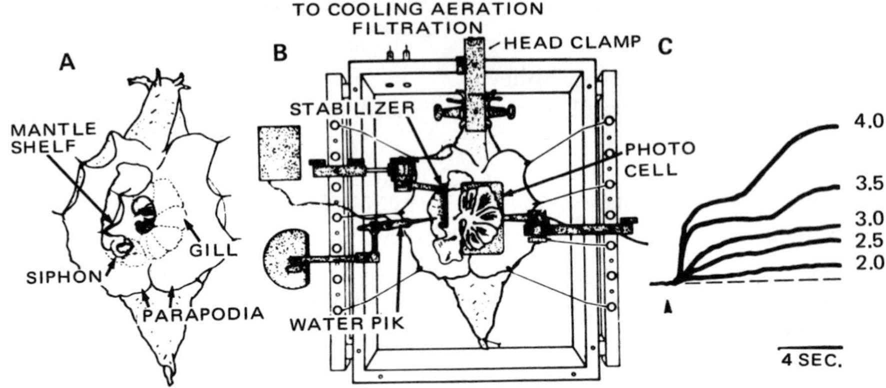

Figure 12.10. Experimental arrangement for testing habituation of gill-withdrawal reflex in *Aplysia.* (a) Dorsal view of an intact animal showing the fully contracted gill. Normally the parapodia and mantle shelf obscure the view of the gill, but they have been retracted to allow observation. The relaxed position of the gill is indicated by the broken lines. The tactile receptive field for the gill-withdrawal reflex includes the siphon and the edge of the mantle shelf. (b) An animal immobilized in the test aquiarium. The tactile stimulus consisted of a brief jet of seawater (via Water Pik). Gill contractions were monitored by a photocell. (c) Gill responses to individual tactile stimuli of different intensities separated by long time periods. The strongest stimuli evoked a late second contraction. (From Pinsker, H., Kupfermann, I., Castellucci, V., and Kandel, E., Habituation and dishabituation of the gill-withdrawal reflex in aplysia. *Science*, March 1970, *167*, 1740–1742. Copyright 1970 by the American Association for the Advancement of Science.)

correlated with spike discharge in these neurons. Secondly, habituation and dishabituation could not be ascribed to peripheral changes in either sensory receptors or gill musculature but rather to changes in the amplitude of excitatory synaptic potentials at the motor neuron, a central process.

The third experiment (Castellucci, Pinsker, Kupfermann, & Kandel, 1970) indicated that both habituation and dishabituation of gill withdrawal involve changes in the effectiveness of a specific set of central excitatory synapses between sensory and motor neurons. Habituation is the result of a decrement in excitability of these synapses. Dishabituation results when an excitatory input to these synapses is relayed over a different afferent pathway and the data suggest that this facilitation operates presynaptically.

These data show that all the characteristics of behavioral habituation obtained in *Aplysia* can be duplicated at the level of specific cells involved in that behavior and can be explained by alterations in excitatory processes in the synapses of these cells. The data also imply that, at least in this case, it is unnecessary to explain behavioral modification by invoking complex fields or distributions of activity in a neural aggregate—in this instance, at least, the changes are a function of specific cells. Second, these experiments indicate that dishabituation is not merely the removal of some decrementing process but that it is an independent, facilitatory process superimposed on the decrement. In this view, dishabituation is seen as a special case of the behavioral notion of sensitization. Finally, these studies strengthen the assumption that analysis of the "wiring diagram" underlying behavior is a prerequisite for studying the behavioral modifications that we ascribe to learning.

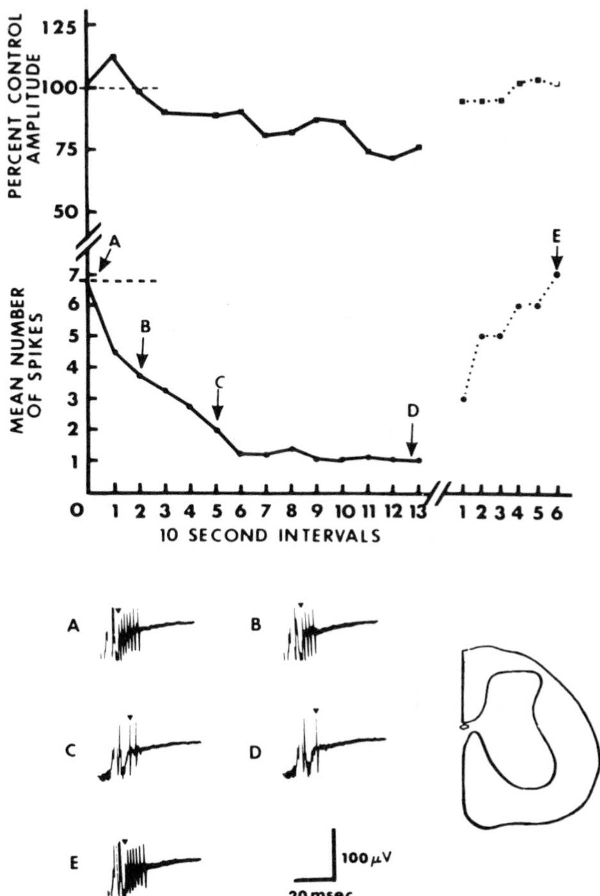

Figure 12.11. A typical type H interneuron. Upper graph represents the amplitude of the flex or twitch of the tibialis anterior muscle, showing sensitization followed by habituation and spontaneous recovery. The lower graph represents mean number of spikes per stimulus of a simultaneously recorded interneuron. Note that the interneuron shows only a progressive decrease in evoked discharges even during behavior sensitization. The position of the electrode tip is shown at lower right. Sample oscilloscope tracings are shown in A through E. (From Groves, P. M., and Thompson, R. F. A dual-process theory of habitation: Neural mechanisms. In H. V. S. Peeke and M. J. Herz (eds.), *Habituation, Vol. II*. New York: Academic Press, 1973, pp. 175–205.)

These results are in remarkable agreement with data and theory derived from the study of habituation of the startle response in the rat and flexion responses in the spinal cat (R. F. Thompson & Spencer, 1966; Groves & Thompson, 1970); such agreement suggests that even data from so primitive an organism as *Aplysia* has general utility for the learning problem.

In the cat spinal cord, Groves and Thompson (1973) have isolated two general classes of neurons whose response characteristics correlate well with the habituation of flexor muscle responses. One class of neurons, Type H, shows a decrementing frequency of spike discharge to repeated elicitations of the muscle response (Figure 12.11). The other class of cells, Type S, first shows an initial sensitization—increased discharge—followed by habituation with further elicitations of the muscle response (Figure 12.12).

Conclusions

We began this review by noting certain deficiencies in behavioral approaches to understanding learning, and we expressed the hope that a physiological approach might clarify some of these problems. Obviously it would be pretentious to imply that we are now in a position to supply many definitive answers. However, it does seem that we are now able at least to ask some potentially productive questions.

It is probably true that learning requires the presence of a sophisticated CNS, although even this is debatable—witness the controversies over learning in paramecia and planaria. What distinguishes trainable from nontrainable neurons is not clear. Thus, the apparently greater plasticity of central, in comparison to spinal, neurons is a topic that requires basic physiological investigation. A corollary question concerns whether CNS neurons differ in their plasticity because of some intrinsic property that each possesses or whether it is the aggregate of neurons that has this property. Thus, while we have seen that single cells show modification, it is by no means clear that they could show this if they were not in the context of other, surrounding, neurons. However, given this neural plasticity, what questions does it imply?

Behaviorally, psychologists distinguish learning effects from sensitization, pseudoconditioning, habituation, and maturation. Will we be able to continue to make these distinctions when we examine neural processes more closely? In one sense, at least, conditioning and extinction are both forms of learning. In experiments reviewed in Chapter 2 it was seen that the functional integrity and responsiveness of CNS neurons was dependent on appropriate stimulus input. Are we premature in discounting this as relevant to learning? We have also seen examples of neural changes that seem to occur as a result of sensitization or habituation; to what extent are these changes really different from those that might be involved in learning? In other words, these processes, at a neural level, may not be sharply distinct. In

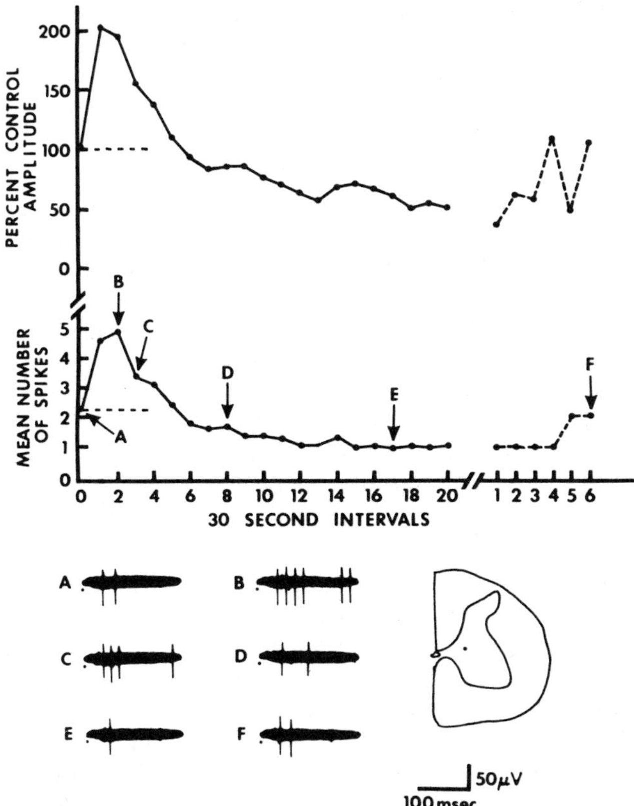

Figure 12.12. A type S interneuron having a firing pattern of one or a few discharges. Upper graph represents the amplitude of the flexor twitch of the tibialis anterior muscle, showing sensitization followed by habituation and spontaneous recovery. The lower graph represents mean number of spikes per stimulus of the simultaneously recorded interneuron. Note that the interneuron shows an initial increase followed by a decrease in evoked discharges. The position of the electrode tip is shown at lower right. Sample oscilloscope tracings are shown in A through F. (From Groves, P. M., and Thompson, R. F. A dual-process theory of habituation: Neural mechanisms. In H. V. S. Peeke and M. J. Herz (eds.), *Habituation, Vol. II*. New York: Academic Press, 1973, pp. 175–205.)

short, the psychologist cannot afford to be unduly selective about the models employed. The only concern is whether they are productive of meaningful research.

Similarly, psychologists frequently characterize learning as the acquisition of new stimulus-response connections. A number of considerations suggest that there may be nothing "new" about learning. Thus, the various EEG and evoked-potential studies that we have reviewed all indicate the widespread access that stimulus information has in the brain. Furthermore, the studies are all similar in showing that unless specific habituation techniques are employed, behaviorally neutral stimuli are accompanied by widespread brain responses. A productive research hypothesis might then entertain the notion that learning involves the activation of previously inhibited connections.

Many of the experiments that we have reviewed here have produced changes in neural activity as a consequence of pairing two stimuli. Such results certainly suggest that, at a neural level, sensory integration (S-S conditioning) is an effective learning procedure. It may be pertinent to ask whether the whole controversy over S-R versus S-S conditioning may not disappear at the neural level simply because neural responses are neural responses regardless of whether they accompany S's or R's; that is, they may not be distinguishable in the CNS.

The single most perplexing issue still pertains to the question of the localization of the engram. We have presented data which suggest that it may be possible to compromise the contrasting notions of an isolated, circumscribed engram versus a diffusely located engram. Be that as it may, a large store of accumulating information suggests that the properties of specific cells *are* of concern in understanding the question of engram storage. Thus, we have seen many instances where only some individual cells have properties and response characteristics that appear to be pertinent to the plasticity of behavior. Storage of the engram would seem to depend on these specific cells.

It also seems appropriate to offer alternatives to the localization issue. Thus, given a relatively circumscribed task, such as discrimination, in contrast to a multisensory task like maze learning, the evidence does suggest that all normal subjects learn the response with the same neural tissue—lesions that are effective seem to be generally effective in all animals. This consistency seems to have been ignored. If the engram were diffusely organized, one might expect that this would not be the case and that some animals would not be affected by a given lesion. What variance there is in performances between animals with lesions in similar loci seems generally to be a function of lesion size—larger lesions produce a greater decrement in behavior. This consistency, then, would seem to imply that there is some specificity to the location of the engram in the normal animal. The fact that animals may relearn the task does not deny such a specificity. Rather, it simply points to the fact that the specific tissue is not essential. This suggests that historically we have focused on the wrong problem. At issue here may not be the question of localization of the engram but rather the mechanisms that govern the hierarchical control over which tissue will be employed in a learning task. To state this another way: There seems to be an orderly priority among different CNS areas that are more or less equally capable of storing the learning of specific tasks. The proper question may thus be, What are the mechanisms that control this hierarchical ordering? One possibility is that some hierarchy of sustained inhibitory processes exists; destruction of tissue higher in the hierarchy frees the lower levels for such storage. In any event, reliance on concepts like mass action and equipotentiality does not answer the questions we are asking—equipotentiality and mass action are themselves problems which require explanation. We need to find out how and under what circumstances they occur.

MEMORY

We infer that learning has occurred if some time after training an organism displays the modified behavior under appropriate stimulus conditions; we say that the organism "remembers" because the correct response is performed. We assume that the prior training experience has caused some relatively permanent modification to occur within the organism and that modification stores the engram or trace of the training experience. Here we shall review some theories about how this storage might occur. The main approach taken to studying memory storage has been to disrupt that storage—only by determining what affects storage can we ascertain its characteristics. A principal finding of such experiments has been the relatively fragile nature of memory. Memory is not necessarily permanent, particularly when newly acquired. Newer engrams seem to be more subject to disruption than older traces. The transition from a weak to a more permanent condition of the memory trace is known as *consolidation* and seems to be a function of the passage of time.

The Consolidation Hypothesis

The history of the consolidation hypothesis has been outlined by Glickman (1961). It stems mainly from human clinical data: Persons sustaining head injuries often demonstrate *retrograde amnesia*—they cannot remember events during the period immediately preceding the injury, although more remote events generally appear unaffected. It has been suggested, therefore, that memory involves some physiological "fixing" or "setting" process that requires time for completion. Immediate recall is believed to be dependent on some transient mechanism that is subject to disruption; left undisturbed, this transient process is replaced by a more permanent storage mechanism. The transient mechanism generally is conceived to be some sort of reverberatory, perseverative activity of the neurons involved in processing the learning (Hebb, 1949). The storage we will be concerned with is the more permanent storage.

It will also be helpful if at the outset of this discussion an obvious point is made: Amnesia is a general term indicating the absence of memory, but memory can be missing for any of several possible reasons. We say people "forget"—implying that the memory is lost because of some gradual weakening of the storage mechanism. Destruction of the trace is just one possible explanation, however. Memory might also be absent because the trace, though still intact, cannot be "retrieved"—for instance, when we have something on the "tip of our tongue" but cannot quite remember it. In considering methods for disrupting memory, we will have to keep these distinctions in mind.

ECS Studies

The basic consolidation hypothesis was advanced as long ago as 1900 (Glickman, 1961), but the first technical method for conducting experimental investigations of it dates back to 1937 when electroconvulsive shock (*ECS*) was introduced into clinical practice. It was immediately apparent that ECS leads to retrograde amnesia. ECS has subsequently become the major tool for the investigation of memory and the consolidation hypothesis. In recent years, however, there has been controversy about the significance of ECS for memory. That ECS produces performance deficits is not to be denied; whether such deficits represent memory impairment is, however, not clear.

A number of early studies (see Glickman, 1961) tested retention of verbal material in patients receiving ECS. These studies generally supported the notion that ECS given soon after learning disrupted retention, while delayed ECS did not. The early studies did not systematically investigate the time course of the effect; the first study to do this was performed by Duncan (1949).

Duncan trained rats to avoid shock to the feet in a shuttle box. Shock came on 10 seconds after the rat was placed in the apparatus; it could be avoided by moving into a lighted "safe" compartment. The rats received one trial per day; in the experimental groups, each trial was followed, after a specific interval, by an ECS. In an additional control series, shock to the hind feet, at comparable intervals after each trial, was substituted for the head shock used to convulse the experimental animals; the latter control was designed to test the assumption that, in effect, the experimental rats were being punished for making avoidances by being given ECS.

Figure 12.13 summarizes the major results of these experiments. ECS (head shock, in the figure) given up to 15 minutes after completion of each trial resulted in a decrement in avoidance. That these results cannot simply be attributed to an aversion to entering the safe area is suggested by the results from the control groups. Only the group receiving leg shock 20 seconds after each trial showed an avoidance learning decrement, and this appears to be smaller than the decrement produced by ECS (but differences between any of these controls and the ECS animals were not tested statistically).

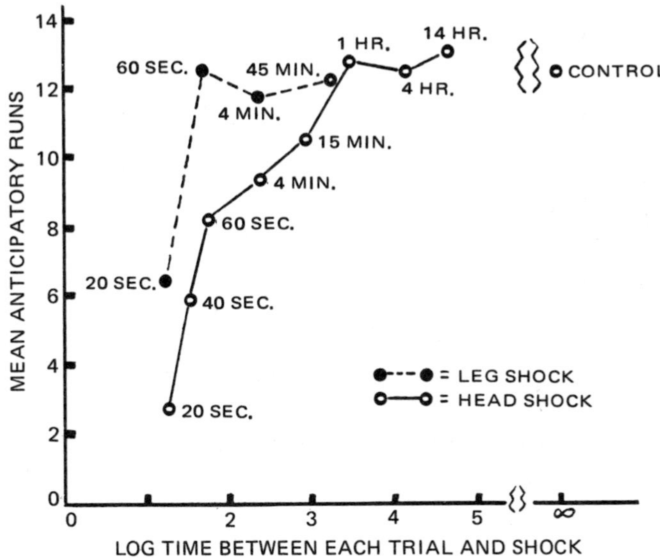

Figure 12.13. Mean number of avoidances over 18 training trials for groups receiving ECS (head shock) or leg shock at various times following each trial. Animals receiving ECS within 15 min after each trial were retarded in performance. In the leg-shock controls, only the 20-sec group showed retardation. (From Duncan, C. P., The retroactive effect of electroshock on learning. *Journal of Comparative and Physiological Psychology*, 1949, *42*, 32–44. Copyright 1949 by the American Psychological Association. Reprinted by permission.)

Figure 12.14 plots learning curves for the ECS animals. Note that over the series of trials, ECS does seem to have an additional cumulative effect, as indicated by the decline in avoidance responding in the latter parts of training in the 20- and 40-second groups. Memory impairment alone should have resulted in a generally lower level of responding but not in a rise followed by a fall. Thus, some additional aversive factors must have also been operating.

Duncan thought his results were in accord with the consolidation hypothesis and suggested that about 15 minutes is necessary for the effects of a single trial in this situation to become consolidated. Substantially the same results were also reported by other investigators in a variety of other tasks, but with disagreement over the length of the consolidation interval. Some studies have found ECS-induced memory decrements even if the treatment was applied as long as an hour or more after learning (see R. Thompson & Dean, 1955).

In recent years, there has been a growing reluctance to accept results such as Duncan's as necessarily indicating the validity of the consolidation hypothesis. A large body of data has been accumulated in an attempt to analyze further the apparent memory failure induced by ECS. Actually, there are two issues to be considered. One concerns the validity of the

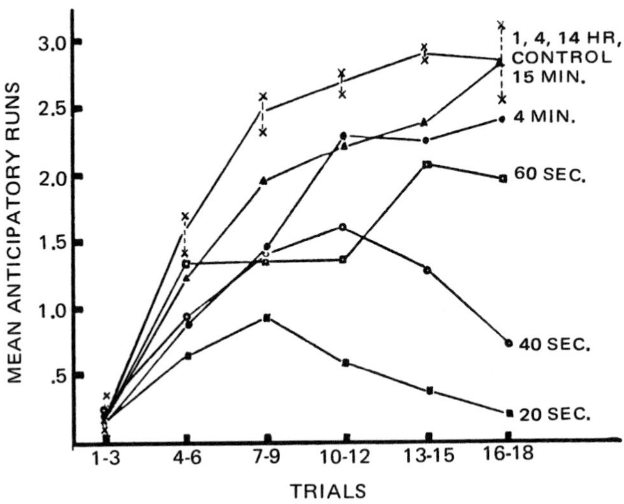

Figure 12.14. Learning curves for animals receiving ECS at various times after each avoidance training trial. Only the ranges of the means for the 1, 4, 14 hr, and control groups are shown. The upper curve connects the midpoints of the ranges. Note the decline in performance in the latter part of training exhibited by the 20- and 40-sec groups. (From Duncan, C. P., The retroactive effect of electroshock on learning. *Journal of Comparative and Physiological Psychology*, 1949, *42*, 32–44. Copyright 1949 by the American Psychological Association. Reprinted by permission.)

consolidation hypothesis itself. This issue has tended to become obscured by the volume of literature concerned with the second issue, analysis of the specific effects of ECS. It should be clear that the validity of the consolidation hypothesis is in fact independent of whether ECS is an appropriate tool for testing that hypothesis.

Beginning in 1960, a large number of studies have specifically challenged the retrograde amnesia interpretation of the effects of ECS. The literature is voluminous and we shall only cite the types of problems raised. The first study to suggest that retrograde amnesia was not a primary effect of ECS was carried out by Coons and Miller (1960). Their experiments concerned the possibility that in Duncan's experiment fear or conflict produced by the ECS prevented the animals from entering the safe compartment and would be indistinguishable from loss of memory. They suggested that Duncan's leg-shock control inadequately sampled this possibility. Other hypotheses have also been offered suggesting that some aspect of the ECS procedure produces effects that interfere with the performance of the tested response (e.g., Lewis & Adams, 1963; McGaugh & Madsen, 1964). Generally, as a result of these studies, the type of experiments testing the consolidation hypothesis has changed. Interference effects seem to be produced if animals are given repeated ECS treatments; therefore, most recent studies have employed variations of passive avoidance training as the experimental setting for testing ECS-induced memory deficits. Passive avoidance learning can be accomplished in one trial and repeated ECS treatments are not required to disrupt the learning.

Assuming for the moment that performance deficits produced by ECS do not result from some external interference such as fear or conflict, do they necessarily represent disruption of consolidation? Several other objections to the consolidation hypothesis have been offered. If ECS does disrupt consolidation, it would be expected that performance decrements would be permanent—yet several experiments suggest that they are not. Some of these experiments suggest a spontaneous recovery of memory; others suggest that treatments designed as "reminders"—supposedly without adding to any learning—can result in the reinstatement of performance that has been disrupted by ECS. As an alternative to the consolidation hypothesis, it has been suggested that ECS disrupts retrieval rather than consolidation (Miller & Springer, 1973; 1974; Gold & King, 1974; Meyer, 1972).

We have previously (Chapter 7) indicated that pairing an external stimulus with a strong shock will produce a conditioned emotional reponse (CER). Brady and his associates (Brady, 1951; Brady, Hunt, & Geller, 1954) have shown that a CER may be alleviated by ECS treatment even if the treatment is given hours or days after the original CER training. In addition, disruption of the CER is not permanent. This suggests that a major effect of ECS may be on the CER rather than on consolidation.

State-dependent or *dissociated* learning are terms applied to a group of findings indicating that memory for a learned task depends on the existence of some special "state" that prevails during training. Thus, for instance, Girden and Culler (1937) trained animals under the drug curare; when tested wihout curare, the responses were absent but subsequently reappeared following administration of the drug. Several experiments suggest that a similar effect may occur with ECS (Gardner, Glick, & Jarvik, 1972; C. I. Thompson and Grossman, 1972). ECS given within an hour *before* training resulted in retention of a passive avoidance response if testing for retention was also preceded by an ECS. On the other hand, when retention was tested in the absence of a prior ECS, it was disrupted. In the latter instance, since ECS *preceded* original training it can hardly be presumed that ECS disrupted memory consolidation.

Conclusions

It is clear that ECS is not an uncomplicated technique for testing the consolidation hypothesis. In addition to the effects already discussed, a single ECS has been shown to reduce operant responding, open-field activity, stepdown latency, and to produce weight loss (Routtenberg & Kay, 1965). If

ECS has amnestic effects, it also has other consequences that may confound the evaluation of these effects.

We have concentrated on ECS since it is the most popular technique employed in the study of memory. Other manipulations have been used to either disrupt or enhance consolidation. With these, it would also appear that further study is required to ascertain whether their effects are on consolidation per se.

Given the above complications, what can be concluded about the consolidation hypothesis itself? Even those workers who maintain that ECS does disrupt consolidation estimate that it is effective only for brief periods after training—10 seconds at most. Thus two interpretations emerge: It may be that consolidation is effectively over within 10 seconds, but it may also be that ECS is an ineffective means for disrupting processes that actually operate over a much longer time period. There is evidence that memory undergoes spontaneous fluctuations over a much longer time period than is commonly conceived of in talking about consolidation.

Storage Mechanisms

Synaptic Conductance Theory

The material to be discussed here is compatible with the hypothesis that memory retrieval depends on alterations in synaptic conduction. Alterations in both cholinergic and adrenergic activity seem to be implicated, though in different ways.

Cholinergic Mechanisms. Deutsch, Hamburg, and Dahl (1966) trained rats in a Y-maze to run into the lighted arm to escape shock; the safe arm varied randomly from trial to trial. After reaching the criterion of 10 consecutive correct choices, the various experimental groups received injections of the anticholinesterase drug diisopropyl fluorophosphate (DFP) in a peanut oil vehicle, while control groups received injections of peanut oil alone. In the first series, relearning tests were conducted in different groups 1, 2, or 5 days after injection of DFP and 1 day after peanut oil. These groups were designed to test whether interference with cholinergic synaptic transmission would cause amnesia and whether there would be spontaneous recovery of the habit with the passage of time. Figure 12.15a illustrates the results: DFP produced a deficit—more trials were required to relearn the task—24 hours after injection; controls and animals retrained 5 days after injection did not differ, indicating return of the habit within that period of time.

In the second series, animals were trained and received their injections at various times following training (the injection-test interval was a constant 24 hours in this series); animals were injected on the day of training, or 3, 5,

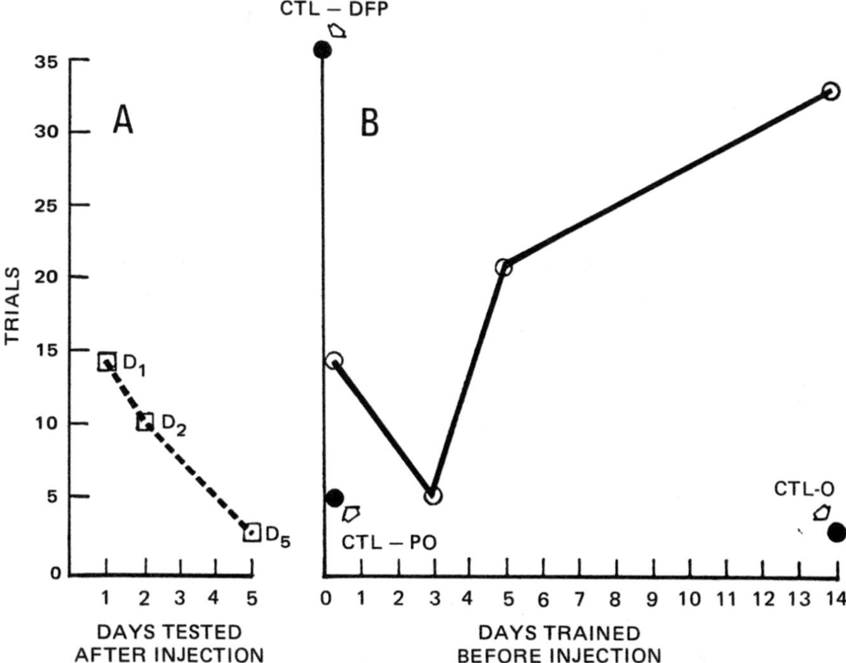

Figure 12.15. Trials to relearn to avoid shock in a Y maze after DFP injections. In (a), initial training occurred 30 min before injection. In (b), training took place the indicated number of days prior to injection, and relearning was carried out 24 hrs after injection. CTL-O indicates animals trained and retested without intervening treatment; CTL-DFP indicates animals injected with DFP without original training. CTL-PO indicates animals trained and injected with peanut oil 30 min after training. (From Deutsch, J. A., Hamburg, M. D., and Dahl, H., Anticholinesterase-induced amnesia and its temporal aspects. *Science*, Jan. 1966, *151*, 221–223. Copyright 1966 by the American Association for the Advancement of Science.)

or 14 days afterward. One control group was used to assess how fast an untrained group could be trained 24 hours after DFP, and another control group was used to assess the amount of forgetting over a 14-day period—the latter group received no injection. The results are shown in Figure 12.15b. DFP given 14 days after training completely eliminated the habit—these animals required as many trials to relearn as the group trained for the first time after DFP. There was no forgetting in the control group maintained for 14 days without treatment. Three days after training, the memory of the habit appeared to be immune to the effects of DFP, while 5 days afterward the disruption was intermediate between the 3- and 14-day extremes. Again, animals injected on the day of training also showed some memory loss. The results from the first 3 days, then, show the familiar retrograde amnesia, but the 5- and 14-day groups show a reversed pattern: Older memories were *less* resistant to the disruption produced by DFP. These results suggest a biphasic process of memory storage. They have been replicated by Hamburg (1967) using another anticholinesterase drug, physostigmine.

These data and those from additional experiments suggest that, as a result of training, an initially nonfunctional synapse is modified so that it releases its chemical transmitter. This increase in transmitter takes time to stabilize. Depending on the relative amount of transmitter available, different effects of interfering with the transmitter supply should be obtainable. Immediately after learning, the transmitter level is sufficient for behavioral evidence of memory, but it is neither so large nor so small that shifts in the level markedly alter the apparent memory. Within the next day, the transmitter level drops and then starts to increase again. In short, there are two ways of producing an amnesia, depending on the relative level of transmitter available: Amnesia can be produced if low levels of transmitter are further reduced or amnesia can be produced if high levels of transmitter are further increased, blocking the synapse.

Several experiments have provided tests confirming these notions (see Deutsch, 1969). In one (Deutsch & Leibowitz, 1966), a 14-day-old habit was blocked with DFP and a 28-day-old, partially forgotten habit was strengthened with DFP. In another (Wiener & Deutsch, 1968), scopolamine was used to block acetylcholine. As expected, blocking acetylcholine produced effects that were opposite to those produced with DFP, which increases acetylcholine. Note that the amnesias produced by these manipulations are temporary; animals trained and treated on the same day but tested after 5 days rather than after 24 hours show complete retention of the habit—the effects of the drug on acetylcholine levels dissipate and retention is shown.

Adrenergic Mechanisms

Recently, similar effects have been produced following manipulations of adrenergic transmitters (Hamburg & Cohen, 1973; Cohen & Hamburg, 1975). The results differed, however, in that norepinephrine depletion or beta adrenergic blockade seemed to prevent the formation of a long-term memory trace if administered within some 3 hours after training. If administered after long-term memory was established, a temporary blockade of retrieval occurred that did not vary as a function of the age of the habit. These results suggest that adrenergic transmitters are involved in an access pathway of long-term memory.

Summary

These studies suggest the operation of cholinergic and adrenergic transmitters in memory. The effects of these systems appear to be related to access to and retrieval from memory. Thus manipulations of these systems do not result in destruction of memory, though long-term store seems to be prevented by interfering with adrenergic mechanisms.

These data suggest the existence of some short-term memory process that occurs between the establishment of the initial trace, about a 10-sec interval, and the more permanent long-term storage mechanism. This suggestion will be repeated in the following section.

There are also other remaining questions. Some of these experiments have employed intracerebral injections while others have employed peripheral, systemic injections; the site of action of the drugs is generally assumed to be central but caution must be exercised. These transmitter systems have been additionally implicated in a variety of motivational and arousal mechanisms so that the effects of these various substances cannot be said to be specific to memory. Nonetheless, these results suggest that long- and short-term memory are physiologically differentiable and that the substrate for long-term memory undergoes changes that occur well beyond the time limits traditionally associated with the consolidation hypothesis.

RNA and Protein Theories

The synthesis of neural transmitters depends on the metabolism of RNA and proteins (Chapter 2). It has been hypothesized that protein synthesis is somehow involved in the storage of learning; for instance, proteins could determine activation patterns in synapses or the formation of new synapses. Protein changes as a result of learning could involve the proteins themselves, e.g., amounts synthesized, locations, etc., or they might be the result of changes in the messenger RNA involved in the production of various newly synthesized proteins.

Transfer Experiments

Much of the impetus for research on the role of RNA in memory stems from experiments in the planarian (marine flatworm). These animals possess the ability to regenerate whole individuals from each of several cut pieces of an animal. In addition, the planarian has been reported to be capable of classical conditioning. These characteristics formed the basis for an experiment (McConnell, Jacobson, & Kimble, 1959) in which planarians were classically conditioned, cut in half, allowed to regenerate into two individuals, and then were retested for conditioning. (Controls for sensitization resulting from the cutting process were also included.) The major finding of this experiment was that individuals regenerated from original tail sections (new heads) showed about equal retention scores on reconditioning as individuals regenerated from original trained head sections. This suggests that the entire nervous system, not just the dominant head, is involved in retention of the CR in the planarian. RNA was implicated in this result by an experiment by

Corning and John (1961). They repeated the McConnell et al. experiment but allowed some of the animals to regenerate in their natural environment of pond water while others regenerated in pond water containing ribonuclease, an enzyme that destroys RNA. Animals regenerating in ribonuclease from tail sections of conditioned animals did not show retention of the conditioned responses, while animals regenerating from head sections did. Animals regenerating in pond water showed retention regardless of whether regeneration was from head or tail sections and only cut animals were affected by the ribonuclease—intact animals were not. These results suggested that RNA is involved in the retention of conditioned reponses in planarians and that some sort of transmission involving RNA occurs between trained and regenerating sections in the case of trained tail sections; transmission to the dominant head is disrupted by ribonuclease.

Planarians are cannibalistic. This led McConnell (1962) to condition planarians, chop them up, and then feed them to naive planarians. Untrained animals showed savings in subsequent training if fed such trained animals but not if they were fed untrained ones. The results suggest the possibility that RNA from the trained animals found its way to appropriate sites in the recipient animals and mediated the more rapid learning.

A more direct test of this notion was attempted in experiments in rats (Babich, Jacobson, Bubash, & Jacobson, 1965; Jacobson, Babich, Bubash, & Jacobson, 1965). In essence, RNA was extracted from the brains of both trained and untrained rats and injected into untrained recipients; rats receiving RNA from trained donors were claimed to show significantly enhanced responding in subsequent tests.

These studies have generated considerable controversy and subsequent work. It should be obvious that memory storage must involve the brain's biochemical systems and that the specific mechanism may, in fact, involve RNA even if these experiments are not valid; they have been examined and criticized extensively. The planarian experiments have been attacked in several ways. First of all, their fundamental assumption—that planarians can be conditioned—has been attacked (Jensen, 1965, presents evidence against conditioning; Corning and Riccio, 1970, present evidence for conditioning). Hartry, Keith-Lee, and Morton (1964) additionally concluded that planarians that cannibalized planarians exposed to the CS only, or handling only, or previous conditioning, did not differ in subsequent CR training. Nutritional changes or metabolic factors could, therefore, account for any apparent transfer of learning.

A large number of experimenters have reported their inability to replicate the transfer of learning with injections of RNA from trained donors (Gross & Carey, 1965; Luttges, Johnson, Buck, Holland, & McGaugh, 1966; Byrne et al., 1966). But work on this problem has continued and some of the positive findings and the technical issues involved have been presented in a book edited by Byrne (1970). Recent transfer experiments have concentrated on the transfer of proteins rather than RNA; two recent examples of claimed successful transfer are provided by Braud and Hoffman (1973) and Webster and Fox (1974). In addition, particular attention should be paid to experiments based on the work of Ungar (1970).

Ungar assumes that the same pattern of learned behavior employs identical or at least homologous pathways in the brains of different individuals. Information is stored in the structure of molecules which "label" genetically organized pathways. Chemical products which result in transfer from trained animals to untrained animals are effective because they seek specific nerve terminals—Ungar draws an analogy here with the chemical specificity postulated to account for development (see Chapter 2). ". . . transfer experiments can now be understood as the reconstitution in the recipient brain of the 'cell assembly' created by training in the donor. The extracts are assumed to contain the labels of the pathways and the connectors of the newly created synaptic junctions . . . These substances must have, by definition, a high affinity for the sites from which they have been extracted and should, therefore, be able to attach themselves selectively to homologous sites in the brain of the receipients" (Ungar, 1970, p. 172).

Experimentally, Ungar employs a passive avoidance conditioning situation—rats are shocked for entering a small, dark compartment. He has isolated a particular protein constitutent, named scotophobin, injection of which causes naive rats to avoid entering the dark compartment. This material has also been synthetically reproduced with comparable behavioral results (Malin, 1974). The effects of scotophobin are claimed to be specific to the stimulus conditions involved in the training of the donor animals, rather than to have a nonspecific emotional effect (Malin, 1974; Malin, Radcliffe, & Osterman, 1976).

Protein Synthesis Inhibition

The synthesis of proteins in the brain may be inhibited by a number of antibiotics; a large number of experiments have been carried out using this technique to produce amnesia. Barraco and Stettner (1976) have comprehensively reviewed this complex literature, so only some illustrative material will be presented here.

Flexner, Flexner, and Stellar (1963) introduced the use of antibiotics to inhibit protein synthesis and produce amnesia. They trained mice to avoid shock in a Y-maze in a single training session. At varying times after training, intracerebral injections of the antibiotic puromycin were made. Some injections were localized to the temporal cortex while others were more extensive so as to involve the entire cerebrum. Retention was measured in retraining 3 days after injection, when protein synthesis was again recovered. Injections made from 1 to 2 days after training resulted in impaired retention even with the localized injections; if injections were delayed until 6 or more days after training, deficits were obtained only with the more extensive injections and this effect was obtainable even weeks after training. Some mice were trained and then received reversal training 3 weeks later. Puromycin was injected 24 hours after reversal training in an attempt to produce amnesia for the reversal training; in tests without shock, all the animals chose the arm of the Y correct during the original training; control animals tested without puromycin, chose the arm correct during reversal training. Finally, Flexner and Flexner (1968) carried out experiments in which mice received additional saline injections after puromycin but prior to retention testing; control mice received the puromycin injections only. In retention testing, the controls showed the usual amnestic effects of puromycin but the experimental animals did not—somehow the saline inections cured the amnesia!

Data such as these suggest that initially memory may be dependent on localizable processes but, with time, there is a "spread of the engram" to encompass more of the brain. In addition, at least some effects of antibiotics may involve disruption of retrieval processes rather than destruction of the engram itself.

Several antibiotics have been used to produce protein inhibition. Biochemically, their modes of action are different and, behaviorally, the amnesias they produce have different characteristics. It is also probable that inhibition of protein synthesis per se is *not* the crucial correlate of the behavioral amnesias produced by antibiotics; several investigations have implicated transmitter effects, for instance. Based on antibiotics and other treatments, short-term and long-term retention may each depend on several physiological processes which have different time courses, and short-term and long-term retention processes may operate in parallel rather than in sequential fashion. Barraco and Stettner propose that antibiotics produce three effects: (1) Puromycin injected long after training (1 or more days) affects adrenergic neurons involved in longer term memory processes; (2) another class of antibiotics, injected immediately before or after training, affects adrenergic neurons which are involved in shorter term processes—minutes to hours; and (3) puromycin injected before or immediately after training interferes with cholinergic neurons concerned with consolidation. The cholinergic neurons mediate storage (memory) and the adrenergic neurons mediate information retrieval and integration (learning). These hypotheses suggest that there are at least three phases involved in the formation of an engram: An initial electrochemical phase, lasting for seconds only, which constitutes the trace of the stimulus events; an early short-term phase involving initial molecular changes; and a long-term consolidation involving permanent storage and retrieval processes.

SUMMARY

Learning and memory are complementary processes involved in what is probably the outstanding characteristic of the mammalian nervous system—its great capacity for changing the organism's behavior based on past experience. This review has revealed that the capacity for altering its functional capabilities is demonstrated widely in the CNS. On the other hand, there do appear to be limits to this property—not all neural elements appear capable of such change. Thus, two issues seem to be paramount: (1) What, if any, are the "boundary conditions" that separate learning from other possible forms of response modification? (2) What distinguishes "trainable" from "untrainable" neurons? It seems likely that the answers to both questions may come from intensive study of the comparative physiology of individual neurons and neural networks. An additional aid here may involve the relative capacity for memory demonstrated by individual neurons.

While many studies have shown that individual neurons show capacity for changes in their functional characteristics, none has gone very far toward showing the relative permanence of such change. Without further evidence of such relative permanence, we cannot term change per se as "learning."

The consolidation hypothesis originally suggested that memory storage takes place in two stages—a temporary, labile form of storage followed by a more permanent storage. The time limits on consolidation originally suggested that the labile process lasted a matter of hours at most and that the two processes were sequential, with long-term storage dependent on the integrity of the labile stage. Newer data have altered our conception markedly.

It seems obvious that the immediate representation of a stimulus situation in the CNS is electrochemical. This trace is probably extremely limited in duration, most likely not exceeding seconds. ECS and drugs may obliterate this trace with a resultant permanent amnesia. During its existence, however, processes involved in more permanent storage are probably initiated. Presently, it appears that there may be several such processes. This more permanent store also shows lability; however, its lability may be characterized as affecting the retrieval of information rather than storage per se. Thus, lability of the trace is not in itself a distinguishing characteristic of temporary versus permanent storage. Furthermore, temporary and permanent processes may very well overlap each other in time and there is the suggestion that they are at least to some extent independent processes.

Finally, there are signs that studies of learning and memory are beginning to converge—evidence from both is beginning to suggest that cholinergic and adrenergic neurons may play specialized roles in these complementary processes.

REFERENCES

BABICH, F. R., JACOBSON, A. L., BUBASH, S., & JACOBSON, A. Transfer of a response to naive rats by injection of ribonucleic acid extracted from trained rats. *Science*, 1965, *149*, 656–657.

BARRACO, R. A., & STETTNER, L. J. Antibiotics and memory. *Psychological Bulletin*, 1976, *83*, 242–302.

BENNETT, T. L. The effects of centrally blocking hippocampal theta activity on learning and retention. *Behavioral Biology*, 1973, *9*, 541–552.

BERGER, T. W., ALGER, G., & THOMPSON, R. F. Neuronal substrate of classical conditioning in the hippocampus. *Science*, 1976, *192*, 483–485.

BRADY, J. V. The effect of electro-convulsive shock on a conditioned emotional response: The permanence of the effect. *Journal of Comparative and Physiological Psychology*, 1951, *44*, 507–511.

BRADY, J. V., HUNT, H. F., & GELLER, I. The effect of electroconvulsive shock on conditioned emotional responses as a function of the temporal distribution of treatments. *Journal of Comparative and Physiological Psychology*, 1954, *47*, 454–457.

BRAUD, W. G., & HOFFMAN, R. B. Specificity of process, response, and stimulus in behavioral bioassays. *Journal of Comparative and Physiological Psychology*, 1973, *84*, 304–312.

BROMILEY, R. B. Conditioned responses in a dog after removal of neocortex. *Journal of Comparative and Physiological Psychology*, 1948, *41*, 102–110.

BYRNE, W. L. *Molecular approaches to learning and memory*. New York: Academic Press, 1970.

BYRNE, W. L., SAMUEL, D., BENNETT, E. L., ROSENZWEIG, M. R., WASSERMAN, E., WAGNER, A. R., GARDNER, F., GALAMBOS, R., BERGER, B. D., MARGULES, D. L., FENICHEL, R. L., STEIN, L., CORSON, J. A., ENESCO, H. E., CHOROVER, S. L., HOLT, C. E. III, SCHILLER, P. H., CHIAPETTA, L., JARVIK, M. E., LEAF, R. C., DUTCHER, J. D., HOROVITZ, Z. P., & CARLSON, P. L. Memory transfer. *Science*, 1966, *153*, 658.

CASTELLUCCI, V., PINSKER, H., KUPFERMANN, I., & KANDEL, E. Neuronal mechanisms of habituation and dishabituation of the gill-withdrawal reflex in *Aplysia*. *Science*, 1970, *167*, 1745–1748.

CHALUPA, L. M., MACADAR, A. W., & LINDSLEY, D. B. Response plasticity of lateral geniculate neurons during and after pairing of auditory and visual stimuli. *Science*, 1975, *190*, 290–292.

CHOPIN, S. F., & BUERGER, A. A. Instrumental avoidance conditioning in the spinal rat. *Brain Research Bulletin*, 1976, *1*, 177–184.

COHEN, R. P., & HAMBURG, G. D. Evidence for adrenergic neurons in a memory access pathway. *Pharmacology, Biochemistry and Behavior*, 1975, *3*, 519–523.

COONS, E. E., & MILLER, N. E. Conflict versus consolidation of memory traces to explain "retrograde amnesia" produced by ECS. *Journal of Comparative and Physiological Psychology*, 1960, *53*, 524–531.

CORNING, W. C., & JOHN, E. R. Effect of ribonuclease on retention of conditioned response in regenerated planarians. *Science*, 1961, *134*, 1363–1365.

CORNING, W. C., & RICCIO, D. The planarian controversy. In W. L. Byrne (ed.), *Molecular approaches to learning and memory*. New York: Academic Press, 1970, pp. 107–149.

DEUTSCH, J. A. The physiological basis of memory. *Annual Review of Psychology*, 1969, *20*, 85–104.

DEUTSCH, J. A., HAMBURG, M. D., & DAHL, H. Anticholinesterase-induced amnesia and its temporal aspects. *Science*, 1966, *151*, 221–223.

DEUTSCH, J. A., & LEIBOWITZ, S. F. Amnesia or reversal of forgetting by anticholinesterase, depending simply on time of injection. *Science*, 1966, *153*, 1017–1018.

DICARA, L. V., BRAUN, J. J., & PAPPAS B. A. Classical conditioning and instrumental learning of cardiac and gastrointestinal responses following removal of neocortex in the rat. *Journal of Comparative and Physiological Psychology*, 1970, *73*, 208–216.

DOTY, R. W., & GIURGEA, C. Conditioned reflexes established by coupling electrical excitation of two cortical areas. In J. F. Delafresnaye (ed.), *Brain mechanisms and learning*. Oxford: Blackwell Scientific Publications, 1961, pp. 133–151.

DUNCAN, C. P. The retroactive effect of electroshock on learning. *Journal of Comparative and Physiological Psychology*, 1949, *42*, 32–44.

DURKOVIC, R. G. Classical conditioning, sensitization and habituation in the spinal cat. *Physiology and Behavior*, 1975, *14*, 297–304.

FETZ, E. E. Operant conditioning of cortical unit activity. *Science*, 1969, *163*, 955–958.

FIBIGER, H. C., PHILLIPS, A. G., & ZIS, A. P. Deficits in instrumental responding after 6-hydroxydopamine lesions of the nigro-neostriatal dopaminergic projection. *Pharmacology, Biochemistry and Behavior,* 1974, *2,* 87–96.

FLEXNER, J. B., FLEXNER, L. B., & STELLAR, E. Memory in mice as affected by intracerebral puromycin. *Science,* 1963, *141,* 57–59.

FLEXNER, L. B., & FLEXNER, J. B. Intracerebral saline: Effect on memory of trained mice treated with puromycin. *Science,* 1968, *167,* 330–331.

GARDNER, E. L., GLICK, S. D., & JARVIK, M. E. ECS dissociation of learning and one-way cross-dissociation with physostigmine and scopolamine. *Physiology and Behavior,* 1972, *8,* 11–15.

GASTAUT, H. The role of the reticular formation in establishing conditioned reactions. In H. H. Jasper, L. D. Proctor, R. S. Knighton, W. C. Noshay, & R. T. Costello (eds.), *Reticular formation of the brain.* Boston: Little, Brown, 1958, pp. 561–579.

GERKEN, G. M., & NEFF, W. D. Experimental procedures affecting evoked responses recorded from auditory cortex. *Electroencephalography and Clinical Neurophysiology,* 1963, *15,* 947–957.

GHISELLI, E. E. The relationship between the superior colliculus and the striate area in brightness discrimination. *Journal of Genetic Psychology,* 1938, *52,* 151–157.

GIRDEN, E.,& CULLER, E. Conditioned responses in curarized muscle in dogs. *Journal of Comparative Psychology,* 1937, *23,* 261–274.

GLICKMAN, S. E. Perseverative neural processes and consolidation of the memory trace. *Psychological Bulletin,* 1961, *58,* 218–233.

GOLD, P. E., & KING, R. A. Retrograde amnesia: Storage failure versus retrieval failure. *Psychological Review,* 1974, *81,* 465–469.

GRASTYÁN, E., LISSÁK, K., MADARASZ, I., & DONHOFFER, H. Hippocampal electrical activity during the development of conditioned reflexes. *Electroencephalography and Clinical Neurophysiology,* 1959, *11,* 409–430.

GROSS, C. G., & CAREY, F. M. Transfer of learned response by RNA injection: Failure of attempts to replicate. *Science,* 1965, *150,* 1749.

GROVES, P. M., & THOMPSON, R. F. Habituation: A dual process theory. *Psychological Review,* 1970, *77,* 419–450.

GROVES, P. M., & THOMPSON, R. F. A dual-process theory of habitation: Neural mechanisms. In H. V. S. Peeke and M. J. Herz (eds.), *Habituation, Vol. II.* New York: Academic Press, 1973, pp. 175–205.

HALL, R. D., & MARK, R. G. Fear and the modification of acoustically evoked potentials during conditioning. *Journal of Neurophysiology,* 1967, *30,* 893–910.

HAMBURG, M. D. Retrograde amnesia produced by intraperitoneal injection of physostigmine. *Science,* 1967, *156,* 973–974.

HAMBURG, M. D., & COHEN, R. R. Memory access pathway: Role of adrenergic versus cholinergic neurons. *Pharmacology, Biochemistry and Behavior, 1973, 1,* 295–300.

HARTRY, A. L., KEITH-LEE, P., & MORTON, W. D. Planaria: Memory transfer through cannibalism re-examined. *Science,* 1964, *146,* 274–275.

HEARST, E., BEER, B., SHEATZ, G., & GALAMBOS, R. Some electrophysiological correlates of conditioning in the monkey. *Electroencephalography and Clinical Neurophysiology,* 1960, *12,* 137–152.

HEBB, D. O. *The organization of behavior.* New York: Wiley, 1949.

JACOBSON, A. L., BABICH, F. R., BUBASH, S., & JACOBSON, A. Differential-approach tendencies produced by injection of RNA from trained rats. *Science,* 1965, *150,* 636–637.

JASPER, H., & SHAGASS, C. Conditioning the occipital alpha rhythm in man. *Journal of Experimental Psychology,* 1941, *28,* 373–388.

JENSEN, D. D. Paramecia, planaria, and pseudolearning. *Animal Behaviour,* 1965, *13,* Suppl. 1, 9–20.

JOHN, E. R. *Mechanisms of memory.* New York: Academic Press, 1967.

JOHN, E. R. Switchboard versus statistical theories of learning and memory. *Science,* 1972, *177,* 850–864.

KANDEL, G. L., & BENEVENTO, L. A. Classically conditioned limb reflexes reinforced by motor cortex stimulation. *Physiology and Behavior,* 1973, *11,* 481–496.

KENT, E. W., & GROSSMAN, S. P. Elimination of learned behaviors after transection of fibers crossing the lateral border of the hypothalamus. *Physiology and Behavior,* 1973, *10,* 953–963.

KNOTT, J. R. Electroencephalography and physiological psychology: Evaluation and statement of problem. *Psychological Bulletin,* 1941, *38,* 944–975.

KUPFERMANN, I., CASTELLUCCI, V., PINSKER, H., & KANDEL, E. Neuronal correlates of habituation and dishabituation of the gill-withdrawal reflex in *Aplysia. Science,* 1970, *167,* 1743–1745.

LASHLEY, K. S. *Brain mechanisms and intelligence.* Chicago: University of Chicago Press, 1929.

LASHLEY, K. S. The mechanism of vision. XII. Nervous structures concerned in habits based on reactions to light. *Comparative Psychology Monographs,* 1935, *11,* 43–79.

LASHLEY, K. S. Studies of cerebral function in learning. XII. Loss of the maze habit after occipital lesions in blind rats. *Journal of Comparative Neurology,* 1943, *79,* 431–462.

LASHLEY, K. S. In search of the engram. *Symposium of the Society of Experimental Biology,* 1950, *4,* 454–482.

LEWIS, D. J., & ADAMS, H. E. Retrograde amnesia from conditioned competing responses. *Science,* 1963, *141,* 516–517.

LIDDELL, H. S. The conditioned reflex,. In F. A. Moss (ed.), *Comparative psychology.* New York: Prentice-Hall, 1942, pp. 178–216.

LIGHT, J. S., & GANTT, W. H. Essential part of reflex arc for establishment of conditioned reflex: Formation of conditioned reflex after exclusion of motor peripheral end. *Journal of Comparative Psychology,* 1936, *21,* 19–36.

LOUCKS, R. B. The experimental delimitation of neural structures essential for learning: The attempt to condition striped muscle response with faradization of sygmoid gyri. *Journal of Psychology,* 1935, *1,* 1–44.

LOUCKS, R. B. Studies of neural structures essential for learning: II. The conditioning of salivary and striped muscle responses to faradization of cortical sensory elements, and the action of sleep upon such mechanisms. *Journal of Comparative Psychology,* 1938, *25,* 315–332.

LOUCKS, R. B., & GANTT, W. H. The conditioning of striped muscle responses based upon faradic stimulation of dorsal roots and dorsal columns of the spinal cord. *Journal of Comparative Psychology,* 1938, *25,* 415–426.

LUTTGES, M., JOHNSON, T., BUCK, C., HOLLAND, J., & MCGAUGH, J. An examination of "transfer of learning" by nucleic acid. *Science,* 1966, *151,* 834–837.

MALIN, D. H. Synthetic scotophobin: Analysis of behavioral effects on mice. *Pharmacology, Biochemistry and Behavior,* 1974, *2,* 147–153.

MALIN, D. H., RADCLIFFE, C. J., JR., & OSTERMAN, D. M. Stimulus specific effect of scotophobin on mouse plasma corticoids. *Pharmacology, Biochemistry and Behavior,* 1976, *4,* 481–483.

MARK, R. G., & HALL, R. D. Acoustically evoked potentials in the rat during conditioning. *Journal of Neurophysiology,* 1967, *30,* 875–892.

MCCONNELL, J. V. Memory transfer through cannibalism in planarians. *Journal of Neuropsychiatry,* 1962, *3,* Suppl. 1, 542–548.

MCCONNELL, J. V., JACOBSON, A. L., & KIMBLE, D. P. The effects of regeneration upon retention of a conditioned response in the planarian. *Journal of Comparative and Physiological Psychology,* 1959, *52,* 1–5.

MCGAUGH, J. L., & MADSEN, M. C. Amnesic and punishing effects of electroconvulsive shock. *Science,* 1964, *144,* 182–183.

MEANS, L. W., HUNTLEY, D. H., ANDERSON, H. P., & HARRELL, T. H. Deficient acquisition and retention of a visual-tactile discrimination task in rats with medial thalamic lesions. *Behavioral Biology,* 1973, *9,* 435–450.

MEYER, D. R. Access to engrams. *American Psychologist,* 1972, *27,* 124–133.

MILLER, N. E. Learning of visceral and glandular responses. *Science*, 1969, *163*, 434–445.

MILLER, R. R., & SPRINGER, A. D. Amnesia, consolidation, and retrieval. *Psychological Review*, 1973, *80*, 69–79.

MILLER, R. R., & SPRINGER, A. D. Implications of recovery from experimental amnesia. *Psychological Review*, 1974, *81*, 470–473.

MILSTEIN, V. Contingent alpha blocking: Conditioning or sensitization? *Electroencephalography and Clinical Neurophysiology*, 1965, *18*, 217–324.

MORRELL, F. Electrical signs of sensory coding. In G. C. Quarton, T. Melnechuk, & F. O. Schmitt (eds.), *The neurosciences, a study program.* New York: Rockefeller University Press, 1967, pp. 452–469.

NEFF, W. D. Neural mechanisms of auditory discrimination. In W. A. Rosenblith (ed.), *Sensory communication*, New York: Wiley, 1961, pp. 259–278.

OLDS, J. Operant conditioning of single unit responses. *Excerpta Medica International Congress*, 1965, *87*, 372–380.

OLDS, J., & OLDS, M. Interference and learning in paleocortical systems. In J. F. Delafresnaye, A. Fessard, R. W. Gerard, & J. Konorski, (eds.), *Brain mechanisms and learning.* Oxford: Blackwell Scientific, 1961, pp. 153–183.

PATERSON, M. M., CEGAVSKE, C. F., & THOMPSON, R. F. Effects of a classical conditioning paradigm on hind-limb flexor nerve response in immobilized spinal cats. *Journal of Comparative and Physiological Psychology*, 1973, *84*, 88–97.

PAVLOV, I. P. *Lectures on conditioned reflexes.* New York: Liverwright, 1928.

PEEKE, H. V. S., & HERZ, M. J. (eds.). *Habituation.* New York: Academic Press, 1973.

PINSKER, H., KUPFERMANN, I., CASTELLUCCI, V., & KANDEL, E. Habituation and dishabituation of the gill-withdrawal reflex in *Aplysia. Science*, 1970, *167*, 1740–1742.

RAMOS, A., SCHWARTZ, E., & JOHN, E. R. An examination of the participation of neurons in readout from memory. *Brain Reasearch Bulletin*, 1976, *1*, 77–86.

ROUTTENBERG, A., & KAY, K. E. Effect of one electroconvulsive seizure on rat behavior. *Journal of Comparative and Physiological Psychology*, 1965, *59*, 285–288.

SAKHIULINA, G. T. Electroencephalograms of dogs in some complex forms of conditioned reflex activity. *Electroencephalography and Clinical Neurophysiology*, 1960, Suppl. *13*, 211–220.

SCHARLOCK, D. P., TUCKER, T. J., STROMINGER, N. L. Auditory discrimination by the cat after neonatal ablation of the temporal cortex. *Science*, 1963, *141*, 1197–1198.

SCHNEIDER, A. M. Control of memory by spreading cortical depression. *Psychological Review*, 1967, *74*, 201–215.

SCHNEIDER, A. M. Stimulus control and spreading cortical depression: Some problems reconsidered. *Psychological Review*, 1968, *75*, 353–358.

SCHWARTZ, M., STEWART, A. L., & SUNENSHINE, H. Evoked responses to the CS during classical conditioning in the rabbit. *Communications in Behavioral Biology*, 1969, *4A*, 35–40.

SHURRAGER, P. S., & CULLER, E. Conditioning in the spinal dog. *Journal of Experimental Psychology*, 1940, *26*, 133–159.

SQUIRE, L. R., & LISS, P. H. Control of spreading cortical depression: A critique of stimulus control. *Psychological Review*, 1968, *75*, 347–352.

THOMPSON, C. I., & GROSSMAN, L. B. Loss and recovery of long-term memories after ECS in rats: Evidence for state-dependent recall. *Journal of Comparative and Physiological Psychology*, 1972, *78*, 248–254.

THOMPSON, R. Localization of the "visual memory system" in the white rat. *Journal of Comparative and Physiological Psychology*, 1969, *69*(4), Part 2, 1–29.

THOMPSON, R., & DEAN, W. A. A further study of the retroactive effect of ECS. *Journal of Comparative and Physiological Psychology*, 1955, *48*, 488–491.

THOMPSON, R. F., & SPENCER, W. A. Habituation: A model phenomenon for the study of neuronal substrates of behavior. *Psychological Review*, 1966, *73*, 16–43.

UNGAR, G. The role of proteins and peptides in learning and memory. In G. Ungar (ed.), *Molecular mechanisms in memory and learning*. New York: Plenum Press, 1970, pp. 149–176.

WAGNER, A. R., THOMAS, E., & NORTON, T. Conditioning with electrical stimulation of motor cortex: Evidence of a possible source of motivation. *Journal of Comparative and Physiological Psychology*, 1967, *64*, 191–199.

WEBSTER, J. C., & FOX, K. A. Altered learning by recipients of brain extracts from trained and retrained donors. *Pharmacology, Biochemistry and Behavior*, 1974, *2*, 209–213.

WIENER, N., & DEUTSCH, J. A. Temporal aspects of anticholinergic- and anticholinesterase-induced amnesia for an appetitive habit. *Journal of Comparative and Physiological Psychology*, 1968, *66*, 613–617.

WYRWICKA, W., & STERMAN, M. B. Instrumental conditioning of sensorimotor cortex EEG spindles in the waking cat. *Physiology and Behavior*, 1968, *3*, 703–707.

YOSHII, N., & MAENO, S. An electroencephalographic study of conditioned salivation. *Folia Psychiatrica et Neurologica Japonica*, 1958, *12*, 296–316.

YOSHII, N., MATSUMOTO, J., OGURA, H., SHIMOKOCHI, M., YAMAGUCHI, Y., & YAMASAKI, H. Conditioned reflex and electroencephalograph. *Electroencephalography and Clinical Neurophysiology*, 1960, Suppl. *13*, 199–208.

13

Cognitive Functioning and Integration

The material considered in the previous chapters of this book concerned behavior and capacities shared by humans and the lower animals. In this and the next chapter, we will consider behaviors that seem to be characteristically human. In this chapter, our main focus will be on language and the integration of cognitive functions with the capacity for language; in the next chapter, we will be concerned with disordered cognitive and emotional functioning. In both instances, some animals display rudimentary capacities for similar behavior or disorders, and animal studies will be an adjunct to our investigation. However, in neither instance can it be said that such behavior is common or expected in the natural behavioral repertoire of animals. Our major data, therefore, will come from human subjects. The availability of much of the relevant data is dependent on the occurrence of disease and injuries and, therefore, these "experiments" rarely contain the niceties of experimental design that one would like. On the other hand, ingenious technical and design considerations have enabled investigators to obtain much relevant information from intact, normal subjects. An important secondary purpose of these two chapters, then, is to demonstrate the degree to which techniques employed in animal research may also be used in human experimentation.

LANGUAGE

Language Development

Languages are learned by their users and the argument has been made, principally by Skinnerian psychologists, that the learning involved in the acquisition of language is, in principle at least, no different from the learning involved in the acquisition of any other skill. Here, we shall suggest otherwise; we shall propose that the development of language by humans is a species-specific, biological adaptation, an adaptation for which the human brain is rather specifically "designed."[1] Lenneberg (e.g., 1969) has particularly pursued this point of view.

Unlike a rat learning to traverse a maze or a person learning to drive a car, the human learning language does not require any very special set of environmental contingencies for the acquisition of language. (Of course, the acquisition of a specific language, e.g., English, is determined by such contingencies, but the acquisition of language per se is not dependent on such contingencies.) In a reasonably constant developmental progression, most human infants spontaneously begin to learn a language. They learn to speak and understand it and employ the intricacies of its rules without explicit instruction. They are able to generate new sentences that they have never heard before. Obviously, circumstances can alter that progression—the children of deaf or mute parents may be handicapped in such development, and

[1]It has been assumed that language capability, in the fullest sense of the term, is uniquely human. Parrots, for instance, do utter human-sounding vocalizations, but it is clear that they do not employ such vocalizations in anything like the manner that human beings do. Six years of intensive effort (Hayes & Hayes, 1952) to teach vocal language to a chimpanzee resulted in the apparent learning of but four sounds that seemed to correspond to appropriate English words. Apes possess a different vocal apparatus and produce only a minimal amount of spontaneous vocal behavior. Recent attempts to teach language to apes have employed the extensive use these primates make of their hands by training in sign language and the manipulation of symbols (Gardner & Gardner, 1969; Premack, 1971). This change in approach seems to be responsible for the remarkable language acquisition that such studies have demonstrated. There can be no doubt that apes can demonstrate the linguistic abilities of young children; their maximum performance levels are still undetermined. Obviously, one would like to see comparative CNS experiments carried out on such trained animals, but at the present time such animals are too few and valuable for the original research purposes for such research to be carried out. However, it does bear repetition that until humans intervened no ape spontaneously developed sophisticated language; thus the human brain does appear to have a unique adaptive specialization.

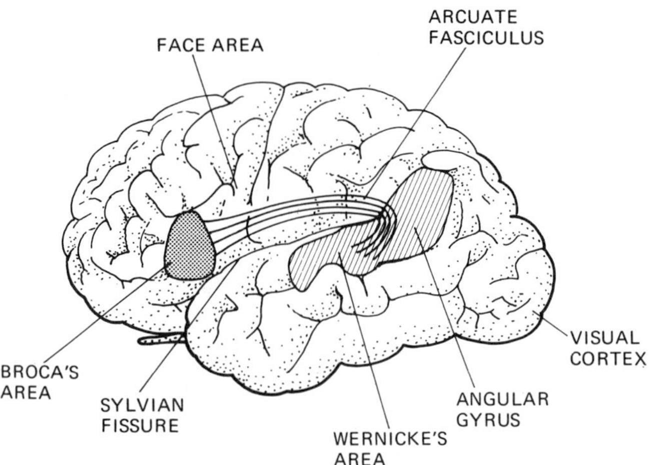

Figure 13.1. Diagrammatic representation of the location of Broca's and Wernicke's areas. (Adapted from Greschwind, N. Language and the brain. *Scientific American*, 1972, *226*, 76-83.)

children with sensory, neurological, or psychiatric disability may not develop language. But the underlying capacity and the utilization of that capacity seem generally to be more products of innate development than of explicit exposure to training.

The acquisition of language, then, appears to be more like the acquisition of walking than it is like the acquisition of instrumental skills such as driving a car. And unlike most instrumental skills, language appears peculiarly dependent on the integrity of certain very specific brain structures. As we saw in the previous chapter, most learned behavior shows considerable capacity for retraining after brain damage; language shows a much more limited capacity.

The Anatomy of Language

Historically, our understanding of the neural basis of language has been rooted in the study of disorders of language resulting from brain damage. A brief survey of this material was presented by Geschwind (1970; 1972).

Two cortical locations, named after the physicians Broca and Wernicke who first described the effects of their lesioning, are the areas of principal concern. They are schematically located in Figure 13.1. Broca's area is adjacent to motor cortex controlling muscles of the lips, jaw, tongue, soft palate, and vocal cords. It apparently coordinates the activities of such muscles in the production of speech. Damage to Broca's area results in slow, labored speech but comprehension is unaffected. Wernicke's area is in the dorsal posterior part of the temporal lobe. It lies between the primary receiving area for auditory stimulation in the temporal lobe and the angular gyrus, which receives both auditory and visual information. Lesions in Wernicke's area result in fluent speech as far as the words uttered are concerned, but content is absent and comprehension of language is lost. Geschwind supplies the following examples of severe speech impairment in persons with lesions. In a patient with a lesion in Broca's area: "Asked to describe a trip he has taken, the patient may say 'New York.' When urged to produce a sentence, he may do no better than 'Go . . . New York'. . . . [I]n repeating words, he has difficulty with certain grammatical words and phrases. 'If he were here, I would go' is more difficult than 'The general commands the army.' The hardest phrase for such patients to repeat is 'No ifs, ands or buts.' A patient with a lesion in Wernicke's area, in contrast, produces speech that may almost sound normal: 'Before I was in the one here, I was over in the other one. My sister had the department in the other one.' . . . The patient fails to use the correct word and substitutes for it by circumlocutory phrases ('what you use to cut with' for 'knife'), . . . substitution of one word or phrase for another, sometimes related in meaning ('knife' for 'fork') and sometimes unrelated ('hammer' for 'paper'). . . . If there are several incorrect sounds in a word, it becomes a neologism, for example, 'pluver' or 'flieber' " (1972, p. 78). Note that these speech defects occur in patients whose hearing of non-verbal sounds and music may be entirely normal.

Wernicke's and Broca's areas are interconnected. When the connection is damaged, speech is fluent and the patient can comprehend words but cannot repeat them.

Cerebral Dominance for Language

To the above facts, it is necessary to add an important feature—cerebral *dominance*. In general, language functioning is controlled by one side of the brain. Which side of the brain controls language in the particular individual may be determined from the effects of cerebral injury. It may also be determined from the unilateral injection of anesthetics into the blood supply to the brain; speech will be blocked temporarily by injection on one side of the brain but not the other. Generally, language is controlled by the left hemisphere and is only roughly correlated with handedness. In more than 90 percent of right-handed persons, speech is controlled by the left hemisphere of the brain; speech is controlled by the left hemisphere in about two-thirds of left-handed individuals; in left-handers with left cerebral injury before the age of 6, speech is controlled by the left hemisphere in only about one-third of the cases; in each of the preceding instances, the remaining persons show either right hemisphere or mixed (bilateral) control of speech, with bilateral control being less frequent (Milner, 1974). The hemisphere controlling language is termed *dominant* and generally is the left hemisphere.

Since control of language is *lateralized*, the integration of the two cerebral hemispheres is critical. This integration is accomplished through the

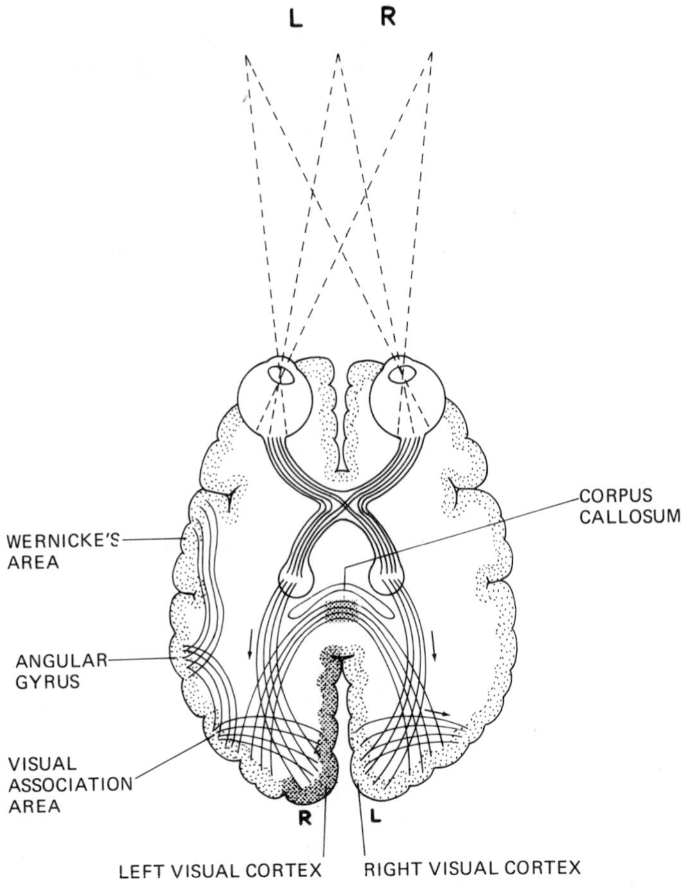

Figure 13.2. Schematic representation of the corpus callosum connecting the two cerebral hemispheres and the location of lesions resulting in an inability to read. (Adapted from Geschwind, N. Language and the brain. *Scientific American*, 1972, *226*, 76-83.)

cerebral *commissures*, tracts linking the two hemispheres. This is shown schematically in Figure 13.2, which indicates the major commissure, the *corpus callosum*. In addition, the figure diagrams the classic case of a patient with damage to the left visual cortex and the posterior part of the corpus callosum, which is responsible for transmission of visual information between the two hemispheres. The patient was blind in the right portion of his visual field; thus, although words in the left visual field were properly received, they were cut off from the language mechanisms of the left hemisphere because of the corpus callosum damage. As a result, words seen by this person remained unreadable. We will return to a fuller discussion of the integration of the functions of the two hemispheres in the next section. Here, however, we have the essentials necessary for a description of the apparent functioning of the language mechanisms.

Comprehension of language seems to be dependent on the integrity of Wernicke's area. Conversions between vocal and visual language involve the angular gyrus and its connections to Wernicke's area. Speech production involves Broca's area and the understanding of vocal speech requires the connection of the auditory cortex to Wernick's area. Depending on the locus of a lesion and how circumscribed it is, a variety of *aphasias* or language disorders may be seen. The clinical literature contains descriptions of individuals whose disability was limited to speech, or reading, or writing, or presented mixtures of these, depending on the lesion.

Finally, in regard to anatomy, Geschwind and Levitzky (1968) found that an anatomically identifiable portion of Wernicke's area was larger on the left side of the brain in 65 percent of the cases examined and larger on the right side in only 11 percent of the cases. Such an anatomic differentiation seems to supply the basis for the known functional lateralization.

Recording Studies

The material reviewed above comes exclusively from patients with abnormal conditions. While such data strongly imply that normal language mechanisms operate in accord with what is seen in these patients, that inference is not necessarily correct. For instance, a lesion that interferes with a behavioral process could block the functioning of another brain area. Thus, it would be desirable to have some independent measure of localization of brain functioning in language that can be applied to nonpatient populations. A number of behavioral techniques, such as the dichotic listening task (Kimura, 1967),[2] have been used for this purpose and suggest that language processing is lateralized, generally in the left hemisphere. Physiologically, recording procedures have also been employed (McAdam & Whitaker, 1971; Teyler, Roemer, Harrison, & Thompson, 1973; Wood, Goff, & Day, 1971). Such studies have generally indicated that comparing left and right hemisphere recordings shows small but statistically significant differences in potentials to meaningful and language related auditory stimuli; meaningless, nonlanguage stimuli, generally do not show any hemispheric differences.

[2]Dichotic listening involves the simultaneous presentation of two different auditory inputs, one to each ear. Usually accuracy of perception of the inputs is greater for one ear, indicating cerebral dominance.

The Hemispheric Disconnection Syndrome

We have generally indicated that the two hemispheres of the brain are linked by several commissures; chief among these is the corpus callosum. Figure 13.2 has indicated the consequence of a lesion in the corpus callosum for one patient: in combination with destruction of his left visual cortex, the corpus callosum lesion rendered this man incapable of reading. The behavioral consequences of interfering with the integration of the two hemispheres are dramatically presented in cases where the corpus callosum has been surgically cut for therapeutic purposes. (Cutting the corpus callosum may provide relief from otherwise intractable epileptic seizures.) These patients are of interest to us for the specialized functions of the two hemispheres that are revealed as a result of the operation. Several descriptive and experimental summaries have been published (e.g., Gazzaniga, 1970; Nebes, 1974; Sperry, 1968).

In casual observations, patients whose corpus callosum have been cut are reported to be remarkably undifferentiated from persons with an intact callosum—there seem to be no gross changes in functioning or intellectual

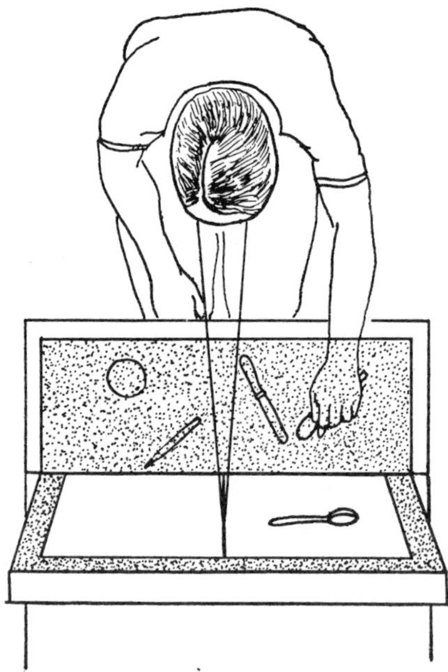

Figure 13.3. Visual-tactile association performed by a patient with a split corpus callosum. The picture of the spoon is seen by the right hemisphere; with the left hand, the spoon is retrieved from behind a screen. Touch information from the left hand projects mainly to the right hemisphere; the weak ipsilateral projection is insufficient to enable him to name (with the left hemisphere) what was retrieved. (From Gazzaniga, M. S. *The Bisected Brain.* New York: Appleton-Century-Crofts, 1970.)

capability. But specialized testing, with sensory input lateralized to one hemisphere, reveals some important differences. For instance, a test situation such as depicted in Figure 13.3 may be used. If a picture of a spoon is flashed in the patient's left visual field, the patient can successfully retrieve a hidden spoon from among several objects, employing the left hand. When asked to name the object retrieved, however, he is unable to do so. Objects retrieved with the right hand, in response to a picture in the right visual field, are named. This result is in accord with our previous discussion of language—information which is sent to the right hemisphere is isolated from the speech mechanisms in the left hemisphere. In this situation, despite the fact that such patients make correct responses with the left hand, verbally they report that they do not know what objects were retrieved nor can they report what was seen in the left visual field; they report seeing nothing. Thus, the left hemisphere (doing the talking) literally does not know what the right hemisphere is doing! With left visual information and working with the right hand, only chance matching of retrieval with the visual information occurs. Thus, in order for appropriate matches to occur, the sensory information from vision and from the hand must come to the same hemisphere. However, as such patients become more sophisticated with their condition and the test situation, apparent exceptions to this can arise. In the crudest instance, if visual information is presented to the left hemisphere, and the patient is allowed to "cue" the right hemisphere by naming the object, the right hemisphere hears this and can respond correctly. Such cross-cuing can become quite sophisticated and subtle. For instance, frowning or shaking of the head, initiated by the right hemisphere receiving the information, can cue the left hemisphere that it is making an incorrect verbal response (which was heard by the right hemisphere).

It is clear that verbal *expression* is dependent on the functioning of the language dominant hemisphere; but as the above material suggests, some language *comprehension* is possible in the other hemisphere. In brief, the right hemisphere can read and understand names of objects and adjectives. It can also respond to abstract descriptions of objects; for instance, it will respond to "select an object that makes things look bigger" by correctly selecting a magnifying glass while the left hemisphere replies "telescope." The right hemisphere's capabilities for comprehension of verbs is more suspect, however. It is not clear whether it cannot respond to verbs, as some of the early evidence suggested; it is possible that the testing methods allowed interference from the language-dominant left hemisphere (see Nebes, 1974, for details).

Minor Hemisphere Functions

While the left hemisphere is generally dominant and superior in language functions, the minor, right hemisphere does show superiority for certain functions. Among these are spatial relations and part-whole relations. For instance, when these subjects blindly feel a three-dimensional form and simultaneously view a number of two-dimensional patterns that can be folded into the three-dimensional form, they are superior in making matches when the information comes to the right hemisphere. The minor hemisphere also seems to be superior in dealing with complex visual stimuli such as faces and nonsense figures. A number of experiments (see Nebes, 1974) have employed so-called chimerical stimuli. These stimuli consist of pictures with two incongruous halves, such as the left side of one face joined to the right side of a different face, or half a flower juxtaposed to half a picture of an eye. Such chimeras are presented to the subject so that half is presented to the visual field of one hemisphere and half is presented to the visual field of the other. If a subject is asked to point to the object seen, he or she invariably points to the object seen by the minor hemisphere, and gives no indication that the stimulus was in any way irregular. (There generally were no instances of responding to both stimuli.) However, if asked to name the object seen, the response is appropriate to that seen by the dominant hemisphere. It has been suggested that all visual stimuli, including words, are perceptually processed by the minor hemisphere. It is only when language transformation of visual stimuli such as words is required that the language-dominant hemisphere enters the perceptual processing.

Conflict Between the Hemispheres

To this point, we have emphasized the relative independence of functioning of the two hemispheres in patients with a sectioned corpus callosum. Motor control by the ipsilateral hemisphere (e.g., left hemisphere–left hand) is possible and instances of such interaction can be shown; these may take the form of interference. For instance, it is possible for such patients to copy simple words with the left hand; however, when instead of copying, the task requires the production of written names of objects, the first few letters are about all that can be produced. The left hemisphere seems to guess at the word and preeempts the writing process: when shown the word "sit" in the left visual field, a patient wrote "si", hesitated, continued with "mp", and said "jump." In contrast, in experiments with chimerical stimuli, when the task called for pointing to the stimulus seen, the minor hemisphere's visual perception controlled the motor output irrespective of which hand did the pointing. These results suggest that which hemisphere dominates is a function of the type of information processing that is required: If visual recognition is called for, the minor hemisphere controls the action; if a verbal transformation of the information is required, the left hemisphere controls the action; i.e., motor actions are controlled by the hemisphere specialized for the task.

Summary

Splitting the brain into two disconnected hemispheres reveals the specialized functions of each hemisphere. Language functions predominate in one, typically the left hemisphere. While the minor hemisphere has some rudimentary language capability, it cannot perform at anything like the level and efficiency of the dominant hemisphere. Nonetheless, the minor hemisphere is capable of constructive conceptual activity. Furthermore, it shows specializations of its own. All of these may not yet have been discovered. Those that have been include superiority for visual processing, particularly for synthesis of part-whole and spatial relations. The evidence suggests that normally the two hemispheres cooperate in integrated fashion and that tasks are carried out under the predominant control of the hemisphere specialized for the information processing required.

Recovery of Language After Lesions

Without reiterating the material presented in Chapter 3 and without going into a detailed examination of the human clinical data, it is appropriate here to make a few remarks concerning recovery of lanaguage functioning after cerebral lesions (see the discussion by Geschwind, 1974).

To begin with, significant recovery of language function does occur in many cases of aphasia due to cerebral injury in adults. But useful recovery is probably not the rule in the majority of adult aphasics. Generally, left-handed subjects are more likely to become aphasic regardless of which hemisphere is damaged; in contrast to left-handers, it is rare for right-handers to become aphasic after right hemisphere injury. But left-handers show better recovery from aphasia; they recover better from right hemisphere lesions than from left but they also recover better from left hemisphere lesions than do right-handers. Similarly, right-handers with left-handers among their biological relatives appear to recover better from aphasia than right-handers without such a family history. Such data suggest that left-handers may be different somehow in cerebral organization.

Comparable lesions in children lead to a different prognosis (Lenneberg, 1969). Lesions of the left hemisphere in children under 2 years of age are no more debilitating of language development than lesions of the right hemisphere. Children incurring left hemisphere lesions quickly reestablish language functions if the right hemisphere remains intact. Such children often seem to retrace earlier stages of language acquisition but the reacquisition is much more rapid. This capacity for recovery may last until the early teens, after which lesions appear to be as effective in producing aphasia as they are in older adults. There is an implication in these data that recovery in young children is really an acquisition process, i.e., acquisition of language by the right hemisphere, and a prolonged period in childhood for this capacity.

Geschwind (1974) suggests that the child may actually learn language with both hemispheres. This implies that *utilization* of right hemispheric capacity for language is what is lost as the child matures. Recovery of language, then, may represent the results of overcoming a suppressive mechanism. In this regard, it may be noteworthy that neurologists generally feel that recovery proceeds independent of whether there is specific training—most recovery of function appears "spontaneous" in adults. In other words, recovery of language functioning may be due to a renewed ability to employ right-hemispheric mechanisms that have previously acquired language.

Be that as it may, the effects of specific language training must also be considered so as to avoid missing appropriate opportunities for increasing recovery. Gazzaniga (1974) has summarized initial attempts to employ sign language training such as has been used with teaching language to chimpanzees. The cognitive capacities of the minor hemisphere, demonstrated in the callosally sectioned patients, and the progress made with chimps, who presumably do not have the brain specilizations for language that humans do, both make sign language training for aphasics a plausible thing to do.

Reading Disability

We cannot pursue the clinical details of dyslexia (reading disability) here; however, it is pertinent in this context to indicate that there is evidence suggesting that the problem involves the maturation of nervous system mechanisms (Satz, Friel, & Rudegeair, 1974). An interesting aspect of this study is its prospective nature. A large group of children was tested prior to any exposure to reading training; their performance on a variety of tests was predictive of *future* performance in reading. The tests which discriminated dyslexics were measures of cognitive and perceptual skill. It is also noteworthy that such tests continued to discriminate even after a subset of good and poor readers were matched for intelligence. Generally, the results indicate that the tests tap maturationally dependent skills that lag in development in the dyslexics. It is also argued that the older dyslexic child has a problem in language processing while the younger child shows a lag in visual-perceptual integration.

Sex, Handedness, and Cognitive Functioning

Much behavioral work has been devoted to the study of sex-related differences in cognitive performance; much of this work turns on the relative contribution of differential training in cognitive skills. Does female superiority in verbal skills, for example, or male superiority in mathematical skills represent differential training? Recent evidence is beginning to suggest that there may be a neural basis for some of these differences.

An animal study by Goldman, Crawford, Stokes, Galkin, and Rosvold (1974) illustrates such differences between the sexes. These researchers tested monkeys for the effects of bilateral lesions of the orbital region of the prefrontal cortex (generally, the inferior portion of the tip of the frontal lobe). Such lesions result in deficits in adult monkeys on object discrimination reversal and delayed response tasks. The present study showed an unexpected sex-related outcome of the placement of such lesions in young monkeys. Generally, male monkeys with lesions were impaired on such tasks as early as 2½ months of age; female monkeys failed to show such deficits until they were from 15 to 18 months of age. These results suggest that the orbital region matures earlier in male monkeys than in females. Goldman et al. draw some parallels between these results and those from humans: For instance, cerebral palsy and dyslexia seem to have a higher incidence among boys than girls. To the extent that perinatal injuries are implicated in such disorders, such injuries may have greater consequence in males than in females because of regional differences in the rate of brain maturation between the sexes.

An analogous finding has been demonstrated in humans (Witelson, 1976). Witelson tested 200 right-handed children for right hemipshere superiority in spatial processing. For this, she checked the accuracy with which the children correctly identified two solid forms, which were simultaneously handled out of view (one in each hand), from among six such shapes visually displayed. Boys ranging in age from 6 to 12 years showed a consistent superiority of performance for objects handled with the left hand (right hemispheric superiority). In contrast, girls of the same age range failed to show any hand difference. It is noteworthy that the children were also tested in a dichotic listening task and both boys and girls showed a left hemispheric superiority, consistent with language specialization in that hemisphere. These results suggest that right hemispheric specialization for spatial processing occurs much earlier in boys than in girls. In girls, there seems to be bilateral control, at least until adolescence. Some studies suggest that participation by the left hemisphere in spatial tasks may persist into adulthood for females. A sexual differentiation in hemispheric specialization could have educational implications; Witelson, therefore, suggested that methods for teaching reading might be differentially effective for the two sexes. She also noted that a more slowly maturing right hemisphere, and a possibly consequent longer capacity for plasticity of function, may underly the fact that women show less impairment than men as a result of left hemispheric damage.

A study by Levy and Reid (1976) showed that females and left-handers who write with an inverted hand position showed a smaller degree of hemispheric differentiation than males or subjects with a more typical writing

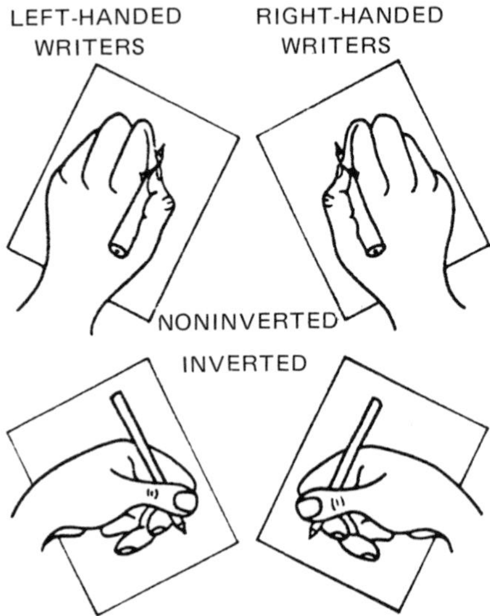

Figure 13.4. Typical writing postures of left- and right-handed subjects using inverted and noninverted hand positions. (From Levy, J. and Reid, M. Variations in writing posture and cerebral organization. *Science*, 1976, *194*, 337–339.)

position. Right-handed subjects generally would be expected to have a left-hemispheric specialization for language and a right-hemispheric specialization for spatial functions; among left-handers; about two-thirds show a similar organization. This study investigated whether writing posture could serve as an index to this organization. Figure 13.4 illustrates the writing postures. Levy and Reid scored their subjects for lateralization of verbal and spatial functioning on the basis of tachistoscopically presented visual stimuli. The subjects were also classified as to whether they were right- or left-handed and whether they used an inverted or noninverted writing posture. Subjects with the normal writing posture demonstrated linguistic superiority in the hemisphere contralateral to the writing hand and visuospatial superiority in the hemisphere ipsilateral to the writing hand; that arrangement was reversed for subjects with the inverted writing posture. The combination of handedness and writing posture correctly predicted the outcome of the tachistoscopic lateralizations tests in 70 of the 73 subjects. But once again, lateralization of language and spatial functions was less strongly demonstrated in female subjects and in left-handers writing with the inverted posture. Left-handed males with the inverted writing posture were the most variable subjects on the spatial test: three outperformed all right-handed subjects using the left visual field but eight were inferior to all right-handed subjects; only one was in the range of the right-handed males.

Finally, Waber (1976) presented evidence that sex differences in cognitive function—female superiority in verbal abilities, male superiority in spatial abilities—may be more a matter of rate of physical maturation of secondary sex characteristics. Waber found that irrespective of sex, early-maturing adolescents performed better on tests of verbal than spatial abilities; later-maturing adolescents performed better on the spatial than the verbal tasks. But late-maturing adolescents showed *more* lateralization for language functioning, in a dichotic listening task, than those maturing earlier. Sexual differences were generally in the direction of female superiority for language and male superiority for spatial tasks, but such differences were overshadowed by relative maturation rate. These results are also congruent with the finding of a lesser degree of lateralizations in females.

Summary

Generally, these studies suggest differential rates of maturation in cerebral mechanisms between males and females. Females seem to show slower attainment of lateralization, greater plasticity of functioning, and less specialization of the involved neural tissue than males. Such differences probably underlie some of the differences in cognitive functioning that have been observed behaviorally. Such neural differences might result from genetic and hormonal differences that operate during early neural development. How writing posture is associated with lesser lateral specialization remains obscure, and whether it too is related to cognitive functioning is presently not known.

MEMORY IN HUMANS

Cognitive integration requires memory—a person with deficient memory literally can become lost in his or her environment. In the preceding chapter, we reviewed the literature that has so far sought in vain to pinpoint the engram to discrete structures. Recent animal studies, however, suggest that more widely conceived systems of neurons may be responsible for engram storage. In contrast to these studies, human clinical data present a somewhat different picture; here it is possible to see some highly specific deficits that, on the face of it, appear to involve memory mechanisms as a result of relatively specific neural damage. Prominent in this literature are the effects of hippocampal damage.

The Hippocampal Memory Deficit

Evidence for involvement of the hippocampus in learning comes almost exclusively from human clinical material. Generally, animal experiments have indicated that hippocampal lesions may result in learning deficits but none that approach the severity seen in humans and none that could not be attributed to "nonassociative" mechanisms. Patients with bilateral hippocampal lesions show no loss of previously acquired skill or knowledge nor do they have perceptual difficulties. Immediate memory appears to be normal, provided that memory span is not exceeded. But these patients appear to be incapable of long-term storage of newly acquired information. One patient is described as follows: "This forgetfulness applies to the surroundings of the house where he has lived for the past six years, and to those neighbors who have been visiting the house regularly during this period. He has not yet learned their names and does not recognize them if he meets them in the street. He has, however, succeeded in retaining a few constant features of his immediate environment, such as the layout of the rooms in the house. On formal testing of this patient, 20 months after operation, it was clear that forgetting occurred the instant his focus of attention shifted. . . . Thus, he was able to retain the number 584 for at least 15 minutes, by continuously working out elaborate mnemonic schemes. A minute or so later, H. M. was unable to recall either the number 584 or any of the associated complex train of thought; in fact, he did not know that he had been given a number to remember because, in the meantime, the examiner had introduced a new topic" (Milner, 1970, pp. 36–37).

The lesions of concern here were produced in patients operated on for epileptic seizures whose focus was in the temporal lobes. Two anatomic considerations are of importance: (1) memory is most affected in bilaterally damaged patients and (2) memory impairment is greater, the greater the apparent involvement of the hippocampus. As a result, more recently performed operations have attempted to spare the hippocampus whenever possible. As we shall see, however, it is still not absolutely clear that the hippocampus is, indeed, the critical locus.

Capabilities of Hippocampal Patients

Despite the profound amnesia resulting from bilateral hippocampal damage, such patients generally show little or no general intellectual loss; in fact, probably because of improvement in their general clinical condition, there may even be some modest gains in intelligence test performance. It should also be noted that since the operation involves the medial portions of the temporal lobe, rather than the lateral surface, there is no aphasia.

One such patient, H. M., has been studied extensively over the years by Brenda Milner and has become a classic example of the selective memory deficit. H. M.'s memory for events and behaviors well-learned prior to surgery remained intact, but he no longer seems generally capable of converting immediate short-term into long-term storage. However, some evidence of long-term memory has been demonstrated. This mainly involves motor skills. In a mirror drawing task, the subject views a star-shaped figure with a border of double lines in a mirror, and must draw a line around the figure, between the double lines, without touching them. H. M. showed improvement in performance within daily sessions and retention of the improvement from day to day. However, after three such sessions, when his performance was practically perfect, he still was unaware that he had ever done the task before and required an explanation of what he was expected to do. Interestingly, H. M. failed to show improvement in learning a visually or tactually guided maze with 28 choice points, although some improvement was manifested with shorter versions of the mazes. H. M. also showed some retention of a task requiring the identification of fragmented pictures or words. Here successive versions of the material are presented with increasingly more detail filled in until the subject can identify the material; he learns to identify it from the least complete version.

Patients with unilateral hippocampal lesions do not show the global memory deficit that H. M. demonstrates. However, they do demonstrate deficits. Generally, the deficits demonstrated are in accord with the hemispheric specializations discussed earlier; that is, patients with left hippocampal damage show some deficit in retention of verbal material and patients with right hippocampal damage show deficits in retention of visual, spatial materal (see Milner, 1974).

It is clear that temporal lobe damage, particularly bilaterally, results in profound memory problems. Following such lesions, there is a deficit in demonstrating long-term retention of new learning. It is clear that the hippocampus itself is not the "repository" of such memory since engrams acquired prior to surgery do survive the lesions. Milner suggests that the hippocampus is somehow involved in mediating the storage of new learning. On the other hand, Warrington and Weiskrantz (1973) argue that the problem is one of retrieval rather than storage. We shall return to this question shortly.

Frontal Lobe Effects

An extremely complex literature involves the effects of lesions in the frontal lobes. Monkeys with frontal lesions are severely impaired in performance on delayed response tasks. Although such tasks were originally conceived as tests of memory, it was noted in Chapter 5 that such deficits in animals seem to be, at least in part, the result of attentional deficits—i.e., high distractionibility. Monkeys with frontal lesions also seem to have difficulty with inhibiting incorrect responses. In humans, the effects of frontal lobe lesions are obscured by the fact that such lesions were primarily employed therapeutically in emotional disorders prior to the advent of tranquilizers. More recently, such lesions have been of some value in the relief of otherwise intractable pain. However, Milner (1974) has summarized some work in

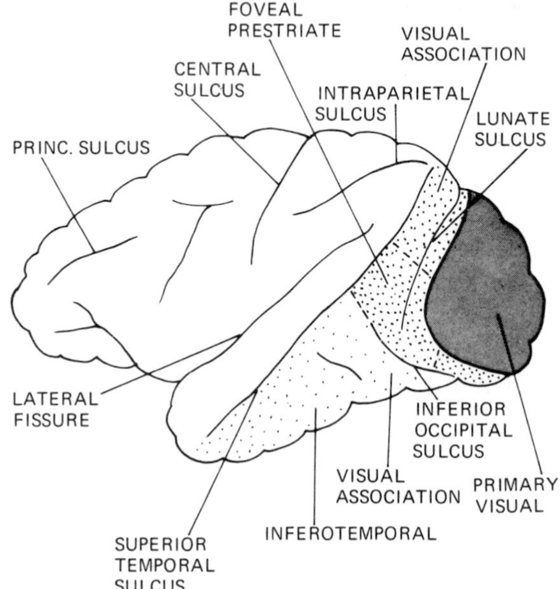

Figure 13.5. Approximate location of inferotemporal and foveal prestriate cortex in the monkey. In man, the hippocampus lies medial to the inferotemporal area in the depths of the temporal lobe. (After Gross, 1973)

epileptic patients with such lesions and suggests that frontal lesions impair processes related to the temporal ordering of events. Thus, such patients may be unable to distinguish which events occurred more recently as compared to earlier in a sequence.

Inferotemporal and Posterior Association Cortex

Because of a possible relationship to the memory deficit produced by hippocampal lesions in people, we will also briefly note here the effects of temporal and visual association area lesions in monkeys. Inferotemporal cortex is association cortex located on the inferior surface of the temporal lobe in primates. In close proximity, caudally, is a related visual association area, termed the foveal prestriate cortex (see Figure 13.5). Lesions in these two areas produce deficits in visual discrimination learning in monkeys. In humans, the hippocampus lies medial to the inferotemporal cortex, within the temporal lobe.

It has been hypothesized that these two areas operate in conjunction in visual discrimination learning (Gross, 1973). Very briefly, there is evidence to strongly suggest that foveal prestriate lesions interfere with the animal's ability to process stimuli in the foveal portions of the retina, those stimuli normally central to making discriminations, and this results in a diffusion of attention. Inferotemporal lesions, on the other hand, may interfere with recognition of critical cues in the discrimination problem. Note that the deficits resulting from these lesions are specific to visual discrimination problems—other modalities are not disrupted. Inferotemporal lesions produce only a relative deficit, i.e., they do not impair learning of easy discrimination problems, nor do they impair the retention of problems well learned prior to the lesions. Furthermore, punishment of incorrect responses, along with reward for correct responses, results in the learning of difficult discriminations as well.

Gross (1973) suggests that these two cortical areas recycle information between themselves in the learning of discrimination problems. He further suggests that the foveal prestriate cortex contains mechanisms involved in attentional aspects of visual learning while the inferotemporal cortex has a memory or associative function. However, another way of characterizing the inferotemporal lesion is to emphasize that it may be the output from memory, rather than the input, which is impaired. That is, the lesion may interfere with the animal's ability to integrate present stimulus conditions with previously stored information. In any event, Gross also suggests the comparison between these lesions in monkeys and temporal lobe lesions in humans. In people, damage to the temporal lobe of the dominant hemisphere produces language disturbances; damage to the nondominant hemisphere affects visual functions in a manner that seems analogous to the effects of inferotemporal lesions in monkeys. This is not to suggest that the human brain is equivalent to the monkey brain with language added to the left hemisphere! However, a recent paper by Horel and Misantone (1976) suggests that the analogy may not be entirely inappropriate either. In this experiment, monkeys were lesioned in a fiber band connecting the temporal lobe with more dorsal and medial subcortical portions of the brain. In two animals in which the cuts were complete bilaterally, there was a severe deficit in retention of a previously learned visual discrimination and the problem was not relearned. Most importantly, the fibers cut in this experiment lie directly in the path of the surgical approach to the hippocampus in humans. Thus, it is suggested that the amnestic effects of temporal lobe lesions in humans may not stem from a dysfunctioning hippocampus but rather from the destruction of temporal lobe connections to subcortical areas of the brain. If such a hypothesis can be verified, it will go a long way toward removing a fundamental disagreement over the functions of the hippocampus between the animal and human literature.

Summary

It is not possible to synthesize the above material into a definitive set of statements about human memory that we can accept with great assurance. However, some trends in these data are discernible.

Though the effects of hippocampal lesions have generally been conceived of as interfering with consolidation of memory, there are some strong suggestions that human memory deficits resulting from lesions might be more a matter of retrieval. In their discussion of this problem, Warrington and Weiskrantz (1973) emphasize several points. One is that the retrograde amnesia found may be underestimated; rather than being limited to a period just prior to incurring the lesion, the amnestic problem may extend back much further, so that remote events are no better remembered than recent events. A related point concerns storage of new material—here the emphasis is on the fact that the failure to learn new material is not so complete as many have emphasized. There is evidence that H. M., for instance, does learn new material. Finally, long-term retention seems to be demonstrable most easily in situations employing "partial information," such as the fragmented stimulus material referred to earlier. It is noteworthy that amnestic patients seem to be differentially aided by such material. One advantage of such material is that it tends to limit incorrect, false-positive responses. Generally, Warrington and Weiskrantz suggest that interference, rather than a failure of consolidation, may be of major importance in producing amnesia as a result of lesions.

Recent analyses of the relevant animal data are also beginning to suggest that the discontinuities between human and animal data may be more apparent than real. Here, again, the data may be interpreted as demonstrating retrieval deficits and problems in linking new with older stimulus material.

SUMMARY

The human brain appears to be uniquely prepared for the learning and utilization of language. That specialization appears to be reflected in the unique lateralization of functioning that occurs in humans. Generally, language comprehension and expression is dependent on the integrity of one hemisphere, usually the left. Destruction of the relevant neural loci produces severe impairments in language functions. The minor, or *non*language-dominant, hemisphere also has its own specialization—it appears to be specifically adapted for complex visual and spatial relationships. The hemispheric disconnection syndrome dramatically emphasizes these specializations: When the two hemispheres are surgically separated, the normal functional cooperation between the hemispheres is lost and cognitive integration between the two halves of the brain can be virtually absent.

In addition to language capabilities, cognitive integration depends on memory. Human memory appears to be susceptible to disruption from lesions in several locations. Particularly severe memory impairment seems to result from lesions of the hippocampus, but whether it is the hippocampus per se that is involved is still unclear. Much emphasis has been placed on the apparent discontinuity between animals and human studies in this regard—i.e., hippocampal lesions do not appear to result in a memory deficit in animals. Recently, however, several lines of evidence are beginning to suggest greater continuity between the animal and human lesion literatures. It is at least possible that both human and animal amnesia resulting from lesions may be explainable in terms of retrieval deficits.

Finally, male-female differences in cognitive functioning have been variously attributed to training differences and to genetic differences. Recent research is beginning to analyze the genetic components in such differences and focuses on differential maturational rates of relevant brain tissue. Such maturational differences may predispose males and females toward differential utilizations of specialized brain areas.

REFERENCES

GARDNER, R. A., & GARDNER, B. T. Teaching sign language to a chimpanzee. *Science*, 1969, *165*, 664–672.

GAZZANIGA, M. S. *The bisected brain.* New York: Appleton-Century-Crofts, 1970.

GAZZANIGA, M. S. Determinants of cerebral recovery. In D. G. Stein, J. J. Rosen, & N. Butters (eds.), *Plasticity and recovery of function in the central nervous system.* New York: Academic Press, 1974, pp. 203–215.

GESCHWIND, N. The organization of language and the brain. *Science*, 1970, *170*, 940–944.

GESCHWIND, N. Language and the brain. *Scientific American*, 1972, *226*, 76–83.

GESCHWIND, N. Late changes in the nervous system: An overview. In D. G. Stein, J. J. Rosen, & N. Butters (eds.), *Plasticity and recovery of function in the central nervous system.* New York: Academic Press, 1974, pp. 467–508.

GESCHWIND, N., & LEVITZKY, W. Human brain: Left-right asymmetries in temporal speech region. *Science*, 1968, *161*, 186–189.

GOLDMAN, P. S., CRAWFORD, H. T., STOKES, L. P., GALKIN, T. S., & ROSVOLD, H. E. Sex-dependent behavioral effects of cerebral cortical lesions in the developing rhesus monkey. *Science*, 1974, *186*, 540–542.

GROSS, C. G. Inferotemporal cortex and vision. In E. Stellar & J.M. Sprague (eds.), *Progress in physiological psychology*, Vol. 5. Academic Press: New York, 1973, pp. 77–123.

Hayes, K. J., & Hayes, C. Imitation in a home-raised chimpanzee. *Journal of Comparative and Physiological Psychology,* 1952, *45,* 450–459.

Horel, J. A., & Misantone, L. J. Visual discrimination impaired by cutting temporal lobe connections. *Science,* 1976, *193,* 336–338.

Kimura, D. Functional asymmetry of the brain in dichotic listening. *Cortex,* 1967, *3,* 163–178.

Lenneberg, E. H. On explaining language. *Science,* 1969, *164,* 635–643.

Levy, J., & Reid, M. Variations in writing posture and cerebral organization. *Science,* 1976, *194,* 337–339.

McAdam, D. W., & Whitaker, H. A. Language production: Electroencephalographic localization in normal human brain. *Science,* 1971, *172,* 499–502.

Milner, B. Memory and the medial temporal regions of the brain. In K. H. Pribram & D. E. Broadbent (eds.), *Biology of memory,* New York: Academic Press, 1970, pp. 29–50.

Milner, B. Hemispheric specialization: Scope and limits. In F. O. Schmitt & F. G. Worden (eds.), *The neurosciences, Third study program.* Cambridge, Mass.: MIT Press, 1974, pp. 75–89.

Nebes, R. D. Hemispheric specialization in commissurotomized man. *Psychological Bulletin,* 1974, *81,* 1–14.

Premack, D. Language in chimpanzees? *Science,* 1971, *172,* 808–822.

Satz, P., Friel, J., & Rudegeair, F. Differential changes in the acquisition of developmental skills in children who later become dyslexic. In D. G. Stein, J. J. Rosen, & N. Butters (eds.), *Plasticity and recovery of function in the central nervous system.* New York: Academic Press, 1974, pp. 175–202.

Sperry, R. W. Hemisphere deconnection and unity in conscious awareness. *American Psychologist,* 1968, *23,* 723–733.

Teyler, T. J., Roemer, R. A., Harrison, T. F., & Thompson, R. F. Human scalp-recorded evoked-potential correlates of linguistic stimuli. *Bulletin of the Psychonomic Society,* 1973, *1,* 333–334.

Waber, D. P. Sex differences in cognition: A function of maturation rate? *Science,* 1976, *192,* 572–574.

Warrington, E. K., & Weiskrantz, L. An analysis of short-term and long-term memory defects in man. In J. A. Deutsch (ed.), *The physiological basis of memory.* New York: Academic Press, 1973, pp. 365–395.

Witelson, S. F. Sex and the single hemisphere: Specialization of the right hemisphere for spatial processing. *Science,* 1976, *193,* 425–427.

Wood, C. C., Goff, W. R., & Day, R. S. Auditory evoked potentials during speech perception. *Science,* 1971, *173,* 1248–1251.

14

Functional Disorders of Behavior

It is estimated that one out of every four hospital beds in the United States is occupied by a person with behavioral pathology—and not all people with behavioral pathology are hospitalized! Behavioral disorders range from those where there is an obvious organic involvement to those in which such involvement is obscure. The behaviors manifested range from impairments of consciousness and motor performance, through a variety of language and memory impairments, to conduct disorders and frank psychosis. In this chapter, we will discuss the so-called functional disorders—disorders of behavior with no *known* organic etiology.

The term "functional disorder" is applied to behavioral disorders specifically associated with the diagnostic labels of neurosis, schizophrenia, manic-depressive psychosis, and personality disorder—that is, behavioral disorders where organic pathology is either obscure or believed to be absent altogether. Over the years, psychology has vacillated between an emphasis on theories stressing either organic or behavioral etiologies in these disorders. It will not be our purpose to try to settle this issue—in fact, it is most likely that both factors are involved. However, in recent years, increasingly impressive evidence for an organic contribution in schizophrenia and depression is accumulating. We shall survey some of the major highlights of this evidence.

Probably the strongest reasons for believing that there are organic factors in the etiology of at least some functional disorders arise from the genetic studies of these disorders (see Chapter 2). Given a strong genetic influence in a disorder such as schizophrenia—and this now seems undeniable—the search for physiological factors becomes understandable. And given that genes operate through the body's biochemistry, an emphasis on biochemical and neural concomitants of behavioral disorder is to be expected.[1]

METHODOLOGICAL CONSIDERATIONS

One of the most perplexing problems in dealing with any disorder is the definition of its essential characteristics—how, for example, to distinguish a schizophrenic from a nonschizophrenic patient. Resolution of the problem is generally a "bootstrapping" operation—constellations of patient characteristics are tentatively grouped into syndromes, etiologies are investigated, presumed disorders of physiological function are isolated and treated, behavioral changes are evaluated, *and* definitions are continually revised. Thus, in our review, we shall see hypotheses derived, for instance, on the basis that certain drugs seem more effective in some patients than in others. However, it is also true that these drugs rarely have especially specific effects; i.e., for either the patients successfully treated or for the biochemical systems that they affect. Without reviewing the definitional question in depth (several papers in Freedman [1975] deal with it), the following generalizations may be offered: Schizophrenia may consist of a spectrum of disorders rather than a single disorder; similarly, the affective psychoses (depressive and manic-depressive) may consist of two subtypes; the affective psychoses and schizophrenia seem to be genetically separable—it is unlikely that monozygotic twins ever show one with schizophrenia and one with an affective psychosis; but the "characteristic" symptoms of the two syndromes do show considerable overlap.

Although there is growing methodological sophistication in this field, many studies have been carried out employing only two groups—an ill group and a "normal" control group. This design is subject to a variety of interpretations of any differences that might be found. In addition to the difference for which they were intially selected—illness versus comparative mental health—it is often forgotten that institutionalized groups may differ from normal controls in their diet, exercise, drug intake, and degree of anxiety. Any physiological differences found between these groups could be attribut-

[1]The recent volume edited by Freedman (1975) is an excellent supplement to the material to be discussed here.

able to one or more of these other variables rather than their differences in mental health. Thus, for instance, while Ferguson and Fisher (1963) found that the injection of plasma from catatonic patients disrupted the performance of monkeys on an operant conditioning task, similar disruption was also produced by the injection of plasma from normals under preoperative stress.

A further implication of this point is that any physiological differences might not be attributable specifically to this particular illness; before specifically attributing a biochemical abnormality to the presence of schizophrenia, it must be ascertained that the abnormality is not also found, for instance, in manic-depressive psychosis.

There is also the problem of causality. If, for instance, one were to isolate a biochemical factor in schizophrenia, and even if injection of this substance into normals produced true schizophrenic symptoms, it would not be certain that the substance was the cause of schizophrenia. It would still be possible that the substance is only a *result* of being schizophrenic, or, perhaps, the result of some still more primary biochemical defect.

Finally, there is the question of the validity of "models." Much of the work in this area has involved the attempt to produce model psychoses, either in animals or in humans. Even if an injected substance produces a psychotic condition in otherwise normal people, to what extent can the psychosis be considered an analogue of schizophrenia, for instance? Even if characterized by acute episodes, a naturally occurring psychosis is a relatively long-term condition that probably involves adaptation by the patient to the condition. In the absence of this developmental history, can a model psychosis effectively reproduce all the essential characterisitics of the disorder?

Keeping these limitations in mind, we shall turn to the empirical data. This material generally falls into two major categories, according to which we have organized this chapter: First, we shall consider how CNS recording has been used in studying the functional disorders; then we shall examine the biochemical approach to their study.

CNS RECORDING STUDIES

The EEG is an invaluable aid in the diagnosis of certain types of brain pathology; for example, certain organic disorders, such as some tumors, result in characteristic electric changes. Hans Berger, the first person to record the human EEG, was a psychiatrist whose primary concern was that the EEG would aid in distinguishing between the various psychotic conditions. This hope has not been fulfilled. There are no EEG signs that can be considered characteristic of psychosis and none which sufficiently differentiate between diagnostic groups. However, while the EEG apparently contains no specific signs associated with psychosis, it may still reveal something about brain function in these disorders.

EEG STUDIES

Generally, the EEGs of psychiatric patients are characterized by a higher incidence of abnormality than nonpatient groups. But schizophrenics show such abnormalities much more frequently than depressives. The interpretation of the incidence of abnormality is complicated, however, by the presence of such variables as institutionalization, medication, and so on. In addition, if EEGs are recorded only when possible brain damage is suspected, a higher incidence of abnormality must be expected simply because such samples are not representative of the general population.

Davis (1940) reported a so-called choppy EEG pattern which has a high incidence in schizophrenia. This pattern is characterized by "disorganized" low voltage, very fast frequencies, and a lack of slower rhythms. The choppy pattern does suggest intense activiation. There is controversy, however, about the possible artifactual nature of this pattern (Hill, 1957).

Goldstein and Sugerman (1969) summarized research indicating that the EEG of schizophrenics does not differ from normals in energy content (that is, integrated voltage) but does differ from normals in relative variability (mean voltage/standard deviation); schizophrenics show less variability. They also indicate that schizophrenics followed over a period of time show a relationship between EEG variability and behavior; that is, with improvement in their behavioral condition, the relative variability is increased. These results also suggest a defect in arousal.

It is also interesting that a number of studies (see Igert & Lairy, 1962) have found that schizophrenics with more normal EEG patterns have the most unfavorable prognosis; persistent and regular alpha activity is associated with poorer therapeutic results.

Schizophrenia and Epilepsy

The relationship between schizophrenia and epileptic disorders is still a matter for discussion among electroencephalographers and psychiatrists. It is interesting to note, however, that the mistaken notion that epileptics do not become schizophrenic was strongly influential in the development of convulsive therapies; electroconvulsive treatment has, of course, proven most effective in depression rather than schizophrenia.

The empirical findings with three EEG abnormalities might suggest a relationship between schizophrenia and epilepsy in that they are found in both groups. Gibbs, Gibbs, Tasher, and Adams (1960) described two var-

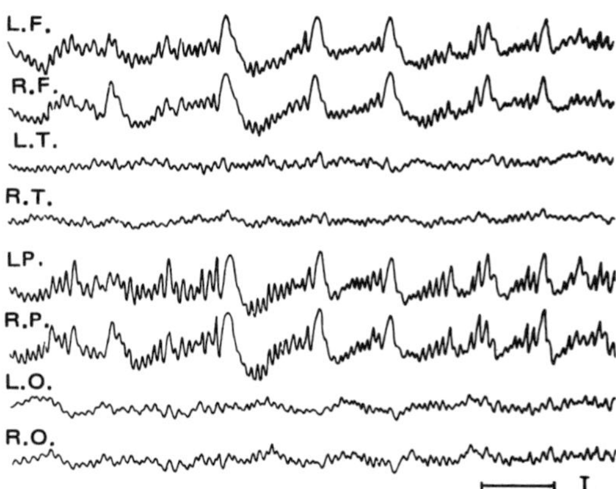

Figure 14.1. B-Mitten EEG patterns. Sleeping male subject, age 32, catatonic schizophrenic. Linked ear reference. F, frontal; T, midtemporal; P, parietal; O, occipital. Calibrations: 1 sec, 50 μV. (From Struve, F. A., Becka, D. R., The relative incidence of the B-mitten EEG pattern in process and reaction schizophrenia. *Electroencephalography and Clinical Neurophysiology*, 1968, *24*, 80–82.)

ieties of EEG discharge whose shape has been likened to that of a mitten, thereby providing the names of A- and B-mitten. (In Figure 14.1, the "thumb" of the mitten is a sharp transient; the following slow wave forms the envelope of the "hand.") A-mittens are distinguished from B-mittens in that the thumb component is of shorter duration in the B-mitten. A-mittens seem to be correlated with Parkinson's disease (see p. 532). B-mittens appear in moderately deep sleep, and they have their highest incidence in epileptics with psychosis (42 percent); among the psychoses, the incidence is highest in schizophrenics (37 percent). Struve and Becka (1968) studied this pattern in process and reactive schizophrenics. *Process schizophrenics* are characterized by an insidious onset of thought disorder with a lack of apparent precipitating factors; there is also a lack of affective turmoil and a history of poor premorbid adjustment. *Reactive schizophrenics* are chacterized by a relatively good premorbid adjustment, a fairly rapid onset (which may be associated with specific precipitating factors), and by affective turmoil, disorientation, and confusion. Only 1 of 10 process schizophrenics showed the B-mitten pattern, whereas 8 of 11 reactives did ($p = .006$); there were no other differences between the groups in incidence of EEG abnormality. Three process and two reactive schizophrenics also showed the pattern of 14- and 6-per-sec positive spikes.

The EEGs of epileptics characteristically contain spike discharges. Patterns of positive spike discharge from the temporal lobes at 6/sec and 14/sec constitute an EEG symptom that has been recorded with relatively high incidence in psychiatric groups, including both schizophrenics and patients with personality or character disorders. It is a phenomenon that appears with disproportionate frequency among children and adolescents (Gibbs & Gibbs, 1963). Headaches, abdominal pain, and autonomic disturbances are associated with its occurrence, and there is also an apparently marked association with aggressive and violent behavior, such as firesetting, acts of rage, and murder. The antisocial behavior of the personality disorders tends to decline with increasing age, and so does the incidence of this particular spike pattern. This suggests a maturational defect.

Heath (1969) reported that during psychotic episodes, schizophrenic patients with implanted electrodes show spiking and slow-wave activity from the septal area. These spikes were generally not seen in recordings from scalp electrodes. Spikes may also be recorded from other limbic structures, but they appeared to be associated with psychotic behavior only if recorded in the septal area. No septal spiking was observed in nonpsychotic patients. Stimulation of the septal area induced general arousal and feelings of well-being and pleasure. Heath interprets schizophrenia to include anhedonia, an impaired ability to integrate feelings of pleasurure, and associates this with septal dysfunction. This interpretation is heavily dependent on the results of animal studies employing electrical stimulation of the limbic system and hypothalamus (Chapter 11).

Pharmacological Agents and the EEG

EEG recordings may be employed to assess the reactivity of subjects to pharmacological agents. One example of such techniques has been employed in an extensive series of studies by Shagass (1958). Intravenous injection of the barbiturate sodium amytal tends to increase the amount of fast activity (15 to 30 Hz) in the frontal EEG. Shagass' procedure involves injecting amytal in standardized amounts over a period of time and measuring the cumulative increase in fast activity; the total dose of amytal which produces the greatest increase in fast activity, and following which there is a tendency to plateau, is defined as the "sedation threshold."

In nonpsychotic subjects, the sedation threshold is correlated with the apparent anxiety of the subjects. It is highest in patients with anxiety states and neurotic depressions and lowest in hysterics. In psychotic subjects, the threshold correlates better with the degree of "ego impairment." The threshold is low in acute schizophrenics and agitated depressive psychotics and lower still in patients with organic psychoses. It is highest in "borderline" and chronic schizophrenics, patients with the least impariment of ego functioning.

On an empirical level, the sedation threshold technique has proven most useful in distinguishing neurotic and psychotic depressives: psychotic depressives are almost uniformly low in their threshold, while neurotic depressives tend to be high. This difference is predictive of therapeutic success with electroconvulsive therapy—low threshold subjects respond better to such treatment.

Summary

While the EEG does show some quantitative differences between patients (particularly schizophrenics) and nonpatients, it is unclear as to whether such differences are anything more than accompaniments of the psychological states occurring in the psychoses. For instance, the EEGs of schizophrenics do suggest a heightened state of arousal. In addition, some relationship to epilepsy is suggested in schizophrenia. It seems unlikely, however, that epilepsy per se is any sort of etiological factor in schizophrenia; more likely, some epileptics may show schizophrenic symptoms or the two disorders share some common mechanisms or manifestations.

Sleep Studies

The discovery of REM sleep and its association with dreaming (Chapter 6) gave renewed impetus to the study of sleep in psychiatric populations. Sleep disturbances are common among psychiatric patients. Also, the apparent similarities between hallucinations and dreams encourage hypotheses concerned with the similarity of their neurophysiological mechanisms.

In addition to the usual interpretive cautions concerned with the adequacy of controls, sleep studies also involve prolonged recordings, entailing experimental arrangements and equipment that are often disturbing to psychiatric patients. Many patients may refuse to participate, thereby introducing possible sampling biases; the severely ill, but more passive, depressive patient may be overrepresented compared to the more negativistic schizophrenic. Finally, institutionalization may itself change sleep patterns; daytime napping might be a more common occurrence in patient groups.

REM in Functional Disorders

Many studies have attempted to examine the simple base-line patterns of sleep in the psychiatric disorders, particularly schizophrenia and psychotic depression. Several studies suggest that both REM and slow sleep are attenuated in acute episodes of schizophrenia and psychotic depressive illness, but the interpretation of this is not clear. Feinberg and Evarts (1969) suggest that such losses are most parsimoniously attributed to an increased arousal level in patients; Kupfer and Foster (1975) suggest that differences within these patient groups can also be discerned and that the sleep changes may be of greater significance. It is perhaps noteworthy that following the reduced REM sleep, there generally is no compensatory rebound effect. This does suggest that there may be changes of significance in the neurotransmitter systems controlling sleep. It has been suggested that REM deprivation in the functional disorders represents a self-healing process—the restoration of needed amine levels (see discussion of the paper by Kupfer and Foster, pp. 161–162).

Summary

Sleep is disturbed in the functional disorders. Clinically, such disturbance is even a distinguishing feature of depressive illness. It seems possible that there is an etiological link between the sleep disturbances and the functional disorder but cause-and-effect relationships are not clear. Probably both the sleep and behavioral disturbances share a primary problem.

Evoked Responses and Brain Excitability

That deviant reactivity or excitability of the brain underlies the psychopathology of mental disorders is implied in just about all theories dealing with CNS functions in these disorders. The problem has been how to measure this excitability in some direct manner without inflicting operative procedures on the subjects to gain access to the brain.

The development of techniques for recording evoked responses from scalp electrodes has provided methods for direct measurement in unoperated subjects. Relative excitability of the brain can be assessed by comparing patients and controls in their evoked-response characteristics. Amplitude and latency of response are one set of measures. Paired stimuli separated by varying time intervals, can also be used to measure a recovery function—the degree of a subject's response to the second stimulus of a pair indicates the degree to which the neural system has recovered its excitability following the first stimulus. Trains of stimuli, which would be expected to stress the recovery mechanisms, may also be employed. Shagass and Schwartz have reported the most extensive series of studies employing such techniques.

Reduction in Brain Excitability

Figure 14.2 represents the type of data obtained in recovery function determinations with paired stimuli. Stimulation was of the median or ulnar nerves at the wrist. Recording was done with scalp electrodes placed over the contralateral somatosensory receiving area. Each tracing is the average response obtained by summing the responses to a series of 50 or more individual stimulation trials. Individual inflection points on these responses have been numbered in sequence as an aid in visualizing the complex cycle of waxing and waning in recovery that occurs for different components of the response.

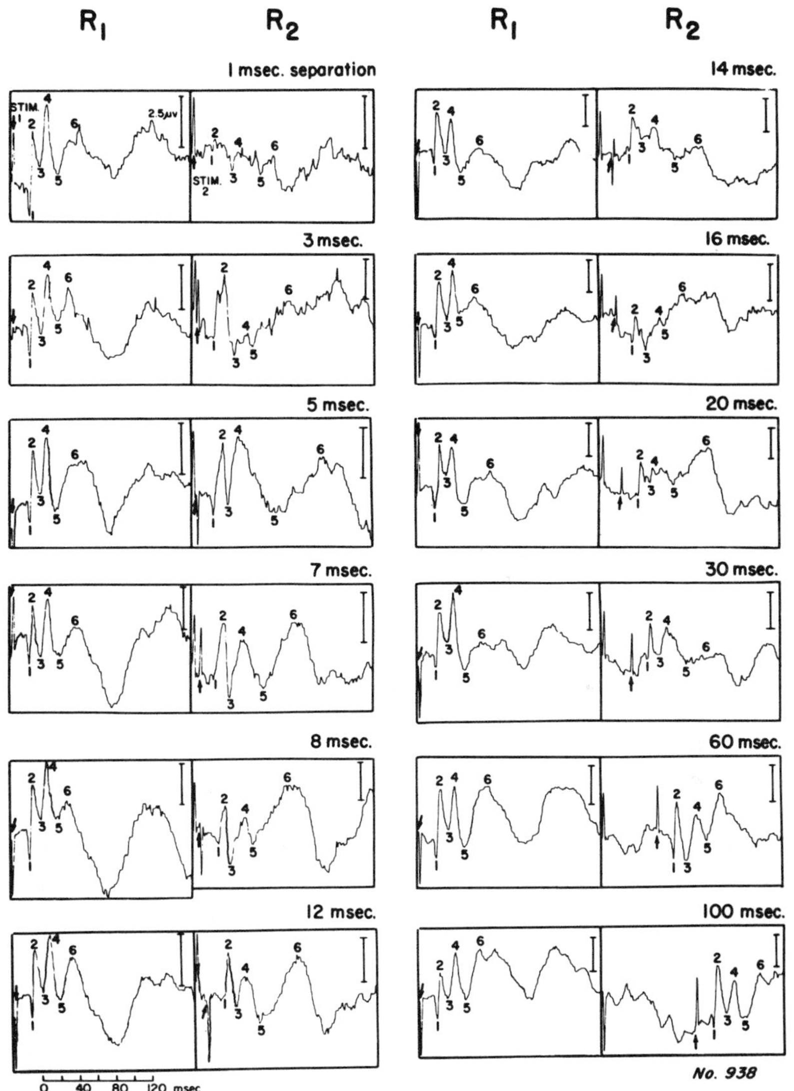

Figure 14.2. Average cerebral evoked responses to electrical stimulation of the median nerve at the wrist in one subject. R_1 is the average response to single stimulations. R_2 is the average response to the second of paired stimuli separated by the time interval indicated at the upper right of each panel; it was obtained by the computer's subtraction of R_1 from the average response to the paired stimuli. Note the waxing and waning of the response components, particularly 1–2, with short time separations between the paired stimuli. (From Shagass, C. and Schwartz, M., Recovery functions of somatosensory peripheral nerve and cerebral evoked responses in man. *Electroencephalography and Clinical Neurophysiology*, 1964, *17*, 126–135.)

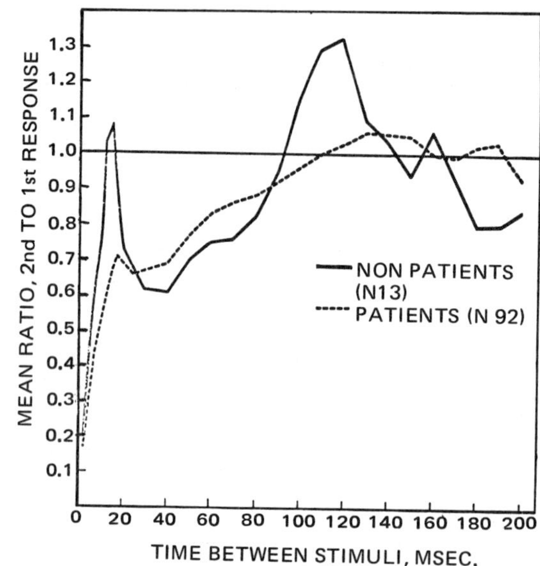

Figure 14.3. Mean recovery curves of somatosensory-evoked responses in psychiatric patients and nonpatients. Curves are based on measurements of responses (component 1–2) as illustrated in Figure 14.2. (From Shagass, C. and Schwartz, M., Reactivity cycle of somatosensory cortex in humans with and without psychiatric disorder. *Science*, Dec. 1961, *134*, 1757–1759. Copyright 1961 by the American Association for the Advancement of Science.)

Schwartz and Shagass (1964) have discussed some of the methodological problems in recording such cycles. In their first reports, Shagass and Schwartz (1961) concentrated on measuring the initial components of these responses, that is, between points 1 and 2 of Figure 14.2. They found a biphasic curve of recovery in control, nonpatient subjects, as shown in Figure 14.3. In these subjects recovery of excitability is characterized by a steeply rising curve, which reaches a maximum of full or near full recovery with delays of as little as 20 msec between the paired stimuli; this peak is followed by a decline and a subsequent return to normal responsiveness at about 100 to 150 msec. Figure 14.3 also shows the curves of a mixed group of psychiatric patients of all types. While their curves are generally biphasic individually, they show less recovery than those of the control group, the amount of early recovery is considerably smaller on an individual basis and there is also great dispersion in the timing of when their peak recovery occurrs. Only 29 percent of the patient group showed full recovery, while only one nonpatient did not show it.

In subsequent studies (Shagass & Schwartz, 1962a, 1962b, 1962c), the patient group was broken down into subcategories based on psychiatric diagnostic categories. Schizophrenics, psychotic depressives, and patients with personality disorders were all found to show attenuated recovery of responsiveness with short separations between the test stimuli; a mixed group of neurotic patients seemed to differ from the rest of the patients in that their recovery functions were more nearly normal.

This general pattern of results was replicated in a subsequent study (Shagass & Schwartz, 1963). It suggests that psychiatric disorder is accompanied by a reduction in brain excitability.

Correlation with Behavior

Does the altered recovery function obtained from psychiatric subjects return to normal when the psychopathaology recedes? A positive answer to this question would support the hypothesis that we are dealing with a characteristic that reflects the functional, behavioral condition of the subject rather than some immutable, predisposing factor.

Psychotic depressive subjects provide a ready means of answering this question, since depressive symptoms are generally readily relieved by electroconvulsive treatments or antidepressant drugs. Figure 14.4 (Shagass &

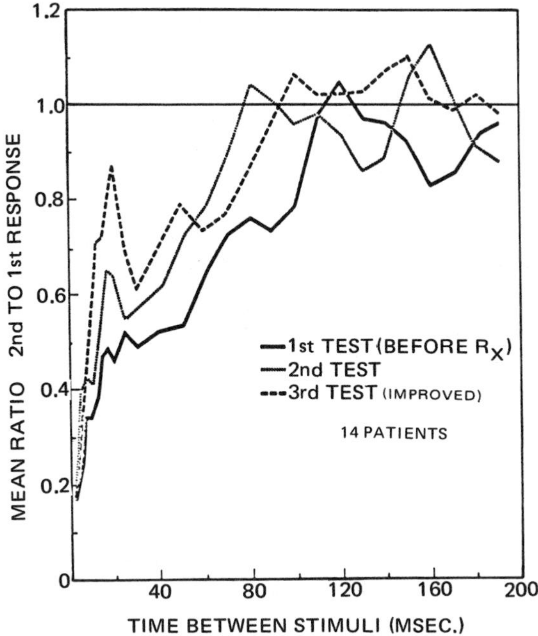

Figure 14.4. Mean recovery curves of 14 depressive patients in three consecutive tests. (1) before treatment; (2) toward the end of treatment; (3) just before discharge from hospital. Note progressively increasing recovery with short interstimulus intervals. (From Shagass, C. and Schwartz, M., Cerebral cortical reactivity in psychotic depressions. *Archives of General Psychiatry*, 1962, 6, 235–242. Copyright 1962, American Medical Association.)

Schwartz, 1962c) shows the results of serial determinations of the recovery function in a group of depressives; three tests were carried out, one before treatment, one during treatment, and one near the time of anticipated discharge from the hospital. It can be seen that there was a progressive increase in responsiveness in the early portions of the curve with improvement in the patients' status. One patient was followed over successive remissions and relapses of symptoms; there was generally a very good relation between her behavioral status and the recovery function; that is, recovery was attenuated during depressive episodes and improved during remission. It should be noted that whether electric shock or drugs were used, the recovery function changes were similar provided the therapeutic outcome was comparable. Thus, to the extent that psychotic depression is representative of all psychiatric disorders, the results suggest that the reduction in brain excitability is not unalterable.

Within Group Differences

The general pattern of results of studies with paired stimuli revealed a relatively nonspecific reduction in brain excitability in the presence of behavioral pathology. In addition, a number of studies from this lab indicated that age and sex relationships to excitability determinations were complicated. More recently, Shagass has employed trains of stimuli to assess excitability (e.g., Shagass, Overton, and Straumanis, 1974). These studies suggest that age and sex variations in evoked-response measurements are different for nonpatients than for psychiatric patients. In addition, there are suggestions that chronic and acute schizophrenics may show some differences. Another important point to be followed up is that fractionating tients on the basis of both evoked responses and characteristics of the resting EEG may add to the diagnostic specificity of the results (Shagass, Straumanis, & Overton, 1975).

Alertness Effects

Evoked responses vary as a function of the state of alertness of the subject. This is particularly striking in the case of the visual response. In Figure 14.5 the response in one subject to a series of single light flashes presented about 3 seconds apart is shown during different sleep stages; in the awake condition there is a prominent after-discharge, at about the frequency of the alpha rhythm, which disappears in all sleep stages (Shagass & Trusty, 1966). The after-discharge is also eliminated during delirium induced by the anticholinergic drug Ditran (Brown, Shagass, & Schwartz, 1964) and is almost nonexistent in patients with chronic brain syndrome as a result of arteriosclerosis (Straumanis, Shagass, & Schwartz, 1965). These results suggest that the after-discharge is reduced in instances involving impaired

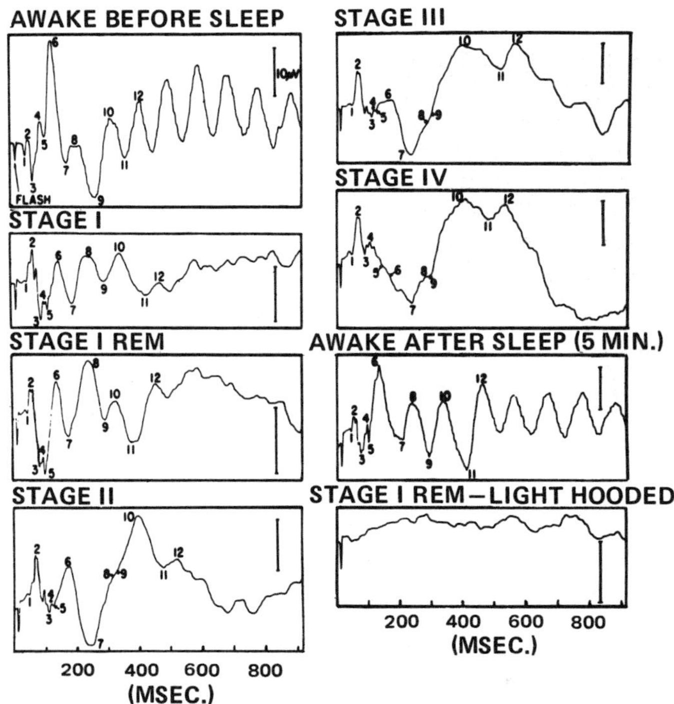

Figure 14.5. Responses evoked by light flash during various stages of sleep in one subject. Note repetitive after-discharge following intitial evoked-response components in the awake condition. This after-discharge disappears during all stages of sleep. "Light hooded" was a control run to test the effect of the slight noise accompanying the photic stimulus. [From Shagass, C. and Trusty, D., Somatosensory and visual cerebral evoked response changes during sleep. In J. Wortis (Ed.), *Recent Advances in Biological Psychiatry*, Vol. III. N.Y.: Plenum Publishing, 1966, 322–334.]

perception of the environment. It is, therefore, of interest that Shagass and Schwartz (1965) also found the after-discharge to be reduced in schizophrenics.

Reticular Involvement

Finally, some results in animal studies may be applicable here. Schwartz and Shagass (1962, 1963) and Schwartz, Shagass, Bittle, and Flapan (1962) studied the somatonsensory recovery function in the cat, and their findings suggest that regulation of the recovery function is influenced by reticular mechanisms. Their most striking finding is illustrated in Figure 14.6 (Schwartz & Shagass, 1963).

The recovery function in the cat is typically a relatively smooth, monotonic curve, with depressed responsiveness lasting 50 to 100 msec.

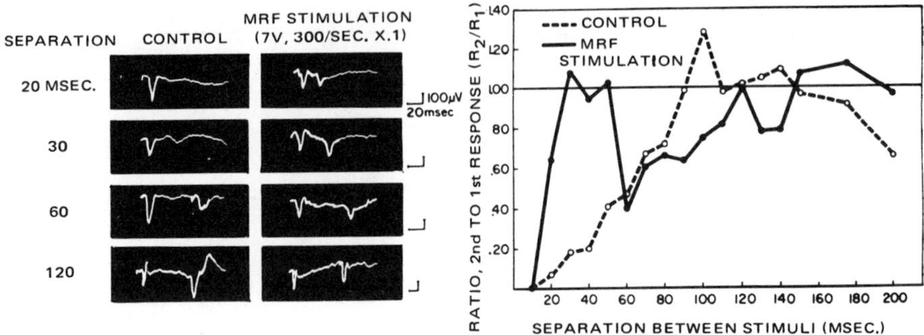

Figure 14.6. Recovery function to radial nerve stimulation in one cat with and without prior reticular stimulation. Note marked augmentation of recovery of second response at separations of 20 to 50 msec by reticular stimulation. (From Schwartz M., and Shagass, C. Reticular modification of somatosensory cortical recovery function. *Electroencephalography and Clinical Neurophysiology*, 1963, *15*, 265–271.)

Stimulation of the reticular system of the midbrain changed that function into a biphasic curve, with an early period of enhanced excitability. The results of reticular stimulation in the cat are so markedly analogous to the curves seen in normal human subjects as to suggest that human psychopathology may specifically involve some reticular dysfunction. This suggestion is also compatible with the findings of observable deficit in after-discharge to visual stimuli seen in psychiatric patients. It is also noteworthy that the effects of reticular stimulation were seen to operate after the thalamic relay nucleus; recordings of the afferent impulses in the medial lemniscus were not affected, suggesting a thalamic site of influence.

Conclusions

The results of these studies indicate that subjects with marked psychopathology also show deviant excitability of the CNS. Whether such deviation represents a decrease in excitatory processes or an increase in inhibitory processes remains to be determined. In fact, the relatively nonspecific nature of the results to date do not necessarily indicate that the same mechanisms operate in all varieties of psychopathology. However, there are indications that greater specificity could be obtained if these evoked-response measures were combined with other electrophysiological and biochemical determinations in the same subjects.

BIOCHEMISTRY OF THE FUNCTIONAL DISORDERS

As indicated earlier, schizophrenia and the affective psychoses are generally conceived to be two disorders (or groups of disorders) that are fundamentally different. Of the functional disorders, they are the two on which most of the biochemical investigations have concentrated. The single most productive source of hypotheses about the etiology of psychotic depression and schizophrenia is the psychiatric clinic itself. That is, treatment of these disorders with different drugs has suggested that certain transmitter systems are differentially altered in each. Beginning in the 1950s, a revolution has taken place in psychiatric practice owning to the introduction of drugs that appear to be relatively specific for the treatment of these illnesses. These drugs apparently have a variety of relatively specific effects on synaptic transmission. In Figure 14.7 the synaptic processes are illustrated by the norepinephrine system, but the principles apply equally well to other transmitters. There are several points at which the system is vulnerable to alteration or disruption: A competitive blocker of norepinephrine at the receptor site (C) will influence transmission across the synapse; interference with the deactivation of norepinephrine in the synaptic cleft (B) or the reuptake of norepinephrine into presynaptic sites (A) will raise the level of norepinephrine in the cleft. Of course, the availability of presynaptic norepinephrine may also be depleted or enhanced through the action of drugs. All such alterations affect the transmission process but each could have different *behavioral* consequences.

Endogenous Psychotogens

Over the last quarter century or more, there has been a gradual shift in emphasis in the biochemical investigations of the functional disorders. Ini-

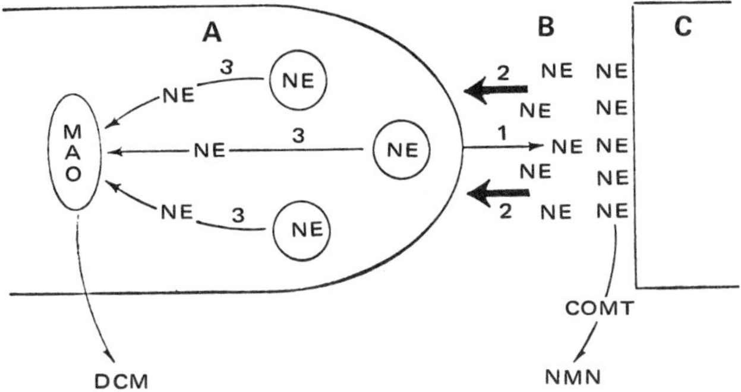

Figure 14.7. Schematic representation of (a) a noradrenergic nerve ending, (b) synaptic cleft, and (c) receptor. *NE*, norepinephrine; *NMN*, normetanephrine; *DCM*, deaminated catechol metabolites; *COMT*, catechol *O*-methyltransferase; *MAO*, monoamine oxidase (within a mitochondrion); 1, discharge of norepinephrine into synaptic cleft and onto receptor; 2, reuptake of norepinephrine from synaptic cleft; 3, intracellular release of norepinephrine from storage granules into cytoplasm and onto mitochondrial monoamine oxidase. (From Schildkraut, J. J. and Kety, S. S., Biogenic amines and emotion. *Science*, April 1967, *156*, 21–30. Copyright 1967 by the American Association for the Advancement of Science.)

tially, concentration was on schizophrenia and the search centered on the isolation of some specific abnormality of CNS metabolism that might produce the disorder. In other words, it was thought that if a specifically abnormal product could be isolated, the etiology of the disorder could be positively identified. Demonstrations of the psychotomimetic effects of drugs like LSD helped reinforce this approach; thus, it was thought that an LSD-like product, occuring naturally in the CNS of some people, would lead to schizophrenia. Over the years, a large variety of proposed endogenous psychotogens has been investigated (see Wyatt, Termini, & Davis, 1971). For instance, work with LSD and other psychotomimetics has suggested that there is some abnormality in the metabolism of serotonin. *Adrenochrome* and some associated compounds are oxidized products of epinephrine, and it is suggested that the natural occurrence of such products could produce schizophrenia. *Taraxein* is a hypothesized abnormal blood protein which might produce an immunological disorder—a self-allergic reaction. In general, however, we can summarize such research efforts in the following ways. First of all, it has been difficult to replicate findings between laboratories—continued apparent research success in one lab is often concurrent with repeated failure in others. Second, most such efforts have not convincingly ruled out the possibility that factors such as diet, other drug treatments, hospitalization, etc. might be producing the results. Furthermore, the specificity of the results to schizophrenia is not clear. Finally, the approach itself, looking for specific abnormalities, may be equivalent to fishing in the ocean—there are so many species of "fish" that it would be hard to know which particular species is the relevant one. More recently, the research strategy seems to be shifting toward concentration on understanding transmitter systems generally and determining their interactions within a specific functional disorder. Thus, rather than seeking a specific end-product, the intent is for more complete understanding of the transmitter system per se.

Affective Disorders and Norepinephrine

Generally, the role of catecholamines, particularly norepinephrine, in emotion and the affective disorders has been deduced from studies of the metabolic changes produced by clinically active psychotropic drugs. Schildkraut and Kety (1967) discussed a variety of clinical studies which are at least compatible with the notion that norepinephrine plays a critical role in affective disorders. Their review demonstrates that some, if not all depressions result from a deficiency of norepinephrine at some functionally important adrenergic synapses while elations and mania can be attributed to an excess of amines. Much of this research is directed at validating that it is specifically norepinephrine rather than serotonin that is critical in these disorders.

Drug-Induced Depression

Reserpine, a drug that is effective in the treatment of hypertension, produces severe depression in at least some patients. Prior to the development of other drugs, it was used in psychiatry in the treatment of mania. Reserpine apparently interferes with the intraneural binding of both the catecholamines and serotonin. As a result of such interference, the amines are freed to diffuse through the cytoplasm and become inactivated by monoamine oxidase (MAO).

In animals, reserpine induces a sedated state that has been proposed as an animal analogue of clinical depression seen in humans. The ability of artificially produced variants of reserpine to induce sedation has been correlated with their ability to reduce cerebral amines. Some separation of the effects of catecholamines and serotonin on reserpine-induced sedation has been achieved by administering their amino acid precursors to subjects previously given reserpine. Generally, administration of the catecholamine precursor reverses the reserpine effect, while administration of the serotonin precursor does not. Similarly, drugs that selectively block synthesis of serotonin or norepinephrine may be administered; here, too, norepinephrine generally appears to be the critical substance in sedative effects.

A study by Redmond, Maas, Graham, and Dekirmenjian (1971) in monkeys tends to support the view that catecholamines rather than serotonin are critical in depression. Prolonged disruption of catecholamine synthesis was produced in a group of monkeys by repeated administrations of alpha-methyl-p-tyrosine. Similarly, serotonin synthesis was disrupted in another group of monkeys by administration of parachlorophenylalanine. Close observation of the health and social interaction patterns of both groups was carried out. Disruption of serotonin synthesis caused profound physical disability but did not disrupt the social behavior of that group of animals. In contrast, the catecholamine-depleted animals appeared relatively healthy, but their social interactions were markedly disturbed and apathetic. The authors suggest that the social behavior of these animals may be a suitable animal model for investigating neurochemical activity in depression.

Antidepressants

In recent years, MAO inhibitors have been employed in the treatment of depression; their effect is presumably related to an increase in intraneural amines. Generally, the effectiveness of MAO inhibitors in animals has been related to the levels of norepinephrine. Similarly, imipramine and related compounds have been found to be effective antidepressants; in this instance, they appear to be effective by reducing the reuptake of norepinephrine; such an action of imipramine might "sensitize" the synapse. Conversely, lithium salts have been employed in treating mania; it has been suggested that they are effective because they increase the deactivation of norepinephrine and allow less to be available at synaptic receptor sites.

Affective Disorders: Multiple Etiologies Model

While the above data would seem to point primarily to the role of norepinephrine in the etiology of depression, a number of considerations suggest that this is too simplified an explanation. A major point involves the treatment of depressives with the metabolic precursors of catecholamines and serotonin: L-tryptophan, the amino acid precursor of serotonin, apparently does have antidepressive properties, while treatment with L-dopa, the catecholamine precursor, has, for the most part, been a failure. Furthermore, there are several reasons for believing that there may be interactive effects between norepinephrine and serotonin and possibly additional interactions with acetylcholine (see Akiskal & McKinney, 1973). Thus, reliance on a single amine theory does not appear warranted.

Reasonable analogues to the human depressive state have also been produced in monkeys with psychological manipulations. Harlow and Suomi (1974) have discussed several methods that are effective, separating infant monkeys from their mothers being a particularly good example for producing behaviors that appear to be close analogues to human depression. The ability to produce such analogues with psychological methods seems to relate to the fact that most, if not all, human cases of depression also seem to reveal relevant psychological precipitating factors. Finally, the implication of genetic trends in the occurrence of depression suggests that there may be biological factors that predispose the organism to vulnerability to one or another type of stress.

Together, then, all these considerations suggest a model of depression in which a predisposed genetic consitution, experiencing certain psychological stresses (particularly bereavement conditions and loss of control over reinforcement), responds with several changes in aminergic neural chemistry; these influences operate on the diencephalic mechanisms mediating reward and reinforcement; the final, behavioral manifestations are the depressive disorders. Within this etiological complex, the specific weightings given to the different sources of influence in particular individuals may determine the exact patterning of the symptoms manifested.

Several recent studies add support for the biochemical-genetic portions of the above formulation. For instance, several studies show that depressives have lower levels of MHPG, a metabolite of norepinephrine (Schildkraut, Keeler, Papousek, & Hartmann, 1973; Post, Gordon, Goodwin, & Bunney,

1973). On the other hand, the distribution of a serotonin metabolite was found to be bimodal in depressives (Åsberg, Thorén, Träskman, Bertilsson, & Ringberger, 1976). Only in patients falling into the lower mode of the distribution was the severity of their symptoms correlated (negatively) with the concentration of the metabolite. These results suggest that depressives are not homogenous with respect to transmitter alterations.

In two inbred strains of rats, Segal, Geyer, and Winer (1975) found that activity levels were differentially affected by intraventricular norepinephrine infusion. These and other data were interpreted to indicate that genetic differences can produce sensitivity differences at the postsynaptic receptors. Genetic-biochemical implications are further highlighted by findings in subjects screened for MAO activity: compared to those in the top 10 percent of the distribution, those in the bottom 10 percent showed more frequent psychological counseling, problems with the law, and an eight-fold increase in suicidal relatives (Buchsbaum, Coursey, & Murphy, 1976). Whether low MAO activity is indicative of more serious clinical and personal vulnerability to psychological disorder will have to be determined from long-term follow-up studies.

Conclusions

The dominant biochemical theory of the affective disorders postulates some sort of disturbance involving adrenergic neural transmitters. Most likely, these disorders involve some genetic predisposition to certain kinds of psychological stress, which is compounded by a disturbance in several transmitter systems. In some patients, it appears that the transmitter systems are of primary importance: Such patients generally show recurrent depressive episodes or cyclical manic-depressive states; maintenance treatment of such patients with drugs that alter the transmitters seems necessary for them to remain relatively symptom free. Other patients show depressive episodes that are isolated in occurrence and more obviously precipitated by specific psychological conditions. Viewed together, there is the strong suggestion that the affective disorders are not homogenous and any catecholaminergic involvement may represent only something they have in common.

Schizophrenia and Serotonin

The suggestion that serotonin is implicated in the etiology of schizophrenia arose largely out of work with psychotomimetic drugs such as LSD. A number of drugs whose structures are analogues of serotinin produce some schizophrenic-like symptoms. In addition, such drugs have also been shown to compete with serotonin for receptor sites in isolated smooth muscle preparations. Because of this competitive activity, it is suggested that a similar CNS action of these drugs is responsible for the mental symptoms they produce.

The serotonin hypothesis (see Woolley, 1962) suggests that faulty metabolism of serotonin is responsible for schizophrenic symptoms. The model is not specific about the exact nature of the metabolic defeat—it could be a failure to produce appropriate quantities of serotonin, or a failure to destroy it at a normal rate, or a defect in receptors causing inappropriate utilization. The administration of the serotonin precursor, 5-hydroxytryptophan, to schizophrenics reportedly resulted in the worsening of their symptoms. This evidence is in dispute, however.

A persistent question that has been raised in connection with the symptoms produced by LSD is whether they indeed mimic schizophrenia. Schizophrenics in remission indicate that the LSD condition seems different from their illness. Furthermore, LSD symptoms are largely hallucinatory, and visual at that. In contrast, thought disorder is considered the cardinal feature of schizophrenia rather than the presence of hallucinations; when they do occur, hallucinations in the schizophrenic are typically auditory rather than visual. It, therefore, seems reasonable to conclude that there are some very important differences between schizophrenia and the effects of LSD. This is not to say, however, that the study of psychotomimetic action is useless for the understanding of schizophrenia. In fact, the psychotomimetic action of another drug class, the amphetamines, is currently considered to be an extremely fruitful "model" of schizophrenia.

Schizophrenia and Catecholamines

Several lines of evidence suggest that it is the catecholamines which are altered or disturbed in schizophrenia. An impressive suggestion comes from the report (Wyatt, Murphy, Belmaker, Cohen, Donnelly, & Pollin, 1973) that MAO activity is lower in both schizophrenic and nonschizophrenic cotwins than in normals and was highly correlated between twins. There was a significant correlation between MAO activity and severity of the schizophrenic disorder. MAO activity might be a marker of the genetic susceptibility to schizophrenia. Animal studies of the self-stimulation effect have suggested that norepinephrine is the catecholamine of primary concern in schizophrenia (Stein & Wise, 1971). On the other hand, the clinical effects of the drugs classed as phenothiazines (e.g., chlorpromazine) appear to be specific for the treatment of schizophrenia and have suggested that dopamine is the transmitter of concern. In addition, stimulant drugs of the amphetamine class also have effects that are supportive of a dopamine model. We shall look at each of these models in turn.

Norepinephrine

Stein and Wise attempted to relate self-stimulation in animals to schizophrenia before the current emphasis on the role of dopamine in self-stimulation (see Chapter 11). While their formulation may require revision as a result, there is some supporting evidence. They suggested that reward mechanisms in the brain are largely mediated by a system ascending through the medial forebrain bundle, connecting lower brainstem mechanisms with those of the hypothalamus, limbic system, and frontal cortex. They assumed that this system is dependent on norepinephrine-containing neurons. They argued, as do at least some clinicians, that the primary impairment in schizophrenia consists of deficits in goal-directed thinking and the capacity to experience pleasure. They attributed such deficits to impairment of the noradrenergic reward system. This impairment involves the conversion of dopamine to norepinephrine in noradrenergic neurons. In essence, normal organisms convert virtually all the dopamine to norepinephrine, while in schizophrenics, a pathological gene results in partial conversion only. In these individuals, the remaining dopamine is released into the synapse where it is converted to a toxic product which, when taken up into the presynaptic terminals, results in their gradual destruction. They hypothesized that the beneficial effects of chlorpromazine derive from its protection of the reward system by blocking the uptake of the toxic substance; thus, although it continues to be produced, the toxic derivative of dopamine can no longer attack the vulnerable system.

The primary substantiating evidence for this formulation comes from a study of postmortem brain tissue from a group of schizophrenic patients and a group of normal controls (Wise & Stein, 1973). Dopamine-β-hydoxylase (DBH) is the enzyme responsible for the final step of norepinephrine synthesis. DBH activity was determined in these two sets of brains and a reduction was found in the schizophrenic group. A reduction in norepinephrine production would be consistent with the proposed model of defective noradrenergic reward pathways in schizophrenia. However, a key factor in evaluating these results revolves around control procedures for the effects of drug treatment, age, sex, hospitalization, etc. Wise and Stein also specifically attempted to control for deterioration of the brains as a function of time since death and failed to find any relationship that would have biased their results. However, this result is presently a matter of controversy (see Wyatt, Schwartz, Erdelyi, & Barchas, 1975; Wise & Stein, 1975). It remains to be seen if some more direct measure of norepinephrine synthesis might be developed and applied to schizophrenics. An independent, but also indirect, test measuring DBH in patients and controls suggested that *increased* synthesis of norepinephine occurs in acute schizophrenics and in the manic state of manic-depressive illness but not in the depressed condition (Rosenblatt, Leighton, & Chanley, 1973). Obviously, the specifics of the Stein and Wise hypothesis will require further scrutiny, but its cardinal feature—the involvement of the reward system—is extremely interesting and has not been contraindicated.

Dopamine

A succinct review of the evidence pointing to catecholamine involvement in schizophrenia has been presented by Snyder, Banerjee, Yamamura, and Greenberg (1974). Much of this evidence seems specifically to implicate dopamine. The evidence stems, on the one hand, from the observed clinical results of certain drug treatments and, on the other, from biochemical analysis. Clinically, there are several observations that are suggestive. First is the relative specificity of certain drugs for the treatment of schizophrenia. Second was the early observation that the efficacy of such treatment seems to be related to the degree with which motor side effects are also produced by these drugs. Finally, a clearly psychotic condition, sometimes mistaken for acute paranoid schizophrenia, can result from amphetamines and related stimulants.

Phenothiazines. Clinically, the phenothiazine drugs appear specifically to affect the fundamental symptoms of schizophrenia—the thought disorder, affect, and autism. Secondary symptoms, such as delusions and hallucinations, are not significantly improved, and nonschizophrenic symptoms, such as anxiety and depression, show no improvement with phenothiazines. The positive results with phenothiazines are not replicated by using sedatives. It is unlikely that a direct reversal of the fundamental biochemical disorder occurs with phenothiazines; rather they appear to exert indirect, palliative effects (Snyder et al., 1974).

The phenothiazines have a prominent side effect—they produce motor symptoms similar to Parkinson's disease. This is intriguing in view of their apparent specificity for schiozophrenia. Parkinson's symptoms include muscular tremors and rigidity, a stiff, propulsive gait, and loss of emotional expression in the face. It is now known that Parkinson's symptoms result from degeneration of a portion of the brain's dopaminergic neurons. The forebrain terminations of these neurons (Figure 8.13) are in the *caudate nucleus* and *putamen*. The caudate, putamen, and the *internal capsule*

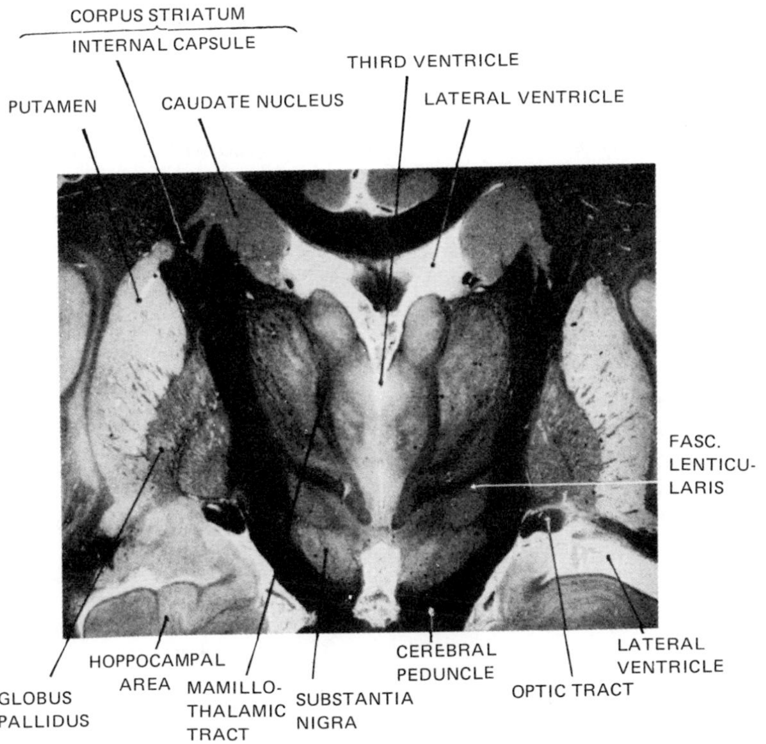

Figure 14.8. Coronal section of the human brain showing the location of corpus straitum. (From Gardner, E. *Fundamentals of Neurology*, 5th ed. Philadelphia: W.B. Saunders, 1968.)

(Figure 14.8), are collectively known as the *corpus striatum*. Along with the *globus pallidus*, the caudate and putamen form the group of nuclei known as the *basal ganglia* and are important for motor functioning. Of importance here is the fact that treatment of Parkinson's involves the restoration of dopamine levels with L-dopa, the amino acid precursor. Thus, a likely hypothesis is that the effectivness of the phenothiazines for schizophrenia results from their effects on dopamine, i.e., the motor side effect of these drugs may be a clue to the involvement of some other dopaminergic system. Note also that psychiatric symptoms sometimes accompany L-dopa treatment of Parkinson's patients. Recently, a reasonable candidate for a dopaminergic system involved in schizophrenia has been identified: Hökfelt, Ljungdahl, Fuxe, and Johansson (1974) demonstrated a new dopaminergic system that is confined to the limbic cortex. This dopamine system could be the relevant one in schizophrenia.

Dopaminergic involvement in schizophrenia is bolstered by additional findings. It is hypothesized that drugs clinically effective in treating schizophrenia block dopamine in some fashion. Blockage would, through feedback mechanisms, result in increased dopamine synthesis; it has been found that the effectiveness of the clinical drugs is correlated with their ability to increase such synthesis. But there is controversy over the specific sites of action of these drugs and the neural mechanisms affected (Groves, Wilson, Young, & Rebec, 1975). For instance, Seeman and Lee (1975) indicate that these drugs block secretion of dopamine while Creese, Burt, and Snyder (1976) presented evidence that their effectiveness was correlated with their ability to block the receptors.

Amphetamines. Low doses of amphetamines exacerbate the symptoms of schizophrenia; in high doses, they induce an acute paranoid psychosis whose hallucinations and delusions are much like those of paranoid schizophrenia. It has been proposed that such a psychosis could serve as a model for study. Drugs effective with schizophrenics are also effective with the amphetamine-induced psychosis. Snyder et al. (1974) have summarized a great deal of evidence that suggests that these effects of amphetamines are mediated by catecholaminergic mechanisms and a primary role is played by dopamine.

Peptides. Peptides are fragments of proteins, structural intermediaries between the constituent amino acids and the proteins formed from them. Several such peptides have been isolated from the brain which have morphine-like biological effects. Such peptides have also been shown to bind to the same receptors that are reached by the opiate drugs. Anti-psychotic drugs seem to show a similar CNS distribution. These results generally suggest that the effective sites of action of these various drugs are, in fact, responding to protein fragments. It is of great interest, then, that two groups of researchers have simultaneously reported that one of these peptides produces a profound catatonic state in rats that appears comparable to that seen in catatonic schizophrenia (Bloom, Segal, Ling, & Guillemin, 1976; Jacquet and Marks, 1976). These results suggest a chemical and behavioral specificity of peptides that has profound implications for the etiology and treatment of the psychoses. It is also of interest that the relevant peptide is a fragment of a pituitary hormone, suggesting that failure of appropriate enzymatic activity of hormones might be involved in psychopathological states.

Conclusions. At the present time, the most viable and strongly pursued theory of the organic substrate of schizophrenia implicates dopaminergic neural systems. Given the complex interactions possible between systems, however, it probably is unrealistic to expect that a single neurohumoral system will prove solely responsible. For instance, in addition to L-dopa treatment, anticholinergic drugs relieve Parkinson's disease and also combat the Parkinson's side effects of antipsychotic drugs. Thus alterations in either dopamine or acetylcholine probably produce compensatory effects. The new results with peptides also suggest that the dopamine system may not be the primary locus of any biochemical effect; a primary defect elsewhere could subsequently manifest itself through the dopaminergic neurons.

SUMMARY

One major purpose of this chapter was to illustrate how the problems and techniques of some of the traditional areas of academic physiological psychology are being brought to bear on some extremely important clinical problems. Concerns with genetics, sleep, self-stimulation, and neural transmission processes were all shown to be pertinent to the possible clarification of the so-called functional disorders. At the least, we must conclude that psychosis can no longer be considered "functional" in the sense of being devoid of organic pathology. And more optimistically, recent research seems to suggest real progress in specifying that pathology. Recordings of CNS activity in these disorders has not revealed any definite qualitative differences specific to them. However, there are strong suggestions that at least quantitative neural characteristics may be disturbed in several varieties of behavioral pathology.

More specific differences seem to be emerging from the study of neural transmitter functions. Both schizophrenia and the depressive illnesses have generally been related to catecholamine activity. More specifically, the dominant theoretical themes implicate norepinephrine disturbance in the depressive illnesses and dopamine disturbance in schizophrenia. In both clinical groups, however, a role for serotonin seems possible, and it is generally considered unlikely that a single amine will ultimately prove solely responsible for either. In fact, since it is probable that these disorders represent complex interactions between genetic predisposing factors and specific psychological conditions, no single etiological factor is likely to prove sufficient. Thus, even if a definitive biochemical defect can be isolated, it will be extremely difficult to differentiate whether it is a cause or an effect—e.g., does the defect cause schizophrenia, or is it a result of being schizophrenic? Ultimately, it may be necessary to demonstrate the entire chain of mechanisms involved in the disorder before such etiological questions can be answered with assurance.

REFERENCES

Akiskal, H. S., & McKinney, W. T., Jr. Depressive disorders: Toward a unified hypothesis. *Science*, 1973, *182*, 20–29.

Åsberg, M., Thorén, P., Träskman, L., Bertilsson, L., & Ringberger, J. "Serotonin depression"—A biochemical subgroup within the affective disorders? *Science*, 1976, *191*, 478–480.

Bloom, F., Segal, D., Long, N., & Guillemin, R. Endorphins: Profound behavoiral effects in rats suggest new etiological factors in mental illness. *Science*, 1976, *194*, 630–632.

Brown, J. C. N., Shagass, C., & Schwartz, M. Cerebral evoked potential changes associated with Ditran delerium and its reversal in man. In J. Wortis (ed.), *Recent advances in biological psychiatry*. New York: Plenum Press, 1964, pp. 223–234.

Buchsbaum, M. S., Coursey, R. D., & Murphy, D. L. The biochemical high-risk paradigm: Behavioral and familial correlates of low platelet monoamine oxidase activity. *Science*, 1976, *194*, 339–341.

Creese, I., Burt, D. R., & Snyder, S. H. Dopamine receptor binding predicts clinical and pharmacological potencies of antischizophrenic drugs. *Science*, 1976, *192*, 481–483.

Davis, P. A. Evaluation of the electroencephalogram of schizophrenic patients. *American Journal of Psychiatry*, 1940, *96*, 851–860.

Feinberg, I., & Evarts, E. V. Some implications of sleep research for psychiatry. In J. Zubin & C. Shagass (eds.), *Neurobiological aspects of psychopathology*. New York: Grune & Stratton, 1969, pp. 334–393.

Ferguson, D. C., & Fisher, A. E. Behavior disruption in cebus monkeys as a function of injected substances. *Science*, 1963, *139*, 1281–1282.

Freedman, D. X. *Biology of the major psychoses; A comparative analysis*. (Research Publications: Association for Research in Nervous and Mental Disease, Vol. 54) New York: Raven Press, 1975.

Gardner, E. *Fundamentals of neurology (5th ed.)*, Philadelphia: W. B. Saunders, 1968.

Gibbs, E. L., Gibbs, F. A., Tasher, D., & Adams, C. B-mittens: An electroencephalography and abnormality correlating highly with psychosis. *Electroencephalography and Clinical Neurophysiology*, 1960, *12*, 265.

Gibbs, F. A., & Gibbs, E. L. Fourteen and six per second positive spikes. *Electroencephalography and Clinical Neurophysiology*, 1963, *15*, 553–558.

Goldstein, L., & Sugerman, A. A. EEG correlates of psychopathology. In J.

Zubin & C. Shagass (eds.), *Neurobiological aspects of psychopathology*. New York: Grune & Stratton, 1969, pp. 1–19.

Groves, P. M., Wilson, C. J., Young, S. J., & Rebec, G. V. Self-inhibition by dopaminergic neurons. *Science*, 1975, *190*, 522–529.

Harlow, H. F., & Suomi, S. J. Induced depression in monkeys. *Behavioral Biology*, 1974, *12*, 273–296.

Heath, R. G. Schizophrenia: Evidence of a pathologic immune mechanism. In J. Zubin & C. Shagass (eds.), *Neurobiological aspects of psychopathology*. New York: Grune & Stratton, 1969, pp. 234–246.

Hill, D. Electroencephalogram in schizophrenia. In D. Richter (ed.), *Schizophrenia: Somatic aspects*. London: Pergamon Press, 1957.

Hökfelt, T., Ljungdahl, Å., Fuxe, K., & Johansson, O. Dopamine nerve terminals in the rat limbic cortex: Aspects of the dopamine hypothesis of schizophrenia. *Science*, 1974, *184*, 177–179.

Igert, C., & Lairy, G. C. Intérêt prognostique de l'EEG au cours de l'évolution des schizophrenes. *Electroencephalography and Clinical Neurophysiology*, 1962, *14*, 183–190.

Jacquet, Y., & Marks, N. The C-fragment of β-lipotropin: An endogenous neuroleptic or antipsychotogen? *Science*, 1976, *194*, 632–635.

Kupfer, D. J., & Foster, F. G. The sleep of psychotic patients: Does it all look alike? In D. X. Freedman (ed.), *Biology of the major psychoses: A comparative analysis* (Research Publications: Association for Research in Nervous and Mental Disease, Vol. 54). New York: Raven Press, 1975, pp. 143–159.

Post, R. M., Gordon, E. K., Goodwin, F. K., & Bunney, W. E., Jr. Central norepinephrine metabolism in affective illness: MHPG in the cerebralspinal fluid. *Science*, 1973, *179*, 1002–1003.

Redmond, D. E., Jr., Maas, J. W., Graham, C. W., & Dekirmenjian, H. Social behavior of monkeys selectively depleted of monoamines. *Science*, 1971, *174*, 428–430.

Rosenblatt, S., Leighton, W. P., & Chanley, J. D. Dopamine-β-hydroxylase: Evidence for increased activity in sympathetic neurons during psychotic states. *Science*, 1973, *182*, 923–924.

Schildkraut, J. J., Keeler, B. A., Papousek, M., & Hartmann, E. MHPG excretion in depressive disorders: Relation to clinical subtypes and desynchronized sleep. *Science*, 1973, *181*, 762–764.

Schildkraut, J. J., & Kety, S.S. Biogenic amines and emotion. *Science*, 1967, *156*, 21–30.

Schwartz, M., & Shagass, C. Effect of different states of alertness on somatosensory and auditory recovery cycles. *Electroencephalography and Clinical Neurophysiology,* 1962, *14,* 11–20.

Schwartz, M., & Shagass, C. Reticular modification of somatosensory cortical recovery function. *Electroencephalography and Clinical Neurophysiology,* 1963, *15,* 265–271.

Schwartz, M., & Shagass, C. Recovery functions of human somatosensory and visual evoked potentials. *Annals of the New York Academy of Science,* 1964, *112,* 510–525.

Schwartz, M., Shagass, C., Bittle, R., & Flapan, M. Dose related effects of pentobarbital on somatosensory evoked responses and recovery cycles. *Electroencephalography and Clinical Neurophysiology,* 1962, *14,* 898–903.

Seeman, P., & Lee, T. Antipsychotic drugs: Direct correlation between clinical potency and presynaptic action on dopamine neurons. *Science,* 1975, *188,* 1217–1219.

Segal, D. S., Geyer, M. A., & Weiner, B. E. Strain differences during intraventricular infusion of norepinephrine: Possible role of receptor sensitivity. *Science,* 1975, *189,* 301–303.

Shagass, C. Neurophysiological studies of anxiety and depression. *Psychiatric Research Reports,* 1958, *8,* 100–117.

Shagass, C., Overton, D. A., & Straumanis, J. J. Evoked potential studies in schizophrenia. In H. Mitsuda and T. Fukuda (eds.), *Biological mechanisms of schizophrenia and schizophrenia-like psychoses.* Tokyo: Igaku Shoin Ltd., 1974, pp. 214–234.

Shagass, C., & Schwartz, M. Reactivity cycle of somatosensory cortex in humans with and without psychiatric disorder. *Science,* 1961, *134,* 1757–1759.

Shagass, C., & Schwartz, M. Excitability of the cerebral cortex in psychiatric disorder. In R. Roessler & N. S. Greenfield (eds.), *Physiological correlates of psychological disorder.* Madison: University of Wisconsin Press, 1962, pp. 45–60.(a)

Shagass, C., & Schwartz, M. Observations on somatosensory cortical reactivity in personality disorders. *Journal of Nervous and Mental Diseases,* 1962, *135,* 44–51. (b)

Shagass, C., & Schwartz, M. Cerebral cortical reactivity in psychotic depressions. *Archives of General Psychiatry,* 1962, *6,* 235–242.(c)

Shagass, C., & Schwartz, M. Psychiatric correlates of evoked cerebral cortical potentials. *American Journal of Psychiatry,* 1963, *119,* 1055–1061.

Shagass, C., & Schwartz, M. Recovery functions of somatosensory peripheral nerve and cerebral evoked responses in man. *Electroencephalography and Clinical Neurophysiology,* 1964, *17,* 126–135.

SHAGASS, C., & SCHWARTZ, M. Visual cerebral evoked response characteristics in a psychiatric population. *American Journal of Psychiatry*, 1965, *121*, 979–987.

SHAGASS, C., STRAUMANIS, J. J., & OVERTON, D. A. Psychiatric diagnosis and EEG-evoked response relationship. *Neuropsychology*, 1975, *1*, 1–15.

SHAGASS, C., & TRUSTY, D. Somatosensory and visual cerebral evoked response changes during sleep. In J. Wortis (ed.), *Recent advances in biological psychiatry*, Vol. VIII. New York: Plenum Press, 1966, pp. 321–334.

SNYDER, S. H., BANERJEE, S. P., YAMAMURA, & GREENBERG, D. Drugs, neurotransmitters, and schizophrenia. *Science*, 1974, *184*, 1243–1253.

STEIN, L., & WISE, C. D. Possible etiology of schizophrenia: Progressive damage to the noradrenergic reward system by 6-hydroxydopamine. *Science*, 1971, *171*, 1032–1036.

STRAUMANIS, J. J., SHAGASS, C., & SCHWARTZ, M. Visually evoked cerebral response change associated with chronic brain syndromes and aging. *Journal of Gerontology*, 1965, *20*, 498–506.

STRUVE, F. A., & BECKA, D. R. The relative incidence of the B-mitten EEG pattern in process and reactive schizophrenia. *Electroencephalography and Clinical Neurophysiology*, 1968, *24*, 80–82.

WISE, C. D., & STEIN, L. Dopamine- -hydroxylase deficits in the brains of schizophrenic patients. *Science*, 1973, *181*, 344–347.

WISE, C. D., & STEIN, L. Dopamine-β-hydroxylase activity in brains of chronic schizophrenic patients. *Science*, 1975, *187*, 370.

WOOLLEY, D. W. *The biochemical bases of psychoses, or the serotonin hypothesis about mental diseases*. New York: Wiley, 1962.

WYATT, R. J., MURPHY, D. L., BELMAKER, R., COHEN, S., DONNELLY, C. H., & POLLIN, W. Reduced monoamine oxidase activity in platelets: A possible genetic marker for vulnerability to schizophrenia. *Science*, 1973, *179*, 916–918.

WYATT, R. J., SCHWARTZ, M. A., ERDELYI, E., & BARCHAS, J. D. Dopamine-β-hydroxylase activity in brains of chronic schizophrenic patients. *Science*, 1975, *187*, 368–370.

WYATT, J., TERMINI, B. A., & DAVIS, J. Biochemical and sleep studies of schizophrenia: A review of the literature—1960–1970. *Schizophrenia Bulletin*, 1971, *4*, 10–44.

Index

MA

MAI